This book is a study of the prose writings of Richard Wagner and their relevance to an understanding of his music and drama, as well as their relation to music criticism and aesthetics in the nineteenth century in general. As a by-product of Wagner's many-faceted career as composer, conductor, cultural critic, and controversial ideologue, the writings are documents of undisputed interpretive value, despite their notoriously problematic style. This study focuses on Wagner's words on music, and interprets them in light of the musical, aesthetic, and critical contexts that generated them. Professor Grey considers Wagner's ambivalence concerning the idea of absolute music and the capacity of music to project meaning or drama from within its own systems of referents. Central themes are Wagner's appropriation of a Beethoven legacy, the metaphors of musical "gender" and "biology" in *Opera and Drama*, concepts of melody, and the critical background to ideas of motive and "leitmotif" in theory and practice.

New perspectives in music history and criticism

Wagner's musical prose

New perspectives in music history and criticism

GENERAL EDITORS
JEFFREY KALLBERG AND ANTHONY NEWCOMB

This new series explores the conceptual frameworks that shape or have shaped the ways in which we understand music and its history, and aims to elaborate structures of explanation, interpretation, commentary, and criticism which make music intelligible and which provide a basis for argument about judgements of value. The intellectual scope of the series will be broad. Some investigations will treat, for example, historiographical topics – ideas of music history, the nature of historical change, or problems of periodization. Others will apply cross-disciplinary methods to the criticism of music, such as those involving literature, history, anthropology, linguistics, philosophy, psychoanalysis, or gender studies. There will also be studies that consider music in its relation to society, culture, and politics. Overall, the series hopes to create a greater presence of music in the ongoing discourse among the human sciences.

ALREADY PUBLISHED
Leslie C. Dunn and Nancy A. Jones (eds.), *Embodied voices: representing female vocality in Western culture*
Downing A. Thomas, *Music and the origins of language: theories from the French Enlightenment*

Wagner's
musical prose
Texts and contexts

THOMAS S. GREY

Stanford University

CAMBRIDGE
UNIVERSITY PRESS

Published by the Press Syndicate of the University of Cambridge
The Pitt Building, Trumpington Street, Cambridge CB2 1RP
40 West 20th Street, New York, NY 10011–4211, USA
10 Stamford Road, Oakleigh, Melbourne 3166, Australia

© Cambridge University Press 1995

First published 1995

Printed in Great Britain at the University Press, Cambridge

A catalogue record for this book is available from the British Library

Library of Congress cataloguing in publication data

Grey, Thomas S.
  Wagner's musical prose: texts and contexts / Thomas S. Grey.
  p. cm. – (New perspectives in music history and criticism)
  Includes bibliographical references and index.
  ISBN 0 521 41738 4 (hardback)
  1. Wagner, Richard, 1813–1883 – Written works. 2. Wagner,
Richard, 1813–1883 – Aesthetics. 3. Wagner, Richard, 1813–1883.
Operas 4. Music – 19th century – Philosophy and aesthetics.
5. Musical criticism. 6. Opera. I. Title. II. Series.
ML410.W19G83   1995
782.1'092 – dc20   94–11417 CIP MN

ISBN 0 521 41738 4 hardback

For my parents
Ann Foote Grey and Spencer Y. Grey

Entnahmt ihr 'was der Worte Schwall?

– Beckmesser

CONTENTS

Contents

Preface

It has long been customary to preface books on Wagner with apologies, and apologetics, for "yet another" – sometimes accompanied by vague comparative statistics about Jesus and Napoleon. Since these statistics (which have usually sounded suspiciously obsolete anyway) have been revealed as yet another mythical Wagnerian motif,[1] and since the apology can by this point be taken as read, I shall concentrate briefly on the apologetics.

Until recently it could be said that Wagner's prose writings, after spawning a sizeable quantity of adulatory mystification in the days of the *Bayreuther Blätter*, the *Revue Wagnérienne*, or *The Meister*, and a more sinister if less exhaustive phase of exegesis over the next generation, had eventually succumbed to a state of near-total scholarly disregard (even if the fundamental articles of their musical-dramatic creed had since become sedimented into a universal critical consciousness).[2] Over the last several decades the situation has changed, however. The same period that saw the critical and academic rehabilitation of Verdi and Rossini, across the 1960s and 70s, also witnessed a revival of serious critical interest in Wagner's literary oeuvre. (I am not proposing any secret, deep-structural link here, aside from the fact that this was a time of much academic rehabilitation in general.) This revived attention to the writings is attributable above all to the large body of work by Carl Dahlhaus from these years addressing certain central themes of Wagner's aesthetic thought and its intellectual-historical contexts, although Jack Stein's *Richard Wagner and the Synthesis of the Arts* (1960) had already revived some interest in Wagner's writings among English-speaking readers before that, and Ernest Newman's *Wagner as Man and Artist* (1911; 2nd edn, 1924) has always stood apart from the routine ideological Wagnerian blather of the early days.

---

[1]   Barry Millington, "Wagnerian Myths and Legends," in *The Wagner Compendium*, ed. Millington (London and New York, 1992), 132.

[2]   Despite the evolutions and revolutions of musical and dramaturgical fashions, Roger Parker submits, "we remain under the influence of Wagnerian ideals about how one might 'read' an opera. This is less often recognized and stated than it should be" ("On Reading Nineteenth-Century Opera: Verdi Through the Looking-Glass," in *Reading Opera*, ed. A. Groos and R. Parker [Princeton, 1988], 291).

Dahlhaus's Wagnerian project began largely as an attempt to discredit the orthodoxy of Alfred Lorenz's famous Wagner analyses, whose compendiousness seemed to have served as a kind of protective armor over the years.[3] Wagner's relatively few, but relatively unequivocal statements on the nature or "secrets" of his musical form were cited and interpreted by Dahlhaus as corroborating evidence to numerous analytical demonstrations of the insufficiency of Alfred Lorenz's architectonic schemes and of the need to take seriously Wagner's assertions that his music absorbed the fluid, open-ended, and often ambiguous designs of drama into its own structures and procedures.[4] This project was largely completed by the mid-1970s, although Dahlhaus continued to return to and modify his points through the next decade. Since then the basic texts of the Wagnerian prose canon have rarely been absent altogether from critical writing on the music. Klaus Kropfinger's *Wagner und Beethoven* of 1974 (trans. *Wagner and Beethoven*, 1991) represents the next and most thorough confrontation with Wagner's writings on musical and aesthetic subjects after Dahlhaus's influential beginnings, followed by Dieter Borchmeyer's *Das Theater Richard Wagners* (1982; trans. *Richard Wagner: Theory and Theatre*, 1991), two essays by Carolyn Abbate from 1989 (in *Analyzing Opera* and the *Cambridge Opera Journal*), and most recently Jean-Jacques Nattiez's *Wagner Androgyne* (1990; trans. 1993), which – under the seemingly esoteric rubric of an "androgynous" motif linking aspects of Wagner's life, thought, and works – involves substantial readings of many of the prose texts, and includes a convenient conspectus of the ever-shifting emphases of poetry, drama, and music in relation to one another.[5]

---

[3]   Dahlhaus seems to have taken a cue here from Rudolf Stephan, who laid out the fundamental objections to Lorenz's compulsive and often irrational rationalizations of Wagnerian "form" in a lecture inquiring: "Gibt es ein Geheimnis der Form bei Wagner?" Though written in 1962, it was not published until 1970 (*Das Drama Richard Wagners als musikalisches Kunstwerk*, ed. C. Dahlhaus [Regensburg, 1970], 9-16).

[4]   The principal texts in question here are Dahlhaus's essay "Formprinzipien in Wagners *Ring des Nibelungen*," in *Beiträge zur Geschichte der Oper*, ed. Heinz Becker (Regensburg, 1969), 95–130, and the monograph *Wagners Konzeption des musikalischen Dramas* (Regensburg, 1971), although a foundation for the critique of Lorenz was laid in the earlier essay, "Wagners Begriff der 'dichterisch-musikalischen Periode'," in *Beiträge zur Geschichte der Musikanschauung*, ed. Walter Salmen (Regensburg, 1965), 179-94.

[5]   Nattiez also includes a comprehensive catalogue of Wagner's writings, including information regarding original publication, and numerous items not included in the sixteen-volume *Sämtliche Schriften und Dichtungen* (*Wagner Androgyne*, trans. Stewart Spencer [Princeton, 1993], 303-22). Because of the availability of this list, as well as those given by Barry Millington (*The Wagner Compendium*, 1992) and John Deathridge (*The New Grove Wagner*, 1984), and because I focus here on a relatively small number of basic texts, I have included only a selective check-list of these as an appendix (see pp. 378-9).

My aim here has been to bring together a variety of leading musical motifs in Wagner's writings and situate them within the larger texture of his aesthetic and critical thought, to analyze them in the manner of a *Gewebe von Grundthemen* or fabric of recurring, transforming, interrelated "fundamental themes," as Wagner characterized his own scores. Some of these motifs have been sounded and variously developed in the work of Dahlhaus and the other writers mentioned here, others may be less familiar. I have been concerned to ground these themes not only in the contexts of Wagner's literary and musical-dramatic oeuvre as a whole, but also more broadly in the aesthetic, cultural, and social contexts of his time (to do for these musical-aesthetic themes something of what Dieter Borchmeyer has done for the principal motifs of the dramas, for instance, in *Richard Wagner: Theory and Theatre*). To some extent such a methodology is inevitable and hence, scarcely unprecedented: no one would think to invoke a Wagnerian "philosophy of music" without also invoking the name of Schopenhauer or Nietzsche, and Kropfinger's study of the *Beethovenmotiv* in Wagner's writings (one of the most prominent and heavily transformed motifs there) has stressed the extent to which this philosophy looked to established figures of cultural authority for support, even as it reconstructed the image of such authority to suit its needs.

All the same, Wagner the *Gesamtkünstler* was remarkably successful in projecting an illusion of intellectual autonomy, a sense that he really had re-invented art and music in his own image, that his oeuvre was indeed a perfected, self-contained whole that was expressly designed to render its context – an imperfect present – obsolete. (Nietzsche caustically summed this up as the three-point guiding principle of the writings as a whole: "Everything Wagner can *not* do is reprehensible. There is much else that Wagner could do: but he doesn't want to, from rigorism in principle. Everything Wagner *can* do, nobody will be able to do after him, nobody has done before him, nobody *shall* do after him. – Wagner is divine."[6]) Even Dahlhaus, who was anything but naive with regard to the historical contexts of Wagner's music and ideas, still tended to approach the works (music and prose alike) as a series of more or less self-contained problems, topics interconnected only, or primarily, within the great artistic monologue of Wagner's career; when Dahlhaus did appeal to a wider context, it was to a relevant but narrowly circumscribed canon of musical, philosophical, and critical texts.

In fact, Wagner did often try and sometimes succeeded in isolating himself from the "corrupt" surroundings of the modern world – on the Wesendonck hillside *Asyl*, behind the tapestried walls of a Venetian palazzo, or in his peninsular Tribschen idyll – and the music that

---

6   Friedrich Nietzsche, *The Birth of Tragedy and The Case of Wagner*, trans. Walter Kaufmann (New York, 1967), 176–7.

emanated from these cloistered sites stands remarkably apart from much else of the time. But in so many other ways, of course, Wagner was deeply engaged with the culture of his century, even programmatically so. And the terms of the musical-cultural critique articulated throughout his writings are (again) inevitably implicated in those of the musical culture critiqued. Indeed, a principal strategy of this critique and of the ongoing brief for a new "musical drama" was, as I shall argue, the appropriation of a popular critical discourse of music and "ideas," "poetic ideas," new means (and forms) of musical representation and signification, and the ideal of an increasingly "determinate" musical semantics. The endless stream of words issuing from Wagner's pen in the form of essays and articles, brochures and treatises, proclamations and rebuttals to the press, letter upon letter, not to mention the dramatic poems – all of this might be read as a kind of collective, almost desperate gesture underwriting the greater project of making music "speak" (to articulate "ideas" and enact dramas). Wagner's prose thus becomes a kind of *supplément* to his music and its aspirations, which crystallized those of the age, even in pressing them to extremes.

The rubric under which I have chosen to approach these Wagnerian texts, as his "musical prose," is meant to designate the admittedly narrow limits of the enterprise. (Although I do occasionally touch on the matter of musical prose in the technical, Schoenbergian sense, I trust that the allusion to that familiar term in my title will not be misconstrued as the principal subject of the book, which it clearly is not.) The greater part of Wagner's published writings are not devoted to musical matters at all, and among those that are, I have largely restricted myself to a central canon that is generally agreed to speak most directly to issues in his own music, and to the reception of the similarly narrow canon of works Wagner was willing to acknowledge as historically significant. In the modern (which is to say postmodern) critical climate it becomes increasingly difficult to segregate strictly musical issues from "extra"-musical ones; and to a certain extent, this permeable border is one of my chief concerns, so far as it engages problems of musical expression, representation, and other forms of meaning. But the possible intersection of Wagner's manifold implication in matters of politics, race, psychology, and cultural ethics – as documented in so much of his writing – with the procedures and sounds of his music is a notoriously elusive thing. Those social, psychological, and ethical matters, as such, have scarcely lacked for attention; how they intersect with the methods of the composer and the music is quite another matter – maybe a real and pressing one, but not one I am prepared to pursue at length in the context of his "musical" prose. (If we dismiss Wagner's diagnosis of "Jewishness" in music as the bigoted drivel it seems to be, how do we go about ascertaining antisemitic traces in his music? The question is not posed as an exoneration of

Wagner, but as a genuine methodological query whose answer seems to me still ambiguous.[7]) On the other hand, some kinds of broad cultural constructions are so obviously engaged by both the writings and the dramas at once that they demand to be recognized even within the discussion of musical-aesthetic issues, which I scarcely want to represent as pure and self-contained. Along these lines I have scrutinized in chapter 3 the familiar metaphors of gender that figure so largely throughout *Opera and Drama*, and propose a reading of how they may be allegorized, both consciously and unconsciously, in the dramatic configurations and musical processes of scenes from *Siegfried* and *Parsifal*. Even so, I am not necessarily sure what the consequences should be (if any) for our evaluation of the music "itself" or of the musical drama, as aesthetic artifact.

Embedded in the designation "musical prose" is the irony that the style of these writings is anything but musical, in the sense of conveying delight through sheer sounding surfaces, lyrical contours, or dancing rhythms. (On the other hand, the prose style does often bear a certain kinship to Wagner's "endless melody," which was often faulted on similar grounds, and both share that marked tendency to motivic recurrence and transformation, mentioned above.) The famous opacity of Wagner's prose style, its overwrought syntax, and often strident rhetorical tone surely reflect something fundamental about the author's character. These points have been sufficiently remarked over the years that there is no need to dwell on them here. (I might just note the long list of neurotic symptoms diagnosed by Max Nordau, of *Degeneration* fame, on the basis of Wagner's prose style, beginning with "persecution mania, megalomania, mysticism, vague philanthropy, and anarchism" – none of them too surprising – and concluding with "graphomania, namely incoherence, fugitive ideation, and a tendency to idiotic punning."[8]) Thomas Mann, who was originally put off by the verbosity of the prose and its over-inflated rhetorical posturings, later came to

---

[7]   The problem (like so many pertaining to operatic music) is of course compounded by the concrete representational stratum of the drama. Barry Millington has recently argued, for instance, that Beckmesser was indeed intended by Wagner as an anti-semitic caricature, on the grounds of both musical and textual evidence ("Nuremberg Trial: Is there Anti-Semitism in *Die Meistersinger?*" *Cambridge Opera Journal* 3:3 [1991], 247-60). Similarly, Sander Gilman's reading of Jewish representations and attendant cultural paranoias in Strauss's *Salome* is predicated on conscious compositional intent, supported and "determined" (as Wagner would put it) by the dramatic text (Gilman, "Strauss and the Pervert," in *Reading Opera*, 306-27). On the other hand, Paul Lawrence Rose's attempts to implicate "the music itself" and the operas more generally in Wagner's anti-semitism – to hear in the music sublimated traces of racial bias and aggression – are not wholly convincing, even if they remain incidental to the biographical, cultural, and historical picture that is his principal concern (*Wagner: Race and Revolution* [London and Boston, 1992]).

[8]   Max Nordau, *Degeneration* (7th edn New York, 1895), 171.

acknowledge behind its "stiffness" and "random, unkempt amateurism" an "astonishing perspicacity and intellectual vigor," both as aesthetic theory and as cultural critique.[9] Wagner's texts, at any rate, give new meaning (so to speak) to deconstructive adages about the undecidability of textual meaning, its "iterability" and endless dissemination, the inevitability of misreading, as well as the fundamental metaphoricity of language (the "prison-house of language" might also come to mind, especially the longer one immerses oneself in the toils of Wagnerian syntax). Though offered as opinion rather than fiction, theory rather than art, these texts force us to linger more than usual at the first stage of interpretation. The "transparent" meaning we might normally posit at this stage is often absent here. For the English speaker, the necessity of translation presses this point further. The reader of Wagner's prose needn't work hard at teasing out latent ambiguities, blind-spots, slippages of figural language, unwitting contradictions and aporias: they grow in rank profusion across nearly every page.

Despite the frequent challenge of establishing just a provisional first-level or intended meaning in these texts, I have tried not to remain insensitive to other levels of interpretation, or to the problematic status of authorial intentions in general. That status has been perhaps over-problematized to a wearying extent by now. But the relation of an author's secondary, critical or reflective texts to primary, creative ones (i.e., Wagner the "author" to Wagner the composer) largely reduces to a simple matter of historical awareness (I won't say objectivity).[10] A moderate dose of skepticism has nearly always been axiomatic in reading Wagner's self-presentations, at least outside of the Bayreuth sanctum of old. Inevitably, I will often have recourse to the usual declarative formulae (Wagner said this, Wagner thought that, Wagner believed . . .). The larger context should make the contingencies of such statements clear

---

9   Thoman Mann, *Pro and Contra Wagner*, trans. Allan Blunden (Chicago and London, 1985), 105. Adorno's comment that Wagner was "the author of his collected works from the first day" is characteristically perceptive and misleading at once. It captures that aspect of the mature Wagner dedicated to creating his own monuments, epitaphs, and memoirs, but thereby misconstrues the essentially random and occasional nature of the writings as a whole. It is this occasional (hence contextual or contingent) nature of the writings that explains, to a great extent, their many lapses of "theoretical" consistency.

10   Carolyn Abbate has reviewed "the problems of taking Wagner's prose as a primer for Wagnerian analysis" in the prefatory remarks to her essay "Wagner, 'On Modulation,' and *Tristan*," *Cambridge Opera Journal* 1:1 (1989), 33-4. The remarks are offered partly as critique, partly as disclaimer. Within the essay she does not dispense with the composer's critical voice, but looks and listens for different ways of hearing it, or the different identities it assumes (in this case, an "anti-symphonic" voice that might be heard as dissonant to that of Beethoven's "heir"). The method is essentially similar to that I have adopted here, while I have tried to bring into the conversation some of the voices around Wagner, as well.

enough, I hope. Part of my project is indeed to interpret what I think Wagner *did* say, think, or believe at a given time, for a given purpose. Another part is to interpret how these attitudes were modified over time (his celebrated reversal on the "absoluteness" of music, for instance). A further part is to suggest how beliefs about the nature of his and others' music respond not only to Wagner's development as a composer – which of course they do – but also to the musical discourses and discourse on music happening around him. Analyzing or otherwise interpreting the music on the basis of his words (prose or poetry) is not the central objective of this book. But where I do attempt this, I don't look to the critical texts for straightforward directives on the interpretation of form and meaning (such directives are not there). Rather, I have tried to put Wagner's words on music into a counterpoint with the music, offering a tentative analysis of the various harmonies and dissonances that result. Such methods of reading the prose as a counterpoint to the music I have also tried to extend to the "musical prose" of Wagner's contemporaries, as an additional contrapuntal strand against those of his music and his prose.

Just as we are exhorted to renounce the illusion of reconstituting authorial intentions and the attempt to found our interpretive acts upon that unsafe ground, a parallel danger exists, I realize, in seeking to supplant author with context, claiming to speak for the many instead of the one. The potential arbitrariness of seizing on a name and date to represent a larger place and time is manifest. But this is hardly a sufficient argument to forgo all speculation about shared ideas and the intellectual physiognomy of the past in any form. The philosophy and method informing the chapters that follow are neatly encapsulated in a passage by George Steiner, which attempts to recuperate the values of historical contextualism from the encroachments of programmatic theoretical uncertainty:

> We must read *as if* the temporal and executive settings of a text do matter. The historical surroundings, the cultural and formal circumstances, the biographical stratum, what we can construe or conjecture of an author's intentions, constitute vulnerable aids. We know that they ought to be stringently ironized and examined for what there is in them of subjective hazard. They matter nonetheless. They enrich the levels of awareness and enjoyment; they generate constraints on the complacencies and license of interpretive anarchy.[11]

---

11   George Steiner, *Real Presences* (Chicago, 1989), 86. In a similar vein, if from a somewhat different perspective, Gary Tomlinson has advocated a music-historical contextualism "that will not circle back narrowly to the notes but will instead *resolutely historicize musical utterance*, exploding it outwards through an imaginative building of contexts out of as wealthy a concatenation of past traces as the historian can manage" ("Musical Pasts and Postmodern Musicologies: A Response to Lawrence Kramer," *Current Musicology* 53 [1993], 22).

To inveigh against the "complacencies and license of interpretive anarchy" may have an uncomfortably authoritarian, even reactionary ring to it. If so, we could censor that. We could even censor "constraints," and be left with "awareness and enjoyment." (To my mind, that may be enough.) But if our theoretical rigor insists that we forgo all that precedes, then we probably have no business lingering about in the past and its artifacts at all.

While my approach to the writings is neither comprehensive nor chronological, I have tried to incorporate at least a rudimentary sense of these values. That is, I have touched on what I take to be representative writings from across Wagner's career, and according to a pattern that generally moves in a historical direction. Chapter 1, on fundamental questions of musical autonomy, form, and content, is the most telescopic, but in addressing the "dialectics" of Wagner's positions on the question of absolute music it necessarily engages the diachronic history of those positions. Chapter 2 again moves across much of Wagner's career, in considering Wagner's absorption of Beethoven's music, mythos, and the critical traditions attendant on these. Here the trajectory is perhaps more evident, moving from the Parisian stories of 1840–1 to the "programmatic commentaries" and reform essays of the Zurich years to a few passages from *Beethoven* (1870). (Since Klaus Kropfinger has already provided a detailed history of Wagner's reception and appropriation of Beethoven in general, I have focused here on just a few *Grundmotiven*, especially on the ways in which Wagner adapted the critical tradition around Beethoven's music to the purposes of his own program.) Chapters 3 and 4 are concerned almost exclusively with Wagner's critical *Hauptwerk*, *Opera and Drama*, from different but (marginally) complementary perspectives. The margin of overlap is located in the figure of "evolution," which itself figures as a central, centering concept for much of what I have to say about Wagner's aesthetics of musical form. That he strove to make his music "evolve" after the manner of the drama, as a deliberate alternative to the "architectonics" of symphonic form was a foundational point of Dahlhaus's critique of Lorenz, and hence of much that grew out of it. I have tried to ground this idea (and ideal) more fully in the metaphors and terminology of the writings. Concern with Wagner's metaphors involves a concern with the kinds of ideological and cultural meanings they embody (here archetypes of gender), and the ways in which these may be transmitted to the music, which might be understood to absorb the metaphors that surround it. Chapter 4 focuses on terminology (the disputed "poetic-musical period") more than metaphor, though they intersect. (Wagner appeals to the poetic-rhetorical origins of the term "period" as a means of transforming its musical applications.) As such, the methods of this chapter are fairly traditional. Chapter 5 revolves around a slightly later text ("*Music of the Future*," 1860) and another

contested and still more famous phrase: "endless melody." As a terminological study, it resembles chapter 4, just as the categories of "period"
and "melody" overlap. But just as the category of "melody" enfolds that
of "period," chapter 5 takes a broader view of the history and aesthetics of
the term "melody," as received by Wagner, and moves to analytical interpretations only at the end. Chapter 6, finally, begins with a later text ("On
the Application of Music to the Drama," 1879), but also moves further
than the preceding chapters into contextual margins and byways, particularly in constructing a history for the term "leitmotif." Although
obviously an authentic Wagnerian practice, with a tentative theoretical
foundation in *Opera and Drama* (Part III), the famous term "leitmotif" is
itself entirely a product of Wagnerian *contexts*, while absent from the
primary texts. How the term and its originating contexts may have a
bearing on our reading/hearing of Wagner's *musical* texts, their forms
and textures, is a question I address in the end of that chapter.

In closing, I would like to thank especially Anthony Newcomb, Paul
Robinson, and Stephen McClatchie for responses to and suggestions on
the form and content of the text. My thanks also to Erik Goldstrom and
Jean Pang-Goyal for their assistance at various stages of work on this
book, to Penny Souster of Cambridge University Press for her patience
with my continual (all too Wagnerian) deferral of closure on this project,
as well as to Kathryn Bailey Puffett and Ann M. Lewis for their careful
scrutiny of the final draft and proofs, respectively. I am grateful for grants
received from the National Endowment for the Humanities and the
Alexander von Humboldt-Stiftung which supported work on the later
stages of writing and the final preparation of the text (fall 1993–winter
1994); and my gratitude also extends to Karol Berger, Klaus Kropfinger,
Barry Millington, and Steven P. Scher for their supportive assistance.

1

Wagner and the problematics of "absolute music" in the nineteenth century

Ideas of absolute music

"The advocates of an absolute music obviously don't know what they're talking about," Wagner insisted, somewhat petulantly, in 1857 (the open letter "On Franz Liszt's Symphonic Poems"), three years after the appearance of Eduard Hanslick's immediately influential brochure on the subject (V, 191).[1] Perhaps Wagner felt justified in issuing such a summary dismissal of Hanslick's *Vom Musikalisch-Schönen* ("On the Beautiful in Music") and its perceived thesis – the advocacy of "absolute music" – on the grounds of intellectual property, since the phrase appears to have its origins in his own writings rather than with Hanslick. Wagner, it seems, coined the phrase "absolute music" in the course of a programmatic commentary he had devised to accompany his performances of Beethoven's Ninth Symphony for the Dresden Palm Sunday concerts of 1846, foreshadowing his famous historical-philosophical reading of this crucial work in the post-revolutionary "Zurich writings" of 1849–51, particularly *The Art-Work of the Future*.[2] (The seemingly casual reference to "absolute music" in the 1846 commentary would multiply at an alarming rate, like Wagner's prose itself, and undergo manifold mutations in the works to follow.) In claiming, in the 1846 commentary on the Ninth, that the instrumental recitative of Beethoven's finale seemed intent on

[1] All citations of Wagner's published writings within the text refer by volume and page number to the *Sämtliche Schriften und Dichtungen* (SSD), vols. I–XVI (Leipzig, 1911–16). Volumes I–X are equivalent to the *Gesammelte Schriften und Dichtungen* (GSD, vols. I–X [2nd edn, Leipzig, 1887]). References to Cosima Wagner's diaries, where no text is specifically cited (either in German or in translation), are given as "CWD" followed by date of entry.
[2] Carl Dahlhaus, *The Idea of Absolute Music*, trans. Roger Lustig (Chicago, 1989), 18–19. Attention was first drawn to Wagner's use of the phrase in 1846 by Klaus Kropfinger; see Kropfinger, *Wagner and Beethoven: Richard Wagner's Reception of Beethoven* (1974), trans. Peter Palmer (Cambridge, 1991), 115.

"transgressing the boundaries of absolute music" (II, 61), Wagner was in fact expressing what was already becoming a widespread critical conviction regarding all of Beethoven's later works and the telos of his oeuvre as a whole (see chapter 2). Although it seems unlikely that this relatively obscure Wagnerian text could have had any significant role in the dissemination of the phrase itself ("absolute music"), the context could not have been more apt: the Ninth Symphony was and remained, of course, the gravitational center of debates about the nature and limits of musical form, expression, autonomy, genre, and meaning throughout the century. And when Wagner penned this soon-to-be-famous phrase, in 1846, this already incipient debate over musical form and meaning was about to inundate the critical landscape to an extent that could scarcely have been predicted – the "thirty-years' war of the music of the future," as Wagner jestingly referred to it in retrospect ("On Operatic Poetry and Composition in Particular," 1879: X, 171).

Just how Wagner hit on the phrase "absolute music" in 1846 is not entirely clear, but the ubiquity of the adjective "absolute" throughout the polemical discourse of *The Art-Work of the Future* and especially *Opera and Drama* certainly suggests the example of Ludwig Feuerbach – the principal philosophical spokesperson for the revolutionary youth of the 1840s ("Young Germany") – whose *Grundsätze einer Philosophie der Zukunft* ("Foundations of a Philosophy of the Future") was an obvious inspiration behind the rhetoric of Wagner's tracts.[3] In referring, in *Opera and Drama*, not only to "absolute music," but to a large family of related species (from absolute melody and absolute poetry down to such exotic ones as absolute recitative and absolute opera singer), Wagner deemed the word "absolute" itself sufficient demonstration of the nullity of whatever object it modified. Egoistic phenomena that refused to participate in the greater communal spirit of the age would be refused the nourishment of the progressive world-spirit and left to wither and die: the inevitable mediocrity of all those sonatas, trios, quartets, and symphonies that composers might continue to produce was a pre-ordained consequence of their cultural irrelevance (thus spake Wagner). To this extent, perhaps Wagner's annoyance at the appropriation of "his" phrase by his formalist opponents is understandable. For in the Feuerbachian context of his Zurich writings the predicate "absolute" was a consciously pejorative alternative to the positively value-laden

---

[3] The context of the 1846 Beethoven commentary, on the other hand, has nothing particular to do with Feuerbachian ideas or vocabulary, although Wagner may have already been familiar with these. The subsequent impact of Feuerbach on Wagner's ideas and writings is discussed at some length by Rainer Franke in *Richard Wagners Zürcher Kunstschriften* (Hamburg, 1983), 189–254.

predicate "pure" that might otherwise serve here, in the formulation "pure instrumental music" – a phrase that had, in fact, been in circulation since at least the beginning of the century. (Hanslick, incidentally, combined both – as "die reine, absolute Tonkunst" – in the unique instance of that term within his book.)[4]

But in 1857 ("On Franz Liszt's Symphonic Poems") Wagner found himself in the awkward position of trying to deny the very existence of a phenomenon he had carried on about at such length in *Opera and Drama*. (Hence, perhaps, the curtness of the riposte.) "Absolute music" is an epistemological chimera, he now insists. And all those sonatas, quartets, and symphonies, we might ask – were they not just mediocre, but altogether illusory? Here, of course, Wagner has recourse to another argument from the Zurich writings, his thesis that all instrumental and operatic forms are elaborations of simple, pre-artistic song and dance. According to Wagner's rather generalized intuitions, everything that we are tempted to consider as "purely musical form" is ultimately dependent on the external shaping forces that dictate music's tempos, rhythms, and phrasing – and, by extension, the "large-scale rhythm" (*Rhythmus im Großen*) which even Hanslick understood as the foundation of music's perceptible forms.[5] Supposedly abstract, autonomous musical form, Wagner argued (rather presciently), is in fact a function of the body, its instinctive binary gestural rhythms and symmetries, or else it inscribes patterns of social behavior: ritualized courtship, as dialogic interaction of gendered principles, for example. Wagner was thus speaking from the lofty perspective of his own, privately intuited musical-anthropological *Geschichtsphilosophie*, an imagined historical genesis of musical forms, where Hanslick (or other "formalists") were taking a more pragmatic view of music in its present condition – that for all practical purposes, music had become fundamentally abstract and autonomous.

Wagner's testy response to Hanslick (or the "advocates of an absolute music") in the 1857 open letter is not so much evidence of irreconcilable premises as it is of his fundamentally problematic relationship to the very concept of absolute music, a persistent cognitive dissonance in Wagner's thought that Dahlhaus has referred to as the "twofold truth" of his aesthetic credo.[6] A traditional view of Wagner's aesthetics, as revealed in the prose writings, has posited a kind of conversion to a metaphysics of

---

4   Eduard Hanslick, *Vom Musikalisch-Schönen* (Leipzig, 1854), 20.
5   Ibid., 32. Cf. Carl Dahlhaus, "Eduard Hanslick und der musikalische Formbegriff," *Die Musikforschung* 20 (1967), 145–53.
6   "The Twofold Truth in Wagner's Aesthetics: Nietzsche's Fragment 'On Music and Words'," in *Between Romanticism and Modernism: Four Studies in the Music of the Later Nineteenth Century*, trans. Mary Whittall and Arnold Whittall (Berkeley and Los Angeles, 1980), 19–39.

absolute music under the influence of Arthur Schopenhauer's *Die Welt als Wille und Vorstellung* ("The World as Will and Representation"), which Wagner first discovered in 1854, the same year in which Hanslick's book appeared. It is sometimes supposed that this forceful encounter with Schopenhauer's ideas had an immediate impact on Wagner's view of the metaphysical and essentially autonomous dignity of music, although there is scarcely any evidence of such a sudden and conscious aesthetic conversion.[7] (The unexceptional rhetorical paean to music as "the highest, most redeeming art" in the letter "On Liszt's Symphonic Poems" [V, 191], sometimes cited as evidence, is not especially convincing.) According to another, fairly traditional view, the conversion was a more gradual one, which was only completed by the time of the 1870 Beethoven essay (the only public context in which Wagner makes any direct reference to Schopenhauer's ideas on music). This view is more amply corroborated by changing emphases in Wagner's writings between 1850 and the 1870s. The idea of a more gradual aesthetic conversion reasonably couples Schopenhauer's purported influence with that of Wagner's internal experiences as composer, the drastic stylistic upheavals of the first decade in exile that produced *Tristan und Isolde* and the first part of the *Ring*. Nietzsche, who is supposed to have become increasingly committed to an ideal of absolute music the more he distanced himself from Wagner, was not above satirizing Wagner's apparent "conversion" to this Romantic ideology. "[Wagner] grasped at once," Nietzsche writes in *On the Genealogy of Morals* (1887), "that with the Schopenhauerian theory . . . *more* could be done *in majorem musicae gloriam* – namely, with the theory of the sovereignty of music as Schopenhauer conceived it . . . With this extraordinary rise in the value of music . . . the value of *the musician* himself all at once went up in an unheard-of manner, too: from now on he became an oracle, a priest, indeed more than a priest, a kind of mouthpiece of the 'in itself' [*An-Sich*] of things, a telephone from the beyond – henceforth he uttered not only music, the ventriloquist of God – he uttered metaphysics."[8]

---

[7] Dahlhaus repeatedly resorts to this formulation (possibly as a convenience). See, for example, the *Wagner Handbook*, ed. U. Müller and P. Wapnewski, trans. and ed. John Deathridge (Cambridge MA, 1992), 303: "Wagner adopted Schopenhauer's philosophy of absolute music after 1854" or "The Twofold Truth," where he states that "absolute music" signified "everything Wagner wanted to separate from musical drama, as the idea of it shaped itself in his mind around 1850 . . . , [but] once he began to read Schopenhauer in 1854 his certainty started to waver" (33). Jean-Jacques Nattiez has identified three "plots" into which the vagaries of Wagner's aesthetic thought have been configured, of which the "conversion" theory (more commonly seen as a gradual process, completed by about 1870) figures as the first. See Nattiez, *Wagner Androgyne*, "La querelle des intrigues," 99–101, and 173–8.

[8] *On the Genealogy of Morals*, trans. W. Kaufmann and R. J. Hollingdale (New York, 1969), 103.

Whatever the precise biographical chronology (or psychology) behind it, some ideological shift of this kind is the basis of that "twofold truth" diagnosed by Dahlhaus: Wagner's evident need to sustain his earlier critique of absolute music in *Opera and Drama* while embracing a broader aesthetic of music as a "noumenal" language above words and mere reflected phenomena, in the spirit of Schopenhauer and the Romantic critical tradition (Wackenroder, Tieck, Hoffmann). "At the same time as Wagner pronounced the doctrine that music is, or ought to be, a means to a dramatic end," Dahlhaus writes, "he also espoused other, contradictory aesthetic principles which reveal that he, hardly less than the 'formalists' who were his opponents in the day-to-day cut and thrust of musical debate, took for granted the truth of the idea of an 'absolute' music which was characteristic of the nineteenth century as a whole."

Opera and Drama, officially his principal theoretical work, propagates an "exoteric" aesthetic, but there is another, "esoteric," Wagnerian theory of aesthetics, the components of which are to be found scattered throughout the later writings. It was a theory for initiates which Nietzsche took as his starting point but then carried to an extreme where it was converted into a critique of Wagner and finally into an outright polemic against him.[9]

In other words, the case of Nietzsche *contra* Wagner could be argued on the evidence of Wagner's own texts. And not only the post-*Beethoven* texts. The Romantic metaphysics of "pure music" – which Wagner grew up with, along with the German instrumental canon that nourished it – is never really absent from Wagner's aesthetic thought, as Dahlhaus also notes,[10] even in such contexts as *The Art-Work of the Future* and *Opera and Drama*, where such metaphysics would seem incompatible with the gospel of music's redemption by the holy trinity of word, drama, and "poetic intent."

The fragmentary text of Nietzsche that occasioned Dahlhaus's reflections on Wagner's aesthetic schizophrenia (a pendant to those musical passages from *The Birth of Tragedy* clearly indebted to Wagner's own *Beethoven* essay) is said to reveal "the latent unity of musical aesthetics in the nineteenth century": a fundamental conviction in the idea of absolute music, "one of the central aesthetic tenets of a century in which art music . . . rose to aesthetic 'autonomy,' that is, no longer had a manifest function to fulfill, but was intended to be listened to for its own sake."[11] Having chosen opera as a professional specialization,

9   Dahlhaus, "The Twofold Truth," 32.
10 ". . . the apologetic construct by which Wagner sought to elevate his own work to the goal of music history, and the romantic inheritance that secretly nourished his concept of music – the contradictions seem like a gaping abyss" (*The Idea of Absolute Music*, 25–6).
11 "The Twofold Truth," 39, 37.

5

but unwilling to relinquish hereditary claims to a recently canonized culture of German instrumental classics, Wagner thus found himself in an anomalous position. The anomaly was partly of his own creation, in that he was committed to overcoming the tendential autonomy even of operatic music (which perfectly well satisfied Schopenhauer). For, aside from the social functions of opera as an institution, it was hardly the case, of course, that its music was always "functionally" subservient to the text. Indeed, music's tendency to resist functional subservience was always and again the starting point for theories of reform, for Wagner as for his predecessors. And, as I will argue here, the difficulties resulting from Wagner's need to sustain a traditional discourse of operatic reform, on one hand, and an allegiance to newer Romantic ideologies of musical autonomy, on the other hand, can be understood to crystallize a broader division afflicting nineteenth-century critical attitudes to music as a whole: a similar schismatic allegiance to organicist notions of the autonomous musical work and to a developing discourse of "ideal" or "poetic" content, the desire to claim for music, too, the determinate objects, tangible meanings, and representational status of the other fine arts.

Questions of autonomy

The story of music's unexpected access to metaphysical dignity in the context of emergent Romantic ideologies of aesthetic autonomy around 1800 is well known.[12] The abstract, non-representational condition of music had traditionally rendered suspect the position of any music that did not set a text or serve some other purposeful function. Gradually,

---

[12] The now standard account is Carl Dahlhaus's *The Idea of Absolute Music* (see n. 2). The first chapter sets out the case for the "paradigmatic" value of absolute music in the Classic-Romantic era in general, and the more or less traditional view of a distinct paradigm-shift (p. 7) as documented in a new critical consciousness of music around 1800. Dahlhaus characteristically avoids presenting the story as a single-stranded, diachronic history, attempting to do justice to the co-existence of opposing musical traditions and aesthetic philosophies. Nonetheless, the figures in his story, and the texts that represent them, are largely the same ones that populate earlier traditional accounts of Romantic aesthetics and the emergence of an idea (and ideal) of musical autonomy, such as Rudolf Schäfke's *Geschichte der Musikästhetik in Umrissen* (Berlin, 1934) and Felix Gatz's *Musikästhetik in ihren Hauptrichtungen* (Stuttgart, 1929). A different approach is represented in John Daverio's recent book, *Nineteenth-Century Music and the German Romantic Ideology* (New York, 1993), which, rather than focusing on Romantic views of (absolute) music, considers broader affinities between Romantic poetics in general (Friedrich Schlegel's in particular) and representative composers and works across the century; these examples are interpreted as carrying out, consciously or not, Schlegel's programmatically "unfinished," evolving aesthetic project of Romantic art.

in the wake of certain European instrumental repertoires (paradigmatically represented by a north-German *empfindsamer Stil* and a Viennese "classical" style), the traditional construction of musical forms as an ingenious but ingenuous, quasi-mechanical play of tones regulated according to a code of affects came to be re-constructed in terms of a language of "pure," self-referential signs. Such an instrumental language might now be understood to mean anything, or nothing in particular. It might be read as an infinite flux of possible meanings, generated in the wordless dialogue between work and listener. The link between the former abject state of music and this present exaltation was a continuing notion of music as a direct, unmediated language of pure, abstracted feelings – a notion shared (with varying emphases) by an eighteenth-century aesthetic of sensibility and Romantic metaphysics alike. But a persistent, rationalistically biased Enlightenment view of instrumental music as a "deficient mode" (song without words) gave way, by the end of the eighteenth century, to the idea of a language "above" speech, a language that transcended the vulgar world of empirical reality and fixed signs.

This Cinderella story of absolute music, grounded in the canonic scriptures of a few central figures of German Romanticism (the essays of Tieck and Wackenroder, E. T. A. Hoffmann's music criticism, passages from Jean Paul and Novalis, and a few aphorisms by Friedrich Schlegel) is, if not strictly a fairy tale, probably an overly "romanticized" narrative. While the aesthetic status of music, as represented by its more ambitious genres, certainly underwent a significant transformation by the early nineteenth century, its abstract, non-referential character remained as problematic as ever. Many composers, critics, and listeners shared something of Wagner's ambivalent, "twofold" perspective on musical autonomy: a desire to reconcile this Romantic idea of a "higher" language of absolute music (with its privileged access to the philosophical Absolute, as essence or "Idea") with a new valorization of music's ability to convey "meaning" of a more concrete (determinate) kind by means of new characteristic, representational, dramatic or narrative capacities (it is scarcely possible to distinguish clearly between these). In traditional historiography of the textbook variety these "un"-Romantic impulses to locate concrete, determinate meaning have often been conflated with Romantic ideologies of musical autonomy. Dahlhaus, on the other hand, tended to distinguish between a "genuine" Romantic tradition (founded in those few canonic texts) and a popular tradition – the legacy of an older "aesthetics of feeling" – eager to relate music to the experiences of life, history, and literature. The two co-exist in the "dialectic" of Wagner's aesthetic ambivalences, as described by Dahlhaus. But I believe that they co-existed much more widely, as well. Even aside from the misgivings a dichotomy of genuine ("pure") and popular traditions is likely to engender today, it seems to me that Dahlhaus's habit of ideal-typing for methodological convenience, as criticized by Philip Gossett, does tend to distort this particular historical picture.[13] Literary figures like Wackenroder, Hoffmann, or Jean Paul might apostrophize the inscrutable mysteries of a hieroglyphic language of tones, but the Romantic yearnings of most musicians and audiences – and not only the benighted dilettantes among them – seemed to be more and more oriented to "content," a category construed in predominantly literary or "material" terms. This yearning was all the stronger for the fact that such "content" had for so long seemed unavailable to music, except through the contorted applications of an increasingly stale theory of imitation. Music's autonomous tendencies were seen more and more as a liability to be overcome than as a unique asset, and not only by philosophical skeptics like Kant or Hegel, but by musical enthusiasts of every stripe. Wagner may have been an extreme example of this divided resistance to musical autonomy, in his role as operatic reform-theorist, but (as in so many ways) he was also an epitome of the culture at large.

The question of art's autonomy in general embraces a host of issues – epistemological, cultural, political – that have been the subject of critical concern throughout the twentieth century, much of it converging in Adorno's *Aesthetic Theory* (1970).[14] These issues can hardly be given a thorough airing here, nor do they need it. It should be enough to acknowledge their scope simply as a preface to some remarks on a fundamental issue for music (and Wagner): the relative autonomy of music from

---

[13] Philip Gossett, "Carl Dahlhaus and the 'Ideal Type'," *19th-Century Music* 13 (1989), 49–56. See also James Hepokoski's review/critique of the theoretical underpinnings of Dahlhaus's work, "The Dahlhaus Project and its Extra-Musicological Sources," *19th-Century Music* 14:3 (1991), 221–46.

[14] Issues of art and autonomy have tended (particularly among Marxists, of course) to concern the relation of art-works to contexts of society, culture, and politics, while the autonomy from a represented content understandably tends to presuppose the more limited areas of certain modernist art and literature, and the peculiar case of music. While the old "New" criticism experimented with treating representational works from this modernist/musical perspective of absolute formal autonomy, most recent music criticism has been occupied with an opposite strategy (following Adorno's lead), asking how even "abstract" music might manifest the same social contingencies as representational art. Some pioneering efforts in this area are represented in the collection *Music and Society: The Politics of Composition, Performance and Reception*, ed. Richard Leppert and Susan McClary (Cambridge, 1987). The burgeoning literature on issues of gender and sexuality in music could also be cited here, of course (see, for example, the positions outlined in the introduction to Susan McClary's volume of essays, *Feminine Endings* [Minneapolis, 1991], 3–34). While probably no composer in history is more thoroughly implicated in issues of society, politics, and culture than Wagner, my immediate concern here is with questions of autonomy "within" the work (regarding the relative independence of its textual levels), although the broader question of music's motivations and meanings inevitably leads toward that of social and cultural significations.

language, or, conversely, its relative contingency on language, culture, and extra-musical "ideas." Is the putative autonomy of absolute music manifested in the individual work, or does it derive from the apparently self-contained, non-referential musical "language" or system? If we accept the practical autonomy of either of these – the work or the system – as an apparently self-generating, internally coherent set of behavioral protocols, syntactic procedures, hierarchical relations and such, do we nonetheless accept the epistemological contingency of the "system" on culturally determined habits of perception, consensual codes of hearing and interpreting, the institutional transmission of the skills of production and of reception, and so on? To what extent is an emphatic concept of autonomy compatible with notions of cultural or historical change at all? Or how compatible is the idea of musical autonomy with any notions of musical signification, expression, or meaning? Is it therefore more useful to think in terms of a relative autonomy, one that accepts (if not simply ignores) historical and geographical parameters as premises requiring no further comment? Music, like language, may convey an impression of an autonomy to those who produce and receive it, while contingencies are revealed with historical, cultural, and critical distance. Production and reception then open up another slew of questions about function, patronage, economic forces, authorial control, and so on (the contingencies are self-perpetuating). Can an intended autonomy be subverted by the practices of listeners who reserve a right to the self-determination of their own experience? This last question is important: just as the text and context of an operatic piece automatically subvert the potential autonomy of its musical structure, the dominating cultural role of opera, drama, poetry, and novels by the early nineteenth century increasingly led consumers of absolute music to listen against the grain of its autonomous appearance, so to speak, to listen for cultural, literary, or otherwise fictive meanings. In this way, the development of a "programmatic" aesthetic by the mid-nineteenth century, like the whole critical discourse of "poetic ideas" feeding into it, was (as Arno Forchert has argued) the result of a dialogic process between composers, critics, and listeners rather than something dictated by the imagination of a few Romantic individuals.[15] The rhetoric of Wagner's aesthetic theory is directly engaged in this dialogue – as I will further argue in chapters 2 and 6 – although the volume of his voice (as of his writings)

---

[15] Arno Forchert, "'Ästhetischer' Eindruck und kompositionstechnische Analyse. Zwei Ebenen musikalischer Rezeption in der ersten Hälfte des 19. Jahrhunderts," in *Rezeptionsästhetik und Rezeptionsgeschichte in der Musikwissenschaft*, ed. H. Danuser and F. Krummacher (Laaber, 1991), 193–203. Some examples of the phenomenon Forchert describes are discussed in my essay "Metaphorical Modes in Nineteenth-Century Music Criticism: Image, Narrative, and 'Idea'," in *Music and Text: Critical Inquiries*, ed. S. P. Scher (Cambridge, 1992), 93–117.

has tended to obscure the other voices and to give instead the impression of a vast Wagnerian monologue.

If the cultural and historical contingency of an intelligible musical "language" as such was hardly an issue in 1800, it was gradually becoming one by the middle of the century, with the rapid increase of historical (and even geographical) awareness, as well as the rapid disintegration of stable stylistic, formal, and generic norms that precipitated Wagner's "thirty-years' war of the music of the future." Already by the 1850s Hanslick – perhaps more so than Wagner – acknowledged the essential contingency of most musical experience. One was more than ever aware of the historical contingencies of musical taste and evaluation. "There is no other art that so rapidly exhausts so many of its forms," Hanslick declared. "Modulation, cadence patterns, intervallic and harmonic progressions become obsolete after thirty to fifty years, such that the sensitive and intelligent composer can no longer employ them, and is continually compelled to discover new, purely musical gestures."[16] (The longevity of taste had apparently not changed much since the time of Tinctoris.) Earlier Hanslick remarked that one need not inconvenience Indians or Caribes, the "usual auxiliary troops" enlisted to demonstrate the "variability of taste." It is enough to look at the European concert audience, one half of which finds its deepest, strongest responses elicited by Beethoven's symphonies, while the rest hear nothing in them but "difficult, intellectual stuff," totally lacking in "feeling."[17] Hanslick's growing conviction in the historical and cultural contingency of musical "beauty" (and even of its expressive value) is evident from accretions to later editions of the book expressing his awareness of the ultimate mortality of so many aesthetic judgements. This was apparently one of the factors that led him to renounce further aesthetic speculation altogether, despite the immediate success (or notoriety) of *Vom Musikalisch-Schönen* .[18]

---

[16] *Vom Musikalisch-Schönen*, 41. Note, though, how the phrase "purely musical features" (*Züge*) re-inscribes the illusion of autonomy even as Hanslick tries to discredit the idea on a historical level.

[17] Ibid., 8. In the fourth and fifth editions of the book (1874, 1876) Hanslick substituted the "late quartets and Bach's cantatas" as exemplars of the more demanding component of the canon and proof of the contingency of appreciation or taste on *Bildung* (see Dietmar Strauß, ed., *Eduard Hanslick: Vom Musikalisch-Schönen*. Teil I: *Historisch-kritische Ausgabe* [Mainz, 1990], 35).

[18] See, for instance, the lengthy footnote added to chapter 3 in the sixth edition (1881), introduced by the assertion that "all music [*Tondichtung*] is human artifact, the product of a particular individual, of a time, a culture and therefore shot through with elements of a mortality that will be visited on it sooner or later." The case in question is that of opera, which has the highest mortality rate, as it were, precisely because it is the most socially contingent of musical genres, as regards both its creation and its evaluation. The once exemplary "classicism" of Hasse and Jomelli is cited as case in point. (Strauß/Hanslick, *Vom Musikalisch-Schönen*, vol. I, 95–6.)

Without ever developing Hanslick's appetite for music-historical facts, Wagner was well enough aware of the contingencies of history and culture affecting the development of musical forms and styles. Clearly, the author of such tracts as *Art and Revolution* – and the tireless propagator of cultural redemption through hybrid genres vaguely patterned after ancient ritual practices – did not promote the autonomy of art from society. In his own terms, he shared with Hanslick and virtually all of their contemporaries a fundamental belief that music, like the rest of the arts, reflected the character, disposition, and spiritual "needs" of its age. Of course, Wagner was inclined to adjust this relationship so that art could lead the way in social progress rather than merely reflect a status quo. Still, neither Hanslick nor Wagner denied the reciprocal relation between culture at large and the seemingly "abstract" and mysterious language of tones. Nothing could be more typical of the period, in fact, than the tendency to read artistic (hence even "purely musical") style as an index of the cultural psyche, just as it was taken to reveal essential characteristics of a nation, or the psychology of a composer.[19]

On the other hand, Wagner and Hanslick were fundamentally agreed in ascribing a relative autonomy to the language of the classical canon and its forms (in Hanslick's case the point is obvious). Both would have concurred that a Beethoven symphony – the paradigmatic musical artwork – is a unified, organic entity that carries within its "sounding forms" all that is necessary for its satisfying aesthetic contemplation. Presumably Hanslick would even have agreed with Wagner (in *"Music of the Future"* and *Beethoven*) that the *Missa solemnis* – a nominally "functional" and indisputably texted composition – is essentially a piece of pure "symphonic" music in a post-classical idiom (cf. VII, 127 and IX, 102). They would probably have further agreed that in abdicating its social function as liturgical accompaniment this work (like all "serious" composition in their century) acquired the same "function" as a symphony, one of providing spiritual edification through aesthetic contemplation. Finally, Wagner and Hanslick were agreed that even opera, for better or worse, tended toward musical absolutism – that the cantabile portion of a Donizetti aria or duet, for instance, was thoroughly comprehensible (not to say reprehensible) as a piece of self-contained musical discourse, quite independent of its text.

---

[19]   A. W. Ambros is a paradigmatic figure here, whose activity as critic and as historian was informed by the style of *Geistesgeschichte* practiced by Jacob Burckhardt. Similarly, Ambros gives a classic formulation of the premises of a biographical hermeneutics in his essay on "The Ethical and Religious Element in Beethoven," where he states: "It is with Beethoven as with Goethe: the works become a commentary to the artist's life ... and the life becomes a commentary to the works" (*Culturhistorische Bilder aus dem Musikleben der Gegenwart* [Leipzig, 2nd edn, 1865], 9).

Wherein did they differ, then, regarding the autonomy of music? We come back to the difference between a pragmatic, empirical view of how music "is" (Hanslick's concerns) and a tendentiously speculative view of how it "came to be" and how it "ought to be" (Wagner's concerns). This same, unfailing tendency of Wagner's to adopt the highest possible ground – aesthetically, ethically, and historically – also let him evaluate the acquired or relative autonomy of modern music differently. He insisted on stressing the contingency of the formal conventions behind this apparent autonomy (the roots of classical instrumental forms in the traditional human activities of song, march, and dance) and in condemning even such apparent or relative autonomy as a liability to music's cultural participation, to its acquisition of greater freedoms, increased expressive scope, and a genuine "ideal content" (a liability to progress, as the New Germans would put it).

Hanslick and Wagner were agreed that music had acquired a level of practical autonomy, while they differed in assessing the aesthetic consequences. Where they did agree, though, we can assume that most of their contemporaries would have, as well. Music was obviously no longer limited to a strictly functional status, but had taken on the higher "function" of aesthetic *Bildung*. Music could dispense with poetic texts, or simply ignore them, and still be both effective and comprehensible. The logic, unity, and emotional effect of a composition were generally predicated on internal, "purely musical" parameters in most current repertories, and not dependent on a text, where one existed. These are some of the premises of what I have called a theory of practical or relative musical autonomy, as opposed to Wagner's epistemological (or *geschichtsphilosophische*) scruples regarding what we might call the anthropological genesis of musical forms. Wagner accepted most of these premises, in the sense of an incontrovertible status quo, and even celebrated (in the Zurich writings) the achievements of absolute music up to the time of Beethoven as a necessary and beneficial stage in the "world-historical" course of the art. Autonomy became problematic, for Wagner, when one considered the price exacted by it (music's cultural isolation), which led him to question its status as a positive aesthetic criterion. In his exposition of the changing accentuation of Wagner's positions over time, Dahlhaus is acutely aware of such ambivalences and their origin in Wagner's divided loyalties to conflicting Romantic ideals of autonomy and synthesis. What he perhaps fails to stress, in an exposition of the larger historical picture, is the extent to which Wagner's ambivalences were in fact characteristic of the musical culture at large, while an unqualified valorization of musical autonomy remained exceptional.[20]

---

[20] The almost unfailingly antagonistic response to Hanslick's *Vom Musikalisch-Schönen* in the musical press is certainly one index of this situation, even if much of it was

The basic question remains that of music's relation to a verbal text. This should be the simplest, as well: absolute music is, first of all, music without text, program, or title – music that is free of words. Yet, as we know, even this basic definition could not be sustained, at least not for Wagner. The (pejorative) paradigm of musical autonomy in *Opera and Drama* was the Rossinian aria, in flaunting the independence of music from poetry, or rather the hegemony of the one over the other. (Here Wagner could count on the support of a whole generation of anti-Rossinian operatic criticism, and not only German.) And in another sense, even vocal music that entered into a properly responsive, intimate relation with its text did not automatically renounce all rights to aesthetic autonomy, at least as regards the final product, as "work." Wagner obviously considered the scores of *Lohengrin*, *Tristan*, and *Parsifal* as unified, coherent, and thus autonomous art-works in a much stronger sense than, for example, his *Columbus* overture, his C-major Symphony, or his various *Albumblätter* for piano. As a musical text, in fact, it is fair to say that the music drama really did aspire to the status of the symphony – a sacrosanct musical score to be protected at all costs against mutilation at the hands of unscrupulous producers, conductors, or arrangers. (In this sense, one could assert the paradox that *Götterdämmerung*, with all its words, is an autonomous work in the way that instrumental "works" such as Siegfried's Rhine Journey or Funeral Music are not.)

But to what degree *should* music sacrifice structural autonomy (and hence integrity?) as self-satisfying artistic form in entering into a collusion with text and drama? The question, of course, was under constant discussion in Wagner's time, as it was before and has been since (*in saecula saeculorum*).[21] Some variations of it are pondered in the

founded on misapprehensions of Hanslick's actual arguments and reacted to what was perceived as a heretical and counter-intuitive denial of music's expressive effect. On some of the responses to Hanslick, see T. Grey, "Richard Wagner and the Aesthetics of Musical Form in the Mid-Nineteenth Century (1840–60)" (Ph.D. dissertation, University of California, Berkeley, 1988), chapter 3, *"Vom Musikalisch-Schönen*: Hanslick's Challenge to the Aesthetics of Feeling," esp. 188–99. On the reception and historical context of Hanslick's work generally see also Dorothea Glatt, *Zur geschichtlichen Bedeutung der Musikästhetik Eduard Hanslicks* (Munich and Salzburg, 1972), Werner Abegg, *Musikästhetik und Musikkritik bei Eduard Hanslick* (Regensburg, 1974), and the editorial commentary included in Geoffrey Payzant's translation *On the Musically Beautiful* (Indianapolis, 1986).

21   The tendency of twentieth-century analysis to "redeem" Wagner's works on the basis of an underlying structural autonomy is, of course, typified by Alfred Lorenz's schematic analyses of the whole music-dramatic oeuvre. While these analyses have been largely discredited since the 1960s for their often willful manipulations of musical "facts" to fit a small repertoire of procrustean formal models, it is worth recalling that Lorenz by no means ignored the text or stage action (even if these, too, were usually pressed into the service of tidy schematics). The critical trope of Wagner's "symphonic" opera is taken up in chapter 6.

course of later chapters. For now, a brief sketch of Wagner's theoretical position(s) on this question can lead us to a few remaining philosophical prolegomena and some concrete exemplifications.

This first and simplest question sounds alarmingly like that perennial and often tedious theme of operatic criticism, "words vs. music." Plenty of strategies can be devised for evading that tiresome theme (as one might evade a long-winded guest), such as invalidating the terms of its formulation (retracting the invitation, as it were), or – as Wagner would try to do – substituting other terms, such as "drama," for "words." One way or another, the theme is likely to return, and is probably most tolerably endured in a series of brief encounters, each one pursuing the issue from some discrete angle. For the moment, let us recall Wagner's most famous contribution to the discourse of "words and music" – the dictum about "means and ends" from *Opera and Drama* – along with a few anticipations and variously distorted echoes elsewhere in his writings.

"The error of the operatic genre," Wagner trumpeted in boldface in the peroration of his preface to *Opera and Drama*, "has been that the means of expression (music) has been made an end in itself, and the proper end of music (drama) has been made instead a means" (III, 231). Under the dispensation of such erroneous beliefs one has even come to the point of imagining that "the genuine drama might be created on the basis of absolute music" (III, 233). In this preface Wagner appeared to be doing little more than digging out the old reformers' credo (*prima le parole*) from the storehouse of operatic polemics and fitting it out with a newly painted legend, now in solid German *Fraktur*, to hang above the critical workshop of *Opera and Drama*. Having set it out here, he by no means ignored it in going about his critical business, although he was at some pains to reformulate the traditional economy of poetic power and musical subservience in gentler terms of a marital partnership rather than the traditional metaphorical economy of master and servant.[22] Of course, one might question whether Wagner's

---

[22] Suzanne G. Cusick has recently analyzed the interaction of the master-servant analogy in the critical discourse of early opera (Monteverdi) with gendered analogies, primarily man and wife ("Gendering Modern Music: Thoughts on the Monteverdi-Artusi Controversy," *Journal of the American Musicological Society* 46:1 [Spring 1993], 1–25). Perhaps in response to the feminizing constructions of the emerging monodic and tonal idioms, she suggests, "musical power needed constantly to be understood as a response to – and as controlled by – the composer's (masculine) intention"; the male composer "within this system of metaphors must make himself understood as manly and in control" (24). The terms of this observation recall, of course, Wagner's category of the "poetic intent," which is likewise male-gendered within his metaphorical universe. This gendered economy of a formative masculine (poetic) "intent" and a malleable female musical substance could suggest how Wagner's polemics against ideals of musical autonomy or "absolute music" were able to assert his own masculine "dominance" (see also chapter 3).

gendering of poetry and music as masculine and feminine agents in his biological metaphor of operatic (re-)production (*Opera and Drama*, Part I, sect. 7) accomplished any significant change in the domestic economy of opera. At least, where Hanslick construed the "morganatic marriage" of words and music in terms of a constitutional inequity between musical nobility and an inferior poetic estate, Wagner's representation was of a more idealized, harmonious union.[23] Music may in some sense submit to poetry in allowing itself to become impregnated or fertilized with a "poetic intent," but after that the metaphor of sexual reproduction breaks down. For the offspring of this union is no separate, newborn entity, but a composite of the same music and words, the compound entity of a "musical drama." (The analogy could only be salvaged if we think of these parents as metaphysical constructions and only the offspring, the musical drama, as corporeal entity.) Even as a metaphysical construction, we are to suppose that music has willingly surrendered its autonomous free will, its (metaphysical) godhead of absolute music Brünnhilde-like to a dramatic-poetic Siegfried (see the instantiation of this allegory proposed in chapter 3). How, then, does the familiar thesis of music as "means" to a dramatic end square with the metaphysical intimations of *Beethoven*, and later texts, that music is the "source" of drama, the enabling condition, as expressed in the claims that music "contains the drama entirely within itself" or represents "the *a priori* capacity of man for the formation of drama altogether" (IX, 105, 106)? Or, as expressed in another famous phrase from the 1872 essay "On the Designation 'Music-Drama'" that constitutes the antithetical counterpart to the apothegm of "means and end," that we witness on stage "deeds of music made visible," a scenic-gestural metaphor for the quintessential drama that emanates from the mystical abyss of the Wagnerian orchestra (see IX, 305–6). Indeed, one would suppose from a passage like the following (from *Beethoven*) that the conjugal bliss of *Opera and Drama* had degenerated well beyond the standoff of Hanslick's morganatic marriage to a point where music and words were ripe for divorce:

We are all aware that music loses nothing of its character when very different words are set to it; and this fact proves that the relation of music to the *art of poetry* is an entirely illusory one; for it holds true that when music is heard with singing added thereto, it is not the poetical thought, which, especially in choral pieces, can hardly be articulated intelligibly, that is grasped by the auditor; but, at best, only that element of it which, to the musician, seemed suitable for music, and which his mind transmuted into music. A union of music with poetry must, therefore, always result in such a subordination of the latter, that

---

[23] Hanslick's original phrase was a "left-handed marriage" (*eine Ehe zur linken Hand*), modified in later editions (see Strauß/Hanslick, *Vom Musikalisch-Schönen*, vol. I, 73).

one can but be surprised at seeing how our great poets considered and re-considered the problem of a union of the two arts, or actually tried to solve it.[24]

One solution to the discrepancy with earlier doctrines is contained in the thesis of Wagner's gradual conversion to a Romantic *Kunstreligion* of pure absolute music through the teachings of Schopenhauer (the first of Nattiez's "three plots" cited in note 7). (The echoes of Schopenhauer in *Beethoven* are beyond dispute, where he is invoked by name and liberally paraphrased.) Another, compatible (and not wholly facetious) answer is that Wagner had simply become a better composer over the years, and accordingly reversed the anti-musical stance of *Opera and Drama* in favor of the Romantic aesthetic of musical autonomy, which had continued to surface from time to time since even the earliest writings (notably in those of the Parisian period around 1840). This thesis draws some sustenance from the fact that Wagner looked forward to occupying himself with the composition of symphonies – albeit of a new Wagnerian genre – upon retiring from the exhausting business of the music drama. As early as 1871 (at the very period in question here) Wagner expressed an urge to be composing "idylls and quartets," and the various traces of this urge are well known (the *Siegfried Idyll*, the speculations about a "Starnberg" quartet and the various unrealized instrumental sketches).[25]

Yet another explanation might allow that Wagner was indulging again in a rhetorical game of ping-pong, bouncing between meta-physical constructs and empirical cases. A general conception of music as a symbolic representation of a dynamic interplay of emotional gestures permits one to imagine it also as a metaphor for the fluid con-figurations of dramatic action. Yet as minuet, character-piece, or musical drama, musical forms are indebted to an extra-musical motivation (model, impulse) from the domains of dance, song, or actual drama. This, at least, would be the explanation that could hope to reconcile the disparate, conflicting components of a larger Wagnerian "theory." The same metaphysical/empirical dialectic that formed the subtext of Wagner's attempt to discredit "the advocates of an absolute music" in the 1857 open letter is invoked by Dahlhaus to explain the paradox that

[24] IX, 103; cited from E. Dannreuther, trans., *Beethoven* (London, 1880), 74. Though offered as a general observation, the context of this passage makes it clear that Wagner is speaking of a traditional status quo and not necessarily an ideal musical-dramatic condition.

[25] See, for example, CWD, 28 July 1871, and the summary by Barry Millington of these projected late orchestral essays and their surviving traces ("Orchestral Music: Plans for Overtures and Symphonies [Uncompleted]; Themes and Melodies," in *The Wagner Compendium*, 312–13), as well as the entries for WWV 98 and 107 in the *Verzeichnis der musikalischen Werke Richard Wagners* (WWV), ed. John Deathridge, Martin Geck, and Egon Voss (Mainz, 1986), 495–6, 519–24.

Wagner's musical score can be determined by the (real, empirical) drama we see unfolding before us (as described in *Beethoven* and later writings) while that same drama can be designated as a "deed" of music and thus a consequence of musical form, a metaphorical reflection of a musical "essence."[26]

Such metaphysical evasions aside, the point remains that the tendency to elevate "drama" (or even music) over words after 1870 need not be at odds with the more text-oriented reform theory of the Zurich writings, but can be understood as a change of focus, or accent. In fact, a certain prejudice against words, as such, is evident in a number of Wagner's remarks on Beethoven's Ninth, the very work traditionally assumed to symbolize the inevitable ascendancy of the "word" in Wagner's theory, the great historical signpost pointing toward the ultimate re-union of *logos* with *rhythmos* and *harmonia* in the *Gesamtkunstwerk*. When the great composer discloses to the young "R." of the Parisian story "A Pilgrimage to Beethoven" his conception of a new symphony with voices, the value of the human voice itself – as a kind of symbolic timbre – is given distinct priority over the contribution of any specific text. "Let me assure you how difficult it has been to overcome the insufficiency of whatever poetic verses I would choose for this purpose," Beethoven confides to his young admirer. "I've finally decided on Schiller's ode 'To Joy'; it's a noble and uplifting poem, at any rate, even if it can't come close to expressing that which no verses in the world could really express" (I, 111). The 1846 "program" or commentary to the Ninth similarly stresses the emergence of the human voice out of the din of instrumental chaos as the fundamental gesture (II, 61). Granted, in *The Art-Work of the Future* the word, as such, acquires a distinct potency, which infuses Wagner's discourse with a pathos of aesthetic clairvoyance. ("This word was . . . the necessary, omnipotent, all-unifying one in which the entire current of the fullest emotions could be poured; the safe harbor for the unstable wanderer; the light that illuminates the night of infinite longing: the word, which redeemed mankind cries out from the depths of humanity's heart, which Beethoven set as the crown on the peak of his musical creation. This word was: *Freude!*" [III, 96–7].) But the quasi-historical constructions of this essay continue to extol the independent achievements of music during its era of enforced isolation, and there is no talk about poetic texts providing in any sense an indispensable framework for composition or a key to comprehension during that era of classical maturation. In *Opera and Drama* the Finale of the Ninth is offered as an object lesson in the

---

[26] *Wagners Konzeption des musikalischen Dramas*, 89–93. The third section of this study ("Musik als 'Mittel' und 'Ursprung' der Musik," 89–121) takes this central conflict of Wagnerian theory as a starting point.

difference between "absolute" melody (the hymn-like theme) and poetically conditioned *Versmelodie* (the rhapsodic intonations of *"Seid umschlungen, Millionen . . ."*), and to that extent the words demand their due. But then in the Beethoven-centenary essay (as we might now expect) Wagner returns to his earlier perspective with greater force:

> . . . for in truth, it is not the sense of the words that takes hold of us when the human voice enters here, but the character of the human voice itself. Nor do Schiller's verses subsequently occupy us as much as the cordial sound of choral singing, inspiring us with the desire to join in . . . It is quite evident that Schiller's words have been somewhat forcibly appended to the principal melody; for on its own, performed by the instruments alone, this melody has already unfolded before us and filled us with an ineffable sense of joy at the paradise here regained.   (IX, 101)

Content and/or/as form

Wagner's words reinforce the fact that by the nineteenth century one could no longer convincingly equate a poetic text with the actual "content" of a musical composition, or at least any such position had become radically undermined. (The many interpretations that took Schiller's text, naturally enough, as the key to the meaning of the symphony did not necessarily take it as "content," but simply as a hermeneutic tool.) The "ineffable sense of joy" Wagner experiences in advance of the textual cues might remind us of Beethoven's appeal to the "topos of inexpressibility" in the 1840 novella – "what no verses in the world could express." Or it might be heard as an echo of the inexpressible *Rührung* of a Heinse or a Jean Paul, the otherworldly intimations of Tieck or Hoffmann, or the "devotional" transports of Herder or Wackenroder, mingling the traditions of sensibility and effect (*Wirkung*) with Romantic metaphysics.[27] Where content had become displaced from linguistic text it was sought in the effect produced by music on the listener, the feelings aroused. But so long as it was construed in reductive terms – as a kind of *précis* of what was signified, re-told, or otherwise expressed by a work of art – musical "content" was difficult to reconcile with the view of musical meaning as transverbal, inaccessible to analysis through linguistic concepts. Prior to the advent of analytical methods whereby Schenker, for instance, could propound the "true content" of the Ninth or the "Eroica" in terms of a purely musical distillate, there was no easy way of accounting for musical content (conceived as some reduced essence)

---

[27] See Dahlhaus, *The Idea of Absolute Music*, chapter 5 ("Esthetic Contemplation as Devotion") as well as chapter 4 ("The Aesthetics of Feeling and Metaphysics," esp. 62–3) on the "topos of inexpressibility" or ineffability (*Unsagbarkeitstopos*).

aside from verbal formulations of music's impact on the feelings and imagination, or else recourse to the schematics of *Formenlehre*, which would not even have satisfied the original practitioners of that discipline as a definition of musical "content."

The common-sense proposition that the content of music resides in the notes themselves, Hanslick's "sounding forms in motion," might seem to render further philosophical debate superfluous. But it cannot satisfy the demand for a reductive, essential content so long as it requires that we accept the totality of a composition as its form and content at once, a structure irreducible to any more compact meaning. Even Hanslick felt compelled, finally, to identify some higher level of content, though he postponed this until the last chapter of his book, where he somewhat reluctantly proposed that one consider the musical *theme* as such an essential or significant content, a content that is "formed" and developed in the course of the complete work. And however willing we may be to collapse the distinction of form and content in music (so as to be rid of it altogether), we should not forget the extent to which the intellectual culture of Wagner and Hanslick alike remained steeped in the binarisms of idealist metaphysics. In this historical context it was far from easy to relax the scruples of categorical thinking so far as to suppose that such a basic dichotomy as form and content might cease to apply to music at all. We can witness this difficulty not only in Hanslick's lingering hesitation to collapse these categories, but also in the vehemence with which the very suggestion of doing so was resisted almost to the end of the century. (While Dahlhaus at one point dismisses the polarity of "formalism" and an "aesthetic theory of content" as a "typical piece of nineteenth-century silliness," he also concedes its usefulness as a heuristic construct, even if "the conflict could at best be a matter of . . . emphasis.")[28]

If we include Hanslick's provocative though incomplete gesture toward the dissolution of a form/content dichotomy as one viable application of it, we might then consider nineteenth-century responses to the problematics of form and content in music according to a broad tripartite model (if only to offer some respite from the binary imperative). (1) Form and content: accepting the operation of this dichotomy in music, as well as other forms of art, one could validate the analysis of a formal object either together with or apart from some notion of content that might be reduced to verbal concepts, including (primarily) some verbal construction of an emotional content. That is, one could seek to preserve traditional philosophical or theological binarisms of essence and appearance, form and idea, body and soul (mind), etc. (2) Form or content: accepting the nominal co-existence of the dichotomy, as just

[28]   *Between Romanticism and Modernism*, 57.

described, one could choose to privilege one side over the other. To privilege "abstract" form over some conception of content was an exceptional stance, especially with regard to music, either before or after Hanslick's proposal. (A few neo-Kantians can be found to take this position, such as Johann Friedrich Herbart, Hans Georg Nägeli, and Robert Zimmermann; while early advocates of a "formalist" aesthetic were, with the exception of Nägeli, mainly philosophers, the whole tradition of "formalist" analysis since the end of the nineteenth century onwards can obviously be fit under this rubric, too.) On the other hand, a distinct majority took it as a matter of course to exalt the significance of "content" (again, normally construed as a content of "feelings," though the construction of content in more overtly literary, visual, or broadly psychological-imaginative terms was also possible). (3) Form as content: following Hanslick's lead, or appealing to earlier Romantic critical and philosophical propositions, one could pursue the significance of music as its own, irreducible essence (content), a system of merely self-signifying signs. The conviction in an affective content might be preserved so long as it could be founded on explicit compositional details. This represents something like the "Schopenhauerian" position Wagner tended to adopt after 1870, although without implementing it in critical practice to any extent. A rigorous pursuit of this view would ultimately lead to the collapse of the dichotomy espoused by such early twentieth-century writers as August Halm, Ernst Kurth, Hugo Leichtentritt, and others.[29] Unlike a strictly formalist privileging of musical structure as autonomous, sounding abstraction, this position tries to preserve something of the traditional idea of an expressive content while discouraging any notions of content or meaning not grounded in analytical observation. The fact that modern critical sentiment accepts this latter view as nearly axiomatic (and as mere common musical sense) should not blind us to the historical fact that it hardly appeared self-evident in the nineteenth century – neither necessarily desirable nor practical. The following, obviously provisional sketch of these alternative attitudes toward a form/content dichotomy in music will also attempt to situate the various positions represented in Wagner's writings, shifting as they do according to context and purpose.

---

[29] Cf. Dahlhaus, *The Idea of Absolute Music*, 39–41. This collapsing of the categories of form and content in music, which now seems to us such a self-evident proposition, has been increasingly applied to other modes and discourses where the distinction has traditionally been seen as logical, even crucial. The counter-claim – that a content of "factual historical events" can rarely be separated from the form of its discursive (narrative) representation – is especially associated with the work of Hayden White (see for example *The Content of the Form: Narrative Discourse and Historical Representation* [Baltimore and London, 1987]).

Form and content

As a conceptual scheme for aesthetic understanding, some version of the form/content dichotomy was a piece of standard intellectual baggage of early nineteenth-century culture. It might be freighted with heavy systematic import, or lightened to the extent that it remained mere ritual terminology, empty baggage. But one way or the other, it was not easily discarded; one didn't travel (philosophically or critically) without it. Even those who take a jaundiced view of the airy artifices of such metaphysical tradition should consider that we can scarcely unburden ourselves of this cognitive model, in some sense, as long as we continue to think in terms of musical "structure" and "meaning" at all, even if the latter is construed in seemingly innocuous terms of style, manner, or effect.[30] It is just this innocuous, philosophically unfreighted version we find Wagner applying in his earlier critical writings, not surprisingly, as when he distinguishes between the repertory of standard, schematic "forms" of which Auber's *opéras-comiques* are composed and the inimitable "content" (*Gehalt*) with which, at his best, he is able to infuse them (this in the Parisian essay on "Halévy and the French Opera," 1842). The content of Auber's music consists of "spirit, grace, and freshness" – in short, a kind of personal *élan* that resides in the details adorning the largely schematic phraseology of his *couplets*, ensembles, and so forth. "What, in God's name, do these forms amount to, if not filled by such content as this? They are reduced to a state of wretched poverty, small and meaningless in the extreme, completely unsuited to the expression of any genuine perceptions (*geistiger Anschauungen*)" (XII, 142).

Musical content, in this sense, is comprised of melodic ideas, rhythmic gestures, an occasional harmonic piquancy, or an inspired touch of orchestration that "fill" the conventional periodic designs, cadential formulae, strophic and ternary models, or piecemeal concatenations of the larger ensemble structures. In a broader sense, it is the sum of Auber's stylistic vocabulary, his personal imprint (*le style, c'est l'homme*). Either a technical or an evocative reading of the style (its impression or effect) might thus convey the content in the sense of a reduced essence, what

---

[30] This perseverance of the old form/content dichotomy in the categories of "structure" and "meaning," as they inform modern-day practices of analysis and criticism, is the starting point for Fred E. Maus's essay on "Music as Drama," *Music Theory Spectrum* 10 (1988), 56–73. The model he develops here for grounding an affective (or "dramatic") reading of a Beethoven quartet in analytical observation is very much congruent with Hanslick's tentatively articulated "theory" of musical processes as a metaphor for the dynamics or "physics" of the mind's life. Its similarity to Wagner's comments on the *Coriolan* overture (see below) also points up the congruity between Hanslick's and Wagner's views on classical instrumental works (at least), especially in the "post-Schopenhauer" years (however we date those).

the details boil down to – an essence which, appropriately diluted with the all-purpose formulae of compositional convention, will satisfactorily fill out the forms in question.

The reductive model of content poses a problem for music, however, as soon as it is forced to accommodate metaphysical constructions of noumenal essence or "idea," on one hand, or the representational content of literary or visual art, on the other (the underlying plot – as *fabula* or *histoire* – of a narrative, epic, or drama that precedes a specific elaboration, or the perceptible natural "object" of visual representations). While the category of "idea" might remain equally vague for any art form, it will naturally tend to lean on a representational content, where one exists. Construed in the terms of literary formalism as a fundamental plot structure or mythic archetype, the content of music might possibly be identified with structural models of fugue, ritornello, rondo, rounded binary, da capo aria, sonata allegro, and so forth (a point of contact that has, of course, been pursued in recent applications of narrative theory to music).[31] On the other hand, the venerable tradition of designating a content of "feelings" in music – whether as a "doctrine of affections" or a looser aesthetics of emotion (*Gefühlsästhetik*) – interpreted feelings or emotions both as an "object" of representation and as the metaphysical essence, content, or "idea" manifested in musical forms, as when Schopenhauer speaks of music's representation of feelings "*in abstracto,* as it were, their essential qualities, without the circumstantial detail, thus without their motivating impulse."[32] As Dahlhaus suggests,[33] an "aesthetics of feeling" and a schematic *Formenlehre* were the complementary sides of a nineteenth-century musical-aesthetic economy, a division of aesthetic labor in which the feelings that resided in details of melody, harmony, figuration, and so forth "fill" any of the available standard forms (something like Wagner's reading of form and content in Auber, in other words).

Examples of a reciprocal form/content dichotomy applied to music in the earlier nineteenth century are legion, of course, whether in philosophical discourse or in everyday criticism. As a professional authority on such matters, Hegel can perhaps be taken also as representative of the "objective," non-musician's view. The discussion of

[31] As proposed by Anthony Newcomb, for instance, in "Schumann and Late-Eighteenth-Century Narrative Strategies," *19th-Century Music* 11:2 (1987), 164–74.

[32] Arthur Schopenhauer, *Die Welt als Wille und Vorstellung,* ed. Arthur and Angelika Hübscher (Zurich, 1977), vol. I, §52, 328. Schopenhauer is suggesting, in other words, that music represents the "content" of feelings abstracted from any empirical manifestation, their "abstracted essence" (*abgezogene Quintessenz*). His suggestion that the representation of such "abstracted," objectless emotional content lacks a "motivating impulse" is a point that would concern Wagner, as discussed in chapter 6.

[33] C. Dahlhaus, "Gefühlsästhetik und musikalische Formenlehre" (1967), reprinted in *Klassische und romantische Musikästhetik* (Laaber, 1988), 335–47.

music in his *Lectures on Aesthetics*, originally delivered between 1817 and 1829, is understandably concerned with the question of musical content and whether music can be understood as representational in any consistent way (representational of any distinct "content," in other words). Where Kant was not even sure about the cognitive status of musical form (hence whether music could qualify as a fine art at all), Hegel had no reservations about its formal character. In more optimistic moments, he was even fairly sure about its content. "Music does have a content," he asserts, "but not in the sense that the visual arts or poetry have; for what it lacks is objective self-formation [*Sichausgestalten*], either forms of real external appearances or the objectivity of mental apprehensions and representations."[34] After temporizing for several paragraphs, as if not yet quite sure what sort of content music *does* have, Hegel gradually formulates two alternative answers: (1) music may derive its content from a text that it sets (the text provides the object of musical expression, the outward representation of music's "sounding inwardness," not unlike Schopenhauer's view of music as will or expression prior to its objectification); or (2) music can attempt to generate an affective content on its own, without textual object, "freely unfolding in the unfettered independence of its own realm."[35] The faint echo of Romantic panegyrics here is hardly capable of disguising a deep-seated suspicion of the preponderance of form "for its own sake" (incapable of manifesting any genuine element of "idea") that dominates the rest of Hegel's discussion of music. Music may illuminate and even enrich some aspects of a textual content (its affective stratum), but it is unclear to what extent it has really acquired a content of its own in the process. However we might assess the level of musical competency underlying Hegel's judgements, the alternative he promoted of a text-based or else an abstractly affective content remained the typical foundation for much critical writing on music through at least the middle of the century.

Adherents of an aesthetics of feeling (*Gefühlsästhetik*) in any of its manifold guises had little difficulty in defining content as those feelings inscribed in or manifested by musical forms. The demonstration of such a content, however, was generally limited to bald assertions of the semantic value of musical figures or appeals to rhetorical analogies. An aesthetics of feeling was also likely to invoke the image of form as a "container" in which a volatile, ethereal content of feelings was somehow captured and preserved. Wackenroder extended this image to all the arts in speaking of them as "monstrances" for the preservation of

---

[34] G. W. F. Hegel, *Vorlesungen über die Ästhetik*, in Hegel, *Werke*, ed. E. Moldenhauer and K. Michel (Frankfurt, 1970), vol. XV, 136.
[35] Ibid., 137.

precious relics of our inner life, but he found this image to be most appropriate to music.[36] A corollary of this conception was the thesis that music (in the absence of a textual object) served as the receptacle for the composer's own feelings, as a record of his spiritual life in the same way that the poetic lyric might be supposed to do so. A characteristic formulation is offered as an alternative to a more formalistic view of content as musical material or thematic ideas by the composer-theorist-critic-*Kapellmeister* Johann Christian Lobe, who (as we will have occasion to see) can be counted on to represent almost any widely-held musical opinion of the earlier nineteenth century, generally unobscured by original insights:

[the content of music] consists first of all in a series of musical ideas brought together into perceptible unity through the application of thematic connections and artistic forms [*thematische Bezüge und kunstgesetzliche Formen*], as a sonata, an overture, etc. It consists secondly in the expression of a feeling, that by which the composer was inspired during the act of composition.[37]

We might take the first part of this passage as an anticipation of Hanslick's makeshift definition of musical content as thematic idea (or even Adorno's notion of the "musical material"), though it also harks back to rhetorical categories of *inventio* and *dispositio* (*Erfindung, Anlage*). In any case, the relation of the musical material to a content of feelings expressed remains unaccounted for, except by the inference that the composer's acts of invention, elaboration, and arrangement serve to channel a psychic emotional content (biographically experienced) into music's sounding forms.

Wagner, too, belongs in this group – at least the Wagner of the operatic reform essays. As noted before, he clearly absorbed the conventional aesthetics of feeling in his early years alongside a Romantic "metaphysics of absolute music." Dahlhaus's attempts to separate one from the other as distinct traditions may be justifiable as a heuristic construction of "ideal types" of music-aesthetic thought, but (again) it tends to misrepresent the extent to which they could and did commingle in the general musical consciousness, as they did in Wagner's. On one hand, an aesthetics of feeling was easily assimilated to the ideology of the musical drama (or to any operatic aesthetic), as its highly visible traces in the Zurich writings demonstrate. On the other hand, while Wagner may have inveighed there against "absolute" music and anything else carrying that predicate, that did not mean he felt obligated to renounce a conviction in the mysterious, ineffable, transcendent attributes of the "language of tones" – only that he was now intent on

[36] See Dahlhaus, *The Idea of Absolute Music*, 74.
[37] J. C. Lobe, "Einige Gedanke über die malende Instrumentalmusik," *Neue Zeitschrift für Musik* 22:41 (1845), 169.

demonstrating the necessity of grounding this language in the all-important element of the "purely human" experience or consciousness.

Wagner's attitudes toward musical form and content in *Opera and Drama* are in fact not far removed from Hegel's views, despite the radical dissimilarity of their intellectual temperaments. Like Hegel, he conceded that purely instrumental music might generate a certain degree of content (conceived primarily as emotional content) within the framework of instrumental forms, the dance-derived forms of the sonata and symphony. But, also like Hegel, he suspected that instrumental music could be pushed too far – too far from the conventions of symmetrical balance, alternation, and reprise, as Wagner saw it – and lose itself in aimless speculations, disfiguring contortions, and generally futile efforts to expand the scope of its content from within. (In *Opera and Drama* Wagner explicitly drew attention to this "problem" in Beethoven's late style and the works of its misguided followers – whoever those might be; it seems likely that Hegel's denunciation of a tendency of "more recent music" to abandon a readily intelligible content was also aimed at Beethoven, whose name is conspicuously absent from the *Lectures*[38]). Like Hegel, Wagner too maintained that any more substantial emotional or "subjective" content must needs be injected from without, by means of the famous "poetic intent" (*dichterische Absicht*) as described in *Opera and Drama* – the logocentric masculine principle whose duty it was to inseminate a feminine-gendered music.

As we have seen, the reproductive metaphor begins to unravel here. It is not clear whether music thus fertilized begets a new, autonomous organism – a baby music drama. Or is music rather infused with a consciousness, a formative will it so far lacked? Is poetry in fact the seed, or just the "fertilizer" that will encourage music to transform itself, take on new shapes, to grow in ever more luxuriant profusion out and around the trellis-work of a dramatic superstructure? Retreating from this metamorphosing metaphor, we can at least see that the text-oriented theory of *Opera and Drama* preserved traditional notions of a poetic text that constitutes the content of music either as an object of expression or as a content of ideas, images, actions, feelings that are somehow transfused into the musical body. In what sense the content becomes the property of the music, if successfully metabolized, remains ambiguous.

[38] Wagner's comments on late Beethoven from *Opera and Drama*, Part I, section 5, are discussed further in chapter 2. Hegel remarks (*Werke*, vol. XV, 145) that "in recent times, especially, music has withdrawn from a clear and direct content (*von einem für sich schon klaren Gehalt*) into its own element" and hence has forfeited a wider interest by concentrating on "purely musical issues of composition and its intricacies, which are a matter for the connoisseur but of less general, humane artistic interest." Hegel's lectures would have coincided with the appearance of Beethoven's later works in the early 1820s.

The exposition of Wagner's nascent motivic "theory" in Part III of *Opera and Drama* involves a somewhat clearer construction of content as meaningful essence or extract which, infused in the fluid matter of music (to borrow from another Wagnerian metaphor, the musical "ocean") assumes an intelligible form. Here the "fundamental motifs" (*Grundmotive*) of the drama are equated with the notion of a "poetic intent" introduced in Part I, and these are said to be transmuted into music motives (*"melodische Momente"* or what we now call leitmotifs) by the composer.[39] In a well-known passage, adumbrating later descriptions of the "symphonic" qualities of musical-dramatic form, Wagner explains how this content, translated from dramatic "motifs" to musical motives, will spread out to define the musical structure as a whole:

> The musician, in realizing the poet's intent, is thus charged with ordering these motifs now condensed as musical ideas (*diese zu melodischen Momenten verdichteten Motive*), in perfect accord with the poetic intent, so that from their mutually conditioned recurrences there will emerge a perfectly unified musical form; the forms arbitrarily pieced together by composers up to now can here be replaced by a necessary, truly unified, and hence truly intelligible form as it is shaped in accordance with the poetic intent. (IV, 201)

Wagner always continued to maintain that music could be fructified or fortified by a poetic-dramatic substance, and hence surpass the limitations of "absolute" forms, although after *Opera and Drama* traditional constructions of a form/content dichotomy become notably scarce.

Form or content

Once accepted as an appropriate conceptual model for understanding music, the dichotomy of form and content might easily tempt its practitioners to privilege one category over the other. It is hardly surprising that any hard-line *Gefühlsästhetiker* would feel compelled to privilege content. So long as one acknowledges some essence or idea as the ultimate meaning of a thing, the soul that animates the form, it would seem callous to do otherwise.

Hegel, as we have seen, approached music with the expectation of finding in it a mutual reflexivity of form and content such as should characterize any fine art. He came away from it feeling unconvinced of a viable balance, suspecting that music was after all too much form and too little content.

[39] Here and throughout the remainder of the text I have attempted to distinguish orthographically between dramatic or conceptual "motifs," on one hand, and musical "motives," on the other, although I have maintained the most common English spelling of "leitmotif" (which also reproduces the German pronunciation). Both Wagner's theory and practice of motives engage the semantic and orthographic ambiguities of English usage in ways that are further elaborated in chapter 6.

[A]s I have said earlier, music has the greatest capacity among the arts not only to free itself from any actual text, but even from the expression of a distinct content, and to satisfy itself in a complete and independent course of juxtapositions, variations, oppositions and mediations, all within a purely musical sphere. But in this case it remains empty and meaningless, and, lacking a principal factor of all art – a spiritual content or expression – it could hardly be considered as art at all.[40]

Later on he reiterates even more explicitly this choice the composer faces and its consequences: in the absence of a text, the composer can aim to generate some sense of representational or emotional content from within, or else risk forfeiting the status of art altogether:

The composer, for his part, can invest his work with a particular significance, a content of representations, emotions, and their complete and organized progression; on the other hand, without bothering himself about such content, he can concern himself only with the purely musical structure of a work and the intellectual qualities of its construction. By this latter course, however, the musical production can easily become devoid of thought or emotion, something requiring no high degree of sophistication or feeling.[41]

Hegel's philosophy of music, as Dahlhaus remarks, "is stamped, in every phase of its development, with the apprehension that emancipating music, and emancipating a soul that retires into itself in 'pure sounding,' will lead off into sterility."[42] The problem lies not only in the potential preponderance of form over content, but in the peculiar nature of musical form. For Hegel, the form of music was characterized, no less than its content, by "subjective inwardness" ("music takes the subjective, as such, for both its content and form," he writes). "Subjective" is an apparently paradoxical modifier of form, but can be explained as an evaluation of the transient, immaterial and temporal nature of form in music. These very qualities had led Kant to question its status as significant "form" at all, since the melodies and chord progressions constituting musical "form" just vanished into thin air, leaving no perceptible (hence measurable) trace. Unlike other predominantly "formal" media such as architecture or ornamental design, musical form tended to defy the organizing perceptual activity of the aesthetic observer (at least, for the non-professional).

Hegel's belief that a composer could choose to privilege either form or content within a work (and ought to choose the latter) was shared by numerous critics of the time – but with a crucial difference. Where Hegel viewed technical complications as a vulgar exhibition of empty, facile virtuosity, critics within the profession would point to the

40   Hegel, *Werke*, vol. 15, 148–9.
41   Ibid., 217.
42   Carl Dahlhaus, *Esthetics of Music*, trans. William Austin (Cambridge, 1982), 49.

increasing differentiation of modern musical means as precisely the source of the augmented "content" they advocated. Chromaticism, textural and timbral variety offered by larger orchestras, "new" harmonic combinations or enharmonic progressions, expanded and loosened periodic structures, the judicious modification of formal prototypes became the means of constructing a more emphatic, more determinate content. For the average "professional" critic, an excess of form or, conversely, a dearth of content normally signified the schematic application of received formal patterns lacking in melodic invention or originality of detail (for example, the kinds of characteristic detail that constituted the *Gehalt* of Auber's music for Wagner). Our trusted jack-of-all-musical-trades, J. C. Lobe, invokes the universally derogatory epithet of "a mere play of tones" in distinguishing music *with* content from music *without*:

A perfectly pleasing form may be present [in a composition] . . . without any clear reflection of an object [of expression], without any truth of expression, that is. In that case the composition is a mere play of tones, which may at best afford an external pleasure through its form, but can never produce any effect on our emotions.[43]

Where Hegel feared that lack of content would result from an "excess" of form, Lobe (like most critics) implies that it is rather a consequence of deficient form, or lack of attention to the details of "inner form" as well as to the framework of "outer form."[44] The fact that Lobe's own compositional treatise of 1844 is well-nigh obsessed with the virtues of thorough thematic-motivic development is sufficient evidence that he perceived an affinity between meaningful content and the elaboration of "inner" form.

A certain discomfort with form as a critical category is by no means alien to professional musicians and critics, as Lobe's comments testify. If schematic or mechanical conceptions of form were, as Dahlhaus posits, a natural corollary of the reigning aesthetics of feeling, it is hardly surprising that professionals and amateurs alike would adopt a disparaging attitude toward the category of form. (Hanslick puzzled over the fact that only philosophers seemed willing to acknowledge the concrete "formal" causes of musical effects.) But suspicion toward the nature of musical form was above all a product of the conceptual opposition between the "science" and "poetry" of music that was

---

43 J. C. Lobe, "Ästhetische Briefe" no. 1, *Fliegende Blätter für Musik* 1:4 (1855), 189.

44 Though this distinction between an "inner" and "outer" form – that between the processive formation of a work on a detailed level and the abstract "structure" that results – does not reflect historical usage, it does recall aspects of a standard form/content dichotomy as represented in the preceding section (the distinction between affective detail and schematic formal paradigms, for example). On the "inner/outer" dichotomy, see also Mark Evan Bonds, *Wordless Rhetoric: Musical Form and the Metaphor of the Oration* (Cambridge MA, 1991), 1–3.

most characteristic of an amateur or non-specialist perspective. Joseph Berglinger, the hero of W. H. Wackenroder's eponymous musical *Bildungsnovelle*, is afflicted by the aporias of this dichotomy in a manner that surely reflects Wackenroder's own misgivings as an enthusiastic amateur. Having patiently acquired skills of the musical profession, Berglinger can only bemoan the disillusionment this drudgery has caused him, as one who used to "soar freely" in the tonal empyrean, without bothering about the details of its molecular composition – "it was a wretched, mechanical business."[45] Berglinger's disillusionment with the *mühselige Mechanik* of music is, on one hand, only one manifestation of Wackenroder's typically Romantic anxiety over the disjunction of "poetry" and "science" in all of the arts. But at the same time, it represents the roots of a strong anti-analytical prejudice that would remain particularly characteristic for critical attitudes toward music for several generations, at least. The prejudice is frequently met in the form of metaphors of anatomical dissection (such as in Schumann's sheepish apology for his analysis of the *Symphonie fantastique*), where analytical scrutiny is regarded as a necessary evil that cannot fully escape the onus of sacrilege against the biological integrity of the artistic organism.[46] Such disclaimers also betray something of the bad conscience of the aesthetics of feeling, however. For Berglinger, the inability to reconcile the poetry and science of music is only a symptom of a broader strain of Romantic cultural anomie resulting from the antagonism between art and life in general, as expressed in the other Berglinger fragments. In listening to music, he exists in a wash of feelings he can hardly account for (like Hanslick's "pathological listener"), nor has any wish to, knowing that they are the products of an artifice he thinks he despises.

Like most nineteenth-century composers who also indulged in the production of literary texts, Wagner condoned this anti-analytical prejudice, at least by negative example: only a tiny fraction of his vast corpus of critical writings is devoted to descriptive analytical discourse of any kind. He also subscribed to a more or less conventional aesthetics of feeling, which serves as a foundation for much of the operatic "theory" of the Zurich writings. *Opera and Drama*, for instance, is thoroughly saturated with conventional adages about music as an "art of expression" or "an unmediated language of the emotions" (*eine Kunst des Ausdrucks, die unmittelbare Sprache des Herzens* – III, 243, 245). It is possible that the discourse of *Gefühlsästhetik* is part of a rhetorical strategy in these

---

45 L. Tieck and W. H. Wackenroder, *Herzensergießungen eines kunstliebenden Klosterbruders* (Berlin, 1797), ed. R. Benz (Stuttgart, 1975), 118.

46 Fred E. Maus remarks on some of the implications of this trope of analysis as "dissection" as it is invoked, again apologetically, even by the "formalist" Hanslick ("Hanslick's Animism," *Journal of Musicology* 10:3 [1992], 289).

writings designed to touch the sympathies of a broad audience of the cultured bourgeoisie, outside the ranks of professional musicians. But there is little reason to doubt that Wagner himself accepted this discourse as a natural and correct one. An aesthetics of feeling was, again, perfectly compatible with almost any theory of vocal music, in which the musical "language of feelings" complements the representation of determinate concepts, images, and situations through words (as for Hegel or Schopenhauer). It was likewise consistent with the perception of instrumental music as limited to a restricted repertoire of conventional forms or formal principles.[47] Wagner cites as proof of the aesthetic bankruptcy of opera since Rossini the fact that its "forms" – its predictably square-cut "absolute melodies" – have become its actual content, while the poetic text (the proper source of a poetic content in Wagner's theory just as in conservative Enlightenment tradition) has been demoted to the role of a mere vehicle for these forms, as so much syllabic material cut to order. "Strictly speaking, it was now [after Rossini] left to the musician to write the drama, to make his music constitute not just an expression [of the drama] but its very content" (III, 243; see also III, 313–14). Paradoxically, a statement which out of context suggests the glorification of the purely musical (musical form as the "content" of the drama) is meant here as a condemnation. The idea that music (form) should usurp the rights of poetry or drama (content) is dismissed as an absurd perversion.

Of course, Wagner would eventually arrive at a very different evaluation of music as the "content of drama" (after 1870), but it is relatively rare to find any critic explicitly privileging musical form over ideas of content in the first half of the century. The "theory of instrumental music" propounded in Hans Georg Nägeli's *Vorlesungen über Musik* (*Lectures on Music*, 1828) has often been cited as an ancestor to Hanslick's "formalism," and, like Hanslick, Nägeli's aim is to correct the misconceptions resulting from an unreflective, amateur perspective. Indeed, the Calvinist sobriety of Nägeli's opinions (he was a Swiss pastor, as well as music theorist, educator, and publisher) seems almost deliberately calculated to forestall the ill effects of Berglinger's effusive *Schwärmerei*, much as the formalist doctrines of a later generation could be understood as a corrective to the hedonistic indulgences of aesthetically undisciplined Wagnerians and their ilk. "Music has no content," Nägeli asserts, contrary to what has generally been supposed, and what people have tried to read into music ("ihr andichten wollte"). "It

---

[47] See Dahlhaus, "Gefühlsästhetik und musikalische Formenlehre" (see n. 33). Dahlhaus also mentions here the trope of structural analysis as anatomical dissection, citing (for example) A. W. Ambros's designation of musical *Formenlehre* as a "comparative anatomy" of music, distinct from the aesthetic analysis of music's "soul" or spirit (335).

has only forms, combinations of tones and scales regulated according to a whole."[48] Rather than reproducing psychological or emotional conditions (*Gemüthszustände*) it reproduces only their movement (*Gemüthsbewegungen*); music is essentially movement and "play." Like Hanslick's notion that music simulates the dynamics of emotional or psychological experience – which is indeed anticipated here – Nägeli's thesis of music as "play" offers a basis for an alternative understanding of musical affect, and one that has been variously explored by twentieth-century writers on the topic of musical expression: music can very well "play at" being (appearing, sounding, behaving) happy or sad, without necessarily arousing real, objective feelings in the listener.[49] Like the conviction I have ascribed to the majority of "professional" critics – even where they did not always fully articulate it – that a more variegated "inner form" will yield a richer affective content, Nägeli proposes that a musical work will be "good and effective" in pro-portion to the quality of its play: "the richer its forms, the more full of play a composition is, the fuller and more accurate (*allseitiger, unfehlbarer*) its effect . . ."[50] Nonetheless, Nägeli's rhetoric of a musical play of tones (*Formenspiel*) was bound to render him suspect in the eyes of most contemporaries, and his immediate influence remained limited to his advocacy of the "Pestalozzi method" applied to musical pedagogy and to miscellanies of simple *Hausmusik* he supplied to the bourgeois market. It remained for Hanslick to articulate a critique of the con-ventional *Gefühlsästhetik* in terms that would effectively challenge it.

With the unequivocal assertion that the "content of music consists purely and simply of sounding forms in motion" Hanslick attempted to collapse the dichotomy by invoking an alternative, rational-empirical definition of content as the material comprising any given object, as opposed to some non-objective "essence" requiring the mediation of interpretive analysis. Such a rational, materialist posture was difficult to maintain consistently, and it is well known that Hanslick did not refrain from waxing metaphysical about music's symbolic reflections of "great universal laws" and "movements" of the cosmos.[51] Empirical

---

48 H. G. Nägeli, *Vorlesungen über Musik mit Berücksichtigung der Dilettanten* (Stuttgart and Tübingen, 1826), 32.

49 This view of representation is developed under the rubric of "make-believe" by Kendall Walton, for instance, in *Mimesis as Make-Believe* (Cambridge MA, 1990).

50 Nägeli, *Vorlesungen über Musik*, 33.

51 Hanslick was subsequently persuaded to remove some of these offending passages at the urging of his "formalist" colleague, Robert Zimmermann; see Rudolf Schäfke, *Geschichte der Musikästhetik*, 380, and Strauß/Hanslick, *Vom Musikalisch-Schönen*, vol. II. Dahlhaus argues that these passages were no mere ornament, accidental remnants of the views Hanslick meant to oppose, but were instead implicit in the very proposition of an autonomous art-work, understood as a "whole perfected in itself," in the words of K. P. Moritz (*The Idea of Absolute Music*, 28–9).

and metaphysical interpretations of the nature of "absolute music" prove to be difficult to keep apart. And, unlike Nägeli, Hanslick was loath to dispense with the category of content altogether, as we have seen, hoping that he could salvage it in some specifically musical sense. In moving from the underrepresented view that would privilege form over content to our third category (the provisional collapsing of the dichotomy), let me focus on the two leading figures of Hanslick and Wagner, and how Hanslick's attempted empirical philosophy of absolute music ultimately harmonizes with the Romantic metaphysics gradually re-assimilated by Wagner, with the assistance of Schopenhauer.

The second chapter of *On the Beautiful in Music* is devoted to a demonstration of the negative thesis that neither feelings nor their representation can legitimately be understood as the content of music. This is also where Hanslick begins to develop his alternative thesis that music might be understood to embody the dynamic properties of feelings or other types of experience in the guise of "musical ideas" that exhibit a structural analogy to these mental processes. For the time being he resists designating these dynamic analogies as "content," perhaps because he has so far insisted on content as representational act and is unsure to what extent his dynamic analogies might legitimately constitute representations. This doubt would be consistent with the conviction that musical properties cannot be attached to any concrete or nameable feeling in a binding, exclusive relationship.

The fact that Hanslick returns to the issue of form and content in his last chapter suggests that he was not quite satisfied with his own earlier equation of content with "sounding forms." At any rate, he must have sensed that this explanation was likely to be resisted by a culture so wholly committed to metaphysical dichotomies of form and content. So, evidently resigning himself to the impossibility of dismissing entrenched epistemologies, Hanslick directs his efforts at finding some analogy to a reductive, essential construction of content in "specifically musical" terms, ultimately arriving at the proposition of a thematic or motivic "content."

One designates as the "form" of a symphony, overture, sonata, aria, chorus, etc. the architectonics of the [musical] details and groups of which the piece consists. More specifically, the form is the symmetry of these parts in their sequential arrangement, contrasts, reprise and development. The content of such architectonics, then, would be the themes on which it is based. There is no more question of content as "object" here, but only of a musical content.[52]

Theme or motive (both terms appear in the larger context of this passage) represent the smallest meaningful unit into which a composition

---

[52] *Vom Musikalisch-Schönen*, 101.

can be divided, whether viewed in terms of rhetorical "invention" or organic seed. (Hanslick's reference to the "organic unfolding of a composition, like the profuse blossoming of a bud" signals his own allegiance to organic doctrines, not surprisingly.) As a parting concession to those who will not be satiated with a content of such paltry motivic grains he does offer a broader alternative category of "substance" (*Gehalt*). Rather than isolated thematic building blocks, this spiritual or intellectual substance (*geistiger Gehalt*) embraces the work as a whole and very much recalls Wagner's earlier use of the same term in describing the "content" of Auber's forms, denoting the overall style or character of a work. Here too, style is read as a manifestation of the composer's musical personality or physiognomy. Beyond this, the "substance" of a work entails such other unquantifiables as the level of overall technical proficiency it demonstrates and the general density of musical thought – the evidence of what Hanslick calls the "activity of the mind within a material suited to it" (*Arbeit des Geistes in geistfähigem Material*).

It is tempting to hear in Hanslick the voice of empirical common sense, a voice which others (like Wagner) tacitly heard and believed, even while they remained unwilling to renounce openly their illusory faith in a transcendent musical content of feelings or ideas. Did Wagner gradually confess, in his later writings, to such a tacit belief in the ultimate autonomy of musical value and meaning, as some have proposed – at least as far as he could do so without appearing to recant his own dogma of the art-work of the future and thereby risk the disillusionment of an ever-growing Wagnerian cult? Specifically, did Schopenhauer's views on music (which Wagner had willingly absorbed in his enthusiasm for the larger philosophical project) in fact open Wagner's eyes to the inherent logic of Hanslick's propositions, despite all the differences of tone, ideology, and personal history between them? Rather than perpetuating a discourse of abstract ideas and recapitulating themes that have been sufficiently developed elsewhere (especially given Wagner's dim view of unmotivated reprises), let me turn to a pair of examples drawn from Hanslick and Wagner, respectively.

Form as content
(Prometheus and Coriolanus, Hanslick and Wagner)

In proposing to demonstrate the vacuity of a "content of feelings" in music Hanslick adduces as a "randomly chosen" test case the opening eight bars of the Allegro molto con brio of Beethoven's overture to *The Creatures of Prometheus*. Two years earlier, Wagner had drafted a "programmatic commentary" to Beethoven's *Coriolan* overture in connection with performances of the work he was to conduct in Zurich. The commentary, together with a pair of letters to two early Wagnerian adepts, Hans von Bülow and Theodor Uhlig, touching on this and related themes, detail Wagner's insights into the "poetic object" of Beethoven's overture, hence its "content" in terms of the predominant aesthetic discourse of the time. In the 1870 *Beethoven* essay Wagner returns briefly to *Coriolan* as an example of the inherently dramatic character of music, or musical form, even as purely instrumental music (the term "absolute music" is avoided). More precisely, he suggests how the "complex of Beethoven's motive-world, with its irresistible penetration and distinctness" offers an analogue to Shakespeare's drama; not to the full text of *Coriolanus* (which Wagner by now seems to realize was not the nominal subject of Beethoven's composition, in any case), but "the innermost kernel of this action or story (*Handlung*)," represented in apparently autonomous musical form. (Wagner speaks of the musical "sphere" and its own "laws of extension [*Ausdehnung*] and motion [*Bewegung*]" – IX, 107–8.) What emerges from these respective assessments of musical content in relation to its form?

Example 1.1 Beethoven, *The Creatures of Prometheus*, Overture (mm. 17–24)

In elucidating the "content" of the opening eight measures of the main Allegro of Beethoven's *Prometheus* overture (Example 1.1), Hanslick indulges in a rare piece of "formalist" analysis. A figure in rapid eighth notes rises and falls around a tonic center, like "pearling drops," answered in a slightly varied consequent phrase beginning on the second degree of the scale and settling on the dominant. The simple sequential model and the rhythmic pattern of the accompaniment (four tonic downbeats with a subdivided third measure) constitute a simple and satisfying piece of variety within unity.[53] The "notes themselves" and perhaps this reassuring impression of aesthetic balance constitute the only discernible "content." Hanslick has only described the opening theme, of course, but that would be consistent with his later thesis of theme as the essential content which is then "formed" by process of addition, contrast, and development. (Hanslick was presumably unaware, as yet, of the proximity of his thesis to Baroque affective-rhetorical constructions of form.) He could easily have extended his purview to include the brief, mock-stately adagio introduction, the motivically significant *sforzando* gesture introduced in the bridge (mm. 37ff) or the second theme (mm. 49ff), airily enunciated by staccato woodwinds and every bit as well-behaved as the first theme. The general picture wouldn't change. We still have a splendidly classical example of that very "play of tones" which conservative formalists were suspected of advocating, and precious little evidence of any emotional content likely to satisfy a hearty Romantic appetite. (Where a *Prometheus* surely ought to serve up a spirit-drenched *flambé* extravaganza, rich and complex, we get something more like cucumber sandwiches or *petit-fours*.)

There is, of course, nothing to stop us from reading a content of feelings here, in the traditional, corrupt manner Hanslick was opposing, or, more broadly, a content in terms of the characteristic impression (manner, tone) generated by themes, phrases, or the composition as a whole, in the sense we have seen adopted by Wagner and others. This content is one of bubbling high spirits, scampering intrigue, and an occasional outburst of comic surprise, dismay, or mere impertinence – in short, the world of *opera buffa*. Not much reflection is needed to conclude that Hanslick was thoroughly disingenuous in speaking of a "randomly chosen example." The discrepancy between title (hence presumed object) and "musical content" is just as apparently egregious here as in the celebrated case of Gluck's "Che farò?", which Hanslick introduced into subsequent editions. What sort of "Promethean" content is this, and coming from that most Promethean of all artists, who had

[53] As Fred Maus notes ("Hanslick's Animism," 291), Hanslick slightly misquotes the example, deferring the subdivided measure by one. Maus suggests that Hanslick's choice of example may not have been "entirely random" (as I will argue here, too), but Maus's suggestion of Hanslick's motive – that he identifies with the eagle of the Promethean myth, "grimly mutilating the music as punishment for its claims to animation and warmth" – seems wildly implausible (whether as conscious or subconscious impulse). Similarly, while the general "animistic" features of Hanslick's language highlighted in Maus's essay are evident enough, the erotics of the text uncovered here require some pretty heavy critical stimulation.

supposedly proclaimed his mission to bring "fire to the hearts of men" (not to mention tears to the women)? We might press the music a little more in hopes of extracting some more suitable content: perhaps the V_2^4/IV that begins the introduction (close kin to the gesture that so often passes for an intimation of revolution in the opening of the First Symphony); perhaps the shadow of *Sturm und Drang* momentarily cast across the recapitulation in the form of a developmental interpolation (mm. 133–64), or the climactic foray to $\flat$VI in the coda (mm. 243–8)? But no, these little disruptions are easily assimilated into the comic-opera vision. Indeed, Beethoven seems to be prophesying little more than Rossini here. (Not only the "content" – or manner – of the Rossinian overture is anticipated here, but even its form – a sonata allegro without development – except for those small developmental touches introduced into the recapitulation.) The rhetorical question Hanslick later posed with reference to the Gluck example is prompted here, as well. Surely music possesses far more appropriate accents ("weit bestimmtere Töne") for the expression of Orpheus's bereavement, or – in the case of Prometheus – for the titanic defiance of Olympian authority, the torments subsequently endured, and (one would hope) an ultimate spiritual transcendence? If Beethoven could get no closer than this, then music evidently has no expressive content worth speaking of. That Hanslick did not spell out these inferences would suggest either a stylistic disinclination to belabor the obvious, or perhaps a certain compunction for choosing such easy targets. (Perhaps he realized, moreover, that in alluding to "more appropriate accents" his argument carried within it the seeds of its own potential destruction.)

Coriolan, on the other hand, has all the appropriate accents (more appropriate to *Prometheus*, as well, as Hanslick might have conceded – and in demonstrating the interchangeability of the titles he would have won half his argument, anyway). Wagner, in 1852, speaks unequivocally of the representation (*Darstellung*) of an object (*Gegenstand*). At one level, this representation is one of "feelings," in terms of conventional music aesthetics. The music represents not the concrete externals of the plot and its "political relationships," Wagner asserts, but only the configuration of emotional or psychological impulses underlying them ("Stimmungen, Gefühle, Leidenschaften und deren Gegensätze.")[54] And true to the interpretation of absolute music expounded in the Zurich writings, the musical representation of this configuration is derived from the structural archetypes of dance movement, i.e., as a confrontation of gendered principles: man (Coriolanus) and woman (the entreaties of mother, wife, and children that he relax his stance of treasonous

---

[54] See the letter of 15 February 1852 to von Bülow regarding the *Coriolan* overture and Wagner's programmatic commentary (Wagner, *Sämtliche Briefe*, vol. IV, 275).

defiance and return to the cause of his Roman fatherland). The conflict of crossed allegiances can only be resolved in Coriolanus's demise (famously depicted in Beethoven's expiring coda). Wagner's commentary does attempt to relate, at least by inference, certain elements of the conceptual drama with specifics of theme (defiant introduction, alternately agitated and still defiant main theme, beseeching second theme), process (the dialogue between beseeching second theme and gestures of resistance [mm. 62–3, 70–1] that initiates a sequential intensification of the theme from E♭ through F minor to G minor), and form (the counterpoint of the dotted rhythmic motive of mm. 19–20, 26–33, etc. with the accompaniment figure of the second group, suggesting the psychological counterpoint of Coriolanus's growing anxiety and indecision against the familial forces of entreaty; recapitulation and coda as renewed yet consistently weakened resolution of defiance; coda as the final collapse and inevitable consequence of relaxing that defiance which is, Wagner says, the veritable substance of Coriolanus's character). While Wagner thus attempts to correlate musical gestures with dramatic motifs, he also explains that Beethoven has necessarily organized these conceptual dramatic motifs in accordance with certain dictates of musical form, that is, by matching musical gestures to such appropriate formal functions as introduction, first or second theme group, development, and the initiation or the resolution of a coda. Dramatic ideas (character and dramatic configuration) might motivate the invention and disposition of musical ideas, but only after the drama has been re-conceived in musical terms (the burden of Wagner's 1857 open letter on the symphonic poem). And to speak of "musical terms" in this sense implies some notion of structural or procedural principles that are "absolute" at least in the sense of being somehow instinctively – or conventionally – suited to the means of tonal music.

Wagner's interpretation of the *Coriolan* overture as the representation of a poetic-dramatic object was designed according to a particular function, to convey the "content" of the work to the audience of his Zurich concerts in a way that would promote their understanding of the composition. There is no reason to doubt, though, his own conviction in the broader validity of these insights or in this manner of constructing them, as the letters to von Bülow and Uhlig testify.[55] In the writings from the immediately preceding years Wagner had been at pains to demonstrate the limitations of "absolute music" with regard to the expression of such a poetic content (or the "realization of a poetic

---

[55] These letters are given in translation in *Selected Letters of Richard Wagner*, trans. and ed. Stewart Spencer and Barry Millington (New York, 1988), 249–53 and 253–5. See also T. Grey, "Wagner, the Overture, and the Aesthetics of Musical Form," *19th-Century Music* 12:1 (Summer 1988), 17–19.

intent"). But here, outside the openly self-serving polemics of the Zurich writings, in a context devoted to the practical appreciation of an instrumental work from Beethoven's still eminently intelligible middle period, Wagner is perfectly willing to confirm the "dramatic" capacities of the mature classical idiom. In what ways, then, do the comments from the 1870 essay confess a "new" or regained faith in the idea of absolute music, inspired by the testimony of the revered Schopenhauer, the inner epiphany of *Tristan und Isolde*, or perhaps even the sharply-worded polemics of Hanslick? It needn't be looked on as special pleading for some higher, inner consistency to Wagner's thought to say that the difference is mainly a matter of emphasis (the same applies to the manifest differences between the 1852 commentary and the ideas on Beethoven and instrumental music propounded in *Opera and Drama*).

The case for a more or less concrete "object" as described in the 1852 program is merely alluded to in 1870, in a more condensed form (the family delegation sent to plead with Coriolanus has been reduced to the mother alone), as the dramatic *Hauptmotive*: Coriolanus's defiance and Volumnia's entreaties.

Beethoven chooses for his drama only these two principal motifs [*Hauptmotive*] which, more distinctly than any conceptual presentation, let us feel the inner nature of these two figures. If we now devote our full attention to the movement evolving entirely from the confrontation of these two motifs and their respective musical characters, and allow ourselves to be affected by the purely musical detail contained in the various gradations, points of contact and departure, and intensifications (*Abstufungen, Berührungen, Entfernungen, und Steigerungen*) of these [musical] motives, then we are also following a drama that expresses in its own way that which the stage-poet's work presented to us as a complicated action involving manifold subsidiary characters.   (IX, 107)

Dramatic "motifs" are transmuted into musical motives in Wagner's prose here through the alchemy of its characteristically distended syntax. The dramatic motifs singled out by Beethoven are imperceptibly converted here into musical motives (further ramifications of this are taken up in chapter 6). The equation is made more explicit later in the paragraph, where the "musician's motives" are said to be "identical in their innermost nature" with the psychological motives at work within the individual characters. Music represents the "innermost kernel" of the dramatic action.

Here, indeed, is Schopenhauer's voice emanating from Wagner's pen. Music "gives the innermost kernel of things" – this was Schopenhauer's message, too. (Music is able to mimic, re-enact, or simulate the "form" of mental processes, subconscious motivations, the variegated and largely unnameable activities of the Will, he proposed.) Wagner is more conscious in the 1870 essay of something he appeared to sense already in 1852: that traditional talk about feelings was not really adequate to the way he understood the representation of the dramatic "object" in this music. And it is perfectly possible that Schopenhauer's musings on the nature of music had contributed to a new manner of formulating his perceptions. One could well begin with emotional attributes of "defiance" or "supplication" in characterizing certain thematic gestures. But what actually goes on in this composition, or in most, is not easily encompassed by a handful of such words, which can describe states of mind, but not the interior action (*Handlung*) they generate. The striking introductory gesture of mm. 1–4 can be said to express an attitude of defiance, the classic Beethovenian posture of the clenched fist and fierce scowl. But what of the particular metrical pattern of arsis and thesis set up at two-measure intervals, so that the main theme itself enters (m. 15) in a weak measure and leaves a strong measure unsettlingly empty (m. 21) after the offbeat "shake of the fist" that articulates the end of the first phrase – or again at m. 28, after the same fist shake, half-restrained? What of the dialogue of strings and woodwinds occupied with Coriolanus's "motive of agitation," if you will, in the development (mm. 118ff)? What of the *echt*-Beethovenian fourth-beat *sforzandi* and the further metrical displacement of the main eighth-note motive to the second beat in the transition (mm. 46–50) and the amplification of this procedure in the recapitulation (mm. 167–76)? Maybe these, too, could be construed as expressive gestures of a kind, and as musical and psychological consequences of other gestures and events. But the more closely one tries to account for them, the further one is driven from the vocabulary of affective characterization to a more "analytical" discourse, or at least one of actions and consequences, in which verbs demand an equal space with adjectives. For Schopenhauer, an "explanation of music, perfectly correct, exhaustive, and descending into minute details," a "comprehensive reproduction of that which music expresses" would be the equivalent of a "true philosophy" and a satisfactory explanation of the world of phenomena and concepts.[56] For Wagner it would describe the essence (hence content?) of the drama. Whether a comprehensive analytical description or some other form of detailed music-theoretical discourse would have struck either of them as philosophy or as drama remains a question. But, though Wagner offers less by way of analysis in his 1870 comments than in 1852, the accentuation of "purely musical detail" or the "movement belonging entirely to the musical character" of the motives and their interaction is unmistakable. In place of affective descriptions we now read of "gradations, points of contact and departure, and intensifications."

This language recalls a description Wagner had given some years earlier of Act III of *Tristan und Isolde*. No one would deny that "feelings"

---

[56] Schopenhauer, *Die Welt als Wille und Vorstellung*, vol. I, §52; cf. Wagner, *Beethoven* (trans. Dannreuther), appendix, 173.

are in some sense expressed in the music of this third act (indeed, feelings run amok). Wagner frames his description of the musical "content" of Act III (up to the moment of Tristan's death) in emotive terms: a range of wild fluctuations between "the most extreme longing for joy" and "the most decisive yearning for death" (the entire gamut of *Sehnsucht*, as it were). But in directing the reader's attention to the musical score and the motivic activity of the *Orchestermelodie*, he changes to a verb-oriented discourse describing "the musical motives restlessly surfacing, evolving, combining, separating, then melting together, growing, reducing, further contesting with each other, embracing, almost devouring one another . . ."[57] This veritable cavalcade of present participles is, like the 1870 *Coriolan* passage, neither a primarily affective description, nor, certainly, a technical analysis. It is a more extensive example of an attempted discourse of musical action or *Handlung*, an attempt to convey something of the parallel Wagner perceived between drama and the processes of musical form.

To this extent it might be fair to say that Wagner had indeed "converted" to a belief in absolute music. In locating the essential qualities of the drama in "sounding forms in motion" (to use Hanslick's phrase), Wagner had effectively cancelled those indignant judgements passed in *Opera and Drama* on operatic music that presumed to constitute "its own content." It may be true that the dramatic end served by the musical means was to be understood there as a musical-dramatic end product, not simply the dramatic text itself. The formula still holds, but the dramatic share now accorded to the score is significantly greater. Of course, it might also be argued that *Coriolan* is not a music drama, and the *Beethoven* essay is – at least ostensibly – not about Wagner, but about Beethoven. Suffice it to say that the neo-Schopenhauerian construction of music as the metaphysical essence of dramatic action leads to the conclusion, in the terms of conventional nineteenth-century aesthetic reasoning, that music is therefore a kind of dramatic *content* and the principal "end" of the musical drama (the poetic text, as motivating factor, could likewise be re-construed as a means).

The inadvertent reconciliation with Hanslick (at an abstract aesthetic level, at least) certainly owes something to the assimilation of Schopenhauer's ideas on music, to which Wagner seems not to have given much attention before the *Beethoven* essay. As a conception of the whole range of activity of the unconscious mind – all its inarticulate appetites, drives, desires, reflexes to pleasure and pain that precede conscious action – the activity of the Schopenhauerian Will is at once

---

[57] "die rastlos auftauchenden, sich entwickelnden, verbindenden, trennenden, dann neu sich verschmelzenden, wachsenden, abnehmenden, endlich sich bekämpfenden, sich umschlingenden, gegenseitig fast sich verschlingenden musikalischen Motive" ("Meine Erinnerungen an Ludwig Schnorr von Carolsfeld" [1868], VIII, 185).

the fundamental stratum of the Wagnerian *Handlung* and the "motion of a psychic process" (according to such dynamic spectra as fast and slow, strong and weak, rising and falling) that Hanslick claimed to be the only point of contact between music and "feelings."[58] Where Hanslick, in pointing out music's limitation to such dynamic analogies, meant to invalidate the notion that music could represent any empirically conditioned feeling ("love" rather than fond flattering breezes or some other appropriate quality of motion), these dynamic properties (like those of the Will) are in Schopenhauer's view more pertinent, more fundamental than the specific concept or instance they might represent (whether "love" as such, Armida's love for Roland, Tristan's for Isolde, or Richard's for Mathilde). For Schopenhauer, the movements of the Will constitute a perfectly valid content for music, one that is essentially congruent with its form. All of Wagner's talk about the importance of drama as action (*Handlung*), gesture, or scenic event will seem ill-founded or simply perverse until we consider "action" in terms of the activity of the Will in this sense – a point that has been made often enough about *Tristan*, but applies to the music dramas in general. The music does most of the acting, leaving the singers little to do but sing (often that's enough), or perhaps cast meaningful glances, as Wagner was always exhorting them to do.

And what about *Prometheus* vs. *Coriolan*? Congruent aesthetic insights do not necessitate a congruence of taste or technique. Schopenhauer, after all, may have preferred to hear the Will reflected in Rossini, Hanslick may have found its dynamic activities most artfully enacted by Schumann or Mendelssohn. There is no reason to suppose that Wagner would have claimed to hear much more than pearly scales, symmetrical phrasing, and a tiny intensification-relaxation pattern in the eight measures of the *Prometheus* overture, the Will in one of its more playful and un-Promethean moods. Hanslick would presumably have agreed that the themes or musical ideas of *Coriolan* are more pregnant with significance than his example, more original, more extensive, more intense. The careless critics Hanslick castigates would maintain that *Coriolan* preserves the same "form" as the earlier overture, but imbues it with "more content" (on reflection, some of them might note formal distinctions here, too).

The content of the *Coriolan* overture is greater than that of *Prometheus* not simply because of a greater quantity of notes or thicker scoring, but because (in contemporary critical terms) it is more "distinct," due to the quality of the musical ideas and their subsequent "formation." "Distinctness" or "determinacy" (*Bestimmtheit*) of expression was a value widely shared, although not easily articulated, especially for

---

[58] "die Bewegung eines psychischen Vorgangs," *Vom Musikalisch-Schönen*, 16.

critics working on the premise that music represented abstract or even "indistinct" (indeterminate) feelings. Schopenhauer, who also shared something like these premises, tried to assert that the musical embodiment of "abstract" emotions need not remain indistinct (voicing, in other words, a general Romantic conviction that music conveyed distinct impressions in its own peculiar, inarticulate way): "Its generality is, however, in no sense that empty generality of [conceptual] abstraction, but of an entirely different order, and is connected with thoroughgoing, clear distinctness."[59] Yet a critical account of this higher "determinacy" of musical expression (or content) remained problematic. How do we reconcile the ineffability of absolute music celebrated by a Romantic poetics with an increasing popular demand for "determinate expression," if we resist Dahlhaus's aesthetic class distinctions of genuine Romanticism and a degenerate, popular aesthetic of emotional content and "ideas"? It was precisely this collision of values that Wagner was able to put to work in his polemical writings at the middle of the century.

Absolute music and "ideas": a new determinacy?

A greater part of musicians, critics, and listeners up to and well beyond the middle of the nineteenth century conceived as the mission of music in their time (to adopt an appropriately imperialistic figure) the conquest of a new world of ideas, first sighted by Beethoven – Wagner's musical "Columbus" – and now to be colonized with the help of modern harmony, orchestration, developmental techniques, and other such contemporary musical technologies. By broad consensus, music was only just now reaching its belated age of majority, a stage reached by its sister arts several centuries earlier (at least in their modern-Christian life cycle). Among the obligations of this maturity was not only a higher standard of technical proficiency, but a capacity for the expression of ideas, to articulate an individual identity. As Kant proclaimed that mankind rose above its state of intellectual "minority" (*Unmündigkeit*) through the perfection of reason, so music's rise to majority, its place among the fine arts, was seen by many as a function of a new-found ability to "speak," to articulate ideas (*mündig* suggesting literally the attainment of voice, the right to be heard). The *Prometheus* and *Coriolan* overtures are emblematic of this change, as paragons of Beethoven's early and middle styles, respectively. The few years separating these two works represent the decisive step in the composer's career, in which he helped music come of age. The innocuous "play on tones" of the earlier work gives way to the distinct expression of "ideas," of an ideal (or for Wagner, dramatic) content. This widely held view –

---

[59] *Die Welt als Wille und Vorstellung*, vol. I, §52, 329.

as extensively promoted by the likes of A. B. Marx or Franz Brendel, as well as Wagner, in his own way – was evidently not wholly compatible with the Romantic poetics of an infinite and indeterminate absolute music, as I have suggested, even if few were willing to renounce the metaphysical dignity bestowed on music by the preceding generation.[60] Post-Beethovenian music entertained a continuing fantasy of overcoming its characteristic condition of objectless expression and infinite longing. (In a certain sense, this fantasy defines that very longing.) As I have also suggested, Wagner would turn this conflict of aesthetic ideals to his own advantage in arguing the historical necessity of a new, hybrid "art-work of the future."

In disposing of the conventional wisdom that music represented "indistinct feelings" as a logical fallacy (on the grounds that what was not distinct did not permit of representation), Hanslick also alluded to another increasingly popular thesis: if music was not yet quite able to represent thoroughly "distinct" feelings or ideas, this at least represented a goal toward which music was progressing. "The many genial locutions one hears regarding the tendency of music to break the bonds of its indeterminacy and become a concrete language, the critical approval showered on works in which such tendencies are presumably manifested – all of this attests to the real currency of this view."[61] Many who took the "literary" impulse in modern music as an index of progress (following Liszt) suspected that the autonomy of "pure instrumental music" had been purchased at the expense of a parochial isolation, or else asserted that the invisible "spirit of the age" was now drawing music out of that isolation, and that whoever resisted it did so at the risk of cultural and historical irrelevancy. For this considerable faction, the notion of musical autonomy was uncomfortably suggestive of the "empty form" of outmoded, classicizing formulae.

These critical tendencies could also be seen as a response to challenges posed by such intellectual authorities as Kant and Hegel to the status of music. It would have been easy to dismiss the misgivings of a Kant or Hegel regarding music's aesthetic value as a product of pedantic bias, a contempt bred of ignorance (ignorance of a literature whose language they scarcely understood). But it was less easy to renounce

---

[60] Jacob de Ruiter makes this point about both the exponents of a "materialist" idealist criticism (i.e., one advocating the expression of "distinct" rather than abstract ideas) and the original exponents of a Romantic aesthetic of absolute music. De Ruiter explains the difficulty faced by the likes of Marx, Brendel, and their generation in reconciling a Romantic metaphysics with the representation of "distinct" ideas, feelings, etc. in terms of a confusion between "distinctness" (*Bestimmtheit*) of expression or utterance, on one hand, and linguistic "determinacy" (*Bestimmbarkeit*) of ideas or concepts, on the other. See *Der Charakterbegriff in der Musik, 1740–1850* (Stuttgart, 1989), 284–98.

[61] *Vom Musikalisch-Schönen*, 25.

the metaphysical charms of the "idea" and the allure of systematic models of thought that suffused an entire culture. Whether Hegel's judgements about music were really systematically grounded or more a reflection of a layman's prejudices, they can be read as representative of a strong tradition of intellectual skepticism regarding the substantial value of music as an art. And among the primary deficiencies Hegel ascribed to music was its inherent lack of "distinctness" or representational determinacy: "As much as music may take up a spiritual content (*geistigen Inhalt*) and make its inward qualities, or the inner movement of a feeling, the object of its expression, this content still remains indistinct and vague, just because it is construed only according to its inwardness, as the resonance of subjective feeling." As a musical layman, Hegel distrusted the ability of variation or development techniques to contribute in any way to the representation of a legitimate content: ". . . [for] musical variation or development is not the same thing as the variation or development of a feeling or the representation of a thought or an individual figure; rather, it tends to be a mere spinning out, autonomous play, and at the same time a means of organization."[62] Complexity of form, in other words, does not guarantee distinctness of content – not for Hegel, at least.

But this is just where Hegel and his kind provided a goad to contemporary critical opinion. "Critical opinion" was not of course always of one mind, but on this matter it generally tried to show a united front. Hoffmann, for one, claimed to recognize a "distinct idea" (*bestimmte Idee*) in Beethoven's *Coriolan* overture, even if this idea was not much more specific than a "tragedy in high style" whose hero will play out his appointed tragic role and meet his destined end. (The character of the work was at least "distinct" enough to suggest to Hoffmann that it would really be better suited to a *Hamlet* or *Macbeth*, or something of Calderón, rather than the dryly reflective verses of Collin's play.[63]) Marx and Brendel, as leading flagbearers of "idea" or ideas in music, were also particularly concerned with the distinctness of their musical manifestations, and not willing to have them remain some unapproachable abstraction, a numinous aureole whose presence might be divined while forever eluding the analytic grasp. Marx is well known for his early campaigning on behalf of Beethoven's works, and especially with regard to their manifestation of "ideas." A typical formulation appears in an 1829 critique of Louis Spohr's Third Symphony (op. 78), which Marx feels has failed to respond to Beethoven's cue: "In his symphonies in C minor and D minor (with chorus) Beethoven has raised the entire genre to a higher level, from an indistinct play of tones and a merely lyrical

---

[62] Hegel, *Werke*, vol. XV, 186.
[63] E. T. A. Hoffmann, *Schriften zur Musik*, ed. Friedrich Schnapp (Munich, 1977), 97–8.

effusion to a more distinct idea, firmly and consciously maintained."[64] By the time Brendel took up the cause of music and "ideas" in the 1840s, both the cause itself and Beethoven's pioneering contribution were universally familiar, if not uncontested, matters. At the same time Wagner was interpreting the Ninth as the gospel of the artistic cult of the future, Brendel was citing the work, and Beethoven's achievement in general, as testimony of the present progress of music in its drive toward the representation of ever more distinct ideas:

Instrumental music proceeds from the indistinct to the distinct, from a mere provocation [of indeterminate feelings] to the representation of fully distinct soul-states; thus the word interposes itself as the final stage of determinacy, not as it existed prior to the musical creation, but as a result of a concentration of musical feeling . . . Thus the words in the Ninth are secondary, subordinate, that which is added in order to assist the continually more pointed expressive element in achieving its ultimate determinacy.[65]

The text, that is, provides the means to an end: a new determinacy (*Bestimmtheit*) of musical expression. Similar assertions of a "new determinacy" of musical expression and ideas abound in Brendel's writings, and they are among the principal leitmotifs of the later chapters of his *History of Music* (first published in 1852 and variously expanded across the remainder of his lifetime). In 1850, for example, we find him proclaiming:

Modern music displays a decisive impulse for distinct expression, the utmost possible degree of character, even in purely instrumental music. The common goal [of today's composers] is the ability to represent poetic soul-states in a way that can be distinctly grasped.[66]

Or, elsewhere, with reference to Beethoven again:

As a consequence of the greater significance of content [in Beethoven's works] we notice a [general] striving for the utmost distinctness of expression (*Bestimmtheit des Ausdrucks*), whereby even pure instrumental music, without words, attains the capacity to represent thoroughly distinct soul-states.

A variation on the now-familiar theme follows: where his classical predecessors had purveyed what was essentially a free play of tones (*freies Tonspiel*) of indeterminate expressive value, Beethoven depicted "distinct situations" and "soul-states," thus elevating instrumental music to a "determinacy of expression it had never previously possessed."[67]

---

[64] *Berliner Allgemeine musikalische Zeitung* 6:28 (1829), 217.

[65] "Haydn, Mozart, Beethoven: Eine vergleichende Charakteristik," part 5, *Neue Zeitschrift für Musik* 28:9 (1848), 52.

[66] "Einige Worte über Malerei in der Tonkunst," *Neue Zeitschrift für Musik* 32:47 (1850), 242.

[67] Franz Brendel, *Geschichte der Musik* (1852), 338f., 509.

Gradually, other composers were charged (in two senses) with the responsibility of carrying forward Beethoven's example: Berlioz, Schumann, Liszt, Wagner. Their respective associations with the cause of "ideas" and a Beethovenian legacy were of course encouraged in various ways by their own contributions to a critical discourse of music and ideas. Schumann's and Liszt's famous apologias for Berlioz's program symphonies (*Symphonie fantastique, Harold en Italie*) are but two more historically prominent examples of an ongoing discourse of ideas and the new musical frontiers to be discovered, explored, and exploited with their assistance. A contribution to the "philosophy of music" under the rubric "Berlioz and the Modern Symphony," and occupying a chronological mid-point between the essays of Schumann (1835) and Liszt (1855), exemplifies the continuity of this discourse of music's aspirations toward poetry: ". . . thus we find now that the symphony – through a similar determinacy of content – begins to take on either epic or dramatic character."[68] Despite Dahlhaus's frequent admonitions that we understand "poetry" or the "poetic" in music (in Schumann's critical vocabulary, for instance) as an abstract aesthetic quality rather than as the emulation of a literary model, it is clear that a large proportion of critics did not share these scruples.[69]

According to one vocal faction, at least, music and its practitioners were increasingly attempting to shed the autonomy they had acquired over the last century or so. For many the idea of absolute music was coming to look obsolete (the outmoded "play of tones," the entertainment of an *ancien régime*), suspiciously hermetic (the abstruse complications of a Bach fugue, or of Beethoven's later experiments in fugue and variation), or too much like a mere commodity (waltzes, polkas, quadrilles, potpourris of operatic airs and other *Haus* and salon music for middle-class consumers). Absolute music was generating an uneasy conscience in the context of modern culture. And here, of course, is where Wagner stepped in. For, aside from beating (somewhat prematurely) his own peculiar operatic drum in the Zurich manifestoes, Wagner was also preaching salvation and utopia to a musical culture increasingly beset with such pangs of aesthetic conscience. In this light, some of the

---

[68] Julius Wend, "Berlioz und die moderne Symphonie: Ein Beitrag zu einer Philosophie der Musik," *Wiener allgemeine Musik-Zeitung* 6:43 (1846), 161.

[69] It should be emphasized that Dahlhaus does allow for the presence of this post- (or "neo-") Romantic counter-discourse of ideas and determinacy, especially under the elusive rubric of "realism" after mid-century (see *Realism in Nineteenth-Century Music*, trans. Mary Whittall [Cambridge, 1985], passim). But aside from the methodological problems of adapting this catchword of mid-century literary-artistic culture to musical contexts, it serves again to cordon off "materialistic," degenerate or otherwise suspect critical practices from a "genuine" Romantic aesthetic, the integrity and purity of whose legacy is to be preserved as far as possible.

extravagant positions of his writings may begin to look a little less perverse – if not less extravagant.

Wagner's polemics did strike most of his contemporaries as extremist, it is true. Nonetheless, few of them would have questioned the relevance of the topics he chose for these cultural sermons – not only the obvious timeliness of his themes of revolution and cultural reform, but also the regeneration of the operatic genre (a sensitive issue for a German musical culture that had witnessed no *bona fide* masterpieces or even respectable hits since the time of *Fidelio* and *Der Freischütz*), and the dilemma of an instrumental culture torn between allegiance to a classical ideal of recent vintage and a conviction in the imperative of material and stylistic progress.

Wagner's earlier writings are largely preoccupied with specifically operatic issues. But even here there is an awareness of critical issues of absolute music that would subsequently fuel the arguments of the Zurich writings. An exposition of the nature of German music and music-making offered to the readers of the Paris *Revue et gazette musicale* ("De la musique allemande," 1840; reprinted in the collected writings as "Über deutsches Musikwesen"), for example, gives an idealized portrait of a German bourgeois culture of absolute music: "here, where one can give rein to one's dreams and fantasies, where one's imagination is not restricted to the expression of a single specific passion, where one can lose oneself in the great realm of indefinite feeling . . ."[70] But the operations of imagination and fantasy are already problematized in a "Fantasie sur la musique pittoresque" (as he originally subtitled the story, "Une soirée heureuse," of 1841, later reprinted as "Ein glücklicher Abend"), which appeared shortly afterwards in the same journal. Here the prototypical German of the earlier article has become a symbolically divided subject (its dual ego cannily labeled as "R." and "Ich"), divided precisely over the issue of the musical representation of determinate "ideas." One of these selves is convinced that Beethoven "must have conceived the plan of his symphonies according to a certain philosophical idea" (*nach einer gewissen philosophischen Idee*), a conviction challenged by the other. This dialogical schizophrenia achieves a provisional synthesis in a near paraphrase (entirely fortuitous) of Schopenhauer's claim that music expresses, if not "ideas," then the abstracted essence of the diverse passions (a.k.a. the Will).[71]

The critical turn taken in the Zurich writings is perfectly logical for a composer whose ambitions had been decisively channeled into an

---

[70] I, 156; translation adapted from Robert Jacobs and Geoffrey Skelton, eds. and trans., *Wagner Writes from Paris . . . Stories, Essays and Articles by the Young Composer* (London, 1973), 41.

[71] I, 145, 148. Cf. Schopenhauer, *Die Welt als Wille und Vorstellung*, vol. I, §52, 328.

operatic cause: all the critical flailings of the post-Beethoven era will be neatly resolved if one just translates those troublesome "poetic ideas" into a "poetic intent" (*dichterische Absicht*) grounded in the drama. If neither Beethoven nor anyone since had yet fully succeeded in grounding such volatile ideas in the material of absolute musical forms, then why not incorporate these ideas into the work itself, as a dramatic text? A genuine, musically sympathetic dramatic text will become the *pretext* for a new kind of music for which neither the nebulous "ideas" of idealist aesthetic speculators nor routine opera texts (with no ideas worthy of the name) have yet provided a satisfactory object. (Traditional libretti, Wagner maintained, only catered to the forms of absolute music.)

With some modifications, this argument will persist through the time of *Tristan und Isolde* ("Music of the Future," 1860) and *Parsifal* (the various contributions to the *Bayreuther Blätter*, particularly "On the Application of Music to the Drama"). The basic thesis is that music is an ungrounded, fluid, and volatile medium of expression. It may be internally grounded by means of simple, conventional forms that (by virtue of their cognitive simplicity or cultural familiarity) provide an intelligible means of formal containment: dances, marches, variations, sonatas. But the aim to intensify expression – to make it more variegated, nuanced, precise – will exacerbate the need for some causal explanation, an object of expression. (Wagner remained unwilling to admit that music could motivate its own forms, or generate "ideas" entirely from within.) And, to extrapolate from these arguments, it is unlikely that a whole new set of widely intelligible conventions will evolve rapidly enough to support the comprehension of any radically new, alternative forms of musical behavior as "absolute music" (a fundamental issue for music since Wagner's time, in fact). Rather than blindly groping for the ideas that might explain why music might behave in perplexing and unfamiliar ways – ideas to explain its enigmatic propositions, its alternating attempts to seduce, to unnerve, to uplift, to mesmerize through the application of enriched harmonic vocabulary and orchestral textures, unsprung forms, and a labyrinthine *melos* – one would do better (Wagner's argument would continue) to ground this behavior in a dramatic conception that can properly motivate it, from the composer's perspective, as well as explain it, from the listener's perspective.[72] If Beethoven's Fifth Symphony had set

---

[72] Aside from *Opera and Drama*, the central texts of this argument (further discussed in chapter 6) are "On Franz Liszt's Symphonic Poems" (with its idea of an extra-musical *Motiv zur Formgebung*, V, 192), "*Music of the Future*" (which postulates the ways in which a composer can answer or forestall the question "Why?" instinctively posed by the listener in response to an expressive-musical stimulus, VII, 112ff.), and "On the Application of Music to the Drama," where this hermeneutic "Why" is reiterated and developed (X, 180).

instrumental music *à la recherche du drame*, as its many commentators seemed to intimate, the symphony had best bring this quest to an end by subjecting itself to the drama as such, rather than continuing to prevaricate with half-hearted replications of the Beethovenian model.

The outline of Wagner's arguments is familiar enough; some of the details will be taken up in later chapters. The point I want them to serve here is this. Aesthetic and critical thought about music in the nineteenth century may well have been dominated (at some level) by a master trope of "absolute music" – once the idea had been recognized, it could not be easily ignored, or forcibly forgotten, and its particular cachet was not likely to be discarded, willingly. But, even if we discount all the "peripheral" (which is to say majority) repertoires of French and Italian opera, sacred and recreational choral music, commercial and popular music and focus solely on a German/Central European instrumental mainstream, the hegemonic paradigm of absolute music is still strained. For all his awareness of these other repertoires and of this internal strain (generated by "idealistic" and programmatic impulses), as well as his commitment to some notion of objectivity, Dahlhaus's view of a "central" music-aesthetic trajectory across the century retains something of the more blatant orthodoxy of many older historical models (Rudolf Schäfke's for instance): a gradual fall from the grace of a "pure" Romantic aesthetic of absolute music, a decadent, "materialistic" interim phase around the middle of the century (with a growing concern for tangible meanings and a crude devaluation of "ideas" from the metaphysical to the literary or picturesque – Dahlhaus's "realism"), to be redeemed not only by Brahms, but even by a prodigal Wagner who gets religion from the prophet Schopenhauer and, with the assistance of the zealous young disciple Nietzsche, passes the new religion on to future generations. (Nietzsche's subsequent apostasy doesn't interfere, since it embraces an even more vehement profession of the new faith of pure music.) I don't mean to take issue with the notion that Wagner tried to articulate a particular view of absolute music compatible with his dramatic ideals in the later writings, and I have argued in favor of that (now more or less standard) view in the preceding section. I simply want to stress here the extent to which the central theoretical agenda of the middle period draws on and responds to these alternative impulses of "idea," character, program, and "determinate" expression that dominate the critical discourse across much of the century (and not only a delimited materialist or "realist" phase) – a discourse whose roots reach well back into the eighteenth century, to notions of imitation, character, tone-painting, and the whole aesthetics of feeling. We needn't subscribe to a dogma of Wagner as "symphonic" composer, or as nurturing a frustrated symphonic ambition, to realize the implications of these instrumental musical issues (musical character, metaphor, sign) for his musical dramas, most obviously the leitmotif.

But the shadow of that great symphonic avatar (Beethoven) has been looming largely over much of the discussion. So before abandoning the problematics of absolute music altogether for those of the musical drama, we had best confront this shadow directly.

2

Beethoven reception and the hermeneutic impulse: "poetic ideas" and new forms

In a lecture entitled "Overinterpreting Texts," Umberto Eco outlines an interpretive phenomenon he designates as "Hermetic semiosis," in which not only sacred, but also culturally sacralized (secular) texts generate a tradition of highly developed, esoteric exegesis.[1] Eco examines the case of Dante in the hands of a number of more or less obsessively mono-maniacal critics going back to Gabriele Rossetti (father of the poet and pre-Raphaelite Dante Gabriel Rossetti), who avidly examined the *Divine Comedy* for encodings of Masonic and Rosicrucian symbolism. Similar patterns can be cited in the interpretive histories of Virgil, Rabelais, or Shakespeare. It is not surprising to find that Beethoven, among com-posers, has produced the closest analogue to this phenomenon in the history of music and its criticism.

The notion that Beethoven, in composing his larger instrumental works, was guided by a "poetic idea" or object which he strove to repre-sent in music is a kind of *idée fixe* of the composer's critical reception from the last decade of his life through much of the nineteenth century. Arnold Schering's efforts in the 1920s and 30s to crack the secret code of what he took to be Beethoven's "esoteric" literary programs represent the belated culmination of this tradition, and Schering's zealous conviction that he was bringing to light incontrovertible truths that had hitherto remained concealed within the sounding hieroglyphs of Beethoven's scores closely parallels the tone and methodology of Eco's Dantean hermeneutes. While Dante's texts invite interpretations of a more overtly religious character, both interpretive traditions (Dante and Beethoven) reflect an attitude originally directed toward sacred texts which "has also been transmitted, in secularized form, to texts which have become metaphorically sacred in the course of their reception."[2] Like Dante, Beethoven himself provided

---

[1]   Umberto Eco, "Overinterpreting Texts," in *Interpretation and Overinterpretation* (Cambridge, 1992), 45–66.

[2]   Ibid., 53. An anonymous (and disgruntled) critic writing in 1854 noted parallels between the modern reception of Shakespeare and Beethoven in this regard,

the impetus to interpretation in explicit, though enigmatic, oracular form. Dante hinted at a deeper strand of signification *"sotto il velame delli versi strani"*; Beethoven revealed to a few elect disciples (Schindler, Czerny, Wegeler and Ries) that many of his works reflected a particular poetic idea, while cannily refraining from committing these "ideas" to a definitive textual form – something which he must have deemed impossible in any case. (In one famous instance, he contemplated putting out a collected edition of his piano sonatas in 1816 with indications of the "poetic ideas" underlying each work; that the project never materialized is one more sign of the composer's understandable ambivalence.)

Aside from such biographically transmitted clues, it was of course the character of Beethoven's own *versi strani* that nourished the belief in a secret subtext of "ideas": the "new" or radically modified forms, the "speaking" recitatives, the fragmentations and dislocations of the late works, the unruly, "bizarre modulations" contemporary critics decried even in the earlier works. Biographical mythography and musical documents or "scripture" collude in creating a new paradigm of music as meaningful text, as a legitimate object of critical interpretation. "The new insight that Beethoven thrust upon the aesthetic consciousness of his age," Dahlhaus writes, "was that a musical text, like a literary or philosophical text, harbors a meaning which is made manifest but not entirely subsumed in its acoustic presentation – that a musical creation can exist as an 'art work of ideas' transcending its various interpretations."[3] Beethoven and his "poetic ideas" naturally became the fulcrum of that larger discourse of musical determinacy sketched at the end of the preceding chapter, just as the major works became the scripture of this new musical faith, the biographical anecdotes and clues the foundation of its mythology.

Schering offered a detailed pedigree for his hermeneutic efforts in the form of a substantial introduction to *Beethoven und die Dichtung* (1936), presenting the critical history of this discourse of "poetic ideas" around Beethoven's works. This history does not lead quite as smoothly to his own "discovery" of the literary pre-texts behind Beethoven's works as Schering would have liked. In fact, he pretty much abandons this critical history after Wagner in favor of an

---

complaining of wildly abstruse and exaggerated "speculations on the 'intentions' which are thought to lie beneath (*zu Grunde liegen*)" the surface beauties of classic works of art, and which "a misplaced comma or a misspelled word might bring to nought. So it went with Shakespeare, not long ago. And now it is the composers' turn. Beethoven has recently become the darling of the musical aestheticians; his works have become a treasure-trove for aesthetic twaddle" ("Beethoven und die Ästhetik," *Süddeutsche Musik-Zeitung* 3:25 [1854], 97).

3 Carl Dahlhaus, *Nineteenth-Century Music*, trans. J. Bradford Robinson (Berkeley and Los Angeles, 1989), 10.

apologetic exposition of his own methods and results. (Naturally, Schering had nothing but contempt for the unhappy formalist impasse in which his contemporaries seemed to be mired.) The interpretation of "ideas" in Beethoven's music hardly ceased with Wagner, of course, though it may have increasingly degenerated in the direction of trivial program notes and popular concert guides. After Wagner, certainly, this hermeneutic tradition lacked distinguished voices, and fell under a shadow of disrepute with the rise of positivistic historical scholarship and formal analysis around 1900 (the approach of Paul Bekker in the early twentieth century represented – for Schering, at least – a diluted compromise between the interpretation of "ideas" and inhibiting doctrines of absolute music).

It would not be difficult to propose an explanatory model for the decline of the earlier hermeneutic tradition according to the history of Wagner's contributions to it. Such a model might look something like this.

1   In his youth, Wagner absorbed a critical tradition that prized the expression of "poetic ideas" in Beethoven's works and his efforts to realize these ideas with ever greater determinacy or distinctness (reaching a problematic culmination in the Ninth Symphony).

2   In trying to formulate a radical aesthetic program for musical drama around 1850, Wagner manipulated the terms of this critical tradition to serve the purposes of this personal agenda, suggesting that the initial success of Beethoven's "new path" in the middle period and the ultimate failure of the later works to achieve popular or critical acceptance indicated the misdirection of his artistic ambitions, which could only be rectified by re-channeling them in the direction of an entirely new genre (one which Beethoven was unable to conceive, though he intimated it in the Ninth Symphony).

3   Finally, from his Schopenhauerian, post-*Tristan* perspective, Wagner came to reject the thesis of an increasing determinacy of musical expression (poetic ideas) in favor of a re-animated faith in the Romantic ideology of "absolute," immanent musical meaning. Viewed from this "reactionary" perspective, Beethoven's music did not develop in the direction of more distinctly expressed "ideas," but probed more deeply the ineffable metaphysical import of a musical language *per se*, a direction that remained for Wagner (with the assistance of dramatic motivations) to explore more fully.

This scenario is partially familiar from the preceding chapter. The scheme of acceptance–rejection–reinterpretation, which can be applied to Wagner's attitudes toward a philosophy of absolute music, could be modified as a scheme of acceptance–reinterpretation–rejection in the case of the critical tradition of "poetic ideas." In either case, the final stage represents something more than (or different from) a restitution of a Romantic ideology of aesthetic "purity." Wagner's adaptation of the critical tradition around Beethoven's works is best read as a dialogue with this tradition and with the broader concerns of a musical culture we may find inscribed therein. This chapter will, among other things, test the validity of this model (the absorption and "sublation" of a critical tradition of poetic ideas in Wagner's thought) in looking at some of the ways Wagner adapted the tradition to his own purposes and changing views.

Beethoven's "poetic ideas": notes on the genesis of a critical tradition

When Wagner offered his two novellistic tributes to Beethoven – "A Pilgrimage to Beethoven" and "A Happy Evening" – to the *Revue et gazette musicale* (in late 1840 and 1841, respectively), Anton Schindler's *Biographie von Ludwig van Beethoven* had just appeared (Münster, 1840). Wagner himself had contemplated collaborating with a fellow expatriate, G. E. Anders, on a study of the composer that would make good the shortcomings of style, coherence, and musical insight of Schindler's unsatisfactory, but putatively authoritative effort. Still, Schindler's personal liaison with the composer obviously gave his biography a certain cachet, and however much his reliability has been impugned by generations of subsequent scholarship, the historical impact of his book remains a fact. Among other things, Schindler's biographical testimony is the cornerstone of the critical tradition of Beethoven's "poetic ideas," if by no means its sole source. On the contrary, Schindler suggests that the notion was already widespread: ". . . regarding the matter of poetic ideas, it is notorious that Beethoven was not constrained by conventional forms in composing, but often circumvented these if the idea that had inspired him demanded some other treatment, or rather, to be clothed in a new fashion."[4] Ries and Wegeler, as Schindler noted, had already published statements about the role of a "determinate object" (*bestimmter Gegenstand*) in Beethoven's works, "though he often scorned and derided musical imitations of a naive sort." Schindler himself had broached the subject earlier in a contribution to the *Wiener Theaterzeitung* (1831), invoking the names of

---

[4]   Anton Schindler, *Biographie von Ludwig van Beethoven* (Münster, 1840), 196.

Shakespeare and Goethe's *Faust* – figures that would continue to inhabit the discourse on Beethoven's "poetic ideas" throughout the century.[5] Schindler was hardly eager that others should presume to interpret the ideas behind Beethoven's compositions, but he maintained nevertheless that the term "poetic idea" was authentic to Beethoven's own time, "and was used by him – along with similar terms, like poetic content – to distinguish [his works] from those that were just a harmonically and rhythmically well-organized *Tonspiel*."[6]

Schindler's claim is corroborated by a philosophically inclined contributor to the Leipzig *Allgemeine musikalische Zeitung*, going by the name "Triest," who was already promoting the musical expression of "distinct ideas" at a time when Beethoven had hardly emerged from the innocuous *Tonspiel* of his first period. Music is most effective, Triest asserted, when the listener is "able to perceive the expression of distinct, yet unarticulated, ideas or feelings (without any of the accessory matter of marches or ballets)," and where the composer himself has tried to express an idea or feeling "as distinctly as possible."[7] Written in 1801, Triest's comments demonstrate that, however crucial Beethoven's works were to the emergence of a discourse of "poetic ideas" and determinate expression in music, neither he nor his biographers were solely responsible for its invention. Rather, Beethoven's music nurtured an impulse already nascent in the musical culture of the time, just as he was surely encouraged, in turn, by the existence of this interpretive impulse in his audience. By the 1820s A. B. Marx was publicly campaigning in support of "ideas" and their innovatory role in Beethoven's music, even if (as Scott Burnham argues) his appropriation of a now *au courant* idealist terminology remained systematically ungrounded (the process is typical, after all, of the fate of theoretical discourse in any period, not least our own).[8]

Chiding Schindler for exaggerating the significance of "poetic ideas" and their supposed authentication by the composer, Carl Dahlhaus has tried to relocate the concept (or the related one of an "underlying idea," passed on by another contemporary witness, Louis Schlösser) in the

---

5   See Arnold Schering, *Beethoven und die Dichtung*, (Berlin, 1936; rpt Hildesheim, 1973), 560.

6   Schindler, *Biographie von Ludwig van Beethoven*, cited from Schering, *Beethoven und die Dichtung*, 26.

7   *Allgemeine musikalische Zeitung* 4 (1801), col. 397.

8   Scott Burnham, "Criticism, Faith, and the *Idee*: A. B. Marx's Early Reception of Beethoven," *19th-Century Music* 13:3 (Spring 1990), 183–92. It is certainly true that the whole discourse of music and "ideas" I am detailing here had little use for the metaphysical substance (as it were) of the Hegelian *Idee*, aside from its cultural prestige; in fact, the "materialist" tendencies of this popular discourse were largely antithetical to genuine metaphysics – hence Dahlhaus's apparent discomfort with them.

domain of musical autonomy, as denoting the kind of specific "compositional problem," in a Schoenbergian sense, that determines the profile of a musical work as an internally significant aesthetic object.[9] (The particular context of Schlösser's phrase, at least [*die zugrunde liegende Idee*], may in fact warrant a more strictly musical reading, as something mediating between theme and the formal "idea" of a movement. In this reading, idea as expressive content or "the succession of aesthetic characters" is secondary to the specific compositional idea, of which these are a function.) Dahlhaus's approach to the underlying "compositional idea" is, in its own way, reminiscent of the "Hermetic semiosis" of Schering's literary decodings; where Schering looked for secret literary keys to musical structure, Dahlhaus reveals esoteric formal "problems" behind musical structures, such as the reconfiguration of traditional functional characters within an exposition, held together by a "network" of contrasting derivations (op. 10, no. 3, first movement), or the interaction of thematic material and divergent formal implications (rondo, sonata rondo, "double-cursus") across different stages of composition in the Finale to the Second Symphony. Beethoven's elusive remark about the "conflict of two principles in dialogic form" as the underlying idea of the op. 14 piano sonatas, as communicated by Schindler, also suggests something closer to the abstracted compositional ideas promoted by Dahlhaus than to Schering's literary programs.

Despite Dahlhaus's criticisms, Schindler himself remained remarkably unsympathetic to the hermeneutic efforts of others (as mentioned) who lacked the benefit of his privileged intimacy with the composer, while for his own part, he can hardly be said to have provided anything like an "interpretation" of Beethoven's works. His few fragmentary reports, in fact, seem calculated more to confound than to enlighten (almost as if this had been Beethoven's own design). The "clue" to the significance of the op. 14 sonatas (which had been "recognized by everyone at the time," as Schindler's Beethoven peevishly asserts, against the prosaic *Zeitgeist* of the 1820s) does not even clarify whether the agents in this "conflict of two principles" are to be understood as whole sonatas, individual movements, thematic characters, specific voices (as A. B. Marx inferred), some combination of these – or something else entirely. Similarly, the famous injunction to "read Shakespeare's *Tempest*" for the interpretive key to *both* the sonatas op. 31, no. 2, and op. 57 would seem to confront the thesis of determinate expression with a gesture of radical indeterminacy: one text for two compositions. While Schindler ventured no kind of critical analysis (he seemed to consider performance as his area of technical expertise), he did make a point of

---

[9] Carl Dahlhaus, *Ludwig van Beethoven: Approaches to his Music*, trans. Mary Whittall (Oxford, 1991), chapter 7: "The Underlying Idea" (143–51).

connecting the existence of underlying "poetic ideas" with the individuality and novelty of Beethoven's musical forms (hence potentially even with the kind of esoteric formal ideas that Dahlhaus proposes.) "By all means the most important and unusual feature of this tone-poet," he writes, "was the manner in which an idea – either from nature or from literature – provided the impetus for composition, whenever such an idea had made a deep impression on his imagination, such that each work would be completely guided by this idea and wrought into fixed, distinctly modeled forms, which had as little in common with conventional forms as they did with one another."[10] By the time Schindler thus formulated the role of ideas in the genesis of "new forms" (only in the third edition of his biography, from 1860) it had become a critical commonplace. By that time, the trope of "new forms" generated by poetic (or dramatic) ideas had been thoroughly absorbed into the rhetoric of the "art-work of the future."

Wagner surely began assimilating the elements of this hermeneutic tradition from the time of his first encounter with Beethoven's works themselves in the late 1820s.[11] By the time of Schindler's biography and Wagner's first written tributes to Beethoven around 1840 the tradition was well established, as I have suggested, and Wagner was in a position to reflect on its implications for his own evolving program. The question of how "ideas" generate "form" in Beethoven's works – unlike the supposedly naive, unreflective application of form in earlier styles – figures centrally in the genial colloquy between Wagner's dialectical partners in the 1841 vignette, "A Happy Evening," as they ruminate on their impressions of an outdoor summer concert. The conjunction of Mozart (Symphony in E♭, K. 543) and Beethoven (Seventh Symphony) in this early example of classical pops programming is anything but accidental; it sets the stage for a modest installment in a continuing critical debate now several decades old. E. T. A. Hoffmann's famous, though non-polemical, evaluation of the differing levels of "Romanticism" manifested in the music of these two composers had since become more sharply focused on the question of form and "ideas." The general consensus – that Mozart's naively inspired lyricism was cheerfully dispensed into received forms while Beethoven's music harkened to the call of higher ideas – is neatly recapitulated in Wagner's dialogue. The two partners assume positions for and against musical representation, but even "R." (who takes up the brief against concrete representation) concedes that Beethoven has endowed his bold

---

[10] Schindler, *Biographie von Ludwig van Beethoven* (3rd edn, 1860), 219.
[11] See the summary account of "Wagner's Knowledge of Literature on Beethoven," in Klaus Kropfinger, *Wagner and Beethoven*, 58–61.

developments of classical forms with a "philosophical consequence," without forsaking the unsullied and "elevated sphere . . . that is the exclusive domain of true music." "Ich," on the other hand, pleads the cause of ideas, and what was by 1840 becoming an orthodox distinction between the foundations of classical and "modern" music. Mozart's musical "effusions" (*Ergüsse*) may indeed emanate from pure musical sources, his inspiration attaching to "an indeterminate inner feeling which, even if he had been possessed of a poet's faculties, he could never have expressed in words, but only in tones." "Ich" thus appeals to the familiar trope of Mozart as the quintessentially (and "purely") musical mind, grasping every detail (*das ganze Tongepräge*) in advance of its execution as musical score. "On the other hand, I can only imagine that Beethoven first conceived and arranged the plan for a symphony according to a particular philosophical idea (*nach einer gewissen philosophischen Idee*) before leaving to his imagination the task of inventing the musical ideas appropriate to it" (I, 145).

Though he feigns an insight born of personal experience here, "Ich" is clearly invoking a timely critical topic, especially considering the recent appearance of Schindler's biography (Schindler himself had been in Paris just a short time before this, where he had involved himself with Maurice Schlesinger and his journal – the *Revue et gazette musicale* – in which Wagner's stories were printed).[12] Schindler himself had traced the hermeneutic response to Beethoven specifically to some comments on the Seventh Symphony in 1819 by a certain Dr. Iken of Bremen, whose interpretive efforts evidently met with Beethoven's – and consequently Schindler's – displeasure. Wagner signals his awareness of the particular hermeneutic challenge posed by the Seventh Symphony in the 1841 story, where the performance of this work sparks allusions to a "peasant wedding" scenario published in 1825 which had also earned the ironizing attentions of Schumann's Florestan in the meantime.[13] Wagner's philosophizing concert-goers turn from the elusive Seventh to the presumably less equivocal case of the "Eroica," recognized pretty much from the beginning as a signal work, not only for the emergence of Beethoven as Romantic individual,

[12] See ibid., 60, and also the additional information included in the original German edition (1974), 67–9.

[13] See the summary of this interpretive history of the Seventh Symphony in T. Grey, "Metaphorical Modes," 93–117. Wagner himself repeatedly returned to a "Dionysian" hermeneutic gloss on the Seventh Symphony, in private (Cosima's diaries), and in the essay "On Poetry and Composition," for instance (X, 147). The original biographical and cultural contexts of this critical tradition of Beethoven's "poetic ideas" have been explored in a number of articles by Owen Jander over the last decade, beginning with his influential piece on the Fourth Piano Concerto, "Beethoven's 'Orpheus in Hades': The *Andante con moto* of the Fourth Piano Concerto," *19th-Century Music* 8 (1985), 195–212.

but (as Marx later formulated it), for the transition from an *ancien régime* of mere *Tonspiel* into a brave new century of musical "ideas."

Poetics, heroics, *funérailles*

Before picking up the thread of Wagner's dialogical vignette I must digress for a moment to sketch a provisional outline of Wagner's musical poetics as a context for his reception of Beethoven, as well as for his adaptation (appropriation) of the critical tradition of "poetic ideas."

If Wagner can be said to have professed a theory of musical form in any sense, or if one could be abstracted from the pertinent observations scattered throughout his writings, it might look something like this. (1) The origin of "absolute" instrumental music in functional, "pre-artistic" dance and march types (similarly of absolute "operatic melody" in monophonic or homophonic folk song) is the source of certain fundamental formal constraints still necessary to insure the purely musical intelligibility of music derived from these types (the auton-omy of such music being merely an illusion founded on internalized con-ventions of hearing). (2) Paramount among these constraints are the principles of thematic reprise and tonal closure, at various levels. (3) Modulation is similarly constrained by convention and by formal function in such closed forms (wide-ranging modulations being normally limited to a position of central contrast or development). (4) The constraints of thematic contrast and reprise (alternation or *Wechsel*) in absolute music can be superseded by an evolutionary, processive or dynamic model of form (*Entwicklung*) analogous to drama, but only when music is applied to the realization of an actual drama (i.e., the "art-work of the future"). (5) The full expressive potential of harmonic modulation (whether local harmonic progression or larger "structural" modulations) can only be exploited by such dramatic means – that is, the potential for unlimited modulation by virtue of enharmonic or chromatic relations inherent in the tonal system will not find adequate scope in absolute forms (where it becomes detrimental to the clarity of expository or recapitulatory functions, for example), whereas a dramatic action might legitimately exploit an expanded modulatory practice, justifying and "explaining" unaccustomed musical behavior.

These claims range from the conventionally axiomatic to the idiosyn-cratically Wagnerian. Examining their validity, applications, and ramifications will be the business of most of the chapters to follow, along with a fuller documentation, interpretation, and contextualization of the relevant texts. For the moment, I only want to emphasize how much of what Wagner believed (or came to believe) about the nature of musical form is founded in his perceptions of Beethoven's music and its relation to his own. Beethoven was for Wagner, as for others at the time, at once the apogee of two centuries of "absolute musical" development and the principal agent of its modern transformation. For Wagner this latter role was interpreted as the prophecy of absolute music's sublation in the musical drama. This construction of musical drama (hence of "dramatized" musical form) as an imperative of historical progress is familiar enough; the point I want to bring out here is how this familiar construction is bound up with the broader contemporary discourse of "poetic ideas" and their role in Beethoven's oeuvre. Ideas and their "determinate" expression through the sensuous immediacy of musical sound were thought to motivate newly individualized yet still integrated musical designs. The individuality of these designs (in Beethoven's case sometimes bordering on the abstruse and enigmatic) provoked interpretation of the underlying "ideas," in turn. Such a conviction in the reciprocal relation of "new form" and the realization of "ideas" led to the new status of musical compositions as signifying "texts" or works in an emphatic sense, as Dahlhaus remarked. Not only did Wagner clearly covet this new aesthetic status for his own operas, as texts worthy of continued exegesis, he also appropriated for his own musical-dramatic project something of the musical characteristics that made Beethoven's works interpretable texts (while the mythic-allegorical nature of Wagner's dramatic texts made the demand for interpretation that much more overt). The process of appropriation can be read both in Wagner's critical writings and – less transparently, but perhaps more interestingly – in his musical texts.

Challenged to defend the notion that Beethoven conceived his symphonies "according to a certain philosophical idea," Wagner's hermeneutically inclined alter-ego ("Ich") in "A Happy Evening" unhesitatingly invokes the "Eroica" as an irrefutable, self-evident case in point. And indeed, the "Eroica" was certainly the cornerstone of this whole hermeneutic tradition (notwithstanding Schindler's remarks about the Sonatas op. 10, no. 3, and op. 14, which, as first-period works, were quickly consigned to tertiary status). The significance of the "Eroica" as the inauguration of a new period in Beethoven's career and of a new musical epoch altogether was axiomatic almost from the earliest stages of its reception.[14] Early enthusiasts such as W. R. Griepenkerl and Wilhelm von Lenz variously apostrophized the work as the dawn of a new musical era, and the work's chronological position on the cusp of a new century – along with the biographical circumstances of its

[14] The point is emphasized by Scott Burnham in his essay, "On the Programmatic Reception of Beethoven's *Eroica* Symphony," *Beethoven Forum* 1 (1992), 2. Burnham also notes the ways in which Wagner's views of the work went somewhat against the grain of the more "reality-bound" programmatic tradition of Marx and other critics discussed here, who refused to relinquish the Napoleonic clues embedded in the work's genesis.

composition, its dimensions, and its musical "content" – have all continued to reinforce such views.[15] (The work commands pride of place in A. B. Marx's Beethoven study, for instance, as the first paradigmatic example of his third and highest stage of historical-musical development, which he refers to alternately as "music of the spirit" or "music of ideas": *Musik des Geistes* or *Idealmusik*.[16])

Yet the problems attending the work's early reception were by no means effortlessly resolved. Like the experience of the Napoleonic era that gave birth to the work itself, the experience of the "Eroica" was at once exhilarating and troubling. Both experiences could be said to conjoin a glimpse of thrilling utopian horizons with intimations of an unstable, deracinated, "artificial" (rather than conventional) yet voraciously ambitious regime – a glimpse, perhaps, of incipient modernity. Wagner naturally concurred with views of the "Eroica" as an epochal work, for Beethoven and for history, even remarking once to Cosima that the cellos' famous C♯ in the eighth measure of the first movement was "the first note of modern music."[17]

Just as the "Eroica" was emblematic of the "new" in the development of nineteenth-century musical consciousness, and consequently an object of some critical ambivalence, its status as representative of the emergence of "poetic ideas" in Beethoven's music was not unproblematic. What *was* the "idea"? And what was the nature of its musical representation? (And here we can rejoin "R." and "Ich" in their postconcert philosophical causerie.) Wagner's more sober and conservative alter-ego in the 1841 novella ("R.") rehearses familiar objections to the

[15] Representative views to this effect expressed by the enthusiastic *Beethovener* W. F. Griepenkerl and Wilhelm von Lenz can be found in a collection of material on the reception of the "Eroica" published by Martin Geck and Peter Schleuning, *"Geschrieben auf Bonaparte." Beethovens "Eroica": Revolution, Reaktion, Rezeption* (Hamburg, 1989). Lenz, who is very much taken up with the Napoleonic background of the piece in his *Beethoven: Eine Kunststudie* (Cassel, 1855–60), apostrophizes the work as the musical herald of the brave new century: "On your knees, old world! Before you stands the image of the great Beethovenian Symphony (*Du stehst vor dem Begriff der großen Beethoven'schen Symphonie*). Haydn and Mozart are only playing the kettledrums in this orchestra. Here is the end of one empire and the beginning of another. Here is the boundary of a [new] century" (translated from the original in Geck/Schleuning, 278–9). "The horn would have been too early for Mozart, too, naturally," Lenz adds with reference to the famous recapitulation (surely as a goad to his critical nemesis and arch-Mozartian, Ulibishev); "too early for you, eighteenth century; but at the right time for the nineteenth."

[16] A. B. Marx, *Ludwig van Beethoven: Leben und Schaffen* (Berlin, 1859), vol. I (Leipzig, 1902), 203ff. ("Die sinfonia eroica und die Idealmusik").

[17] CWD, 17 June 1871. In the 1869 essay *On Conducting*, Wagner argues that Beethoven's major works after the "Eroica" belong to the sphere of "sentimental" rather than "naive" art (referring to the famous Schillerian dichotomy), and accordingly demand a new level of flexibility and nuance in performance (VIII, 286ff).

naive pictorialism associated with meretricious battle pieces of the Napoleonic era, arguing that the "idea of heroic strength striving mightily for the sake of a noble cause" can be entirely subsumed within the domain of pure music.

Can you point to a single passage which could be taken to describe an event in the young [Bonaparte's] career? Why the Funeral March, why the Scherzo with hunting horns? Why the Finale with its interwoven, meltingly expressive Andante? Where is the bridge at Lodi, the battle of Arcola, the march on Leoben, the victory of the Pyramids, the 18th Brumaire? . . . I leave it to others, more learned than I, the task of deciphering the battles of Rivoli and Marengo from the secret hieroglyphics of the score.[18]

"R." directs his scorn at the cruder manifestations of a "Hermetic semiosis" ("the secret hieroglyphics of the score"), offering what would seem the sensible alternative view that Napoleon's example (the "idea" of Napoleon, or simply of "the heroic") provided the creative impulse for a work of heroic character and unprecedented proportions. The conversational partners reach a harmonious accord on this note, which also provides the point of departure for Wagner's 1852 "programmatic commentary" to the work (V, 169–72). (There, "ideas" are rescued from the prosaic banality of political history and preserved at a higher level, as analogues to the "purely musical." This 1852 program was widely commended, in fact, by the likes of Marx, Lenz, Alexander Ulibishev, Ernst von Elterlein, and others for its tactful restraint in matters of idea and representation – even where those same critics had often been less restrained themselves.)

"Why the Funeral March, why the Scherzo with hunting horns? Why the Finale . . . ?" Despite the apparent reconciliation at the close of Wagner's music-critical vignette (a requisite of its literary form, here), we can imagine these questions continuing to echo through the cool night air of its setting as the concert-goers linger on over their steaming *Punsch*. These questions continued to occupy "Eroica" exegetes for some time. Such patently naive concerns with a storybook dimension of narrative representation – Who fights whom in the first movement? Who dies in the second movement? Why is the Scherzo happy? What happens at all in the Finale? – might scarcely seem to warrant attention. But they were hardly uncommon; almost every commentary throughout the nineteenth century (Wagner's included) felt compelled to offer some kind of explanation for the sequence of movements in terms of a "logical" and interrelated series of events. Moreover, these impertinent, even childish queries ("Why? Why? Why?") can be seen to touch on some of the fundamental points of Wagner's critique of absolute music in relation to his theories of musical form and "motivation."

[18]   I, 148; trans. Jacobs and Skelton, *Wagner Writes from Paris*, 185–6, 187.

The "motivation" of musical behavior, the question "why" a composition proceeds as it does is perhaps the most fundamental issue of Wagner's "theory of form," as far as one can be constructed. (Any analytic inquiry proceeds from the same concerns, of course, so far as it seeks to explain the rationale or inner "logic" of musical structures.) For many of Beethoven's earlier interpreters, the question was a first step toward the divination of those secret meanings *"sotto il velame delli versi strani,"* beneath the veil of the music's sounding surfaces. For Wagner, the question was the crux of his argument for the musical drama as historical imperative. Thus his remarks on the "Why" of musical forms in *"Music of the Future"* head in the usual direction of his arguments: toward musical drama. At the same time, they are germane to his (and others') critical perceptions of Beethoven, whose symphonies have just been adduced in the preceding paragraph of the 1860 essay as an example of the enabling condition (a flexible, developmental motivic-musical language) of the great synthesis to come:

Poetry will . . . acknowledge its own deep longing for an eventual merging with music as soon as it realizes that music itself has a need which only poetry can fulfil. To explain this need we have to remind ourselves of the human mind's ineradicable impulse, when confronted by an impressive phenomenon, to put the question: Why? Even when we are listening to a symphony the question cannot be completely suppressed and, since the symphony is least of all able to provide an answer, the question puts the listener's faculties, bound to the laws of causality, into a state of confusion.[19]

Several years earlier, in the open letter "On Franz Liszt's Symphonic Poems," as we may recall, Wagner had broached this issue at a similar juncture between classical symphonic forms, "program music," and (tacitly) musical drama. There Wagner had spoken of a motive (or motivation) to formal construction (*Motiv zur Formgebung*), which was at the same time a rationale for the "behavior" of a musical work (V, 191). This line of argument – that classical forms presuppose the collective internalization of the "corporeal movements of the dance or march" – extends back to the earlier Zurich writings, and needn't be pursued here, except to note that all of these contexts lay the groundwork for the axiom of *"Music of the Future"* that radical departures from internalized conventions of musical form will demand a justification which the immanent musical context can no longer provide. In its distress, music (the eternally "feminine") awaits rescue at the hands of poetry and drama (cf. chapter 3).

A corollary of this position is Wagner's view of modulation and its role both in the constitution of "form" and on a local syntactic level. The theoretical implications of these (as always) tendentious views are

---

[19]   VII, 111–12; trans. Robert L. Jacobs, *Three Wagner Essays* (London, 1979), 28.

too problematic to follow up in any detail just now, beyond a suggestion of their pertinence to the nexus of issues around form, "poetic ideas," and drama (see also chapters 4 and 6). The intelligibility of conventional forms, Wagner argued, depended on the limitation of modulatory activity to a circle of closely related keys in most formal contexts (introductions and developments might presumably be exempted, though Wagner did not bother to go into such matters). Where a conventional melodic period, fulfilling an expository function, was generally predicated on the logic of a simple tonic–dominant relation, a dramatically conditioned or determined musical passage (i.e., the "poetic-musical period" of *Opera and Drama*) would be given poetic license to pass freely through any key areas that might suit its expressive purposes (its "poetic intent"). What exactly determines the expressive appositeness of one or another key, and what guarantees that the resulting shape will satisfy as "musical form" – as opposed to aimless recitative, for instance – are questions Wagner answered only in music, not in prose. But he stuck fast to the premise. In a stray fragment from about 1856 he noted:

On modulation in pure instrumental music, and in the drama. Fundamental difference. Rapid and distant transitions are often as necessary in the latter as they are impermissible in the former, due to lack of motivation.[20]   (XII, 280)

Affecting the seasoned conservative and bemusedly ironic tone characteristic of his later writings, Wagner re-phrased this fragment in 1879 ("On Operatic Poetry and Composition in Particular") as a cautionary message to over-eager disciples of the "music of the future": "[H]e who indulges in bold and strange modulations without cause (*ohne Not*) is no better than a rank amateur (*ein Stümper*); but he who misses the opportunity for a bold modulation in the proper place is – a 'senator'" (X, 174: the allusion is to a euphemism of Shakespeare's Iago). The "proper place" (*am richtigen Ort*) is evidently defined dramatically, or by some "idea," over and above the "purely musical." Like much of Wagner's "theory," his ideas on modulation leave almost everyone else in a no-win situation. (To whom does one apply to learn where a bold modulation is *am richtigen Ort*? To the *Meister* alone, apparently.) But Beethoven was always a special case, and these few tenets about form and modulation can help us in charting Wagner's position with regard to Beethoven's music and its critical traditions.

---

[20]   The fragment, its original context in the *"Tristan"* sketchbook, and its critical implications are discussed by Carolyn Abbate in "Wagner, 'On Modulation,' and *Tristan*". As Abbate notes, Wagner's idea of "modulation" embraces what we would normally think of as local progressions or inflections, as well as the longer-range tonal phenomena we now designate by that name (see also chapter 4, below).

Wagner's approach to the "Eroica" was, again, a generally cautious one. He knew better than to indulge in the kind of biographical-historical hermeneutics against which "R." had railed in "A Happy Evening." And as the profile of his own theoretical position gradually took shape Wagner did, in fact, seem to feel increasingly obliged to defend Beethoven's innovations in the name of a Romantic purity. Isolated transgressions of musical "autonomy" (or its appearance) might be interpreted as pointing in the direction of musical drama, but Wagner felt increasingly compelled to validate Beethoven primarily on the grounds of his "purely musical" achievements. Thus the 1852 programmatic commentary seeks to explain the "heroism" of the Third Symphony as a heroic "deed of music" (to anticipate the famous honorific later bestowed by Wagner on his own works). The idea had been adumbrated in 1841: "[Beethoven] was a musician, and saw how he might accomplish in his own domain something of what Bonaparte had accomplished on the battlefields of Italy . . . And is not this symphony just as great a testament to the powers of human creativity as Bonaparte's glorious victories?" (I, 148). The 1852 commentary makes no more mention of the "creative genius" of Napoleon's military campaigns, but only of Beethoven's personal and musical "heroism." Later allusions to the "Eroica" as a model for Wagner's conception of "infinite melody" (see chapter 5) have only to do with technical innovations, broadly construed, that became part of the symphonic inheritance of the musical drama, and no longer with putative "ideas" at all (by now the exclusive property of drama).

Other critics were less circumspect, but their reactions to the work also speak, if often bluntly, to issues relating to Wagner's construction of symphonic *vis à vis* dramatic musical forms and procedures. Let us consider here some contemporary views of two famous nodal junctures – one in each of the first two movements of the "Eroica" – and their significance for the critical junctures of form and meaning, analysis and hermeneutics in Wagner's "theory of form."[21]

Hermeneutic skirmishes with the development and "new theme"

First, the celebrated "new theme" and ensuing E-minor episode in the development of the first movement. The spot has always been a provocative one, but in our time it has generally provoked explanations

---

21 For a complementary survey of interpretive responses to several other signal events in the first movement (opening phrase, "new theme," recapitulation, and coda) and their relation to contemporary analytical perspectives, see Burnham, "Programmatic Reception." Burnham's essay, which appeared after this chapter was originally drafted, treats a number of the same figures discussed here, such as Lenz, Marx, Ulibishev, and Schering.

about how the substance of this unorthodox interpolation in the development might be related to (or derived from) the material of the exposition. Does such a pedigree, if established, "explain" the gesture of thematic and tonal intrusion? To posit a motivic provenance for the theme in this way is not necessarily to answer Wagner's hermeneutic query "Why?"

Just as striking as the intrusion of the E-minor theme, if not more so, is its emphatic preparation across three dozen measures of unrelenting cross-rhythms and hemiola, culminating in the movement's second-most-famous dissonance (after the re-transitional clash of tonic and dominant), the four measures of Neapolitan (F_5^6, mm. 276–9), as they are subsequently interpreted by the cadence to E minor: "thirty-six measures of nineteenth century!" exclaimed Griepenkerl, in a swoon of *Fortschritts-Pathos*.[22] Surely the phenomenal energy of the preparation – the climactic moment of the entire development and hence the gravitational center of the movement's entire musical orbit – has something to do with the reason "Why?", whether buried in the enigmatics of the "purely musical" or requiring the mediation of "ideas."

This is one of the few moments to which Wagner's 1852 program specifically alludes. There he speaks of the "leading idea" of the movement (in suitably abstract terms) as that of "energy" (*Kraft*): a kind of physical or dynamic affect, as it were, that serves to unify, according to a classicist aesthetic, all the subsidiary affective moods of the work that Wagner enumerates here in alliterative pairs (*"Wonne und Wehe, Lust und Leid, Anmut und Wehmut, Sinnen und Sehnen, Schmachten und Schwelgen, Kühnheit, Trotz, und ein unbändiges Selbstgefühl"*).[23] This governing energy, he continues, "gathers itself near the center of the movement into a force of annihilating power, and in its defiant proclamation [of this power] we imagine before us one with the might to trample whole worlds, a titan who struggles with the gods" (V, 170). Indeed, the E-minor episode emerges with its new theme out of a gesture of apocalyptic destruction, which seems in some sense to account for the subsequent feeling of tonal alienation, the air of quiet despondency, exhaustion, and perhaps the thematic disguise or difficulty of recognition (is it a stranger, or

---

[22] W. R. Griepenkerl, *Das Musikfest oder die Beethovener* (1838); cited from Geck and Schleuning, *Geschrieben auf Bonaparte*, 243. More precisely, it is the organist Pfeiffer in Griepenkerl's novella of musical enthusiasm who says this. Pfeiffer, one of the instigators of Griepenkerl's *Musikfest*, has blocked out this passage in red pencil in his score, inscribed with the following commentary: " . . . and here there followed upon the basses' B of the breakthrough (*Durchbruch*), with the defiant ninth above, leading into the heavenly spheres of E minor and A minor and then to the main theme again, bright and triumphant in C major."

[23] "Joy and sorrow, pleasure and pain, grace and melancholy, brooding and longing, languishing and wallowing, boldness, defiance, and an unbounded self-assurance" (V, 170).

someone so changed we fail to recognize him?). The convergence of Wagner's text (with its familiar echoes of "spirits" and "struggles") and the puzzling emergence of the new theme recalls A. W. Ambros's image for Beethoven's hermeneutic provocations more generally:

This music struggles powerfully for determinate expression, it is like a captive spirit whose freedom hangs on the enunciation of a certain word – the spirit himself may not speak it, and we behold this apparition with dumb amazement, searching with a passionate sense of sympathetic engagement for the right word.

(Diese Musik drängt mit gewaltigem Ringen zu bestimmtem Ausdrucke, sie ist wie ein gebannter Geist, dessen Erlösung an das Aussprechen eines einzigen Wortes geknüpft ist – er selbst darf das Wort nicht sagen und der andere steht stumm, rathend, ja mit leidenschaftlichem Antheil nach dem rechten Worte suchend vor der Erscheinung.)[24]

Yet Wagner, in his commentary on the work, evades the question his own theoretical precepts would bid him pose here, the question "Why?"

For A. B. Marx the development section represents the real fray of the metaphorical or "ideal" battle waged across the first movement of the "Eroica" as a whole. His lengthy analytical commentary (1859) may itself represent the originary moment of that since rather tired trope of developmental processes as musical battlefields. Like Wagner's still more generalized "leading idea" of musical (and symbolic) *energeia*, Marx's figure of the musical battle permits him to move freely between associative imagery and large stretches of conventional musical description (all manner of tonal and thematic conflicts, skirmishes, hand-to-hand combat, concerted sorties, temporary truces, and ultimately decisive victory). The net result is more a phantasmagoria of martial motifs embellishing a descriptive analysis than any kind of self-sufficient metaphorical narrative. But at this critical juncture in the development (from the misfired fugato of mm. 237ff through the accumulation of cross-rhythms and up to the new theme of the E-minor episode) Marx does pause to take stock, now that the *musical* "plot" has gone astray. So far, the musical battle has progressed according to plan; only the overall proportions have been expanded, in accordance with the dignity of the epic conception. Up through the intensely

---

[24] A. W. Ambros, *Die Grenzen der Musik und Poesie* (Leipzig, 1855/6), 131. The critic and aesthetician Adolf Kullak (perhaps inadvertently paraphrasing Ambros's text) attributed the "melancholy and grandiose pathos" characteristic of the "modern" idiom in general (Wagner's operas, as well as the program music of Liszt and Berlioz) to the effect of this tragic struggle for articulate expression: "Es ist ein sich *Heranringen* der Töne zum Worte; diese Sphinx blickt so wehmütig, ihre Gebehrden sind so flehend, so beredt, und ihr Mund bleibt stumm, ihre Thränen, ihr Sehnen, ihre Verzweiflung ringen nach Verständniß, und wenn sie es erhascht zu haben meint, streckt sich immer wieder die eherne Hand dazwischen, welche Ton und artikulirtes Wort getrennt hält" ("Ueber Herrn von Bülow's Orchester-Concert und die moderne Richtung der Musik," *Berliner Musik-Zeitung Echo* 9:9 [1859], 66).

syncopated passage climaxing in the "evil" dissonance of mm. 276–9 (*auf einem bösen Akkorde, a–c–e–f*) it has been combat-as-usual, if on an intensified scale. But the collapse of the developmental process and the emergence of the new E-minor theme finally provoke a moment of hermeneutic reflection: ". . . is it sorrow for the sacrifice incurred? Is it a prophetic warning, not yet understood? Is it a voice of recollection heard from the distance?" In describing the character, voicing, and instrumentation of the moment Marx underscores its uncanny, quizzical properties with incantatory repercussions: "a strange song is sounded . . . , the flutes join their monotone, tired and empty sounding B to the rhythmic hovering of the first violins, while the bass undergirds it all with quiet, drum-like strokes." Marx eventually poses the question, if not precisely "Why?", then at least *what* is signified here: "What is this? – It is one of the mysteries of the human heart, one of those enigmatic voices that occasionally penetrate the sphere of human affairs (*die bisweilen hineintönen in die Geschicke des Menschen*), like the words Brutus once heard whispered from the lips of Caesar as he lay slain; such secrets resist the 'common intelligibility of things'."[25]

It is simply an enigma. "This has no place in the life of the hero," Marx opines. With the C-major unison statement of the main theme in m. 300 the music (or the hero?) promptly begins to exorcise this enigmatic incursion and to forge ahead on the path to recapitulation, resolution, and victory. Following the famous moment of crisis at the point of reprise (the newly awoken voice of heroic resolve resounds above a faint chorus of fear and doubt, as Marx imagines it), the battle resumes its course and the *telos* of strife and victory recommences. Here the battle trope proves to be apt enough, since such activity can plausibly return to its starting point, recover the same territory a second time, trace and retrace similar patterns as long as its heroes and adversaries remain to play things out. The ultimately random teleology of the battle trope is easily subsumed again within the descriptive discourse of "purely musical" form.

But what of the (musically) anomalous episode, the incursion of E minor and the new theme? Marx's apparent dismissal of the enigmatic moment is perhaps not quite the gesture of hermeneutic defeat it seems. "It is one of those enigmatic voices . . . , like the words that Brutus once heard whispered from the lips of Caesar as he lay slain."

---

[25] "Was ist das? – Es ist eines der Rätsel in der Menschenbrust, eine dieser Rätselstimmen, die bisweilen hineintönen in die Geschicke des Menschen, wie damals das Flüsterwort, das Brutus von den Lippen des erschlagenen Cäsar vernahm. Solche Geheimnisse entziehen sich der 'gemeinenen Deutlichkeit der Dinge'" (A. B. Marx, *Ludwig van Beethoven*, vol. I, 196). Marx evidently refers to Caesar's famous dying words in Shakespeare, "Et tu Brute? – Then fall, Caesar." On Marx, see also Burnham, "Programmatic Reception," 7ff.

We are reminded of Wagner's words about the "annihilating force" in the wake of whose musical destruction the new theme emerges. The allusion to Caesar (though this is no battle of his, of course) puts us in mind of the violence of the moment, whether it betokens an assassination or some nameless victim of war. Further, Marx's earlier queries about the new theme open up a wider frame of temporal reference, more appropriate to the leitmotivic drama, or the novel, than to the normally present-tense discourse of symphonic time: "Is it a prophetic warning, not yet understood? Is it a voice of recollection from the distance?" Though the answer is deferred, finally, we are alerted to a potential stirring of the impulses behind the Wagnerian musical drama – even if Wagner himself seems to have suppressed them in his own commentary.

The Russian critic Alexander Ulibishev had established an international reputation as a leading reactionary with his *Nouvelle biographie de Mozart* (Moscow, 1843), where he notoriously championed the ideals of a musical classicism at the expense of the glorious Beethovenian revolution. His polemical Beethoven monograph of 1857 (*Beethoven, ses critiques et ses glossateurs*) appeared in German translation two years later, simultaneously with Marx's study. Throughout much of it Ulibishev seems to take an impish delight in tweaking the sensibilities of high-minded idealizing critics of Marx's ilk with outrageous suppositions (for instance, that the Finale of the Fifth Symphony had originally been intended for the Third), uncensored flights of interpretive fancy, and all manner of eccentric critical *obiter dicta*. As a Russian and a musical enthusiast with a highly charged imagination, Ulibishev was very much engaged with the case of the "Eroica" and its Napoleonic resonances (while he seems largely unfazed, strangely enough, by its now iconic status as the *coup-de-grâce* to a Mozartian musical culture).

Ulibishev also takes the expected battle scenario as a point of departure. In his explication of the musical action he veers between the constraints of an apparently naive narrative logic (the repeat of the exposition parallels a military strategist's reprise of an outlined battle plan, or the troops' repeated passing in review) and phantasmagoric hallucination. The development, of course, is again the real fray of the battle, the crux of the action ("Oh maintenant, ce n'est plus comme à la parade!"). Ulibishev follows the heated course of the campaign with sympathetic attention – a good musical field reporter, like Marx. The tonal and thematic peripeteia of the "new" episode and its preparation provokes his most intense interpretive involvement:

The invisible phalanx is no longer marching straight and proud; it twists like a wounded serpent, moving across a frenetic modulation; it advances, rises up in rage, and suddenly it stops. Its forces are broken by a superior resistance, but one which Beethoven does not reveal to us. Is it God, is it the enemy? I don't know.

The musical skirmish sparked in the fugato of mm. 237ff has revolved around the matter of a second-beat rhythmic accent (a legacy of the exposition), and this, together with the concomitant hemiola, is primarily what leads to the climactic issue of the "new theme," where the metrical conflict is at last resolved. (Wagner's more abstract reflections on the accumulation of a [self-]annihilating "energy" really come somewhat closer to revealing the musical forces at work here, where Ulibishev is at a loss to identify a motivating agency.) Ulibishev does not doubt the significance of the critical moment, however, even if its signification remains problematic for him.

The orchestra [now] produces nothing but notes without melody or harmony – a repeated "e" against "f," raucous and lacerating, a death-rattle expressed with a too-real realism that becomes a lie with respect to art (*exprimée avec cette verité trop vraie qui devient un mensonge par rapport à l'art*). But what can be signified by these terrifying dissonances that cease so abruptly and remain unresolved? Did Beethoven alarm himself here, or is it perhaps the prophetic glow of the conflagration of Moscow illuminating some future disaster in the [clairvoyant] mind of his hero?

As in Marx's account, the violent extremity of this juncture threatens to shatter temporal continuity: present and future (musical and "historical") are confounded under the impact of this violence of dissonant accent and harmony and the maximal displacement of the action from the tonic orbit (from E♭ major to E minor). Ulibishev registers the musical (tonal) displacement of the new theme in stylistic and "geographical" terms, struck by its Otherness: the new melody is said to have an "oriental" character, "melancholy and a little savage." It is as if suddenly a new mental tack sends the hero's thoughts back in time:

to Egypt, or maybe India, whose conquest he proposes to an ally too magnanimous to be tempted by such rich and easy prey. After a few measures of preparation – the equivalent of a moment's silence – we suddenly hear a melody of oriental color, intoned by oboe and cello in the manner of a trio.[26]

Temporal perspective is unloosened, as is the narrative perspective itself (the reference to a "magnanimous" conquest of India suggests that the hero may be Alexander now, in place of Napoleon). While Ulibishev responds to the unorthodox placement of a new theme in this context he does not attempt to explain it away, nor to dismiss it as one of the "chimerical" whims he denounces in the late works later in the book. The principle he later enunciates with reference to the striking gesture of harmonic expansion that opens the coda (the move from E♭ through D♭ and C, mm. 551–66) could be invoked, perhaps, in

[26] This and the preceding quotations are from A. Oulibischeff [Ulibishev], *Beethoven, ses critiques et ses glossateurs* (Leipzig and Paris, 1857), 177–8.

explaining the anomalies of the development: "it's not very agreeable to the ear, I admit it; but here the poetic idea (*l'idée poétique*) comes to assist the musical idea, or rather, supplements it." Or, as he succinctly sums up there: "C'est étrange, mais c'est frappant."[27] The fact that both Marx and Ulibishev are finally at a loss to "determine" the poetic idea whose presence they intuit in the events of Beethoven's development would seem to lend support to the Wagnerian thesis that such poetic ideas could not be fully "realized" by music alone.

The Marcia funebre *as instrumental "drama" (voices in the crowd)*

Wagner's 1852 commentary on the "Eroica," however, generally stresses immanent, "purely musical" values over any perceived representational impulse or unrealized expressive ambition. (It was written as an appreciation and not a polemic, after all.) His resistance to popular Napoleonic programs (whether prosaic or "poetic") is readily comprehensible, though the generality of his remarks – and his consequent evasion of the movement's more provocative details – suggests a deliberate attempt to preserve the work's symphonic autonomy against the misguided transgressions of the later works, as Wagner understood them around 1850. Ulibishev, for all his unrestrained fancy, followed a similar strategy: "It is on an ideal level rather than that of genuine action that this picture (*tableau*) often appears to be dramatic," he asserts of the "Eroica"; "without owing anything to the forms of drama, it is composed, instead, in the truest and grandest symphonic style."[28] Yet others insisted on the dramatic tendencies of the work. Marx construed each movement of the symphony as an "act" within a larger symphonic drama – although having done so, he contrived to absent himself from the last act, suggesting a certain embarrassment about his ability to interpret the outcome.

Ulibishev, like Berlioz before him, found the more specifically dramatic qualities of the work concentrated in the second movement – "a complete drama," in Berlioz's words (*la marche funèbre est tout un drame*),[29] and a drama with four acts of its own, according to Ulibishev. The funeral march is certainly the central locus of the symphony's poetic idea, as the

---

27 Ibid., 178, 179. "From this example and many similar ones," Ulibishev observes, "we can draw an important conclusion, and one that has been as yet too little noticed: that things [apparently] defective in themselves may be transformed into relative beauties by the application of a poetic idea or a given program" (179). Thus, contrary to the classicist aesthetic he generally subscribes to, Ulibishev here invokes the principle of contextually "relative" beauty (*le beau relatif*).

28 Ibid., 175.

29 Berlioz, "Etude critique des symphonies de Beethoven," in *A travers chants* (Paris, 1862), 21.

71

solemn commemoration of the anonymous "hero" of its eventual title. By means of generic reference Beethoven is able to endow the movement with an initial level of expressive "determinacy," which can then be further shaped by details of form, melodic gesture, and the like. As a march, on the other hand, the movement exposes the primitive, abstractly ceremonial roots of instrumental forms altogether (according to Wagner's theory), and from this perspective, any dramatic ambitions imposed on it will risk transgressing the inherent constraints of such form.

Up to a point, Beethoven's march obeys the strictures of Wagner's conservative instrumental poetics, presenting a stately hierarchy of contrasting, complementary phrases and periods. In his 1852 commentary Wagner narrated the initial progress of the movement (these rudimentary periodic contrasts) in characteristically gendered terms, reminding us that, for him, even such fundamentally "absolute" forms exhibit traces of their anthropological origins. Of the first hundred measures, encompassing the C-minor A section and contrasting, major-mode B section, he writes: ". . . the lament begins in a tone of deeply earnest, virile sorrow, which yields to a more tender sensibility, recollection, tears of love, an inner exaltation, and finally to spirited acclamations" (V, 171). With reference to the central, developmental episode (the fugato) through the varied reprise of the march (mm. 173ff), Wagner continues:

From out of this sorrow springs a new force (*Kraft*), filling us with a sublime warmth: as if to nurture this [new force], we instinctively turn again to feelings of sorrow; we yield to this impulse even to the point of expiring in sighs; but precisely at this point we muster all our strength (*Kraft*) again: we will not surrender, but endure. We do not repress sorrow, but bear it aloft on the strong waves of a stalwart, virile heart. (V, 171)

Wagner's account of the movement is that of a "succession of soul-states," in the typical critical vocabulary of Beethoven's time. As such, it is historically "authentic" enough, encouraging us to view the movement from within the safe confines of an instrumental *Gefühlsästhetik*, fenced off from the dynamics of drama. There are no characters in Wagner's script: in the classicistic tradition of an aesthetics of effect (*Wirkungsästhetik*) it is "we" who are filled alternately with sorrow, compassion, and exaltation, or at least are given to experience the aesthetic simulation of these conditions. Wagner even cuts his account short (before reaching the famous thematic disintegration of the final bars) with an appeal to the topos of inexpressibility, entirely in the spirit of the musically absolute: "Who could possibly describe in words these infinitely manifold, and just for that reason inarticulate feelings . . . ? Only the tone-poet could do so, [as he has] in this wonderful composition" (V, 171).

72

"From out of this sorrow springs a new force . . ." To this extent Wagner registers the emergence of the central developmental episode from the (interrupted) reprise of the march theme ("sorrow"). But in decoding his text to this movement, we will notice that Wagner has largely suppressed any mention of its formally subversive gestures, such as the deflection of its "attempted" reprise here. He suppresses, that is, the fact that the protocol of orderly alternation (*Wechsel*) befitting the march form is resisted from within, by what we might interpret as evolutionary (dramatic) tendencies.

It is precisely the march's resistance to the ceremonial decorum of its genre that elicits admiration of its "dramatic qualities" from other writers. The most striking of such gestures is the second "deflected" reprise, following the central developmental episode, beginning from m. 154. In this case the apparent deflection turns out to be rather a deferral and correction: the march theme enters faintly (*sotto voce*), half-heartedly in G minor, after a suspiciously flat-footed cadence in that key in the strings. This deflection/deferral serves to relocate the theme in the tonic, C minor, where it recommences, surrounded by a pulsing sextuplet accompaniment (Wagner's "strong waves of a stalwart, virile heart"), energized and slightly destabilized by an implied G pedal in the bass. The faint-hearted G-minor quasi-reprise is overtly "dramatized" – in the colloquial sense – through its interruption by an extravagantly melodramatic gesture: the violins break off the theme and sustain for two beats an exposed a♭². This fragile, isolated tone is answered by a sudden roar of 'cellos and basses three and four octaves below, followed by a cataclysmic interjection from the horns and trumpets (see Example 2.1).

Wagner's faithful admirer and pen-pal of the early Zurich years, Theodor Uhlig, drew attention to the passage in an essay on the Beethoven symphonies published in the *Neue Zeitschrift für Musik* in 1850, between the time of *The Art-Work of the Future* and *Opera and Drama*. He cites mm. 151–76 as an example of certain exceptional excursions within this symphony into the domain of "descriptive music" (*malende* or *schildernde Musik*): "not because the designation of the movement (*Marcia funebre*) may itself serve to call up specific representations (*bestimmte Vorstellungen*) of external appearances, but because such passages point toward particular, individualized representations [in the mind] of the composer himself; because their significance can only be explained from the perspective of musical description (which is never the case with pure music)."[30] The specific representation imagined by Uhlig here is rather less dramatic than we might expect: "the

---

[30] Theodor Uhlig, *Musikalische Schriften*, ed. Ludwig Frankenstein (Regensburg, 1913), 193.

Example 2.1   Beethoven, Symphony No. 3 ("Eroica"), second
movement: *Marcia funebre* (mm. 151–76)

appearance of a grand funeral convoy and its stately progression onto some great plain." He exculpates this mild hermeneutical indulgence with a piece of Wagnerian theoretical rhetoric, diverting the blame to the composer's transgressions. "Such representations should not really occur to the listener of an untexted composition: but then, an instrumental work should not depart from the ordained confines of the genre in the first place."[31]

In addition to formal transgressions and overtly characteristic features (the funeral topos as such, the heroic fanfare-acclamations of the *maggiore* episode, the deflected and deferred reprises, the fragmentations of the coda), the movement also provoked exegesis as a scene of drama through its multiple evocations of voices, both choral and solo. What apparently begins as a ceremonial beating and strumming of lifeless instruments is progressively endowed with palpable vocal qualities that animate the formalistic ritual and potentially simulate the presence of those prerequisites of drama that Wagner would deny to instrumental forms: human agency, psychological motivation, a conscious will, and the quality of human actions directed to a goal or purpose.[32]

A. B. Marx had identified the "Eroica" as the first significant example of an animating or "vocalizing" principle already in his early (1824) essay "On the Symphony and Beethoven's Accomplishments in this Field":

Soon [the instruments] were no longer merely a lifeless means for him, which by means of an appropriate selection and deployment might serve to express one's subjective feelings and might thus at best stand in place of human speech and song (that is, as musical speech). They now appeared to him in the light of a finely limned personality (*Persönlichkeit*), and the orchestra assumed the role of an animate chorus engaged in dramatic activity (*ein belebter, in dramatischer Thätigkeit begriffener Chor*).

---

[31] Ibid., 194.
[32] Joseph Kerman identified the instrumental projection of a human (singing) voice as a special preoccupation of Beethoven's late quartets – a feature which indeed has much to do with their contribution to the larger hermeneutic tradition under discussion here (see the chapter entitled "Voice" in *The Beethoven Quartets* [New York, 1966], 191–222). Such instrumental projection of a vocal "persona" is of course one of the ideas explored in Edward Cone's *The Composer's Voice* (Berkeley and Los Angeles, 1974). Carolyn Abbate distances such musical imitations or evocations of "literal" vocality from her concerns with narrative or other figurative voices (as well as objective operatic ones) in the introductory chapter to *Unsung Voices* (Princeton, 1991 [see p. 19]); nonetheless, the phenomenon plays a role (inevitably) in her interpretational activities, for instance in construing the second (*"Gesang"*) theme of Mahler's *Todtenfeier* movement as a "vocal" intrusion from outside of the instrumental-symphonic sound world (151). Like the variety of vocal projections in Beethoven's music, the gesture recalls Rousseau's notion of the (human, singing) voice in itself as a sign of human presence, or, for Wagner, the (intended, if not realized) projection of a conscious human will or motive.

This animation of instrumental voices, Marx continues, was of course not without precedent in earlier music, or in Beethoven's own works (the projection of human vocal quality onto instrumental artifice is surely one of the most venerable tropes of musical criticism). "But it is just as certain that Beethoven, far from abandoning the example of these earlier tendencies, rather consolidated them [in the aim of achieving] a psychological evolution (*psychologische Entwickelung*), allied to a sequence of external conditions, represented in the thoroughly dramatic activity of the orchestral instruments."[33]

"Il est écrit en style dramatique" – with this assertion Ulibishev brings Marx's intuitions about the dramatizing tendencies of Beethoven and the "Eroica" in general to bear on the funeral march in particular (echoing Berlioz's similar contention). The first of its "four acts" is the "march itself, executed by a military band on stage, following the funeral cortège" – thus, stage music without voices. In the "second act" (the *maggiore* B section), the cortège has passed from sight: "a character within the drama intones, in the major mode, a hymn in which the idea of historical immortality dominates that of death, and whose soothing accents penetrate the general mourning like a consoling ray of hope." Individual voices are raised (oboe, flute), although Ulibishev passes over the strongly choral quality of the *tutti* acclamations without comment. The significance of the contrapuntal development eludes him, but he finds "more than sufficient compensation" in the last "act," a *scène dramatique sublime*. "Returning in G minor . . . , the march theme has not yet completed its first phrase when the violins emit a searing cry, followed by a general pause. With this cry and this silence one senses the approach of those who come to lament the man, rather than the hero." Ulibishev sketches a scene with new characters: the hero's family and veteran comrades, who emerge from the faceless crowd. Finally, the expressive fragmentation of the final bars transforms the lugubrious *musique militaire* of the march into a living voice:

. . . the march is silenced and a human voice – that of the wife, now forever widowed – pronounces the last farewell. In repeating this farewell address, the voice grows weaker and weaker, until it breaks against a suspended chord, deprived of resolution. Sublime, I say again; it lacks only words. Yes, words, scenery, and a *prima donna* – a fine singer and actress – in place of the oboe, as I've said before and as I still believe.[34]

---

[33] A. B. Marx, "Etwas über die Symphonie und Beethovens Leistungen in diesem Fach" (1824), cited from Stefan Kunze, ed., *Ludwig van Beethoven: Die Werke im Spiegel seiner Zeit* (Laaber, 1987), 637.

[34] This and the preceding quotations are from Ulibishev, *Beethoven, ses critiques et ses glossateurs*, 180–1.

Ulibishev's last remarks are probably another instance of the calculated provocations in which he was wont to indulge, even if the phrases *"prima donna"* and *"bonne chanteuse"* were not originally meant to convey the ironic tone we might hear in them. Here, at least, is one piece of evidence confirming Schindler's otherwise unlikely assertion that people often heard Beethoven's symphonies as "operas in disguise" (*verkappte Opern*).[35]

Ulibishev's dramatic voices are prefigured in a nearly contemporaneous description of Beethoven's funeral march by A. W. Ambros, which will also return us to Wagner and his theoretical compunctions regarding the expressive content of Beethoven's music. For Ambros, like Ulibishev, the initial *minore* march is an "instrumental" prelude to the drama. While this opening period-group establishes "a general character of great pathos," it remains within the boundaries of its genre, not yet aspiring to "an inner evolution that concerns itself analytically with its fundamental idea."[36] Such an "evolutionary" process begins only with the turn to major.

With this *maggiore* the evolution [*Entwickelung*] is set in motion . . . – The quietly beginning, slow and measured step of its animating sextuplets suggests "the approaching ray of hope" [a citation from Schindler], the shattering *fortissimo* thunder of the cadences to this section, with their ominous trumpet-calls, are an unmistakable call to resistance. The march that means to return here is interrupted and repulsed, then in the *fugato*, forces are assembled from all quarters – yet remain mired in sullen resignation – when suddenly there sounds a summons to a terrifying battle of annihilation, a titanic offensive – but in vain! – From the heights they [?] tumble lower and lower, irresistibly pulled downward until their ever weaker resolve yields to the funeral march, which, brooking no more resistance, now resumes like the annunciation of some merciless imperative; a last diversionary tactic is attempted in the deceptive cadence to A♭, but finally it all comes to an end in the empty sepulchral stillness of C minor – crushed and fragmented, the theme dissolves into the void.[37]

The rambling parataxis of this narrative (which I have deliberately tried to preserve in translation) suggests that the story enacted here lacks the kind of causal, conceptual coherence we would expect of a dramatic narrative in poetry or prose. Ambros has insisted on the "evolutionary" quality of the movement as a whole (precisely the quality that distinguishes drama from "pure music," for Wagner), yet his account is not really so different from Wagner's "anti-dramatic" reading as a string of alternating psychic conditions. Both of them, for instance,

---

[35] A. Schindler, *Biographie von Ludwig van Beethoven* (1840), 196; see also Schering, *Beethoven und die Dichtung*, 565.

[36] ". . . nicht aber eine innere *Entwickelung*, welche sich analytisch mit ihrem Grundgedanken befaßt" (A. W. Ambros, *Die Grenzen der Musik und Poesie*, 133).

[37] Ibid., 133–4.

light on identical terms to describe the apocalyptic moment preceding the second (or first successful) reprise, with their talk of "annihilation" and "titanic" upheavals.

In one respect crucial to the constitution of "drama" Ambros differs from Wagner, however. Ambros hears "an unmistakable call to resistance" in what he describes as the "ominous trumpet calls." In the sequence of his account this would appear to refer to the fanfares closing the B section, mm. 90ff, but as a description it is much more apposite to the apocalyptic explosion at m. 160, preceding the second, complete reprise; it may be that he confused or conflated the two moments in his mind. Similarly, "the march that means to return" (*der Marsch, der wieder eintreten will*) but is "interrupted and repulsed" evidently refers to the first, aborted reprise of the main march idea following the major-mode B section, although it could equally well describe the events prior to the second, ultimately successful reprise. In either case, Ambros attributes to the music something that (for Wagner) may obtain to animate voices – as representations of living presence, or conscious dramatic agents – but normally not to mere "lifeless" instruments: instruments employed in the execution of a musical design, without will or motive of their own. These two subversive junctures between the larger units of Beethoven's march (the deflected and deferred reprises, respectively) connote for Ambros the presence of an active will that can "resist" its ordained musical-formal destiny (even if it is ultimately reduced, Wotan-like, to a state of tragic resignation). When untexted music attempts to transgress the formal-behavioral norms that guarantee its perceptual intelligibility, as Wagner maintained in "*Music of the Future*," it provokes the hermeneutic query "Why?" According to Wagner's precepts, we need to be *shown* an answer to this, or at least hear it spoken (sung). In any case, the answer is not one that instruments alone are able to speak. Any attempt to insinuate "dramatic pathos" into a symphonic form will only end by confusing us, prompting "questions without answers," as Wagner still insisted in 1879 ("On the Application of Music to the Drama," X, 180). Or, as he put the matter in an oblique criticism of the Fifth Symphony and its historical consequences (in *The Art-Work of the Future*), music as such does not act of its own accord: "it may accompany an ethical, human deed (*sittlichen Tat*)," provide a certain sonic rhetorical emphasis, "but it is not the deed itself; [likewise,] it can present us with an alternation of feelings and moods, but cannot develop (*entwickeln*) one mood from out of another with any sense of inner necessity: it lacks the moral will" (III, 93).[38]

---

[38] Note the apparent contradiction to the famous phrase about "deeds of music made visible" ("Über die Benennung 'Musikdrama'," 1872) – further evidence of the tortuous dialectics of Wagner's "evolving" aesthetics.

Symphonic interludes as choral laments

Theoretical objections aside, there is reason to suppose that Wagner did not appreciate a kind of dramatic impulse in Beethoven's funeral march – not only in its tentatively subversive formal gestures, but also in its projection of dramatic voices, as identified by these other critics. While his 1852 comments generally suppressed such metaphorical vocal presence, his own adaptations of this genre of funereal-processional lament in *Götterdämmerung* and *Parsifal* draw explicitly on the "choric" role of the orchestra, an idea which he developed at some length in *Opera and Drama* and elsewhere.

In Wagner's theoretical model, the orchestra was intended to absorb the mediating, reflective role of the ancient Greek (and modern operatic) chorus. It was enabled to perform this role thanks to a newly acquired faculty of "speech" (*Sprachvermögen*) that was a principal legacy of Beethoven's accomplishments. On the other hand, the traditionally subordinate, accompanimental role of the operatic orchestra made it possible for the orchestral "chorus" to keep up the kind of running commentary for which the Wagnerian orchestra (with its well-stocked storehouse of topical leitmotifs) is so widely renowned. What gives Wagner's orchestra the right to speak up – what empowers its participation as an active voice or as omniscient narrator, as it is often construed – is the existence of a palpable dramatic object in the singers and stage action, without which we would obviously have no basis for interpreting this ongoing stream of orchestral oratory (or what, for instance, motivates the many contrasting tones it strikes, from the high oratorical to the ironic, fussy, and prattling).[39] The transitional "symphonic" funeral processions in the third acts of *Götterdämmerung* and *Parsifal* are instructive here. Both involve the stage presence of a real dramatic chorus (although in *Götterdämmerung* it remains silent). But as instrumental "arch-forms," in essence, both passages are tendentially regressive, illustrating the point of contact between Wagner's full-fledged "symphonic drama" and the antique choric ritual perceived in Beethoven's dramatizing symphonic movement – a movement to which Siegfried's funeral music surely pays homage.

---

[39] On the role of the orchestra as "chorus" see *Opera and Drama* (IV, 190–1) and *"Music of the Future"* (VII, 130). Dieter Borchmeyer has discussed this motif of Wagner's operatic-dramaturgical theory and its role in Nietzsche's *Birth of Tragedy* in *Richard Wagner: Theory and Theatre*, trans. Stewart Spencer (Oxford, 1991), chapter 12: "Choral Tragedy and Symphonic Drama." In *Unsung Voices* Carolyn Abbate generally fights shy of traditional notions of orchestral "narration" or choric commentary, although the figure of orchestral narrator does occasionally crop up, for instance as a means of establishing temporal distance from the characters' own dramatic narration (169–70).

Although Wagner had proposed the "choral" identity of the *Ring* orchestra *in toto*, he was conscious of the more explicit analogy he had established in the context of Siegfried's funeral music:

"I have composed a Greek chorus," R. exclaims to me this morning, "but a chorus which will be sung, so to speak, by the orchestra; after Siegfried's death, while the scene is being changed, the Siegmund theme will be played, as if the chorus were saying: 'This was his father'; then the sword motive; and finally his own theme; then the curtain goes up, Gutrune enters, thinking she has heard his horn. How could words ever make the impression that these solemn themes, in their new form, will evoke? Music always expresses the direct present."[40]

Wagner's remarks to Cosima confirm the common critical intuition that Siegfried's funeral music functions as a kind of pocket heroic-musical *Bildungsroman*. But this is not so much the story of his life (which Siegfried has just finished recounting, after all), as it is a genealogy of the hero in an epic or Biblical manner. Its concision is due, in part, to the omission of any reference to the hero's encounters with his adversaries (Mime, Fafner, Hagen, and the Gibichungs) that would only distort the high-toned dignity of the moment – these matters are dealt with in the more prosaic context of Siegfried's autobiographical narrative ("Mähren aus meiner jungen Tagen") preceding his murder. Even Brünnhilde is conspicuously absent from this heroic musical eulogy; her ghostly, disembodied leitmotivic presence only intrudes afterwards, as the procession fades into the distance, displaced from the glorious past to the doom-laden present of the following scene.

As either "Greek chorus" or symphonic interlude, Siegfried's funeral music falls somewhere between formalized ritual and genuine drama. Its "poetic idea" is precisely that of Beethoven's *Marcia funebre* (cele-brating the memory of a fallen hero), and its musical-dramatic context is at least faintly analogous, in that both precede a final, affirmative musical resolution, for which each might be said to serve a preparatory cathartic function. The gendered motivic and instrumental contrasts (and implicit scenario) Wagner read in the "Eroica" funeral march can be recognized again in Siegfried's funeral music. Wagner's words on the initial expressive–musical phases of Beethoven's march are, in fact, remarkably apposite to his own music. An expression of "serious, virile sorrow" yields to a more "tender [feminine] sensibility, to

---

[40] CWD, 29 September 1871 (vol. I, 417–18). An 1859 review of *Lohengrin* in Berlin – possibly reflecting the influence of Wagner's own theorizing – identifies Wagner's orchestra as an "omniscient chorus" ("ein allwissender, in die Zukunft und in die Vergangenheit schauender Chor [der] die Personen des Stückes umgiebt"). Just like the spirits of fallen warriors who continue to fight out the battle in the sky, so the orchestral discourse here "shadows" that of the drama on stage ("so trägt sich hier das ganze Drama noch einmal im Elementarreich der Instrumente zu") ("*Lohengrin* von R. Wagner," *Berliner Musik-Zeitung Echo* 9 [1859], 45).

remembrance, to tears of love," and then gradually to "inner exaltation" and "spirited acclamations" ("Programmatic Commentary," V, 171). And so, exactly, are Siegmund's serious and melancholy motives intoned by the "virile" choir of Wagner tubas, subsequently reinforced by trumpets, *pianissimo* and *ausdrucksvoll.* This performance directive, "expressively" (*ausdrucksvoll*), is multiplied throughout the parts as the "tender" feminine compassion of Sieglinde's motives emerge (she who represents at once sister, wife, and mother in this intimate genealogy) in the expressive timbres of English horn, clarinet, and oboe, in turn, while Siegmund's music continues to emote quietly in the cellos and basses. Wagner, like Beethoven, begins with a funereal tattoo of "lifeless" (unvocalized) instruments. Here the dead drumbeats rap out the emblematic rhythm of the motive first heard at the moment of Siegfried's murder, and again after his dying words ("Brünnhild' bietet mir Gruß!"). Like Beethoven, Wagner proceeds to trace a symbolic sequence of "male" and "female" voices through to combined choral acclamations, the great *tutti* hurrahs that transform the rhythm of the lifeless funereal tattoo into the symbolic voice of collective humanity.

Wagner's symphonic interlude assumes a compact, somewhat cautious "evolutionary" form as befits an intermediate genre, crossing the primitive instrumental march with elements of choral drama and mimed action (the visible but silent cortège that carries Siegfried's corpse away). It is appropriate that Wagner's orchestral "chorus" attains its full voice at just about the same point that the mute human chorus of vassals disappears from view, in a kind of dramatic-musical "voice-exchange" (if this metaphorical adaptation of the technical term might be permitted).[41] The music progresses at a deliberate, measured pace and in periodic phrasing, appropriate to the instrumental genre. Short (leit-)motivic phrases of discrete melodic and harmonic shape pause sedately on secure points of tonal articulation: tonic, subdominant, and dominant. The brief form is held together by the rhythmic refrain of its opening measures (the funereal tattoo of the "dead-march" proper). Transformed into the triumphant acclamations of the central climax, this rhythm alternates with Siegfried's motives: that which prophesied his birth in *Die Walküre* and the heroic variant of his horn-call from the prologue of the present opera.

Despite its apparent formality, this march follows the lead of Wagner's other dramatic transitions rather than holding strictly to the dictates of instrumental form (as construed by Wagner). That is, it debouches into the next and final scene without distinct tonal closure or formal

---

[41] Wagner's stage directions specify that the procession should have disappeared from view in the passage leading up to the arrival of C major, with the sword motive and the *tutti* acclamations.

reprise.[42] The processional music dissolves along with the Wagnerian stage mists, enlisted one last time to effect a "naturalistic" change of scene. Where the resistance to reprise and sectional closure in Beethoven was occasioned by the intervention of unknown agents, provoking hermeneutic puzzlement, Wagner's music is peopled by familiar motivic acquaintances, all of them previously dramatically "determined" and hence leaving no semiotic lacunae. We've seen who dies, we know his story, and are able to recognize it again in this eulogistic précis. As in Beethoven's movement, the final stages of the choral eulogy are dissolved. Or we might say that our aural view of the procession (as it trails off into the distance) is interrupted by the appearance of other musical events. But unlike the invisible forces that interrupt the progress of Beethoven's march, the new musical presence that intervenes here assumes a concrete identity (Brünnhilde), as she emerges from the parting mists to enact a brief musical pantomime of her nocturnal colloquy with the Rhine-maidens prior to Gutrune's (physical) appearance. Now with human presence reinstated on stage, the orchestral "chorus" steps back, as it were, into its discreet invisibility below the action. Wagner's procession dissolves, like Beethoven's, into a silent void, at least momentarily, but one that is explained visibly and audibly by the empty spaces of Gutrune's monologue. The "poetic idea" of this bit of instrumental stage music (the funeral procession) has been rendered "determinate" (*bestimmt*) by its dramatic context.

Titurel's funeral cortège in Act III of *Parsifal* occupies a position and function closely analogous to Siegfried's funeral music as an instrumental transition to the final scene of the drama. In this position they both also serve as a prelude of sorts to these respective culminating scenes – somber instrumental introductions to transcendent vocal finales. The style and context of both passages present (as I have already suggested in the case of the *Götterdämmerung* music) analogies to the figurative distinction, as implied in those early critical readings of Beethoven, between an introductory instrumental "dead-march" in the "Eroica" second movement and the dramatized "vocal" and/or "choral" qualities of the middle and end. These distinctions between instrumental and vocal styles find still closer analogues in the case of the *Parsifal* music: its contrast between the hollow pealing of the ostinato bell figure or the lugubrious rotations of the crawling, stepwise

---

[42] Tonal closure in C minor is actually implied where the heroic variant of the horn-call returns in muted, minor-mode guise, at the moment of Gutrune's entrance. But by this point, both the scenic and musical elisions with the new scene have been fully established. On the question of tonal closure versus "dissolution" here, see also Christopher Wintle, "The Numinous in *Götterdämmerung*," in *Reading Opera*, ed. A. Groos and R. Parker (Princeton, 1988), esp. 230–4.

motive in the cellos and basses, on one hand, and the keening motive of "Desolation" (*Öde*) in the upper strings, brass, and woodwinds, on the other. (Although the latter is also an orchestral motive throughout the opera, it is an emphatically "vocal" gesture, stylistically, while the ostinato motives are emphatically instrumental.) As with the thematic material of Beethoven's march, the semantic value of these motives – ritual mourning and personal lament – is easily decoded, even without the aid of precise verbal or scenic determination. The form of this processional music, if we include the bifurcated chorus that emerges with the beginning of the ensuing final scene, is again loosely rounded or arch-shaped (that favorite architectural category of Lorenzian analysis finds a natural habitat here within the Grail temple). The figurative "voice-exchange" between real, though mute, chorus and chorus-of-instruments in the *Götterdämmerung* music is replicated here in reverse (and more fully realized) as the chorus picks up and completes the wordless orchestral lament to the text of the funeral catechism, "Geleiten wir im bergenden Schrein . . ." A solemnly hieratic character of formal ritual suffuses the Grail temple scenes in *Parsifal* altogether, of course, and this episode is perhaps even further removed from dramatic action than was the music of Siegfried's obsequies. The tone, moreover, is one of lament throughout, without the element of paean that Christopher Wintle notes as a generic admixture in *Götterdämmerung*.[43] Thus the "poetic idea" differs slightly from that of Beethoven's march and of the processional music of the earlier opera. Instead of the hero's memorial, we have an act of pure mourning, moving entirely to the gloomy gait of a Mahlerian *schwerer Kondukt*.

The musical progress of this interlude involves a free but orderly succession of motivic ideas, as in the *Götterdämmerung* music, glued together here by the continuous stratum of ostinato figures (the bells and rotating bass motive). Again, the formal procedure could be tagged as something between a balanced "alternation" of brief motivic periods and an overall, modest "evolution" toward the climactic antiphonal cries of *Wehe* that crush dissonantly against the fixed pitches of the bells, forced into an uneasy, quasi-Phrygian resolution on E.

With its clearly identifiable motives and simple, ritual actions the episode is hermeneutically transparent enough, offering little interpretive challenge, aside from the matter of tonality. The quizzical E minor of our earlier (first-movement) "Eroica" example was emphatically prepared and realized, but in a formal context that offered no clear *raison*

43   Wintle, "The Numinous in *Götterdämmerung*," 203. Wintle also notes the function of Siegfried's funeral music as musical and affective prelude the the final scene as a whole (204). The designation here of the march as a "synopsis of action that is still unfolding" seems to me problematic, however (the procession is an "action," to be sure, but the leitmotivic "genealogy" – as eulogy – is a retrospective gesture).

d'être, at least not from the perspective of a Wagnerian instrumental poetics. By contrast, the E-minor tonality that launches and rounds out Titurel's funeral cortège is only faintly articulated, at first, and is re-attained at the end only by means of an extreme gesture of tonal *Gewaltsamkeit*, wrenched from the chromaticized B♭ minor that dominates the processional music as a whole (this move being precipitated by the re-entry of the tolling bells with their fixed pitches, C–G–A–E). Such a drastic tonal rupture is just what Wagner had expressly proscribed in the context of instrumental forms, to be permitted only on the basis of poetic-dramatic license. If the ostinato pitches of the bells can be identified as a literal "cause" behind this wrenching modulation, what about the poetic or dramatic motivation, as required in Wagnerian theory?

Taken as a whole, the two sections of the funeral music in *Parsifal* (the instrumental transition proper and the antiphonal chorus) trace a fourfold traversal of the tortured (tritonal) intervallic space between B♭ and E♮. The longer episodes in or around B♭ minor do indulge in far-flung "modulations," too (construed in the loose Wagnerian sense of the word that embraces local progressions or temporary tonal shifts), and this also without any verbal point of reference. The broader tonal trajectory here – two round-trips between E minor and B♭ minor – could be explained in terms of a more or less esoteric compositional idea (in the manner of late Beethoven), as the composing-out of a central surface feature of the music: the descending tritone (B♭ to E) of the *Öde* motive, recalled here from the Prelude to Act III (see Example 2.2). This internal musical explanation is given some force by Wagner's determined highlighting of this intervallic fragment of the motive, precisely at the junctures between these two key areas where the motive itself participates in effecting a tonal rupture that can hardly be called "modulation" in

Example 2.2 Motivic B♭/E♮ tritone ("Desolation"/*Öde* motive) in
Parsifal Act III
(a) *Parsifal* Act III, Prelude (mm. 1–4)

(b) *Parsifal* Act III, scene 2

the terms of normal functional harmony (see Example 2.3). Such a structural *Auskomponierung* of an emblematic surface interval might be interpreted as the generation of a new "form" from a poetic idea (that of the dirge or lament, of which the tritone interval and the *Öde* motive as a whole constitute a sonic image and a musical-formal motivating force). In Wagner's treatment, the emblematic interval achieves a concrete determination – if one is needed – in the wailing reiterations of the word *Wehe!* (woe!) set to this interval, as embedded in the climactic wrenching of the key back to E minor (see Example 2.4). The

Example 2.3 *Parsifal*: Titurel's funeral cortège (Act III, mm. 833–42: "retransition" to Grail temple)

Example 2.4 Textual "determination" of motivic B♭/E♮ tritone (*Wehe!*)
(a) *Parsifal*: Titurel's funeral cortège (Act III, mm. 907–19)

89

(b) *Parsifal* Act III, mm. 922–7

insistent F♯/F♮ cross-relation, which at once intensifies and undermines the resolution to E minor, can be read as a lingering consequence of the unresolved B♭-minor pole of this dissonant tonal axis, F♯ (G♭) and F♮ representing strong diatonic functions of ♭$\hat{6}$ and $\hat{5}$ in that key.

What, then, of the local harmonic peregrination of this music? Or what, particularly, of the wide-ranging and abrupt "modulations" within the instrumental transition itself? From this point of view, the passage could recall Wagner's words (contemporary with the composition of *Parsifal*) about the similarly "modulating" phrases of Elsa's Dream in *Lohengrin*: "The motive [*sic*] consisting almost exclusively of a fabric of distant harmonic progressions that the composer of *Lohengrin* appended as a closing phrase to the opening arioso of Elsa, as she is possessed (*entrückt*) by a dream-like vision, would appear quite contrived and unintelligible in the context of a symphonic Andante, while here it suggests itself quite naturally" ("On the Application of Music to the Drama," X, 191). How convincing this line of reasoning really is may be a moot point (we will return to it in chapter 6). The underlying argument is simple enough, in any case: the enharmonic (here thoroughly triadic) excursions of the phrase accompany a pantomime of blissful *Schwärmerei* and virginal candor. The sense of the musical sign – the "modulations" – is determined by the simple acting-out of its signification or semantic content. We needn't lose ourselves in idle speculation as to how or why Wagner gets from A♭ to D (♮) and back again in eight measures. For we can see that these characteristic progressions must represent innocent, virtuous exaltation, a maidenly vision of chivalric salvation (and not, for example, a sunrise, a swan, a stray page from some student's notebook of adventuresome harmony exercises, or whatever else it might conjure up).

In *Parsifal* we are retrospectively informed by the ensuing scene to think in terms of a formal dirge: the loosely strophic shape of the choral procession bearing Titurel's corpse, the design and content of the choral "catechism," and the stage picture itself make this function unmistakably clear. The preceding orchestral transition, then, can be understood as a musical-affective "anticipation" of something as yet not dramatically determined, while it also awakens recollections of familiar sounds (the bells of the Grail temple, the "descriptive" prelude of Act III with its intimations of Parsifal's tormented wanderings). The sense of the tortuous, "wandering" progressions from B♭ minor to E minor (touching on D minor, E major, and E♭ minor within much diminished-chord activity and a high incidence of other non-harmonic tones) is "determined" by the images of the prescribed scene change, with its proto-Einsteinian conflation of *Raum* and *Zeit* (prefigured in the first act). But unless we consider the unscrolling of a painted backcloth (as Wagner intended to accompany this transition) as somehow a suitable motivation of explanation of these progressions, their justification requires an intuitive application of "poetic ideas" (Parsifal's lacerating remorse, general distress over Titurel's demise) that are not literally present during this interlude.

As in *Götterdämmerung*, Wagner's transitional procession here effects a compromise between the primitive structuring codes of the march or dance and the dramatic imperative of "evolution." The instrumental transition returns strongly to its (initially faint) E center for seventeen measures as the new scene materializes. The second return to E minor is more painfully, and more desperately, accomplished and the result is weaker (pain and weakness being also the terms that constitute the condition of Amfortas, who now appears). On a larger level, the whole episode can be understood as a preludial dissonance to be resolved by Parsifal's return and the luminous consonances of the closing Grail ceremonies. (There the dissonant E♮ resolves to E♭ within the context of A♭ major, if one accepts the idea of such long-range pitch relations.)

In a broad sense, then, the final scenes of both of these third acts replicate a process Wagner had read in the Finale of the Ninth Symphony. The funeral marches touch back to the primitive roots of symphonic form in formalized ceremonial (the march) and re-enact the progress toward a state of musical emancipation – epitomized in the musical *vers libre* of the hymnic "Seid umschlungen" in the Beethoven symphony or in the rhapsodic apotheosis of Brünnhilde's immolation scene at the end of *Götterdämmerung*, which thoroughly eschews the conventional codes of symphonic behavior.[44] The roots of this formal

---

[44] See *Opera and Drama*, Part III (IV, 149–51), where Wagner contrasts the strictly limited tonal ambitus of "patriarchal melody" (Beethoven's *Freude* theme) with the poetically motivated transgression of this ambitus in the hymnic ecstasies of "Seid umschlungen, Millionen!"

emancipation and its "poetic" motivation can be discerned in the funeral march of the "Eroica," among the first paradigmatic manifestations of "poetic ideas" in Beethoven's oeuvre and a cornerstone of that critical tradition.

Fear of the Fifth: the uncanniness of instrumental speech

"Beethoven's music sets in motion the lever of fear, of awe, of horror, of suffering, and wakens just that infinite longing which is the essence of Romanticism."[45] E. T. A. Hoffmann's famous words on Beethoven's romanticism and its traits of the fearful, the sublime, and the uncanny introduce what is probably the first real classic of musical criticism. Like a genuine classic, Hoffmann's essay on Beethoven's Fifth Symphony (in its revised form, as published in the *Fantasiestücke in Callots Manier* in 1814–15) has remained in continuous circulation. A. B. Marx already referred his readers to it in 1824 ("Etwas über die Symphonie und Beethovens Leistungen in diesem Fache"), and references to Hoffmann and his essay are rarely absent from literature on Beethoven and the Fifth from that point on. (Without citing Hoffmann by name, Wagner's preliminary comments on the significance of Beethoven's symphonies in *The Art-Work of the Future* are suffused with the language of "infinite longing," "inexpressible expressivity," desire and fear – the whole passage, indeed, reads like an overwritten paraphrase.[46]) Aside from some passing suspicion of romantic hyperbole regarding Hoffmann's characterization, in the course of a hundred-odd years of "Classic or Romantic" debate, few have really questioned its essential aptness to the tone of the Fifth Symphony – the merciless rhythm of fate in the first movement, its ghostly permutations in the third, or the fleeting gesture of insecurity between the two themes of the Andante, for instance.

---

[45]   E. T. A. Hoffmann, "Beethoven's Instrumental Music," trans. Oliver Strunk, in *Source Readings in Music History* (New York, 1950), 777.

[46]   The passage, describing Beethoven's contribution to the expressive powers of "absolute music," includes such variants of Hoffmann's original phraseology as: "the expression of boundless longing" (*Ausdruck des unergränzlichsten Sehnens*), the "burden of artistic longing" (*Wucht des künstlerischen Seelenverlangens*), the "storm of wild impetuosity" (*Sturm [des] wilden Ungestüms*), the "expression of immeasurable heart's desire" (*Ausdruck des unermesslichen Herzenssehnens*), "the infinitude of this expression" (*die Unendlichkeit dieses Sehnens*), and "storms of infinite longing" (*Stürme unendlicher Sehnsucht*) – see III, 92. The larger context of these phrases within *The Art-Work* represents something that had become a veritable genre unto itself in music-historical criticism, following Hoffmann: the "comparative analysis" or critique of Haydn, Mozart, and Beethoven, with a view to demonstrating Beethoven's fundamental contribution to a new musical epoch. See, for instance, Franz Brendel's "Haydn, Mozart und Beethoven. Eine vergleichende Charakteristik," *Neue Zeitschrift für Musik* 28 (1848).

"Fear, awe, horror, suffering." What exactly was Hoffmann afraid of? Even in the original 1810 review of the Fifth Symphony as an individual opus, Hoffmann's words are not attached to any specific movement or passage. Later, the generality of this characterization is underscored by the generality of the revised title, "Beethoven's Instrumental Music." In the original, more detailed review Hoffmann passes over the overtly meaningful, threatening return of the third-movement theme within the Finale almost without comment, while seizing, instead, on an exceptional moment of apparently jocular high spirits (see Example 2.5). Of this momentary "stammering" of the basses and cellos in the third-movement Trio, he remarks: "To many, this may seem comical; in this reviewer, however, it stirs an uncanny feeling (*ein unheimliches Gefühl*)."[47]

Example 2.5 Beethoven, Symphony No. 5 in C minor, third movement (mm. 161–70): "stammering" cello-bass figure

Hoffmann was similarly disturbed by the final measures of the symphony:

The final chords are handled in a peculiar manner: following the chord which the listener takes to be the final one [there is] one measure of rest, the same chord, one measure's rest, the chord again, one measure's rest, the chord for the length of three measures (in quarter-note values), one measure's rest, the chord, one measure's rest, and a unison C struck by the whole orchestra. The feeling of complete resolution that has been achieved by means of a series of cadential figures is undone by these isolated chords, hammered out between

---

[47] Hoffmann, *Schriften zur Musik*, 46. Joseph Kerman has commented on this passage and Hoffmann's sensitivity to Beethoven's "stammering repercussions" (which Kerman identifies as a kind of affective–stylistic motif throughout the Fifth) as a possible sign of the "terror of the unknown, the inchoate, and the inarticulate" ("Taking the Fifth," in *Das musikalische Kunstwerk: Festschrift Carl Dahlhaus zum 60. Geburtstag*, ed. Hermann Danuser, et al. (Laaber, 1988), 489.

pauses, which recall those singly attacked chords in the [first] Allegro, and the listener is thus put back into a state of expectation. They have the effect of a fire which one believes to have been extinguished, and yet continues to flare up in bright flames.[48]

It is not surprising that Hoffmann should have reacted to the tonic excess of this coda; critics have continued to voice subdued protests from time to time about this triumph that itself protests too much, that risks bombast and rhetorical overkill. Wagner, for one, ridiculed its disproportionate influence on subsequent symphonists, who found it all too convenient to re-trace Beethoven's unsubtle progress from "minor-mode tribulations successfully withstood" to "glorious major-mode celebrations."[49] Yet Hoffmann's response here is no rejection of bombast in the name of moderation or *bon goût*. Rather, he suggests that our confidence in the outcome of the movement is undermined by its very vehemence. The flames that burn here are no symbolic beacon of victory or a new dawn – they are flames one thought to be safely extinguished (destructive flames). Hoffmann's verbal "transliteration" of the closing measures into words (". . . the same chord, one measure's rest, the chord again . . .") seems calculated to drive home the disconcertingly obsessive quality of the coda, a compulsive repetition belying some inner doubt ("which one believes to have been extinguished, and yet continues to flare up").

As the *auctor classicus* of the literary uncanny, Hoffmann can speak with some authority. Several motifs identified with the idea of the uncanny and its manifestations in Hoffmann's fiction, as considered in Freud's famous essay of 1919, also resonate with Hoffmann's evocation of these "uncanny" moments in the Beethoven Fifth. A motif noted in an earlier essay by Jentsch which provided the starting point of Freud's inquiry (but reasonably dismissed by Freud as of merely secondary significance to the "uncanniness" of Hoffmann's "Der Sandmann") has to do with "doubts whether an apparently animate being is really alive; or conversely, whether a lifeless object might be in fact animate" – the case in point being the mechanical doll, Olympia, of Hoffmann's tale.[50] Looked at through the right interpretive spectacles of a musical-critical

---

48 Hoffmann, *Schriften zur Musik*, 49–50. Hoffmann evidently intends to draw here a parallel with the end of the development section of the first movement (see mm. 195–252), which might similarly evoke this image of a fire "flaring up" when it had seemed to be extinguished.

49 "Who was less satisfied with this victory than Beethoven himself? Did he feel the urge to try it again? Perhaps the hordes of thoughtless imitators were pleased to follow suit, preparing a continuous series of victory feasts in the form of major-mode triumphs following upon minor-mode tribulations (*die aus gloriosem Dur-Jubel nach ausgestandenen Mollbeschwerden sich unaufhörliche Siegesfeste bereiteten*), but not the master himself, whose mission it was to write the world-history of music in his works" (III, 93).

50 Sigmund Freud, "The 'Uncanny'," in *On Creativity and the Unconscious*, ed. Benjamin Nelson (New York, 1958), 132.

Coppelius, such unsettling doubts might attach to almost any piece of instrumental music. Jentsch further noted the related effect of "epileptic seizures and [certain] manifestations of insanity, because these excite in the spectator the feeling that automatic, mechanical processes are at work, concealed beneath the ordinary appearance of animation."[51] Hoffmann's two "uncanny" moments in the Fifth are just such fissures in the projection of a musically "animate" being, where Beethoven seems to have perversely, deliberately revealed the machine – the automaton of notes, chords, strings, and pipes – responsible for the impression of a living heroic "subject" within the symphony.[52] For just a brief moment in the Scherzo, the apparatus threatens to break down, to unwind (like Offenbach's version of Olympia in *Les Contes d'Hoffmann*). In the coda of the Finale, on the other hand, the mechanism threatens to burst from overwinding: heroic affirmation becomes "uncanny" in its excess, and the illusion of a triumphant human will is (nearly) exposed as the product of a vast mechanical apparatus running out of control. Freud himself, although not initially interested in the motif of the automaton, remarks later in his essay on the factor of "involuntary repetition" in effects of the uncanny, which he traces to the phenomenon of a repetition-compulsion and its roots in infantile psychological development ("whatever reminds us of this inner *repetition-compulsion* is perceived as uncanny").[53] He further equates the uncanny with the re-activation of an early "animistic stage" of human cultural development (characterized by the impulse to attribute life-like properties to inanimate objects) and with the re-awakening of latent superstitious impulses generally. Both phenomena might attach to the uncanniness in the final measures of the Fifth Symphony, as heard by Hoffmann. (Either as machine or as ghost, the music elicits and then challenges the universal instinct to interpret musical sounds as animate beings, signs of life.)

In *The Art-Work of the Future* Wagner seems to have pursued Hoffmann's somewhat vague misgivings about these closing measures (which, on the surface, could be read as a simple observation about metrical proportions and listeners' expectations) in a direction that ties

---

51 Ibid.
52 Another striking instance of Beethoven's highlighting the "mechanical" character of a musical composition by exposing the threat of malfunction can be seen, it seems to me, in the sudden irruption of E♭ across the first double bar of the scherzo in the op. 135 String Quartet (mm. 16–25); the radical disruption of the steady rhythmic process, in conjunction with the unmediated introduction of the foreign pitch, produces the effect of a smooth-running machine suddenly sabotaged. On the idea of the "mechanical" as a source of aesthetic wit in Beethoven, see also Janet Levy, "'Something Mechanical Encrusted on the Living': A Source of Musical Wit and Humor," in *Essays in Honor of Leonard G. Ratner*, ed. Wye J. Allanbrook et al. (Stuyvesant, NY: Pendragon Press, 1992), 225–56.
53 Freud, "The 'Uncanny'," 145.

in with the "uncanniness" of the stammering moment in the trio: the discomforting apprehension of music trying to speak without language, to act without "motive" or will (here in a non-Schopenhauerian sense). It was an apprehension Wagner would go on to develop with respect to the vocal and representational impulses in Beethoven's late works in *Opera and Drama* (see below, "Beethoven's 'sketches'"), but which already serves as a foundational point in the musical *Geschichtsphilosophie* under construction in *The Art-Work*, and which will lead to the familiar thesis about the Ninth Symphony and the "manifest destiny" of the musical drama.

What inimitable art Beethoven applied in his C-minor Symphony in trying to guide his [musical] ship out of the ocean of infinite longing (*unendlichen Sehnens*) toward the harbor of fulfillment! He *almost* succeeded in lifting musical expression to the level of moral resolve, yet not to the point of articulating this in the music itself. After each effort of the will, and deprived of any firm ethical grounds (*ohne sittlichen Anhalt*), we find ourselves troubled by the possibility that this [final] triumph might just as easily regress back to a state of suffering. In fact, such a regression must strike us as really more plausible than the morally unmotivated triumph which occurs here, less as a convincing achievement than as an arbitrary gift of grace; hence it must ultimately fail to provide an ethically grounded sense of exaltation and satisfaction, such as we really desire in our hearts.   (III, 93)

Following a prolix paraphrase of Hoffmann's Romantic credo about the infinite, unfathomable, and ineffable expressive qualities of "pure music" (immediately preceding these comments on the Fifth Symphony) Wagner had turned the tables and branded the objectlessness of music a liability, a failing:

The transition from a mood of infinitely excited longing to one of joyful satisfaction cannot be accomplished without the resolution of that longing in some *object*. With respect to a character of infinite longing, such an object must necessarily be a finite one, something that will admit of concrete sensible and ethical representation. But here is where absolute music meets its strictly defined boundaries; without imposing arbitrary conditions there is no way that, of itself, it can achieve a clear, distinct representation of a sensibly and ethically determined human object . . .   (III, 93)

To some extent, Wagner's theorizing here – as throughout the Zurich writings – deals in variations of classical music-aesthetic motifs. Music without an intelligible conceptual object will necessarily regress toward pleasant noise. Such an object must be integrated within the body of the art-work, and not arbitrarily imposed; hence serious musicians can do no better than aspire to a restitution of the syncretistic Greek *mousike*, while taking advantage of all the technical sophistication of the modern era. To return to these classicistic convictions after the metaphysical turn of Hoffmann's generation might seem itself regressive (and indeed, a growing historical awareness exposed the evident parallels of Wagner's thinking to over two centuries of operatic reform-theory, thus rendering them suspect by progressive criteria). On the other hand, Wagner's demand for an objective grounding of musical expression could be explained in the spirit of such post-romantic developments as Young German sensual empiricism and Feuerbachian humanistic philosophical "anthropology" – both of which left their mark on Wagner's thought and writings, of course. The thesis of musical drama as cultural imperative, that is, can easily be grounded in a materialist, anti-idealist spirit of the 1848 generation rather than (or as well as) in the resuscitation of classicistic reform theory. The demand for material fulfillment has displaced ideals of indistinct longing, of spiritual or physical desires infinitely deferred.

This may sound incongruous applied to the future author of *Tristan und Isolde*. It could be taken as the basis of an argument, however, as to why *Tristan* needs its words and singers, why *Tristan* isn't a symphony. *Tristan* may be the ultimate paradigm of infinite longing and deferred consummation, musically encoded; yet desire here has a name, a face, a story – an object. This recalls Nietzsche's suggestion (in the *Birth of Tragedy*) that text and drama in *Tristan* act merely as a screen, Apollonian sunglasses to mute the Dionysian glare of the music itself.[54] Wagner himself, though, even in the post-Schopenhauer years, would not have retracted the essence of his "materialist" argument about the function of a real, palpable dramatic object. Despite traditional apostrophes to its symphonic and "absolute" musical values, it remains true that the design and sense of the *Tristan* score depend much on the articulations of the dramatic text, the "fabric of its words and verses" (VII, 123).[55] And despite the vaunted "immateriality" of the motives in *Tristan*, largely shunning any crudely overt semiosis, they still operate in a necessary hermeneutic "counterpoint" with dramatic objects: the characters, their situations and motivations. An hour's musical raving (as in the third act) ought, in Wagner's view, to be explained.

The fact that Beethoven was evidently stirred by the urge to rave in music, from time to time, and the problematic nature of the results – these were for Wagner proof of the need for real, dramatic objects to contain and justify such transgressive impulses, in themselves natural and inevitable. With some of these instances, such as the *Große Fuge* or the Finale of the "Hammerklavier" Sonata, Wagner was apparently never able to fully reconcile himself. His feelings toward the more

---

[54]   Cf. Nietzsche, *The Birth of Tragedy and The Case of Wagner*, §21 (124–30).
[55]   This is the gist of Carolyn Abbate's argument in "Wagner, 'On Modulation,' and *Tristan*" (see n. 20).

rhetorically focused passion of certain middle-period works, like the Fifth Symphony or the "Appassionata" Sonata, seem to have been ambivalent, at best. On one hand, a work like the *Coriolan* Overture (another member of this family) demonstrated Beethoven's sound instinct that music could and should aspire to the representation of "poetic objects" and the dynamics of dramatic process. On the other hand, Wagner saw fit to argue that the Fifth Symphony was a relatively exceptional work in the master's oeuvre (*eine der selteneren Konzeptionen des Meisters*) in its attempt to master a dramatic progression, one that posed a risk to the "purity" of the genre:

Here lyric pathos nearly enters the arena of an ideal dramaticism, in a more specific sense. And while we may wonder whether this might not already endanger the purity of the musical conception, since it would seem to seduce us (*uns . . . verleiten*) into calling up representations foreign to the spirit of music (*Vorstellungen . . . , welche an sich dem Geiste der Musik durchaus fremd erscheinen*), it must nonetheless not be overlooked that the master was guided here not by any aberrant aesthetic speculation, but solely by an ideal instinct stemming from the most genuine sphere of music.   (IX, 99–100)

Wagner has come typically close to tying himself up in a knot of self-contradiction in these remarks from the *Beethoven* essay, but the knot is an instructive one for understanding his adaptation of the Beethovenian critical tradition. On one hand, the impulse toward real, human drama in the Fifth Symphony is interpreted as a danger to the "purity" of the genre, rooted in the elaboration of "idealized dance figures" (X, 178) and the fairly stylized modes of affective content suited to these. On the other hand, Wagner claims that the transgression from the symphonic into the dramatic is the result of an insight into the "genuine sphere of music" (*dem eigensten Gebiete der Musik* – IX, 100). Both views (as voiced in these later writings) go back to the historical construction of the Zurich essays, where Wagner had been arguing that Beethoven was instinctively drawn toward dramatic expression, but thwarted by the limitations of his native instrumental culture of sonata and symphony. In "On the Application of Music to the Drama" (1879) Wagner was still maintaining that "dramatic pathos" and the character of a "dramatic action" remained entirely off limits to the nature of the symphony, as this had been established by Haydn and essentially preserved by Beethoven (X, 178). If what Wagner had previously referred to as the "lyric pathos" of the Fifth Symphony (in *Beethoven*) was pushed there to the brink of "drama," as he also claimed, then Wagner would evidently have to interpret the Fifth as more a misguided transgression of, rather than triumphant transcendence of, the natural boundaries of its genre. For a symphony to indulge in gestures of heroic tragedy would be to risk an effect of the "uncanny" that was evidently alien to Wagner's aesthetic canon.

Wagner's argument against the dramatic capacity of symphonic music in the 1879 essay ("On the Application of Music to the Drama") would appear to contradict directly the claims of 1870, surrounding the *Coriolan* Overture example, that music embodied in itself man's "*a priori* capacity for the making (*Gestaltung*) of drama" (IX, 106). To resolve the contradiction we would have to have recourse again to the distinction between a metaphysical concept of music as an "essence" (what music hypothetically might have been, or could be) and the empirically conditioned realities, and limitations, of received symphonic forms. Wagner's arguments – like Beethoven's Fifth, in his reading – probably defy satisfactory resolution. As Edwin Evans, a first generation Wagnerian and true believer, pointed out long ago in his brief exposition of *Wagner's Teachings by Analogy*, it is not easy to reconcile the claim that music only achieved its modern expressive capacities through the history of its development as "absolute" music (in the symphony and sonata) with claims that such instrumental genres had now suddenly to yield up their secrets to the musical dramatist and beat a hasty, self-effacing retreat from the stage of the "world-history" of music, their part having been played out.[56] A provisional answer to this paradox would be that the symphonic development of simple, dance-based structures had produced those techniques of complete harmonic flexibility (by chromatic and enharmonic means) and motivic development (fragmentation and re-combination) which were to contribute to a new, dramatic language, but which could never really achieve "drama" within the confines of the instrumental genres that nurtured their early growth.[57] In the symphony "there can be no conclusion, no intent, no achievement (*keine Konklusion, keine Absicht, keine Vollbringung*). Thus it is that these symphonies [i.e., symphonies in general] maintain a consistent character of sublime cheerfulness" (X, 178).

Even as a general proposition the contention seems much exaggerated. What work could possibly convey a stronger sense of "conclusion, intent, and achievement" than the Fifth Symphony, after all? But this is precisely the basis of Wagner's theoretical objections to the work: all

---

56 See Edwin Evans, *Wagner's Teachings by Analogy: His Views on Absolute Music and of the Relations of Articulate and Tonal Speech, with Special Reference to "Opera and Drama"* (London, n.d. [c. 1885?]). Evans discusses this apparent contradiction – between Wagner's construction of the historical development of music and its present calling – under the rubric of "the higher musical problem" (39–62).

57 Thus Wagner's metaphor of Beethoven as musical Columbus: he sighted the shores of a new musical world (musical drama) without ever recognizing, or admitting, what he had discovered. Having discovered the route to the new world, he persisted in taking it for a new route to the old (instrumental music). See III, 277–8 (*Opera and Drama*, Part I), where Wagner develops this metaphor of Beethoven as musical Columbus, originally proposed in *The Art-Work of the Future*.

its restless striving and noisy affirmations are to no avail, its gestures of triumphant "conclusion" and "achievement" remain empty gestures (betrayed by their very excess, verging as it does on the disturbing and uncanny), so long as we are unable to ascribe to the work any real, human "intent," the compelling presence of a human agency that can legitimately motivate such evidently impassioned musical goings-on. The argument may still seem merely dogmatic, for all that. And there is a suggestion that Wagner – as performer and listener – was not really convinced by Wagner the aesthetic polemicist. In the essay *On Conducting* of 1869, a year before the Beethoven centenary essay, Wagner commented on a small epiphany regarding the first movement of the Fifth. The sense of the movement had become entirely clear to him from an understanding of one prominent detail, the little oboe cadenza that blossoms dolefully from the fermata in the opening thematic period of the recapitulation (m. 268) – a detail to which the conductor must pay its full rhetorical due. Wagner does not elaborate on the significance of this hermeneutic crux, but it is easy enough to suppose that it has something to do with the overt projection of a vocal persona by this declamatory interpolation, the oboe being typecast once again as a plangent vocal stand-in. The emergence of such an implied vocal presence is able to project the sense of a dramatic agent, a subject in which to ground all the hitherto abstract raging of the impersonal musical forces of fate.[58] The voice is an isolated presence here, but a presence that is nonetheless able to engage a question of drama and form of particular interest to Wagner. With its tone of weary exhaustion it seems to enter a feeble protest against the "inexorable" process of recapitulation now underway, a protest rendered all the more pathetic and futile by the emphatic teleology of Beethoven's middle-period developmental procedures. (Apparently the same "voice" returns momentarily in the closing measures of the movement, incidentally, to utter a couple of despairing semitone "sighs" prior to the brutal conclusion: see the newly interpolated oboe part of mm. 486–7 and 490–1 as compared to the original close of the exposition.) This tentative voice of "dramatic pathos" begins to project, however faintly, an intentional human subject in the music, such as Wagner considered indispensable to drama, musical or otherwise. But

---

[58] In "Taking the Fifth" (see n. 47) Kerman cites Thomas Mann's evocation of the "naked human voice" in connection with this detail (483). The association of a given instrumental part with an anthropomorphizing "persona" recalls, of course, Edward Cone's influential model in *The Composer's Voice*. It is important to this pseudo-Wagnerian reading of the movement (as to that of the "choral" element in the *Marcia funebre*) that the instrumental part in question projects specifically vocal (hence human) qualities, which is not essential to Cone's broader model of the instrumental "persona."

this feeble voice is silenced by Beethoven, or by the ruthless imperative of the symphonic form: the recapitulation brooks no resistance.[59]

This feeble *vox clamantis* of the Fifth's first movement will eventually make itself heard more forcefully in the Ninth. The Ninth Symphony, of course, furnished Wagner with just the material he needed to complete his now universally familiar justification of the musical drama as a historical-aesthetic inevitability in the spirit of Hegelian world history. The human incarnation of the Finale's instrumental voices renders the religious metaphor of Wagner's construction almost a foregone conclusion: "the redemption of music from out of its own peculiar element into a communal art form (*zur allgemeinsamen Kunst*)" and "the human gospel of the art-work of the future" (III, 96). As observed in the previous chapter, Wagner tended to lay greater emphasis on the emergence of the human voice as such in the Ninth (or here, in *The Art-Work*, on the "word" as a symbolic entity), while downplaying the significance of Schiller's text as verbal artifact. The instrumental rehearsal of the accumulating voices in Beethoven's Finale (from recitative to solo melody to choral hymnody) supports a Wagnerian reading of the symbolic transfer of voice from the orchestra to the real human voice as a sign of the human presence prerequisite to drama. Moreover, the famous trajectory of Beethoven's Finale (encapsulating that of the symphony as a whole) from nightmarish chaos to luminous order serves Wagner – as it did many of his contemporaries – as a parable for the progression from a state of inarticulate "longing" to solid, determinate expression of a utopian message. (Instrumental music's search for its lost "object" in human speech might invite certain psychoanalytic constructions as well.)

The fear and dread unleashed in the first movement of the Fifth and not fully extinguished in its Finale flare up again in the Ninth, most drastically in the "harsh outcry" of this Finale's opening measures, as described in Wagner's 1846 program – the "terror fanfare" (*Schreckensfanfare*, the name bequeathed to critical posterity by Wagner's 1873 article on performing the Ninth) or "cry of fear upon waking from a frightful dream," as he imagines these opening measures in the spirit of Schopenhauerian notions of the clairvoyant subconscious in the 1870 essay.[60] In each case, the terror of this famous outburst is occasioned by

---

[59] The timbral and registral associations of the oboe with the tragic female voice, in particular, and its audibly implicit role here as victim of what Susan McClary notoriously described as Beethoven's furious "pelvic thrusting" suggest a gendered subnarrative of the rape and/or silencing of a feminine/individual principle at the hands of a masculine/group aggression obvious enough to require no further comment.

[60] See, respectively, II, 60 (*wie mit einem grellen Aufschrei*, 1846), IX, 241 (*Schreckensfanfare*, 1873), and IX, 110–11 (*Angstschrei des aus dem bedrängenden Traumgesichte des tiefen Schlafes plötzlich Erwachenden*, 1870).

something more than its manifest dissonance and metrical chaos. Simply as a rhetorical gesture, at this point in the symphonic cycle, Beethoven's instrumental outburst presses issues crucial to Wagner – the questions of "will," motivation, agency, and anthropomorphic teleology – to the fore. The music "departs from the fixed character of instrumental music maintained in the first three movements, which manifests itself in infinite and indeterminate expression (*der sich im unendlichen und unentschiedenen Ausdrucke kundgibt*); the progress of this musical poem presses toward decision, a decision such as can only be expressed by human speech" (II, 61).

In a brief series of notices published in the *Dresdener Anzeiger*, prefatory to the 1846 Palm Sunday concert and its accompanying program, the personal tragedy of Beethoven's deafness becomes the subject of a brief parable in which Beethoven's aural disability parallels the ultimately tragic inability of music to make itself thoroughly understood. "Once there was a man who felt himself driven to express everything he thought and felt through the language of tones, as passed down to him by great masters of the art; to speak this language was his innermost need, to perceive it himself was his greatest happiness on earth . . ." (XII, 206). Struck by deafness, Beethoven enacts in his works another tragedy, that of music striving for an articulate voice that it can never fully obtain. Wagner enjoins his audience to sympathize with the plight of the deaf composer and his mutely expressive art, "the poor man who calls so beseechingly to you (*euch so verlangend anruft*)," and not to evade him, even if, "to your perplexity, you cannot at first understand his speech, if it seems so strange and new to you at first that you ask youself 'what does he want, this man?' (*Was will der Mann?*)" (XII, 207). Thus the *Schreckensfanfare* of the Ninth, the fearful cry of distress of the dreamer upon waking, becomes an expression of shock at the discovery of music's "anarthric" condition, its inability to speak, hence to project a will, human motive, or purpose. The parable of the deaf man condemned to speak through inarticulate, though uniquely expressive, musical signs achieves its redemptive closure in the symphony itself, where language is symbolically regained. Such a parable of music's anarthria, its loss of speech, and its ultimate redemption (in the music drama) can be grounded in the anthropological mythology of *Opera and Drama*, drawing on that of Rousseau and Herder, which posits a poetic-musical *Ursprache*, an originally articulate musical language that served the communicative needs of humanity so long as it remained in a state of primal grace and innocence (see chapter 5).[61]

---

[61] The instinctive, wordless musical communication that often transpires between Wagner's heroes and heroines (Senta and the Dutchman, Siegmund and Sieglinde, Kundry and Parsifal) resonates with this Enlightenment mythology of a primal musical language.

The dream from which Beethoven's Finale is awoken with such a terrifying start is apparently no nightmare. At least, the nightmarish visions of the first movement have since yielded to peaceful, even blissful images in the third movement, where the B♭ Adagio and the D-major Andante drift in and out of one another in a gentle if abrupt, unmediated manner, thoroughly characteristic of a dream state. Yet here, too, there is a moment of hermeneutic provocation where the music slips from the fixed course of the double-variation plan, its pattern of alternating periods, in Wagner's terms. The two briefly inter-polated fanfare gestures near the end of the movement (m. 121, m. 131; see Example 2.6) might recall a similar gesture in the slow movement of the Fifth Symphony, the fanfare-like second theme in C major that breaks through the quiet surface of the movement with its resplendent trumpets and drums (Example 2.7). Both gestures have a proleptic quality, suggesting an anticipatory vision of some momentous future. But in both cases, the unexpected quality of the event, the sense of disruption in the even flow of musical time, occasions an admixture of unease with the sign of hopeful anticipation. "I would imagine that most listeners have always been shocked and disturbed, even frightened by it," Lawrence Kramer remarks on the C-major theme of the Fifth Symphony Andante; "it is sudden, aggressive, and deliberately over-emphatic as a gesture, and seemingly quite irrational in what it emphasizes."[62] Although the disruptive fanfares in the Ninth Symphony slow movement do not themselves disrupt the tonal plane, they are perhaps more disturbing as a formal gesture. The second, C-major theme of the Fifth Symphony movement is given a distinctly dramatic-rhetorical preparation, and as the second idea of a double-variation set it becomes integrated into the formal process of the form from the beginning. In the Ninth, the interruption comes at a point when we expect the movement to be drawing to a close. And although these brassy admonitions (to what?) stay within the orbit of the home key, the strings respond, the second time, with a flustered tonal dislocation to ♭III (D♭), and the second violin continues to whisper the brass rhythm (♩₈² ⁷⁷⁷ ♫ ♩ ⁷⁷⁷ ♫ | ♩ ⁷) as it cautiously searches its way back to the fifth degree (F) of the tonic.

The force of the brass interruption, its belated formal context, and the distinctly troubled response of the strings all seem to press more urgently Wagner's hermeneutic query, "Why?" In *"Music of the Future"* Wagner had described as one of the functions of the mythical material of his dramas the transportation of the audience to a "dream-like state which soon becomes a clairvoyant vision: the phenomena of the world

[62] L. Kramer, *Music and Poetry: The Nineteenth Century and After* (Berkeley and Los Angeles, 1984), 235–6.

Example 2.6 Beethoven, Symphony No. 9 in D minor, third movement (mm. 130–7)

are then perceived as possessing a coherence they do not have for the inquiring mind in its ordinary waking state, forever asking 'Why?' in order to overcome its fear of the incomprehensible world – that world it now perceives so clearly and vividly."[63] So long as Beethoven's slow movement has succeeded in inducing a similar trance-like state, it may persuade us to defer the questions raised by this episode, at least until the rude awakening of the next movement. However, with no mythic allegory explicitly provided within the text of Beethoven's symphony – so far – it is not certain that (from a Wagnerian perspective) the listener's clairvoyant aural vision can really continue undisturbed and unreflective.

The suggestion that these disruptive fanfares push the listener to move between two levels of time, to step outside the continuum of real musical time (*temps duré*) in order to perceive a narrative anticipation of future events, alerts us to a fundamental point of contact between Beethoven's formal experiments and Wagner's musical-dramatic methodologies, even though it is one that Wagner himself never addressed as such in his writings: an analogy between Beethoven's overt and possibly covert networks of musical forecasts and reminiscences across movements and Wagner's system of leitmotifs, or motifs of "anticipation and recollection." Beethoven's recollection of discrete thematic identities from preceding movements within the Finales of the Fifth and Ninth represented, for Wagner, an overt transgression of the boundaries of instrumental form in the direction of drama. Leaving aside the question of other more subtle techniques of forecast and reminiscence that have been attributed to Beethoven in these and other works, the few explicit instances of thematic recurrence across movement boundaries (the Fifth, the Ninth, and the Sonata in A♭, op. 110, for example) have this in common: in each case, the recurring material acts as a formal and expressive intrusion that must be exorcised in order that the music can proceed toward its stable, affirmative goal. Such thematic revenants suggest the gothic-Romantic trope of the "numinous intruder,"[64] precisely because of the surprising and inexplicable effect

---

[63] VII, 121. Cited from Jacobs, *Three Wagner Essays*, 34.

[64] The figure of "numinous intruder" that maintains a leitmotivic (not to say numinously intrusive) presence throughout various portions of Carolyn Abbate's *Unsung Voices* is most prominent in chapter 4 ("Mahler's Deafness"), where it is metaphorically transferred from its multiple guises in Mickiewicz's *Todtenfeier* to the apparent intrusions of "phenomenal" music (song) and "distant music" in Mahler's movement (parallel to the thematic intrusions under discussion here). Earlier in the chapter Abbate attaches the figure of deafness, drawn from the vignette Mahler proposed toward the elucidation of his *Fischpredigt* Scherzo, to the ultimate "impossibility of locating meaning *within music*. Deafness is an inability to interpret the sounds that thrash in the air, or the black notes that wind across the pages of the score" (125). The image might be re-constituted in the present context (the difficulties of giving musical voice to "poetic ideas") in terms of music's ultimate "muteness," its inability to articulate precise meaning, and the sense of

Example 2.7   Beethoven, Symphony No. 5, second movement
(mm. 27–49)

of these apparitions outside of their proper sphere of existence: ghostly images of themes whose existence ought to have ceased with the last cadence of their respective movements. Wagner could claim to have explained and motivated the host of thematic revenants that populate his scores (as leitmotifs), to have redeemed those wandering musical souls through a continual act of dramatic absolution, as it were. Unlike Beethoven's lost themes, their meaning and purpose are determined (if only gradually) by a real, "human" dramatic context, and thus a new element of semantic definition toward which the melodies of absolute music could only look longingly from afar, like the ondines of Romantic fiction.

Of course, Wagner had no real wish to rid his music of every trace of the "uncanny." Fear, doubt, and all the peculiar, indeterminate *Ahnungen* of absolute music are crucial effects for him, too. The dramatic role of the orchestra is hardly limited to providing a clarifying editorial commentary on the action and its motives; it also serves to raise doubts, questions, surmises, and even fears. Wagner creates a kind of hermeneutic double counterpoint of questions and answers, in which the musical and dramatic strata continually shift positions, and this, of course, goes a long way toward compensating for the frequently attenuated character of the actual dramatic action (what Wagner tried to justify as its necessary "condensation"). His practical aim was not so much to exorcise the "uncanniness" of indeterminate instrumental expression as to channel it (rather like Hans Sachs's aim to channel *Wahn* to the higher purposes of *Meistergesang*) to the "higher" purposes of drama.

fear or the uncanny that can follow on this perception, as I have tried to suggest. (Abbate has developed a similar transposition of the motif of musical "deafness" to "muteness" under the figure of interpretation as "ventriloquism.")

Beethoven's "sketches" (poetic intentions and musical consequences)

> In the works of the second half of his creative life Beethoven is least intelligible – or rather, most misunderstood – where he tries hardest to express a particular, individualized content. Here he exceeds the perceptual bounds of absolute music as established by common consensus (that is, a recognizable relation to familiar dance and song forms), and attempts to speak a language that gives the impression of random whimsy. Apparently unconstrained by the codes of purely musical coherence (*einem rein musikalischen Zusammenhange unangehörig*), this language seems instead to be connected only according to some poetic intention (*nur durch das Band einer dichterischen Absicht verbunden*), but one that music is unable to articulate with the clarity of genuine [verbal] poetry. The majority of Beethoven's later works must be viewed as manifestations of this instinctive attempt to formulate a language suited to conveying these [more individualized] expressive impulses. They often give the impression of sketches for a painting for which the master had a clearly conceived subject (*Gegenstand*), while he had not yet determined the exact details of its composition (*dessen verständlichen Anordnung*). (III, 279)

Wagner's analogy for the late works in this passage from *Opera and Drama* may strike us as ironic, even perverse, in view of the central role of Beethoven's actual *compositional* sketches in our current picture of the composer and his creative process. It is difficult to know how much, if anything, Wagner knew of Beethoven's sketching habits at this time (1851), though it seems likely that he had at least a notion of them. Beethoven's musical sketching could have served Wagner's point equally well, as graphic representation of the titanic struggle for *le motif juste*, "the compulsion to give precise expression in his music to a distinct content drawn from the realm of his own feelings and perceptions," as Wagner puts it in the preceding paragraph. Wagner claims, however, that in the more extreme, problematic cases Beethoven's *finished* compositions are figurative "sketches," conveying the impression of something unfinished, of palpable *intentional* meanings that remain unrealized. Thus the primal scream of the Ninth Symphony's Finale speaks for the late works as a whole. There Beethoven reveals to the public audience of the symphony the terrifying discovery of music's anarthria or loss of true speech, offering a provisional resolution to that dilemma that was not open to the private genres of sonata and quartet (i.e., the intervention of the word, or the human voice). The pathos of the late sonatas and quartets, then, lies not only in the biographical picture of their deaf and isolated composer, but also in his poignantly futile, sincere determination to make these absolute instrumental forms speak and sing.

In representing Beethoven's late-period works as an unfinished project – one as vital to the present history of music as it was unrealizable –

Wagner adopted a familiar line of conservative critical discourse around 1850, but re-interpreted so as to serve his own overtly radical agenda. That is, he advertised the widely acknowledged difficult and even "unintelligible" qualities of the late works as proof of the historical imperative of the musical drama, over and above the evidence of the Ninth Symphony. In retrospect, this critical maneuver may appear more duplicitous than it perhaps was. Over the following decades proponents of the progressive "New German" party often hailed Beethoven's late works as a *Zukunftsmusik avant la lettre*, prophetic anticipations of the subsequent avant-garde musical experiments of Berlioz, Liszt, and Wagner. Yet the biographical evidence indicates that at the time of *Opera and Drama* Wagner genuinely was, like the greater part of his contemporaries, still uncomfortable with most of the late works (aside from the Ninth and perhaps the *Missa Solemnis*). An early fascination with the late sonatas (opp. 101, 106, and 110, to judge from some possible traces to be detected in his instrumental juvenilia) probably subsided with the beginning of Wagner's operatic career, and a remark in the 1857 Liszt essay suggests that hearing Liszt play "the two great sonatas, in B♭ and C minor, op. 106 and op. 111" (V, 185) had only recently rekindled his appreciation of them (this would have been some time after 1853). His epiphany regarding the late quartets – op. 131 in particular – is dated at 1853 by Wagner himself, with reference to performances by the Maurin-Chevillard Quartet in Paris and subsequent private readings with local players in Zurich.[65]

In any case, for the two essential points behind Wagner's arguments about the significance of the late works he could count on the nearly unanimous support of contemporary opinion: 1) that the striving for more distinct, "determinate" representation of "poetic ideas" or content in music characteristic of the present age (along with such technical side effects as expanded harmonic practice or cyclic integration) had been decisively inaugurated by Beethoven, and 2) that the problematic nature of this enterprise had been brought to an impasse already in the composer's late works, and that subsequent compositional confrontation with these was an important gauge in the evaluation of contemporary works and their solutions to modern critical problems. The first point has been addressed already in the preceding chapter and at the beginning of this one. To substantiate the second of these claims (and reinforce the first) as economically as possible let me air a few representative voices with a minimum of commentary.

---

[65]   On the compositional traces of the late sonatas in Wagner's early music see Kropfinger, *Wagner and Beethoven*, 170–90. The account of the ear- and mind-opening rendition of the C♯-minor quartet, op. 131, in Paris was recorded in *Mein Leben* (see *My Life*, trans. Andrew Gray and ed. Mary Whittall [Cambridge, 1983], 503; cf. Kropfinger, *Wagner and Beethoven*, 46–9).

A. B. Marx, as we know, had been promoting the epochal significance of "ideas" in Beethoven's music since the 1820s. In doing so, he evidently thought to be emulating Hegelian doctrines of the progress of the world spirit in art, which he (like many others) tended to translate into more pragmatic corollaries of material "progress": the more diversified and sophisticated the musical means of the new era became, following Beethoven's example, the closer musicians would be able to approach the perfect realization of "ideas" in sensible, sounding form.[66] At the same time, the very idealization of Beethoven's achievements by Marx and his kind tended to support – perhaps inadvertently – a more troublesome tenet of Hegelian thought, that in the evolutionary development of the arts a phase of classical perfection would be followed by inevitable decline, and that the "end of the era of art" in the history of modern culture was already at hand. Thus, while conservative critics of the earlier nineteenth century might dismiss Beethoven's late style as an aberration due merely to biographical circumstances (one with a perverse appeal to certain rebellious instincts of the present generation), even critics like Marx portrayed the legacy of Beethoven's "progress" in a problematic light. "The last indisputably permanent achievement in the area of musical progress is that associated with the name of Beethoven," Marx could still write in 1855; "that is the spiritualization (*Durchgeistigung*) of instrumental music in raising this to the level of determinate representation, of the idea (*zur bestimmten Vorstellungen, zur Idee*). If there has been any further progress since then, or if we should expect any, that remains a real question."[67] Marx's tripartite model for the development of music in the modern era was, as mentioned earlier, no proper dialectical triad, but simply a progressive scheme that made no real provision for further stages of "progress." A retrospective observation on the phases of Beethoven's career (reflecting the three-part scheme of music's recent evolution in general) from Marx's 1859 Beethoven study plays all too easily into the hands of Wagner's musical historiography, which may have left its mark here (even though Marx kept a skeptical distance from the Wagnerian cause):

Thus our initial survey of [Beethoven's] works has led us to recognize a continuous series of constructs, leading from the point of an animated play of tones to the expression of determinate feeling, to the evolution of a firmly controlled progression of emotional states, which – once set in motion – brings us to the point of desiring articulate speech, since conscious thought has been so clearly and distinctly evoked here that it is hardly to be satisfied with anything less than the precision of words.

[66] On Marx's appropriation or misappropriation of fashionable Hegelian categories, see Burnham, "Criticism, Faith, and the *Idee*" (n. 8).

[67] A. B. Marx, *Die Musik des Neunzehnten Jahrhunderts und ihre Pflege* (1855; 2nd edn, Leipzig, 1873), 100.

110

(So hat uns der erste Hinblick auf die Werke eine stetige Reihe von Gebilden erkennen lassen, die sich von dem Standpunkte beseelten Tonspiels zum Ausdruck bestimmter Empfindung, zur Entwicklung festgehaltener und fortschreitender Gemüthszustände, – gleichsam angeregt, – bis dahin fortführt, wo man nach dem Wort verlangt, weil das Bewusstsein so bestimmt und klar geworden, dass es kaum anders als durch das präzise Wort sich genugthun zu können meint.)[68]

By the time Marx wrote this, of course, such sentiments had become a commonplace of "progressive" critical thought, tirelessly (sometimes thoughtlessly, and often thanklessly) propagated by the likes of Franz Brendel, Richard Pohl, Hans von Bülow, and other Lisztians, along with Liszt himself – with the difference that, for these Lisztians, the desire for "words" could be successfully sublimated in poetic programs and the ever more distinct musical representation of "ideas" as such. "Instrumental music since Beethoven," Brendel writes in 1856, as Liszt's symphonic poems are first appearing in print, "has moved in the direction of ever greater distinctness of expression. Any composer who wishes to escape the meaningless repetition of old forms now looks to the representation of psychological processes, determinate portrayals, and contact with a poetic program."[69]

Such views were by no means limited to partisan fanatics. Even a moderate-to-conservative figure like J. C. Lobe, earlier invoked as critical representative of the *vox populi*, can be heard advancing similar models of "progress" which posit the representation of "distinct content" as a cultural imperative of the age. Writing at the time of Wagner's *Opera and Drama*, for instance, Lobe also proposes a tripartite scheme of musical progress, of which the third stage constitutes "works with distinctly recognizable, determinate, intelligible content, and consequently producing a stronger, more distinct effect."[70] Somewhat earlier we find the one-time *Davidsbündler*, Hermann Hirschbach, advocating a five-point program of progress, tracing the same familiar trajectory from "mechanical" classicism or pseudo-classicism ("a mere technically correct assemblage of phrases") to articulate expression ("poetic portraits of a fairly strictly defined character" – the Beethoven symphonies – and music so constructed that, "although it does not absolutely require an indication of its content in words, it will at least permit one").[71]

---

68 *Ludwig van Beethoven: Leben und Schaffen*, vol. I, 144.
69 ". . . Darstellung psychischer Vorgänge, Bestimmtheit der Schilderung, Anlehenen an ein poetisches Programm" (Franz Brendel, "Programm-Musik," *Anregungen für Kunst, Leben, und Wissenschaft der Tonkunst* 1 (1856), 82.
70 "[Werke] mit deutlich erkennbarem, bestimmtem, verständlichem Inhalt und folglich mächtiger, bestimmter Wirkung" (Johann Christian Lobe, "Fortschritt in der Musik," in *Musikalische Briefe. Wahrheit über Tonkunst und Tonkünstler, von einem Wohlbekannten* [1852; 2nd edn, Leipzig, 1860], 109).
71 Hermann Hirschbach, "Wozu komponirt man ein Instrumentaltonstück?" *Neue Zeitschrift für Musik* 9 (1838), 47.

Determinacy or distinctness of character, however, presupposes a certain degree of accessibility, and thus even a cultural liberal like Hirschbach feels compelled to classify the late Beethoven quartets one step below the symphonies, due to their excessive degree of "intellection" (*Überwiegen des Künstlerverstands*). A more cautious personality, such as Lobe, could outline a model for musical progress based on the criterion of increasing "determinacy of expression," and yet withdraw support from the immoderate fancy of Beethoven's late style. As long as he can account for the expressive element in Beethoven's music in the conventional, somewhat antiquated terms of a "principal mood" (*Hauptstimmung*) displayed in all its various modifications or through the organic phases of its "growth and development" Lobe can maintain an appreciative tone. But the exaggerations that an originally healthy expressive impulse undergoes in Beethoven's late style raise precisely the kind of objections (still very common) that served Wagner's arguments in *Opera and Drama*. In his desperation to articulate his feelings and ideas in musical form, the deaf Beethoven strove to invest his late works with an intensified eloquence, but through methods that proved finally counterproductive, such as tortuous polyphony and unnaturally distended melodic periods:

Such are his [later] compositions, in which every voice claims equal prerogative to speak at once, each with its own melody . . . But in trying to provide every voice with its own particular melody he only succeeded in suppressing any truly engaging melody. He put in too much, and the result was too little, that is, too much that is unintelligible . . .

In the beginning, under better conditions, he was able to construct complete forms and their periodic articulation in a clear, recognizable, and intelligible manner, down to the last detail; now [in the later works] he departed from this: he constructed artificial, confused periods and then enmeshed them with one another in such a way that one can only detect their beginning, continuation, and conclusion at best with one's eyes [i.e., in the score], and often only with great effort, while in performance even the best trained ears will not always succeed in this.

(So sind seine Compositionen, in denen alle Stimmen gleichzeitig und gleichbedeutend sprechen sollen und jeder Stimme eine eigene Melodie zugetheilt ist . . . Dadurch, daß er jede Stimme eine entsprechende Melodie geben wollte, unterdrückte er selbst die ansprechende. Er legte zu Viel hinein, und so mußte zu Wenig, d.h. ein unverständliches Zuviel, herauskommen . . .

Im Anfange, wie in seiner besten Zeit, hatte er die ganze Form und die Gliederung, den Periodenbau, bis ins einzelne klar, deutlich erkennbar und verständlich gebildet; jetzt ging er auch davon ab: er baute kunstvolle, verwickelte Perioden und flocht und schlang sie oftmals so in- und untereinander, daß man ihren Anfang, Fortgang und Ende allenfalls, wenn auch häufig mühsam, mit den Augen heraussuchen und finden kann, bei der Aufführung aber durch das Gehör, und wenn es noch so sehr geübt ist, durchaus nicht immer zu erkennen vermag.)[72]

However imprecise the technical terms of Lobe's critique of the late style, its essential congruity with Wagner's critique in *Opera and Drama* is unmistakable – as is, ironically, its anticipation of a widespread critique of Wagner's new dramatic music and its "endless melody," just now emerging.

Wagner's and Lobe's critiques also harmonize perfectly with regard to the putative ill effects exerted by Beethoven's late style on recent and contemporary composers (for Wagner this seems to have meant Berlioz; for Lobe – who was rather partial to some of Berlioz's music – it surely meant Wagner, as well). Worse than the eccentricities (*Verirrungen*) of Beethoven's late works themselves, according to Lobe, have been the effects of these works on his "blinded admirers" – a widely acknowledged though rarely identified "cult" of the late works – who have perpetuated an example that would be better set aside. The willful syntactic confusion that Lobe found characteristic of the late style seems to be vaguely implied in Wagner's description (in *Opera and Drama*) of the "interweaving" or superimposition of contrasting affective gestures that are part of Beethoven's baleful legacy to the misguided musical thrill-seekers of the present generation:

The desire to formulate a new musical language in these [late] works had frequently resulted in contorted features which these later composers naturally regarded as unusual, bizarre, and entirely new, if nothing else. Those accents of sorrow and joy, delight and despair in rapid alternation, interwoven or even sounded simultaneously, which the master transmuted into such unusual harmonic and rhythmic configurations in the aim of expressing a distinctly individual emotional content through a new expressive musical vocabulary – all of these peculiarly Beethovenian procedures were liberally plundered by later composers in hopes of enriching their arsenal of technical means with which to impress a public eager for novelty. While our older generation of musicians can still only accept that element in Beethoven's works which least belongs to his real nature (merely a remnant of an earlier, untroubled musical era), our younger generation has deliberately sought to imitate the external peculiarities of Beethoven's later manner.   (III, 280–1)

This last remark might make us wonder if Wagner isn't perhaps letting slip a reactionary critical mask he has just donned for the occasion: not only does he distance himself from the narrow-minded perukes who hold fast to the early-period Beethoven, but he seems to imply that something of the "real" Beethoven does indeed inhabit the late works, not merely their isolated "external peculiarities." Such nuances of tone betray the gulf separating Wagner's premises from those of Lobe and

---

[72] Lobe, *Musikalische Briefe*, 204–5.

the critical *juste milieu* he represents, but the fundamental proximity of these two cautionary critiques – Lobe's and Wagner's – remains. The following summary remarks from the conclusion of Lobe's "letter" perfectly exemplify the line of middle-brow critical opinion Wagner chose to invoke in *Opera and Drama* with respect to the object-lesson of Beethoven's career:

> When, on the other hand, [Beethoven] transgressed the fundamental rules of his art and imposed on music more than could be expected from it, such as the articulate expression of overly individualized thoughts and overly subtle nuances of feeling, when he meant to convey some conceptual content through every voice – then his compositions lost the general validity, transparent intelligibility, appealing beauty, and thus to some extent their affective power . . . [Here] he demonstrated the incapacity of music altogether to convey a detailed narration of all that transpired in his heart and – his mind. As he proved here, even the greatest master of the art of tones could not accomplish this, nor could any listener ever properly comprehend such an impossible musical discourse.

> (Als er dagegen über die Grundregeln der Kunst hinausging, der Musik mehr und Anderes zumuthete als sie überhaupt zu leisten vermag, wie das Aussprechen und Ausdrücken gar zu individueller Gedanken und kleiner subtiler Gefühlsnüancirungen, als er durch jede Stimme gleichsam einen *Begriff* verdeutlichen wollte, – verloren seine Compositionen die allgemeine Wahrheit, die durchsichtige Klarheit, die anmuthige Schönheit und damit wenigstens zum Theil ihre Wirkungskraft . . . oder er zeigte doch die Mangelhaftigkeit der Musik überhaupt, durch welche er der Welt detailliert erzählen wollte, was in seinem Herzen und in seinem – Kopfe vorging. Dies vermag, wie er bewiesen hat, auch der größte Meister im Reich der Töne nicht und eben so unmöglich ist es dem Hörer, eine solche Tonsprache zu verstehen.)[73]

The fractured idiom of Beethoven's late music, melodically and harmonically saturated and yet "unsatisfying," is suffused with palpable poetic *intentions* which it can never hope to articulate fully and distinctly. It was just this verdict, frequently expressed by Lobe and his ilk, that was so easily adapted to Wagner's rhetoric of intentions that must be "realized" for the ear, eye, and mind alike in the musical drama.

It would be a mistake to attribute any too clearly articulated, unequivocal sense to Wagner's term "poetic intent" (*dichterische Absicht*) itself, however (just as it is usually a mistake to attribute genuine theoretical status to Wagner's "theory" in general).[74] We should be alerted to this

---

[73]   Ibid., 210.
[74]   This problem is evident in Frank W. Glass's *The Fertilizing Seed: Wagner's Concept of the Poetic Intent* (Ann Arbor, 1983), which does not so much describe a coherent theory of the "poetic intent" from Wagner's writings and operas as it settles for the axiomatic cliché that Wagner took seriously the setting of his dramatic texts to music, seeking to do full musical justice to their psychological and dramatic content (although this by no means invalidates his commentaries on the music dramas).

lack of a single, precise meaning by the very casual way in which Wagner introduces the phrase in *Opera and Drama*. It appears without fanfare or even so much as a provisional definition several times in Part I (with reference to such diverse phenomena as the operas of Mozart/Da Ponte and Meyerbeer/Scribe, as well as Beethoven's instrumental works). The term only begins to come into clearer focus toward the end of Part II, where it is connected with the biological metaphor of the poetic-dramatic "insemination" of music (see also chapter 3). Its incidence finally escalates at a great rate across Part III, as Wagner begins to outline his own creative vision in earnest and the heat of his artistic imagination rises perceptibly. By the end of Part III, indeed, the phrase "poetic intent" is resounding with leitmotivic frequency, as if what had been in Part I a tentative "motive of anticipation" – to put it in Wagnerian terms – is gradually "realized" only in the final scene of *Opera und Drama*. (Or one might say that the history of this term in Wagner's text faithfully embodies his melodic ideal of gradual "becoming.")

The particular wording of this locution "poetic intent" is significant. In substituting "intent" (*Absicht*) for the "idea" of standard critical parlance, Wagner emphasizes the necessity of fulfillment, completion, or "realization" (as he put it). Unlike the more nebulous "idea," assumed to be transcendently ever-present to those able to divine it, an "intent" or intention implies realization. The distinction between the "realization of a poetic intent" in Wagner's terminology and the Hegelian formula of art as the "sensual appearance of the idea" (*sinnliches Scheinen der Idee*) might seem like pedantic casuistry. But in *Opera and Drama*, at least, it allows Wagner to distinguish between the imperfectly realized "intent" of Beethoven's later works and the new genre of musical drama, where such poetic intents might (belatedly) find adequate musical scope, or "realization."

Between the time of *Opera and Drama* and *Tristan und Isolde* Wagner's attitude toward the later works of Beethoven underwent a radical revision (in a sense this parallels a larger critical turn in Germany and elsewhere regarding the status of the "difficult" late works across the middle of the century). As mentioned earlier, this change of heart was initially precipitated by revelatory performances of the late quartets by the Maurin-Chevillard Quartet in Paris (1853), and evidently by Liszt's performances of some of the late sonatas between 1853 and 1856.[75] The

---

[75] *My Life*, 503–4 (see n. 65 above). I assume that the E♭ quartet referred to in *My Life* is op. 127 rather than the "Harp" Quartet, op. 74. Like the earlier Beethoven epiphany of hearing the Ninth Symphony under Habeneck in Paris around 1840, this second epiphany immediately preceded an intense phase of compositional activity in a

works Wagner specifically recalls having heard in Paris – the Quartets in Eb, op. 127, and in C♯ minor, op. 131 – were precisely those to which he became most partial; he rehearsed the latter work with musicians from Zurich on more than one occasion, and the "program note" he jotted down for a resulting (private) performance in 1854 was later incorporated into the 1870 *Beethoven* essay. The impact of this second Beethoven "epiphany" may have been more gradual than that of hearing the Ninth Symphony under Habeneck a dozen years before (also in Paris), but the consequences were perhaps more profound. Whether Wagner continued to subscribe to the view of the late works as "sketch-like," as expressed in *Opera and Drama*, is uncertain. At any rate, it has been proposed that the beatific Adagio variations of op. 127 served as an inspirational sketch, of sorts, for the famous central episode of the Act II duet in *Tristan und Isolde* ("O sink hernieder, Nacht der Liebe"), and it would be possible to hear a resonance of the opening movements of the op. 131 Quartet (and the "poetic idea" Wagner discerned here) in the musical-dramatic conception of the beginning of Act III of *Tristan*. By way of a speculative conclusion to his discussion of Wagner's Beethoven, then, we might consider how these passages in *Tristan* could be understood as a response to the musical and hermeneutic challenges of these late Beethoven works, and how Wagner has realized here a "poetic intent" similar to that suggested in Beethoven's enigmatic "sketches."

It is not difficult to recognize in the gently throbbing, nearly a-pulsatile introductory measures of the Adagio movement of op. 127 (rising up from the fifth degree, Eb, of the Ab tonic) and in the gentle, stepwise ascent of the melody in the first violin an embryonic image of the opening of Wagner's duet[76] (Example 2.8). For all the breathtaking

radically new idiom. Wagner heard the concerts of the Maurin-Chevillard Quartet in October 1853, just several weeks before finally beginning work on *Das Rheingold*. In the 1857 open letter on Liszt's symphonic poems Wagner mentions having first truly appreciated the "Hammerklavier" and C-minor sonatas (opp. 106, 111) after hearing private performances of them by Liszt (V, 185); it can be inferred that such perfor-mances occurred during one of Liszt's visits to Zurich in 1853 and 1856, at the same time Wagner was becoming familiar with Liszt's own new compositions.

76 Of course, the duet had already been "sketched," in the form of the song, "Träume," from Wagner's settings of Mathilde Wesendonck's poems. The similarity of these two openings (op. 127 and "O sink hernieder") is noted by Klaus Kropfinger in *Wagner and Beethoven*, 209–17, taking a cue from a footnote to Heinrich Porges's short mono-graph on Wagner's opera (*Tristan und Isolde* [Leipzig, 1906], 40). The footnote there cites a diary entry by Porges of 10 Dec. 1875: "The musical model [*Urbild*] of 'Sink hernieder, Nacht der Liebe' is the Adagio of the Beethoven Quartet in E-flat major, op. 27 [*recte*: 127]." The observation may reflect a conversation between Porges and Wagner himself. At any rate, Wagner had been acquainted with Porges's essay on *Tristan* since the later 1860s (it had originated at the behest of Ludwig II in 1866–7), and he expressed particular admiration for the commentary on Act II (see the letter from Wagner included in the preface to the publication of Porges's monograph, iii).

Example 2.8
(a) Beethoven, String Quartet in E♭, op. 127, second movement
(Adagio), opening

Adagio ma non troppo e molto cantabile

intricacies of the melodic and rhythmic surface of Beethoven's movement, the theme and most of its variations remain within the ambitus of the simplest tonal relations: tonic and dominant, with a brief but important touch of subdominant in the cadential phrases to the theme, mm. 17 and 19. In this respect a comparison of this movement with the luxuriant modulations of Wagner's scene, as it progresses, would confirm Wagner's strictures about the nature of tonality and form in instrumental versus dramatic genres. Beethoven carries out his introspective, atomizing melodic "analysis" entirely within the confines of a classical harmonic-metrical phrase structure, as befits an instrumental *cantabile* (although the underlying regularity is somewhat disguised by

(b) *Tristan und Isolde* Act II, scene 2: love duet, opening

tempo and texture). Wagner's scene takes a similar musical point of departure, but plunges into the remotest tonal regions as the two singers explore the depths of their emotional being, as newly disclosed to them in this moment of Schopenhauerian nocturnal clairvoyance.

Beethoven, in his instrumental reverie, does transgress the boundaries of absolute musical etiquette at one crucial moment, where the third variation (adagio molto espressivo) precipitously sinks to the flat submediant (F♭ major, rendered enharmonically as E major). The ♭VI relationship was, of course, a common enough gesture in the expressive arsenal of early nineteenth-century style. But its deployment as the key of an entire variation is less conventional. Furthermore, Beethoven underscores the surprise value of the move in deliberately wrenching the music out of the A♭ tonic – where the second variation has been dithering in a busy, seemingly purposeful way around its final cadence – and forcibly displacing all four parts up a semitone from C to C♯ (Example 2.9). This abrupt musical "spasm," as Joseph Kerman calls it, is really no modulation at all (as Kerman also notes), but simply a tonal dislocation, a change of key effected by fiat rather than by functional progression.[77] Such a spasmodic, deliberately unprepared tonal rift is undoubtedly the kind of thing that led Wagner to speak of the late works as "sketches." (In the same part of *Opera and Drama* he also refers to "those powerful, painful, yet captivating oracular *spasms* and stutterings": III, 279 [emphasis added].) Such a gesture might also recall Wagner's prose jottings, from the time of his own first sketches for *Tristan*, on the inadmissibility of "bold and strange" (*stark und fremd*) modulations in instrumental music (XII, 280), cited earlier, and the later admonition that "he who indulges in such bold and strange modulations without cause is just a bungler" (X, 174). To determine whether or not Beethoven's abrupt move to E has a just and sufficient "cause" would

[77] Joseph Kerman, *The Beethoven Quartets*, 214, 216.

Example 2.9   Beethoven, String Quartet, op. 127, second movement
(mm. 59–62)

necessarily involve an interpretive act, whether regarding structural design or "poetic intent." The very abruptness of this unmediated (non)modulation – and of the subsequent return to A♭ – would have to play a part in either such interpretation.

A poignant recollection of the contrasting key in the coda (mm. 124–6, see Example 2.10) seems to offer a retrospective explanation of the enharmonic function of E as ♭VI (F♭) by revealing the enharmonic equivalencies of F♭/E and A♭/G♯ (the latter equivalency also happens to play a considerable role in the course of the *Tristan* duet). But does such a retrospective harmonic gloss speak to "causes," or to effects? From the perspective of Wagner's dramatic-musical poetics the move to E major raises the suspicion of a "poetic intent" that inevitably lacks

Example 2.10 Beethoven, String Quartet, op. 127, second movement (mm. 124–6)

a distinct motivating object, so long as it resists interpretation on the basis of musical convention or some internally generated sense of structural logic.

Yet the "poetic" effect of this move is easy enough to sense. The ecstatic tranquillity of the hymn-like E-major variation and its tonal distance from the original tonic are reinforced by the breath-taking jolt (in a quasi-literal sense) of the sudden rupture of this C–C$\sharp$ rise. The radical paring-down of rhythmic values combines with this tonal alienation to create the effect of a contrasting island within the movement, so that the third variation also functions, implicitly, as a central episode – one which is surely heard as the emotional core of the movement and hence of the work as a whole.[78] The impression of transcendent "apartness" created here (a tranquil counterpart to the role of the "new theme" in the "Eroica") is thus easily related to formal attributes: the simplified, song-like melodic surface, the abruptness of the move to the new and distant key, and the central, episodic position the variation occupies within the movement.

The means and effect are, in fact, similar to those of a familiar Wagnerian "poetic intent," the expression of an ecstatic, visionary, trance-like moment of *Entrücktheit*, as encountered in the modulating phrases of Elsa's Dream in Act I of *Lohengrin* or throughout the central duet of *Tristan und Isolde* Act II. These characters express their visionary transports in continually widening progressions that have no parallel – it is true – in the restricted tonal ambitus of Beethoven's individual variations. But in *Tristan* the interpolated episodes of Brangäne's "Watch Song" create an effect roughly analogous to that of Beethoven's

[78] This is also how Kerman hears the third variation (ibid., 216).

121

"episodic" E-major variation. The episodic formal function of Brangäne's song and its sense of tonal separation – as if meant to draw the music out of the self-deceptive complacency of the lovers' flat keys into a shifting orbit of sharp keys – parallel her physical, spatial distance from them on stage (hence "motivating" the musical procedure, which in turn "realizes" the theatrical situation). As the explanatory or retrospective reference to E major in Beethoven's coda can be viewed as a conciliatory gesture that (retrospectively) bridges the tonal excursion of the third variation with its tonal surroundings, the tonal excursions of Brangäne's song are similarly met with conciliatory, rather than oppositional, tonal responses from Tristan and Isolde: after both Brangäne's principal episode and its brief reprise, the two lovers calmly accept her cadential tonality as a new point of departure for the developing variation of their enraptured discourse (F♯/G♭ major at Isolde's "'Lausch', Geliebter!" and G major at Tristan's parallel response, "Soll ich lauschen?"). Far from supporting the minatory message of her words, the new tonal spaces opened up by Brangäne seem instead only to encourage the luxuriant tonal promiscuity of the musical behavior of the lovers, who take full advantage of the "poetic license" for unlimited modulation offered them by Wagner's doctrine of poetically emancipated tonality.

Compared with such modulatory abandon (which will of course continue its trajectory through to B major before its catastrophic interruption), the excursion to ♭VI in Beethoven's variation is a modest gesture. Wagner's remarks about the unrealizable excess of poetic "intent" in the late works may have been sooner prompted by such other movements as the following scherzo in op. 127, or that of op. 135, where a radical break-down or short-circuiting of melodic-thematic continuity evidently betokens the presence of some enigmatic, concealed "poetic idea." "The inquisitive listener," as he wrote in *Opera and Drama*, "could never hope to interpret these powerful, painful yet captivating oracular spasms and stutterings, since this musical oracle himself lacked the means to make himself properly understood" (III, 279). Still, the momentary "spasm" in the op. 127 variations and the dislocated lyric episode it precipitates could not have failed to make an impression on Wagner. These gestures, too, Wagner presumably interpreted as misplaced signposts on the road to the musical-dramatic art-work of the future, where Beethoven's objectless ("rootless") expressive experimentation could be profitably cultivated in the rich, sustaining soil of drama.

Wagner did leave some indication of what he perceived to be the "poetic idea" of the C♯-minor Quartet, op. 131 (if not for op. 127), in the form of his 1854 program note and its revised appearance in the *Beethoven*

122

essay. The earlier version is particularly succinct. On the first two movements, it reads:

(Adagio) Melancholy morning thoughts of a deeply suffering mind: (Allegro) a pleasant apparition, awakening new longing for life.

[(Adagio) Schwermütige Morgenandacht eines tiefleidenden Gemütes: (Allegro) anmutige Erscheinung, neue Sehnsucht zum Leben erweckend.   (XII, 350)]

This is hardly a bold interpretation. (The punctuation does register, at least, the importance of the two movements' interrelated status.)

In the expanded paraphrase of these words Wagner interpolated into the *Beethoven* essay the quartet is read as a musical allegory of the inner life of the composer. Here the first two movements are interpreted (still in very general affective terms) as the expression of two complementary psychic states which, taken together, suggest the gradual "awakening" of Beethoven's creative consciousness:

The long introductory Adagio – surely the most melancholy thing (*wohl das Schwermütigste*) ever expressed in tones – I would describe as waking up on the morning of a day that "in its long course will not fulfill one wish, not one!" Yet at the same time it is a penitential prayer, a colloquy with God about faith in the eternally good. – The inward-turned eye now looks toward a consoling vision, visible only to itself (Allegro 6/8), in which longing becomes a bittersweet reflexive game (*zum wehmütig holden Spiele mit sich selbst*): the innermost dream vision awakens in the form of a delightful recollection.   (IX, 96–7)

The poetic idea, as further glossed here in the 1870 essay, appears as a piece of "inner biography."[79] In the new version of the "program" as a whole Beethoven's artistic persona is rendered as that of a holy mystic, a combination of saint and sorcerer. The quartet itself is now revered as a kind of Grail-like sacred object, a testimony to its creator's mysterious powers, which embrace at once the divine and the occult.

In *Opera and Drama*, a similar idealized musical "autobiography" had been invoked to explain the aesthetic failings of the late music, as Wagner then construed them. There Wagner was still adopting what appears to have been a widely held view, that an obsession with detailed psychic self-representation in this music was the underlying cause of its refractory qualities:

The less he devoted himself simply to making music – expressing a spectrum of generalized emotions that range from the pleasant to the gripping and impassioned – and followed instead a compulsion to give precise expression in his music to a distinct content drawn from the realm of his own feelings and perceptions (*einen bestimmten, seine Gefühle und Anschauungen erfüllenden*

---

[79]   On this passage in Wagner's *Beethoven* and its relation to nineteenth-century traditions of biographical hermeneutics, see also Hermann Danuser, "Biographik und musikalische Hermeneutik," in *Festschrift Rudolf Stephan* (Laaber, 1990), 585–6.

Inhalt), . . . all the more must Beethoven make the impression of a madman, if a divinely inspired one. (III, 279)

J. C. Lobe, in his *Musikalische Briefe* of 1852, cited earlier, concurs with Wagner's position in *Opera and Drama* that Beethoven's efforts to represent in the late works the psychic detail of his inner life only exposed the limitations of absolute musical expression: "one noticed [here] his lack of technical proficiency, for instance in all his fugal movements, which lack the unconstrained Mozartian manner and natural sense of voice-leading (*natürliche Stimmengang*), or rather, he demonstrated the incapacity of music altogether to convey a detailed narration of all that transpired in his heart and – his mind."[80] In addition to condemning Beethoven's failed fugal ambitions, Lobe had, in the passage just before this (see above, p. 114), also accused Beethoven more generally of overloading his musical textures with intended signification, or in Wagnerian terms, unrealized (unrealizable) poetic intent: "[Beethoven] trangressed the fundamental rules of his art and imposed on music more than could be expected from it, such as the articulate expression of overly individualized thoughts and overly subtle nuances of feeling, when he meant to convey some conceptual content through every voice (*durch jede Stimme gleichsam einen **Begriff** verdeutlichen*) – then his compositions forfeited their general validity, transparent intelligibility, appealing beauty, and thus to some extent their affective power."[81] Along the same lines, Wagner wrote of "those accents of sorrow and joy, delight and despair in rapid alternation, interwoven or even simultaneously sounded, which the master transmuted into such unusual harmonic and rhythmic configurations in the aim of expressing a distinctly individual emotional content" (III, 280).

Neither Wagner nor Lobe illustrate just what they understand by this multiplicity of signifying voices in the late music. (Both accounts, on the other hand, read very much like a prescient description of the leitmotivic "fabric" [*Gewebe der Grundthemen* – X, 185] of Wagner's own "infinite melody" – a Beethovenian affinity that would eventually be highlighted by both Wagner and his critics, alike: see chapter 5.)[82] Since the first movement of op. 131 is a fugue, and even a fairly well-behaved one, it would seem exaggerated to accuse its polyphony of excessive

---

80 "…durch welche er der Welt zu detailliert erzählen wollte, was in seinem Herzen und in seinem – Kopfe vorging" (Lobe, *Musikalische Briefe*, 210).

81 Ibid.

82 An anonymous critic writing in 1875 referred (already) to Wagner's "leitmotivic fabric" in *Tristan* and *Die Meistersinger* as a species of "dramatic counterpoint": "Das aus Leitmotiven gefügte Gewebe, das wir *dramatischen Contrapunkt* nennen möchten (da er allerdings nicht immer identisch mit dem rein musikalischen ist) . . . " (Anon., "Neue Opern," *Allgemeine musikalische Zeitung* 10:43 [1875], col. 676; orig. emphasis).

representational intent, even though the semitone appoggiaturas of the subject do denote a consciously "expressive" gesture, and the famous four-note chromatic configuration these derive from can be said to attain an arcane leitmotivic status, of sorts, between the outer movements of the quartet and in the context of the late quartets as a group, as often noted. With op. 131, Wagner seems to respond most immediately to a kind of figurative "counterpoint" of moods, successive rather than simultaneous. Beethoven highlights this emotional "counterpoint," of course, through the unbroken succession of movements in performance.[83] (One might extend this figurative counterpoint to the contrast between the despairing gesture of the subject and its exposition, on one hand, and the ethereal, prayer-like tone of the episodes, spun from the tail of the subject, on the other) In the work as a whole Wagner presumably recognized an impulse to unify a continuous musical cycle by means of a differentiated "poetic intent," as reflected in his sketch of it as a piece of "inner biography." (A paragraph of commentary appended to the original 1854 note on the quartet underscores the continuous, cyclical quality of the "idea" by stringing together evocations of the various moods to form a single syntactic trajectory, tracing an arch from meditative dejection through "pleasant, engaging, and exhilarating" thoughts, "feelings of joy, delight, longing, love, and surrender," finally to fierce, sorrowful resignation in the Finale [XII, 350].)

It would be possible to view the opening sequence of musical-dramatic events of Act III of *Tristan und Isolde* as a Wagnerian "realization" of the poetic intent "sketched" in the opening movements of op. 131, as Wagner understood it. The first principal segment of Act III, a larger Lorenzian "period" in F minor/major (extending through the textural dissolution of the Kareol motif following Kurwenal's lines, "darin von Tod und Wunden / du selig sollst gesunden"), encompasses a progression or "evolution" (*Entwicklung*) along similar lines to that represented by the contrast (*Wechsel*) between Beethoven's opening two movements (to employ the Wagnerian formal terminology).

Both the orchestral prelude and the Shepherd's *alte Weise* express much the same mood of melancholy desolation as Wagner identified in Beethoven's Adagio fugue – a slow and despondent awakening. Kurwenal, however, greets Tristan's awakening as a "consoling vision" (Beethoven's Allegro, in Wagner's program), which he desperately

---

[83] Note that in the 1870 essay Wagner specifically designates the Adagio as a "long introduction" to the D-major Allegro. In his remarks on this quartet in *On Conducting*, Wagner is emphatic about the rhetorical significance of the musical link between the movements, the echo of the final C♯ octave rise that introduces the Allegro (D–d).

tries to encourage with the robustly cheerful F-major strains of the Kareol music. Within the prelude itself the contrast of the opening phrase (Wolzogen's compound "solitude" motive, tapering off in the high exposed thirds of the violins) and the descending sequence of its consequent response (variously labeled "distress" or "anguish") conveys an alternation of despondency and prayerfulness similar to that which Wagner identifies between the exposition and central episodes of Beethoven's fugue. The solo *alte Weise* embodies even more distinctly the "melancholy morning thoughts of a deeply sorrowful mind," in the words of Wagner's 1854 note (*schwermütige Morgenandacht eines tiefleidenden Gemütes*). Like its counterpart in Act I, the unaccompanied Sailor's song, the monophonic *alte Weise* is gradually woven into the "verse" and "orchestral" melody of this act as it unfolds. One could say that this weirdly melancholy tune functions as an extended "subject" of the musical-dramatic counterpoint of the ensuing scene, in a way that combines both literal (musical) and figurative (dramatic) senses of the contrapuntal idea.

The literal counterpoint is spare and fragmentary, at first. (While not contrapuntally imitative, of course, we could perhaps speak of a counterpoint that is aesthetically "imitative": imitative of sonic imagery and psychological process.) Like Beethoven, Wagner splits off the tail of his initial subject – the fifth to seventh measures of the *alte Weise* – for further sequential development, if only in the most tentative way, sounding beneath the Shepherd's first two lines. Subsequently, fragments of this melancholy "subject" mingle briefly with other lines in an explicit counterpoint of signification – the very device Lobe and Wagner claimed to have detected in Beethoven's late style. As Tristan first gains consciousness, for example, the opening strain of the *alte Weise* is heard against a faint echo of the "solitude" motive of the prelude, *pianissimo* in cellos and basses (see Example 2.11). Further on, Tristan's confusion of time and place is aurally rendered by the intermingling of the same figure – the head-motive of the subject, as it were – in the oboe ("Was erklang mir?") with the initial fragment of the Kareol motive (see Example 2.12).

The *alte Weise* plays a relatively minor role in the earlier part of this scene, before its extended reprise in the center (harmonized by tremolo strings). In the music of Tristan's "Delirium" (from "Nein! Ach nein! So heißt sie nicht") through to the moment of his death the motive is much more extensively incorporated into the full orchestral texture, a passage that includes perhaps the most extended and virtuosic examples of such leitmotivic counterpoint in any of Wagner's operas.[84] But even

---

[84]   The words of Tristan's recollections, as triggered by this reprise of the *alte Weise* ("durch Morgengrauen bang und bänger, als der Sohn der Mutter Los vernahm"), suggest again a proximity of mood to the "poetic idea" of op. 131, as sketched by Wagner.

Example 2.11   *Tristan und Isolde* Act III, scene 1

its modest role in the orchestral fabric of the first phase of this scene begins to suggest something of the way Wagner might have thought to have "realized" a poetic image or idea he perceived as latent in one of Beethoven's late "sketches." In particular, Wagner has distilled the extreme contrasts of Beethoven's opening movement pair and interwoven them across the opening of this scene according to the motifs of exhaustion and hope "polyphonically" mingled here in the alternation of Tristan's questions and Kurwenal's answers. The diachronic "affective counterpoint" generated by the succession of (sometimes fragmentary) movements in op. 131 finds a broader scope in the context of Wagner's *Tristan*, where motivic signification can be dramatically determined and contrasting musical moods can be not only freely juxtaposed, but also "evolved" at length out of one another, as Wagner had already prophesied in the *Art-Work of the Future* (III, 93). The hermeneutic impulse provoked by Beethoven's late style has, perhaps, generated a productive critique from Wagner, who believed he understood at last what Beethoven had been trying to say.

At the time of the Zurich writings Wagner had sided with his own future opponents in condemning what they collectively regarded as the transgressions of "absolute" musical intelligibility in Beethoven's late works and the kinds of "Hermetic semiosis" (to recall Eco's term)

127

Example 2.12 *Tristan und Isolde* Act III, scene 1

these consequently elicited, even encouraged. But already now, Wagner's objections differed categorically from those of his genuinely conservative colleagues. He condemned what he perceived as misguided responses to aesthetically valid, even historically inevitable impulses. In this, he sided after all with those progressive advocates of the "poetic idea" who were his natural allies. Perhaps this aspect of Wagner's critical position in *Opera and Drama* involved a convenient polemical strategy of appearing to side with his opponents' premises only in order to make a very different point of his own (that music drama was the answer to the late-Beethoven "question"). In doing so Wagner, like many other critics, exaggerated one element of the late style – its enigmatic disruptions and the occasional mimicry of recitative elements – as evidence of the music's "poetic intent." Still, he was probably sincere in his conviction that his newly envisaged musical-dramatic "art-work of the future" answered problems that Beethoven's late works really did raise for him, as for his contemporaries. The semantic determination of musical signs (as leitmotifs), the dismantling of schematic phrase and period structure in favor of rhetorically "speaking" melody, and the substitution of continuous, evolving formal designs patterned after the trajectories of dramatic action for those bound by the ritual formalities of dance and march – all of these things could be understood as a legitimate response to the musical-hermeneutic aporias that Beethoven posed to Wagner and his generation.

3

Engendering music drama: *Opera and Drama* and its metaphors

Die Musik ist ein Weib.
(Music is a woman.)
             – *Opera and Drama, Part I (III, 316)*

Metaphors of gender, and others

A passion for extravagant clothing, in life, finds a parallel in Wagner's passion for extravagant metaphor in his prose. Before he had the proper means to indulge the former fetish, he could at least afford the latter. And he certainly did so during the impecunious days of his early Swiss exile, when he produced his most notoriously prolix essays on musical and broadly cultural issues, in which no intellectual expense was spared in decking himself out in a luxuriant profusion of figurative language. Throughout the Zurich essays Wagner treats his abundant stock of metaphors rather in the fashion of musical leitmotifs: they continually reappear, transform, combine, and re-combine to suit the needs of the argument (which was, with Wagner, truly an improvisatory act). And like the fundamental motives of the *Ring* – what Wagner later designated as its malleable or plastic "nature motives" (*plastische Natur-Motive*, VI, 266) – the basic metaphors of the Zurich writings also derive largely from the natural world: harmony as "ocean," melody as its rippling surface (boldly charted by Beethoven-as-Columbus), folk song as "wildflower," drama as organism or human body. Since the musical drama, as the perfected "communal art-work of the future," is the ultimate object of Wagner's theoretical inquiry, it is this last organic, or rather physiological, figure (drama as organism) that supports the most extensive metaphorical complex in these writings, particularly in *Opera and Drama*. This physiology of the musical drama elicits, in turn, a gendered construction of its parent elements, poetry and music, as male and female, whence derives the familiar representation of the "poetic intent" (*dichterische Absicht*) as the fertilizing seed received and nurtured by the womb of music.

130

Wagner's metaphors of organicism and gender are entirely con-sonant with the predominant modes of cultural representation of his era, as are the details of their application. To this extent the metaphorical language of *Opera and Drama* embodies broad cultural norms and stereotypes in ways that are, if hardly surprising, at least highly pro-filed. Some of these themes are still more prominent within the dramas themselves, their characters and configurations – above all in that omnipresent figure of the unconditionally loving, self-sacrificing, all-redeeming, eternally-feminine Woman. But beyond demonstrating the participation of Wagner's theoretical writings (as well as his operas) in a broader cultural discourse, his metaphors may also provide some interpretive links between the writings and the operas with respect to music, drama, and "ideas." Thus my proposal here is twofold: first, that an analysis of the leading metaphors of *Opera and Drama* is one logical step toward interpreting this famously opaque text, and, second, that the congruence of these leading metaphors (primarily those of gender and sexuality) with prominent psychological-dramatic motifs (in *Siegfried* and *Parsifal*) may provide a hermeneutic window, to use Lawrence Kramer's phrase, on their musical realization – the realization (*Verwirk-lichung*) of the "poetic intent," in Wagnerian terms.[1] At the same time, the play of these interrelated tropes on multiple levels of critical, dra-matic, and musical text is some measure of Wagner's complexly textured contribution to the cultural discourse of the nineteenth century in general, in which he played such an out-sized role.

Music is a woman. The metaphorical equation is set out this way in its simplest form, italicized but syntactically unadorned, near the end of Part I of *Opera and Drama*, where it stands revealed as the logical consequence of a developing organicist discourse on the gestation of melody, also forming the theme for a metaphorical finale or coda on the typology of operatic-musical "woman." The theme of music-as-woman is an old one,[2] and in developing it Wagner employs a number of familiar variants. In particular he plays on what has been identified as a polarizing trope that divides women into opposite extremes of idealized and degraded femininity: music as goddess, muse, or saint,

---

[1] Lawrence Kramer, *Music as Cultural Practice, 1800–1900* (Berkeley and Los Angeles, 1990), 1–20 ("Tropes and Windows: An Outline of Musical Hermeneutics").

[2] In much French feminist writing (notably Julia Kristeva's) the traditional female gendering of music is grounded in more general associations between aurality (vocality) and the maternal, a state of being preceding language and articulate thought. The same set of associations reaches back to the Enlightenment "anthro-pology" of musical origins (informing Wagner's ideas of melody, as discussed in chapter 5) that views music, melody, or song as the matrix of language (music or song standing for the vocalization of "feelings" or experience at an instinctive level). Here, too, is the pedigree of music's status as a system of natural or "motivated" signs.

131

Engendering music drama

on one hand, and music as corrupting courtesan (herself the product of social corruption), on the other hand, embodying all that is shallow, cheap, false, and morally bankrupt in modern commercial culture.[3] This polarization of the woman-as-music metaphor obviously serves Wagner's critical agenda here of distinguishing between a corrupt operatic tradition and the redeeming promise of the "art-work of the future." But submerged beneath the explicit critical agenda we can also detect something of Wagner's unspoken ambivalence on the whole issue of absolute music ("pure music," as its champions would still more likely refer to it at this time) and its claims within the operatic domain. This ambivalence assumes either conscious or unconscious allegorical shape in the relationship of Wagner's two heroic *ingénus* – Siegfried and Parsifal – to the "unstable, " labile female characters of Brünnhilde and Kundry, representatives of the two opposing poles of feminine good and evil. In the second part of this chapter I will suggest how these contrasting relationships might allegorize, on both dramatic and musical levels, Wagner's theoretical ambivalence toward "pure music." I might remark in advance, however, on the telling irony that while in the metaphorical constructions of his theory, and in what I propose as a conscious allegory of "pure music" in the figure of Brünnhilde, Wagner strove to represent only the classically idealized woman (whatever her innate needs and lacks), the reception of his own music consistently aligned it with the inverted type represented by Kundry (and her music): the frenzied, hysterical, and dangerously unaccountable female subject, forever at the mercy of her sensual being and her polymorphous psychopathology.

For Wagner, music resembles woman in its capacity for feeling (and its incapacity for thinking), in following the laws of instinct rather than reason, in its alleged affinity with nature and the natural, and in

[3] Kramer identifies elements of this polarizing of feminine ideal and "dangerous contrary" in Liszt's musical "character portrait" of Gretchen in the *Faust Symphony*, although not without considerable strain, it seems to me ("Liszt, Goethe, and the Discourse of Gender," in *Music as Cultural Practice*, 102–34). On the background of the dichotomous trope itself he cites the now classic work of feminist literary history, Sandra M. Gilbert and Susan Gubar, *The Madwoman in the Attic: The Woman Writer and the Nineteenth-Century Literary Imagination* (New Haven, 1979), 1–44, as well as the Freudian male defense mechanisms understood to project this division of the female persona. Bram Dijkstra's iconographic study, *Idols of Perversity: Fantasies of Feminine Evil in Fin-de-Siècle Culture* (New York, 1986), is naturally oriented toward the negative side of this dichotomy, which Dijkstra sees as becoming increasingly predominant in artistic representations of women as the century progresses. Nonetheless, he chronicles the whole spectrum of types in the course of the book, which begins with a survey of idealized, submissive, and self-sacrificing portrayals, primarily in domestic contexts (chapter 1, "Raptures of Submission: The Shopkeeper's Soul Keeper and the Cult of the Household Nun," 3–24).

lacking the means – or even the moral right – to independent existence. Poetry, or language in general, resembles man for the obverse reasons: it deals in thought, understanding, and rational concepts; it begins where civilization departs from nature; and while it clearly is able to lead an independent existence, it feels itself drawn toward a complementary union with music, or at least it ought to feel this. Music lacks the will or motivation to shape itself; poetry can provide music with the structuring motivation it lacks. This economy describes the general circumstances of music and poetry with relation to one another. But there remains the potential division between ideal and corrupt conditions of music or femininity. (Not surprisingly, the fault behind a fall from a unitary grace is ascribed, implicitly, more to female music than to male poetry.)

Music, then, may resemble woman in both her highest and lowest estates. Wagner's vision of these opposing conditions of woman and his moral evaluation of them are thoroughly characteristic of the age, as will already be obvious, even while he applies them to a radical critique of the musical status quo. (Apparently his participation in the revolutionary socialist fervor of 1848–9 did not extend to the contemporaneous beginnings of an emancipatory women's movement.[4]) Ideally, music resembles woman in its selflessness, its pliability, and its readiness to surrender itself to a higher cause. Wagner's account of the "nature" of woman, as metaphor for the nature of music, begins as a veritable casebook in patriarchal subjugation, and moves in the direction of outright hostility: first in speaking of the necessary "annihilation" of the woman's individual identity as a consequence of her surrender to man (*"Vernichtung"* – the word that figures notoriously in the conclusion of

---

[4] While the early stirrings of a feminist consciousness in Europe appear in the context of progressive socialist thinking of the 1830s and 40s, the relation between the two was far from stable. Pierre-Joseph Proudhon, for instance, one of the leaders of the socialist movement in France who exerted a pronounced influence on Wagner's revolutionary tracts, became a staunch opponent of women's rights; his anti-feminist stance received its strongest formulation in work not published until after his death, entitled *Pornocracy, or Woman in Modern Times* (Paris, 1865). On Proudhon and the interrelation of women's causes and early socialist thought see Marguerite Thibert, *Le féminisme dans le socialisme français de 1830 à 1850* (Paris, 1926), Leslie F. Goldstein, "Early Feminist Themes in French Utopian Socialism: The Saint-Simonians and Fourier," and Angus McLaren, "Sex and Socialism: The Opposition of the French Left to Birth Control in the Nineteenth Century," both in *Race, Class, and Gender in Nineteenth-Century Culture*, ed. M. C. Horowitz (Rochester, NY, 1991), 195–212, 213–30; and L. J. Rather, *Reading Wagner*, 246–59: "Wagner, Proudhon, and George Sand." Rather's other chapter, on "The Insurrection of Woman," has remarkably little to say about Wagner's social or political (or artistic) views on women's issues, unfortunately. Jean-Jacques Nattiez, on the other hand, has compiled a variety of derogatory remarks made by Wagner from 1870 on that reveal an almost virulent misogyny in the composer's later attitudes – attitudes which the self-abasing Cosima was all too ready to encourage in him (*Wagner Androgyne*, 167–9).

Judaism in Music), and finally in turning to his characterization of national operatic genres as types of degenerate women (*entartete Frauen* – III, 318).

The whole passage in question – the conclusion of Part I of *Opera and Drama* – makes for a sociological document of some interest. If the cultural attitudes expressed here are typical and unsurprising in themselves, the bluntness of their expression is still striking. It is worth quoting this evocation of music's feminine nature at some length, in any case, since it forms the core of Wagner's extended metaphorical gendering of music, thereby situating music (or Wagner's views on it) explicitly within a discourse of contemporary social values.

Music is a woman.

The nature of woman is *love*: but this is a *receptive* love, one that *surrenders itself* unreservedly.

Woman achieves full individuality only at the moment of surrendering herself. She is like the *ondine* (*Wellenmädchen*) who floats about aimlessly in the waves of her native element, without a soul, until she finally receives one through the love of a man. The look of innocence in the woman's eyes is the infinitely clear mirror in which the man can only recognize the general capacity for love, until he is able to recognize in it his own image: when he has done so, then too is the woman's polymorphous capacity for love condensed into a pressing need to love this man with the full ecstasy of surrender. (III, 316)

In just a few lines we are inundated with a veritable torrent of Romantic-bourgeois tropes of feminine ideality. Both male and female gender identities may be construed as incomplete, complementary halves, but clearly the female is less than half, more incomplete. Woman is conditioned by nature to yield her less stable, less completely formed identity to a more stable, defining male counterpart. She realizes her "true" identity only upon giving up her imperfect feminine identity to this higher union. In the Feuerbachian rhetoric of the Zurich writings, it is true, the "egoistic" character of either gender alone is evaluated as incomplete prior to its communion with the complementary other half. But there is no question that this complementary difference is skewed in favor of a more definitive ("determinate") male identity. The floating "soul-less *ondine*" receives soul and stability from the male principle (the fluid musical element is grounded in poetry, or some "form-motive" derived from material existence, as Wagner argues in the Liszt essay of 1857).

This image of the "floating woman," whose visual representations in the nineteenth century have been catalogued by Bram Dijkstra[5] (strangely omitting any mention of Wagner's musical Rhine-maidens), carries another classic symbol of gender relations in tow: the male "gaze," or more particularly, here, the narcissistic "specular" gaze that seeks and finds the reflection of its own image in the feminine object of desire.

---

5   Dijkstra, *Idols of Perversity*, chapter 4: "The Weightless Woman; the Nymph with the Broken Back; and the Mythology of Therapeutic Rape" (83–118).

"The look of innocence in the woman's eyes," Wagner writes, "is the infinitely clear mirror in which the man can only recognize the general capacity for love, until he is able to recognize in it *his own image.*" Lawrence Kramer, who has sought to analyze musical instantiations of the phenomenon of the controlling and consuming male gaze in the polar contexts of the idealized and demonized feminine identities, respectively, of Goethe's (or Liszt's) Gretchen and Wilde's (and Strauss's) Salome, calls attention to this particular Lacanian variant, the narcissistic, specular gaze: "what the gazer both seeks and is authorized to find is a 'specular' image: an image in which the subject's privileged sense of self is crystallized."[6] However problematic the application of such psychological constructions to an "objectless" musical discourse, they receive explicit embodiment both in Wagner's theoretical metaphors and – as we shall see – in a variety of his poetic images and dramatic configurations. The narcissistic gazes described by or exchanged between such characters as Senta and the Dutchman, Siegmund and Sieglinde, Siegfried and Brünnhilde, or Tristan and Isolde figure prominently in Jean-Jacques Nattiez's thesis of a motif of "androgyny" central to Wagner's oeuvre and to his own creative identity.[7] I will return later to Nattiez's androgyny thesis and its implications for the interpretation of Wagner's metaphorical imagery, and to some of the larger problems facing a critical application of this whole discourse of gender to the musical texts. But for the moment, let us pursue the fundamental terms of Wagner's theoretical metaphor itself.

"The true woman loves unconditionally," Wagner continues, "because she must." She has no choice, no will, no prior identity. He proceeds to engage in some obscure psychology, the upshot of which is that, after a certain amount of interior struggle, the woman comes to the realization that she has "neither power nor will" outside of her communion with the "beloved object," and through this communion she herself is eventually "annihilated" (*vernichtet*).

The open recognition of this [necessary] annihilation is the act of sacrifice in the form of the woman's final surrender: her pride is consciously dissolved in that one thing she is able to both feel and think, the thing she herself is, finally: the love for this one man. (III, 317)

---

6   Kramer, *Music as Cultural Practice*, 111. Cf. "Culture and Musical Hermeneutics: The Salome Complex," *Cambridge Opera Journal* 2:3 (1990), 269–94. Isolde Vetter discusses the thematics of the "narcissistic gaze" in *The Flying Dutchman* in her essay, "Senta und der Holländer – eine narzißistische Kollusion mit tödlichem Ausgang," in A. Csampai and D. Holland, eds., *Richard Wagner: Der fliegende Holländer, Texte, Materialen, Kommentare* (Reinbek, 1982), 9–19. Kramer returns to the thematics of gazes and mirrors in "*Carnaval*, Cross-Dressing, and the Woman in the Mirror," in *Musicology and Difference*, ed. Ruth A. Solie (Berkeley and Los Angeles, 1993), esp. 315–23.

7   *Wagner Androgyne.*

Thus is woman "by nature." Modern society has created types of women (those anti-types of the idealized woman) as diametrically opposed to the symbolic feminine ideal as modern operatic genres are to the unsullied essence of Wagner's musical ideal. What they have in common is the failure or inability to surrender themselves wholly, body and soul. After limning the ideal "nature of woman" as character model for music, Wagner passes in review the depraved modern anti-types as emblems of modern operatic genres and their abject condition. (Wagner's gesture of "passing in review" ["Führen wir uns die charakteristischen Typen solcher Frauen vor!"] seems consciously to evoke some scene of female degradation – the oriental slave market or the convicted whores being led to deportation at Le Havre in *Manon Lescaut*.) Italian opera is a common strumpet [*Lustdirne*] – she yields her body in a commercial transaction, but necessarily remains emotionally impassive, psychically absent. (Her one redeeming feature, Wagner notes, is that she "at least continues to fulfill the physical function of the female sex" – III, 317). French opera is the coquette (Wagner takes the *opéra comique* as a paradigm here, rather than the grand opera he had excoriated at length in preceding chapters). Her aims are profit and adulation, but her soul-less egoism exceeds that of the Italian operatic woman, since she resists as far as possible any physical embrace. Wagner's evocation of this "type" again underscores the polarizing phenomenon, while also touching back on the theme of the specular "gaze": "in her, the nature of woman," he writes, "is inverted into a horrible antithesis of itself (*zu ihrem widerlichen Gegenteile verkehrt*), and from her cold smile, in which we see only our distorted image reflected, we turn in despair back to the Italian strumpet" (III, 318).

In the moral code of Wagner's gendered aesthetics, as we see, sexual promiscuity is not the cardinal sin. That consists, rather, in the woman's refusal to surrender herself completely, physically *and* spiritually – to "annihilate" her individual ego by subordinating it to the embrace of a male identity. Hence the most "repulsive" of these degenerate metaphorical females (*entartete Frauen*) is the hypocritical "prude" emblematic of contemporary German opera.[8] (Wagner exempts Weber here, thus leaving the genre rather scantily represented, as he acknowledges in a footnote.) The purity and virtue to which this prudish woman pretends are likened to the smug sense of superiority indulged in by the German opera composer when he contemplates the shortcomings of the popular foreign styles. Both the metaphor and its critical object recall Wagner's "Young German" affiliations of the 1830s, when moral prudery and sterile musical "science" were vigorously rejected as manifestations of

---

8 William Ashton Ellis renders the phrase *"entartete Frauen"* freely but suggestively as "unsexed dames," paraphrasing Lady Macbeth (*Richard Wagner's Prose Works* [London, 1892–9], vol. II, 113).

narrow-minded German hypocrisy. The strumpet and the coquette might still, by chance, fall under the redeeming influence of some individual man, as Italian or French opera sometimes contains passages of genuine musical inspiration, thanks to exceptional poetic or dramatic circumstances. The prudish woman (like the German opera) secretly lusts after the pleasures of the flesh (the sensual enjoyment offered by French and Italian operatic styles), but its false pride condemns it to sterility (*Unfruchtbarkeit*).

This metaphorical typology of "degenerate women" is little more than a whimsical, if perhaps offensive, by-product of Wagner's central figurative construct, however: the procreative union of male and female principles, poetry and music, that begets the ideal dramatic "art-work of the future." Before turning to his historical analysis of poetry and drama in Part II of *Opera and Drama*, he briefly recapitulates the role of the ideal woman, as metaphorical embodiment of music in its relation to poetry. This woman surrenders herself unconditionally to the man who loves her. Her role is above all to become impregnated, to nurture and bear new life. She acts best when she acts without thinking, instinctively.

To bear gladly (*froh und freudig*) that which is received, this is *the deed* of the woman, – and to accomplish such deeds it requires only that she be exactly what she is; there is no question of "wanting," for she can want only one thing: *to be a woman!* Thus woman is for man the infallible measure of nature (*das ewig klare und erkenntliche Maß der Untrüglichkeit*), for she is most perfect when she does not transgress the sphere of beautiful instinct (*Unwillkürlichkeit*), the sphere which holds her in thrall by virtue of the one thing that brings her joy, the necessity of love. (III, 319–20: original emphasis)

This idealizing denigration of the status of music as the abjectly selfless bourgeois help-mate sums up very well the apparent position of music in *Opera and Drama* as a "means" subordinate to the higher "end" of drama, an end that can be effected only through the willing subjugation of music to the formative power of words and a "poetic intent." While the situation may be perfectly consonant with the social structures of nineteenth-century bourgeois patriarchy, it seems disturbingly dissonant with the more liberal musical aesthetics of the Romantic tradition, according to which music was supposed to be an absolutely independent, self-determining subject and no longer the chattel of poetic, conceptual discourse or material imitation. (Wherein resides the "purity" of music? If music is a chaste goddess in the context of Romantic aesthetics, it becomes here a Wagnerian heroine, who finds redemption in self-sacrifice or "annihilation," the mythological apotheosis of the middle-class housewife. Wagner realizes that "purity," too, is a cultural construction.) On the other hand, the corollary of Wagner's gendered metaphor and its ultimate source is the quintessential Romantic trope of organicism. Wagner assigns gendered identities to music and poetry in order to engage in explicitly sexual, physiological metaphors of reproduction and organic growth, gestation, development, or evolution (*Entwicklung*). In the process, the metaphorical status of gender and that of biological sexuality become increasingly confounded, as does the aesthetic status of music "herself."

Natural sciences: reproductive biology and a theory of "evolution"

While Wagner draws his metaphors from the whole range of the natural world, his organicism is essentially that of human biology (rather than of the lower orders of the plant and animal kingdoms), as befits the value-system of the Zurich writings in which the "purely human" (rather than the merely organic) reigns as the final measure of perfection. The gendering of music and poetry in *Opera and Drama* – for all that it partakes of a cultural discourse of social roles, stereotypes, and moral judgements – inevitably reverts to a "scientific" discourse of biological sexuality and human anatomy, an organicism centered on the image of the human body. The musical-dramatic *Gesamtkunstwerk* is both gendered and engendered. More precisely, it is *engendered* by the gendered contributions of its component (parental) media, music and dramatic poetry. At the center of this metaphorical engendering is Wagner's familiar notion of the "poetic intent" (*dichterische Absicht*) as the "fertilizing seed" by which the musical womb is impregnated in order to give birth to the musical drama.

This idea of dramatic poetry as the "fertilizing seed" of musical drama is the axis of a large and diffuse complex of metaphorical constructions in *Opera and Drama*, as Frank Glass rightly suggested in his study of Wagner's writings and music under the aegis of this phrase.[9] And, as Nattiez has pointed out,[10] *Opera and Drama* as a whole can be understood to be loosely structured around the idea: Part I concerns the history and status of opera up through Wagner's time as dominated by the independent development of musical form and expression (hence a "feminized" art-form, in that it is determined foremost by the "female" principle of music); Part II analyzes the "male" principle of

9   Frank W. Glass, *The Fertilizing Seed*.
10   Nattiez, *Wagner Androgyne*, 38. Wagner summarizes the structural role of this guiding metaphor in a letter to Theodor Uhlig (cited here), written in December 1850. See further 35–7 for a translation and gloss of the same passage from the end of Part II of *Opera and Drama* I am concerned with here, where the sexual metaphor for the union of music and poetry is most fully elaborated. The letter to Uhlig was written when Wagner had just completed Part II , thus at exactly the time he had been elaborating upon this metaphor.

drama, from various historical and critical perspectives; and Part III then evokes the coupling of music and poetry in the ideal musical drama. (Wagner introduces Part III with a kind of voyeuristic invitation to observe or eavesdrop on [*belauschen*] the act of conception and/or birth [*den Akt der Gebärung*] – IV, 103.) Yet even as the crux of his theoretical metaphors, this idea of the poetic insemination of music develops rather haphazardly in the course of the book, evidence of the highly improvisatory process characteristic of Wagner's critical writings in general. While the gendered imagery at the end of Part I is all predicated on the explicitly sexual metaphor of biological repro-duction, the identification of a poetic intent as "fertilizing seed" does not occur until the end of Part II. The drive of the poetic "understanding" to communicate the significance of some concentrated action or series of actions to the emotional faculty,[11] Wagner explains here, necessitates a productive union with music, as the "language of feeling."

> Understanding is thus pressed, of necessity, to marry itself with an element that will absorb its ["his"] poetic intent as a fertilizing seed (*befruchtenden Samen*) and will be capable of nurturing and forming this seed according to its own [i.e., music's feminine/musical] nature in order to bear [give birth to] it as an actualized, redeeming emotional expression. (IV, 102)

Music itself was the hypothetical "feminine, maternal element" from which language is supposed to have evolved according to the mytho-poetic historiography of *Opera and Drama* and its antecedents (see chapter 5), just as all organic life forms evolved from the tepid primeval sea. The impulse of language to be re-united with the element of musical tone is thus a partially incestuous Oedipal drive, as Wagner explicitly acknowledges in a half-ironic footnote pointing to the birth of the "redeeming" character of Antigone from the union of Oedipus and Jocasta (see IV, 103n.).

The drive to achieve a more perfect, complete communication is manifested in the eventual impulse of language to be both "embraced" and "mirrored" by music (*umfasst, wiederspiegelt*) – both terms appealing to Wagner's ambiguous psychological representation of music as mother and wife in one. For Wagner, writing in 1850, this problematic duality of the female role is rationalized through an invocation of that virginal icon of secular Romanticism, *das ewig Weibliche*. For Wagner's purposes, however, the saintly image has to be converted to a profane one, with license to solicit desire. The male principle (poetry, language, intellect) is "enticed" out of his egoistic state by the mysterious, irre-sistible attractions of the "eternal feminine":

[11] " . . . die Darstellung der verstärkten Handlungen seiner [des Dichters] gedichteten Gestalten durch Darlegung ihrer Motive an das Gefühl" (IV, 101). The phrase describes the actualization or "realization" (*Verwirklichung*) of the poetic intent.

The attraction that awakens this impulse [of language to recognize itself in and join with music] and excites it to the highest pitch resides . . . in the object of desire [i.e., music, or tone] . . . This attraction is the effect of the "eternal feminine," which entices the egoistic masculine intellect (*Verstand*) out of its isolation. (IV, 102)

Wagner's choice of image and verb here (*herauslocken* – to lure or entice) evokes the *ondines* or sirens of myth – his Rhine-maidens, for example – whose charms embody precisely this ambiguous role in which sexual attraction is merged with blandishments of maternal affection (cf. Kundry), the promise of a regression to the womb-like security of the watery depths. The implicit confusion of sexual roles is further confounded by a blurring of gender identities: the "eternal feminine" manifested in musical tone – former mother and future wife – effects its seduction of language (or intellect, understanding) by awakening an androgynous consciousness in the "male":

It is able to achieve this [enticing of the masculine intellect] only by appealing to the feminine element within the intellect. This common element shared by feeling and intellect alike is the *purely human*, that which constitutes the essence of the human *species* as such. Both masculine and feminine partake of this purely human essence, and only when united by love do both together become *human*. (IV, 102)

Of course, the idealized sexual act celebrated in Wagner's metaphor is not to be associated with the base commercial transactions of those fallen "operatic women" held up to public censure at the end of Part I, nor with "that frivolous, indecent (*unzüchtige*) love in which the man seeks only pleasurable satisfaction" (IV, 103). The metaphorical insemination of music by the "poetic intent" is at once a physical act, with physiological consequences, and a gesture of metaphysical transcendence, in which the two parties relinquish their individual identities in favor of a single, "higher," and more complete one.

Such a synthesis of physical and metaphysical love, and the consequent sublation of individual identities into a mystical one-ness, may put us in mind of such Wagnerian heroic couplings as Siegfried and Brünnhilde or Tristan and Isolde (even if they mostly remain barren of offspring, as Nietzsche felt compelled to point out). The poetic language in which both of these mythical marriages are consummated also resonates with the merging of or transcendence of gendered identities evoked in *Opera and Drama*, and both relevant scenes (*Siegfried* Act III, scene 3, and *Tristan und Isolde* Act II, scene 2) thus figure largely in Nattiez's case for the idea of androgyny as a central Wagnerian motif. The wider Oedipal confusion of sexual roles implicit in Wagner's metaphorical discourse also recalls the scene of Brünnhilde's awakening and wooing by Siegfried, as it does that other famous Wagnerian scene of sexual awakening through psychologically ambivalent seduction, that between Kundry and Parsifal. I will return to both of these scenes below, arguing that the *Siegfried* scene, in particular, can be interpreted as an allegorical enactment of the whole metaphorical congeries of the aesthetic theory in *Opera and Drama* (an allegory that becomes problematized, however, once we extend it to *Parsifal*). But before pursuing these issues of sexuality, gender, fusion, and confusion into drama and music, let me continue for a moment my attempt to sort out the tangled metaphorical fabric of *Opera and Drama* and its aesthetic consequences.

The terms of Wagner's metaphor appear to press beyond the gendering of music and drama according to generalized cultural attributes and to insist on the biological determinants of sexuality. Certainly the central image of sexual reproduction suggests that this is so. But if we follow these metaphorical terms to their logical consequences, we find that the "objective" structures of natural science are still inextricably bound up with cultural constructions of gender, just as the supposedly distinct biological and gender-roles of mother, father, and offspring become confounded in ways that recall the Oedipal and incestuous motifs of Wagner's dramas, or that drive us from the realm of natural science to the mythical, alchemical, and allegorical realms inhabited by the androgynous figures analyzed by Nattiez.

The "biological" image of the fertilizing seed itself – especially in its metaphorical function here as symbol of the procreative male "word" of poetry or rational, linguistic thought – appears to derive more from symbols of ancient mythical cosmology than from modern natural science (reminding us how the explanatory models of science and of myth become increasingly indistinguishable as one moves back in time). Although I cannot say whether Wagner might have been conscious of the derivation or not, his metaphor of the poetic word as "fertilizing seed" seems to be clearly linked to the *logos spermatikos* of Stoic cosmology, later revived by Jung in his gendered psychological theories of the creative mind. This concept of a procreative (male) "spermatic word" can be traced back to Aristotle and forward through the writings of the fathers of the early Christian Church (underlying, for instance, the pronouncement of St. John: "In the beginning was the Word") and to medieval scholastic thought. Christine Battersby has pointed out the role of this concept within the tradition, stretching from ancient to modern times, that ascribes explicitly male attributes to the figure of "genius." "In the Stoic elaborations of this Aristotelian idea," she writes, "*logos* was the formula contained within the male seed that enables the father to reproduce his own likeness in his offspring" – hence, "a kind of mystical (genetic) code, which only males carried."[12] This may explain why Wagner, writing before the advent of modern genetics and presumably little informed on current research in human biology, can ascribe an actively procreative force to the male (verbal) seed alone, to which the female womb provides a nurturing receptacle for incubation, but without any active, determinative share in the process of conception. (Battersby refers to the Aristotelian "flower-pot" theory of reproduction, according to which the woman contributes only "the soil and container in which the seed will grow.")[13] The detailed vocabulary of the metaphor reinforces this archaic notion of the reproductive process, according to which the male seed functions analogously to a botanical seed, containing the entire form of the future organism *in nuce*. The phrase often translated as "fertilizing seed" – as I have continued to do here – would be more accurately rendered as "procreative seed," as it is indeed by the always literal William Ashton Ellis:

The necessary bestowal, the seed that only in the most ardent transports of Love can condense itself from his noblest forces – *this procreative seed* (zeugende Samen) *is the poetic Aim* (dichterische Absicht), *which brings to the glorious loving woman, Music, the Stuff for bearing.*[14]

Other details of Wagner's sexual biology are also informed by theory more ancient than modern. At the end of Part II of *Opera and Drama* (immediately preceding the passage just quoted) he speaks of "the seed which is to be emitted, and which is distilled from [the man's] noblest powers in the heat of amorous excitement (*der nur in der brünstigsten Liebeserregung aus seinen edelsten Kräften sich verdichtende Samen*)" (IV, 103). According to the views of traditional, "pre-scientific" theory, the male semen is distilled in the heat of intercourse. Likewise, a certain

---

12   Christine Battersby, *Gender and Genius: Towards a Feminist Aesthetics* (London, 1989), 49. Thomas Laqueur also comments on the symbolic affiliation of the male seed or sperm with "intellection" for Aristotle, and its implications for patriarchal social structures: "The *kurios*, the strength of the sperma in generating new life, is the microcosmic corporeal aspect of the citizen's deliberative strength, of his superior rational power" – recalling Wagner's male poetic principle – "and of his right to govern" (Laqueur, *Making Sex: Body and Gender from the Greeks to Freud* [Cambridge MA, 1990], 54–5).

13   Several weeks after Cosima had given birth to Wagner's son, and during the time he was completing the last act of *Siegfried* (see below), Wagner reflected on the fact that woman is "like the earth in the relation to the sun: she is entirely passive, and all that comes out is what Man puts in . . . Orientals rightly regard Woman as the plowed field in which they scatter the seed" (CWD, 22 June 1869). Wagner was commenting on the fact that Cosima's elder children resembled von Bülow rather than her.

14   Wagner/Ellis, *Prose Works*, vol. II, 236 (Wagner, IV, 103), original emphasis. Stewart Spencer also maintains this distinction in his translation of the passage, in Nattiez, *Wagner Androgyne*, 37.

increased level of bodily heat was perceived as a prerequisite for the success of the reproductive process as a whole (the fertilization of the female).[15] Metaphorically, this heat necessary to conception is that produced by the poet-dramatist's heightened desire to communicate more fully to the emotional faculties of his audience, the point at which he is instinctively driven to embrace musical tone. This metaphor, too, I will suggest below, is played out allegorically in the text, "action," and music of the closing scene of *Siegfried*.

Perhaps the major obstacle to literal (scientific) analogy posed by Wagner's metaphors of gender lies in their androgynous implications, whether consciously developed by Wagner (as they appear to be in some places), or an inadvertent product of a metaphorical discourse run amok (as they appear to be elsewhere). Wagner himself cautioned against an overly scrupulous demand for metaphorical consistency – this in a footnote to a later passage in *Opera and Drama* where he has recklessly switched images in mid-metaphorical stream, transforming the orchestra from an ocean-going vessel into a body of water (a lake) in order to picture "verse-melody," in turn, as a boat floating upon *orchestral* waters.[16] The androgynous implications of Wagner's gendered metaphors are difficult to assess, in any case, since they are generated as much by improvisatory accident as by rhetorical design.

The figure of androgyny, which Nattiez interprets as a potential key to Wagner's creative mind and works alike, is affiliated by nature and by tradition with the realms of myth, symbol, and metaphysics, and as such it seems to be at odds with the natural sciences (reproductive biology, human physiology, geography, and a smattering of botany) that otherwise inform his metaphorical constructions. Nonetheless, the idea of androgyny does appear to be explicitly invoked in several important contexts from the period of *Opera and Drama* and the conception of the *Ring*. In discussing (rather abstractly, as usual) Beethoven's contribution toward a more "organic" approach to melody in *Opera and Drama*, for example, Wagner ascribes an androgynous character to the composer's creative persona: "In order to become fully *human*, Beethoven had to become a complete, composite person, at once subordinate to

---

15 On the role of "heat" in the process of intercourse and reproduction as understood from classical times through the Renaissance and beyond, see Thomas Laqueur, "Orgasm, Generation, and the Politics of Reproductive Biology," in *The Making of the Modern Body: Sexuality and Society in the Nineteenth Century*, ed. C. Gallagher and T. Laqueur (Berkeley and Los Angeles, 1987), 1–41 (esp. 4–5, 7–11) and also Laqueur, *Making Sex*, 43–52 ("Orgasm and Desire").

16 "An object will never correspond exactly to another one with which it is compared; the similarities may be pursued in one particular direction, but not in every direction" (IV, 171n.).

143

the determinants of both male and female gender" ("... *ein ganzer,*
d. h. gemeinsamer, den geschlechtlichen Bedingungen *des Männlichen
und Weiblichen* unterworfener Mensch werden – III, 312: original
emphasis). This sounds something like a proto-Jungian construction of
the bisexually compounded psyche, *animus* and *anima*, an admixture of
psychological gender traits that Jung himself viewed as fundamental
to the (male) creative mind, especially. For Wagner, as Nattiez rightly
points out,[17] this transcendence of gender identity is equated with the
quasi-Feuerbachian idea of the "purely human" that figures largely in
the social and aesthetic philosophy of the Zurich writings, a condition
that Wagner also construes as epistemologically anterior to the division
of male and female. Yet this androgynous formulation of Beethoven's
persona seems also to be the chance by-product of the organic, physiological, and "functionally" sexual metaphors Wagner is tentatively
exploring at this point, several pages before he expounds more fully
the idea of music-as-woman, cited at the beginning of this chapter. To
the extent that he raised music out of its "feminine" condition as
absolute music and infused it with newly formative "poetic intent,"
Beethoven (like Wagner) subsumes both male and female roles of poet
and musician.[18] At the same time Wagner appeals here once again to
his favorite example of the Ninth Symphony and the revelatory, prophetic force of its vocal finale, effected by Beethoven's decision to enlist
the outside aid of the poetic word. This elicits from Wagner the rather
incongruous image of Beethoven "throwing himself into the arms of
the poet, in order to accomplish that act of *conceiving* that unmistakably
true and redeeming melody," that is, the *Freude* melody of the Finale
(III, 312). Symbolic androgyny and the organic metaphor of sexual
reproduction make for strange bedfellows.

---

[17] *Wagner Androgyne*, 41.
[18] In *A Communication to My Friends* Wagner had stated explictly that the "absolute
artist" (hence absolute musician) is to be regarded as "feminine" (IV, 247). While this
evaluation clearly harks back to the terms of *Opera and Drama* with its distinction
between male (pro)creativity and female receptivity and nurture, Wagner appeals
to another element of the contemporary social discourse of gender here: the idea that
the woman's sphere was naturally dissociated from the "real world" of public life,
as typified by Marlowe's assessment of woman's domestic "dream-world" in
Conrad's *Heart of Darkness*. See also Ruth Solie, "The Gendered Self in Schumann's
Frauenliebe Songs," in *Music and Text: Critical Inquiries*, ed. S. P. Scher [Cambridge,
1992], esp. 223–6. The absolute artist, Wagner writes in the *Communication*, exists "in
an artistic world entirely cut off from life, a world in which art is merely a self-
referential play [lit. 'art plays with itself'], retreating from any contact with reality –
not only the reality of modern life but also the reality of life altogether, which it feels
compelled to regard as absolutely inimical to it and its cause ..." (IV, 247). Painting
is most guilty of this disengagement from "real life," according to Wagner
(evidently innocent of the debate being waged over "realism" in France at this
moment), followed by music.

Several years later Wagner again invokes the figure of androgyny as symbol of the trans-gendered "purely human" ideal in the famous letter to August Röckel of 25–6 January 1854, elucidating the symbolic import of the *Ring* drama and its characters:

The highest satisfaction of individual egoism is to be found in its total abandonment, and this is something which human beings can achieve only through love: but the true human being is both man and woman, and only in the union of man and woman does the true human being exist, and only through love, therefore, do man and woman become human.[19]

It is almost as if Wagner wishes to embody in the redundantly chiastic structure of this formulation (human – man and woman / man and woman – human) the very androgynous union he describes. Several pages later in this essay-length letter he applies this same formula of the androgynous complementarity of gender to the figures of Siegfried and Brünnhilde:

Not even Siegfried alone (man alone) is the complete "human being": he is merely the half, only with *Brünnhilde* does he become the redeemer; *one* man alone cannot do everything; many are needed, and a suffering, self-immolating woman finally becomes the true, conscious redeemer: for it is love which is really the "eternal feminine" itself.[20]

The androgynous formula is thrown together here, somewhat confusingly, with the socialistic rhetoric of the earlier Zurich writings and the "self-immolating" heroine we encountered in *Opera and Drama* as a metaphor for music yielding to a poetic *force majeure*. But what becomes clear is that Wagner insists on the physically sexual component of his own brand of the "metaphysics of sexual love" (to adopt Schopenhauer's title), just as he does in *Tristan und Isolde*. Even in the context of the Röckel letter, where he is not constrained by the "materialistic," empirically organic metaphors of *Opera and Drama*, Wagner nonetheless insists on the essentially physical, sexual nature of this idealized (symbolic) union of male and female: "[I]t is the union of man and woman, in other words, love, that creates, physically and metaphorically, the human being, and just as the human being can conceive of nothing more creatively brilliant than his own existence and his own life, so he can never again surpass that act whereby he became human through love; he can only repeat it." Throughout this portion of the letter Wagner continually insists on the epistemological priority of physical, sensual love over philosophical abstractions deriving from it. "[T]he full reality of love is possible only between the

---

19   *Selected Letters of Richard Wagner*, 303.
20   Ibid., 307.

sexes: only as *man* and *woman* can we *human beings* really love."[21] Wagner, still in full Feuerbachian/Young German mode, emphatically rejects any intellectual devaluation of the senses in favor of idealistic abstractions. Even where he seems to appeal to a symbolic androgyny, he steadfastly refuses to relinquish the biology of sexual difference and the model of the natural sciences.

Where does this leave us with regard to the gender-identity of the musical drama, of its creator(s), or, finally, the aesthetic implications of this identity? If music is a "female organism," as Wagner maintains (III, 314), and poetry the male, creative or "procreative" principle destined to mate with it, what sort of thing is engendered by their productive intercourse? Conventional opera, dominated strictly by musical concerns, is a feminine entity for Wagner, as testified by his disparaging typology of national operatic styles as a gallery of "degenerate women." It provides entertainment without thought or emotional conviction. Modern drama is male, on the other hand; whether it treats of history, politics, social relations, or even ostensibly amorous or other emotional subjects, it speaks to the rational mind and not directly to the "feelings." (Even the admixture of incidental music, as a kind of feminine ornament, would not substantially alter the male gender-identity of the spoken play, we can assume.)

At this point Wagner would presumably feel compelled to invoke his authorial right to ban metaphoric proliferation. Despite his insistence on the terms of sexual reproduction, the metaphorical coupling of these gendered aesthetic agents defies the logic of natural principles. Their offspring is androgynous, by inference, since it partakes of the essential aesthetic gender traits of both parents; but to persist with logical inference would lead us to the conclusion that the "true" musical drama was some kind of sterile hybrid, the same peculiar aesthetic *Zwittergattung* that unsympathetic criticism had seen in opera since its inception. While it is true that Siegfried and Brünnhilde or Tristan and Isolde achieve their ideal, "purely human" status only through a complete mutual submersion of their individual identities (and eventually self-annihilation – the men's by accident and the women's by choice), one can't help but recall again Nietzsche's observation that Wagner's heroic couples remain childless. Is the Romantic motif of the union or the "becoming-one" of complementary opposites (man and

---

[21] Ibid., 303. It is difficult to reconcile Nattiez's hypothesis of a more-or-less consciously developed androgynous ideal in Wagner's thought with the obviously disparaging assessment of the oratorio genre in *The Art-Work of the Future* as a "genderless operatic embryo" (*diese geschlechtslosen Opernembryonen* – III, 101), or the equally disparaging reference to a "hermaphroditic *Volksballet-Theater*" from a discussion of the plight of modern German theatrical conditions in *On Actors and Singers* (IX, 185).

woman) in fact androgynous in nature, or does it insist on the fact of biological sexual difference, which, as scholars like Laqueur claim, had only recently become the accepted paradigm?[22] The aporia of Wagner's gendered metaphor of music and poetry may not finally merit extensive reflection for its own sake. But it is as typical a product of the culture of Romanticism, in its way, as the more general trope of organicism, from Goethe on; like the organic metaphor itself, Wagner's is an unstable compound of paradigms drawn from the natural sciences and metaphysical speculation. Perhaps Wagner shares a certain Romantic disinclination to accept that nature and science were *really* the same thing, after all.

Whatever subconscious ambivalences he may have harbored, Wagner showed no reticence in deploying "real," scientific, empirical nature as a model for the production and evaluation of art. *Opera and Drama* is of course shot through with the discourse of organicism, often in a crudely physical or physiological form, and the metaphors of gender and sexual reproduction are grounded in this broader organicist discourse. It is not surprising that Wagner should appropriate the by now well-established ideology of organicist aesthetics in presenting his brief for a new kind of musical drama, but in doing so, he exposed a certain irony that was always inherent in the application of this organicist ideology to music. That is, he makes it quite clear that music (for all its affinity with nature and woman) has to *become* more like nature than it presently is. Music has the potential to become a complex, evolving organism, but it needs to be trained in this capacity, and trained out of the confining artifice that has dominated its forms up to now. Music is to be liberated from such artificial behavioral constraints, of course, by the drama, which teaches it to behave "like nature," to grow and evolve naturally. To "become" more like nature, music has to unlearn the predictable routines acquired from a culture of artifice, fashion, and commerce and to learn instead how to "become," that is, to emulate the evolutionary processes of natural things, eschewing the mechanics of mass-production.

The opposition between conventional (dance-based) forms rooted in the principle of alternation (*Wechsel*) and reprise and a new ideal of musical form based on the dramatic principle of development or evolution (*Entwicklung*) – already encountered in the previous chapter –

22 The previous "hierarchical" paradigm (as Laqueur calls it) inherited from classical doctrines was based on perceived homologies between the male and female anatomy, with the female interpreted as an imperfect variant of or deviation from the male, by inversion, for instance (prefiguring the psychoanalytic interpretations of the feminine as a lack or absence, and feminist critiques of a phallocentric ideology deriving from this). See Laqueur, "Orgasm" and *Making Sex*, chapters 2–4.

was central to Wagner's musical-aesthetic program.[23] The organicist ideal of "evolutionary" form was hardly unique to Wagner, of course, even though its role in his polemical arguments for musical drama might seem to claim it as his exclusive property. In analyzing the nexus of historical and ideological ties among the three figures who shaped the intellectual life of the later nineteenth century – Darwin, Marx, and Wagner – Jacques Barzun drew attention to the universal influence attained by the evolutionary paradigm well before the appearance of Darwin's *Origin of Species* in 1859, through the contributions of such figures as Bonnet, Buffon, Lamarck, and Herbert Spencer. Already by the early nineteenth century, Rousseau's influence had (Barzun says) "replaced mechanical explanations by vitalist [ones] in every realm of thought." Romanticism was, among other things, "a reassertion of the living principle in all things. Evolution thereby became the general law of existence." The effect of this new ascendancy of natural science as an epistemological and aesthetic paradigm – what Barzun refers to as the "biological revolution" of this era – was to posit a new system of value, grounded in the example of natural forces:

This meant preferring the organic to the inorganic; the fluid and flexible and growing to the solid, rigid, and inert. For the Romanticists, the world was a scene of diversity, change, and contradiction, not a formal dance of fixed elements following a geometrical pattern, as the worshippers of Newton and Locke imagined.[24]

This elevation of the organic principles – "the fluid and flexible and growing" – and consequent denigration of mechanistic world-views as "a formal dance of fixed elements following a geometrical pattern" is echoed almost verbatim in the terms of Wagner's aesthetic critique of musical form, as represented by the opposition of *Wechsel* (dance, artifice) and *Entwicklung* (drama, life-like growth). Even the political paradigm of abrupt change through revolution came to be challenged by a "more rational" (because more natural) paradigm of "continual change by small increments."[25] Again, the terms are apposite to Wagner's musical procedures – much more so, in fact, than to his second-hand political ideologies, or even to his own role as an art-historical figure

---

[23] The terminological opposition is presented succinctly in the essay Wagner wrote to accompany his concert-ending for Gluck's overture to *Iphigénie en Aulide* in 1854 (V, 119) and developed slightly in the open letter on Liszt's symphonic poems (V, 189–90).

[24] Jacques Barzun, *Darwin, Marx, Wagner* (New York, 1941; 2nd edn, 1958), 47. Barzun adduces evidence of the extent to which the concept of the biological evolution of species had entered the popular consciousness between the 1830s and 1850s (52–5). Herbert Spencer's views on the principles of evolution ("The Development Hypothesis" and "Progress – its Law and Cause") were published between 1852 and 1857.

[25] *Darwin, Marx, Wagner*, 40.

(where the revolutionary paradigm does apply). Unlike Barzun, who makes no attempt to extend this conceptual model to Wagner's music, Paul Bekker claims the "evolutionary hypothesis" dominated all aspects of Wagner's thought *and* work, as the "formative principle of drama" and epistemological foundation of the leitmotif technique, a network of temporal relationships in which present musical motives constantly mediate between past and future.[26]

Thus Wagner could assert the aesthetic superiority of an "evolutionary" model without fear of contradiction. Melody or musical form that "grows" and whose growth we are actually able to witness (hence truly comprehend) is categorically privileged over melody or form that is fixed in advance according to conventional schematic patterns (see IV, 192). The same distinction applies to drama, and it is the example of drama, as I have suggested, that is meant to enlighten music. For Wagner, drama should provide the aesthetic paradigm of "becoming" that the Romantic theory of Schlegel, Goethe, and company had discovered through the natural sciences:

A finished, ready-made [dramatic] situation will remain as unintelligible to us as nature did so long as we only perceived it as a finished product; whereas we are able to understand it now that we recognize its being as a continuous becoming (*wo wir sie als das Seiende, d.h. das ewig Werdende, erkennen*) – as a being whose "becoming" is present in every phase, from the most proximate to the most distant. (IV, 192)

The dramatic poet is similarly able to make us witnesses to the "organic growth" of his creation, in a way that the visual artist is denied. A cardinal error of the "absolute musician" has been, consequently, his mistaken emulation of the visual or plastic arts (painting, sculpture, or architecture) in presenting a finished, closed form instead of an organically evolving one ("das Fertige anstatt des Werdenden zu geben" – IV, 192). "Organic 'becoming'," Wagner continues, in the spirit of contemporary biological science, "is always growth from below to above, the emergence of higher organisms from lower ones, the synthesis of incomplete elements into a complete whole" ("die Verbindung bedürftige Momente zu einem befriedigenden Momente" – IV, 193). "The synthesis of incomplete elements into a whole" – we know, of course, what that means.

Despite the Darwinian tone of this latter passage, Wagner's model of an "evolutionary" process presumably had less to do with the evolution of plant and animal species over vast periods of time (let alone natural selection) than with simpler ideas about the development of organisms from conception to embryo to birth and maturity, or perhaps some-

---

[26] Paul Bekker, *Richard Wagner: His Life and Work*, trans. M. M. Bozman (New York, 1931), 231–3.

thing gleaned from Goethe's ideas on botanical "metamorphosis." His point of reference remains the physiology of the human body; as nature's most advanced and "perfect" creation, it serves as a metaphorical embodiment of the aesthetic teleology that strives toward the perfect, "purely human" musical-dramatic art-work. Melody itself is likened at one point to the complete human body, the constituent elements of harmony and rhythm standing for its components, "blood, flesh, nerves, bones, and the various inner organs" (III, 309). Thus the "folk" invented its melodies – just as it "conceives and begets new human life through the instinctive act of sexual coupling (*den unwillkürlichen Akt geschlechtlicher Begattung*)" (III, 309) – in the coupling of music and poetic text.

But according to Wagner's peculiar perspective on the natural history of music, such natural instincts died out from the art-music tradition, and Beethoven was compelled to re-enact the "natural" engendering of melody or musical form by artificial means. There was, as we saw, some confusion regarding his metaphorical sexuality. In fact, Wagner suggests that Beethoven was forced to simulate organic growth through the merely "mechanical" means at his disposal, that is, the classical sonata and symphony. In Beethoven's instrumental works we witness "the most astounding struggle of the mechanical to become human" (*die ungeheuersten Anstrengungen des nach Menschenwerdung verlangenden Mechanismus* – III, 311). Or later, "it was in a certain sense his aim to fabricate this organism" – the "inner organism" of absolute music – "by mechanical means (*aus der Mechanik herzustellen*), to vindicate its inner vitality, and to present it to us at its most vital in the very act of being born" (III, 315).[27] Beethoven, it would seem, is none other than the "modern Prometheus" imagined by his contemporary, Mary Wollstonecraft, in the person of Dr. Frankenstein, here seeking to infuse the *disjecta membra* of absolute music with the vital forces of his musical genius. But it turns out that Beethoven (lacking a proper spouse in art, as in life) anticipates a more plausible scientific innovation,

---

[27] " . . . *im Akte der Gebärung zu zeigen.*" It is not absolutely clear whether the word *Gebärung*, which Wagner uses frequently in this metaphorical capacity, is meant to signify the gestation process, the moment of birth, or perhaps both of these things. Nietzsche, incidentally, criticized Wagner's pretensions to "organic evolution" in his music in terms that recall this account of Beethoven's struggle to "appear" organic, though obviously with derogatory intent: "How wretched, how embarrassed, how amateurish is his manner of 'development' (*seine Art zu 'entwickeln'*), his attempt to piece together what has not grown out of each other . . . That Wagner disguised as a principle his incapacity for giving organic form, that he establishes a 'dramatic style' where we merely establish his incapacity for any style whatever, this is in line with a bold habit that accompanied Wagner through his whole life: he posits a principle where he lacks a capacity" (*The Case of Wagner*, trans. Walter Kaufmann [New York, 1967], 170–1 – translation amended).

artificial insemination: "That with which he fertilized this organism," Wagner continues, "was still just absolute melody . . ." (III, 315). Beethoven nonetheless sensed the impracticality of this arrangement, leading him ultimately to seek the "procreative force of the poet" (Schiller), at least in a tentative way. Which guides Wagner back to his leading metaphor:

Just as the folk-melody is inseparable from the living folk-song or poem . . . , so can the musical organism give birth to real, living melody only when it is fertilized by the poet's thought (*Gedanken*). The music bears the child, the poet begets it (*die Musik ist die Gebärerin, der Dichter der Erzeuger*); music had thus reached the very pinnacle of insanity when it sought not only to bear, but even to *beget*.

Wagner is, as usual, carried away by his own metaphorical discourse. (Does Beethoven, too, represent this pinnacle of insanity? Does even Wagner want to represent the entire instrumental repertoire as a collection of misbegotten freaks?)

It is problematic, as we have seen, to press this discourse for logical consistency; it may prove no less difficult to press it into the service of critical interpretation, especially when the pertinence of *Opera and Drama* at all as a key to understanding the subsequent music dramas has long been suspect. Nevertheless, the emphatic role of the gender metaphor in Wagner's book is incontestable, and its resonance with certain highly charged configurations of gender roles in the dramas can be detected on several levels. Let us consider two cases in point.

Music mastered, poetic reason (nearly) seduced: allegory and antithesis

At the beginning of this chapter I referred to the polarized tropes of feminine virtue and evil commonly identified with deeply divided attitudes toward sex and gender in nineteenth-century culture. Something of these two antithetical types – woman as either redeeming ideal or accursed, deadly siren (*femme sacrale* or *fatale*) – informs, respectively, two famous scenes of sexual confusion, panic, and awakening: scenes imbued with the full measure of Wagner's proto-Freudian perspicacity. In Act III, scene 3, of *Siegfried*, Brünnhilde is undoubtedly representative of the "ideal woman" apostrophized at the end of Part I of *Opera and Drama* as a metaphor for the musical partner of the ideal "art-work of the future." In Act II of *Parsifal*, the central scene between Kundry and Parsifal portrays Kundry in her archetypal role as beautiful, wily, seductive, and destructive enchantress – kin to the "degenerate" courtesans also described at the end of Part I of *Opera and Drama* as icons of modern opera. Brünnhilde redeems her male suitor by forfeiting her previously divine powers and her autonomy, and by "annihilating" her independent ego in the act of surrendering herself (*froh und freudig*, following the directives of *Opera and Drama*) to Siegfried. Kundry, on the other hand, has to beg redemption for herself from the ideal male figure (Parsifal), a redemption she also believes must come in the form of sexual communion, though it is refused her. In both scenes a male hero undergoes a frightening, enlightening encounter with a representative of the *ewig Weibliche*, embodying elements of mother and wife at once. Brünnhilde yields, gradually but totally, to Siegfried; *he* kisses *her*, and she submits to his desire and will. Kundry, on the other hand, tries actively to seduce Parsifal, to lull his defenses and take him unawares; *she* kisses *him*, and he resists violently (or "manfully," as the saying sometimes goes) in order to save his soul from perdition. In different ways, both Brünnhilde and Kundry lack "human" souls which – like the "soul-less" musical *ondine* of *Opera and Drama* – they seek from the embrace of a man. It is an implicitly sexual embrace, and the "soul" they seek will evidently be imparted to them, as to the "soul-less" metaphorical-musical *ondine*, in the form of a "fertilizing seed." These two polarized scenarios are blatant enough as commentary on accepted gender roles within the culture. How might they reflect on the implications of the metaphors of sex and gender in *Opera and Drama*?

Whether we are justified or not in reading these metaphors of gender into the "actual" roles and situations of Wagner's dramas is a large methodological question, of course. The answer is different in each case, I think. The closing scene of *Siegfried*, as I will argue (following a cue from writers such as Paul Bekker and Nattiez), probably enacts a conscious allegory of Wagner's gendered metaphorical representation of music and poetry in *Opera and Drama*, developing other metaphorical images from there as well. Any deliberate connection between the *Parsifal* scene and the metaphors of *Opera and Drama* is far from likely, on the other hand. (Beyond the antithetical set of gender relations represented here, *Parsifal* lacks the chronological proximity with the theoretical essay that we find in the case of *Siegfried*, drafted in nearly final form as *Der junge Siegfried* just a few months after the completion of *Opera and Drama* in early 1851.) Yet the scene between Parsifal and Kundry makes an interesting counterpart to that of Siegfried and Brünnhilde. If it is true, as usually supposed, that Wagner's aesthetic evaluation of music and poetry underwent a radical reversal between the time of the early Zurich writings and the music dramas from *Tristan* onward, then a consequent reversal of allegorical representation makes perfect sense; if the representation of the reversal is effected only subconsciously, that would be only appropriate. In any case, the inversional parallel between the scenes warrants attention, as Paul

Bekker noted.[28] And since, as we have seen in the preceding two chapters, Wagner was at all times highly ambivalent toward the idea of
"absolute music," it seems justified to read for signs of this ambivalence
within the works, as well as in his metaphors. Indeed, just such a
radical ambivalence toward absolute music, as idea or ideal, was a
fundamental feature of nineteenth-century musical thought in general,
I believe, finding its most extreme expression in Wagner (like so much
in the nineteenth century). The ambivalence is important to a historical
understanding of the music – his and others' alike.

Siegfried and Brünnhilde

> *"'Here everything is symbolic,' Wagner said."*
> *– Heinrich Porges,* Wagner Rehearsing the Ring
> (*on* Siegfried, *Act III, scene 3*)

The whole extended action of Brünnhilde's awakening and her mystical
mountain-top marriage with Siegfried at the end of Act III of *Siegfried* is
one of those scenes particularly frustrating to naturalistic dramaturgical
sensibilities. Like its nocturnal counterpart in the second act of *Tristan*,
it is an "action" in which nothing really happens (in the case of the
Tristan scene, Wagner later admitted that almost "nothing but music"
goes on – IX, 307). The single important event is the union of the
drama's heroic couple: but apart from the momentary sexual confusion
and panic issuing from Siegfried's initial discovery of Brünnhilde's sex,
the psychological symbolism of the scene is generally less developed
than that of the *Tristan* scene (or of the scene between Parsifal and
Kundry). The earliest version of the scene, in *Der junge Siegfried* (*The
Young Siegfried*, 1851), had been designed to include a lengthy narrative
exposition of the events of the not-yet-conceived *Walküre*: Siegfried's
parentage, Brünnhilde's attempt to intervene for Siegmund, and her
rescue of the embryonic hero in Sieglinde's womb. Without this background narration (one of the few Wagner actually brought himself to
eliminate), the dramatic function of the scene seems to be small, at least
in proportion to the quantity of words and music Wagner still lavished
on it. Some dramatic justifications remain, of course: Brünnhilde is
awakened from her punitive sleep, Siegfried is initiated into manhood
through his discovery of woman, and the end of the old order is
ordained in their closing duet ("Zerreißt, ihr Nornen / das Runenseil! /
Götterdämmerung, dunkle herauf!"), whose invocation of "laughing

---

[28] "There is a very profound connection between this final work and the third act of
Siegfried" (Bekker, *Richard Wagner*, 400). Bekker actually notes a wider set of parallels:
the conjuring of Erda by Wotan and that of Kundry by Klingsor, "the lesson Parsifal
learns from Woman," the maternal motif, and of course, that of the kiss.

death" and annihilation is surely meant to do double duty – as Robert Donington noted – as proleptic image of the impending *Götterdämmerung* and as the conventional poetic metaphor for orgasm.[29] Much of the actual "action," language, and imagery of the scene can be understood as a consciously developed allegory of the gendered metaphor of music and poetry in *Opera and Drama*, finished just a few months before Wagner drafted the text of his *Young Siegfried* (the sexual congress implied at the end of the scene becomes the natural goal of this allegorical rite of passage). After considering the basic terms of the scene as allegory, and the metaphorical motifs it draws on, I will address questions of how the allegory might be embodied in the musical events and design of the scene. Does the abstraction of this scene, as allegory, reduce (or elevate) it to the status of "nothing-but-music" conferred by Wagner on the central scene of *Tristan*, or at least "mainly music"? Does the musical setting bear out, or contravene, the thesis of a late conversion to an aesthetic of absolute music, hinted at in the *Beethoven* essay, nearly coeval with the composition of the scene? (Certainly as a musical structure it lacks the continuity of the *Tristan* scene, being marked instead by violent ruptures and unexplained intrusions – notably that of the *Siegfried Idyll* music at Brünnhilde's "Ewig war ich.") What is signified by Brünnhilde and her "destiny" in Siegfried's hands as an allegory of "pure music" in the hands of poetry or drama? What kind of music (or rather musical drama) is engendered by this allegorical mating?

As background to this scene, we need to recall for a moment the aquatic metaphors of music that had played a large role in *The Art-Work of the Future*. The affinity between the image of the musical ocean and that of the musical woman is easily recognized. The ocean is a magnified image of the female womb, with its mysterious, dark, nurturing depths. The secrets of "evolution" are concealed in the depths of the musical ocean, as they are in the woman's womb: the musical sea fills man, appropriately, with "intimations of the infinite" (*Ahnung des Unendlichen*) and of the "unfathomable depths of [nature's] eternal germination, procreation, and desiring (. . . *den unermeßlichen Grund ihres ewigen Keimens, Zeugens und Sehnens*)" concealed within (III, 83). Here, in *The Art-Work of the Future*, music is also identified as the life-blood of the *Gesamtkunstwerk*, nourishing the "body" of artistic man as a whole (III, 81). Music is essentially fluid, and fluidity is feminine, where solid, fixed structure is masculine: hence the natural tendency of music to seek containment in the structures provided by the ordering principles of language and rational thought. Although Wagner has not yet ascribed the explicit gender roles to music and poetry we find in *Opera and Drama*, they are unmistakably implicit here. Music is an ornament to poetic

29 Robert Donington, *Wagner's "Ring" and its Symbols* (London, 1963), 199–200.

thought, contributing sensual beauty and feeling to the rational content of language and to the visible outlines of the plastic arts – or here, dance and gesture. Content and form are inscribed in music by the agency of the poetic text (or conceivably, by that of "poetic ideas"?): a "meaningful sequence of clearly profiled words (*die sinnvolle Reihe scharfgeschnittener ... Wörter*) intelligibly arranged according to their meaning and measure into a thought-bearing physical body to contain its [music's] infinitely fluid tonal element (. . . *als gedankenreich sinnlichen Körper zur Festigung ihres unendlich flüssigen Tonelementes*)" (III, 82).

In Part III of *Opera and Drama*, then, Wagner returns to the metaphor of sexual reproduction introduced there toward the end of Part I (the engendering of music drama from the gendered principles of feminine music and masculine poetry) and merges the metaphor of music as female body with that of the musical "body of water" – the mysterious, fluid, formless depths of musical harmony (in particular), whose sunlit, visible surface is melody, the immediate point of contact between music and word. Elements of both metaphors inform details of the Siegfried-Brünnhilde scene throughout. Here in *Opera and Drama* Part III, section 3 Wagner is preparing for his exposition of the "poetic-musical period," his attempt to formulate a theory of how melody, modulation, and hence musical form are to be guided by the "poetic intent" and even the details of poetic diction in his new musical drama (see chapter 4). Moving, in the course of the discussion, "from language (*Wortsprache*) back to music (*Tonsprache*)," he writes: "we have arrived at the horizontal surface of harmony, in which the poet's verses are mirrored back as musical melody." In outlining the immediate aim of his theoretical exposition at this point Wagner channels one metaphor into another, drawing out the latent gender implications of the earlier fluid imagery in terms that will resonate distinctly in the final scene of *Siegfried*. He aims to demonstrate how,

starting from this [melodic] surface, we are to master (*bemächtigen*) the unfathomable depths of harmony, that aboriginal womb of all tones, and apply them to an ever fuller realization of the poetic intent, thus plunging this poetic intent, as the procreative principle (*als zeugendes Moment*) into the full depths of that Ur-maternal element in such a way that every atom of this terrifying emotional chaos (*dieses ungeheuren Gefühlschaos*) is determined as part of a conscious, individual communicative action of unlimited, ever-expanding scope.   (III, 145)

The progression from the terrifying *Gefühlschaos* of untamed musical energies to a clear, calm melodic surface under the "mastering" influence of a poetic text – all of this is prefigured in Wagner's familiar allegorical reading of Beethoven's Ninth. Wagner noticed this point, too:

so we find to our surprise, upon closer examination, that the melody I am describing [i.e., as the musical "reflection" of a poetic text on the mirroring surface of the harmonic "depths"] is identical to the one that pressed upward to the surface from the unfathomable depths of *Beethoven's* music to greet the bright sunlight of day in the Ninth Symphony. The appearance of this melody on the surface of the harmonic sea was made possible, as we have seen, only by the desire of the musician to look the poet directly in the eye. Only the poet's verses were able to keep this melody afloat . . . (IV, 146)

Again, the musical sea becomes the musical woman, as Wagner continues:

This melody was the woman's loving greeting (*Liebesgruß*) to the man; and here the all-embracing "eternal feminine" proved itself truer than the egoistic masculine principle, since the former is love itself . . . , whether it be revealed in male or female form. (IV, 146)

Beethoven's example, however, was but a fleeting premonition of what might be, since it lacked the full, active participation of a man (the poet): "what was for this woman the ultimate pleasure of a lifetime, enshrouded in sacrificial incense (*der höchste, opferduftigste Genuß eines ganzen Lebens*) was for the poet merely a passing affair (*nur ein flüchtiger Liebesrausch*)." But, as we know, Wagner insisted on the principle of love (and sex) as an act of mutual "redemption," whether in theory, in drama, or in life. Siegfried and Brünnhilde are destined to carry through, in allegorical form, what Beethoven and the spiritually absent Schiller were not quite up to (or what Wagner would accomplish as a single "androgynous" creator, as Nattiez sees it). And again, the details of that allegorical union are presaged in the metaphors of Wagner's theory:

The poet is now initiated into the deep, infinite secrets of feminine nature through the redeeming kiss of this melody: now he sees with different eyes and feels with different senses. The bottomless sea of harmony, from which this inspiring apparition has surfaced to meet him, is no longer an object of timid awe, of fear, of terror as it had previously seemed, when it presented itself to him as a foreign, unknown quantity. (IV, 146)

By the end of the passage, woman and water are fully confounded. But man has mastered them both, in any case:

The woman has been driven from the lonely, vast expanse of her maternal home to await the man's arrival; now he dives down in the company of his new bride to acquaint himself with all the wonders of the deep. His reasoning mind penetrates everything clearly and rationally, down to the deepest point, from whence he orders the pattern of waves as they are to rise up toward the sunlight, where they now will ripple gently in its rays, now softly plash amidst the murmuring zephyrs, now mount up in virile manner against the stormy north winds. (IV, 147)

The breath of these winds is the breath of that "infinite love, by whose delight the poet is redeemed, and by whose power he becomes the ruler of nature" – which is also to say, of course, the ruler of woman (and her music).

The poet is "initiated into the secrets" of music's feminine nature, and successfully overcomes his fears of this unknown element, this vast symbolic womb. It ceases to be "an object of timid awe, fear, or terror" (*kein Gegenstand der Scheu, der Furcht, des Grausens mehr*). The terms can be perfectly transposed to Siegfried's experience on Brünnhilde's rock. Indeed, the term *Scheu* (timidity or shyness) is, if anything, still more apposite to young Siegfried's condition. I don't doubt for a moment Wagner's immediate interest in exploring the psychology of awakening sexual consciousness in this scene (the full extent of the Freudian anticipations in Wagner's scenario and symbols, including the defiance of Wotan's father-figure and the phallic contest of sword against spear in the preceding scene, is nothing less than uncanny, as many have remarked). But at the same time, Wagner recognized in this proto-psychoanalytic parable a fitting allegory for his recent aesthetic theorizing, and it is the congruence of psychology, aesthetic allegory, and (perhaps) musical form, that is my concern here. The basic terms of this allegory were intimated, if somewhat obscurely, by Paul Bekker, and they are further developed in Nattiez's chapter interpreting "The *Ring* as a Mythic Account of the History of Music."[30] If not entirely convinced by the larger allegorical complex constructed by Nattiez there (despite some intriguing details), I obviously accept the allegorical interpretation of Siegfried and Brünnhilde, which can be developed still further, I believe.

How does Brünnhilde represent music? Among the female characters in the *Ring* she is surely the "ideal" one (in the terms of Wagner's aesthetic sociology), hence the ideal candidate for this allegorical honor. She is endlessly vital, energetic, but without a "will" of her own: she describes herself as a projection of Wotan's will (until her transgression), after which she eventually surrenders herself to Siegfried. Music, according to the Zurich writings, similarly lacks a will of its own, the power of formal self-determination.[31] In the scene of her

[30] Bekker identifies Siegfried with the "Will" and Brünnhilde with "Emotion." "From their embrace Melody must be born, and this evocation of melody from dream-emotion into form is the true subject of the drama of *Siegfried*" (Bekker, *Richard Wagner*, 395). Cf. Nattiez, *Wagner Androgyne*, 53–90 (esp. 76–84), and chapter 4, "Art as a Metaphor for Itself" (91–6). This latter, brief chapter is offered as methodological support for the preceding interpretation of the *Ring* as allegory of a Wagnerian history of music, taking note of Wagner's general propensity for "staging" aesthetic debates in his operas (as in *Die Meistersinger*). The fact that the "history" of music invoked in the earlier chapter ends up being more an amalgam of mythic "prehistory" and modern operatic practices would seem to reflect the idiosyncratic representation of history in Wagner's writings.

[31] See, for example, III, 93 (*The Art-Work of the Future*), where Wagner says that music "lacks the moral will" to develop feelings in a natural, realistic manner, without the input of poetry or external "poetic ideas" (see also "Fear of the Fifth" in chapter 2, above).

awakening, her voice is repeatedly identified as "singing" rather than speaking, as Nattiez notes. It is significant, in this regard, that Siegfried – who is still in the process of discovering the "foreign and unknown" thing that is woman (and music) – is mesmerized by the effect of her "song" but fails to comprehend its meaning; before her union with Siegfried, Brünnhilde is still "pure" music, semantically unconditioned:

Wie Wunder tönt,	How wondrous the sound
was wonnig du singst, –	of what you joyfully sing, –
doch dunkel dünkt mich der	yet methinks its meaning's
Sinn.[32]	obscure.

Siegfried responds to her *physical* presence with all his senses:[33]

Deines Auges Leuchten	The light of your eyes
seh' ich licht;	I see brightly;
deines Atems Wehen	the touch of your breath
fühl' ich warm;	I feel warmly;
deiner Stimme singen	the sound [singing] of your voice
hör' ich süß:	I hear sweetly:

But the meaning of her music remains a mystery:

doch was du singend mir sagst,	but what you say to me in song –
staunend versteh' ich's nicht.	perplexed, I understand it not.

As he explains to her, to excuse this obtuseness, he is so preoccupied with the sensory experience of this discovery of woman/music that his rational mind (emblematic of the "male" intellect of language and poetry) momentarily fails him. This momentary failure of thought and nerve is produced by a mixture of sexual panic and intoxication. Both conditions, Wagner suggests, are equally appropriate to the poet (or the poetic/linguistic psyche) when confronted with the real nature of music, undisguised and undiluted.

[32] Siegfried's reaction to her "singing" follows Brünnhilde's enigmatically condensed account of his origins and of her punishment for defying Wotan. (It is quite reasonable that Siegfried should fail to understand Brünnhilde's story in this condensed form – even as verbal text, rather than "music".) This was the point in the earliest verse draft of *The Young Siegfried* where Wagner originally had Brünnhilde narrate the story of *Die Walküre* at some length. While the surrounding text there differs somewhat from the final version, it insists just as much (or more) on the fact of Brünnhilde's *singing*, which would lend support to Carolyn Abbate's thesis of Wagnerian narrations as "phenomenal" musical performances (*Unsung Voices*, chapter 5, "Wotan's Monologue"; and chapter 2, "Cherubino Uncovered"). For the text from *Der junge Siegfried* see Otto Strobel, ed., *Richard Wagner: Skizzen und Entwürfe zur Ring-Dichtung* (Munich, 1930) 185 (Siegfried: "O rede, singe! / töne in worten! . . . töne mir wunder, / singe mir wonnen") and 188, following Brünnhilde's extended narration (Siegfried: "deiner stimme singen / hör' ich süß").

[33] Recall the statement in *Opera and Drama* that, in becoming "initiated into the deep, infinite secrets of feminine nature," the secrets of the harmonic depths, the poet will "see with new eyes and feel with new senses" (IV, 146).

Brünnhilde herself invokes the traditional binarism of feeling vs thinking (as Nattiez also notes) when she explains how she had simply "felt" or intuited Wotan's thoughts rather than interpreting his literal words ("der Gedanke . . . / den ich nicht dachte, / sondern nur fühlte"). The same opposition is subsequently re-iterated ("weil ich nicht ihn dachte, und nur empfand") to her so-called motive of "Justification" first heard at the end of *Die Walküre*. Wagner had stated the case quite categorically elsewhere in *Opera and Drama*: "Music cannot think" (IV, 184). Whether or not Wagner believed that *woman* could think, he clearly didn't see this as her natural sphere of activity. (If he didn't voice any essentialist claims along these lines, others had already done so for him, such as Schopenhauer in his notorious essay "On Women.")[34] In any case, the identification of music as a medium of "pure feeling" for Wagner and most of his contemporaries was axiomatic. Wagner's rejection of the legitimacy of the concept "absolute music," at least through the 1850s, was predicated on his own emphatic version of this common dogma, in a sense. Without some input from the phenomenal world (dance gestures or the rational syntax and rhetoric of poetic texts, for instance) music was incapable of determining any "form" of its own, he maintained, just as so-called "musical ideas" were not capable of conveying any truly distinct content ("ideas") if they were not somehow semantically conditioned from without.

The Oedipal ambivalence of the initial encounter between Siegfried and Brünnhilde also has a direct parallel in the structure of Wagner's aesthetic metaphor. *Opera and Drama* appeals to the strand of speculative anthropology, popular since the eighteenth century, that recognized the origins of language in an imagined kind of primitive "song," the inarticulate vocal utterance that preceded language as such (see note 2 and chapter 5). Music or song nurtured language in its infant stages. Hence the allegorical significance of Brünnhilde's reference to her attempted intercession in the battle of Siegmund and Hunding and her subsequent rescue of the pregnant Sieglinde:

Dich zarten nährt' ich,	I nurtured you tenderly,
noch eh' du gezeugt;	even before you were conceived;
noch eh' du geboren,	before you were born
barg dich mein Schild:	my shield protected you:
So lang' lieb' ich dich, Siegfried!	That long I have loved you,
	Siegfried!

---

[34] "One only needs to see the way she is built to realize that woman is not intended for great mental or great physical labour. She expiates the guilt of life not through activity but through suffering, through the pains of childbirth, caring for the child and subjection to the man, to whom she should be a patient and cheering companion" (Schopenhauer, *Essays and Aphorisms*, trans. R. J. Hollingdale [Harmondsworth, 1970], 80–1).

The rediscovery of music by language awakens a subconscious memory of these maternal origins, just as, upon discovering Brünnhilde's female identity, Siegfried's thoughts involuntarily turn to the mother he lost at birth ("Mutter! Mutter! Gedenke mein!"). The allegorical reading also clarifies, I think, something of the psychological sense of the famous Oedipal motif here, as in the scene between Parsifal and Kundry. Neither Siegfried nor Parsifal continues to regard the woman as a mother figure once he has recognized her true identity. (After Brünnhilde's words just quoted, Siegfried asks "softly and timidly" whether she is perhaps his mother, whereupon Brünnhilde corrects his misapprehension.) For each, the recollection of his mother is a crucial transformational step in the awakening of an adult sexual consciousness, but the maternal image ultimately remains embedded in the past. So, too, the maternal role of music with respect to poetry – historically or mythically – is ultimately distinct from its present role as submissive wife. (The moment of confusion and panic engendered in the boy at this threshold of sexual awareness is real enough, nonetheless, even if Wagner presumably felt that most poets, aside from himself, never even reach this point of aesthetic maturity.)

Although Brünnhilde is up in the air, according to the stage setting, high on her rocky mountaintop, the language of her dialogue with Siegfried repeatedly engages the metaphor of the musical ocean or body of water. Poet and musician meet on the water's surface, as we will recall, where the poet's words are mirrored back to him as melody. The "Joy" melody of Beethoven's Ninth, anticipating the genuine melody-of-the-future, was described as "pressing upward from the depths of Beethoven's music to greet the bright sunlight of day" (IV, 146). When Brünnhilde covers her eyes, overcome by disorienting anxieties often diagnosed in the case of nineteenth-century brides facing their first sexual experience, Siegfried exhorts her:

| Tauch' aus dem Dunkel und sieh': | Rise ["dive up"] from the darkness and see: |
| sonnenhell leuchtet der Tag! | sunlight illumines the day! |

The mysteries of musical harmony, like those of woman's nature, lay concealed in the depths of the sea, according to Wagner's metaphors. Brünnhilde, representing at once the secrets of music and of the "eternal feminine," is concealed by fire rather than water – but opposites are easily transposed. Wotan warns Siegfried of the "sea of flames" (*ein Lichtmeer*) protecting the object of his quest. Siegfried apostrophizes Brünnhilde's face (while still unaware of her actual sex) as a "bright heavenly lake" (*hellen Himmels-See*) and her flowing tresses as "wave-like clouds" (*Wogengewölk*), embellishing this transposition of sea and sky.

The music that accompanies Siegfried's penetration of the protective ring of fire – compounded of numerous motives from the end of *Walküre* – is imbued with gestures of both rising and sinking. Indeed, the impression of the "magic sleep chords" (sounded across this transition) is predominantly one of "sinking," as into sleep, conveyed by the descending chromatic upper line over the *misterioso* harmonic progression. The "Slumber" motive conveys the same thing, by simpler means. And where Siegfried "sinks" (musically), Brünnhilde rises. (This reciprocal motion is mirrored in the moment of her awakening: in kissing her, Siegfried "sinks, as if dying" on to her sleeping form, after which Brünnhilde, of course, rises to greet the sunlight.) Across the opening of the scene Brünnhilde's feminine identity is continually hinted at by the motive that has by now absorbed multiple connotations of Freia, of "woman" generally, and of nature (who is also woman, of course). The rising contour of this figure is deployed at the opening of the scene as the first half of a vast arching line (paired with the sinking motion of the "Slumber" motive, in downward sequence). The motive literally (well, figuratively) rises up from the musical depths here to reach skyward – toward the light, as it were. Siegfried, it is true, has been ascending; but the music here appears to describe the site he has reached (the *selige Öde* of Brünnhilde's rock) rather than his climb, which has already been accomplished. And the same figure describes a still vaster ascent of musical space at the very point of Brünnhilde's awakening, from the low D of the bass clarinet to the reiterated high b^3 of the violins (see Example 3.1). This same contour is unmistakably echoed in the ritual gestures of Brünnhilde's awakening, a threefold welling up of diatonic music from the registral depths of the orchestra up to its most transparent heights. (Note that the tail-figure of this musical series recurs later when Siegfried exhorts her to "emerge from the dark" into daylight ["Tauch' aus dem Dunkel und sieh': / sonnenhell leuchtet der Tag"].)

Later in the scene, as Brünnhilde makes a final effort to resist Siegfried's advances, she explicitly likens herself to a body of water, alluding also to the motif of the poet's (man's) reflection, the narcissistic gaze:

Sahst du dein Bild	Did you ever see your image
im klaren Bach?	in the clear brook?
Hat es dich Frohen erfreut?	Did you rejoice in it, joyful one?
Rührtest zur Woge	If you then stirred up the
das Wasser du auf,	water into waves,
zerflösse die klare	if the brook's clear surface
Fläche des Bachs, –	were thus disturbed, –
dein Bild sähst du nicht mehr,	no more would you see your image,
nur der Welle schwankend	but only the rippling waves! –
Gewög! –	
So berühre mich nicht,	So do not touch me,
trübe mich nicht!	disturb me not!

161

Example 3.1 *Siegfried* Act III, scene 3 (ascending contour described by "Freia/Woman" motive)

But inflamed by passion, Siegfried is all heat, fire to Brünnhilde's water. He has, as he tells her, "internalized" the fire he passed through ("die Glut, die Brünnhilds Felsen umbrann, die brennt mir nun in der Brust"). To extinguish it, he must immerse himself in her:

so brenn' ich nun selbst,	so I myself burn,
sengende Glut	to cool in the waves
in der Flut zu kühlen;	the raging heat [within me];
ich selbst, wie ich bin,	just as I am,
spring' in den Bach: –	I'll leap in the brook:
o daß seine Wogen	oh, that its waves
mich selig verschlängen,	would swallow me up,
mein Sehnen schwänd' in der Flut!	my desire were quenched in the stream!

Siegfried's wish to be "swallowed up in the waves" is accompanied, oddly enough, by a brief appearance of the Slumber motive in the orchestra, underscored by a sudden tonal slippage from A♭ up to A. This gesture would seem to confirm the semantic transference (or slippage) of the motives of Brünnhilde's sleep onto Siegfried's metaphorical "sinking" across the transition to this scene, as I have suggested (Brünnhilde, after all, is wide awake now).

As in *Opera and Drama*, the implicitly gendered image of water (though reduced here from ocean to stream) flows back into the sexual metaphor. Siegfried's and Brünnhilde's biology is appropriately archaic, couched in the classic literary trope of corporeal fire or sexual "ardor," which reflects, in turn, traditional beliefs about the reproductive process.[35] A certain degree of bodily heat, as mentioned earlier, was understood as a prerequisite to successful conception. Kindling this fire is ordinarily the man's responsibility. Wagner had alluded to this notion in *Opera and Drama*, where the poet's "seed" (the "poetic intent") is produced by the aesthetic "heat" generated by his mounting desire for a more complete, perfect communication to all the senses. Siegfried's preoccupation, once he has mastered his initial panic, is to warm up Brünnhilde, who suddenly gets cold feet, assailed by virginal anxiety over the consequences of the act.[36] And his passionate rhetoric is successful. Forgetting her pleas to remain untouched ("Ewig war ich," etc.),

[35] Lawrence Kramer's chapter on "Musical Form and Fin-de-Siècle Sexuality" (*Music as Cultural Practice*, 135–75) relates the musical embodiment of desire in *Tristan* to a modern (Freudian) libidinal model, as it comes to displace the classical trope of heat (ardor) and what Kramer identifies as an instinctive/subjective model associated with Romantic and bourgeois culture of the earlier nineteenth century. It is perhaps appropriate that where the essentially "modern" figures of Tristan and Isolde enact the modern (libidinal) model of desire, the more archaic-regressive types of Siegfried and Brünnhilde remain true to the classical model.

[36] Peter Gay examines various facets of such wedding-night trauma in records of nineteenth-century society in *Education of the Senses* (New York, 1984), 278–94.

Brünnhilde suddenly becomes again the hot-blooded Valkyrie, the *wild, wüthende Weib* of whooping war-cries, augmented triads, and whirring strings: "Does my arms' embrace not set you on fire?" she now challenges him. "By the heat of my blood in its passionate surge, a fire is kindled – do you not feel it?"[37] This trope of sexual heat can be seen as an essential component of the "poetic intent" that engenders the shape of the scene, dramatically and musically. As such, it also constitutes a point of contact between Wagner's aesthetic metaphors of gender and his compositional practice.

Unlike *Tristan*, where the sexual act itself (or, one might argue, the male experience of it) figures as the poetic image or idea informing the central musical events, the final scene of *Siegfried* is more concerned with the process leading up to it, the rituals of sexual awakening and courtship. (Compared with *Tristan*, there is a certain chasteness to the "white heat" of the final C-major duo and its *Meistersinger*-like sunny diatonicism.) Despite a few vestiges of "operatic" form – the parallel duet-style verses at the end of the scene and in the brief passage after Brünnhilde's awakening ("O Heil der Mutter, / die mich [dich] gebar!") – the scene is diffusely structured. Still, it is not difficult to discern a number of distinct dramatic phases within the scene, and these, as usual, provide the principal cues for articulation of musical sections. As usual, too, one could argue as to the precise number or hierarchical disposition of such dramatic-musical phases: Wolzogen proposed four principal phases, Patrick McCreless identifies five of them, Lorenz divides it into nine "periods" (the last one subdivided into three further independent forms).[38] I don't intend to offer any precise mapping-out of the scene here. But in order to situate the motifs of our gendered allegory within the overall dynamic design of the scene I might propose the following significant phases:

---

37 "Wie mein Arm dich preßt, / entbrennst du nicht? / Wie in Strömen mein Blut / entgegen dir stürmt, / das wilde Feuer, / fühlst du es nicht?" (translation slightly amended from *The Ring of the Nibelung*, trans. Andrew Porter [New York, 1976], 242).

38 Wolzogen's phases are 1) up to Brünnhilde's awakening, 2) Brünnhilde's joy, 3) her struggle with Siegfried (*der Liebeskampf*), and 4) their mutual conciliation (*der Liebessieg*) (Hans von Wolzogen, *Der Ring des Nibelungen: Ein thematischer Leitfaden durch Dichtung und Musik* [Leipzig, 1911], 71–6). McCreless divides the scene into three "movements" (out of five in the act as a whole) which he further breaks down into five larger parts and a larger number of sub-sections (*Wagner's "Siegfried": Its Drama, History, and Music* [Ann Arbor, 1982], 210–19). The scene constitutes Periods 8–15 of Act III in Lorenz's analysis (*Das Geheimnis der Form bei Richard Wagner*, vol. I [Berlin, 1924]).

1 Siegfried arrives on the mountaintop and observes Brünnhilde's sleeping form. (mm. 824–923)
2 Siegfried realizes her true sex and is overcome by sexual confusion and panic (invoking his unknown mother); he masters his fear and kisses Brünnhilde. (mm. 924–1066)
3 Brünnhilde awakens, greets the sun (and Siegfried); they sing together. Brünnhilde explains, elliptically, her role in Siegfried's birth (originally the narrative history of Valkyries and Volsungs in the first draft of *The Young Siegfried*). He hears her but cannot understand. (mm. 1067–278)
4 Brünnhilde reflects on the symbols of her past existence. She becomes distanced and "cooler," while Siegfried grows warmer ("ein zehrendes Feuer / ist mir entzündet"). (mm. 1279–360)
5 Brünnhilde actively resists him, she is overcome with anxiety (*Angstgewirr*). (mm. 1361–477)
6 Brünnhilde is suddenly calm, and entreats Siegfried to leave her undisturbed. (mm. 1478–559)
7 Siegfried's heat rises, unabated, and finally ignites her, too (they embrace). (mm. 1560–718)
8 They sing the closing duet, and Brünnhilde "throws herself into Siegfried's arms." (mm. 1719–89)

The motivic and tonal content of these phases is perhaps too various to warrant their designation as "poetic-musical periods."[39] Phase 3, nonetheless, contains several strongly articulated "structural" cadences in C major, the tonal goal of the scene as a whole. The tonal "polarity" or pairing of E and C that can be seen to operate throughout the scene is also introduced as a local effect here[40] (in the three-part series of Brünnhilde's awakening), as are the principal "thematic" motives of the overall scene: those designated by Wolzogen as "Love's greeting" (*Liebesgruß*), "Love's delight" (*Liebesentzückung*), and the "World-inheritance" (*Welterbschaft*) theme – (see Example 3.2, a–c). The transformed reprise of these motives in C major in the final duet constitutes the principal unifying gesture of the scene. More specifically, the two vestigial operatic duets ("O Heil der Mutter, / die mich [dich] gebar!" and that following "lachend zu Grunde geh'n'"), with their emphatic C-major cadences, mark the scene's two points of equilibrium. Musically and dramatically, the dynamic of the scene is geared to the attainment of these two points.

---

39 McCreless suggests that the concept might apply still in the first two acts of *Siegfried*, composed in the 1850s, but no longer here, where the smaller musical-textual units that would correspond in scope to "poetic-musical periods" are now tonally open, almost invariably (*Wagner's "Siegfried,"* 188). The issues surrounding this term are analyzed in the following chapter.
40 On the role of this tonal polarity in the scene, see McCreless, *Wagner's "Siegfried,"* 212ff.

From Siegfried's point of view then, the scene is comprised of two psycho-sexual trajectories: 1) his sexual awakening (corresponding to Brünnhilde's literal awakening, as Siegfried himself points out),[41] the ensuing phase of panic and confusion, and his eventual mastering of this fear, culminating in the first brief C-major duo with Brünnhilde; and 2) the arousal of his sexual desire (embodied in the trope of physiological "ardor"), his attempt to overcome Brünnhilde's sudden resistance, and his eventual success in igniting a mutual ardor in her. This framework provides Wagner with the type of emotional-psychological "wave" pattern so conducive to his musical-formal sensibilities.

The first trajectory moves from the stasis representative of the physical setting to the agitation of Siegfried's psychological awakening. It begins with the long arching solo line evoking the *selige Öde* of Brünnhilde's rocky heights and moves to the tranquil recollection of various woman- and Valkyrie-related motives: the motive sung by Fricka in anticipation of a new reign of domestic bliss ("herrliche Wohnung, wonniger Hausrath") is twice lingered over and led into textually cued, *sotto voce* citations of the Valkyrie's equestrian emblem, as if hinting at the imminent taming of Brünnhilde. The calm tempo and long dominant prolongations characteristic of this first phase give way to an agitated stop-and-go pacing, rapidly shifting key areas, and appropriately agitated motivic material after Siegfried recognizes Brünnhilde as a woman: particularly the gestural diminished-chord

Example 3.2 *Siegfried* Act III, scene 3: principal motives
(a) Love's greeting (Wolzogen), mm. 1131–4

[41] "How to end this fear, how to muster courage? I must awaken the maid, so as to awaken myself" (*Wie end' ich die Furcht? | wie faß' ich Muth? | daß ich selbst erwache, muß die Maid ich erwecken*).

(b) Love's delight (Wolzogen), mm. 1147–9

(c) World-inheritance (Wolzogen), mm. 1197–200

figure designated by Wolzogen as "Love's pleasure" or desire (*Liebeslust*) and the agitated transformation of the Volsung motive (responding to Siegfried's cries of "mother!"), which Wolzogen gave the fitting appellation of "Love's confusion" (*Liebesverwirrung*). Characteristic of this section – phase 2 of the scene – is not so much the increased tempo and rate of harmonic (and motivic) change *per se* as the continual fluctuation of pace that mirrors Siegfried's psychological uncertainties. (To the extent that these features are vestiges of an operatic recitative idiom, we could take them as emblematic of a "pre-musical" condition, prior to Siegfried's union with Brünnhilde.)

The second trajectory is longer and more complex, but makes use of a similar alternation of musical urgency and restraint. To the extent that Wagner works by simply alternating sections or "periods" of a "quiet, relaxed nature" with more "lively, animated ones," his procedure could be said to approximate the foundation of simple instrumental forms he had opposed to dramatic, "evolutionary" ones in 1857 (as *Wechsel* versus *Entwicklung*). At the broadest level, Brünnhilde contributes an impulse of musical restraint or stasis to phases 4 and 6 of the scene, while the others are dominated by Siegfried's animating impulse. But of course, the process is not so neatly divided as this. Phases 4 and 7, particularly, are marked by a shifting dialogue between the characteristic musical impulses and motives of the two figures, a process of dialectic change by "small increments" that Wagner's notion of dramatic development shares with the contemporary paradigm of biological evolution. (Phase 5 is largely transitional, musically, and phase 6 stands apart as being symbolically self-contained.)

The rapid, incremental contrasts within phases 4 and 7 – as well as their role within the larger scheme of contrasts – might be understood as a musical realization of the "poetic idea" or "intention" of the scene: the process of generating a mutual degree of "heat" requisite to the successful act of conception (the allegorical insemination of music with the "poetic intent" itself, in other words). According to the traditional biology that still informs the poetic tropes of Wagner's text, this heat is produced by the friction of mutual contact, and "irritation of the common human flesh." "Coitus is a generalized friction culminating in a corporeal blaze. Intercourse and orgasm are the last stage, the whole body's final exaggerated huffing and puffing, violent, stormlike agitation in the throes of producing the seeds of life."[42] Laqueur's account of this classical view of the initial stages of reproduction describes rather well the latter stages of the final scene of *Siegfried*, both musically and allegorically. Particularly in the final stages of their musical "dialogue," as Brünnhilde at last succumbs to Siegfried's ardor, the faster tempo, rhythmic accompaniment, increased harmonic and even "motivic" rhythm in Siegfried's statements produce a kind of musical "friction" against Brünnhilde's more broadly paced responses which eventually ignites, as it were, with the sudden recollection of her animated Valkyrie music and finally the closing duet itself.

[42] Laqueur, *Making Sex*, 45–6. This classical view of the sexual act was itself originally susceptible to symbolic reading (a point developed also by Battersby in *Gender and Genius*). As Laqueur puts it here: "Sexual heat is an instance of the heat that makes matter live and orgasm, which signals the explosive release of the seed and the heated pneuma, mimics the creative work of Nature itself" (46).

What, then, of Brünnhilde's perspective, as allegorical representative of "pure music"? In drafting the original text Wagner surely responded to the ready analogy between her sacrifice and what he had demanded of the absolute musician in his theoretical writings. The instrumental composer (or for that matter, the composer of "absolute" operatic melody) had achieved an unprecedented status in modern times, a hitherto unimaginable autonomy – a status that (in Beethoven's case, for instance) at last approached the immortality accorded to masters of the other arts in the past. He ("she") would naturally hesitate to sacrifice the autonomy of "pure music" and the promise of immortality to enter into the artistic matrimony of Wagner's *Gesamtkunstwerk*, whose conditions were an unknown quantity, and whose issue was still obscure. So Brünnhilde, too, sadly contemplates the loss of autonomy and divine status. For a moment, she is disinclined to sacrifice her pure state. Yet the sacrifice is of course "inevitable," from the perspective of Wagnerian dramaturgy and aesthetics alike.

But when Wagner came to set his text to music, almost two decades after drafting it as *The Young Siegfried*, his feelings toward "pure music" had evidently softened from the dogmatic rigor of *Opera and Drama* days. Now the musical setting of Brünnhilde's plea to remain autonomous and untouched (phase 6 of the foregoing outline, beginning at her lines "Ewig war ich, ewig bin ich") embodies the voice of "pure music" in a precise way that Wagner could not have envisioned when writing the text, or even at the time of composing Acts I and II in the 1850s. This passage forms a self-contained musical interlude within the progress of the scene, based primarily on two non-leitmotivic themes familiar now from their deployment as the principal themes of the *Siegfried Idyll* (composed the following year, late in 1870). Both themes exhibit the "instrumental" regularity of phrase structure common to the other brief ideas Wagner jotted down later in life as potential material for the short symphonic essays he hoped to compose after his retirement from music drama (see Example 3.3, a–b). The strict four-part texture of both themes and their scoring for strings alone in *Siegfried* led Ernest Newman to surmise that the passage preserved the music of a string quartet Wagner had possibly composed at Lake Starnberg in 1864, in the early days of Ludwig II's patronage (and the budding affair with Cosima). Although it appears unlikely, now, that this "Starnberg Quartet" was ever realized as such, the earlier origin of the themes is confirmed by a sketch for the opening theme (dated 14 November 1864) and several entries in Cosima's diaries, particularly the following:

Before lunch R. plays for me what he has written and is delighted that several themes which date from the "Starnberg days" and which we had jokingly earmarked for quartets and symphonies have now found their niche ("Ewig war ich, ewig bin ich").[43]

And why else would this music have "found its niche" precisely here – where its motivic and formal autonomy remain strikingly unintegrated with the musical fabric of the rest of the scene or the opera at all – if it

Example 3.3 *Siegfried* Act III, scene 3: *Siegfried Idyll* themes
(a) theme a (mm. 1478–85)

[43] CWD, 19 May 1869. An entry from 30 January 1871 also identifies the main theme of the *Siegfried Idyll* with "a theme that had occurred to [Wagner] at Starnberg, and which he had promised me as a quartet." Given the evidence of the theme's association with Cosima, its implementation in the instrumental context of the *Siegfried Idyll* (which originally bore the heading "*Symphonie*"), the remarks in Cosima's diaries, and radical isolation of this theme within the context of the *Ring* score as a whole, there seems to be no reason to question its genesis as a theme intended for instrumental music (cf. Deathridge, *et al.*, *Verzeichnis der musikalischen Werke Richard Wagners und ihrer Quellen*, 509, where it is suggested that the scoring and date of the existing sketch fail to support the thesis of a "Starnberg Quartet").

(b) theme b (mm. 1497–505)

had not struck Wagner that Brünnhilde embodied here the spirit of "quartets and symphonies," the spirit of "pure music"?

The interpolation of this oasis of musical calm and cool also serves the larger dramatic, "evolutionary" strategy of the scene as the weightiest of the several "restraining" episodes within the overall dialectic of dynamic and static episodes. In a modest way it participates in the evolutionary procedures that otherwise characterize Wagner's style by this time. A small central "development" emerges at Brünnhilde's description of the reflection distorted by troubled waters ("Rührtest zur Woge / das Wasser du auf"), where motives from outside the episode are subjected to brief sequential agitation – both motives associated with Siegfried's earlier experience of sexual panic (Slumber and Love's confusion). Despite a clear tonal and motivic reprise ("Ewig licht") and a closing cadence in E, the episode climaxes in a brief, triumphant statement of the main theme in C major, as if anticipating the tonal goal of the larger context. But while these details respond to the sense of the text, the formal design of the episode – with its two principal themes, its development and reprise, and its symmetrical major-third relations (E and A♭/G♯ in the "exposition," E and C in the "reprise") – displays a fully autonomous musical logic, too (and a logic not particularly consonant with the design of the text). "Leave, ah, leave me in peace! Come not to me in thy furious frenzy, force me not with thy mastering might," Brünnhilde pleads (in Frederick Jameson's venerable translation).[44] Brünnhilde's plea is also argued by her music: music *could* still thrive on its own, perhaps even learn the secrets of dramatic "evolution," with time? Brünnhilde *could* remain single.

Parsifal and Kundry

The allegory of Siegfried and Brünnhilde affirms an accepted cultural order. "Masculine" poetry discovers the nature of music, which is feminine. This nature is at first alarmingly "Other" – frightening, but fascinating. Poetry soon masters its fear of this medial difference, and sets about mastering music, which, after a brief show of resistance, joyfully submits to the superior strength of rational discourse. The "language of feeling" submits to the semantic discipline of ideas, concepts, character, and drama. The encounter between Parsifal and Kundry in Act II of *Parsifal* inverts the gender relations of the earlier scene – woman is the aggressor/seducer, and the innocent youth resists – but the outcome is in its way equally affirmative of societal norms: the woman's attempt to usurp the active role is punished with failure. Because I don't propose that Wagner deliberately invested this scene with any allegorical significance in relation to the metaphors of *Opera and Drama*, in the way he did (I think) in the final scene of *Siegfried*, I don't mean to press one upon it. Yet the close parallel between the two dramatic configurations (partly direct, partly by inversion) may at least justify a brief speculative postscript to the foregoing allegory. Is

---

[44] "Laß', ach, Laß' / Lasse von mir! / Nahe mir nicht / mit der wüthenden Nähe, / Zwinge mich nicht/mit dem brechenden Zwang!" (translation from Richard Wagner, *Siegfried* [vocal score, New York: G. Schirmer, 1904], 319–20).

there anything in the musical realization of this later scene that could be said to reflect Wagner's later attitudes toward the earlier gendering of musical and poetic/dramatic discourses?

While in many respects Kundry is portrayed as the degenerate anti-type of Brünnhilde, she nonetheless embodies distinct qualities of Wagner's metaphorical musical woman. She seems to exist in a world of wild, inchoate, ungrounded "feelings," and she is forever at the mercy of these, or else of her provisional master, Klingsor. (The relation of Klingsor to Kundry is also in a sense a parallel anti-type to that of Wotan and Brünnhilde.) She lacks the "moral will" necessary for self-determination, as Wagner said of music (III, 93). She longs, ultimately, for redemption from her aimless wandering through the intercession of a male redeemer. Her guiding impulse is to serve, but this impulse may be channeled either negatively, as service to Klingsor, or positively, as service to the Grail knights. (In the creed of operatic "reform" from the beginning, music is to be the obedient servant of the words, we recall.[45]) Parsifal perceives her as an object of fascination and dread, an embodiment of the unknown female "other" and momentary surrogate mother, as Siegfried does Brünnhilde. But there is no place in *Parsifal* for a redemptive woman, nor for a redeeming procreative act. (Kundry begs Parsifal to redeem her through physical love – "If my kiss has made you clairvoyant, then surely the full embrace of my love will make you divine" – but Parsifal sees through this as a stratagem for his undoing.)[46] Kundry is portrayed as a dangerously unstable, divided personality, the victim of psychological delusions or *Wahnsinn*. Her attempt to manipulate Parsifal is one manifestation of this neurosis. Similarly, Wagner had described as a symptom of cultural insanity (*Wahnsinn*) the domination of drama by music, with reference to his apothegm of operatic ends and means:

> ... so we must regard as the very essence of this delusion (*des Wahnes und endlich des Wahnsinns*), exposing the operatic genre as the thoroughly unnatural and even ludicrous thing it is, this situation in which *that means of expression wanted to determine, for its own part, the purpose of the drama (die Absicht des Dramas)*.   (III, 308, original emphasis)

---

45 On the gender implications – both grammatical and cultural – in the classic formulation of this creed by Monteverdi's brother Giulio Cesare, see Suzanne G. Cusick, "Gendering Modern Music." Kundry's temporal wanderings and her yearning for salvation-through-surcease also present, of course, a parallel to the male figure of the Flying Dutchman, as Dieter Borchmeyer discusses in his chapter on "The Transformations of Ahasuerus: *Der fliegende Holländer* and his Metamorphoses," in *Richard Wagner: Theory and Theatre*, trans. Stewart Spencer (Oxford, 1991), 190–215.

46 "So war es mein Kuß / der welthellsichtig dich machte? / Mein volles Liebes-Umfangen / läßt dich dann Gottheit erlangen" (*Parsifal* Act II).

What has come to appear as natural through the force of convention – the reign of "absolute melody" in opera – is exposed by Wagner as unnatural and degenerate.

Wagner's "actual" attitude toward the idea of absolute or symphonic music by the time of *Parsifal* is complex and probably not susceptible to the dualistic criteria of aesthetic value that operate in *Opera and Drama*. Part of him apparently longed to found a new genre of "Wagnerian" symphony, and was even willing to entertain the idea of symphonic poems or characteristic "overtures" based on themes from his dramas or from classical literature.[47] Part of him insisted on the "symphonic" character of his music dramas, but part of him continued to argue the incommensurability of dramatic and instrumental musical procedures. Like Kundry, he was deeply divided. Acts I and III of *Parsifal* associate the realm of the Grail with a realm of "pure music," represented in a language of etherealized marches and choral hymns. But in Act II, Kundry and the Flower Maidens could be said to represent the simple harmonies, lilting phrases, and self-contained forms of "pure" or absolute music as an *illusion*: an alluring vision without real substance, a seductive conjurer's trick in which artifice merely apes the ideal of nature. Thus the Flower Maidens, who are neither real plants nor real women, but the products of necromantic artifice; thus Kundry's disguise "in transformed shape," as Parsifal discovers her lying in a flowery bower. The Flower Maidens' music, with its little aromatic arabesques and sensuously mild chromatic inflections of a smooth harmonic exterior, is the musical equivalent of the exotic Parisian scents and fabrics by which Wagner was seduced, particularly in later years – the commercial products of a culture he never tired of condemning from a higher moral ground. After Kundry sends them packing, she substitutes a similar product in the music of her narrative about Parsifal's mother, Herzeleide.

This begins as a kind of Oedipally tinged *berceuse* in simple, quasi-strophic form. The harmony is firmly anchored in G major, but the melodic surface is riffled with insinuating chromatic inflections similar to those of the preceding choral section (the Flower Maidens). The rhythms and melodic contours are smooth and rather sing-song, monotonous and lulling. The tactic is to lull Parsifal into a dreamy complacency by singing him scenes of his childhood to the music of childhood, a lullaby (Example 3.4).[48] Cunning psychologist that she is, Kundry

---

[47] For the evidence of these plans and the occasional sketches they generated, see the entries for WWV 98 (*Romeo und Julie*) and WWV 107 ("Pläne zu Ouvertüren und Symphonien") in *Verzeichnis der musikalischen Werke*, 495–6, 519–24, as well as CWD, 24 January and 10–16 February 1874.

[48] The generic allusion to "lullaby" in the music of Kundry's narrative is noted by Frank Glass in his discussion of this scene (*The Fertilizing Seed*, 251–68).

Example 3.4 *Parsifal* Act II, scene 2 (Kundry's "lullaby")

begins to inject these reminiscences with motives of guilt, already in the second verse, and the change of affect leads the piece away from closure toward contrast ("Den Waffen fern, der Männer Kampf und Wüthen") and intensification ("wann dann ihr Arm dich wüthend umschlang"). The story ends sadly and off-key, or "away from home" (in D rather than G), with Herzeleide's death. The music of the lullaby is replaced by reiterations of the so-called "sorrow" motive (though not really leitmotivic, as it remains confined to this scene). The security of stable tonality and closed forms is revealed as an illusion, a manufactured product (what Adorno would call "phantasmagoria") that merely conceals the true nature of things.

Even before Kundry "awakens" Parsifal with the shock of her kiss the formal texture of the scene starts to become loose and unfocused. Her lullaby was of course an act of musical dissembling. But soon glimpses of her real musical nature slip through: the wild, melodically uncontainable musical gesture of her "laugh" (Example 3.5a) belies her attempt to re-stabilize harmony and texture here. When, after her kiss, Parsifal's eyes (and ears) are suddenly opened, the destructive fury of this "formless" motive is revealed in its full force (Example 3.5b). From the conclusion of Kundry's narrative through the moment of her kiss, the tonal and motivic cohesion already becomes strained (reiterations of static fragments of the "sorrow" motive provide the only element of consistency). After the kiss, however, the music remains in a nearly constant state of flux until Klingsor's intercession effects a peremptory return to B minor toward the end of the act.[49]

Example 3.5 *Parsifal* Act II, scene 2: infiltration of Kundry motive (a)

(b)

The polymorphous motive of her demonic "laughter" echoes through-out this long concluding section, dominated dramatically by Kundry's tortured self-revelations; but this motive can hardly be said to carry the force of a structuring refrain, since it lacks any semblance of tonal or metrical stability. Wagner regarded Kundry's laughter as the crucial emblem of her character, which seems to embody all the problematic antithetical qualities of the "eternal feminine" in the minds of Wagner and his contemporaries. The motivic identity of her laughter becomes

[49] Arnold Whittall comments on a discontinuity of styles across this part of the scene and a "jarring" motivic insertion ("des einz'gen Heiles wahren Quell") that "reinforces one's feeling that the music here is not wholly focussed in style" ("The Music," in Lucy Beckett, *Parsifal* [Cambridge, 1981], 78).

emblematic of the analogous qualities of "pure music" in the allegorical scheme of its feminine personification. The motive, in its aimless, anxious wanderings through the scene, can be taken to represent the qualities implicit, to a considerable extent, in Wagner's metaphorical constructions. Shorn of the tawdry trappings of conventional form that contain music in most of its modern cultural manifestations, it is revealed as a volatile, endlessly mutable kind of psychic energy. If not properly grounded by some rational, ordering principle external to it (which could range from trivial dance steps to the Wagnerian drama), this stuff of "pure feeling" is a potential threat to psychological well-being, as Kundry is to Parsifal. Interpreted in this way Wagner's scene becomes, ironically, an allegorical staging of a rapidly emerging discourse that condemned his own music in these very terms: as a seduction of moral reason, a threat to aesthetic sanity, and a symbol of that ener-vating, feminizing "degeneration" that preoccupied so many minds of the *fin-de-siècle*. The curse Kundry utters against Parsifal, in her rage,

> Irre! Irre! / Mir so vertraut!   Wander! Wander! / Share in my fate!
> Dich weih' ich ihm zum Geleit!   Wander like me evermore![50]

is a curse of "formlessness," a perpetual loss of direction and hence the failure of the teleology – certainly male-gendered – symbolized by Parsifal's "mission."

Consciously or not, on Wagner's part, Kundry becomes a plausible allegorical antithesis to Brünnhilde, embodying the dark, irrational, unstable aspects of music, as the language of "pure feeling," a free-flowing, ungrounded emotional current – ungrounded in the structures of rational thought. She is the Dionysian alter-ego to the Apollonian spirit of "pure music" celebrated in Brünnhilde's "Ewig war ich."[51] Like Brünnhilde (or Erda), she spends much time in the bonds of sleep, immersed in the subconscious. But with Kundry, the inarticulate condition of music is one of nightmarish anxiety (recall Wagner on Beethoven's Fifth and Ninth, in chapter 2):

[50] Translation by Andrew Porter, in *Parsifal*, Opera Guide 34 (English National Opera), ed. Nicholas John (London and New York, 1986), 116. Kundry's lines are grammatically ambiguous. "Irre!" at first suggests an imperative verb form (a command to wander or stray), but the subsequent lines seem to suggest its re-interpretation as a masculine noun ("madman," deranged one, or perhaps simply an apostrophe to "madness" or mental distraction).

[51] Nietzsche perhaps best expressed his sense of the Dionysian element in Wagner's musical imagination when retracting it, in "Nietzsche contra Wagner": "I [once] interpreted Wagner's music as an expression of a Dionysian power of the soul; I believed I heard in it the earthquake with which a primordial force of life, dammed up from time immemorial, finally vents itself, indifferent to the possibility that everything that calls itself culture today might start tottering" (trans. Walter Kaufmann, *The Portable Nietzsche* [New York and London, 1968], 669). But this was, he adds now, part misreading, part self-projection.

Da lach' ich, lache,	I laugh then, laugh then,
kann nicht weinen,	I cannot weep,
nur schreien, wüthen,	but crying, raving,
toben, rasen	storming, raging,
in stets erneueter Wahnsinns	I sink again into madness's
Nacht,	night,
aus der ich büssend kaum	from which, remorseful,
erwacht.	I scarcely woke.[52]

If her counterpart, Brünnhilde, can be identified to some extent with the music of her own voice, such as the wild, "invisible" laughter of the Valkyrie-cry that introduces her in the *Ring* (an element in Carolyn Abbate's construction of a "voice-Brünnhilde"),[53] Kundry is even more closely identified with the primal music of her wild laughter. But, paradoxically, the voice of her laughter is *instrumental*: its range, contour, and rhythm defy vocal performance. (At her famous line, "und lachte . . . ," Kundry approximates the instrumental motive, but only by describing its perimeter.) If she were to represent music, it would be as the inchoate, seething sea of infinite modulatory and sequential possibilities that Wagner had discovered in his *Orchestermelodie*, a sea of expressive potential always seeking containment and then threatening to burst it. Her forced submission to the spells of Klingsor's sorcery recalls the favorite Romantic trope of instrumental music as a mysterious, magical tonal substance pressed into service by the conjurations of the composer-magician (another potentially gendered opposition of female and male principles). Kundry embodies all those aspects of music's explosive potential that Brünnhilde's maidenly song ("Ewig war ich") tended to conceal, as did the Flower Maidens' songs or Kundry's own lullaby-narrative (at first). If Brünnhilde's embrace awakens Siegfried to the infinite expressive capacity of Wagner's musical "ocean," Kundry's alerts Parsifal – inadvertently – to its dangers. Brünnhilde surrenders herself to Siegfried, and the act ends in a celebration of consonant harmony, motivic counterpoint, and even the discipline of melodic imitation. Parsifal rejects Kundry's advances, but she persists; the scene descends toward chaos and increasing disintegration, enacted by the literal disintegration of the scenery as Klingsor's magic castle collapses at the final curtain of the act. A weak semblance of closure is established only when Parsifal grasps control in the form of the spear (enough said), as it materializes *ex machina*. In the end, of course, Kundry is completely silenced, while Brünnhilde sings on, triumphantly, after Siegfried's death.

---

[52] Translation by Andrew Porter (*Parsifal*, 114), amended.
[53] Abbate, *Unsung Voices*, chapter 6 ("Brünnhilde Walks by Night"), 206–49.

There is no reason, finally, to expect all of the gender-related archetypes of Wagner's dramas, or even of his theoretical metaphors, to
translate perfectly into the music. Wagner would presumably consider
both scenes, despite their antithetical representations, to have been
"engendered" by the complementary, gendered principles of poetic
thought and musical expression and to "evolve" according to the different nature of this dialectic in each case.[54] Even if the closing scene of
Siegfried is consciously developed as an allegory of the gender metaphors
in *Opera and Drama* (as I believe it is), the allegory comes to an end here.
Siegfried's and Brünnhilde's love-making engenders nothing, except
perhaps the problems they face in the next opera (their music, it is true,
bore that musical tribute to Wagner's own offspring, the *Siegfried Idyll*).
Kundry fails to seduce Parsifal, but their encounter nonetheless produces some of Wagner's more intense pages of music, if not his most
coherent. It is not literally – or not only – the interaction of dramatic
characters that engenders the musical-dramatic "organism," according
to *Opera and Drama*, rather the fertilization of musical materials with a
poetic-dramatic "intent." At the time he was working out these metaphors Wagner was still a novice regarding the physiology of the "art-
work of the future." He ventured a brief and tentative hypothetical model
there, however, in the notion of the "poetic-musical period," whose
elusive anatomy I will undertake to examine in the chapter that follows.

---

[54] Wagner regarded even the disintegrative, fragmented process of the Parsifal-
Kundry scene as an "evolution," to judge by one of the stage-direction comments
recorded by Felix Mottl (reproduced in the C. F. Peters editions). At the moment
where Parsifal promises Kundry "love and salvation" if she directs him to Amfortas,
Wagner notes that she should listen with marked attention: "Here is the turning
point of the whole development (evolution)" (*Hier ist die Wendepunkt der ganzen
Entwicklung*).

180

4

The "poetic-musical period" and the "evolution" of Wagnerian form

The paradox attending Wagner's attempt to limn the structural principles of his ideal musical drama in Part III of *Opera and Drama* is that these principles had as yet no empirical artistic object. The haziness of so many of the theoretical prescriptions in the Zurich writings is a consequence not only of Wagner's overwrought prose style, but also of the peculiar context of these writings in the creative vacuum of the early years of exile. As has often been pointed out, the ideas of *Opera and Drama* are awkwardly situated between the "no longer" of *Tannhäuser* and *Lohengrin* and the "not yet" of the *Ring*. The shadowy nature of this "theory," then, is explained to some extent by the fact that it is a theory of non-existent works, unrealized ones: *Siegfrieds Tod* and *Wieland der Schmied*. (The abortive musical sketches for *Siegfrieds Tod* from 1850 are a logical counterpart to the hazy theory of the contemporary essays, not so much because composition couldn't proceed for lack of theory, but the reverse: Wagner couldn't offer a fully coherent, detailed "theory" of works that he had yet to compose.) While Wagner did have in the text of *Siegfrieds Tod* a concrete object for his observations on *Stabreim* – however fanciful they may sound – he had none as yet for the specifically musical component of his proposals, most prominently the embryonic theory of "leitmotifs" (the motives of "anticipation" and "reminiscence" expounded in sections five and six of Part III of *Opera and Drama*) and the concept of a "poetic-musical period" proposed in section three. Wagner's thoughts about an expanded network of associative musical "reminiscence" motives at the time of *Opera and Drama* can be reconstructed to some extent by a comparison of the motivic techniques of *Lohengrin* and those of the earlier *Ring* operas, as attempted by Dahlhaus, among others.[1] The same procedure can help to shed some light on the more elusive concept of the "poetic-musical period."

---

[1] Dahlhaus, "Zur Geschichte der Leitmotivtechnik bei Wagner," in *Das Drama Richard Wagners als musikalisches Kunstwerk*, ed. Carl Dahlhaus (Regensburg, 1970), 17–36.

The "poetic-musical period" and "evolution"

Described by Wagner in Part III of *Opera and Drama* on the basis of a brief example, the "poetic-musical period" has been an object of critical contention mainly since Alfred Lorenz appropriated the idea as the theoretical foundation of his exhaustive analyses of all of Wagner's music dramas according to series of tonally and thematically defined units or "periods." Wagner's exposition of the concept in *Opera and Drama* provided Lorenz with his criterion of tonal closure, but little else. Wagner otherwise concentrated on the hypothetical treatment of *Stabreim* in the musical setting, while remaining vague as to the musical procedures involved. (This imbalance is reflected in Part III of *Opera and Drama* as a whole, and not surprisingly so, when we recall again that Wagner had the details of his text at hand, but no clear idea of the music.) Since the time of Lorenz's analyses there has been intermittent discussion of what might constitute such "periods" in the practice of the *Ring* or the later operas, particularly with regard to levels of tonal closure, for which Lorenz made such frequently outlandish claims. In re-reading this passage from *Opera and Drama* yet again I would propose a backward glance at the score of *Lohengrin* (which surely figures as a reference point for Wagner's understanding of textual-musical "periods" here as it does for his speculations about an amplified network of reminiscence motives) in addition to considering the evidence of the earlier *Ring* dramas usually brought to bear on the theories of *Opera and Drama*. Contemporary theoretical discourse offers another context for evaluating the concepts of "period" and "modulation" as understood in the mid-nineteenth century. Above all, I would propose a shift of perspective: rather than attempting to gauge the true dimensions of the individual poetic-musical period according to some "authentic" interpretation of the term, I suggest we pay more attention to the role of such hypothetical periods (whose precise dimensions may remain indeterminate) within the larger "evolutionary" designs invoked by Wagner's text and – as we have seen – fundamental to his understanding of "dramatic" or dramatized musical form.

Periode and *Entwicklung*

As described in Part III of *Opera and Drama*, the "poetic-musical period" amounts to little more than a theoretical – and rather unlikely – correlation of alliterative verse (*Stabreim*) with patterns of harmonic progression within a musical phrase of unspecified proportions. This correlation of text and tonal design may extend over a larger series of such phrases or periods. (Rather than summarizing here the generally familiar details of the entire passage in question I have included a translation of it as an appendix: see pp. 375–7.) Wagner's hypothetical

182

Periode *and* Entwicklung

"period" begins with a single poetic line of unified affect: "Die Liebe gibt Lust zum Leben" (Love gives pleasure to life – IV, 153). This single line is modified and extended to encompass an internal affective contrast (emphasis added):[2]

> Die Liebe bringt Lust und Leid;   (Love brings pleasure and
>   sorrow;
> doch in ihr Weh auch webt sie   but with its pain are mingled joys.)
> Wonnen.

The alliterative consonants of Wagner's *Stabreim* provide a kind of sonorous envelope for individual lines of text. It is the role of harmonic "modulation," he proposes, to extend this unifying impulse to larger levels of phrase or period. In the present case, a return of the initial tonic note or chord at the end of these lines would serve to underscore the affective chiasmus outlined by the words *Liebe – Leid / Weh – Wonnen*, which the alliteration alone is unable to articulate. Wagner suggests that the word *Lust* will function as a kind of emotional pivot between *Liebe* and *Leid*, and should be set accordingly:

the musician would need to match the contrasting emotions of the alliterated words by modulating from the original tonality into a contrasting, related one appropriate to the contrasting sense of the [third] word . . . [T]he note to which the word *Lust* is sung would naturally tend to function as a leading-tone, determining and necessarily drawing us into the new tonality appropriate to the expression of sorrow (*Leid*).   (IV, 152)

Similarly, the word *webt* (mediating between the contrasting affective pair *Weh* and *Wonnen*) can function as the pivot or leading-tone of an emotional and musical modulation back to the original key of the period.

The poet, by means of his *Stabreim*, can only represent this return to our sensible and emotional faculties as a unified progression from pain (*Weh*) to joys (*Wonnen*), but not as a return to the genus of feeling originally represented by the word "love." The musician, on the other hand, can intelligibly connect the entire pair of lines by returning to the original key, distinctly indicating in this way the family relationship between these contrasting emotions – an impossibility for the poet, who must continue to alternate the alliterative syllables of his *Stabreim*.   (IV, 153)

Clearly when he speaks here of "modulation" away from and back to a principal tonality within such a brief span – presumably no more than four to eight measures of music in the case of these two (or three) lines – Wagner must understand the term to embrace local phenomena such

---

2   At the time of *Opera and Drama* (and *Siegfrieds Tod*) Wagner conceived of his alliterative verse form in alternating lines of three and four stresses, the four-stress lines divided by an internal caesura. According to the ultimate layout of the *Ring* text, the extended example would constitute three rather than two lines.

as Neapolitan inflections, parallel minor or major, minor subdominant, or fleeting tonicizations of the third or sixth degrees, for example. What Simon Sechter would designate several years later as an *auskomponierte Nebenstufe* (such as a parenthetical Neapolitan or flat-VI relationship, for instance) would thus have counted as a modulation in Wagner's primitive technical vocabulary, as Dahlhaus suggested.[3] We can assume therefore that Wagner understood the tonal peregrinations of the "wandering tonality" characteristic of the freer, declamatory portions of the *Ring* scores as a continuously "modulating" melodic discourse. The German terms *Rückung* and *Ausweichung* – suggesting a momentary harmonic shift or deceptive resolution – would also be encompassed by Wagner's understanding of word "modulation." A passage elucidating the principles of "melody" in Gustav Schilling's *Versuch einer Philosophie des Schönen in der Musik* (1838) bears a striking resemblance to Wagner's text on the "poetic-musical period," but substitutes, in fact, the term *Ausweichung* for Wagner's *Modulation*. "It should be kept in mind," Schilling writes, "that in the progression of a melody, as long as the expression of the emotion does not require movement away from the tonic (*keine Ausweichung fordert*), the melody should remain as strictly as possible within that key or close by it . . ."[4] A typical early complaint about Wagner's music (even the operas of the 1840s) was directed at its restless "modulations," by which critics normally understood the local harmonic motion of "wandering tonality." An early critic of the *Lohengrin* score bemoans the tiring effect of its "continuous, and often quite unmotivated change of keys (*Wechsel der Tonarten*)." "Within ten measures," this critic continues, "one might easily encounter fifteen different keys [!] . . . – granted, [Wagner] can always find his way back to the principal key (*Haupttonart*) by means of a single move, yet he leaves it so often that one can scarcely keep it in one's ears."[5]

---

3   "Wagners Begriff der 'dichterisch-musikalischen Periode'," in *Beiträge zur Geschichte der Musikanschauung im 19. Jahrhundert*, ed. W. Salmen (Regensburg, 1965), 180. (On Wagner's notion of "modulation" see also Arnold Whittall, "Musical Language," in *The Wagner Compendium*, 254.) Dahlhaus's example is a "period" of thirty measures from scene 2 of *Das Rheingold* (Fasolt: "Lichtsohn du, leicht gefügter!"), which begins off of F minor, touches on E♭ minor, D♭ major, E♭ major, and returns momentarily to F minor. He returns to the same example in "Tonalität und Form in Wagners *Ring*," *Archiv für Musikwissenschaft* 40 (1983), 165–73.

4   "bei dieser [Fortschreitung] der Melodie ist zu merken, daß man, so lange der Ausdruck der darzustellenden Empfindung keine Ausweichung fordert, sich so streng als möglich in der Grundtonart oder deren Nähe halten muß" (G. Schilling, *Versuch einer Philosophie des Schönen in der Musik* [Mainz, 1838], 215).

5   ". . . er ist frelich mit einer einzigen Wendung wieder in seiner Haupttonart zurück, allein er verlässt sie so oft, dass man sie kaum mehr im Gedächtniss behalten kann" (review of *Lohengrin* in Würzburg, signed "B–r.," *Süddeutsche Musik-Zeitung* 5 (1856), 62.

Periode *and* Entwicklung

We should recall, all the same, that the size of Wagner's example is obviously limited for practical reasons, and that he subsequently exhorts the reader to "imagine the content of the above two-line example expanded to a larger scale," where, between the departure from the initial key (and affect) and its eventual return, "a long series of lines" might intervene, "expressing the most varied intensification and admixture of intermediate emotional stages . . ." (IV, 153–4). Here Wagner is envisioning precisely that "wandering tonality" that would characterize the new style of his music after *Rheingold*, as suggested above, although the eventual return to a tonic or *Haupttonart* – if it occurs at all – by no means consistently carries the structural significance Lorenz wished to attribute to it. (It might even be fair to say that the central points of the theoretical proposal – the correlation between affective nuance and "modulation" and the tonal and affective "rounding" of the period – were eventually discarded in practice, leaving only the side-effect of continuous modulation or "wandering tonality" as a means of supporting rhetorical declamation.)

A simple example from scene 4 of *Das Rheingold* (whose text happens to resonate with the hypothetical lines from *Opera and Drama*) might suggest something of what Wagner had in mind in attempting to describe a "poetic-musical period" in its rudimentary form, or what the *Opera and Drama* example might look like if set to music. Sung by Froh in anticipation of Freia's imminent return, the first four lines of the text maintain a single affect:

Wie liebliche Luft	How lovely the air
wieder uns weht,	that wafts to us again
wonnig Gefühl	joyous feelings,
die Sinne erfüllt!	filling our senses!

The musical setting closely follows the dictates of Wagner's theory, never leaving the G-major triad (see Example 4.1). The various alliterative and assonant combinations – *liebliche–Luft, wieder–weht–wonnig, Gefühl–erfüllt* – are all encompassed within a single diatonic scale in the vocal line (recalling Wagner's gloss, earlier in this section of *Opera and Drama*, on the "patriarchal" or strictly scalar ambitus of Beethoven's *Freude* melody). The following pair of lines presents a contrasting supposition, marked by the alliteration of "sad" and "separated" (*traurig, getrennt*) on the downbeats of the strong measures of the four-measure phrase:

Traurig ging' es uns allen,	Sad it would be for us all,
getrennt für immer von ihr,	apart from her
die leidlos ewiger Jugend	who grants the triumphant pleasure
jubelnde Lust uns verleiht.	of eternal youth.

185

Example 4.1 *Das Rheingold*, mm. 3240–55 (scene 4)

(The foreground has become bright again and the aspect of the gods regains in the light its former freshness. The misty veil, however, still covers the background so that the distant castle remains invisible)

This central phrase of the "period" effects a simple modulation to C, touching on the subdominant harmonies of vi, IV, and ii, and capped by the mild dissonance of the $\flat\hat{6}$ appoggiatura (A$\flat$) to the dominant. The final pair of lines returns to both the initial alliteration and affect of the period (*leidlos–Lust–verleiht*), but balances the initial four measures of G with four measures of the new tonic, C (continued in the orchestra). The modulation to C actually rounds out a prolonged cadential motion in that key (I$^6_4$–V–I), beginning thirty-two measures earlier (m. 3208), following Alberich's curse and melodramatic exit. (This larger tonal entity might suggest a larger "period" entirely in C, mm. 3208–52.) Otherwise, the shorter passage, as given in Example 4.1, follows the particulars of the *Opera and Drama* example in nearly every particular. The textual unit itself, furthermore, represents a single "period" in the original rhetorical-poetic sense of the word, comprising a single coherent statement by a dramatic character (here, as eight lines of text, divided into equal sub-groups of two- and three-stress lines). The musical structure of this short excerpt is also periodic in a conventional musical sense, its three four-measure phrases being rounded out to an even sixteen by the orchestral extension.

In scene 2 of *Das Rheingold* the first statement of the motive of Freia's "golden apples" ("Gold'ne Äpfel / wachsen in ihrem Garten") follows the prescription of *Opera and Drama* still more closely, with a peremptory return to the original tonic (D) in the last two measures, although the final line of text ("Ihrer Mitte drum sei sie entführt") forms an ironic

Example 4.2 *Das Rheingold,* mm. 1111–26 (scene 2)

antithesis to the neutral-natural affective tone of the opening description of Freia's Edenic garden (see Example 4.2). The phrase structure is even more conventionally periodic than that of the preceding example, its eight-plus-eight-measure phrases dividing neatly into complementary two-measure sub-phrases. The text again constitutes a poetic-dramatic "period" in the sense of an individual speech by one character forming a single, coherent proposition. The first eight lines of text (eight measures of music), describing the rejuvenating powers of the golden apples, remain firmly rooted in the tonic, D major, over a stationary A pedal. The contrasting text ("Siech und bleich / doch sinkt ihre Blüte") elicits a tonal parenthesis in the Neapolitan, E♭, further colored by chromatically

189

altered neighbor chords and a chromatic progression to IV of the Neapolitan at "alt und schwach / schwinden sie hin." In this case, the abrupt tonal return seems to be motivated more as an expression of Loge's ruthless, scheming character than by any legitimate affective return in the text (compare the similarly perfunctory D-major cadence that closes Loge's narration to the gods in the same scene, at the words "Nun löste Loge sein Wort"). Dahlhaus, who also cites "Gold'ne Äpfel" as an example of a poetic-musical period, suggests that, while a perception of the Neapolitan relationship of E♭ to D is necessary to establish its expressive character as a darkening disturbance (*Trübung*), the relation to the tonic is really less functional than "centrifugal," in Ernst Kurth's terms: "Yet the accent here falls not so much on the subdominant function that obtains to E♭ in the context of D major – it would be difficult to justify six measures of subdominant preceding one measure of dominant and two of tonic harmony – but instead on the [expressive] coloring assumed by E♭ against the background of D."[6] The concept of a "centrifugal" relationship of subsidiary key areas to a central tonic is undoubtedly apposite to Wagner's account of the free-ranging "modulation" within a poetic-musical period, in which "every key touched on would appear in a specific relation to the original key, conditioning the particular expressive light shed by these various tonalities."[7] Yet in this case, the skewed proportions of the functional cadential harmony (♭II–V–I) are precisely the point, underlining the ironic detachment of Loge's words and his peremptory conclusion. The proportions that Dahlhaus finds difficult to "justify" (*zu motivieren*) from the perspective of a conventional harmonic period are justified – or motivated, as Wagner would say – by the "poetic intent" of the period as a whole.

Both of these examples suggest that, in any case, the movement through "the most diverse tonalities" (*die verschiedensten Tonarten*) within a period covers not only genuine modulations, but also all manner of local inflections, parentheses, and the attributes of "wandering" and "centrifugal" tonal behavior that become so characteristic of Wagner's idiom beginning with *Das Rheingold*.[8] Early exegetes of Wagner's theo-

---

[6]   "Wagner's Begriff der 'dichterisch-musikalischen Periode'," 181.

[7]   The entire passage, in the original German, reads as follows: "Hier würde die musikalische Modulation, um die dichterische Absicht zu verwirklichen, in die verschiedensten Tonarten hinüber und zurück zu leiten haben; alle die berührten Tonarten würden aber in einem genauen verwandtschaftlichen Verhältnisse zu der ursprünglichen Tonart erscheinen, von der aus das besondere Licht, welches sie auf den Ausdruck werfen, wohl bedingt und die Fähigkeit zu dieser Lichtgebung gewissermaßen selbst erst verliehen wird" (IV, 154).

[8]   The larger context of the first example, incidentally, provides a good illustration of how "real" modulations as well as local inflections might be understood to appear in the expressive "light" of a principal key. Following Wotan's line, "Gönn' ihm die

retical writings certainly perceived (and generally distrusted) in them just such an emphasis on the response of the musical accompaniment to details of text rhythm and accent, affective nuance, and so forth, in the tradition of the "obbligato recitative" and hence at the expense of "rational" (absolute, pure, pleasing) melodic phrase structure at the larger level. Although one could argue that such early critics were mistaken in reading *Opera and Drama* as advocating some kind of latter-day *stile rappresentativo*, it can't be denied that these critics could easily have supported their claims with examples from *Das Rheingold* (had they known it then), tending as it does toward a piecemeal or "mosaic-like" formal texture. Yet what Nietzsche later dubbed Wagner's musical "miniaturism" is here probably as much a consequence of a compositional technique still in its experimental stage – the idea of creating a musical fabric of associative musical motives – as of a doctrinaire approach to the musical declamation and representation of textual detail.

Louis Köhler, an enthusiastic but misguided young admirer of the composer, exemplifies this common misreading of *Opera and Drama* in a short book entitled *The Melody of Speech* (*Die Melodie der Sprache*, 1853), evidently intended to derive a practical example from Wagner's rather abstract philosophies of operatic reform. Köhler takes as a starting-point the text of Wagner's hypothetical poetic-musical period ("Die Liebe bringt Lust und Leid," etc.) and works out a musical setting based not so much on the details of the *Opera and Drama* passage itself as on ideas harking back to Rousseau and Herder about the origins of melody in the natural accents and pitch modulations of speech (or rather, the origins of speech in "melody").[9] (Köhler cites as a kind of ethnological evidence the Lithuanian street cries of his native Königsberg.) The four-measure phrase (period?) that Köhler gradually constructs by coaxing out the "natural" melody latent in the words is not only comically inept, as music, but also fails to obey the strictures of the original passage, such as they are (see Example 4.3a). Köhler

geifernde Lust!," the music settles on a long G pedal, supporting a prolongation of C_4^6 (m. 3208). The effect of the secondary dominant (V of V) over the pedal note (at "Fasolt und Fafner nahen von fern" and "Aus der Riesen Haft naht dort die Holde") is clearly anticipatory; the chromatic neighbor tones of C$\sharp$ and E$\flat$ (Fricka: "Bringst du gute Kunde?"; Loge: "dort liegt was Freia löst") effect a brief note of anxiety and threat, in conjunction with the syncopated motive of the "Nibelungs' Hate." The temporary resolution to G ("Wie liebliche Luft / wieder uns weht") creates a provisional sense of repose that is fully realized when the larger tonal "period" finally cadences in C ("jubelnde Lust uns verleiht").

[9] Wagner does appeal to the Roussellian notion of an original, naturally musical *Ursprache* in his anthropological justification of *Stabreim* earlier in Part III of *Opera and Drama*, but not in the account of the poetic-musical period. (See also "Melody, origins, and utopias of regression" in chapter 5, below.)

does manage to set *Leid* and *Weh* to minor triads, but misplaces his E♭ "pivot" tone (by which term I think we can interpret Wagner's use of the word *Leitton* or "leading-tone")[10] on the word *und* rather than *Lust*, as prescribed by Wagner, and ends not on the original tonic, but on ♭III (E♭). As a foil to this bit of natural song (the preferred harp accompaniment is evidently meant to underscore its enlightened innocence), Köhler adduces three examples of a corrupt operatic setting of the text, in the manner of Rossini, Auber, and Meyerbeer – this much, at least, is true to the spirit of *Opera and Drama* (these parodistic settings are reproduced as Examples 4.3b–d). Of these, only the setting *à l'Auber* bears the slightest resemblance to the intended target of its satire. Ironically, the preposterous Meyerbeerian sample (Example 4.3d) unwittingly conforms rather more closely to Wagner's original prescription

Example 4.3 "Natural" and parodistic settings of Wagner's text example for the hypothetical "poetic-musical period," from Louis Köhler, *Die Melodie der Sprache* (Leipzig: J. J. Weber, 1853)
(a) "natural" setting

---

[10] Alfred Lorenz, incidentally, interpreted Wagner's term *"Leitton"* along these same lines, as any member of a pivot chord rather than the major seventh degree, specifically, "which would have exercised an overly artificial influence on the natural flow of the melody" (*Das Geheimnis der Form*, vol. I, 18).

than Köhler's "proper" example, returning successfully to C after appropriately tonicizing ii (D minor) around the word *Weh* – which serves at the same time as a pre-dominant chord for the tonic cadence – so that the word *webt* serves exactly the pivotal role assigned to it by Wagner.[11]

Neither these two excerpts from *Das Rheingold* nor certainly Köhler's practical exegesis of the "poetic-musical period" are likely to convince anyone of the significance of the concept in understanding Wagner's greater achievements. Still, they tell us something. If the aphoristic and somewhat primitive quality of the *Rheingold* excerpts is in fact a consequence of an attempt to implement the theoretical speculation of *Opera and Drama*, then these examples invite us to consider what Wagner himself might have found unsatisfactory with his experiments

(b) "in the manner of Rossini"

(c) "in the manner of Auber"

(d) "in the manner of Meyerbeer"

in operatic reform by comparison with earlier and later examples. The aesthetic poverty of Köhler's pseudo-Wagnerian example raises the same question (to the extent that Köhler thought he was realizing Wagner's "poetic intent"), but the accident that one of his operatic anti-examples seems to fit the prescriptions of Wagner's model just as well as or better than the experiment in "musical naturalism" raises the possibility that conventional operatic practice (Wagner's or others') may also assist in interpreting the "poetic-musical period" and its premises. Let me consider these proposals in reverse.

194

Even in the maligned genre of conventional opera a composer might, of course, succeed in establishing some correlation between the tonal design of traditional musical "periods" and the affective course of the text set (as even Köhler's "Meyerbeer" demonstrates). Such a correlation was, after all, the norm for metrically a-periodic accompanied or "obbligato" recitative or *scena* styles, as mentioned. But it was hardly exceptional even in structured aria or ensemble contexts. Just as the development of Wagner's compositional idiom in general from *Lohengrin* through *Das Rheingold* is easily construed in terms of an increasing synthesis of open, non-metrical recitative or *scena* style, arioso, and regularly periodic aria styles, we could also suppose that the "poetic-musical period" was in some sense conceived as a rapprochement between these different levels of operatic discourse, hence a rapprochement between a recitative or "prose" style oriented to the rhetorical "periodicity" of the dramatic text (so to speak) and an aria style preserving elements of the internal periodicity of "absolute melody." A correlation between harmonic modulation and the modulation of sense or affect within the dramatic text might be achieved in either idiom, though the incorporation of recitative, *scena*, or "prose" style into that of the periodic aria or ensemble naturally tended to increase the potential for a correlation between harmonic and rhetorical-affective modulation in these latter contexts.

A "period," understood in the broadest terms of its original rhetorical application, denotes an utterance that can be understood as complete and intelligible in itself, a complete semantic unit between the level of a sentence and a paragraph of prose, for instance, or between a line and a stanza of verse. Thus a "poetic" period of such proportions (two or four lines of metrical verse, for instance) could be understood to correspond ideally with a metrical musical period. Such a correspondence between poetic and musical "periodicity" is sometimes implicit in the application of the term by Wagner's contemporaries as well as by the preceding generation, especially prior to the acceptance of A. B. Marx's definition of the small-scale antecedent–consequent period as the standard sense of the term.[12] Wagner himself most often seems to use the term "period" to refer to any aspect of conventional, metrical-

---

[12] Some examples of the range of usage of the term "period" by Wagner and others up through about 1860 are catalogued by Peter Petersen in "Die dichterisch-musikalische Periode: Ein verkannter Begriff Richard Wagners," *Hamburger Jahrbuch für Musikwissenschaft* 2 (1977), 105–24 (see esp. 105–9). Petersen notes in particular the similarity between H. C. Koch's use of the term *Hauptperiode* or "principal period" to designate the scope of a sonata exposition, development, or recapitulation (*Versuch einer Anleitung zur Composition*, 1787; *Musikalisches Lexikon*, 1802) and Wagner's use of the term in the 1857 Liszt essay. In both cases, the extended scope can be easily understood by analogy to the extension of the periods of a simple binary form into the two- or three-part model of sonata form (see also chapter 5 below, "Melody as form").

The "poetic-musical period" and "evolution"

harmonic phrase structure – generally at the level of the individual phrase or composite melody, it is true. (Wagner seems, in fact, to favor the word *Periode* over *Satz* in referring to the musical phrase.) But there is at least one piece of evidence that Wagner also entertained the idea of a musical period, in an operatic context, as defined primarily by the rhetorical thrust of the text, specifically in the case of otherwise musically non-periodic recitative. In an 1837 review of Bellini's *Norma*, performed in Königsberg, he refers to the "periods" of Norma's "great recitative" (evidently the scene "Sediziose voci, voci di guerra," preceding "Casta diva") in this oratorical rather than metrical sense:

The great recitative in which [Norma] exhorts the people to remain at peace and to defer the battle of liberation was executed with fitting dignity by Fr. Grosser; but it exhibited her accustomed failing in the execution of recitative, due especially to an excessively regular and dragging delivery that fails to distinguish important words or even syllables from insignificant ones. In this way not only is the significance of the recitative forfeited, but the resulting mass of undifferentiated syllables, vowels, and consonants makes it quite impossible to grasp even the words themselves. In the performance of recitative the *periods* need to be much more forcefully articulated and thus more independently highlighted.[13]

Given the obvious importance of a synthesis of recitative, arioso, and aria idioms in Wagner's "Romantic" operas, through *Lohengrin*, it is not difficult to conclude that the "poetic-musical period" might well have been meant to convey an ideal synthesis of the rhetorical-declamatory "periodicity" of recitative models (very much dependent on the theatrical sensibilities of the performer, as testified by Wagner's remarks here and by his adulation of Schröder-Devrient's histrionic talents) and the immanent, though more formalized, musical rhetoric of the harmonic-metrical phrase. The key (as it were) to exploiting the expressive and rhetorical potential of the latter lay especially in a freer, more extensive manipulation of its harmonic trajectory ("modulation," in the looser nineteenth-century sense of local harmonic progression), opened up by the enharmonic and chromatic vocabulary of nineteenth-century practice. A couple of examples from Wagner's own repertoire as operatic conductor will suffice to show how his description of the "poetic-musical period" might be predicated to some degree on fairly traditional contemporary operatic practices, as well as on his adaptation of them in his own "Romantic" operas.

[13] " . . . Die *Perioden* müssen im Recitativ weit getrennter und somit selbständiger werden" (cited from Friedrich Lippmann, "Ein neuentdecktes Autograph Richard Wagners: Rezension der Königsberger 'Norma'-Aufführung von 1837," in *Musicæ scientiæ collectanea: Festschrift für Karl Gustav Fellerer* [Cologne, 1973], 375, emphasis added). I would like to thank John Deathridge for bringing this text to my attention.

196

Periode *and* Entwicklung

Heinrich Marschner's *Der Vampyr* (1828) is among the works Wagner knew well from the beginning of his professional career (having collaborated with his brother on a production in Würzburg in 1833), and a work generally acknowledged to represent the stylistic point of departure for Wagner's own early operas from *Die Feen* through *Der fliegende Holländer*. The scene and aria (no. 6, "Heiter lacht die gold'ne Frühlingssonne") that introduce the principal heroine, Malwina, in Act I of *Der Vampyr* can be viewed as a typical example of a sectional operatic number in which changes of tempo, thematic material, and key are made to harmonize with the uncomplicated rhetorical "periodicity" of the text in a manner that can be read as an implicit background to Wagner's theoretical construct. The text of this number, given below, has been divided according to the larger "rhetorical" periods observed in Marschner's setting:

Heiter lacht die gold'ne Frühlingssonne	Gaily laughs the golden sunlight
auf die buntgeschmückte neu belebte Flur.	upon the colorful, re-animated fields.
Ach Alles, was ich sehe, ist nur Abglanz	Ah, all that I see is but a reflection
von meines Herzens niegefühlter Wonne;	of my heart's unprecedented joy;
die Flur im bunten Festgeschmeide,	the fields in all their festive colors,
der Baum im duftigen Blüthenkleide,	the tree in its scented cloak of blossoms,
der Vögel Chor, der mich umklingt,	the chorus of birds that surrounds me
und jubelnd auf zum Himmel dringt –	and presses joyously toward heaven –
Ach Alles jauchzt und theilt mein Glück.	Ah, everything rejoices with me.
Heute wogt es in mir auf und nieder,	Today I feel transported,
ja "heute" schallt's von Aussen wieder,	yes, "today," it resounds from afar,
ja heut' kehrt der Theure dir zurück.	yes, today your dearest returns to you.
O! schwing' auch du, mein liebend Herz,	Oh, rise, too, my loving heart,
dich dankerglühend himmelwärts,	glowing thankfully, towards heaven,
und in dem Lust- und Freudendrang	and filled with all these joyful feelings,
lall' deines Schöpfers Lobgesang.	sing the praises of your maker.

197

Vater, Du im Himmel droben,	Father, who art in heaven,
Du, den alle Welten loben,	You, whom all the world praises,
Vater, Du im Himmel droben,	Father, who art in heaven,
Hör' auch deines Kindes Stimme.	Hear this your child's voice.
Still! Wer naht sich dort der Pforte?	Hush! Who approaches at the gate?
Er sieht herauf, es ist sein Blick,	He looks up, it is his glance,
er ist's, er ist es, Edgar!	it's he, it's he, Edgar!
Ach, verzeihe mir die Sünde,	Ah, forgive my sin,
wenn aus freudetrunk'ner Brust	if from my overflowing heart
ich zum Dank nicht Worte finde	I can find no words of thanks,
in dem Übermaß der Lust.	in the excess of my happiness.
Nichts kann ich fühlen, als dies Glück:	I feel nothing but this gladness:
es kehrt der Theure mir zurück (etc.).	my dearest returns to me (etc.)

After twenty-one measures of orchestral introduction (Andante con moto, D major), Malwina expresses her happy condition in a bit of suitably florid accompanied recitative, modulating to V. The aria proper takes off from the dominant, resolving to the tonic seventeen measures further on, where it remains for another thirty measures, culminating in a rising suspension-chain and pre-cadential chromatic bass ascent from the Neapolitan sixth, *stringendo* and *crescendo* (to the text "Heute wogt es in mir auf und nieder, / ja 'heute' schallt's von Aussen wieder, / ja heut' kehrt der Theure dir zurück" – mm. 71–83, see Example 4.4). The harmonic inflections thus serve merely to accentuate the overall tone of happy anticipation in suggesting something of the elated dynamic of Malwina's "swelling breast." Interpolated between this musical strophe and a cabaletta-like return to the same material and key in a faster tempo (mm. 131ff) are two tonally contrasting "periods," one modulating from D through B♭ (flat submediant) to F (♭ mediant), in which the pious girl turns her thoughts heavenwards (the modulation) and offers an efficient little paternoster (a period of eight plus nine measures with introduction, in F: "Vater, Du im Himmel droben" – the first phrase is included in Example 4.4, mm. 103ff). Her prayers are cut short by the sight of her betrothed, precipitating a quick return to the tonic and the accelerated reprise. This cabaletta-like reprise of the original aria is drawn directly into a duet of reunion in B♭ (with the oxymoronic tempo marking "Allegro affetuoso"), which includes a similar internal "period" of contrasting key and tempo (E♭, 6/8, Andantino: "Ach! entfernt vom Heimatlande stand ich klagend oft") in which the two reflect on their days of separation.

There is nothing particularly outstanding about this example, though it represents well enough how a German composer of around 1830 thought to compose a musical structure whose tonal and "periodic" design responsibly reflected the tenor of the text. Wagner never expressed any great regard for Marschner's talents, in fact, but the design of Malwina's scene and aria and its conjunction with the ensuing re-united lovers' duet (whose B♭ tonality links up with the first contrasting "period" of the preceding aria) can easily be recognized in the opening scene of *Tannhäuser* Act II, or even, at a great distance, Act II of *Tristan und Isolde*. Most importantly, for our purposes, it can be seen as a typical model for the way a larger operatic-dramaturgical unit could have been construed, in Wagner's terms, as an interlocking or even crudely "evolving" series of text-based periods. The point is thus a very general one, and in no way limited to this particular example; any number of similar ones could easily be adduced from virtually any opera in Wagner's early conducting repertoire.

Just one other might be mentioned, as one of two pieces from the oeuvre of the otherwise anathematized Meyerbeer that Wagner was willing to admire: the Act IV *grand duo* from *Les Huguenots*, "Ciel! Où courez-vous? . . . Tu l'as dit: oui, tu m'aimes!"[14] The unwonted critical dispensation granted to this particular number can perhaps be understood in retrospect if we notice the distinct resemblance between the musical dramaturgy (though hardly the music) of the central moment of this scene and the drinking of the fatal draft in *Tristan und Isolde*. An escalating psychological conflict between the leading soprano and leading tenor is suddenly derailed by an unexpected mutual confession of love, yielding to a brief moment of private lyric transport (here the G♭ duet), prior to the renewed onset of an irresolvable dilemma regarding the newly discovered lovers' conflicting obligations to social structures of the outside world. The scene as a whole divides into conventional periods of arioso, recitative (or rather fragmentary declamation), and fully structured duet (the ABA' cantabile "Tu l'as dit" and the similarly structured cabaletta or *stretta* in F minor with dramatized coda, "Plus d'amour, plus d'ivresse"). The modulations within this overall series are neither subtle nor complex, but they are effective all the same. The principal tonal contrasts are those between

---

14 The other instance being the preceding scene of the same opera, the "oath and benediction of the daggers" (no. 23). Wagner's praise of this ensemble scene comes from an essay written at the time of *Rienzi* and the first Parisian sojourn (see n. 15), thus before Wagner had identified Meyerbeer as a sworn enemy and artistic anti-Christ. His praise for the *grand duo*, on the other hand, figures in *Opera and Drama*, the principal locus (after "Judaism in Music") of Wagner's anti-Meyerbeer polemic: "I would recall here in particular several features of the familiar, pathos-laden love scene from the fourth act of the *Huguenots*, and above all that wonderfully gripping melody in G♭ major which, as one of the most fragrant blossoms to spring from a situation that touches every fiber of the human heart, bears comparison only with a very few of the most perfect musical creations" (III, 306).

Example 4.4 Modulating "periods" in Malwina's aria from Act I of
Marschner's *Der Vampyr*

various segments (periods) of agitated F minor and the central lyrical episode in G♭, in addition to two shorter passages in F major in which Valentine twice implores Raoul to desist from his vengeful mission (once before and once after the moment of confession). An evolving – or at least contrasting – series of musical and rhetorical-dramatic "periods" variously departs from and returns to its central tonic (F minor), in accordance with a "poetic intent." Or, to adopt Wagner's words, between the opening and closing lines of the scene we pass through "a long series of other lines . . . , expressing the most varied intensification and admixture of intermediate emotional stages – some stronger, some more conciliatory – before finally returning to the [affective or dramatic] point of departure" (cf. IV, 153–4). "In order to realize the poetic intent of these lines," Wagner's text continues, with reference to his hypothetical "Lust und Leid" example, "the musical setting would modulate through the most varied tonalities; yet every key touched on would appear in its specific relation to the principal tonic key, conditioning the particular expressive light shed by these various tonalities, and to some extent making that light possible in the first place" (IV, 154). This description certainly applies to the effect of G♭ in Meyerbeer's duet, even apart from any inherent qualities we might wish to ascribe to that key. And if we accept the briefly articulated F minor that begins the scene (and that also returns in the scene's second larger "period," at "Le danger presse et le temps vole") as the "principal tonality," then its overall tonal trajectory follows very neatly the prescription of *Opera and Drama*.

All this is not to prove that Marschner and even (*horribile dictu*) Meyerbeer ought to be recognized as prophetic exponents of Wagnerian reform; only that, stripped of the particulars of *Stabreim*, Wagner's conception of a dramatic scene compounded of "poetic-musical periods" does not necessarily constitute such a radical departure from the immediate background of his own operatic experience, both receptive and productive. (I should stress, incidentally, that even though the issue of *Stabreim* dominates the exposition of the "poetic-musical period" idea in *Opera and Drama*, I consider it a red herring with respect to any pragmatic interpretation of this piece of text – which is not to say, of course, that Wagner's *Stabreim* doesn't perform other, analyzable roles in the setting of Wagner's dramatic poetry in general.) Discounting, then, the hypothetical correlation of *Stabreim* with modulatory procedures across the "period," the passage in *Opera and Drama* amounts in large part to a reformulation of familiar prescriptions for the harmonizing of textual and musical structures, although couched in terms that would lead many of Wagner's readers to fear that the requisites of intelligible and pleasing musical form were to be sacrificed to a dogmatic and misplaced faith in the generative powers of a poetic text. Despite the specter of formlessness and anarchy raised by such subversive allegiance to textual (rather than musical) authority, Wagner's proposals have precedents not only in classical traditions of operatic reform theory, as has always been recognized, but even in the practice of contemporary, "unreformed" operatic practice, such as that of Marschner or Meyerbeer. This applies not only to the conventional adaptation of "periodicity" and modulation to the sentiments of the text in question, but, more significantly, to Wagner's stated ideal of creating a larger "evolving series" of periods.

What had particularly (and genuinely) impressed the younger Wagner in *Les Huguenots*, for example, and led him to reject the looser experiments of German Romantic opera, for a time, was the way in which the musical dramaturgy of Scribe's and Meyerbeer's conception allowed smaller lyrical or recitative "periods" to be successfully subsumed into larger levels of scene and even act. During his earlier Parisian days Wagner had written admiringly of "the gigantic, almost oppressive expansion of forms [in *Les Huguenots*], and the masterful disposition (*Anlage und Anordnung*) of musical ideas across large ensembles and scene-complexes."

To actively support such claims I need only mention that greatest of achievements, in this regard, the famous conspiracy-scene from the fourth act of *Les Huguenots* [the "Conjuration et bénédiction des poignards"]. Who can fail to be amazed by the disposition and execution [*Anlage und Durchführung*] of this tremendous piece, and how the composer has managed to maintain a continuous intensification throughout the astonishing length of this number, never once letting up, but only after a tumult of raging passions reaching its most extreme point of expression, the very ideal of religious fanaticism.   (XII, 29–30)[15]

For Wagner, Meyerbeer's achievement lies not so much in the musical expression given to individual words or sentiments, but in the larger dynamic shape he has managed to impress on a series of musical "periods" in which, individually, the accommodation of text to musical phrase may be relatively conventional.

Similarly, the more far-reaching significance of Wagner's notion of the "poetic-musical period" for his own practice, I believe, is not in its re-formulation of the traditional critical trope of a text-music harmonization at a level of local detail, but in the implicit re-conceptualization of how these individual harmonizing textual-musical periods (whether tonally and melodically closed lyrical periods or, now, open "periods" of recitative-arioso synthesis in the newer Wagnerian idiom) might be

---

[15] The exact date of this originally unpublished essay ("Über Meyerbeers *Hugenotten*") is unclear. It was first printed, in excerpted form, by Max Kalbeck in the *Neue Wiener Tagblatt* in 1886, and later by Julius Kapp in *Die Musik* (April 1911). Richard Sternfeld (editor of Wagner's posthumously re-printed writings: see SSD XII, 422) and Ernest Newman (*The Life of Richard Wagner*, vol. I [1933], 224–6) have argued that the essay was written as early as 1837, when Wagner was hoping to prepare the way for a successful entry into the Parisian musical scene. Yet part of their argument – that Wagner would never have written about Meyerbeer in such glowing terms by 1840 – is not entirely tenable: he still praises Meyerbeer as the heir to Handel and Gluck in "Über deutsches Musikwesen" (On German Music), published in 1840, although the passage was deleted from the collected edition of 1871 and subsequent editions (compare GSD I, 166, and R. Jacobs and G. Skelton, trans. and eds., *Wagner Writes from Paris* . . . , 50, where the original text is given in translation). In the "*Hugenotten*" essay, Wagner went so far as to praise Meyerbeer for the "world-historical" cultural contribution of his cosmopolitan universalism and for his veritable "deeds of music" (*Taten der Musik*, XII, 27) – ironically anticipating the phrase he famously coined to describe his own music dramas in 1872 (IX, 306).

arranged according to a forward-directed dramatic or "evolutionary" dialectic, less beholden to the hierarchical musical designs that still dominate Meyerbeerian grand opera to a large extent. As soon as Wagner has presented his hypothetical two-line "period" example in *Opera and Drama* he goes on to exhort the reader to imagine "a longer series of verses containing the most varied intensification and mixture of intermediate . . . emotions" (IV, 153–4). It is with regard to this unspecified "longer series" of verses, in fact, that Wagner stresses the variety of corresponding musical modulation. The same emphasis on the resulting interdependent complex of smaller "periods" recurs throughout this passage of Wagner's text, and especially toward the end. Following the progress of the drama as a whole, these mutually "conditioned" periods will "*evolve* . . . into a rich overall artistic manifestation of human nature . . . , a realization of the highest poetic intent . . ."[16] In the concluding paragraph of Part III, section 3, Wagner condenses these ideas from their rather diffuse context in the sentence just cited and speaks of "the mutually conditioned *evolution* of many such necessary periods" ("das Drama, wie es aus der gegenseitig sich bedingenden *Entwickelung* vieler nötiger solcher Perioden zu erwachsen hat" – IV, 155, emphasis added).

From this perspective, Carl Dahlhaus's objection to Lorenz's "inappropriate" application of Wagner's concept of a poetic-musical period to large expanses of music (sometimes several hundred measures in length) is perhaps misplaced, even if semantically justified. Following the lead of Rudolf Stephan, Dahlhaus criticized the immoderate variety of proportions among the periods designated by Lorenz, ranging from brief phrases of one to two dozen measures up to vast "composite" periods of over 800 measures in length. Lorenz, it is true, made no attempt to relate his formal analyses to details of the *Opera and Drama* passage (aside from the questionable criterion of tonal closure), or to any other instances of contemporary usage. But while Lorenz's terminology may seem arbitrary, and his indefatigable cataloguing of strophic, "Bar," and "arch" forms undoubtedly strains the bounds of analytical common sense in far too many cases – often (though by no means always) short-changing the formative role of text and stage action – his larger or "composite" periods do nonetheless reflect an important aspect of Wagner's procedures that Dahlhaus, in turn, tends to overlook: the emphasis in *Opera and Drama* on the "evolutionary"

---

[16] The original text of this passage reads as follows: "So können wir vorläufig das Kunstwerk als das für den Ausdruck vollendetste bezeichnen, in welchem viele solche Perioden nach höchster Fülle sich so darstellen, daß sie, zur Verwirklichung einer höchsten dichterischen Absicht, eine aus der anderen sich bedingen und zu einer reichen Gesamtkundgebung sich *entwickeln*" (IV, 154, emphasis added).

cohesion of smaller units (periods) into musical-dramatic scenes or even acts. Whether or not Wagner might have conceived such larger articulations at the level of the scene or sub-sections of scenes as "periods," he certainly implies in *Opera and Drama* that his "poetic-musical periods" will bear a relation to this larger level of the scene analogous to the hierarchical relation of traditional periods to the formal divisions of a traditional absolute-musical movement. So we may concede the semantic propriety of Dahlhaus's identification of six periods in the first scene of *Götterdämmerung* Act II (Hagen's dream) in place of Lorenz's single period, but there is obviously no doubt that the scene as a whole represents the operative measure of musical-dramatic form, the whole into which Dahlhaus's (sometimes rather arbitrarily defined) shorter periods coalesce or "evolve."[17] Like Wagner's hypothetical "longer series" of poetic-musical periods, the overall scene maintains a central tonality or *Haupttonart* of B♭ minor in Alberich's refrain, "Schläfst du, Hagen, mein Sohn?" – to which the multiplicity of other tonal areas stands (as Dahlhaus rightly notes) in a "centrifugal" relation rather than one of continuous functional subordination.

Even the largest of Lorenz's periods, at least in absolute number of measures, exhibits significant elements of coherence in its overall tonal design and above all in the audibly structural recurrences of a principal motivic group (*Siegfried* Act I, scene 2, mm. 342–1181). The introductory unit of this long passage – the sixty-four measures beginning with Siegfried's intemperate outburst, "Da hast du die Stücken, schändlicher Stümper" – functions as a kind of sectional refrain or ritornello, encompassing the several internal, contrasting song-like episodes of Lorenz's rondo structure into a perceptible larger entity.[18] And Lorenz can only have been inhibited from extending the form even further to its logical conclusion at m. 1220 (as Siegfried storms offstage, " . . . dich Mime nie wieder zu sehen!") by the fact that it would disturb the tonal symmetry of the overall "period," ending in the relative major (B♭) of the proclaimed G-minor tonic.

Even Lorenz, one supposes, can hardly have failed to realize that any remotely conventional sense of the term "period" has ceased to

<hr>

[17] Dahlhaus, *Wagners Konzeption des musikalischen Dramas*, 77. Both here and particularly in the following analysis of the scene between Brünnhilde and the be-Tarnhelmed Siegfried/Günther (*Götterdämmerung* Act I) Dahlhaus naturally does acknowledge the coherence of smaller periods at the level of the scene. But in neither case does he give much thought to the principles by which these smaller poetic-musical periodic units might be understood to generate a larger "evolutionary" design reflecting the dramatic shape of the scene in question.

[18] Lorenz, *Das Geheimnis der Form*, vol. I, 223–4. See also Anthony Newcomb's proposal of a sectional ritornello-style refrain structure in several other Wagnerian scenes, "*Ritornello ritornato*: A Variety of Wagnerian Refrain Form," in *Analyzing Opera: Verdi and Wagner*, 202–21.

obtain in a passage of these dimensions. And it is precisely a case like this one that points up a more serious objection to this extended usage. For not only Lorenz's criterion of tonal closure (for which he can claim the authority of Wagner's text), but also that of motivic-thematic parallelism or symmetry is predicated on the model of a classical periodicity which obviously no longer obtains as a foundation of the leitmotivic idiom of Wagner's music dramas. This misapplication of classical "architectural" criteria to the evolutionary, "logical" or developmental principles of Wagner's later works is another fundamental point of Dahlhaus's critique of Lorenz. Quite apart from the question of dimensions, Lorenz has overlooked another main point behind Wagner's neologism, the implied alternative to classical instrumental periodicity accomplished by the re-integration of poetic (rhetorical or dramatic) formative principles with those of melodic structure and large-scale musical form. Contrary to the apparent emphasis on the role of a governing "central tonality" or tonic in the *Opera and Drama* passage, the real point of the larger "period" or period-complex identified in Lorenz's period 3 of *Siegfried* Act I must be that its audible musical closure (Siegfried's exit) corresponds with the arrival of new motivic material in a new key: the evolution of smaller, sometimes even distinctly song-like poetic-musical periods arrives at a goal that differs from the point of departure (reflecting Siegfried's growing impatience with his domestic situation and his new resolution to explore the world outside). The tonal and motivic return, in which Lorenz still seeks to ground the "forms" he analyzes, yields here to a process of transformation and substitution. Lorenz's instinct for the dimensions of the formal process is accurate, but he interprets it according to principles of simple "alternation and return" rather than those of "dramatic evolution," as Wagner might have put it.

It may not be possible to reconstruct precisely what Wagner understood by the term "period" at the time of *Opera and Drama*. (His understanding was in any case probably not a "precise" one at all, as I've suggested.) In criticizing Lorenz, Dahlhaus invoked the terminology of A. B. Marx, who recognized as the model of a simple period (*einfache Periode*) an antecedent–consequent phrase of four plus four measures, articulated by half and full cadences and motivic correspondence between halves, which could be doubled to sixteen measures and "extended" by another eight or so.[19] Marx's definition is cited in confutation of Lorenz's "irrational" extension of the term to cover hundreds of measures, while

[19] "Wagners Begriff der 'dichterisch-musikalischen Periode'," 179–80. Dahlhaus provisionally equates Wagner's terminology with Marx's "extended period" (*erweiterte Periode*), citing an example of twenty-two measures. He could equally well have

in the case of Wagner's "poetic-musical" period Dahlhaus himself disallows the criterion of tonal closure (even though it remains consistent among early definitions of "period"), and leaves the other conventional theoretical criteria – binary structure and motivic correspondence – out of the picture altogether. Wagner's own use of the term, as surveyed by Peter Petersen, varied considerably over time.[20] For the most part, it seems to have connoted for him any aspect of traditional "absolute-musical" phrase structure, balanced metrical relations and harmonic complementarity of phrase members, though he also used the term – in a sense similar to Heinrich Christoph Koch's term *Hauptperiode* – to designate an entire sonata exposition or recapitulation. Petersen's specific conclusions regarding *Opera and Drama* are debatable, however. He argues that a poetic-musical period should, according to the evidence of Wagner's text, be defined as a unified segment of *Versmelodie* – the conjunction of vocal line and text in a given passage. He further attempts to equate the concept, through a series of indirect textual parallels, with the rather vague concept of a "dramatic situation" brought up later in *Opera and Drama* (IV, 196), and finally to raise the potential status of the individual period to the level of an entire scene, thus returning us to the same situation we find in the larger periods of Lorenz's analyses.[21] In either case, the inflation of the term to cover the dimensions of a whole scene is unnecessary, since nothing prevents us from analyzing a scene as a series of constituent periods, whether or not a continuously functional tonic is maintained. Many of the smaller

pointed to Marx's concept of the tonally open-ended (modulating) period or *Periode mit aufgelöstem Nachsatz* (characteristic of opening groups from later classical sonata-form movements), which would also provide an exception to the older rule of tonal closure.

[20] Peter Petersen, "Die dichterisch-musikalische Periode." To H. C. Koch's use of the term *Hauptperiode* (see note 12 above), we could add the modified version of this usage in E. T. A. Hoffmann's review of the Beethoven *Coriolan* overture: what Hoffmann here calls the first "period" clearly designates the opening group through the change of key; the second "period" consists of the second theme through the end of the exposition (see Hoffmann, *Schriften zur Musik*, 100).

[21] Petersen, "Die dichterisch-musikalische Periode," 112–13. See also the response by Dahlhaus, "[Zur Diskussion:] Was ist eine 'dichterisch-musikalische Periode'?," *Melos/Neue Zeitschrift für Musik* 4:3 (1978), 224–5, and the subsequent reply by Petersen, ibid., 403–4. Petersen's chain of textual parallels, by which he attempts to equate the scope of a "poetic-musical period," with either a scene or a (vaguely defined) "dramatic situation" becomes entangled in contradictions: the original description of the musical drama (*Opera and Drama*) as comprised of "*many* such [poetic-musical] periods" is made to correspond to a reference from *A Communication to My Friends* in which the drama is described as embracing "a *few* . . . scenes or situations" constituting its "easily surveyable members" (see Petersen, "Die dichterisch-musikalische Periode," 113; emphasis added). At any rate, the excerpt from *Siegfried* Act III, scene 1, that Petersen finally chooses to analyze (taken over from Dahlhaus's essay, and even slightly abridged), consists of merely sixteen measures.

passages analyzed by Dahlhaus, on the other hand, may correspond to a more plausible sense of "period," while they too often fail to take account of the emphasis of the original passage in *Opera and Drama* on the possibility of an evolving, interlocking and "mutually conditioned" series of periods as a counterpart to the dialectical and teleological principles of classically conceived dramatic action (dialogue).

Ultimately, once we discard the overly restrictive details about *Stabreim* and modulation as remnants of an artificial utopian theorizing, we are left with a fairly loose set of basic (implicit) principles, which we might interpret and paraphrase as follows. The architectonic periodicity of classical instrumental forms is to be superseded (in the music drama) by a looser, more "prose-like" approach to melodic structure engendered by a sensitivity to textual rhythm, accent, and rhetorical declamation, while the restricted tonal ambitus of the classical antecedent–consequent period will be opened up to a "wandering tonality," taking full advantage of chromatic and enharmonic relations.[22] Variety of "modulation" or harmonic progression, both within individual phrases and across larger musical expanses, will underline affective "modulation" within the dramatic action, but the effect of such modulations will necessarily continue to depend on their contextual relation to a controlling *Haupttonart* or principal key (whether functional or "centrifugal"). Above all, these harmonically and metrically emancipated text-music units will distinguish themselves from the aimless wandering of recitative by coalescing into larger "evolving" series (presumably up to the level of the scene), defined by a mutually conditioning co-operation of dramatic and musical principles. It is this last aspect of the passage in *Opera and Drama* that particularly deserves to be emphasized, again, and that has been least noted by previous commentators.[23] Whatever we take to represent its dimensions as an

[22] Wagner himself does not invoke the term "musical prose" in this section of *Opera and Drama* (a term he had himself coined earlier in the book, but in a negative context). Nonetheless, the substitution of the metrical freedom of prose for the schematics of verse within the "poetic-musical period" is suggested clearly enough by Wagner's comparison, just prior to the "poetic-musical period" passage, of the "absolute," hymn-like setting of the *Freude* melody from Beethoven's Ninth Symphony and the subsequent, metrically and tonally emancipated, setting of the lines "Seid umschlungen, Millionen" (IV, 149–51).

[23] The term has been cited in countless discussions of Wagner's writings and music, of course, and occasionally glossed. Among those who (briefly) mention the term in discussing Wagner's writings might be mentioned Jack Stein (*Richard Wagner and the Synthesis of the Arts* [Detroit, 1960]), Frank Glass (*The Fertilizing Seed*), and Rainer Franke (*Richard Wagners Zürcher Kunstschriften*). Among those – aside from Lorenz and Dahlhaus – who have applied the category to analyses of Wagner's music are Robert Bailey ("The Genesis of *Tristan und Isolde*: A Study of Wagner's Sketches and Drafts for the First Act" [Ph.D. dissertation, Princeton University, 1969]), Patrick McCreless (*Wagner's "Siegfried"*), and Werner Breig ("The Music," in *Wagner Handbook*).

individual unit, the formal significance of the "poetic-musical period," like that of the conventional, "absolute-musical" period, must necessarily lie in its capacity to be integrated within, or (in this case) to "evolve" into larger meaningful structures.

"Evolving" period-complexes and Wagner's evolution: three dialogues

The music historian's impulse to construct evolutionary models and discover stylistic missing links is nowhere more sorely provoked and frustrated (at once) than by the seemingly inexplicable gap between *Lohengrin* and *Das Rheingold*, mirroring in a sense the frustration experienced by Wagner himself during the long hiatus between these works. To a large extent, the simple absence of intermediate works of any significance renders futile an attempt to speak of the "evolution" of Wagner's style across these crucial years between 1848 and 1853. On the other hand, the radical and mysterious upheavals taking place in Wagner's creative mind during this time did leave substantial verbal, if not musical, traces in the form of the prose writings. The vexing imprecision of Wagner's scattered "technical" formulations in *Opera and Drama* or the *Communication to My Friends* is thus not only a consequence of a problematic prose style, but also of the vagueness with which musical details of the *Ring* project presented themselves in Wagner's mind as yet: the very (musical) "sketchiness," or lack of significant musical profile, of the *Siegfrieds Tod* sketches from about 1850 seems to confirm this.[24] As a result, the music of *Lohengrin* must have continued to provide concrete images, perhaps only half-inadvertently, for Wagner's theoretical speculations – a point that has occasionally been acknowledged, though not specifically with reference to the "poetic-musical period," probably because of the prominent role of *Stabreim* in Wagner's exposition of the idea in *Opera and Drama*. Wagner's musical procedures in the *Ring* may be only imperfectly, sometimes confusingly, adumbrated in *Opera and Drama*. But if we interpret this text not as an infallible key to the later works, but instead as a verbal trace of the "unrealized" intermediate stages that separate

---

[24] These sketches for the Norns' scene in *Siegfrieds Tod* show that Wagner was already attempting to realize some of the structural implications of the text that would eventually inform the final version in *Götterdämmerung*, such as the refrain element and certain parallelisms in the verse (see Robert Bailey's transcription and discussion of the sketches, "Wagner's Musical Sketches for *Siegfrieds Tod*," in *Studies in Music History*, ed. H. Powers [Princeton, 1968], 459–94). But, as Bailey notes, both the declamatory vocal lines and the harmonic language of the accompaniment have more in common with the idiom of *Lohengrin* than with that of the *Ring* as it came to be written (470).

the "Romantic operas" from the "music dramas," we might come to a closer understanding of how Wagner achieved this, his "greatest transition" (to paraphrase Arnold Whittall).[25] Thus, while the poetic-musical period described in *Opera and Drama* may not find any exact counterpart in Wagner's works, an attempt to relate it to ideas of musical and dramatic "period structure" in *Lohengrin*, on one hand, and the earlier *Ring* operas, on the other, might help us to imagine something more of that mysterious and musically undocumented evolution that transpired in Wagner's mind between these works, and to arrive at a fuller understanding of the "evolutionary" ideal of musical-dramatic form hinted at in the theoretical writings of this time.

An essential premise of this evolutionary ideal of form, although not thematized at any great length in *Opera and Drama*, is the centrality of dialogic structure to dramatic form (hence also to the "true" musical drama) and the possibility of establishing a counterpart to this dialogue principle – as a dialectic of confrontation and resolution – in the musical form itself. The "reforming" impulse behind the *Ring*, and already evident in much of *Lohengrin*, is much less a matter of naturalistic declamation (as it was so often thought to be) than of the realization of this fundamental principle of the drama within the opera. According to Dahlhaus, it is this application of a dialogic dramaturgy to musical form which, in addition to the fully developed leitmotif technique, significantly distinguishes the music dramas from the pre-1850 works.[26] Traditionally viewed as poorly adapted to the requisites of musical expression, and hence banned to the arid zones of recitative, Wagner sought to recuperate dramatic dialogue for the melodic-motivic core of opera, and thereby dignify it with the status of "musical drama." Such a recuperation necessitated something more than simply supplying musical accompaniment to dramatic dialogue, as in the idioms of *Melodram* or accompanied recitative. (And while the idea of a musical [instrumental] "dialogue" is familiar enough as a sub-species of the common tropes of music as language and rhetoric, going back a century or more, the conventional means of such instrumental "dialogue" – in which a second voice might variously echo, complete, or otherwise complement the melodic statements of a first voice – would not meet the requirements of a truly dialectic dramatic model.) Wagner's celebrated vanquishing of the closed number involved the devising of a meaningful, compelling musical grammar of motives, phrases, periods, and paragraphs that could actively partake in the dialectic progression of a dramatic argument, rather than serving

---

[25] A. Whittall, "Wagner's Great Transition?: From *Lohengrin* to *Das Rheingold*," *Music Analysis* 2:3 (1983), 269–80.

[26] *Wagners Konzeption des musikalischen Dramas*, 33 ("Dialog und tönendes Schweigen").

merely as emphatic underlining or sonic amplification. Experiments in this direction may be seen in two of the principal dialogue scenes in *Lohengrin* (Ortrud–Friedrich in Act II, scene 1, and Elsa–Lohengrin, Act III, scene 2), while the "annunciation of death" scene in *Die Walküre* (Act II, scene 4) represents one of the most successful realizations of a classically structured dramatic dialogue in the new idiom of Wagnerian musical drama.[27] The musical realization of the dialectic progression toward a climax and resolution (whether the synthesis effected represents triumph or catastrophe) can in each case be analyzed in terms of an evolving progression of "poetic-musical periods." A comparison of these efforts might suggest, if not what this elusive theoretical construct "meant" or "was," in any definitive sense, at least how the idea evolved in the first place, and what eventually became of it, in practice.[28]

Lohengrin *Act II, scene 1 (Ortrud and Friedrich)*

The nocturnal dialogue between the outcast couple, Ortrud and Friedrich, that opens Act II of *Lohengrin* has often been singled out as the one scene from Wagner's earlier operas that most anticipates the style and procedures of the later music dramas. Wagner himself seems to have thought highly of his achievement at the time. At the beginning of 1852, not long after the completion of *Opera and Drama*, he wrote to his friend Theodor Uhlig (who had been charged with producing a vocal score of *Lohengrin* and who was currently promoting Wagner's cause in the pages of the *Neue Zeitschrift für Musik*), directing Uhlig's critical attentions to the Ortrud–Friedrich scene in terms that reflect Wagner's current compositional preoccupations, as documented in Part III of *Opera and Drama*:

Looking through the *Lohengrin* score recently it occurred to me that, since you have been taking an interest in these things, you might write something about the thematic-formal fabric (*thematische Formgewebe*) of the work, and how in this style it continuously leads to new formal structures (*Formbildungen*). The first scene of Act II, among other passages, brought this idea to mind.[29]

The novel thematic-formal structures or "fabric" (*Formbildungen, Formgewebe*) Wagner implicitly boasts of here are foremost a function of the opera's most highly evolved, malleable or "plastic" motive group, the

---

27   The remaining dialogue scene in *Lohengrin* (Ortrud–Elsa, Act II, scene 2) could be discussed in the same terms, though it is less clearly shaped as a whole than the two scenes described here.

28   Werner Breig also draws attention to the potential significance of the dialogue principle for the "poetic-musical period" idea, and to the implication that traditional, "absolute-musical" periodicity is to be supplemented or complemented by a rhetorical-poetical "periodicity" ("The Music," in *Wagner Handbook*, 442).

29   Letter of 1 January 1852 (*Sämtliche Briefe*, vol. IV, 241).

complex of diminished-seventh contours associated with Ortrud's sinister machinations, introduced in the monophonic cello line of mm. 3–17 of the orchestral introduction (see Example 4.5). At the same time, this scene represents the most concentrated attempt, up to this point in Wagner's works, to implement a thoroughly dialogue-based dramaturgy across the length of an entire scene. (In *Mein Leben* Wagner recounts a visit he made to Ludwig Tieck in Potsdam in 1847, during which Tieck is said to have voiced reservations about the feasibility of realizing "scenes such as that between Ortrud and Friedrich" in "operatic" form, thus eliciting a lively demonstration of Wagner's "ideal of musical drama," which, Wagner claims, succeeded in arousing the enthusiasm of this literary *éminence grise* for the possibilities of this scene, in particular.[30]) Whereas the character and structure of the operatic duet-scene is generally determined by the situation given at the outset (or "mechanically" turned about by the introduction of some new information inserted between its principal musical sections), a true dialogue scene should "evolve" as a series of statements and counterstatements, propositions, and refutations, leading to some goal that is not clearly fixed from the beginning. Hence a challenge posed by the music drama was the devising of a new kind of musical "periodicity" somehow analogous to the rhetorical periods or statements of the dramatic argument, an arrangement of phrases and periods that could be understood as tracing such an evolving dialogue rather than one based merely on sectional contrast and complementarity.

Of course, as Dahlhaus and others (especially Guido Adler) have noted, Wagner's attempts to establish a dialogic dramaturgy did not preclude the survival of numerous relics of operatic tradition within his works.[31] In Act II, scene 1, of *Lohengrin* there is no mistaking the role of two such operatic pillars that support the scene as a whole: Friedrich's "rage aria" near the beginning ("Durch dich mußt' ich

---

[30] *Mein Leben*, 360.
[31] *Wagners Konzeption des musikalischen Dramas*, 34. Although Adler made a point of exposing all the vestigial aria-like structures still embedded in the music dramas (whose presence ought to have been plain enough, though it was suppressed by an increasingly doctrinaire Wagnerism by Adler's time), he was one of the first to draw attention to Wagner's efforts to realize a genuine musical "dialogue." "The great value of the formal execution of *Lohengrin*," he wrote, for instance, "lies, apart from a few closed structures, in the musically unified treatment of the [complete] scenes, among which the dialogue scenes, such as that between Telramund and Ortrud, further that between Elsa and Ortrud and the love-scene in the bridal-chamber, are especially strong examples. As freely as the latter scene appears to be structured, it is nonetheless very carefully calculated in the relation of its individual parts" (G. Adler, *Richard Wagner: Vorlesungen* [2nd edn, Munich, 1923], 117; see also 119). Adler's intuition about the "individual parts" of the scene could be translated into an analysis of (proto) poetic-musical periods, as I will suggest.

214

Example 4.5 *Lohengrin* Act II, scene 1 (mm. 1–23): Ortrud's motive-complex

verlieren / mein Ehr', all' meinen Ruhm") – an appropriately regressive gesture, perhaps, to accompany what Ortrud dismisses as childish ranting – and the concluding duo, "Der Rache Werk sei nun beschworen," in which the two figures join in conspiratorial octaves to signify their renewed unanimity of purpose and thereby the resolution of the preceding conflict. Both of these traditional formal "periods" maintain a single tonic (F♯ minor) which establishes an overarching – if not continuously functional – tonality for the scene as a whole, justified by the continuity of scenic and psychic character: night-time, vengeful brooding, sorcery, and conspiracy. (Thus the key appears to correspond to what Wagner referred to as a *Haupttonart* – a controlling or dominant tonality – around which the "poetic-musical period" would revolve.) Up through Friedrich's aria the scene can easily be construed in terms of orchestral introduction, dialogue-recitative and solo aria. Similarly, the scene as a whole could reasonably be read along the lines of a *scena, aria, e duetto*, the kind of scene-complex one can readily find in French or Italian operas from the second or third quarter of the nineteenth century. But while the intervening portion of the scene, from aria to concluding duo, still relies fairly heavily on free recitative or *scena*-style idioms, the whole (including the duo) also traces a continuous evolutionary progression, rooted in the dialogue structure and held together by patterns of tempo, tonality, and motivic recurrence.

Altogether, we might locate three formal levels in this scene, each of which could be identified in some way with Wagner's account of the poetic-musical period.

1 The entire scene could be said to constitute a period of (larger) Lorenzian proportions, as abjured by Dahlhaus, though condoned – in principle, if not in practice – by Peter Petersen (see note 21). The whole revolves around a single *Haupttonart* (F♯ minor), as mentioned, reflecting a governing mood of evil nocturnal brooding. Subsidiary keys and emotions are colored by or shown "in light of" this principal tonality, in the terms of *Opera and Drama*. (The D-major offstage fanfares and modulating Elsa motive that punctuate the orchestral introduction, mm. 53–63, are an example of this, just as numerous instances of D-major harmony as VI in F♯ minor can be cited throughout the scene, in which the "bright" quality of the chord is tempered by its function as either minor sixth or Neapolitan of the tonic or dominant, respectively.)[32]

2 An intermediate level of period is represented by those traces of operatic tradition I have mentioned – rage-aria and revenge-

[32] Compare also the analogous offstage fanfare that follows the close of Friedrich's aria (m. 166), replicating this juxtaposition of F♯ minor and D major.

duo – to which we can add the orchestral introduction and a smaller central "pillar," the nineteen-measure, tonally closed duo-arioso "Du wilde Seherin" (again in F♯, with motivic reminiscences of the introduction). This also signals the turning-point within the dialogue: Friedrich is, despite himself, once again entrapped by Ortrud's heathen wiles (mm. 254–72 of the scene).

3 Finally, these mid-range periods or quasi-numbers break down into more or less conventional periodic combinations of four, eight, or sixteen measures (except for passages in more purely recitative style), sometimes extended or elided. Friedrich's aria, for instance, contains seven phrases of roughly eight measures each, and the vocal lines of the concluding duo consist of three phrase-pairs of 5 + 5, 4 + 4, and 4 + 5 measures, in turn. The arioso-period, "Du wilde Seherin," comprises two eight-measure phrases, elided in m. 261 and extended by four measures of orchestral postlude (a diminution of the initial chromatic descending figure suggestive of Ortrud's arcane powers).

The accompanying table (Figure 4.1) divides the scene into eight mid-range periods, in which the four more structured "pillars" alternate with freer recitative or *scena*-style periods. This level seems to be closest to the description of the poetic-musical period in *Opera and Drama*, while it also demonstrates the probable manner in which Wagner's concept was rooted in the traditional scene-complex of early and mid-nineteenth-century opera, as suggested above with reference to the example from Meyerbeer's *Huguenots*. Such potentially multiple levels of poetic-musical periodicity, on the other hand, have some affinity with the open-ended nature of Wagner's theoretical account of the thing, looking forward to the more fluid formal procedures of the subsequent music dramas.

In referring to the "formal fabric" of the scene (*thematische Form-gewebe*) in the letter to Uhlig, Wagner must have had uppermost in his mind the manner in which the sinuous monophonic motive-complex of the introduction weaves its way throughout, surfacing in six of the eight "periods" I have outlined here. Wagner treats the complex somewhat in the manner of a sectional ritornello, comprised of three more or less discrete entities (marked a, b, and c in Example 4.5).[33] As first introduced, these three elements can even be said to fulfill the beginning, middle, and end functions normally associated with a ritornello group, although "a" obscures the key almost as soon as it has defined it, and "c" can hardly be interpreted as a cadential idea, even though it is

---

[33] The notion of a leitmotivic "ritornello" procedure is borrowed from Anthony Newcomb's analysis of "ritornello" structures in *Tristan und Isolde* (Act II, scene 1) and *Siegfried* (Act I, scene 2) cited in n. 18 above.

Figure 4.1   Lohengrin Act II, scene 1 (mid-range "period" divisions)

period/key(s) (mm.)	motivic material	text/dramatic motif (Ortrud "motive-complex")	tempo
1 orchestral intro. (f#) (1–71)	Ortrud (a)–(b)–(c) *Frageverbot*, stage music (Exposition)	Ortrud and Friedrich, brooding	*Mässig langsam*
2 recitative (72–101)	(b)	dialogue: Friedrich vents anger at Ortrud	*Sehr lebhaft*
3 "aria" (f#) (102–70)	(b), (c) variants and stage music	Fr.: "Durch dich mußt' ich verlieren / mein Ehr', all' meinen Ruhm"	
4 recitative/*scena* (171–253)	(c)	Ortrud–Friedrich conflict	
5 arioso (F#–f#) (254–72)	(c)	Fr.: "Du wilde Seherin!"	*Mässig langsam*
6 *scena* (273–335)	(a)–(c), *Frageverbot* (Quasi-reprise)	Ortrud convinces Friedrich of Lohengrin's deceit	
7 *scena*, continued (336–73) transition (f#–C#–f#) (374–83)		Friedrich's response: "Entsetzlich, ha! Was muß ich hören?"	*Sehr schnell*
8 duo (f#) (383–423)	(a) (Resolution)	Both: "Der Rache Werk sei nun beschworen!" (vengeance pact)	*Mässig langsam*

initially led to a tonic cadence coinciding with the fragmentary statement of the *Frageverbot* in m. 18. This conjunction underscores a rhythmic and intervallic similarity between motive "a" and the opening of the *Frageverbot* (we might expect a return of motive "a" here, at first), creating a gestural ambiguity between the Ortrud and *Frageverbot* ideas that remains operative throughout the scene and in later parts of the opera, as well. This resemblance is also imbued with portentous dramatic ramifications, since Ortrud's primary objective in Act II is to plant the seed of suspicion in Elsa's mind that will eventually lead her to disobey Lohengrin's solemn injunction never to ask his "name or kind."

Wagner's deployment of this motive-complex across the scene contributes, like the recurrent F♯-minor *Haupttonart*, to a loose overall coherence, even if there is no justification to speak of a "symphonic" continuity here, since recurrences of the motive-complex and the key are separated by intervals of non-thematic *scena* and ungrounded, wandering tonality. Key and motive do, however, participate in mirroring the evolutionary progress of the confrontation between the two characters, resulting in a musical design that is, if not "symphonic," nonetheless compelling. The essential dynamic of the scene lies in Friedrich's attempt to wrest himself from Ortrud's malign web of deceit, only to become once again entrapped by the end. Thus, not only does Ortrud's motive-complex (whose sinister, web-like character was noted by Liszt)[34] envelop the first two periods (introduction and *scena*), but it also insinuates itself into the center of Friedrich's aria (period 3), which is thoroughly infused with the diminished-seventh contours of Ortrud's motives (see Example 4.6). Despite his vehement bluster, Friedrich is unable to extricate himself from Ortrud's baleful influence, or, likewise, from the snares of her musical motives.

The dramatic crux of the scene falls in period 6, where Ortrud gradually convinces Friedrich that he is the victim of an unholy fraud. In the course of this heightened *scena*-style exchange Wagner recapitulates the whole of Ortrud's motive-complex, including the juxtaposition with the *Frageverbot* and subsequent sequential development of the "c" member, just as had occurred within the introduction (compare the orchestral introduction with mm. 276–308, beginning from Ortrud's line, "Was gäbst du doch, es zu erfarhen?"). Now the tentative development of this figure in the introduction is carried further, through a process of rhythmic diminution (Example 4.7), as Ortrud works on Friedrich's sense of indignation. In the following turbulent and climactic

---

[34] Describing Wagner's deployment of recurring motives, Liszt draws attention to "the phrase in the first scene of the second act, which winds its way throughout the opera like a poisonous serpent, now ready to coil about its victim, now fleeing from the sight of her holy champion" (F. Liszt, "Lohengrin und Tannhäuser von Richard Wagner," *Gesammelte Schriften*, vol. III, part 2, ed. Lina Ramann [Leipzig, 1881], 94).

Example 4.6 Suggestions of Ortrud's motive-complex (b, c) within Friedrich's "aria," "Durch dich mußt' ich verlieren": *Lohengrin* Act II, scene 1, mm. 119–34

Example 4.7   Rhythmic diminutions of Ortrud motive (c): *Lohengrin*
Act II, scene 1, mm. 308–11, 336–7

period 7 the force of Friedrich's rage pushes him, Osmin-like, outside his established tonal orbit from F♯ minor into a cadence in F minor ("O Weib, das in der Nacht ich vor mir seh"). Ortrud brings him quietly and firmly to his senses, and back to F♯ minor for their concluding duo. Just as this formal revenge-duo signals the resolution of the foregoing confrontation, so Ortrud's head-motive ("a") is correspondingly led to full tonic cadence (at "Der Rache Werk . . ."), which forms the springboard for this brief concluding "number" (see Example 4.8).

The recapitulation-*cum*-development that constitutes period 6 is initially articulated by a brief figure from the introduction that also serves to articulate the final period or coda to the scene (period 8): in each case, the figure is stated twice and then followed by Ortrud's motive "a" (see Example 4.9, a–c: figure marked "x"). The structural weight accorded to period 6 by its motivic recapitulatory function corresponds to its decisive dramatic position (Ortrud convinces Friedrich that he has been deceived). At the same time – as in so many instrumental forms of the later nineteenth century – the recapitulatory force is undercut by new developmental activity, here manifested in the rhythmic transformations of Ortrud's material and in the move from four-bar phrasing to a-metrical recitative and *scena* styles across the end of period 6 and the beginning of period 7. Along with this metrical instability, the initially stable F♯ tonic is also destabilized across period 6. In the next, rhythmically still more agitated period (7) Friedrich's rage rouses him into recuperating the forceful periodicity of his earlier aria, as he also recuperates a firmer tonal ground (this penultimate period, apart from Friedrich's momentary transgression into F minor, acts as a kind of prolonged dominant preparation for the final F♯-minor resolution finally effected by Ortrud's lines, "Ha, wie du

221

Example 4.8 *Lohengrin* Act II, scene 1 (cadential resolution of Ortrud motive at beginning of closing duo)

rasest! – Ruhig und besonnen! / So lehr' ich dich der Rache süße Wonnen"). As in many of Liszt's instrumental forms from this time, the real sense of resolution here is only effected by the "coda" to the overall structure (period 8), the point at which the dialectical confrontation of the two characters is at last resolved. Only here is Ortrud's brooding spite, like her restless motive-complex, momentarily discharged.

As a whole, the scene encompasses two gradual intensifications, each culminating in a violent outburst by Friedrich and capped by a musical-rhetorical peroration effect (the end of periods 3 and 7). Accordingly, the tempo rises consistently over the course of both of these larger sections, from an initial *mässig langsam* (Andante moderato) to a much faster tempo (*sehr lebhaft* in period 3, *sehr bewegt und schnell* in period 7), returning to the original *mässig langsam* tempo for the resolution in period 8. The more "structural" than referential use of motives across the scene might look forward to Wagner's mature leitmotif technique (although it is just as likely a remnant of traditional operatic practices, where a stretch of free *scena* is often loosely bound

Example 4.9 *Lohengrin* Act II, scene 1: articulating gesture (x)
(a) m. 28

(b) m. 272

(c) m. 383

together by some recurrent gestural accompaniment figure). And the way in which small or mid-range periods – corresponding to phases of a dialogue confrontation – are bound together by means of key, tempo structure, and the development and reconstitution of an initial motive-complex might represent a prototype of the evolving series of "mutually conditioned poetic-musical periods" envisioned in *Opera and Drama* (IV, 154–5).

Lohengrin *Act III, scene 2 (bridal-chamber scene)*

The fatal consequences of Ortrud's scheming are played out in the bridal-chamber scene of Act III, at once the beginning and untimely end of conjugal bliss for Elsa and Lohengrin. The structure of this "duet" or dialogue resembles that of Act II, scene 1, in its alternation of more-or-less discrete lyrical periods with intervening recitative/*scena* material. Or, as described by Dahlhaus, the scene "can be broken down . . . into melodic periods without leitmotifs [alternating with] recitative-like

223

interruptions that incorporate motivic citations."[35] The dialectic or teleological character of this dialogue is still more emphatic than in the earlier scene. Here the lyrical, operatic duet as such forms the starting-point of the scene rather than its culmination ("Fühl' ich zu dir so süß mein Herz entbrennen," preceded by an introductory arioso), just as the basic dialectic trajectory is reversed, progressing here from initial con-cord to division and catastrophe. Lohengrin's often excerpted "reproach" to Elsa, "Athmest du nicht mit mir die süßen Düfte?," represents the only other fully formed, independent piece of the scene – a central formal "pillar" analogous to Friedrich's "Du wilde Seherin!" in their earlier scene. The decorous tone and structure of this fixed piece can be under-stood as manifestations of an underlying dramatic idea or "poetic intent": Lohengrin's attempt to persuade Elsa to abide by a code of behavioral restraint and to suppress her self-destructive (feminine) impulses. As the scene progresses inexorably through heightened conflict toward catastrophe, rather than reconciliation, it culminates accordingly in musical-formal disintegration, a passage (following the ambush of Lohengrin by Friedrich and the four nobles) of incipient "musical prose," in Dahlhaus's words.[36] The orderly domestic idyll of the opening duet – reflected in a regular periodicity and tonal closure which Lohengrin vainly tries to uphold in "Athmest du nicht" – yields to disorder and fragmentation. (The honeymoon is indeed over, precipitously terminated by the forbidden question.)

The outlines of this scene are diagrammed in Figure 4.2 along the same lines as for the Ortrud–Friedrich duet. Generally, these period divisions correspond to a single poetic or dramatic-rhetorical "period" in the form of a single statement by one character (in some cases shorter, internal periods have been designated, corresponding to two or four lines of text within a speech, where the setting displays some motivic and/or tonal independence). While purely declamatory, recitative-like textures are largely avoided in this scene, it makes less use of motivic and tonal recurrence as unifying devices than did the Ortrud–Friedrich scene. Dahlhaus suggests that here – in the absence of a continuous motivic network, on one hand, and of larger structuring reprise elements, on the other hand – the musical continuity of the scene depends more on the continuous presence of regular periodicity within these small arioso units.[37] Plausible as this analysis of the situation is, it seems worth asking not only how Wagner varies the

---

[35] "Zur Geschichte der Leitmotivtechnik bei Richard Wagner," 24; cf. *Wagners Konzeption des musikalischen Dramas*, 51–4. The analysis of this scene in the latter context is concerned primarily with variations of melodic periodicity on the local level, and not so much with the design of the scene as a whole.

[36] "Zur Geschichte der Leitmotivtechnik," 24.

[37] *Wagners Konzeption des musikalischen Dramas*, 51ff.

Figure 4.2 Lohengrin *Act III, scene 2 (bridal-chamber scene)*, *"period divisions*

period/mm.	key(s)	musical material/motives	text/dramatic motif	tempo
1 (1–56)	E	introduction and duet	Lohengrin and Elsa express their mutual contentment ("Fühl' ich zu dir," etc.).	*Sehr ruhig*
2 (58–72)	A	"knightly" accompaniment figure in strings, clarinet	Loh.: ("Honor and love drew me to you.")	*Etwas bewegter*
trans. (72–82)	E – C – A♭	Lohengrin motive	Elsa recalls her vision of Lohengrin.	
3 (82–90)	D♭	flowing accompaniment, periodic phrasing	Elsa: "Da wollte ich vor deinem Blick zerfliessen."	*Lebhaft*
4 (93–117)	A . . . F	arioso, broken phrases	Elsa begins to press Lohengrin to reveal his name.	*Immer lebhafter*
5 (117–70)	C	closed "aria" (a a′ b c)	Loh.: "Athmest du nicht mit mir die süßen Düfte?"	*Ruhig bewegt*
6 (174–90)	d	arioso, with slightly agitated accompaniment	Elsa continues to press for Lohengrin's confidence.	*Ruhig*
7 (190–227)	. . . E♭ . . . F	accompanied recit./*scena*	Elsa continues . . .	
trans. (227–44)	. . . A	rhetorical gesture of warning, trombones	Lohengrin admonishes Elsa of her promise to him.	*Langsamer*
8 (244–79)	A	varied repetition of four-measure model	Lohengrin attempts reconciliation with Elsa.	*Viel bewegter*
9 (279–329)	D . . . A	"knightly" figure, trumpets; Ortrud (a) and *Frageverbot*	Lohengrin re-assures Elsa, but repeats warning.	*Sehr ruhig – Etwas langsamer*
10 (340–462)	e	introduction–arioso–*scena*: Ortrud (c) developed, *Frageverbot*	Elsa, overcome by anxiety, poses the forbidden question; Lohengrin is attacked.	*Sehr lebhaft – Schnell*
11 (463–500)	e	final cadence, deferred from period 10 recollection of period 1 (duet) "judgement" motive, Ortrud (a)	Lohengrin stunned, Elsa faint	*Langsam*
12 (501–53)	A/a	*Frageverbot,* fragmented	Elsa is led away.	*Ruhig bewegt*

harmonic and metrical parameters of conventional periodicity within these units (Dahlhaus's principal concern), but also what dramatic-musical strategy governs the concatenation of these ("poetic-musical"?) periods at the level of the scene. What principle does Wagner substitute for the classical hierarchical organization of periodic structures?

The answer, again, is an "evolutionary" principle, derived from the dialogue structure itself with its confrontation of opposing wills. Indeed, this dialogue between Elsa and Lohengrin presents a paradigmatic example of such a dialectic confrontation, climactic catastrophe, and cathartic aftermath. The dramatic trajectory moves, as mentioned, from a point of tranquillity and repose in the opening period (the introductory duet) to the climactic agitation of period 10, in which Elsa finally poses the forbidden question and Lohengrin is simultaneously (indeed symbolically) ambushed by his foes, as if on cue. The concluding two periods – Dahlhaus's passage of incipient "musical prose" – constitute a coda/transition following the structural cadence to the scene (Lohengrin: "Weh', nun ist all' unser Glück dahin"). In executing this trajectory in musical form, Wagner dispenses with unifying motivic substance or large-scale reprise (as Dahlhaus pointed out), although important and now familiar motivic ideas such as the *Frageverbot* and Ortrud's motive-complex establish an increasing, dramatically motivated presence in the later periods. And while the scene begins in E major and concludes in E minor (m. 475, taking Lohengrin's above-quoted words as the principal closing articulation), the key cannot be said even to fulfill the loose, refrain-like structuring role played by F$\sharp$ in Act II, scene 1.

Instead, Wagner has devised a kind of "dialectical" tonal plan here, mirroring the dramatic progress of the scene and reinforced by other musical parameters. The outer periods, in which Elsa and Lohengrin participate together, are tonally closed in E major and minor, respectively, and can to that extent be compared to the formal pillars identified in the Ortrud–Friedrich scene. Where the first period comprises a balanced, decorous exchange of poetic verses and melodic phrases, the exchange in the latter period outlines a desperate acceleration, really more a speech by Elsa with interpolated protestations from her partner. The intervening periods correspond to a single, solo utterance by either character, thus to a rhetorical period or phase within the dialectical confrontation. Lohengrin's periods – numbered here as 2, 5, 8, and 9 – tend toward metrical regularity and all exhibit tonal closure, with a marked preference for his "native" key of A (see periods 2, 8, and 9; the latter two can be interpreted as a single unit in A, despite the subdominant opening of period 9). Three of Elsa's four periods, on the other hand, lack tonal closure (periods 4, 6, and 7), and her music exhibits a consistent gravitational pull to the flat side. Her first solo period (3) is in D$\flat$; period 4 wavers – symbolically, perhaps – between

A (Lohengrin's key) and F major; period 6 centers around D minor (with a prominent role for the minor Neapolitan, Eb minor); period 7 moves between Eb and F. Lohengrin's central C-major arioso, "Athmest du nicht?," might be understood as attempting to mediate between these opposed tonal tendencies. Such a mediating role might even be read in its own internal harmonic activity – the initial modulation to the dominant, in the first phrase, being followed by a large tonal parenthesis in Eb across the second phrase ("So ist der Zauber, der mich dir verbunden") before returning to the tonic.

Dahlhaus remarks of this scene that "schematic periods [eight- or sixteen-measure phrase pairs] exist alongside more differentiated ones, tending to dissolution of conventional structure."[38] Indeed, precisely this juxtaposition contributes to the overall sense of a dialectical progression: just as Elsa parries Lohengrin's sharp-side keys with flat keys, and (after period 3) answers his tonal closure with tonal indecision, so do her periods increasingly tend toward metrical instability. Without falling into straight recitative, her period 4 already resists regular scansion. Period 6 (as Dahlhaus also notes) contains neither rhythmic nor motivic correspondence between its two halves, in the vocal line. And while the following period (7) retains a basic two-measure unit, it, too, fails to scan into regular phrases or periods beyond that level.

Tempo contrasts also participate in the musical dialectic in a manner similar to their role in Act II, scene 1. Nearly every period designated here is articulated by a change of tempo. As in the earlier scene, tempo climaxes are reached near the center of the scene (period 4, *immer lebhafter*) and in the final, critical phase (period 10, *sehr lebhaft*). The actual catastrophe is followed by a moment of almost total stasis and silence (a fermata, and four measures of solo timpani, Adagio), and a synthesis of sorts in the cathartic coda (*ruhig bewegt*).

The agitated tempo of the climactic period 10 is at first counterbalanced by a regular 8 + 8 periodicity (Elsa: "Das Los, dem du entronnen"), lending an articulative emphasis to this beginning. But the periodicity is soon abandoned as Elsa's *Wahn* reaches its fatal peak. As the culmination and turning point of the overall confrontation, period 10 also constitutes the scene's longest continuous passage in a single key (E minor), maintained for 154 measures (mm. 337–491). The subtle but distinct incorporation of Ortrud's motive ("c") from Act II into the melodic contours of Elsa's line further contributes to the climactic emphasis of this period, especially as the preceding periods were largely bare of motivic references. The scene as a whole is bisected by Lohengrin's "Athmest du nicht?" (period 5), as mentioned before. Each of the two larger phases thereby defined (periods 1–5, 6–10) is characterized by a

---

[38] Ibid., 52.

gradual increase in the size and musical weight of its component periods. Period 10, finally, is scanned by two strongly prepared but abortive cadences in E minor (m. 401, m. 450). The deferred resolution of the second cadence (m. 475: "Weh, nun ist all' unser Glück dahin") – following the conspirators' ambush of Lohengrin and coinciding with the abrupt turn to stasis and silence – is both dramatically apposite and musically convincing. Just as this scene inverts the dramatic progress (from discord to concord) of the Ortrud–Friedrich scene, it accordingly inverts the musical goal of a re-established tonal and metrical stability (conjured, as it were, by Ortrud's admonition to Friedrich: *ruhig und besonnen*) to a final condition of fracture and disorder (the shards of Elsa's and Lohengrin's shattered bliss, or *Glück*), embodied in what Dahlhaus described as its musical "prose-like" character. But, like the earlier scene, this too suggests something of the musical background to the evolving complex of "poetic-musical periods" Wagner attempted to describe in *Opera and Drama*.

Die Walküre *Act II, scene 4 ("annunciation of death" scene)*

A fundamental ambition of Wagner's musical-dramatic ideal, as we have seen, was to bridge the gap that existed between the dialogue principle (the underlying structural principle of classical drama) and operatic traditions, which had always tended to relegate dramatic dialogue to the musical peripheries, as recitative.[39] Wagner's aim was not to be realized simply in stretching out sung dialogue over real, periodic melody, however, after the manner of operatic *parlando* (as frequently found in contemporary operatic styles, and in Wagner's own earlier works). Something of his ideal had been anticipated, on the other hand, in Mozart's ensembles, which Wagner later praised as a genuine "dialogicization" of music.[40] In the brochure *On Actors and Singers* (1872) Wagner reflected on the flaws of a traditional operatic economy whereby real dramatic dialogue was either relegated to recitative or merely spoken. Thus in the scene between Kaspar and Max in Act I of *Der Freischütz*, for example, Weber segregates the real dramatic substance, as spoken dialogue, from musical substance, which is channeled into Kaspar's vengeance-aria of a rather conventional cut (Wagner speaks of "all the nonsense of the monologic aria," IX, 208). Hearing the dialogue performed to Berlioz's recitatives, in Paris, only made Wagner aware of how "not even the most animated recitative" was an adequate solution to the musical realization of a

---

[39] *Wagners Konzeption des musikalischen Dramas*, 33.
[40] (X, 154): "Der Dialog wird hier ganz Musik, und die Musik selbst dialogisiert" ("On Operatic Poetry and Composition in Particular," 1879).

scene of this sort: "rather, an entirely different means of development was needed, according to which the dialogue itself should be raised to a level of music (*der Dialog selbst . . . zur Musik erhoben worden wäre*) that would make the appendage of a fixed aria, such as Kaspar's here, completely unnecessary."

The raising of the dramatic dialogue to the principal object of the musical treatment, just as it is the most important and truly engaging component of the drama, would therefore determine also the purely musical structure of the whole, from which the individual vocal numbers traditionally inserted between the dialogue portions would now disappear altogether. Instead, the musical essence [of this new musical dialogue] would help to maintain the continuous fabric of the whole, indeed, it would be extended to constitute the whole.

But the key to overcoming the unfortunate division of labor between dialogue and music in traditional opera, Wagner now realizes in retrospect, lies not only in the loosening of metrical period structure into a freer "prose-like" idiom, but, more significantly, in the availability of a repertoire of flexible leitmotifs. If only Weber had thought to deploy motives from the surrounding musical numbers, Wagner suggests (Kaspar's demonic *Trinklied* or the subsequent vengeance aria),

how significantly he could have expanded [this material] and added to it, by working it into a musical setting of the entire dialogue scene [originally separating these numbers], and this without sacrificing a single word of the dialogue to the supposed demands of operatic aria. To accomplish this, we would have to suppose that Weber . . . would not use the orchestra merely to accompany the dialogue in the manner of a recitative, but instead to support that dialogue in a symphonic style, continuously suffusing the dialogue just as blood suffuses the veins of the body . . . (IX, 208–9)

While Wagner was perfectly well aware of Weber's use of recurring "characteristic motives" (as he acknowledges in this same passage of the 1872 essay), he highlights the fundamental difference between Weber's (or his own) occasional reminiscence motives and a consistent application of "leitmotif" that would allow the orchestra full participation in the dramatic dialogue.

Leitmotif, then, turns out to be the missing ingredient in Wagner's formula of the "poetic-musical period," the ingredient that would permit such "periods" to evolve along the same lines as the interacting "periods" of phases of a dramatic dialogue. In our *Lohengrin* examples, the impression of a musical dialogue or argument is still confined to the middle and larger level of "period," without infiltrating or "suffusing" the actual fabric of the musical body at the melodic level. Recurring figures such as Ortrud's motives or the *Frageverbot* audibly recall for us the underlying motives or motivations at work, but without constituting the subject-matter of a continuous argument.

By the time of *Die Walküre* Wagner had come considerably closer to the realization of this goal of a true musical dialogue, or a "dialogic" musical form. The fourth scene of Act II, the so-called "annunciation of death" (*Todesverkündigung*) by Brünnhilde to Siegmund, represents another classically structured dialogue argument or dialectic confrontation which can now genuinely be said to generate (or engender) a parallel musical "dialogue" – a musical dialogue in which motive, tonality, tempo, accompaniment, and so forth all participate to a much fuller extent than in the two *Lohengrin* dialogues. Whether the music here must be understood as mirroring the dramatic dialogue, or whether we might imagine that aspects of the confrontation between Brünnhilde and Siegmund are in some sense motivated by the musical "action" (or some other configuration of mutual implication) is a hypothetical question that can be left open, for now.[41] The co-ordination of dramatic and musical dialogue in this scene can, in any case, serve as one exemplary instance of how a mature Wagnerian dialogue scene might (still) be construed in terms of "poetic-musical periods," as an evolving series of textual and musical units whose coherence lies not so much in any perceptible, diagrammable formal design, but in the psychological trajectory mapped by an escalating conflict of wills leading to a climactic resolution.

The "annunciation of death" scene in *Die Walküre* reverses the dialectic pattern of our previous example, the bridal-chamber scene in *Lohengrin* (thus returning us to something like our first model). Here the scene begins not with sweet and happy concord, but with a dire prophecy of doom, which Siegmund counters with determined resistance. The conflict eventually progresses to a brief but glorious moment of ecstatic, harmonious consensus. The progress of this encounter can be divided into three fairly distinct phases (which closely correspond, as it happens, to the three "periods" described by Lorenz in this scene).[42] The first of these phases consists of Brünnhilde's formal annunciation to Siegmund that he has been chosen to join the ranks of fallen heroes in Valhalla, provoking a series of questions posed by Siegmund in order to clarify the meaning of this unwelcome oracle. In this series of

---

41 Wagner's notion of the orchestra as an active participant in the dramatic dialogue (as intimated in the passage from *On Actors and Singers*) has suggestive ramifications for the whole line of recent operatic criticism growing out of ideas about the cognitive rapport between singer and orchestra first explored in Edward T. Cone's *The Composer's Voice* and subsequently in "The World of Opera and its Inhabitants," in *Music: A View from Delft* (Chicago, 1989), 125–38. This cognitive rapport, as I have called it, between voice and accompaniment is a recurrent theme in Carolyn Abbate's discussion of operatic narratives (rather than dialogues) in *Unsung Voices*, and is also the subject of a critical dialogue (argument, anyway) between Peter Kivy and David Rosen in vols. 3 and 4 of the *Cambridge Opera Journal* (1991–2).

42 See A. Lorenz, *Das Geheimnis der Form*, vol. I, 179–84.

terse, two-line questions, Siegmund inquires who Brünnhilde is; where he is to follow her; if he will find *Walvater* (Wotan) alone in Valhalla; if he will find his own father there; if a woman will be there to greet him. Siegmund accepts the answers to these questions without comment, up to the last of them. Dissatisfied with the evasive response to this last question that Wotan's "Wish-maidens" will attend the fallen hero in Valhalla, Siegmund comes directly to the point in a final question, this one rhetorically augmented to eight lines of text: will Siegmund find Sieglinde there?

Brünnhilde's negative response, coinciding with a striking musical disjunction (V^7 of E minor resolved deceptively to E♭[D♯] minor $^6_4$: "Erdenluft muß sie noch atmen"), initiates the second phase of the dialogue. Here begins the explicit conflict of wills, the argument. Siegmund refuses to accept these tidings. Brünnhilde insists that he must. This central phase is interrupted, in turn, by Siegmund's sudden concern for the unconscious Sieglinde ("Schweig, und schrecke / die Schlummernde nicht!"), and a momentary interlude in which he addresses her – apostrophically, in a sense – and the evil circumstances that face them both. Brünnhilde is moved by this display of passionate temperament (*erschüttert*, the stage directions describe her altered bearing). Now it is her turn to ask a question ("So wenig achtest du / ewige Wonne? / Alles wär dir / das arme Weib . . . ?"). Here begins the third and final phase of the confrontation, as Brünnhilde is progressively persuaded by Siegmund's inflexible resolve, and ultimately by his desperate threat to kill both Sieglinde and himself. At first Brünnhilde pleads to Siegmund to entrust his sister to her. Failing this, she ultimately decides to disobey Wotan's unwilling decree and to protect Siegmund in battle, after all ("Halt ein, Wälsung, / höre mein Wort! / Sieglinde lebe – / und Siegmund lebe mit ihr!"). The conflict of wills leads, in this case, to a reversal of the original situation. The solemn angel of death is transformed back into the spirited Valkyrie, the ebullient Brünnhilde who first swooped on-stage at the outset of Act II.

According to the quasi-naturalistic aesthetic of *Opera and Drama*, the musical realization of such a dialogical confrontation – leading as it does to a new and unforeseen resolution – should eschew formal reprise in favor of an evolutionary process that can track the transformation of the dramatic situation rather than subordinating it to an artificially rounded closure. In a somewhat cruder way, the conventional cavatina-tempo di mezzo-cabaletta series of solo or duo scenes in Italian opera was adapted to similar ends, permitting a concluding phase (cabaletta) that was programmatically contrasted to the initial or central phase (cavatina) in terms of key, tempo, material, instrumentation, and so forth. The mid-range periods described in the two *Lohengrin* scenes, as suggested above, still bear a vestigial relation to these traditional operatic divisions: the multiplicity of small, clearly formed contrasting "periods" in the bridal-chamber scene of *Lohengrin* could be viewed as a kind of atomization of the Italian model, while the earlier Ortrud-Friedrich duet in *Lohengrin* bears a still stronger imprint of the conventional operatic scene-complex. The model of the Italian operatic scene, however, did not impose any overarching tonal closure, but, on the contrary, more often involved a deliberately radical contrast of keys between its principal sections, forfeiting any claims to tonal "unity" (and to this extent anticipating the tonal freedom and text-responsiveness advocated by Wagner's description of the poetic-musical period, at least on a very broad scale). Wagner, on the other hand, seems even in the Romantic operas of the 1840s to have been at some pains to effect a compromise between bold, dramatically motivated contrasts, linear and goal-directed (dramatic) trajectories, on one hand, and some vestige of large-scale musical closure at the level of the dramatic scene, on the other. Where the tonal unity of the Ortrud– Friedrich scene is dramatically justified, it is unclear whether Wagner might have expected the E-minor cadential "period" of the Elsa– Lohengrin confrontation (Act III, scene 2) to be perceived as a tonal rounding of the scene, which began in E major. In any case, the later scene suggests one reasonable alternative to straightforward reprise in an evolutionary or teleological dramatic context, and an alternative very much in tune with the compositional *Zeitgeist*: a transformational reprise, typically involving a shift of mode and tempo, as is the case here. The "annunciation of death" scene in *Die Walküre* makes much more extensive use of such transformational techniques, which it applies to a motivic refrain-complex along the lines of that in the Ortrud–Friedrich scene (here, the hieratic music of Brünnhilde's "oracle"). To a limited extent, it also applies a more innovatory process of motivic and tonal substitution, something Wagner had experimented with in parts of *Das Rheingold* as a means of reconciling dramatic and musical "logic."[43]

[43] The first scene of *Das Rheingold*, for instance, could be construed as a process in which C minor is gradually substituted for E♭, while the "Renunciation of Love" and Ring motives are substituted for the songs and refrains of the Rhine-maidens that dominate the opening of the scene. (The descriptive, flowing accompanimental figures of the strings serve to bind the whole together, of course.) A similar substitution process can be identified in the end of scene 3 of *Das Rheingold*, beginning from Loge's words, "Hohen Mut verleiht deine Macht" (mm. 2354–416), where, again, a new refrain (a parodistic variant of the Valhalla motive) substitutes for an initial refrain, derived from Loge's motive. Here, too, is one of many cases in which a larger unit identified by Lorenz (his fifteenth period) is indeed audible as a formal entity, while his scanning of its putative interior form obscures the subtlety of an "evolving" design in favor of artificial symmetries – an "architectural" model of form is imposed on Wagner's "logical" model, in the terms Dahlhaus borrows from Jacques Handschin. On these passages see also T. Grey, "Wagner and the Aesthetics of Musical Form in the Mid-Nineteenth Century," 327–31.

Example 4.10   *Die Walküre* Act II, scene 4 ("annunciation of death" scene): opening Bar (mm. 1–12)

(Brünnhilde, leading her horse by the bridle, comes out of the cave and advances slowly and solemnly to the front.)

The first phase of the dialogue opens with a formal exposition of motivic material (and key, though the tonality is already characterized by incipient "centrifugal" tendencies). The formality of this exposition corresponds, of course, to the grim ritual of the Valkyrie's solemn office. In fact, the principal motives here – the twofold (sequential) "Fate" motive followed by the more melodically distinct *Sterbegesang* phrase (as Wolzogen labeled it) – form a genuine miniature *Bar* form which, when repeated one step higher and closed by a fragment of the Valhalla motive, combines to form a larger twenty-nine-measure *Bar* in F♯ minor (the smaller *Bar*, described by the two principal motives of the scene, is shown in Example 4.10 – [mm. 1–12]). The near-repetition of this series in mm. 30–55, as Brünnhilde first sings, naturally led Lorenz to extend the nesting *Bar* forms he discerned here to yet one higher level. (In fact, the multiplicity of *Bar* forms he discovered in the scene

233

as a whole compelled Lorenz to invent the delightfully Nietzschean designation of *Über-Stollen* and *Über-Abgesang* for the very highest level, corresponding to what I have identified as the three principal phases of the overall dialogue process.) This next higher-level formal interpretation is plausible to the extent that mm. 67–133 of the scene – the remainder of the opening question-answer group that follows the initial exchange – are united by a refrain-like recurrence of the "questioning" phrase (the *Sterbegesang*), set each time to the same syncopated accompaniment.[44] Brünnhilde's answers form episodic contrasts to Siegmund's questioning refrain. The tonal contrast of these "episodic" responses is reinforced by clear motivic contrasts (generated by textual associations), creating a dialogue of smaller "periods" that can be roughly paraphrased as follows:

Siegmund:	"Where do you lead the hero?" (Question motive, F♯ minor)
Brünnhilde:	"To Walvater, who has chosen you . . ." (Valhalla motive, A – E)
Siegmund:	"Will I find him alone there?" (Question motive, A minor C)
Brünnhilde:	"Fallen heroes will also greet you" (Valhalla and Valkyrie motives, D)
Siegmund:	"Will I find there Wälse, my father?" (Question motive, B minor – V of E)
Brünnhilde:	"The Wälsung will find his father there" (Valhalla, C)
Siegmund:	"Will a woman greet me there?" (Question motive, A – V of D)
Brünnhilde:	"Wish-maidens will serve you there" (Freia/Woman motive, D♭)
Siegmund:	"Fair and holy as I perceive you . . ." (rhetorical preparation of last question): "Will the brother be accompanied by his conjugal sister? Will Siegmund embrace Sieglinde there?" (Question motive, F♯ minor – V of E)
Brünnhilde:	"Earthly air she must still breath; Siegmund will not see Sieglinde there" (E♭ minor, non-motivic).

[44] The designation applied by Wolzogen and Lorenz to the opening ("Fate") motive of the scene, *Schicksalsfrage* or "fate-question," evidently responds to the interrogative intonation this figure adopts from the vocabulary of traditional recitative. In the subsequent dramatic context of this scene, however, the designation "fate-question" would be more appropriately applied to the second motive (Wolzogen's *Sterbegesang*) – which also incorporates the "questioning" half-cadence gesture of the first motive – because of the way it accompanies systematically each of Siegmund's questions to Brünnhilde. The origins of this "questioning" gesture in traditions of eighteenth- and nineteenth-century operatic recitative are discussed by Deryck Cooke in *The Wagner Companion* ("Wagner's Musical Language"), ed. P. Burbidge and R. Sutton (New York, 1979), 225ff. In the following discussion, and in the accompanying

The tonal contrasts between these small periods could recall Wagner's account of the poetic-musical period in that short, contrasting dramatic statements move freely between relatively distant tonalities, in accordance with the shifting emotional perspective of the speaker. Brünnhilde answers Siegmund's first F♯-minor refrain in the relative major and its dominant. When she seeks to evade his question about the female inhabitants of Valhalla, Brünnhilde slips from V⁷ of A into D♭ (♭III) – a key and/or relation evidently intended to sound soft and "feminine" (underscored by high woodwinds and harps, as well as the motive associated with Freia and womanly charms in general) – but the tonal evasion is in any case an apt reflection of this stage of the dialogue process (Brünnhilde's evasive response).[45] Similarly, the striking tonal disjunction of Brünnhilde's last, negative response ("Erdenluft muß sie noch atmen"), created by the substitution of E♭ minor for E♮, constitutes a six-measure "period" in E♭ minor of the (implicitly) miniature dimensions of the original *Opera and Drama* example. The immediate gesture is the kind of "modulation" (or *Ausweichung*) that could only be dramatically motivated, according to Wagner. It is one of many cases in the *Ring* where such a harmonic *Ausweichung* – literally "evasion" – assumes a kind of metonymic relation to the text (other examples can be found in Loge's music in *Das Rheingold*, as we might expect).

Striking, momentary gestures are likely to pall, however, if they merely accumulate as a mass of free-floating particles, ungrounded in any larger musical design or process. Thus the placement of this sudden tonal disjunction between E minor and E♭ minor, as suggested above, is by no means random, but serves to articulate – even motivate – the second larger phase of the dialogue. This phase, beginning after m. 157 (Siegmund: "Zu ihnen folg' ich dir nicht!"), is readily construed as a transformed reprise of the opening of the scene, developed from the same miniature *Bar*-form conjunction of Fate and Question (or *Sterbegesang*) motives, now intensified by an agitated turn-figure in the violas and a gradually amplified orchestration. Most significantly, the ritual formality of the opening is now undermined by the rhetorical thrust of the dialogue, on both sides. Brünnhilde twice interrupts the normal course of the Question motive (having arrogated it to herself) with a new, angry and emphatic octave gesture over diminished-seventh harmony (" . . . mit ihr mußt du nun zieh'n!" . . . "[Tod] dir zu künden / kam ich her"). Siegmund, for his part, introduces the sword motive – emphatically but to no avail. And finally he takes his own turn to

Figure 4.3, I have chosen to designate this second, more developed melodic figure as the "Question" motive, and Wolzogen's *Schicksalsfrage* simply as "Fate" (as it is usually dubbed in English).

[45] The same scoring, motive, and key (written as C♯ major) return momentarily when Siegmund mentions the "Wish-maidens" again slightly further on, in mm. 153–5.

interrupt the progress of the dialogue ("Schweig, und schrecke / die Schlummernde nicht!"), initiating the brief interlude that recalls the music of the previous scene (the siblings' flight). Throughout the second phase, the musical formality and self-control of the interlocutors are progressively eroded.

Another transformational reprise initiates the third and last phase of the dialogue, in which Brünnhilde is ultimately persuaded to protect Siegmund, in flagrant disobedience to her appointed office. This second "reprise" develops only the second motive (the Question motive, or *Sterbegesang*), in rhythmic diminution (reflecting the accelerated dramatic pulse) and with further amplification of orchestral texture. Functioning now as an initiating gesture, rather than as *Abgesang* to the Fate motive, the Question motive might be heard as a reprise of Siegmund's question-series rather than of the opening of the scene itself. As if to support the motive in this new structural role as initiating gesture, it is provided with a rhetorical anacrusis derived from the so-called "Flight" motive (*pace* Deryck Cooke) of the preceding interlude. The new anacrusis is consistently woven into the texture of the following periods, while the Question motive is further reinforced by a new consequent extension. "Question" is thus transformed into "statement": Siegmund is no longer asking questions, but issuing desperate ultimatums. (The anacrusis and expanded form of the Question motive are shown in Example 4.11.)

While the musical weight of the second quasi-reprise is augmented by the addition of the anacrusis, consequent extension, motivic accretions (the agitated violas of the first "reprise" expand their activities here), increase of rhythm and tempo, orchestral texture, and so forth, stable metrical periodicity is by no means maintained. The ritual formality of Brünnhilde's initial appearance to Siegmund and of their question-and-answer exchange has been thoroughly ruptured by now. The rapid musical gesticulations that accompany Brünnhilde's sympathetic conversion are scarcely recognizable as transformations of the solemn Question motive, though they do in fact derive from it (see Example 4.12). In place of the ritualized, hierarchical *Bar* forms of the scene's opening, the formative element of its last pages is a strong cadential drive, at first toward F$\sharp$ major, and then toward A major. The "centrifugal" tonal tendencies of the opening, moving out from an F$\sharp$ center, are replaced by a "centripetal" tendency (towards A), here and across the brief orchestral postlude/transition that prolongs the cadential A$_4^6$. Thus, in addition to the process of motivic transformation across two principal "reprises" (in phase 2 and phase 3 of the dialogue, respectively), the musical structure of the scene is loosely plotted along the lines of a substitution process: the (transformed) secondary motive of the opening complex, the Question (*Sterbegesang*), gradually usurps the priority of

Example 4.11 "Annunciation of death" scene: expanded variant of Question (*Sterbegesang*) motive with anacrusis (mm. 255–61)

[Siegmund: "So jung und schön erschimmerst du mir: doch wie kalt und hart erkennt dich mein Herz!"]

the Fate motive sequence, and in the final phase of the dialogue A major gradually substitutes for F♯ as the tonic key. (This process of motivic and tonal substitution is sketched approximately in Figure 4.3.) The refrain element of the Ortrud–Friedrich scene and the elements of transformation and substitution in the bridal-chamber scene of *Lohengrin* are synthesized and further developed in the course of this more fully "evolving" musical dialogue in *Die Walküre*.[46]

---

[46] Another point of comparison for the "annunciation of death" scene as an evolution of musical periods after the dialogue model would be the final scene of *Die Walküre* Act I. The culmination of both scenes is infused with a dynamic instability through a vacillation between traces of the original minor key of the scene (E minor, F♯ minor, respectively) and the drive to establish the relative major as ultimate tonal goal (G major, A major). In both cases, but more emphatically in Act I, the overall tonal trajectory is deflected toward flat key areas across the center of the process, corresponding to a deflection of the dramatic trajectory (the moonlight, Siegmund's "Spring Song" and its consequences, in the first case; Siegmund's brief apostrophe to the sleeping Sieglinde, in the second).

Example 4.12 "Annunciation of death" scene: final transformation of Question motive (mm. 324–7)

[Brünnhilde: "Und Siegmund lebe mit ihr!"]

Figure 4.3 Die Walküre *Act II, scene 4 ("Annunciation of death" scene)*

Ft = Fate motive
Qu = Question motive (*Sterbegesang*)

1st "reprise"

motive:	Ft–Qu		Qu Qu Qu Qu		Qu	Ft–Qu	Ft–Qu
key area:	...f♯ (G♭)	f♯	a	b	A ...D♭	F♯	f♯	g–c

measure no.   50   100   150

2nd "reprise"   (new   "Coda"
                   material)

Ft		Ft	Qu Qu Qu				
V/f♯	V/b♭	...V/f♯	f♯	b	a	A...	F♯	A...

200   250   300   350

But does the rather dense assembly of musical and dramatic detail presented here finally resolve itself into some rational, surveyable series of (poetic-musical) "periods"? I have avoided tallying these by number and key, as attempted in the case of the preceding *Lohengrin* examples, since I believe that the closer Wagner came to realizing the principles intimated in *Opera and Drama* – in this case, his notion of "poetic-musical periods" – the further he drifted from the terms of their theoretical formulation. This is hardly an original insight, I confess. It has always been a commonplace of Wagner criticism that the composer successively "overcame" the limiting strictures of his own reformist theories. But perhaps the Hegelian figure of sublation (*Aufhebung*) would be more apt, a process whereby theory is not so much resisted or rejected as it is dissolved into a subtler, more differentiated practice. It only stands to reason that the vague, "objectless" and occasionally misguided theorizing of *Opera and Drama* should find some points of contact in Wagner's eventual practice without providing anything like a full and perfect account of it. Already in the eighteenth century when writers such as Mattheson and Koch first appropriated the rhetorical category of the "period" to designate units of musical thought or "speech," its theoretical relation to larger musical forms had been elusive.[47] Wagner's adaptation of the category a century later can be understood as an attempt to reach back beyond the now ossified theoretical applications of the term in nineteenth-century theoretical discourse (the Marxian four- or eight- or sixteen-measure period) to its rhetorical, "poetic" origins, as a means of illuminating experiments in dramatically conceived or "motivated" musical processes, such as that of the dramatic dialogue or argument.

It would be a mistake to couch these issues entirely in terms of the invidious dichotomy of theory versus practice, in which theory will always lose out. The "theory" of the poetic-musical period (like the provisional theory of leitmotif in *Opera and Drama*) was partly predicated on the practice of Wagner's "Romantic" operas (especially *Lohengrin*, as I have tried to demonstrate), even while it struggled to imagine a practice for the unwritten *Ring*. Already in *Lohengrin*, however, the dialogue scenes are easily scanned as a series of motivically and tonally defined "periods," often exhibiting the tonal closure apparently prescribed by the *Opera and Drama* example, in addition to traits of conventional metrical-harmonic periodicity. That Wagner should have worked to minimize conventional periodic closure in his subsequent practice is perfectly in accord with the theoretical spirit of *Opera and Drama*. The account there of short, freely modulating, but tonally closed periods had also proclaimed an ideal of "many such periods"

---

[47] See Mark Evan Bonds, *Wordless Rhetoric*, 79.

evolving over larger spans of dramatic-musical time, a process that would evidently subordinate periodic closure to some larger teleology at the level of a dramatic scene or act. In fact, a closer look at the end of this text reveals that Wagner does not speak of any species of "musical form" resulting from this evolving series of periods, but only of "the drama" ("the drama, as it will grow from the mutually conditioned evolution of many such necessary periods").[48]

Wagner insists that music can and must look to drama for a model of evolutionary process, as perhaps its sole means of historical salvation. But if we are to take Wagner's metaphors of biology and natural science seriously (see chapter 3 above), the "evolution" of a musical scene-form ought be generated also from within, not merely from without. Music, after all, is said to be the nurturing matrix of the "perfected drama of the future." A convincing musical evolution or "dialogue" process must do more than merely follow a set of verbal cues, mirroring or shadowing the dialogue of the characters on stage. The tonal progress of a scene, the manner of its motivic transformations (or substitutions), patterns of tempo change, textural growth and contrast, and so forth must give the impression of a legitimate – if not exactly pre-determined or inevitable – evolution in its own right. It was of course an aim of an earlier generation of analysts (Lorenz, Kurth, and August Halm) to demonstrate that the music of the music drama had such a life of its own. But "the impression of a legitimate evolution in its own right" (the aim I have imputed to Wagner's musical development) need not be construed as a strict autonomy. Wagner himself never went so far as to advocate the virtual autonomy of the music to his dramas, even in later years. At most, perhaps the (sexual) intercourse of poetry and music imagined in the metaphors of *Opera and Drama* gave way to something more like a dialogue, in which the power relations implicit in the earlier gendered model became less clearly (pre-)determined.

The attributes of the "purely human" (*rein-menschlich*), "instinctive" (*unwillkürlich*), and natural freed from the corrupt, restrictive, and "arbitrary" (*willkürlich*) dictates of fashion or convention – this complex of oppositions informs Wagner's ideal (or illusion) of his musical form at all levels. All these variations of an underlying, all-pervasive binarism of nature versus culture are readily exposed as products of rhetorical artifice, on Wagner's part, as far as the historical substance of his music is concerned. But the opposition of empirical "truth" and rhetorical artifice may be no more tenable, in the last analysis. The terms in which Wagner sought to construct his music and the larger cultural project in

[48] " . . . das Drama, wie es aus der gegenseitig sich bedingenden Entwickelung vieler nötiger solcher Perioden zu erwachsen hat" (IV, 155).

which it was to participate can still provide a window on both the music and the larger project themselves. And the same conceptual oppositions that distinguish such formal ideas as the "poetic-musical period" (nature, evolution) and the dialogue idea (human relations, interactions, development) from what is perceived as conventional, mechanical, and arbitrary figure again within the broader category of "melody," in which the individual "period" is subsumed (in Wagnerian and conventional theory alike). Some reflections on a still more famous and more contested locution from the Wagnerian lexicon – "endless melody" – will serve to put the issues raised by the "poetic-musical period" in a broader musical and cultural perspective.

5

Endless melodies

Beckmesser.	*Zwar wird's 'ne harte Arbeit sein:*
	wo beginnen, da wo nicht aus noch ein?
	Von falscher Zahl, und falschem Gebänd'
	schweig ich schon ganz und gar;
	zu kurz, zu lang, wer ein End' da fänd'!
	[. . .]
Several masters.	*Man ward nicht klug! Ich muß gesteh'n,*
	ein Ende konnte keiner erseh'n.
	[. . .]
Kothner.	*Ja, ich verstand gar nichts davon!*
Beckmesser.	*Kein Absatz wo, kein' Coloratur,*
	von Melodei auch nicht eine Spur!

– Die Meistersinger *Act I, scene 3*

Wagner and his critics around 1860 (Wagner's melody – all or none?)

Even before *Tristan* (or *Die Meistersinger*) had reached the public's ear through staged performances, the complaint that Wagner's music suffered from a dearth of perceptible "melody" had become a *Grundmotiv* of anti-Wagnerian criticism. This charge of "lack of melody" was bound up, understandably, with the related charge of formlessness, both at the level of the closed number as a whole and at the level of individual phrase units and harmonic-metrical periodicity. Thus an important strategy of Wagner's response (primarily in *"Music of the Future,"* 1860) to a growing body of hostile criticism was, first, to re-define the nature of "melody" and, second, to assert the functional equivalence of melody and form (where there was one, there was the other). Both components of this defensive critical strategy are grounded in Wagner's perceptions of his own "evolving" musical procedures (in both senses), but at the same time both – the reassessment of the nature or essence of melody and the identification of melody with "musical form" – could draw on the authority of a long tradition of Enlightenment discourse on the origins of music and language (in

242

vocal melody) as a system of "natural signs" for human feelings, and a theoretical–pedagogical tradition that viewed musical form as a function of "melody" according to a hierarchical progression from motive and theme through phrase and period to section and movement. Before pursuing further the aesthetic and theoretical background of Wagner's *apologia pro melodia sua* in "*Music of the Future*," as well as his adaptation of the melody–form equation to his own music, let me begin by considering some examples of the criticism to which these things were meant as a response.

In voicing their perplexity at Walther's "Trial Song" in Act I of *Die Meistersinger* the masters, led by Beckmesser, loudly complain that there seems to be "no end in sight" ("zu kurz, zu lang, wer ein End' da fänd'!" – "ein Ende konnte Keiner erseh'n"). The apparent endlessness they decry here could apply, in fact, both to form (the *Bar* form they are expecting to hear) and to melody on the level of individual phrase: Walther's "improvised" contrast sections to his *Stollen* (e.g. "In einer Dornenhecken . . . ") have expanded the formal model beyond the masters' recognition, while the more-or-less regular four-measure phrases that begin each *Stollen* are themselves expanded (though only slightly) as he approaches the tonic cadence, prior to which root-position tonic chords are avoided. Eduard Hanslick himself, whose fame is now irreversibly linked to his operatic alter ego in Beckmesser, complained of the "restless accompaniment and excessive modulation"of the "Trial Song" (as if unwittingly rising to the bait, and stepping directly into Beckmesser's notorious shoes).[1] W. H. Riehl strikes an aptly *meisterisch* tone in an oblique criticism of Wagner, among other would-be epigones of the "late Beethoven style," for their "endless" spinning-out of melodic periods: "for an infinitely long melody ceases to be melody at all, just as an endless succession of little melodic fragments does, since a principal appeal of any melody lies in its being neither too long nor too short (*nicht zu lang und nicht zu kurz*), and that one can comfortably grasp a beginning, a middle, and an end."[2]

But "endlessness" – especially due to lack of clear harmonic-metrical "punctuation" ("Kein Absatz wo," as Beckmesser puts it) – had been a theme of Wagnerian criticism even before the coining of the phrase "endless melody" in 1860, which then naturally provided an irresistible

---

[1] In a review of the Munich premiere (1868), which was slightly revised for first Viennese production two years later. See Henry Pleasants, trans. and ed., *Vienna's Golden Years of Music* (New York, 1950), 119.

[2] W. H. Riehl, *Musikalische Charakterköpfe* (5th edn, Stuttgart, 1878), vol. III, 47. Riehl makes his allusion to Wagner even more explicit when he adds: "Viele glauben aber jetzt das erstere und meinen ihre Melodien seien dann erst voll und ganz wenn sie zerrissen sind und nennen ein endloses Melodiegebröckel die *endlose Melodie*" (emphasis added).

target for further satire. In his review of *Lohengrin* after its first performances in Vienna in 1858 Hanslick pointed out two principal evils
that lay at the root of such melodic amorphousness: an immoderate
insistence on declamatory recitative- and arioso-based styles, and an
abuse of deceptive cadences to effect syntactic elisions. In *Lohengrin*,
Hanslick maintains, Wagner continually resorted to declamatory vocal
writing and striking orchestral coloring in place of genuine melodic
invention and design. A dramatic dialogue whose musical realization
attempts to trace its every turn with "perpetual modulation" produces
in *Lohengrin* a musical language of "half-recited songs . . . which never
stay four measures in the same key but, with infinite evasiveness,
continue from one deceptive cadence to the next until the ear,
exhausted and resigned to its fate, lets them go where they will." The
result of this is a music without any "skeletal" framework. Wagner's
musical "organism" is scarcely more than an oozing sonorous proto-
plasm. In this vein Hanslick describes

those extended scenes in which one takes in little more than a continuous
fluctuation of featureless, fluid tonal matter. Melody, self-sufficient song, from
which alone the intrinsic musical body can be constructed, is lacking.[3]

Later, in his review of the *Meistersinger* premiere (1868), Hanslick
specifically invokes "Wagner's dry technical expression, 'infinite melody,'
since everyone knows by now what is meant." Ten years after his
review of the Vienna *Lohengrin* he is still likening Wagner's a-melodic
musical creations to invertebrate organisms, although they seem to
have moved up a few small steps on the evolutionary ladder:

The "infinite melody" is the dominant, musically undermining power in *Die
Meistersinger*, as in *Tristan und Isolde*. A small motive begins, and before it can
develop into an actual melody or theme, it gets twisted, pinched, set higher or
lower by continual modulation and enharmonization, enlarged and reduced,
repeated or echoed, now by this instrument, now by another. Anxiously
omitting every conclusive cadence, this boneless tonal mollusk floats on
toward the immeasurable, renewing itself from its own substance.[4]

Wagner's "peculiar principle" remains "the intentional dissolution of
every fixed form into a shapeless, sensually intoxicating resonance; the
replacement of independent, articulate melody by vague melodization."
    Not surprisingly, the chorus of critical opprobrium on the theme of
"endless" (or non-existent) melody became considerably augmented
with the appearance of *Tristan und Isolde*. (Wagner had doubtless
anticipated this in writing *"Music of the Future,"* which may have been
motivated partly as a pre-emptive critical defense of his new work,

---

[3] Review of *Lohengrin* (1858), in *Vienna's Golden Years*, 59.
[4] Review of *Die Meistersinger*, ibid., 127–8.

although it hardly succeeded in this.) The fundamental evils identified in *Tristan* are essentially those Hanslick (among others) had already diagnosed in *Lohengrin* – excess of musical "declamation" and modulation – only now intensified to a vastly higher power. After hearing rehearsals for the Munich premiere in 1865, one (anonymous) critic claimed that the mania for expressive declamation was regressing toward a state of primitive, inarticulate, pre-musical vocalization:

Richard Wagner has pushed to the limit here his propensity to eschew all melody and instead to synchronize as fully as possible a purely declamatory music and appropriate instrumentation with the sense and diction of the dramatic action (*dem Sinne und Wortlaut des dramatischen Vorgangs*). There is no longer any real song to speak of in this so-called opera: the singers' voices as well as the mightily engaged orchestra are simply condemned to follow the often nonsensical libretto by sighing and lamenting, shouting and rejoicing, seething and roaring (*zu seufzen und zu klagen, zu jubeln und zu jauchzen, zu wüthen und fast zu brüllen*). The music is nothing but the accompaniment to emotional or passionate words.[5]

Another critic at the time of the premiere translated the melody problem into one of rhythm, or really the obscuring of metrical periodicity ("Of any rhythm representing musical order not a trace is to be found in *Tristan*"), and yet another summed up the absence of intelligible melody as "the fundamental objection to *Tristan* that crops up in thousands of variations"[6] (endless variations on a critical theme, as it were).

As early as 1853 (during the initial critical confrontation with *Lohengrin* and the Zurich writings) one Friedrich Hinrichs already anticipated these responses to *Tristan*, and on similar grounds. Wagner's emphasis on music as dramatic gesture, Hinrichs argues, inevitably leads to a fragmented, disjunct melodic idiom, since physical gestures, as expressive signs, lack the formative syntactic principles of a real language. He connects Wagner's emancipation of melodic "expressivity" with the

---

[5] "Actenstücke aus München," *Niederrheinische Musik-Zeitung* 13 (1865), 158.
[6] J. J. Abert, "*Tristan und Isolde* von Richard Wagner. Eine musikalische Skizze der Gegenwart" (orig. in *Land und Meer*), *Niederrheinische Musik-Zeitung* 13 (1865), 222; J. B. Allfeld, *Tristan und Isolde von Richard Wagner – Kritisch beleuchtet mit einleitenden Bemerkungen über Melodie und Musik* (Munich, 1865), 6. Another, anonymous, response to *Tristan* in the year of its premiere speaks in similar terms of the "elemental wildness" that constitutes the predominant character of the music, which "rushes past us like the waves of the ocean whipped up by storms." Yet this critic senses the presence of some palpable, if elusive, organizing principle in the music (those waves, perhaps?), as well as a great number of real melodic "beginnings" (*Ansätze*); "and in the way these individualized motives rapidly subside again into the elemental primal motion (*elementarischen Urbewegung*) or into some differently formed motive there lies, at any rate, a significant art of melodic, harmonic, and especially rhythmic formation (*Gestaltung*)" ("Die Aufführung von R. Wagner's 'Tristan und Isolde' in München," *Blätter für Musik, Theater und Kunst* 11 [1865], 190).

Endless melodies

gendered metaphors of *Opera and Drama* analyzed in chapter 3, noting the (metaphorical) consequences – the musical equivalent of the anathematized "new woman":

He [Wagner] cultivates rhapsodic, self-contained musical figures (*rhapsodische, abgeschlossene Wendungen*), his reckless melody mocks our logical reflection. He is fond of comparing the melodic to the feminine: and yet, his own forms so often know neither measure nor restraint (*weder Maß, noch Zurückhaltung*), and in this his melody resembles rather the *emancipated* woman, who exchanges logic for eccentricity, who may perhaps achieve a certain level of geniality this way, but more often succumbs to her own confusion.[7]

The cultural link, also intimated here, between Wagnerian opera and the "irrational," even hysterical, woman – both victims of an uncontrolled expression of destabilizing subconscious impulses – is one we tend to associate with later criticism (such as Nietzsche's), and with later works, particularly *Tristan*. But if *Lohengrin* and *Tannhäuser* hardly provoked the same levels of resistance as *Tristan* or the *Ring*, and even achieved a significant measure of popularity by the time of the Paris production of *Tannhäuser* in 1860, these earlier operas nonetheless continued to be perceived, to a surprising extent, as a real threat to the foundations of an existing musical order.

Drawing attention to the historical contingency of the category of "melody" and what is accepted as such, one of the *Tristan* critics quoted above recalled how ten years earlier the Munich audience of an early *Tannhäuser* performance emitted an "enharmonic cry of pain" on hearing "those six semitones" in the opening phrase of "O du, mein holder Abendstern," while today (1865) no one doubted any longer that this was, indeed, a real melody.[8] At the same time the Munich audience was cringing at Wolfram's seemingly innocuous tune, the critic and theorist J. C. Lobe subjected the music of *Tannhäuser* to more scholarly analysis, and diagnosed the "Venusberg" music of the overture as excessively "aphoristic," lacking syntactic coherence as melody. (Lobe, who considered himself something of an authority in matters of periodic construction and motivic development, identifies eleven units or periods within the first sixty-one measures of the allegro, but also refers to them dismissively as fragmentary "images" [*Bilderchen*] or "thoughts" [*Vorstellungen*].)[9] Hanslick, who had written enthusiastically

---

[7] Friedrich Hinrichs, *Richard Wagner und die neuere Musik. Eine Skizze aus der musikalischen Gegenwart* (Halle, 1854), 63 (emphasis added).
[8] Allfeld, *Tristan und Isolde von Richard Wagner*, 10–11.
[9] J. C. Lobe, "Briefe über Richard Wagner an einen jungen Komponisten," no. 5, *Fliegende Blätter für Musik* 1:8 (1855), 450. We may recall his similar critique of the faulty "punctuation" in Beethoven's late style cited in chapter 2 (see "Beethoven's 'sketches'"), which, like Riehl's criticisms (n. 2 above), posited an unwholesome predilection among modern composers for the late works.

246

about *Tannhäuser* at the time of its original Dresden production, declared that in *Lohengrin* Wagner had become "fanatic in his tunelessness." And he was by no means the only critic to disparage this opera for its lack of "coherent melody." An 1854 review of *Lohengrin* in Leipzig concedes a certain generalized "melodic" quality to the music, but is disturbed by a predominance of "melodic aphorisms" (recalling Lobe on *Tannhäuser*): an "overabundant variety of small, correctly conceived declamatory phrases, [which are] often agreeable in themselves, [but] rarely coalesce into larger formal unities."[10] Again, an overly scrupulous (even "fanatic") preoccupation with natural declamation is perceived as the root cause of melodic decline. (Yet in a sense such criticisms speak to Wagner's own concerns with respect to the idiom of his "Romantic" operas, as suggested in the preceding chapter: the need to organize "poetic-musical periods" into larger, persuasive musical trajectories along the lines of a dramatic dialogue, for instance.) In a lengthy critique of the same Leipzig production Otto Jahn considered that a typical neo-Romantic zeal for the "characteristic" was to blame for many of the opera's shortcomings, and he cites "a critic in one of our daily papers" (possibly paraphrasing the review just quoted?) that Wagner's solution to the problem of conventional "operatic melody" consists in being "melodic, but without melody."[11]

The perception that Wagner's style represented a dangerous affront to traditional musical values, even to some sense of aesthetic "morals," increased proportionally as the post-*Lohengrin* works came to be known and heard. But Wagner had already contributed significantly to such perceptions of a dangerously radical agenda inscribed in his music through his writings, as well as through his much publicized involvement with the 1848–9 uprisings. The contemptuous dismissal of "operatic" and "absolute" melody altogether in *Opera and Drama* probably did much to provoke criticism of Wagner's alleged tunelessness, as did certainly the whole (apparently regressive) discourse there of "natural" vocal melody generated by the sound and sense of poetic speech. Long after his political activities had ceased to be a concern to anyone, the implications of Wagner's assault on the musical order – and especially that of healthy, rational, "objective" melodic structure – continued to inspire ethically tinged warnings against the consequences

---

[10]   Review of *Lohengrin* [anon.], *Signale für die musikalische Welt* 12:4 (1854), 26. "... es sind fast durchgängig melodische *Aphorismen*. Eine überreiche Mannigfaltigkeit kleiner, stets richtig, ert zugelich angenehm melodisch declamirten Sätzchen verbindet sich selten zu einer grösseren Formeinheit."

[11]   Otto Jahn, "*Lohengrin*. Oper von Richard Wagner," originally published in *Die Grenzboten* (1854); reprinted in *Gesammelte Aufsätze über Musik* (2nd edn, Leipzig, 1867), 139.

of his example (even Lobe's early critique of the *Tannhäuser* overture took the form of an admonitory "letter to a young composer" from one who knew and valued the importance of the classics). The cultural threat posed by Wagner's "endless melody" is a principal burden of Nietzsche's late critiques (for example in the first section of "Nietzsche contra Wagner," entitled "Wagner as a Danger"), which also satirize Wagner's own attempts to brand conventional melody as an agent of cultural degeneracy (*Der Fall Wagner*, section 6). Even from well beyond the other side of the great modernist divide Igor Stravinsky, in his *Poetics of Music*, still felt compelled to polemicize against Wagner's "endless melody" in terms that are almost indistinguishable from those of Hanslick and his generation:

The system of infinite melody perfectly translates this tendency [i.e., trying to "fill the spaces left by a lack of musical order"]. It is the perpetual "becoming" of a music that has no more motive to begin than it has a reason to conclude. Infinite melody thus appears as an outrage to the dignity and even the function of melody, which is, as we have said, the musical song articulated by phrase and cadence. Under Wagner's influence the laws that guarantee the life of song have been transgressed, and music has lost the smile of melody.[12]

Even Stravinsky still denounces Wagnerian "endless melody" as an aesthetic "outrage," a "transgression of natural laws," and an affront to the rules of musical grammar and punctuation. It is difficult not to attribute a certain disingenuousness to the author of *The Rite of Spring* in thus chastising Wagner's transgressions against a natural musical order (even from the vantage-point of a neo-classical "regeneration" of healthy musical values). But it is testimony, all the same, to the power of Wagner's emancipatory melodic project that it continued to elicit, from adherents and detractors, these conflicting responses of intoxicated passion and sober resistance for such a long time. And it is one more example – out of hundreds that could be cited – of the enduring fascination of the locution Wagner himself devised for this project: "endless melody."

Wagner wrote his essay *"Music of the Future"* in 1860 for publication (in French) as a foreword to translations of the libretti to *Der fliegende Holländer*, *Tannhäuser*, *Lohengrin*, and *Tristan und Isolde* for the benefit of the Parisian public prior to the ill-starred French production of *Tannhäuser*. The essay is composed of some general reflections on national operatic and musical cultures, some autobiographical notes on the composer's aesthetic and musical *Bildung*, a somewhat shamefaced

---

[12] Translated from Stravinsky, *Poétique musicale* (Cambridge MA, 1942), 43. Cf. also *Poetics of Music*, trans. A. Knodel and I. Dahl (Cambridge MA, 1942), 62.

précis of *Opera and Drama*, only a few perfunctory remarks on the four operas in question, and a sizeable excursus on the nature of musical "form" and "melody" by way of a coda (though Wagner does return briefly to *Tannhäuser* at the very end). The excursus on melody would appear to be the least relevant to what is designed as a preface to his dramatic texts, but Wagner justifies his concern with the topics of melody and form here (which are so mutually implicated as to be nearly synonymous, he argues) by explaining that the novelty of the "melodic form" of his works is largely a consequence of the novel conception of the operatic poems themselves.

An underlying motivation for this closing digression, however, is clearly the desire to refute mounting criticisms of the absence of melody in his operas. And if Wagner suspected that the French might have some difficulty in discerning the "melodies" in *Tannhäuser* on first hearing, he was also anticipating the far greater public bafflement that was sure to greet *Tristan* once that work began to circulate. (Wagner explicitly informs his readers that his evocation of an "endless melody," resembling the finely nuanced textures of sound encountered in a natural environment, applies to his newest work, not to *Tannhäuser*.) In either case, his strategy – however unlikely it was to forestall negative criticism – was simply to re-define the concept at hand. If melody was indeed the *essence* of music, Wagner argued (in the spirit of Rousseau and many more ancient authorities), then the commercially manufactured tunes of modern musical culture no longer deserved the title, while the project of his "musical drama" was to re-generate a kind of melody worthy of the name – on the one hand by returning music to language, "feeling," and expressive gesture, in which "melody" had its putative origins, and on the other hand by following the example of Beethoven's quasi-anatomical experiments with the motivic cell-tissue of music in attempting to fabricate a new symphonic organism (see also "Natural sciences" in chapter 3, above).

Those shrill cries for "melody, melody!" so often raised nowadays by the superficial dilettanti in our midst only serve to convince me that their conception of melody is drawn from works where, along with melody, you have a dearth of melody which makes the melody they cry for so very precious . . . Imagine such an audience [i.e., one accustomed to Italian opera] suddenly confronted with a work that demanded their full attention throughout its entire length, and in every part! You couldn't blame it for feeling rudely torn out of its listening habits – how could it possibly be expected to recognize its beloved "melody" in a thing which at best it might be able to identify as a refinement of that musical noise [i.e., the symphony] which in its more naive state served the purpose of promoting pleasant conversation? And, what is more, this stuff now positively demands to be listened to! . . .

Truly, what may be perceived as opulence from such limited horizons as these will appear as a poor thing indeed to a more cultivated mind. One can pardon the general public for its error, but not the critics.   (VII, 124–5)[13]

Indeed, Wagner was never much inclined to be forgiving of "the critics." A distinct note of exasperation emerges in his development of this point, that there is much more to "melody" than is dreamt of in their philosophy. What seems particularly to exasperate Wagner is that so many critics, claiming to speak as musically educated authorities, could remain so firmly wedded to a "naive" view of melody:

> *melody is the only form of music* . . . To say that a piece of music has no melody is in a higher sense tantamount to saying that the composer has failed to create a form that grips and stirs our emotions; and that this is so because his lack of talent and originality has forced him to fall back on hackneyed melodic phrases that make no impact. Delivered by an uncultivated opera-goer, though, such a judgement would refer only to melody of that specific, narrow type . . . belonging to the childhood of the art – for which reason the exclusive pleasure taken in it actually does seem childish. What is involved here is not so much true melody as melody in its limited original pure *dance-form*.   (VII, 135; Jacobs, 37)

In Wagner's aesthetics, as in his sociology, "convention" is the root of all modern malaise and the inexorable alienation from all that is genuine, true, and natural. (At the same time, he recognizes the indispensable role of convention in the formation of a classical musical language, as in the formation of language *per se*, even as he denounces its stultifying and "alienating" effects on music and language in modern culture.) Hence the more formulaic elements of current musical idioms are interpreted as a detriment to the integrity of true, expressive melody. Recitative of the plainer sort is dismissed as "absolutely unmelodic" and "scarcely better than mere noise" (this despite the fact that Wagner's unmelodiousness was so often attributed to a dependence on the a-metrical, declamatory idioms of recitative). The busy passage-work and "steadily recurring, noisy and expansive half-cadences" that fill out the periodic framework of a classical symphonic movement – more often with the "Italianate" Mozart than with Haydn – are likened to the comings and goings of servants at a princely table, another species of meaningless musical "noise." Since Wagner does not go so far as to deny altogether the status of "melody" to either the traditional styles of operatic aria or sonata and symphony movements, it becomes apparent that he understands the essence of "melody" to lie in the motivic-thematic substance of such pieces rather than in the periodic phraseology of their presentation. "Elaboration," to use the vocabulary of the musical rhetoricians, is valid as melody only

---

[13] Translation adapted from R. Jacobs, *Three Wagner Essays*, 36–7. Subsequent references to this translation will be given in the text.

insofar as it preserves the integrity of melodic (motivic) "invention" and doesn't dilute it with formulaic patter. Hence formulaic exposition and recapitulation of ideas in a traditional periodic framework are devalued with respect to development (the "architectural" presentation of ideas with respect to their "logical" evolution).

This emphasis on motivic invention and development as the "genuine" components of melody is reinforced by Wagner's well-known description, in this same context, of "the construction of a first movement from a Beethoven symphony":

> What we see is a dance-melody split into its tiniest fragments, each one of which – it may amount to no more than a couple of notes – is made interesting and significant, either by rhythmic or by harmonic means. The fragments are continually being reassembled in different formations – coalescing in a logical succession which here pours forth like a stream, there disperses as in an eddying vortex. Throughout one is riveted by their vivid expressiveness, absorbed by the excitement of sensing melodic significance in every harmony, even in every rest. And the completely novel outcome of this procedure was the expansion of a melody, through the richly various development of all its constituent motives, into a continuous large-scale piece of music, which itself constituted no less than a single, perfectly coherent melody.
>
> (VII, 127; adapted from Jacobs, 38)

True, it is hard to read in the "eddying vortex" of Wagner's impressions any very clear account of the "construction" of a symphonic movement he claims to offer. But while this account remains typically generalized (Wagner does not claim to be describing any one particular movement), two other closely related contexts support the likelihood that the first movement of the "Eroica" was Wagner's paradigm here. When Felix Draeseke, an aspiring young musician of the future, was visiting Wagner in Lucerne during the summer of 1859 (just at the time Wagner was putting the finishing touches to the score of *Tristan*), Wagner serenaded his guest on one of their walks with the first movement of the "Eroica." He sang without stopping up to the end of the exposition, Draeseke recalled. "There! Is not melody pure and simple enough for you?" he demanded; "must you always have your crazy harmonies (*verrückten Harmonien*) on top of that?" Draeseke was perplexed at first. "But then he explained to me more calmly about the inexhaustible melodic flow in Beethoven's symphonies, and how one could recall the entire symphony [movement] to mind by means of this single melody [line]."[14] (The jibe about *verrückten Harmonien* was evidently aimed at Draeseke himself – who had brought along some compositions to show the master – and reflects Wagner's characteristic impatience with the harmonic audacities considered *de rigeur* among would-be Wagnerian

[14] Cited (and translated) from Erich Roeder, *Felix Draeseke* (Dresden, 1932), 106.

251

epigones, which he evidently tended to find poorly motivated or integrated within a larger context; similar comments are recorded in his correspondence with the young Hans von Bülow.) Later, in a passing gloss on the formal character of "the Beethoven symphonic movement" in general, in "On the Application of Music to the Drama" (1879), he speaks of the "unimagined variety with which these [motivic] elements can be broken apart, newly configured, and endlessly re-assembled: the first movement of the 'Heroic' Symphony demonstrates this, even to the point of confounding the uninitiated listener, whereas this same movement particularly impresses the initiate with the essential unity of its thematic character" – the subject of Wagner's discussion here (X, 178).

In turning from the example of the Beethoven symphonic allegro to the issue of musical-dramatic form, back in *"Music of the Future,"* Wagner intimates (to say "explains" would be an exaggeration) how the continuous motivic significance of this symphonic idiom might be transferred to the context of a musical drama, which would provide a still far greater scope for the free unfolding of such melodic resources. It is the role of the new, ideal poet, in fact, to encourage such a newly unfettered melodic discourse. "Boldly extend your melody," the poet will now exhort the musician, "so that it pours through the entire work in a continuous stream; say through it that which I have left unsaid, because only you could express it . . ."

> In truth, the measure of a poet's greatness lies in that which he does not say, in order to leave us to speak silently to ourselves that which is inexpressible. It is the musician who brings this "unspoken" element to sounding life, and the unmistakable form of this resounding silence is *endless melody*.
>
> (VII, 130; cf. Jacobs, 40)

The immediate context of this famous phrase demonstrates that Wagner identifies the "endless melody" of the musical drama primarily with the role of the orchestra, or the "orchestral melody" (in the vocabulary of *Opera and Drama*). Beyond that, it is reasonably evident that the perceived affinity between this new ideal of melody and that of Beethoven's symphonies is their common aim of a continuously significant, musically "meaningful" presentation and development of motivic ideas.

While Wagner probably did not succeed in converting many of those narrow-minded critics from their commitment to "narrow" operatic melody (as Wagner also termed it) to the splendors of "endless melody," the phrase certainly did succeed in capturing their attention. Its continuous appeal since that time can be attributed to the way it evokes just what these critics found to be the undoing of Wagner's melody, or the reason for its absence: the persistent evasion of full cadences by means of deceptive resolutions, or other types of harmonic interruption or elision. (Hanslick claimed that Wagner's obsessively evaded cadences simply constituted a new type of musical pedantry, in radical guise.) Avoidance of cadential closure has continued to inform most interpretations since then.

Carl Dahlhaus, on the other hand, resisted this traditional notion of "endless melody": "Bemused by the word 'endless,' people have forgotten to inquire what Wagner understood by 'melody'."[15] Consequently, Dahlhaus's exegesis of "endless melody" appeals to Wagner's concept of melody altogether, especially what we might call the apologetic "transvaluation" of the term in *"Music of the Future."* This interpretation (reiterated in numerous contexts) takes its cue from the account of the paradigmatic Beethovenian symphonic structure – manifested in the "Eroica" first movement – as a "single, perfectly coherent melody," in which every measure is of musical (motivic) significance, down to the silences. From this perspective Dahlhaus equates Wagner's "melody," or "endless melody," with Schoenberg's idea of a "musical prose," whose primary determinant is the "emancipation" of motivic substance from periodic metrical formula (Wagner's "dance-melody"), but which is also defined as a melodic line or texture in which the condition of motivic "meaning" is ever present:

[W]hat is musically eloquent and meaningful is "melodic" in this positive sense, what is formulaic and unexpressive is "unmelodic." Schoenberg's reputedly "unmelodic" musical language is consistently "melodic" by Wagner's criteria. A melody is "narrow" (to use the terminology of *Music of the Future* again) if the truly melodic is forever breaking off, as in Italian opera, to be replaced by "unmelodic" filling out.[16]

Dahlhaus's view of the matter would appear to find corroboration in the texts I have cited here regarding the "melodic form" of Beethoven's symphonic allegros, and in several related texts, such as this gloss on the same subject in the 1870 *Beethoven* essay:

The factor in Beethoven's musical form (*in dem musikalischen Gestalten Beethovens*) that is of such great historical significance is just this: that every

---

15 Dahlhaus, "Issues in Composition," in *Between Romanticism and Modernism*, 55.
16 Ibid. Cf. p. 56: "Thus the primary meaning of the term 'endless melody,' which is often misused and should by no means be treated exclusively as a technical expression, is not that the parts of the work flow into one another without caesuras but that every note has meaning, that the melody is language and not empty sound. The technical characteristic, the absence of formal [full] cadences, is merely a consequence of the aesthetic factor: cadences are regarded as formulas, syntactic but not semantic components – in short, they express nothing and are therefore to be avoided or concealed." See also *The New Grove Wagner* (New York, 1984), 114–15. One significant modification there, however, is the admission that the "significance" of this melody, in the music drama, may depend on dramatic context or association, rather than being musically immanent: "A melody is infinite when every note 'says' something, and it 'says' something when every note of the music has dramatic relevance as well as being inwardly linked to other moments" (115).

secondary or accidental feature of the art (*jedes technische Accidenz der Kunst*) or conventional means by which the artist aims to communicate with the world around him is here raised to the highest level of significance, as an immediate outpouring. As I have expressed this elsewhere, there is here no more filling-out, no [artificially symmetrical] framing of the melody (*keine Zuthat, keine Einrahmung der Melodie mehr*), but everything has become melody, every accompanimental voice, even the pauses. (IX, 87)

The "eloquence" ascribed even to the rests – here and in the earlier essay – does indeed suggest the emancipation of melody from quadratic metrical formulae, in which the empty beats may be essential, but are hardly expressive. And like "musical prose," this new post-Beethovenian melody is more an aesthetic quality or condition than a discrete quantitative entity. In Wagner's music there are no more "melodies" because everything has become "melody."

This distinction between "melody" as an ideal, a condition (that which is infinite does not permit plural constructions) and the popular sense of melody as a finite, infinitely reproducible tune was elucidated by several of Wagner's supporters, such as Hans von Wolzogen and Henry T. Finck.[17] The distinction also points up the deliberate paradox of my title ("Endless melodies"), which is meant to suggest several things: the plurality of meanings Wagner himself attributes to melody; the abundance of related melodic neologisms he coined (especially in the course of *Opera and Drama*); the plurality of meanings later exegetes have attributed to Wagner's terminology; and the variety of levels that I will propose here in applying the idea of melody to Wagner's musical form.

No doubt the distinction of infinite "melody" from finite tunes does fairly represent something of what Wagner was attempting to circum-scribe in his writings, and to realize in his music. And no doubt Wagner often did not receive a fair reading, or hearing, from his critics at the time. Still, his effort to re-define the essence of melody leaves open some legitimate questions, and it is possible that Dahlhaus's exegesis settles the controversy a little too patly in the composer's favor. Meaning and expression, after all, are contingent on reception. This applies to Wagner's music, no less than to his terminology. Critical or polemical catchwords, as Dahlhaus was surely aware, can often take on indelible

---

[17] See, for example, the section "Melody versus Tune" in Finck's chapter on *Tristan und Isolde* in *Wagner and his Works* (New York, 1897), vol. II, 154–61. In Hans von Wolzogen's dialogue for the instruction of aspiring Wagnerians, "Ein Gespräch nach der Oper" (1873), a well-schooled initiate educates a reluctant neophyte in the distinction between conventional, isolated (plural) "melodies" and the singular genus of the "ever-blooming *melos* of the drama . . . , a living evolution (*Entwicklung*) representing the progression of the drama from moment to moment" (Hans von Wolzogen, *Wagneriana* [Leipzig, 1888], 24).

meanings quite apart from what their author may have intended, and from this perspective it seems fairly futile to protest a "popular" association of endless melody with the seamless continuity effected by deceptive or elided cadences (to the extent that "seamlessness" really is projected), even if for the sake of promoting a broader view. And is it, after all, an indubitable fact that the elimination of metrical regularity (symmetrical phrasing), harmonic cadential formulae, or other aspects of melodic convention in either Wagner or Schoenberg has universally guaranteed a heightened, uninterrupted quality of "meaning" as a consequence? Taken as a whole, the reception of these composers could almost suggest the opposite. (By emphasizing the status of "endless melody" as a primarily aesthetic rather than technical category, it is true, Dahlhaus leaves open the possibility that it represents an ideal not always consistently realized.)

Finally, the passage quoted above from Dahlhaus's essay "Issues in Composition" contains a slight, but perhaps not insignificant, misreading of the statements on melody in *"Music of the Future."* While it is true enough that Wagner was contemptuous of the "narrow" or schematic melody that often predominated in Italian or French operatic idioms of his day, he did not in fact refer to the continual "breaking off" or "unmelodic filling out" of melody in the cantabile sections of such operas. Rather it is very clear, both in the context of his initial discussion of operatic melody here and again toward the very end of the essay, that Wagner refers to the still persistent dichotomy of recitative and formal song in traditional opera. What particularly annoys Wagner, it seems, is the continued acceptance of a class of music – the operatic recitative – with absolutely no pretension to musical interest or expression. It is this class of music that is charged with continually "breaking off" and filling out the musical substance of the opera (however variable the quality of the "melodic" formal numbers, as such), and which he denounces as "absolutely unmelodic," meaningless noise (VII, 126, 134). Recitative styles may be formulaic in their own way, but they also possess features of "musical prose" (metrical freedom, if not motivic significance), and represent precisely the root of Wagner's melodic error, as it was commonly perceived: the substitution of "natural" declamatory rhythms for regular, structuring harmonic-metrical periodicity. In aspiring to "endless melody" Wagner clearly strove to divest himself of the ponderous legacy of "absolute recitative" as well as that of "absolute aria" (to cite two more Wagnerian locutions – see VII, 134). Many passages in *Lohengrin*, even *Das Rheingold* or *Die Walküre*, might fairly be called "unmelodic," not because they lapse into old-fashioned cantabile, but because they fail to enliven their declamatory-recitative foundations with real motivic or rhythmic interest. (Faceless recitative-like passages can be used to articulate larger designs, on the other hand, as a kind of punctuating *Luftpause*, as Wagner demonstrates in parts of *Tristan und Isolde*.)

The problem common to both tuneless recitative and mindlessly tuneful arias, for Wagner, was that each in its own way remained a purely conventional language which could be produced and received with scarcely any conscious reflection, feeling, or other interpretive activity. Under the influence of the social theorists of the 1848 revolution, Wagner remained convinced of the alienating forces of conventional codes, in art as in life. Thus the metaphorical "forest melody," invoked at the end of *"Music of the Future"* to convey the effect of endless melody, situates this experience in the bosom of nature, far from the distracting urban scene of the opera house and its conventional, convention-bound fare.[18] This natural "melody" embodies an ideal that is infinitely complex, layered, and finely nuanced yet thoroughly natural and instinctive. Walther von Stolzing, who learned the art of song from "finches and titmice," as Beckmesser caustically observes, apostrophizes this same "forest melody" in his Trial Song, while Beckmesser and the other masters mistake nature's voices for untutored chaos:

es schwillt und schallt,	it grows and resounds,
es tönt der Wald	the forest rings
von holder Stimmen Gemenge;	with a throng of lovely voices;
nun laut und hell	now strong and clear
schon nah zur Stell',	and closer still,
wie wächst der Schwall!	how the sound increases!
Wie Glockenhall	Like the peal of bells
ertost des Jubels Gedränge!	the joyous cries ring out!

In his lilac-scented monologue in the following act, Sachs's halting recollection of Walther's song underscores the parallel to that natural "forest melody" itself:

Ich fühl's – und kann's nicht versteh'n;
kann's nicht behalten, – doch auch nicht vergessen;
und fass' ich es ganz, – kann ich's nicht messen! –
Doch wie wollt' ich auch messen,
was unermeßlich mir schien?

I feel it – and yet can't fathom it; –
can't quite retain it, – and yet can't forget it;
and if I were to grasp the whole thing, – I couldn't measure it!
But then, how should I measure that
which seemed to me immeasurable? [i.e., "infinite"]

18 The discourse of "nature" and natural melody here is related to Wagner's "evolutionary" trope, discussed in chapter 3 – for instance, the axiom that only the melody or "form" that grows before our eyes/ears is truly "intelligible," while ready-made quadratic melodies remain, like the products of industrial commerce they are, "alienated" from our natural emotional faculties.

Wagner sought to represent musical progress not so much under the aegis of an inexorable Hegelian world spirit as in the guise of a return to natural conditions, cleansed of the accretions of historical convention, which had only served to alienate mankind from its own, essential nature. This dichotomy of nature and convention had been at the heart of Wagner's rhetoric of artistic regeneration in the Zurich writings, where "melody" was construed against the background of Enlightenment and Romantic speculations about the common origins of language and music in some primeval, Edenic condition. The lengthy justification for the necessity of poetic *Stabreim* in *Opera and Drama*, and the evocation of a "verse melody" that would be naturally derived from the sounds and significations of dramatic poetry all hark back to earlier notions of a poetic-musical *Ursprache* in which music and language formed an indistinguishable unity, and vocal signs conveyed meaning directly, not merely as mediating, conventional abstractions. Music, in modern times, has undergone the same process of neutralization through the impact of conventional regulation as language had done in ancient times (as Wagner saw it).[19] Wagner's ideal of art tends always to regress toward the imagined roots or origins of things, toward a utopia of absolute, unmediated expressivity, even while it remains, in practice, thoroughly committed in so many ways to the techniques and technologies of modern culture.

Melody, origins, and utopias of regression (melody as the origin of speech and poetry in *Opera and Drama*)

When languages are conceived of as departing from an origin, the difference in question is that between an undifferentiated point in space and time (the origin) and some force of effraction that breaks with and breaks up unified space. And that is why stories about origins so frequently end up being fables about lost wholeness.
　　　　　　　　　　　– *Peggy Kamuf, "Origins (1754? Rousseau Writes His*
　　　　　　　　　　　Essai sur l'origine des langues)"[20]

Weia! Waga!
Woge, du Welle,
Walle zur Wiege!
Wagalaweia!
Wallala weiala weia!
　　　　– Woglinde (Das Rheingold, *scene 1*).

---

[19]　*"Music of the Future"* (see VII, 110–11 or Jacobs, *Three Wagner Essays*, 27–8, as well as n. 30 below).
[20]　*A New History of French Literature*, ed. Denis Hollier (Cambridge MA, 1989), 455.

Like many programs of aesthetic regeneration before it, the ideal musical-dramatic "art-work of the future" theorized at such length in *Opera and Drama* fantasizes the restoration of a natural, original, pre-cultural condition. As always, classical Hellenic culture is the principal model, but Wagner's thoughts are also informed by the speculative linguistic anthropology of Enlightenment figures such as Condillac, Rousseau, and Herder regarding the origins of language itself. From this tradition he drew the notion of some common source of speech and song that would vindicate the imperative of their modern reunion in a perfected, "purely-human" genre of musical drama. Both Nietzsche and Adorno were sensitive to, not to say suspicious of, such an atavistic or regressive strain in Wagner's aesthetic ideology, while also recognizing it as a function of his particular historical context, an early sign of related "atavistic" tendencies of a subsequent modernist culture. Nietzsche also identified this regressive strain with Wagner's tendency to simulate "meaning" by means of rhetorical, theatrical gesture rather than to generate ("authentic") meaning through rational form.

[T]his is the point of departure for our concept of "style." Above all, no thought! Nothing is more compromising than a thought. Rather the state preceding thought, the throng of yet unborn thoughts, the promise of future thoughts, the world as it was before God created it – a recrudescence of chaos. – Chaos induces intimations . . . (*Chaos macht ahnen* . . .)
To speak the language of the master: infinity, but without melody.[21]

The general trope is familiar enough, of course: the ideals of a lost, golden age will be restored, but necessarily modified according to the conditions of a new era. The significance of the trope, in this case, is that it could be used to vindicate Wagner's re-definition of melody. If melody is the eloquent, immediately expressive principle in music, this status is ultimately derived from its common origin with poetry or speech, the mutual origins of music and language in some irretrievable, pre-cultural moment. Such an origin may be nothing more than myth, but for that very reason it represents a higher truth, for Wagner. The "verse melody" and "orchestral melody" of the music drama are both part of a utopian project to restore something of the natural musical speech of a lost or mythical era, newly grounded ("improved," as it were) in the achievements of modern instrumental and vocal technique.

The anthropological mythology of melodic-linguistic origins invited Wagner, in *Opera and Drama*, to bypass the somewhat shopworn model of the union of *melos*, *rhythmos*, and *logos* in ancient Greek drama (a model that remains very much at the center of *The Art-Work of the Future*), and delve back into the imaginary well-springs of human expres-

---

21 Nietzsche, *The Case of Wagner*, trans. Walter Kaufmann, 167; cf. *Der Fall Wagner*, ed. Dieter Borchmeyer, 105.

sion altogether. *"Music (Tonsprache)* is the beginning and end of language *(Wortsprache),"* he asserts in *Opera and Drama,* "just as *feeling* is the beginning and end of understanding, *myth* is the beginning and end of history, and *lyric* the beginning and end of literature [*Dichtkunst*]" (IV, 91). The familiar binary oppositions – *Tonsprache/Wortsprache,* feeling/understanding, myth/history, lyric/prose (or "literature") – apparently catalogued in this passage are represented instead as complementary terms. In the telos of Wagner's aesthetic mythology, the original terms (music, feeling, myth, lyric) are both "beginning and end," the point of origin that must be regained.

Wagner could appeal to a century-old tradition of philosophical speculation regarding the common origins of melody and speech, although he chose not to do so. (He once confessed his aversion to the "pedantry" of documented citations, and in the Zurich writings he seems particularly determined to pose as the sole source of all his ideas; indeed, the mania for tracing everything back to a point of natural origins seems to inform the methodology and the content alike.) But there are enough parallels between the discourse of musico-linguistic origins in Rousseau's *Essay on the Origin of Languages* and that of *Opera and Drama* for us to conclude that Wagner must have had some familiarity with Rousseau's text, directly or otherwise. (Perhaps he sensed that Rousseau's reputation as a musical dilettante, despite any claims to scholarly erudition, might only be detrimental to his own cause.)[22] Both Rousseau and Wagner are fundamentally concerned with gestural and vocal signs as the root of human communication. For both, some system of immediately intelligible signs – appealing directly to the senses and minimizing the need for reflective, interpretive activity – represents the common point of origin for music and language, as visible gestures, audible cries, or other primitive vocal utterances. Even without the benefit of grammar or writing, the earliest language was "poetic" in its direct appeal to the feelings. It was poetic precisely because of this directness, which it shared with singing. Passion, rather than the prosaic demands of survival, generated the earliest vocal signs, according to Rousseau, "and so it had to be." "One does not begin by reasoning, but by feeling." Hunting and gathering, he suggests, require no speech. "But for moving a young heart, or repelling an unjust aggressor, nature dictates accents, cries, lamentations. There we have the invention of the most ancient words; and that is

---

22 Rousseau is scarcely mentioned in Wagner's writings, although one comment recorded by Cosima suggests his awareness of the *Essay*: "[H]e frequently invokes Buddha and Rousseau; the first, who never said what he knew about the beginning and end of things, the second, who could not say what had been his inner vision" (CWD, 1 October 1882). The Bayreuth house tutor, Heinrich von Stein, had also written an essay on Rousseau that met with Wagner's approval.

why the first languages were singable and passionate before they became simple and methodical."[23] The affinity of signifier with signified was direct, immediate, and sensible, as far as possible (the relation Tzvetan Todorov designates, rather clinically, as "intransitive signification"). While the development of a more complex semantics would have to depend on conventional agreement about the meaning of vocal sounds, language would gradually sacrifice the "poetic" and musical immediacy of these earliest stages, as it evolved. The closer language remained to its natural origins, the closer it remained to music, as a system of directly expressive sounds.

Since sounds, accents, and number, which are natural, would leave little to articulation, which is conventional [i.e., artificial], it [the first language] would be sung rather than spoken. Most of the root words would be imitative sounds or accents of passion, or effects of sense objects. It would contain many onomatopoeic expressions.[24]

Rousseau returns to these initial propositions of his essay in the later chapters, devoted to the nature of music and melody, specifically in order to prove his thesis about the expressive primacy of melody over harmony. "With the first voices came the first articulations of sounds formed according to the respective passions that dictated them," he writes at the beginning of chapter 12 ("The Origin of Music and its Relations"):

Thus rhythm and sounds are born with syllables: all voices speak under the influence of passion, which adorns them with all their éclat. Thus verse, singing, and speech have a common origin. Around the fountain of which I spoke, the first discourses were the first songs. The periodic recurrences and measures of rhythm, the melodious modulations of accent, gave birth to poetry and music along with language. Or, rather, that was the only language in those happy climes and happy times, when the only pressing needs that required the agreement of others were those to which the heart gave birth.[25]

In *Of Grammatology*, Derrida meditated at length on the implications of Rousseau's *Essay* regarding the relative ideological status of speech and writing. Derrida's concern with the immediacy or absolute "self-presence" of the speaking voice (as opposed to the written word) is easily extended to distinctions between a hypothetical original "musical" tongue (in which all discourse was "melodic") and subsequent stages of linguistic development, in which the increased role of "conventional" elements, syntactic complexities and abstract conceptualization inevitably alienated language from its musical roots. (Indeed, Rousseau him-

---

[23] J.-J. Rousseau, *Essay on the Origin of Languages, Which Treats of Melody and Musical Imitation*, trans. John H. Moran, in *On the Origin of Language: Two Essays* (Chicago, 1966), 12.

[24] Ibid., 15.   [25] Ibid., 50.

self gives the cue for this interpretive extension.) Similarly, a remark Derrida makes regarding Rousseau's distinctions between gesture and voice, visible and audible signs, can be applied to the anthropological value-system of Rousseau and Wagner alike: "Natural immediacy is at once origin and end, but in the double sense of these words: birth and death, unfinished sketch and finished perfection. From then on, all value is determined according to its proximity to an absolute nature."[26]

As we have seen, Wagner repeatedly insisted on the "natural," the "instinctive" (*das Unwillkürliche*) and the original as fundamental criteria for all values, musical and otherwise, throughout the writings of his early exile. This rhetoric of natural and "purely human" is perhaps at its densest in *The Art-Work of the Future*, but it returns in full force in the third part of *Opera and Drama*, where it contributes to the gradually developing exposition of a new Wagnerian construction of "melody." As a key element of the greater project of cultural regeneration outlined here, the new Wagnerian melody will work to restore the natural expressive foundations of both speech and music, which have continuously eroded over history. In the last chapter of Part II Wagner moves from the history of drama and literature back to the "origins of language" itself (*Entstehung der Sprache*) by way of preparing the ground for Part III, "Poetry and Music in the Drama of the Future." The discourse of linguistic and musical origins here and throughout Part III (especially in the opening two chapters) recalls much in Rousseau's essay, though some of it could easily derive from Herder's later essay on the subject (*Über den Ursprung der Sprache*, 1772), or perhaps simply from the popular dissemination of such ideas since the eighteenth century. (As Herder had pointed out, the basic proposition of an original, musical tongue that was at once "melody" and "poetry" of some primeval sort had been a philosophical topos since antiquity.)

"The most primitive (*das Ursprünglichste*) expressive organ of man's inner nature," Wagner asserts, for example, "is the language of tone (*die Tonsprache*), as the instinctive mode of expressing some inward feeling motivated from without" (IV, 91). Vowel sounds, as Rousseau, Herder, and others had maintained, represent the remnants of such an instinctive musical speech. Pure vowel sounds, variously inflected, can suggest to us something of "the first language of feelings, in which excited, intensified feelings could only have been communicated as the linking-together of such expressive intonations (*in einer Fügung tönender Ausdruckslaute*), and which would in this way represent themselves as a natural melody" (IV, 92). The feeling for the musical phrase originates

---

[26] Jacques Derrida, *Of Grammatology*, trans. Gayatri Chakravorty Spivak (Baltimore and London, 1976), 233.

in the natural constraints of breathing patterns, as musical rhythm originates in the articulation of these expressive vocalizations by means of accent and consonants, as well as accompanying physical gestures. While Herder did not share Rousseau's (or Wagner's) romanticizing conviction in the aesthetic perfection of such natural "musical" speech, he could supply corroboration of the Wagnerian theory of *Stabreim* and emotionally related root-syllables. Among a list of canonic propositions Herder provides with supportive glosses in his essay are two stating that: "The older and the more original languages are, the more is [an] analogy of the senses noticeable in their roots," and likewise: "The older and more original languages are, the more feelings intertwine in the roots of words."[27] Along the same lines, Herder offers support for Wagner's contention that language inevitably became distanced from its immediate, sensual impact on the feelings the more it had to provide a means for the communication of abstract concepts or any of the more complex information necessary to more developed stages of society.

Like these predecessors, Wagner conceded that language developed according to the dictates of societal needs, but because (like Rousseau, but unlike Herder) his arguments are meant to serve the ends of a personal aesthetic creed, he appeals (like Rousseau) to the mythic-religious scheme of a fall from an original grace and the promise of a future redemption. This theme of fall and alienation, and the subsequent yearning for redemption, re-integration, and wholeness is subjected to endless variation in Wagner's oeuvre. In the context from which I have just been citing, music – as always, the feminine principle – is implicitly the womb of language, and melody is explicitly represented as the "nourishing maternal breast," those primordial musical vocali-zations (*"tönende Laute"*), the "mother's milk" from which language had gradually to be weaned, in order to make its way independently and serve the requirements of reason, commerce, and the rest (IV, 93, 96). However inevitable this maturing process of independent language, the resulting alienation from its natural, physical origins is felt as an irreparable loss. The further language departed from a simple lexicon of emotionally direct root-syllables toward increasing levels of com-plexity and abstraction, "the more contumacious and estranged it became with respect to that original melody (*Urmelodie*), to the point where it finally lost even the most distant recollection thereof, collapsing in the faceless, droning hubbub of modern prose, devoid of [any real feeling for] breath and tone" (IV, 97).

In one sense, Wagner's whole "theoretical" exposition of the develop-ment of language and music and his outline for their redemptive

---

[27] J. G. Herder, *On the Origin of Language*, trans. Alexander Gode, in *On the Origin of Language: Two Essays*, 147–9.

unification in the "art-work of the future" play out a fantasy of regression toward an infantile state, back at the nurturing breast of that maternal *Urmelodie* – an infantile state of "passionate cries" and immediate physical stimuli in which language is just an instinctive babbling, and such vocal sounds are the purely natural signs of the emotions they signify. At moments of highest emotional pitch, Wagnerian heroines (though seldom heroes) will sometimes revert to something like this state, as in the climactic shrieks or wordless exhalations of Isolde (the interrupted tryst, the moment of Tristan's death), Brünnhilde (her surrender to Siegfried/Gunther in *Götterdämmerung*), or especially Kundry, whom Wagner endows with her own personal dialect of animal-like cries and groans. The anonymous reporter on the rehearsals of *Tristan*, cited earlier, seems to have read in the violent, unconstrained emotional contours of its music just this sort of reversion of language and music to a pre-cultural condition: "the singers' voices as well as the mightily engaged orchestra," he proclaimed, "are simply condemned to follow the often nonsensical libretto by sighing and lamenting, shouting and rejoicing, seething and roaring. The music is nothing but the accompaniment to emotional or passionate words."[28] Wagner, in other words, has successfully realized the fantasy of returning language and music to a state of primitive expressive utterance. The *Stabreim* of the *Ring* text explicitly participates in this same fantasy of anthropological regression, under the aegis of modern philology and authentic historical color (an "operatic" value that Wagner never repudiated). Indeed, it is the case for *Stabreim* as the necessary and only possible poetic mode of the new dramatic art-work that motivates Wagner's investigation into the "melodic" origins of language in the first place in *Opera and Drama*. By drawing attention to audible relationships between root-syllables, *Stabreim* could awaken some subliminal feeling for the (putative) phonetic and semantic ties that once united families of words and allowed speech to communicate directly with "feeling," as only music is any longer able to do.

So music, of course, must finally come to the rescue (although its role would be more appropriately construed as that of female redemptrix than chivalric champion). It remains for music, in modern times, to re-animate the "deceased organism" (*abgestorbener Organismus*) of language, the lifeless corpse that has been dissected for us by science

---

28 "Actenstücke aus München," 158 (see n. 5). The moments of reversion to such primal screams on the part of Wagner's characters are discussed by Philip Friedheim in an essay on "Wagner and the Aesthetics of the Scream," in *19th-Century Music* 7:1 (1983), 63–70. Some similar reactions to *Tristan* and other music of Wagner are cited by Peter Gay in a section on sensual, "pathological," and even "regressive" traits in the later nineteenth-century reception of this music. See *The Tender Passion* (New York, 1986), vol. II, 259–70.

(scholarship), but that awaits a new, higher poetic vitality from music, which is called upon literally to "breath life" into language once more (IV, 127). Evidently this is more a matter of a miraculous resurrection than of mere medical experiment. In any case, Wagner's lengthy exposition of his ideas on *Stabreim* revolves around the notion that musical tone will restore precisely that vitality and emotional immediacy that once obtained in the vocalized sounds of language, but has long since been lost. Language, or rather poetry, seeks to return to the element of pure, expressive vocalized "tone" from which it first developed. The poet, like any good Wagnerian, "yearns for redemption" – his warm breath melts a small spot amidst the "snowfields of pragmatic prose" that surround him everywhere, revealing the still living remnants of the "roots" he had given up for dead, striving upwards toward the air and sun (IV, 127–8). The metaphorical scenario of rebirth (Wagner cannot resist invoking the biological-organic connotations of linguistic "roots") jostles with that of regression toward origins – a return to the maternal bosom – as an alternative redemptive teleology.[29] Recognition of the latent, atavistic musical element in the roots of speech encourages the restoration or revitalization of that element (even if by artificial means): "In dissolving the vowel-sounds of the accented, alliterated root-word into its maternal element – musical tone – the poet has decisively entered into the domain of music (*Tonsprache*)" (IV, 137). Since vowel-sounds, whether spoken or sung, have long since lost their original expressive capacity, it remains for the modern or future composer to use all the musical means at his disposal to restore this lost quality to them, to "redeem" language.

Of course, it is not language as such that one can hope to redeem this way, any longer – even Wagner never envisioned a society populated entirely by Heldentenors and Heldin-sopranos, one assumes – only poetry, and that for the purposes of drama. The premises of this redemptive project to restore language and music to their unitary origins as "melody" are purely artificial, after all: its simulation of a "natural" musical language is designed to speak not to Neolithic man,

---

[29] The regressive impulse toward the maternal breast, or even womb, combines at one point with Wagner's familiar gendering of (female) music and the (male) "poetic intent" (or "feeling" and "understanding") to produce an instance of the figurative androgyny that Nattiez sees as fundamental to Wagner's thinking. In the closing pages of Part II of *Opera and Drama* (IV, 102) Wagner writes: "This element [i.e., music, which the male "poetic intent" should impregnate with its fertilizing seed] is the same feminine mother-element from whose womb (the ur-melodic capacity of expression), when fertilized by the objects of the natural world around it, there issued words and language, just as the intellect (*Verstand*) grew from feeling. In this way language, like reason, represents the synthesis of an [emotional] female principle with a male principle, capable of communication (*die Vedichtung dieses Weiblichen zum Männlichen, Mitteilungsfähigen*)."

but to *fin-de-siècle* man (or especially woman, according to some), and their culturally-specific redemptive needs. What we might call the logic of supplement behind this project is limited to the thoroughly artificial realm of opera, however much Wagner might have striven to erase the taint of artificiality that clung to the name of opera, along with the name itself. The lost musicality of language can be supplemented by music only as art, not as life, especially if music entails modern chromatic harmony, the late-Romantic orchestra, and only the most robust of operatic singers. Life, on the other hand, must be satisfied with second-hand redemption through the religion of art.[30]

The speculative pseudo-anthropology of *Opera and Drama* (like its earlier versions in Rousseau or Herder) obviously defies empirical confirmation, and perhaps even resists intuitive confirmation. It is difficult, that is, even to imagine any remotely "factual" basis to it (although Herder, as suggested, conveys a slightly greater sense of scientific plausibility than does Rousseau or Wagner). But aside from the desire to confront the enigma of human speech and its origins, which so provoked and fascinated the inquiring Enlightenment mind, such speculations offered the opportunity to construct a humanistic myth of origins, or at least to contribute to a mythic nexus around these. To people like Rousseau or Wagner this was also a means of validating (very different) personal aesthetic convictions. For Rousseau, it supported a conviction in the authenticity of simple, pleasing melody, and that the aesthetic value of a melody was naturally determined by the "musicality" of the language that engendered it (hence the monstrous birth that was the Lullian *tragédie lyrique*). For Wagner it supported a conviction in a melody radically emancipated from the constraints of conventional metric-harmonic periodicity, and one that might suffuse all fibers of the musical texture, as it had once suffused the fibers of language itself. For both of them, and for many others in the meantime, such hypotheses about the "melodic" origins of music permitted an imaginary contact with a pre-cultural, authentic, "purely-human" condition of origin, which – in Wagner's case – seems to have been a necessary stage in the exhaustive psychological preparations for the *Ring*.

---

[30] Wagner in fact suggested in *"Music of the Future"* that the vastly increased role of music in contemporary society since the eighteenth century could be attributed (aside from immediate sociological and technological factors) to its "supplemental" value along the lines I have discussed here from a more abstract viewpoint. That is, in its present state of development (despite all the faults Wagner is forever finding with it), music in the nineteenth century offers its practitioners and audiences the experience of immediate, direct sensual communication of "feeling" which has been sapped from literary modes of communication, as from linguistic communication altogether, Wagner maintained (see VII, 110–11 or Jacobs, *Three Wagner Essays*, 27–8). Thus modern music developed precisely as a "supplement" to language, which had increasingly lost the capacity for the physically direct communication of feelings.

Indeed, the link between such speculative ruminations on linguistic and musical origins and the *Ring* project itself is explicitly manifest in the opening of *Das Rheingold*. The prelude to *Das Rheingold* has, of course, always been glossed as a musical creation myth, in which the sustained "fundamental" of E♭ gives rise to the major triad by tracing the opening pitches of the overtone-series, and gradually filling in the rest of the major scale. But beyond this, the move from the prelude to the action of the first scene is nothing less than a compact *mise-en-scène* of the mutual origins of language and melody. (The latter, *pace* Rousseau, is shown to emerge from harmony, following Wagner's metaphorical imagery of harmonic ocean depths and melodic surface.) As Woglinde's "natural" melody (based on the triad with added sixth) emerges from the crest of the prelude's vast tonic surge, her words move tentatively from playful nonsense syllables to articulate speech, and back ("Weia! Waga! / Woge, du Welle, / walle zur Wiege! / Wagalaweia! / Wallala weiala weia!"), experimentally conjoining the various "musical" vowel sounds with – aptly enough – the "liquid" consonant "L" and the vowel-like "W". If the *Ring* includes, among other things, a musical-dramatic encoding of Wagner's mytho-poetic view of the history of music, as Jean-Jacques Nattiez contends (starting from this same example), it is also a righting of historical error, through the imaginary re-writing of history.[31] Returning to the very origins of music, Wagner is able to bypass all the errors of history and channel these pure waters directly into his perfected, purely human dramatic art-work. In a matter of measures, music has (re-)evolved from its primitive origins into the music of the future.

As validation of the *Ring* project, and of the musical audacities he was even now contemplating around 1850 (and would be defending within another decade, in *"Music of the Future"*), such fantasies of cultural regression toward natural origins – or the restoration of the values they embodied – could depend, in turn, on the authority of a long tradition of aesthetic thought, indeed of ancient lineage. The tradition had remained very much alive from Rousseau's day to Wagner's, and it may be assumed that much of Wagner's attempt at a theoretical defense of his "melody" derived, directly or indirectly, from recent aesthetic discourse that continued to underscore the morphological relation of melody to language, and hence the generalized status of melody as the "eloquent," "poetic," or "speaking" principle in music. Several examples (from many possible) may suffice to demonstrate.

---

31   See Nattiez, *Wagner Androgyne*, chapter 3 ("The *Ring* as a Mythic Account of the History of Music"), 53–96, in particular 53–60. Nattiez also pursues this phonetic genesis of language further into the opening scene of *Rheingold* (58–60).

Rousseau himself, to begin with, spoke for many of his day in asserting that melody achieved its expressive force in "imitation" of the speaking voice. This would appear to subordinate melody to speech, which it is supposed to have preceded. Rousseau, however, naturally wants to believe that melody possesses an eloquence superior to speech, even as an "imitation" of it:

By imitating the inflections of the voice, melody expresses pity, cries of sorrow and joy, threats and groans. All the vocal signs of passion are within its domain. It imitates the tones of language and the twists produced in every idiom by certain movements of the soul. Not only does it imitate, it speaks. And its language, though inarticulate, is lively, ardent, passionate; and it has a hundred times the vigor of speech itself.[32]

There is an element of cognitive dissonance here, albeit a mild one. Melody is expressive in the imitation of something that it once *was* (real language), but no longer is. The apparent contradiction between melody as the original source of language and language as the original model for melody's expressive character might be explained by the fact that the closing chapters of the *Essay* seem to have been appended to the rest without any attempt at integration. We might also appeal to Derrida's distinction, with regard to the *Essay*, between what Rousseau "declares" and what he "describes" (a basic source of such slippages between intention and meaning as first invited deconstruction). This paradox at the source of melody's eloquence invites, in any case, an interpretation in the spirit of our mythological *telos* of origins, loss, and redemption. The pathos of this auditory spectacle, this sounding dumb show, derives from the atavistic memories awakened in us of the former splendor, the lost paradise of a poetic-musical *Ursprache* or *Urmelodie*. Melody moves us by its inherent attempt to recuperate an irretrievable past, a lost wholeness of speech and song.

In one form or another, the identification of melody as the essential principle of eloquence in music, through a morphological analogy with language, and hence the justification of its potential status as "poetry" maintained a distinguished aesthetic pedigree down to Wagner's time. The entry on "melody" in Johann Georg Sulzer's widely read *Allgemeine Theorie der schönen Künste* (1791–4) amplifies the ideas on melody in Rousseau's *Essay* (as well as the *Dictionnarie de musique*), beginning with the aesthetic primacy of melody over harmony (melody being the "end" to which harmony is an accessory "means"), and suggesting that, in listening to a melody, one should be able to imagine that one is

---

[32] Rousseau, *Essay*, 57 (translation slightly amended). On problems regarding the genesis of the essay, its context, and the readings by Derrida and Paul de Man, see John Neubauer, *The Emancipation of Music from Language* (New Haven, 1986), chapter 6 (85–102), as well as Peggy Kamuf, "Origins" (see n. 20).

hearing human speech, suffused (*durchdrungen*) with a particular emotion.[33] (Here again is the "supplemental" logic I have attributed to Wagner: musical tone restores the direct emotional appeal that has been sapped from spoken language.) The ideas from Sulzer's *Allgemeine Theorie* were kept in circulation into the next century by Gustav Schilling, who paraphrased them in a treatise on musical aesthetics and a musical encyclopedia, both from the 1830s:

> Melody must at all times represent an inner feeling, and in such a way that whoever hears it will imagine that he hears a human discourse, suffused with a particular emotion and striving to communicate this through externally sounding signs (*durch äußere tönende Zeichen kund zu thun*). For this reason, too, it is a product of genius and inspiration.[34]

Hegel, whose specific points on music in the *Lectures on Aesthetics* are similarly derivative of a general tradition, echoes these familiar figures, stating that "melody is the poetic element of music, the language of the soul (*Seelensprache*) which pours into tones the inner joys and sorrows of the heart (*Gemüt*)," and further, "the higher, poetic side of music, the realm of true artistic invention, also as regards the application of its other elements."[35] Schopenhauer took somewhat greater pains to adapt traditional conceptions of melody to his own system of aesthetic thought, identifying melody with the "highest level of the objectification of the Will, the self-aware life activity (*das besonnene Leben und Streben*) of mankind." This view is situated within the context of a rather elaborate metaphorical reading of musical "levels" (bass line, harmonic inner voices, upper melodic line) as representations of the "Will" and its levels of manifestation in the natural world. Schopenhauer's dithyrambic exegesis of melody and its expressive character works its way back to the familiar point of origin: melody as a language of the feelings (corollary to a verbal language of reason).

> [Melody] thus narrates the history of the Will as illuminated by consciousness, whose impress (*Abdruck*) in reality is the series of its deeds. But it says more – it narrates its most secret history (*erzählt seine geheimste Geschichte*), too, depicting every motion, every striving, every gesture of the Will, everything that reason comprehends under the broad, negative concept of feeling and is unable to absorb any further into its abstractions. Thus it has always been said that music is the language of feeling, as speech is the language of reason . . . [36]

---

[33] J. G. Sulzer, *Allgemeine Theorie der schönen Künste*, vol. III (4th edn, Leipzig, 1793), 371.

[34] G. Schilling, *Versuch einer Philosophie des Schönen in der Musik*, 211–12. Cf. *Enzyklopädie der gesammten musikalischen Wissenschaften*, vol. IV (Stuttgart, 1837), 644.

[35] G. W. F. Hegel, *Vorlesungen über die Aesthetik* (III.2.2. section c), from *Werke*, vol. XV (Frankfurt, 1970), 187, 185.

[36] A. Schopenhauer, *Die Welt als Wille und Vorstellung* (part I, §52), vol. II, 326.

Eventually Wagner's own extensive divagations on the analogies between speech and melody in *Opera and Drama* spawned a whole new era of critical confrontation with this theme. That literature is perhaps best left undisturbed for now, although I might recall the effort of the young Louis Köhler to demonstrate the practical implications of Wagner's insights in a study of "the melody of speech" (*Die Melodie der Sprache*, 1853), cited in the preceding chapter for its attempt to divine the "natural melody" within Wagner's textual example for the "poetic-musical period." Köhler went on to illustrate how one might proceed from the example of street cries and folk songs to intuit the "natural" melodies inherent in any poetic verse. (The results – in a "natural" setting of "Kennst du das Land" – are scarcely convincing; they might fairly be called original, though, or even infantile: Köhler took the "regressive" aspect of Wagner's agenda much too literally, as he did the whole discourse of *Tonsprache* and *Versmelodie*.)[37] Easy as it is to ridicule Köhler's naïveté, his efforts raise a legitimate question as to what the practical consequences, if any, of this traditional discourse might be. For all his appeals to history and pre-history, after all, Wagner claimed to be preparing the future. In one very concrete matter Köhler anticipated a claim that Wagner made explicit in *"Music of the Future,"* though it was already hovering about in Part III of *Opera and Drama*: that musical form could (and should) be derived from a poetic or dramatic text, and that such form could be construed as "melody" (Köhler had boldly asserted that the "form" of a song was always latent in the poem).

The relation of a text to the categories of "melody" and musical "form" can be interpreted at many levels, some banally evident, and others arcane. In certain ways Wagner's contention that form is a function of melody could rely on the support of aesthetic/theoretical traditions similar to those behind his discourse of the mutual origins of melody and speech, as well as some very pragmatic pedagogical views. In other ways Wagner's equation of melody and form tends to evaporate into metaphysics, as does the idea of "endless melody" itself. Or, like so much of Wagner's achievement, we might say that "endless melody" mediates between musical facts and metaphysics, between sound and symbol, form and "content." To illuminate this claim let us consider more closely the equation of "melody" and "form."

[37] Köhler's book was (predictably) lampooned in a review by Ludwig Bischoff (*Niederrheinische Musik-Zeitung* 1:14 [1853], 106–9) but discussed very much in earnest (equally predictably) by Franz Brendel somewhat later (*Anregungen für Kunst, Leben und Wissenschaft* 1 [1856], 10–28). Traditional speculations on the mutual origins of language and music, incidentally, were soon to become the object of a new positivist scientific inquiry in the work of such famous "evolutionists" as Spencer and Darwin. See, for example, the excerpts given by B. Bujic in *Music in European Thought, 1851–1912* (Cambridge, 1988), 309–26.

Endless melodies

Melody as form

Wagner identified melody (and hence "endless melody") as a principle of form, while his detractors identified his "endless melody" (or absence of melody) as a principle of formlessness. Moreover, just as the hypothetical poetic *Urmelodie* would have necessarily been indistinguishable from the "form" of language, or of the individual "speech act" (their common grammar and vocabulary grounded in nature alone), the "endless melody" of Wagner's musical drama was to pattern itself after the dramatic text and/or action: the form of the melody was to be "motivated" entirely by the drama. Here, too, the critics understood a principle of formlessness. Let me begin here by reviewing Wagner's several statements to the effect that melody is the essential "form" of music, and offering a few interpretive remarks. Just as Wagner's broader aesthetic constructions of melody resonate with a long line of speculative and critical discourse (since the eighteenth century) that offered support for such a melodic reading of musical form as an aesthetic construct, I will suggest here how a more or less technical understanding of melodic "form" in his writings can be grounded in earlier theoretical discourse on melody. Finally, I will consider some of the ways the forms or procedures of Wagner's own music have been, and might be, understood as a function of "endless melody."

The equation of melody with form is variously reiterated throughout Wagner's writings, although the terms of this equation become more elusive when he moves from conventional, "absolute" melody to the new ("endless") species that inhabits the music drama. "It is undoubtedly melody that we have to understand as the form of music," he states, in unusually lapidary style, in "On the Destiny of Opera" ("Über die Bestimmung der Oper," 1871).[38] One year earlier, in *Beethoven*, he refers to melody as "the principal form of all music" (*Hauptform aller Musik* – IX, 102). In *"Music of the Future"* we read that melody is "the only form of music" ("Setzen wir zuerst fest, *daß die einzige Form der Musik die Melodie ist"* – VII, 125; original emphasis). And the equation is implicit in a statement that precedes this one by a page or so, that Wagner will turn his attention to the subject of "musical form, or melody" ("Ich will . . . endlich nur noch die musikalische Form, *die Melodie*, ins Auge fasse[n]," VII, 124; original emphasis). Only in this latter statement does Wagner actually speak of "musical form," rather than the "form of music." Wagner's prose may generally lack the rigor that would justify this kind of semantic hair-splitting; yet the distinction here is

---

[38] "Als die Form der Musik haben wir zweifellos die Melodie zu verstehen" (X, 147). Cf. *Opera and Drama* (III, 309), where Wagner identifies melody simply as the "essence" of music (". . . wenn wir das Wesen der Musik kurz und bündig in den Begriff der *Melodie* zusammenfassen").

potentially a fundamental one, as it has the power to invalidate our whole enterprise. If "form" here is to be understood simply as "form of being" – the condition or quality of music *tout court* – it does not automatically follow that melody defines the structure of a composition in any way that might satisfy the canons of formal analysis. For example, when Wagner designates "endless melody" as the "unerring form" in which the musician realizes that which the poet has pointedly left unsaid (VII, 130), he speaks only of a quality or a condition (music), not of any particular structure. Similarly, when he asserts in this same context "that without melody the very idea of music is impossible, and that music and melody are strictly indivisible concepts" (VII, 125), Wagner is simply identifying melody as the invariable substance of music, like scales and pitches, or rhythm.

On the other hand, two already familiar propositions within *"Music of the Future"* seem to confirm a reading of "form" not merely as ontological condition, but also as structure or "formation." Beethoven's symphonic form (of which the first movement of the "Eroica" stood as the presumed paradigm) is construed as the "expansion of melody (*Ausdehnung der Melodie*) . . . into a continuous large-scale piece, which itself constituted a single, perfectly coherent melody" (VII, 127; Jacobs, 38). Somewhat earlier the same phrase is applied to the music of *Tristan*, where the "entire expanse of the melody (*Ausdehnung der Melodie*)" is now dictated by the "fabric (*Gewebe*) of the words and verses, or in other words, the design of this melody is poetically predetermined" (VII, 123). In the following paragraph we encounter a paraphrase of this interpretation of the *Tristan* music, substituting "form" for "melody," where we read of "the musical form as it is predetermined by the poem" (*die im Gedichte vollständig bereits vorgebildite musikalische Form* – VII, 123). In either case – the Beethoven symphony or *Tristan* – it seems possible to construe the melodic "form" of which Wagner speaks *either* as an ontological condition (form of being, i.e., the claim to continuous, genuinely "melodic" status) *or* as empirical structure, in some as yet rather nebulous sense. I will defer the attempt to interpret this nebulous structural reading for the moment, in order to show how Wagner had already absorbed a fairly traditional theoretical construction of form as melody by this time, since it is likely that Wagner's construction of melody-as-form is predicated to some extent on this more concrete traditional background.

One of the predominant conceptual leitmotifs of the Zurich writings, by now a familiar one, is the foundation of classical instrumental forms in a rhythmic or rhythmic-harmonic "dance-melody." (In this sense, Wagner had argued, even supposedly "absolute" musical forms were ultimately grounded in extra-musical gesture: visual, corporeal symmetry and motion.) Essentially Wagner's point is the unexceptionable one that the sonata form, like the other movement types of classic-Romantic instrumental genres, derives from the model of simple binary dance-forms, and these models were generally distinguished by homophonic textures – what Wagner calls the "harmonized dance-melody" – and unified by repeating rhythmic motives, as suggested by the similar phrase "rhythmic dance-melody" (see, for example, *The Art-Work of the Future*, III, 90–1).[39] The basic repertoire of classical movement types, in other words (sonata form, ternary forms, variations, minuet or scherzo, rondo), could all be explained at some level in terms of the alternation of contrasting, complementary melodic periods, variously expanded from pairs of simple four-, eight-, or sixteen-measure phrases. The genesis of classical forms from the model of the simple melodic period proposed in the Zurich writings is succinctly restated in *"Music of the Future"*:

> It is extremely interesting and at the same time enlightening with regard to the nature of all musical form to observe how German composers (*deutsche Meister*) have taken the simple dance melody . . . and sought to impart to it a gradually richer and broader development (*Entwickelung*). The melody originally consisted of a short four-bar period that could be either doubled or quadrupled. It seems to have been the chief aim of our composers to expand this single melody into a broader form, which thereby provided the opportunity for a richer harmonic development, as well. (VII, 108–9)

Wagner's concern with this pedigree of instrumental forms was not so much heuristic as polemical. In this context he is accounting for the superiority of the "developed" dance-melody in the German instrumental classics over the "undeveloped" dance or song forms that live on in modern opera. Beyond that, his larger aim (here as before) is to demonstrate both the historical and epistemological contingencies of "absolute" musical forms, and hence their inherent limitations, which might be transcended if the gestural foundations in dance were traded for those of drama (traded for a more worthy set of contingencies, that is).[40] The highly abstract level at which Wagner carried out this demonstration is characteristic of the Zurich writings and their world-historical posturings, reducing all historical and cultural phenomena to immutable

---

39   Wagner's dance-based theory of classical forms is discussed in T. Grey, "Richard Wagner and the Aesthetics of Musical Form," 296–309. This complex of ideas in the Zurich writings and its relation to contemporary essays by Wagner's friend Uhlig are also discussed by Klaus Kropfinger in *Wagner and Beethoven*, 70–91, esp. 86–91.

40   The same historical construction occurs in the following passage from *Opera and Drama*, for instance (Part I, section 5), where it is adapted to the larger polemical argument:

> While operatic melody, without the fructifying contact of poetry, could only just barely sustain a wretched and sterile existence, stumbling from one forced and artificial incarnation to another, instrumental music had gradually developed into a true language of its own by breaking up its foundations in simple homophonic dance- and song-forms (*harmonische Tanz- und Liedweise*) into ever smaller

principles and inevitable consequences. But behind the neo-Hegelian façade is a century-old theoretical tradition, one that evolved alongside the forms its describes, and construes musical forms in terms of a hierarchy of melodic elements of motive, theme, phrase, period, and section.

Paradoxically, theorists and aestheticians alike had been consistently loath to allow that "melody" could be susceptible to elucidation by theoretical or "scientific" precepts at all, insofar as it was understood to belong within the purview of "invention," poetic inspiration, and genius. Pedagogy focused instead on the principles of counterpoint and harmony (as thoroughbass). Nonetheless, the earliest attempts to codify the principles of classical sonata form – in H. C. Koch's *Versuch einer Anleitung zur Komposition* (1782–93) – occur, as Mark Evan Bonds points out, within the context of "extended discourses on melody," which he notes as being typical of the era.[41] And it is only reasonable that the study of melody – understood to begin with the study of motives, themes, and phrase structure – can provide a better access to principles of organization at the level of a movement than could the rules of counterpoint or figured bass. (The harmonic reading of sonata form, on the other hand, is necessarily more descriptive than generative.) That the closest approach to an explanation of musical forms in the eighteenth century, whether for taxonomic or instructional purposes, is to be found in discussions of melody is demonstrated at some length by Bonds, with reference to Mattheson, Riepel, Daube, and Galeazzi, in addition to Koch. Galeazzi's exegesis of sonata form, for instance, falls within the heading "On Melody in Particular, and on its Parts, Sections, and Rules," recalling the situation with Koch.[42] A melodic approach to form in most of these cases need not be confused with the issue of thematically-oriented definitions of sonata or other forms, although they may eventually intersect. That is, the starting point for these earlier theorists was not, of course, the identification of first, second, and closing themes, but the more fundamental idea that a dance-form, rondo,

---

fragments, which were in turn extended, abridged, and re-combined in manifold new configurations. Yet this language could only remain arbitrary, failing to express any purely human content in any higher aesthetic sense, so long as the formation of these melodic speech-elements (*die Gestaltung jener melodischen Sprachtheile*) was not guided by the need to convey distinct, individual human feelings (III, 277).

41 Bonds, *Wordless Rhetoric*, 2–3.
42 Ibid., 43. On the various theoretical correlations of melody and form, see further 43–50, 71–80, and 90–118. Bonds is also concerned with restoring a greater emphasis to the thematic articulation of forms, even from an eighteenth-century perspective. By Wagner's time, of course, the formal function of thematic identities had assumed an unmistakable prominence, as is often observed, and as the phenomenon of the leitmotif will remind us. (Recall that Hanslick eventually thought to define the "content" of a work in terms of its thematic material, as mentioned in chapter 1.)

or sonata movement, as well as an aria, can be viewed as a concatenation of melodic phrase units, within some loosely hierarchical framework.

However difficult it may have been to articulate the underlying principles of a melodic-formal syntax above the phrase level, an instinctive appreciation of them was central to many views of form, as Wagner's ideas testify. His intuition of the formal derivation of sonatas and symphonies from simple dance melodies is already clearly formulated by Johann Friedrich Daube at the end of the eighteenth century when he explains, encouragingly, that a movement in a symphony or a concerto differs from a simple minuet only in the manner, or scope, of the working-out (*Ausführung*) of its thematic ideas.[43] But while Daube, addressing an audience of late-eighteenth-century amateurs, evidently viewed the relation of simple to complex forms as one based on the internal expansion of individual phrase and period units, Wagner's conception of form as the "expansion" of a melody (*Ausdehnung der Melodie*) – whether in a Beethoven symphonic allegro or in *Tristan* – emphasizes developmental processes and the possibility of implementing these in all sections of a movement. Both, however, see the larger form as an expansion of a simpler, hypothetical melodic model.

This affinity should come as no surprise, if we consider the continuity of the pedagogical views of melodic form between such eighteenth-century writers as Koch and Daube and those closer to Wagner's generation, like J. C. Lobe or A. B. Marx. The composition treatises of Lobe and Marx, as the predominant examples of the genre through the 1840s and 50s (and beyond, in the case of Marx), were both still oriented toward a "periodological" view of form, as Dahlhaus identifies it.[44] Lobe's conception of form, in particular (as we saw in chapter 4), is entirely based on the division of a movement into constituent periods and the appropriate development of melodic or motivic ideas within these. Marx made a greater effort to rationalize a hierarchy of melodic levels that could provide the basis for a more or less organic theory of form. Elementary units of "motive," "passage," and "phrase" (*Motiv*,

43 Ibid., 50. See also George Buelow, "The Concept of *Melodielehre*: A Key to Classic Style," in *Mozart Jahrbuch* 1978–9 (Cassel, 1979), 195, and Daube, *Anleitung zur Erfindung der Melodie und ihre Fortsetzung* (Vienna, 1797–8), 43–7, 48–51. For a recent, fuller account of some of these same issues, see Joel Lester, *Compositional Theory in the Eighteenth Century* (Cambridge MA, 1992), chapter 6, "Mattheson and the Study of Melody," 158–74; chapter 10, "Riepel on Melody and Phrases," 258–72; and chapter 11, "Koch: Toward a Comprehensive Approach to Musical Structure," 273–99.

44 Carl Dahlhaus, *Die Musiktheorie im 18. und 19. Jahrhundert*, vol. I (Darmstadt, 1984), 8, 20. Dahlhaus notes that Marx never fully succeeded in achieving a theoretical mediation between such "periodology" and an account of form at the length of a full movement (the same stumbling block, that is, faced by the authors of eighteenth-century *Melodielehren*).

Gang, Satz), constitute the seeds of larger structural levels: the basic antecedent–consequent period, the larger divisions of *Hauptsatz, Seitensatz, Schlußsatz,* and finally the division into overall sections or parts (*Teile*) of exposition, development, recapitulation, and coda. To the extent the "invention" of motivic ideas sets the process in motion, this view of form is still melodically oriented. And to the extent that Marx or Lobe looked to sonata-form movements (especially those of Beethoven) as a culminating ideal, their theories of form encouraged a re-tracing of the progression from the clearly "punctuated" melodic forms of simple binary or ternary models to those in which thematic ideas avoided distinct closure. Implicit already in classical sonata form, in other words, is Wagner's ideal of a "continuous," coherent melody (brought out by the example of the "Eroica"). Instead of the individual, discrete melody of the "theme" (for variations) or of popular song, melody is increasingly dissolved into melodic *process*, so that finite "melodies" give way to ongoing "melody." According to this view, then, Wagner could legitimately maintain that "endless" or infinite melody was not invented, but evolved. (And this is precisely what he does assert, if loosely, in the course of *"Music of the Future."*)

If it is true, as Bonds suggests, that the word "melody" was commonly associated with the entire length of a movement (or, more precisely, its "outline"), then it could also be said that Wagner, consciously or not, preserved this more rarefied aspect of earlier tradition in defiance of the standard sense of an isolated theme or tune. The identification of "melody" with movement-form as a whole haphazardly implied by Koch, for instance, is still represented as one possible sense of the term in Anton Reicha's 1814 *Traité de mélodie* (where he first expounds such formal taxonomies as his often-cited *grande coupe binaire*, later incorporated into the more methodical composition treatise of 1824–6).[45] Or, if "melody" is not necessarily equated with the entire substance of a movement in all earlier usages, it is, "as the predominant voice, . . . capable of at least representing a complete outline of a movement."[46] This was apparently the very point Wagner aimed to demonstrate to his young admirer, Felix Draeseke, when he regaled him with the first movement of the "Eroica" as solo song, or when he spoke of the Beethovenian symphonic paradigm as a "single, prefectly coherent melody." (Along the same lines, Wagner also referred to the underlying melody or *melos* of such other formally and texturally complex works

45 On Koch, see Bonds, *Wordless Rhetoric*, 91. "Among German theorists, the term *Melodie* carried many meanings and connotations throughout the eighteenth century, one of the most important of which relates it to the outline of an entire movement."

46 Ibid., 150.

as the op. 131 Quartet or the first movement of the Ninth Symphony as the key to aesthetic comprehension and executive interpretation alike.)[47]

Form as melodic *outline* could take us all the way back to Rousseau, who appealed to melody not to explain the structure of musical works, but to explain the effect of melody (rather than harmony) as "imitation" or its capacity to constitute musical "signs." The brief chapter "On Melody" in the *Essay on the Origin of Languages* is devoted entirely to the analogy between melody and "line" or drawing in painting, and to a reciprocal analogy between color and harmony. "The role of melody in music," Rousseau declares, "is precisely that of drawing in painting. This is what constitutes the strokes and figures (*les traits et les figures*), of which the harmonies and the sounds are merely the colors."

Music is no more the art of combining sounds to please the ear than painting is the art of combining colors to please the eye. If there were no more to it than that, they would both be natural sciences rather than fine arts. Imitation alone raises them to this level. But what makes painting an imitative art? Drawing. What makes music another? Melody.[48]

"Imitation" is thus a matter of form and expression at once, in painting and music alike. The visual (or audible) lines that serve to "imitate" an object or feeling also determine the emotional effect upon the viewer/listener.

The word for drawing, *dessin* (or *dessein*), was later defined by Rousseau in the *Dictionnaire de musique* as something like the "design" of a movement or composition, specifically as this emerges from the deployment of the principal thematic ideas in the course of the work. Later writers also used the term to signify the individual theme itself, and Reicha applies it even to the subthematic motive.[49] This latter meaning of *dessin* as theme or motive is not easily reconciled with the sense of large-scale thematic "design," it might seem. And yet it opens up an ambiguity that could be productively applied to Rousseau and Wagner alike, however incommensurable their practical senses of melody must be. As thematic or motivic unit, the *dessin* is that melodic "sign" that so interested Rousseau[50] (without his having tried to develop

---

[47]   See Wagner, *My Life*, 503, on op. 131, and *On Conducting* (VIII, 274 and Jacobs, *Three Wagner Essays*, 57) regarding Habeneck's rendition of the Ninth Symphony in Paris.

[48]   Rousseau, *Essay*, 55.

[49]   See Bonds, *Wordless Rhetoric*, 92–3 and Ian Bent, "Analysis," in *The New Grove Dictionary of Music and Musicians*, ed. S. Sadie (London and New York, 1980), vol. I, 346 (Bonds does not refer to Reicha's use of *dessin*). See Bonds, *Wordless Rhetoric*, 113, incidentally, for a reference to a later *Handbuch* by Koch (1811) that speaks of melody as "the ideal of a composer, or at the same time the sketch of the musical picture," recalling Rousseau's *dessin* and the relation between "melody" and the "design" of a whole composition.

[50]   "The sounds of a melody do not affect us merely as sounds," he asserts in chapter 15 of the *Essay*, "but as signs of our affections, of our feelings. It is thus that they excite in us the emotions expressed by those images we recognize in it" (Rousseau, *Essay*, 59).

an actual musical semiotics), and which is the basis for the larger melodic "design" of a composition – the composite "drawing," or form. And for Wagner, of course, these signs are motives, or leitmotifs. (However much we resist the decoding of leitmotifs as simple, univocal signs, it is obviously futile to deny their fundamentally semiotic aspect.) The "design" traced by his "endless melody" is a design made up of that intricate "network" of such musical-dramatic motives (*Gewebe der Hauptthemen, Gewebe von Grundthemen*) as it spread itself across the "entire drama, in the most intimate relation with the poetic intent" (IV, 322), bountifully dispensing the "unity of a symphonic movement" throughout the vast expanse of the drama (X, 185). Beyond this, Wagner was hardly any more precise than Rousseau regarding the principles structuring the big picture, the *dessin* as a musical whole, or as musical "form." (As a composer and an undisputed *génie*, Wagner felt no more obligation to propound scientific principles than Rousseau had.)

As was the case with Rousseau's thoughts on the origins of melody and language, we find that his analogies of melody and drawing – what we might call his theory of melodic "delineation" – had also been preserved in later aesthetic (if not theoretical) discourse. Friedrich Vischer – the most highly regarded philosophical aesthetician of the mid-nineteenth century, and sometime acquaintance of Wagner's in Zurich – seems to draw directly on Rousseau in his *Ästhetik oder Wissenschaft des Schönen* (the volume in question appeared in 1857):

everything else [beyond the fundamentals of rhythm and harmony] – the direct expression of mood or feeling, character and life – is the product of melody. Only melody gives to the coloration of harmony: light, outline, drawing (*das Licht, den Umriß, die Zeichnung*), the vitality and inner movement of the art-work.[51]

Summarizing both the aesthetic and theoretical traditions we have been surveying here, Vischer adds: "Melody is not just one of the constituent elements of music . . . , but its essential form as it comes into being; it is the form of the musical art-work, as the formation of shapes is that of the plastic arts . . . The study of musical forms is identical with the study of melody."[52] Vischer also brings out another

---

[51]   F. T. Vischer, *Ästhetik oder Wissenschaft des Schönen* (2nd edn, Munich, 1923), vol. IV, 176. In the same paragraph Vischer speaks of melody as "absolute form." It is generally agreed that the musical chapters of Vischer's *Ästhetik* were co-authored by Karl Köstlin, although it seems plausible that this more generalized discourse stems from Vischer himself (as the proximity to Rousseau might also suggest).

[52]   Vischer continues: "Melodie ist nicht eine spezielle Form innerhalb der Musik neben andere Formen, sondern sie ist die allerdings durch Rhythmus und Harmonie bedingte und unterstützte wesentliche Form . . . , sie ist die Form des musikalischen Kunstwerks, wie Gestaltenbildung die des plastischen . . . ; Lehre von der Form des musikalischen Kunstwerks und Melodik sind identisch" (ibid., 169).

potential meaning of Rousseau's analogy with "line" and drawing: that melody could not only be understood as the composite "outline" of the work, but even represent an analogy to the very act of drawing – the line or outline of form *in statu nascendi* (form as the process of formation, experienced in time). While Wagner interpreted Beethoven's melody more or less on the basis of the theoretical-pedagogical traditions enumerated above, it was this broader aesthetic notion of melodic "delineation" (as well as Rousseau's notion of melody as a system of expressive "signs") that better served his defensive strategy in *"Music of the Future"* of re-defining melody simply as the "meaningful" or expressive in music, and as the only meaningful substance of any music at all. This loose kinship between Wagner's and Rousseau's ideas of melody (whether owed to a first-hand acquaintance or mediated by Vischer and the like) brings us back to the unresolved question of "endless melody" and the nature of its "form" or forms it generates.

Whatever forms might be "delineated" or outlined by Wagner's endless melody, they are obviously of a substantially different order than those described by theorists from Mattheson and Riepel through Reicha, Marx, and Lobe (or Wagner himself) as expanded versions of a single periodic-melodic model. In fact, Wagner's revision of the very concept of "melody," discussed at the outset of the chapter, is a logical consequence, in a way, of the "poetic-musical period" in *Opera and Drama*: in each case, Wagner seeks to extend a category of musical structure (the period, as a local unit, and melody, as a global phenomenon) by appealing to an earlier, broader signification wherein the musical sense merges with a linguistic one (the rhetorical period and the Greek *melos* or the mythical-anthropological trope of a prelapsarian poetic *Urmelodie*). In recuperating the ancient, "authentic" meanings of these categories, however, Wagner refashions them to suit the needs of his thoroughly modern music drama.

The forms or musical-dramatic designs that were now loosely "outlined" by a continuous network of leitmotifs are less and less subject to the hierarchies governing traditional notions of melodic form. The "hypotactic" model of form implied by Hanslick's notion of a "large-scale rhythm" (in which phrases and periods stand in either a principal or a subordinate relation to the formal "sentence" as a whole) gives way to a more "paratactic" model of form, in which "poetic-musical periods" are more or less freely strung together.[53] We assume that some principle of musical, as well as dramatic, design guides the way such units are "strung together" – for example, the dialectic model of dramatic dialogue form proposed in chapter 4. (A broader problem

53 Carl Dahlhaus, *Nineteenth-Century Music*, 199–200.

with Lorenz's analyses, beyond the questionable criteria whereby he determined the shape of his individual "poetic-musical periods," is the general lack of concern for how the over-determined forms of these periods are conjoined at a higher level.) In a certain sense, any effort to describe the shapes of Wagner's dramatic music is implicated in an interpretation of "endless melody." Putting the matter this way underscores the potential tautology inherent in Wagner's own equation of melody and form. Even so, the equation will at least yield a corollary that is supported by much of the post-Lorenzian analytical literature: if melody can be construed as the basis of traditional forms, then "endless (infinite, non-finite) melody" naturally yields "non-finite" forms, that is, the open-ended, "evolving" forms whose ideological foundations were touched on in chapter 3, and whose compositional genealogy (or one line of it) was proposed in chapter 4. Before finally advancing a few practical exemplifications of the term, let me conclude this overview of its critical history and pre-history with a look at some of the musical meanings that have been ascribed to it.

For a long time after Wagner coined the term "endless melody," it was generally taken as an outright admission of formlessness, as testified by a number of the comments cited at the beginning of the chapter. As early as 1862 some of the more "advanced" passages in Gounod's *Faust* (!) elicited from the Parisian critic Scudo an allusion to the insalubrious new "doctrine of continuous melody, . . . the melody of the virgin forest and the setting sun, that constitutes the charm of *Tannhäuser* and *Lohengrin*, a melody that may be compared to Harlequin's letter: 'as for periods and commas, I don't give them a thought, I leave it to you to put them wherever you wish'."[54] Harlequin's letter nicely situates for us the problematic transition between the older pedagogical traditions of melodic form and the elusive "form" of Wagner's endless melody. As we saw, the analogy to punctuation had been a standard component of earlier linguistic and rhetorical metaphors for form. Nearly every eighteenth-century writer on the subject, as Bonds notes, "makes some kind of comparison between this hierarchy of cadences and the conventions of verbal punctuation: the full, authentic cadence is the equivalent of a period; the half cadence is like a colon or semi-colon; and weaker points of articulation are analogous to commas." "There is," he adds, "a consistent emphasis on the underlying need for such points of articulation. Without them, individual phrases would be

---

[54] *Revue des deux mondes* (1862), cited from Stravinsky, *Poetics of Music*, 14–15. (Stravinsky is quoting Scudo ironically, of course, in a polemical digression about "the critics," but he is also voicing an implicit solidarity with Gounod, the well-bred melodist, against the real perpetrators of endless melody.

indistinguishable from one another; a movement consisting of unintelligible phrases would be unintelligible as a whole."[55] These same grammatical analogies continue to inform criticism of Wagner's endless melody for several decades, as a constant refrain lamenting the absence of those *Ruhepunkte* (points of repose) essential to melodic intelligibility. This refrain begins with responses to *The Flying Dutchman*, if not earlier, and naturally reaches a climax with *Tristan*.[56] It is easy enough to see why so many earlier listeners were nonplussed by Wagner's musical "stream of consciousness" or *vers libre*, though of course there were many more who found it exhilarating. But it was not until the era of Ernst Kurth and Alfred Lorenz that anyone seriously attempted to subject this apparently *ungebundene Rede* to critical analysis.

Lorenz took the "poetic-musical period," rather than "endless melody," as a (nominal) starting point for his analytic methodology – notions of infinity or endlessness were hardly useful to his agenda to rationalize the formal designs of Wagner's music dramas that had so long remained obscured by the mystical incense of "endless melody" and endless meaning. Kurth, on the other hand (prone as he was to a certain "modern" psychological brand of mysticism) was less interested in discovering secrets of architectonic form and more interested in the musical sources of such infinite depths of Romantic expression, and his lengthy explorations of the "crisis" of Romantic harmony (rather than the secret of Romantic form) culminates in a 127-page chapter on Wagner's "endless melody."[57] For Kurth, the category of "endless melody" represents an area of fundamental psychic impulses, a source of the primitive musical "energies" that motivate harmonic progressions and resultant forms – in short, something vaguely akin to the whole philosophy of melodic "origins" sketched above. Kurth apostrophized a "regenerative force" operating in Wagner's harmony and melody alike, a force by means of which "the genius is able to grasp phenomena by

---

55 Bonds, *Wordless Rhetoric*, 72.
56 Ludwig Rellstab, for example, decried the general lack of "repose" in the music of *The Flying Dutchman* following the Berlin premiere in 1844 – expatiating on the aesthetic values of such "repose" in a way that suggests an encoded homily to the bourgeois social values of the *Vormärz* (see Jürgen Rehm, *Zur Musikrezeption in vormärzlichen Berlin* [Hildesheim, 1983], 89). In his 1865 brochure on the phenomenon of *Tristan*, with "introductory remarks on melody and music," J. B. Allfeld exclaimed: "of leading tonalities or meters, musical points of repose, cadences that might mitigate the continuous, nerve-wracking rhythmic upheavals: not a trace" (*Tristan und Isolde von Richard Wagner*, 31).
57 E. Kurth, *Romantische Harmonik und ihre Krise in Wagners "Tristan"* (Berlin, 1923), 444–571. See also the chapter on "Kurth's Concept of Form" (and particularly 199–212 on "Form in *Romantische Harmonik*") in Lee A. Rothfarb, *Ernst Kurth as Theorist and Analyst* (Philadelphia, 1988), 190–212.

280

their deepest roots – an affinity for the most authentic (*das Ursprüng-lichste*) and simplest things and their secret powers."[58] ("According to Kurth," writes Lee Rothfarb, "Wagner's endless melody represents a 'regaining of an ancient principle, but in new, unique forms'.")[59] Once again we encounter the mythic trope of returning to an original state, or rather restoring "original" values or principles within a new, modern (or even "future") context. At one level, Kurth identified in Wagner a modern revival of the fluid melodic idioms of Baroque *Fortspinnung* techniques, an emancipation from the constraints of classical periodicity (while also "sublating" such classical contributions as the structuring potential of broad harmonic progressions). At a more fundamental level, Kurth concerned himself with discerning the principles of motivic and linear "energy" that operate, in different but related ways, in the music of Bach as well as that of Wagner, in the phenomena he identified variously as "Ur-motives" and "developmental motives" (*Urmotive, Entwicklungsmotive*). In Wagner's music, these operate at a generally sub-leitmotivic level where melody (or motive) and harmony converge, as in the paradigmatic case of the "Tristan" chord and its linear-motivic components. Whether in Bach or in Wagner, the charac-teristic features of such developmental motives belong "to a primitive stage of musical formation," a "subconscious realm."[60] Kurth's account of the technical components of Wagner's endless melody often seems designed to vindicate the "regressive-utopian" fantasy of its aesthetic and ideological premises by providing it with analytical support.

Formation better describes Kurth's interpretation of endless melody as a structural category. His is less interested in identifying large-scale patterns (conventional or otherwise) than in developing what we might call a kind of "physics" of melodic motion and contour. For Kurth, the key to endless melody resided in the moment-to-moment genesis of expressive musical gestures, a dynamic process of melodic and harmonic formation (recalling the notion of melody as "outline" or delineation, as implied by Rousseau – form as an abstraction or hypothetical reification of the processes of linear, directional formation).[61] In any case, the basic

---

58   Kurth, *Romantische Harmonik*, 450.
59   Or, as Rothfarb also notes, "For Kurth, endless melody . . . leads back to the very genesis of music, psychic energies" (*Ernst Kurth*, 50).
60   Ibid., 68. See 68–75 on "Developmental Motives in Wagner's Music."
61   In his Bruckner monograph Kurth states at one point that musical form is a function of tensions, not repose, and is "always the reciprocal balance of energy and its confinement within an outline (. . . *die im Schwebe gehaltene Wechselwirkung von Kraft und deren Bezwingung in Umrissen*)" (*Bruckner*, vol. I [Berlin, 1925], 234). Slightly later he modifies this statement in proclaiming that form in music is "neither [all] flow nor outline (*nicht Fluß noch Umriß*), neither just motion nor its surveyable, fixed and frozen shape," but "the vital battle to capture within a fixed grasp that which is flowing (. . . *die Erfassung des Fliessenden durch Halt am Festen*)" (239).

musical techniques Kurth was concerned with are essentially those that figure in most later attempts to describe the actual mechanisms of endless melody: the infinite variety of deceptive cadences (and related techniques of elision or interruption), the interlocking of motives and phrases, an often concomitant ambiguity of meter and phrase, and other such means of "transition" and *Fortspinnung* contributing to the overall objective of perpetual continuity.[62]

If we assume, as Kurth seems to have, that "endless melody" encompasses all or most of Wagner's music from *Das Rheingold* on, it is unlikely that one could arrive at any simple comprehensive technical explanation. In some of the German Wagner literature from the early 1970s the question was tossed around whether the phrase should be construed in technical terms at all, or whether it was not primarily an aesthetic, metaphorical construct. Fritz Reckow argued that the original context of the phrase supported a purely aesthetic interpretation.[63] In further support of the argument he adduced a number of largely irrelevant instances of other locutions – in and out of Wagner's writings – involving "endlessness" or infinity, scrutinizing semantic distinctions among them ("unending" vs. "endless"), and even assessing other instances of forest imagery in Wagner's writings, with regard to the forest metaphor in *"Music of the Future."* (Reckow's conclusion – on the basis of further dubious textual parallels – that endless melody signifies a melodic idiom transcending the historical contingencies of style and taste is certainly wide of the mark, by any reasonable standard of interpretation.) In another essay from the same volume, Stefan Kunze took more seriously Wagner's equation of melody and form ("musical structure and the concept of melody condition one another and therefore may hardly be separated in the context of analysis"), and proposed specific standard units of text and melody (*Versmelodie*) as the basis for analyzing the music of the *Ring*.[64] Arbitrating between these views a few years later, Klaus Kropfinger pointed out that the broader context of *"Music of the Future"* supported both of them, since the essay ranges from observations on the "technical" basis of Beethoven's symphonies (as melody) to a distinctly metaphorical discourse nearer the end of the essay (the forest metaphor).[65]

62 See Kurth, *Romantische Harmonik*, 454–62, and Rothfarb, *Ernst Kurth*, 47.

63 Fritz Reckow, "Zu Wagners Begriff der unendlichen Melodie," in *Das Drama Richard Wagners*, 81–103. Reckow also mentions the conspicuous absence of the phrase from Wagner's own writings after 1860 and from the "approved" literature of the early Bayreuth circle, such as the compendious *Wagner-Lexikon* of Glasenapp and Heinrich von Stein. But surely the explanation for this absence has to do with the critical and satirical appropriations of the phrase during Wagner's lifetime.

64 S. Kunze, "Über Melodiebegriff und musikalischen Bau in Wagners Musikdrama," in *Das Drama Richard Wagners*, 111–44.

65 Kropfinger, *Wagner and Beethoven*, 100–14. Kropfinger, too, traces a variety of parallel locutions in Wagner's writings and in some contemporary critical literature, citing a

Dahlhaus's view of the matter, mentioned earlier, also mediates between aesthetic and technical readings. Even in equating endless melody (and Wagner's concept of "genuine" melody, or "melody in the strong sense") with Schoenberg's "musical prose," Dahlhaus considered it foremost as an aesthetic category, although one with technical ramifications. That is, the criterion of "continuous, unbroken significance" is an aesthetic postulate, and cannot be automatically converted into any ready compositional formula.

The gap between aesthetic criteria and musical practice (or reception) raises certain critical aporias regarding both Schoenberg's "musical prose" and Wagner's endless melody, as far as we accept the parallel between them repeatedly proposed by Dahlhaus. Does melodic or motivic status automatically guarantee expressivity or meaning, as distinguished from "empty padding" or vacuous formulaic patter? On the other hand, what becomes of form (or musical meaning) when just such a conventional form is shorn of its punctuating flourishes (those "noisy half cadences" Wagner disdained in the Mozartian symphony)? As the precepts of rhetoric will tell us, even apparently empty gestures may serve an indispensable purpose in articulating the argument as a whole. What guarantees that the eradication of all conventional turns of melodic phrase, symmetrical repetitions, and metrical filling-out will result in an unceasing stream of musical eloquence? Quite apart from the case of recitative (which Wagner himself dismissed as "mere noise"), we have seen ample testimony that much of Wagner's earlier audience claimed to find his music often devoid of meaning or expression – and this includes figures of high musical literacy, like Hanslick, who was far from a doddering pedant, after all. Of course, the presumptive "meaning" or significance of musical prose in Brahms or Schoenberg is tendentially a "purely musical" kind, deriving from the internal logic of motivic development or "developing variation." The leitmotivic substance of Wagner's "musical prose" or "endless melody" (still maintaining Dahlhaus's equation of the two) may also be subjected to developmental, evolutionary musical procedures, but few would maintain that its unceasing "meaning" is entirely derived from "purely musical" means alone.

In fact, even Dahlhaus, in his later glosses on the subject, tended to concede a greater role to the semantic conditioning of motivic material

suggestive statement by Champfleury (which happens to predate Wagner's essay by several months) that "every one of Wagner's operas is simply one vast melody, akin to the spectacle of the sea" (114). Champfleury's prescient figure of speech is all the more striking when we consider that the programs of Wagner's Paris concerts consisted mainly of such popular excerpts as the "Entry of the Guests" from *Tannhäuser* and the "Wedding March" from *Lohengrin* (though granted, the *Tristan* Prelude was also programmed).

by poetry and drama. Recapitulating his familiar reading of Wagner's melodic concept in the *Wagner Handbook* (1986/1992), for instance, Dahlhaus includes the following parenthetical qualification: "The Wagnerian concept of melody . . . adheres . . . to the substantiality and the eloquence of the motifs and successions of notes (which are never exclusively musical but are always dramatically based, as well)." Describing the "art of transition" in this same context as "the technique of conjoining diverging motifs without a discernible break and of making it seem that they emanate from one another with compelling logic," he adds that "this should not blind us to the fact that the constituent elements of unending melody, according to abstract musical criteria . . . , often stand unrelated side by side."[66] The "compelling logic" of Wagner's style is exposed as something like a conjurer's trick – in the spirit of Nietzsche's late critiques – and his absolute musical authority once again begins to erode. In *Nineteenth-Century Music* (1980/1989), Dahlhaus still contends that Wagner's music shares with Beethoven's developmental idiom (or with the element of musical prose in later instrumental composers) "a type of musical form that emerges from motivic logic rather than . . . a balance of melodic periods," but here, too, a note of uncertainty creeps into the language: Wagner "attempted to use formal logic to fill the void left by the demise of 'foursquareness'," and thereby to confront the "danger of formal disintegration" that follows upon the abandonment of classical formal principles: "The nexus of leitmotivs was intended to impart a continuity no longer vouchsafed by the syntax."[67] The choice of words here – "attempted" or "was intended to" – seems to raise a specter of doubt as to the actual results. (Wagner, at any rate, was not one to be satisfied with "intentions" that remained unrealized.) And if the "meaning" attaching to Wagner's endless melody, as well as the "form" outlined by it, become increasingly implicated in the words and action of the drama, then another danger starts to loom, attendant on that of "formal disintegration": Wagner risks forfeiting the honorary status of "absolute musician" conferred upon him by his enthusiasm for Schopenhauerian aesthetics and by various attempts from Lorenz to the present to demonstrate the inner musical "logic" of his endless melodic discourse. Or worse yet, perhaps, Wagner criticism may risk a reversion to the leitmotivic exegesis of the old-fashioned Bayreuth school. Needless to say, I don't mean to depict these as serious dangers, whether realized or not. (The relation of leitmotif to the status of Wagner's musical forms in historical and current criticism is something I will return to in the last chapter.)

---

[66]   *Wagner Handbook*, 307–8.
[67]   *Nineteenth-Century Music*, 199–200.

Thus far I have succeeded in deferring any practical demonstration of Wagner's "endless melody," on my own part – a deferral I might hope to pass off as an elaborate textual metaphor of the thing itself (the perpetual evasion of "concrete" forms, the endless deferral of closure). This hesitation arises in part from a fear of having to state the obvious. We all have a perfectly adequate intuitive sense for the "endless melody" of the *Tristan* prelude, or of Isolde's *Liebestod* ("Transfiguration") and it requires but little analytical prowess to translate this intuition into a technical description of motives, their development and interrelation, the exploitation of appoggiaturas and harmonic ellipses, "endless" sequential intensifications, and the overall trajectory or formal "outline" by which Wagner describes the flooding and ebbing of elemental desire. Beyond such passages in Wagner to which we instinctively attach the idea of endless melody (an instinct that surely explains something of the phrase's enduring fascination, and why it is futile to deny its "technical" connotations), I am constrained by the potential tautology of a broader reading that would identify all of Wagner's music with endless melody, or else the striving toward it. Evidently the "technique" is as fluid, protean, and elusive as the aesthetic concept. The following examples, then, are proposed simply as a kind of tentative (and by no means exclusive or exhaustive) typology of endless melody, representatives of several characteristic states of "endless melody" within the overall continuum of Wagner's practice.

The prelude to *Das Rheingold*, mentioned already as an enactment of musical origins (followed by those of melody and speech), represents already a kind of endless melody, an aqueous analogue to that metaphorical "forest melody" of *"Music of the Future."* But this is necessarily an exceptional case, and it is hardly melody, perhaps not even by Wagner's standards, as it precedes (allegorically) even the origin of melody, as song. (The music projects endlessness in an obvious sense, as the infinite flux of elemental natural forces, but paradoxically it relies on a rigorously "quadratic" framework of two-, four-, and eight-measure groupings of its tonic-key figurations to achieve this effect.) After this point, *Rheingold* offers any number of examples of the evolution of Wagner's "musical prose," and thus of what Dahlhaus considered the basic meaning of endless melody.

We can observe *in nuce* the evolution of a such a leitmotivic "musical prose" from out of recitative and arioso idioms in a passage analyzed by Dahlhaus on several occasions: Loge's brief narrative report to Wotan in scene 2 of *Das Rheingold*. Dahlhaus divides the narration into three musical sections, beginning with a non-motivic, recitative-like introduction ("Immer ist Undank Loges Lohn"), followed by an "arioso-cantabile period" comprised of two brief parallel strophes in

D major ("So weit Leben und Weben, in Wasser, Erd' und Luft" and "Doch so weit Leben und Weben, verlacht nur ward meine fragende List"), and concluding in a longer, freely modulating series of phrases based on a changing leitmotivic accompaniment ("Nur einen sah ich"), ending in C major with a citation of the "Rheingold-call" and its flowing scalar accompaniment.[68] Dahlhaus cites the passage as an example of "old and new" compositional techniques existing side by side at this early stage of the tetralogy; only in the third section do we find the leitmotivically-based "musical prose" that will eventually become its compositional *lingua franca*. One might extrapolate further here a kind of dialectical model for the "evolution" of this free motivic "prose," as a synthesis of the recitative and arioso elements represented in the first and second sections, respectively (except that neither section offers the multiplicity of leitmotifs required by the third style). All three sections, though, contain some ingredients of the Wagnerian endlessness. The plain, chordal recitative style of the first section is a basic source of the "wandering tonality" and non-symmetrical phrasing of Wagner's more developed language. The polyphonic interplay of simple, triadic figuration in the second section (motivated by Loge's phrase "Leben und Weben" and the reference to natural elements, "water, earth, and air") recalls the character of the elemental prelude and other passages where Wagner describes the continuous warp and weave of the natural world (the *Waldweben* in *Siegfried*, Act II, for instance). In the third section, finally, the free alternation of key areas and leitmotifs represents a more fully emancipated "prose" idiom, as Dahlhaus puts it, that responds intimately to the poetic text in the choice of motives and keys. In both second and third sections the "melody" is determined by aspects of the text: the repeated text phrases in section two ("Leben und Weben," "Wasser, Erd' und Luft"), the series of textual cues in section three (Rhine-maidens, Alberich, Rhine-gold, Ring, Rhine-maiden's lament, anticipated restoration of the gold). A half-cadence gesture associated with the text "Weibes Wonne und Werth" occurs once in each section, tying all three sections together with a faint suggestion of a refrain. In the move here from arioso to "musical prose" the "meaning" or eloquence of the melody (carried primarily by the orchestra) shifts from an unmediated musical

[68] Dahlhaus, *Wagners Konzeption des musikalischen Dramas*, 71–2. Dahlhaus acknowledges the "appendix" quality of the three lines that follow the C-major cadence ("Dir's zu melden / gelobt ich den Mädchen: / nun löste Loge sein Wort"), but in trying to attribute a "darkened" Neapolitan quality to C major in light of the fleeting B-minor cadence figure here, he misses the main point: the utterly perfunctory cadence in D that actually rounds out the narrative ("löste Loge sein Wort") creates a facetious gesture of closure in the key of the preceding arioso; Loge has "kept his word" only in the same perfunctory, facetious manner.

level to one more dependent on the textually determined semantic content of leitmotifs. Although the arioso section (part two) is punctuated by a figure identified with Freia and woman in general (later with Brünnhilde as paradigmatic and allegorical woman, as we saw in chapter 3, for instance) this is treated in the manner of a ritornello figure, not associatively. Perhaps even the third section manages to cohere "as music" by virtue of transposed repetitions of the "Rhine-gold cry" and the Rhine-gold motif proper; but the provisional conclusion in C major makes no sense if divorced from the illusion of the Rhine-gold restored to the river. This is a "deceptive cadence" of a higher order: Loge knows that the resolution he speaks of ("that you, Wotan . . . , return the gold to the water, forever to remain there") is not about to happen, and both melody (motives) and tonality hark back to the first scene. Despite the apparent (musical) autonomy of Loge's speech, nothing is resolved, musically or dramatically.

The *Ring* also includes examples of leitmotivically-based instrumental passages, without text, that likewise balance elements of musical prose with vestiges of conventional formal principles. The prior semantic conditioning of motives may play some role in establishing the continuity of meaning or significance that is supposed to obtain in endless melody (as in the case of Siegfried's Funeral Music, discussed in chapter 2), but more weight will necessarily fall to the role of an interior musical logic or process. Such is the case in the prelude to Act II of *Siegfried*, that little essay in the aesthetics of the grotesque or "ugly" – as it had recently been theorized by Karl Rosenkranz (*Die Ästhetik des Häßlichen*, 1853) and in the French debates over "realism" – which also exhibits the influence of Liszt's new orchestral works.[69] Here, too, is a music of "origins," but of a dank, oozy primeval chaos rather than the harmonious cosmic order of the *Rheingold* prelude. Though on one hand the Act II prelude in *Siegfried* is just an innocuous bit of musical illustration, a fairy-tale picture of some dark "cursed spot" in the woods, the imagery of caverns and dragons is easily susceptible to interpretation as metaphor of fears and fixations of primitive subconscious origin, along the lines of Jungian archetypes (as better befits the psychological dignity of "endless melody," perhaps).

This is just the sort of music early critics denounced as hopelessly obscure, fragmented, chaotic, and anti-melodic, although to a certain extent these transgressions might have been pardoned on the grounds of "characteristic" intent. (We are reminded, too, of the pre-

---

[69] Rosenkranz, incidentally, saw the "ugly" as necessarily resolving itself into the comic, just as the mock-evil grotesquerie of Wagner's prelude can be heard to do in the course of the ensuing scene and act, which largely maintain the comic tone of *Siegfried*'s first two acts as a whole.

Schoenbergian signification of "prose-like" music, documented by Hermann Danuser, involving the deliberate transgression of the canons of "poetic" musical beauty for characteristic purposes.[70]) But "character" here manifests itself also in specific techniques ascribed to endless melody. Most striking is the all but complete evasion of the implicit tonic sonority, F minor. Aside from one full cadence in m. 29, Wagner manages to avoid even the preparation of a tonic cadence, choosing instead to hover about the C–G♭ (or C–F♯) tritone – an altered dominant sonority – as a kind of substitute tonal center or axis, which also serves as an enharmonic pivot to B minor across the two statements of the "Curse" motive in mm. 55–72. (This particular C–F♯ tritone relationship is prominent throughout the *Ring* as an emblematic sonority, and its initial statement here, to the rhythms and contour of the Giants' motive, is meant to signify Fafner's malign metamorphosis as serpent.) Although the fundamental motivic materials of the prelude – the distorted Giants' motive in the timpani and the serpentine Fafner/Dragon motive in the bass tuba – constitute regular two- and four-measure units, they are consistently subjected to the phrase-overlapping processes (see Example 5.1) that William Rothstein, for instance, considers as the most basic constructive device of endless melody.[71]

There are larger melodic parallelisms underlying the design of the prelude, too, as a partial concession to the demands of instrumental form. The whole-step sequence of the Fafner/Dragon motive (mm. 6, 12) is replicated at mm. 29 and 36, initially resolving the prolonged dominant of the opening paragraph (the first sequential pair begins off of C, the second off of F), but eventually opening out to the modulation to B minor with the Curse motive. The tortuous chromatic descent of the bass from m. 43 to m. 49 constitutes a loose parallel to the cadential descent of mm. 25–8 and a very audible closure to this first section of the prelude as a whole, which it leads back to the tremolo dominant pedal and emblematic tritone of the opening (the G♭ now being sustained as a pedal-note, as well). The tritone pedal reinforces the centrality of this sonority as "tonic substitute," and, being sustained through m. 64, effects a transition to the next phase of the prelude (Curse motive). Tritone pedal and timpani return at the end of the prelude, as a coda gesture and/or introduction to the ensuing scene.

---

[70] Hermann Danuser, *Musikalische Prosa* (Regensburg, 1975).
[71] Rothstein, *Phrase Rhythm in Tonal Music* (New York, 1989), 277ff. Rothstein sees "endless melody" as a broad stylistic tendency in Romantic music from Chopin through Wagner. While the overlapping of phrase members either implicitly, within a single line, or explicitly, between separate polyphonic lines, is represented as the principal means of achieving this style, Rothstein also offers as a broader, provisional definition of endless melody as a compositional technique "the avoidance of any points of simultaneous harmonic and melodic closure" (278). The mere presence of deceptive cadences, in other words, will not guarantee the desired effect of continuity without a concomitant elision or overlap within the melodic line(s).

Melody as form

For all these small-scale symmetries and recurrences, the formal logic of the prelude is an evolutionary one, and – as with other preludes in the *Ring* – continues to unfold across the scene it introduces. At first, the prelude as a whole appears to grow simply by leitmotivic accumulation: Fafner motives sequenced; hints of the Ring; Curse

Example 5.1 *Siegfried* Act II, prelude (mm. 1–18)

motive sequenced; "Nibelung's hate" (the syncopated 12/8 material) with now stronger hints of the Ring; and a climactic statement of the "Despair" or "Servitude" figure (*Fron*) and a Ring-variant, leading back to the opening tritone material. The tritone material thus loosely fills a refrain function; but notice that the third occurrence (m. 96) corresponds to the instrumentally amplified second occurrence (m. 49, with new Gb pedal added to the C), rather than to the beginning. When Alberich starts to sing, as the curtain rises, the "Nibelung's hate" figure that had formed an unintegrated motivic contrast within the prelude (mm. 73–85) returns ("In Wald und Nacht, vor Neidhöhl' halt ich Wacht"), reminding us whose motivic property it is, of course, but also completing the (tritonal) move from F minor into B minor that had merely been intimated in the prelude.

In characteristic Wagnerian fashion, formal implications of the prelude continue to multiply (evolve) outward in ever-increasing spans, although the "outline" of these formal implications becomes increasingly vague as it expands. The Curse sequence of the prelude, for instance (mm. 54–72, see Example 5.2), returns at the same pitch after the B-minor episode in which Alberich detects Wotan's approach (Alberich: "Das Licht erlischt, der Glanz barg sich dem Blick: Nacht ist's wieder"). Following a long stretch of "wandering tonality" (including Wotan's "Wanderer" chords themselves) very loosely centered around F minor, Wagner returns to the "Nibelung's hate" series of the prelude, which had returned in fragmentary form at the scene's opening, and reiterates the entire climax of the prelude (about twenty measures' worth) almost verbatim, except that it is now brought to a raucous conclusion in B minor/major (Alberich: "Das sehrt dich mit ew'ger Sorge!" through "der Welt walte dann ich"). Finally, the persistent C–Gb tritone of the prelude, as we might expect, continues to punctuate the scene (finally reverting to its pedal-form) along with fragments of the bass-tuba melody of the opening paragraph, to close out the scene. This is a different order of "punctuation" than the regular hierarchies of cadential articulation that scanned the discourse of classical melody, to be sure, and no better than the haphazard practice of Scudo's Harlequin, from a classical perspective. The "punctuation" of endless melody occurs here at the broader level of dramatic-rhetorical form, so that Wagner has in effect returned the categories of musical form to their linguistic origins, in accordance with his larger aesthetic program.

There is no denying that the scene is filled out with a certain amount of declamatory and gestural "noise," whether as remnants of recitative or as promiscuously solicited leitmotifs spun out to meet the rhetorical or declamatory needs of the moment. But we can also find corroboration of Wagner's later claim (in *"Music of the Future"*) that the dramatic poet may anticipate and encourage the broad expanse of the musician's endless melody in a way that will even provide sustenance for "form" – that poetry will "pre-determine" the shape of the melodic discourse. For instance, Wotan approaches, at beginning of the scene, to the same scenic effects as accompany his departure – storm-wind and eerie nocturnal glow – and this retrograde performance at the scene's end provides a logical impetus, or encouragement to musical form. Wagner not only follows his own dramatic cue here, further enhancing Wotan's stormy riding music with superimposed progression of the "Wanderer chords," he also reinforces the formal idea suggested in the action by continuing this retrograde impulse yet further. Here at the end of the scene the Curse sequence itself is reversed, moving from B minor up through the C–F♯ tritone through a third statement, resolving toward F minor (compare Examples 5.2 and 5.3). The progression from Curse sequence to the tritone "motto" of the scene can be read as yet a further consequence of the retrograde impulse, reversing the progression of mm. 49–72 of the prelude (and thereby "regressing" back to the point of origin, that chaotic tritonal miasma out of which the scene evolved). The endlessness obtainable by the simple conjoining of leitmotivic material, by the wandering tonality of obbligato recitative, or by various elisions and compressions of "normal" melodic periodicity is refined by the "purely musical" instincts of Wagner the composer, but also by the enabling foresight of Wagner the dramatic poet, who has already imbued the "fabric of his words and verses" with the composer's musical instincts, as Wagner claimed for *Tristan* (VII, 123).

There is a certain irony that the remarks on *Tristan* in "*Music of the Future*" relating to melody, form, and "endless melody" all have to do with the determining role of poetry and drama. For it has always been the example of *Tristan* – the prelude, the vast love-duet, or Isolde's *Liebestod* – that has encouraged the view of Wagner's ultimate emancipation from text and theory, and has encouraged the intuitive reading of endless melody as a primarily musical phenomenon. Even Wagner seems to have sanctioned this view when he later conceded (in 1872) that "almost nothing transpires but music" in the second act ("On the Term 'Music Drama'," IX, 307). It was, of course, this second act that embodied the new "art of transition" Wagner had revealed to Mathilde Wesendonck (in 1859) as the essential "secret of musical form" in his latest works. (Like endless melody, this art of transition has normally been interpreted as a more or less "purely musical" phenomenon, even though it may derive its motivation from a broadly conceived "poetic intent.") Leaving aside the largely autonomous brand of endless melody of the *Tristan* prelude or *Liebestod* as a sufficiently familiar, if relatively exceptional, type, I would call attention to a more characteristic hybrid in which such seamless motivic *Fortspinnung* collaborates with poetic

Example 5.2 *Siegfried* Act II, prelude (mm. 55–72): Curse sequence

Example 5.3 *Siegfried* Act II, scene 1: Curse sequence reversed
(mm. 496–507)

text, and how the musical form generated by this collaboration might be construed as a function of both "transition" and endless melody.

The motive that emerges at the center of the Act II love duet (Isolde: "Lausch', Geliebter!"), following Brangäne's Watch Song, appears to be one of the very earliest musical ideas of the score. As Ernest Newman noticed, it was this theme Wagner must have been referring to when he reported in a letter of December 1856 to Marie Wittgenstein that ideas for *Tristan* had lured him away from his efforts to continue with the *Siegfried* score, "in the shape of a melodic thread which, though I fain would have quitted it, kept on spinning itself, so that I could have spent the whole day developing it."[72] "For the moment," he prefaced this confession, "music without words: several things I would rather treat in music than in verse." Wagner's confession and the sketch that confirms it, dated "19 Dec. 1856," are among the key pieces of evidence

---

[72] Letter of 19 December 1856, quoted in Newman, *The Wagner Operas*, vol. I (New York, 1949; rpt 1983), 193. For a longer excerpt from the letter, and a detailed account of the numerous sketches that grew from this fertile idea, see Robert Bailey, "The Method of Composition," in *The Wagner Companion*, 308–15.

(along with the apparently "autonomous" conception of the prelude) for the case of Wagner as convert, *malgré lui*, to a Romantic aesthetic of absolute music under the mutual influences of Schopenhauer and the discovery of his own, hitherto undreamt-of, musical resources in the decade of *Tristan*. Indeed, the idea of a "melodic thread" that keeps on "spinning itself" for hours on end might be taken as the sensible, empirical definition of endless melody that Wagner perversely withheld from *"Music of the Future,"* where he still insisted on giving the text its due. The musical idea in question is quite clearly a "theme" rather than a real leitmotif, in both its original musical contours and its function within the scene (this despite the obvious significance of its motivic components, above all its first three notes). The full idea is first formally presented as an eight-measure orchestral idea (see Example 5.4); it is developed and reprised in an essentially "instrumental" fashion within this scene, and it recurs only once outside of the scene, near the end of the act (Tristan: "Wohin nun Tristan scheidet"), more like an old-fashioned "reminiscence motive" than a proper leitmotif.[73] The indecision regarding the theme's leitmotivic label (it has been variously designated *Liebesruhe, Schlummer*, or *Todestrotz*) is typical of the motives in *Tristan* altogether, but it is also symptomatic of the autonomy of this theme's genesis and its lack of any distinct textual or dramatic association.

Given what we know of the theme's origins, its eventual implementation within the Act II duet might well exemplify Wagner's description, in *Opera and Drama*, of the "representation of the birth of

Example 5.4 *Tristan und Isolde* Act II, scene 2: *Lauschen* theme

[Isolde: "Lausch', Geliebter!"]

---

[73] The idea does recur significantly in Act III, of course – but this time so transformed as nearly to escape recognition (the music of Tristan's ecstatic anticipation of Isolde's arrival).

melody" (*Vorführung des Aktes der Gebärung der Melodie*) witnessed in Beethoven's symphonic allegros – another significant anticipation of the motif of endless melody. Beethoven's characteristic procedure, Wagner claimed (perhaps with the example of the "Eroica" in mind, again), was to present us with the complete melody "only in the course of the piece," although the complete form of the melody is understood to have been present in the composer's mind from the outset (III, 315).[74] The earlier version of this theme, as Newman mentions, appears as a setting of the text "o Sink hernieder, Nacht der Liebe" in another early sketch, suggesting that Wagner had conceived it as the principal idea for the entire slow section of the scene.[75] In the final composition, he defers its "authentic," formal exposition until after Brangäne's Watch Song, where it accompanies the lovers' semi-oblivious "response" to her cautionary voice. Yet Wagner has also planted it, in a form more closely resembling the genetically prior one of the sketches, near the end of the first phase of the slow section (Isolde: "Herz an Herz dir, Mund an Mund"), and then again shortly afterwards, concealed within the lush accompaniment to Brangäne's song itself (the oboe line against her text, "die den Schläfern Schlimmes ahnt, bange zum Erwachen mahnt" – see Example 5.5, a and b).[76] The "finished" melody in G♭, as it is spun out across the center of the duet, is thus presented as a consequence of earlier, fragmentary intimations, motivic "seeds" planted in advance. But the documentary evidence, and the eight-measure form of the full theme itself, reveal the organic process as a product of calculated artifice (as all musical "organicism" necessarily becomes, when stripped of metaphor). In the *Opera and Drama* passage, Wagner had aimed to demonstrate that the organicism of Beethoven's melodic processes could be only an illusion (the "re-enactment" of birth, but not the genuine phenomenon) due to the absolute-musical foundations of

---

[74] "Beachten wir das Charakteristische, daß, wenn der Meister uns wohl erst im Verlaufe des Tonstückes die volle Melodie als fertig hinstellt, diese Melodie dennoch beim Künstler von Anfang herein schon als fertig vorauszusetzen ist." Dahlhaus has glossed this passage with relation to the "Eroica" in "Zur Wirkungsgeschichte von Beethovens Symphonien," in *Gattungen der Musik und ihre Klassiker*, ed. Hermann Danuser (Laaber, 1988), 224–7.

[75] Newman, *The Wagner Operas*, vol. I, 254–5, n. For fuller details, see again Bailey, "The Method of Composition," 308ff. The original 1856 sketch, including ideas for what became the opening of the prelude, bore the heading "Love Scene. Tristan and Isolde," further reinforcing the likelihood that Wagner had originally conceived the motive as the principal "seed" for this central scene.

[76] In the early sketches the melody of "Herz an Herz dir, Mund an Mund" is conflated with an arpeggiated ninth figure that occurs a few measures earlier in the final version ("leuchten lachend Sterne der Wonne" and "vor deinen Augen süß zerronnen"). Thus, what had functioned as the continuation of the basic motive in several of these sketch ideas (see Bailey, "Method of Composition," Examples 34, 38, 42, and 45, pp. 309–14) now leads into it, as a separate idea.

his melody and the inherent limitations of these. Yet the same illusion persists in the music drama.

Of course, the deployment of this theme across the center of the duet as a whole – its contribution to the "form" – is also textually determined. In the broadest possible terms, Brangäne's Watch Song and the lovers' unresponsive response form a large episode or mid-section (or perhaps "transition") between the formal cantabile of "O sink' hernieder, Nacht der Liebe" and the ecstatic neo-cabaletta or stretta that evolves from the *Liebestod* material. Although the theme itself continues to resist any

Example 5.5 *Tristan und Isolde* Act II, scene 2: anticipations of *Lauschen* theme
(a) mm. 1174–84

Melody as form

(b) mm. 1234–41

(*sehr zart und ausdrücksvoll*)
[Brangäne: "... die den Schläfern Schlimmes ahnt,

bange zum Erwachen mahnt!"]

fixed association, two of its three principal occurrences do correspond to parallel passages of text. The first time it precedes and accompanies Isolde's dreamy exhortation, "Lausch', Geliebter!" (Listen, my love!), to which Tristan responds succinctly, "Laß mich sterben!" (Let me die!). Later, following the fragmentary reprise of Brangäne's warning, the theme returns a half-step higher (following the transpositional model of Brangäne's reprise), and Tristan echoes Isolde's earlier text, inquiring whether he should heed it still ("Soll ich lauschen?"). This gentle irony – if one can speak of irony at all in this context – is evidently persuasive, and Isolde responds on cue, "Laß mich sterben!", taking over Tristan's original part.[77] (The textual parallel will perhaps justify dubbing this figure the *Lauschen* theme, since Wagnerian motives want names, after all, whether or not they behave as leitmotifs.) In each passage the development of the *Lauschen* idea from finite theme into "endless melody" is effected through its conjunction with a "real," textually motivated leitmotif: that sometimes given the awkward label of "second Death motive." This alternation of the *Lauschen* theme with the second Death motive dutifully mimics the languid stichomythia of the lovers' exchange:

Isolde.	Lausch', Geliebter!
Tristan.	Laß mich sterben!
Isolde.	Neid'sche Wache!
Tristan.	Nie erwachen!
Isolde.	Doch der Tag / muß Tristan wecken?
Tristan.	Laß den Tag dem Tode weichen!

[77] Frank Glass points to this exchange of parts as a manifestation of what he reasonably identifies as the central "poetic intent" of the scene, the idea of intertwining identities motivated by the desire to become "one," realized in both textual and musical imagery (*The Fertilizing Seed*, 137–46).

297

The death wish expressed in each of Tristan's lines ("Let me die," "Never awaken," "Let the day yield to death") consistently elicits the appropriate motive (or in any case, defines it as such), which thus enters into a musical dialogue with the *Lauschen* theme (see Example 5.6). The same motivic dialogue is taken up with the quasi-ironic reversal of text roles later on:

Tristan.	Soll ich lauschen?
Isolde.	Laß mich sterben!
Tristan.	Muß ich wachen?
Isolde.	Nie erwachen!
Tristan.	Soll der Tag / noch Tristan wecken?
Isolde.	Laß den Tag / dem Tode weichen!

Such a linking of motives, or motivic dialogue (*Dialogisierung der Musik*) is also invoked by Dahlhaus, along with "musical prose," as a characteristic of Wagner's endless melody.[78] This linking of motives also involves a simple application of the phrase-overlap technique that William Rothstein identified as the key to an endless melodic technique (see note 71): the anticipated fourth measure of the second Death motive is elided each time with the re-entry of the *Lauschen* theme by a dominant-seventh harmonization of the resolving root. (While the second motive finally resolves – in a full cadence, no less, at the end of Example 5.6 – this resolution is withheld in the "reprise" section, where the music pushes forward toward the final phase of the scene with an acceleration of tempo, a new interjection of the "Day" and *Liebesjubel* motives, and a further motivic spinning-out of the *Lauschen* theme.) Throughout all this, the larger, formally constitutive disposition of the "melody" is directly motivated by that of the poetic text, itself motivated by an intuition of musical possibilities. Not only is this true of the broader outlines – the reprise of Brangäne's music and the lovers' solipsistic "response" – but even the local interlocking of motives (*Lauschen*, second Death motive) within this lovers' discourse is modeled on the pattern of the text.

If the exposition and reprise, so to speak, of this bi-motivic "period" (the conjunction of *Lauschen* and second Death motives) are textually motivated, however, the internal occurrence (Isolde: "Doch un'sre Liebe, heißt sie nicht Tristan und Isolde?") might be said to obey an

---

[78] See, for example, *Wagner Handbook*, 306–8 ("Melody as Dialogue"), or *Wagners Konzeption des musikalischen Dramas*, 33–8.

Example 5.6 "Dialogue" of *Lauschen* and second Death themes

imperative of *musical* logic in fulfilling the role of development section, thereby also reinforcing the formal identities I have assigned to the flanking periods as exposition and reprise. In the absence of the proper textual cues, the *Lauschen* theme is left to develop freely, detaching itself from the strict motivic dialogue it was pressed into by the text of the original period ("exposition"). Here, beneath Isolde's metaphysical ruminations on the conjunction "and," the *Lauschen* theme is stated again as a complete eight-measure phrase, though melodically varied, then further spun out and set in counterpoint with itself and other material. Through a process of developing variation the spinning-out of the theme's continuation becomes a running eighth-note figure in the accompaniment to Tristan's reply and continues to propel the music toward the next major articulation, the beginning of the *Liebestod* series (Tristan: "So stürben wir, um ungetrennt"). Indeed, almost the whole expanse between the "expositional" period and this new (*Liebestod*) music can be interpreted as "development" of this principal idea,

Example 5.7 Variants of *Lauschen* theme across developmental phase of dialogue.

(c)

(d)

utilizing the developmental techniques of *Fortspinnung* and developing variation – which are also those of endless melody, read as an empirical, musical phenomenon. (Example 5.7, a–d shows four forms assumed by the *Lauschen* theme across this so-called developmental phase of the dialogue.)

But what of the *Liebestod* series that intervenes here? We can hardly press this unmistakably new material into the service of our development, merely for the sake of a tidy ABA or quasi-sonata operation. (Even the weariest or most unwary listener won't fail to perk up on hearing the arrival of this well-known music, which Wagner precedes with a "punctuating" half-cadence of major proportions.) That brings me to my final point about melody, form, and endlessness, which also brings the "art of transition" into play, for good measure.

The organicizing artifice of planting the "seeds" of the *Lauschen* theme within earlier phases of the duet – in the opening cantabile and

Brangäne's Watch Song – points to a persistent phenomenon within this scene, and one that I would propose is central to the "art of transition," of which this scene was cited by Wagner as the finest exemplar. The entire concluding portion of this nearly "endless" scene, from "O sink' hernieder" through the catastrophic interruption, is characterized by an elaborate interlocking of sections or "poetic-musical periods." The idea is common enough in Wagner's music (we've seen something like it in the "annunciation of death" scene, in chapter 4), but it is treated here with a combination of subtlety and tenacity that justifies Wagner's private boasting. For example, the central, developmental period based on the *Lauschen* theme (Isolde: "Doch uns're Liebe, heißt sie nicht Tristan und Isolde?") acquires a strong re-transitional character starting with Tristan's reply and the "developing variation" of the theme, over a very distinct dominant prolongation on E ("Was stürbe dem Tod, als was uns stört"). Isolde interrupts this, and presses the dominant pedal down to E♭, that is, the proper dominant for the "period" as a whole (A♭). Tonally, this might signal a return of the opening of the period, or even of the original cantabile material ("O sink' hernieder, Nacht der Liebe"). Instead, an entirely new melodic period begins off of A♭ here – the *Liebestod* music ("So stürben wir, um ungetrennt"), whose modulating sequences convey a suppressed urgency that clearly points away from thematic closure. This "period" is beautifully elided with the reprise of Brangäne's warning refrain, "Habet Acht!" (transposed a half-step higher), bringing in tow the lovers' motivic dialogue again, as already described. This partial reprise is clearly "prefigured" in the poem, as we have seen (*dichterisch bereits konstruiert*, as Wagner put it in *"Music of the Future"*). But interestingly, the composer's instincts revised the poet's original formal cues here: in the musical setting, Wagner deleted fourteen lines of text (following the last line of the dialogue quoted above) that would likely have implied a fuller structural parallel to the earlier dialogue, from the expositional period of the *Lauschen* theme up to its development. The musical and "dramatic" logic of the abridged reprise have supplanted the architectural, "musical" symmetry originally suggested by the poet. The logic of the abridged (and transposed) reprise, as suggested before, is the drive toward the climactic "stretta" that follows. And here the process of interlocking thematic periods culminates with the fast-tempo "reprise" of the *Liebestod* music, itself transposed up a half-step to B major (Tristan: "Wie sie fassen, wie sie lassen"), initiating the final, inexorable drive toward climax and catastrophe.[79]

---

[79] Note also the emphatic double statement of the second Death motive that initiates the final "stretta" phase (Both: "O ew'ge Nacht, süße Nacht!"), providing a link with the motivic dialogue of the *Lauschen* period. The overall tonal trajectory of the duet,

The overlapping phrase structures, identified by Rothstein as the basis of endless melody, and the related linking or interlocking of leitmotifs with which Dahlhaus identifies the "art of transition" ("the technique of conjoining diverging motifs without a discernible break and of making it seem that they emanate from one another with compelling logic") can both be seen to operate here on a larger level of "form." This interlocking of thematic *periods* constitutes a very close analogy to the process of leitmotivic overlap (the *Liebesjubel* and Day motives) across the opening two dozen measures of the *Tagesgespräch* back at the beginning of scene 2 (in musical "defiance" of the text) that Dahlhaus offered as a paradigm of Wagner's transitional art.[80] And here, I propose, is where we can find an analogy to the hierarchy of melodic levels underlying earlier conceptions of form-as-melody. Where the traditional model described the expansion of the simple melodic period into a tonally regulated, systematically "punctuated" hierarchy of phrases and periods, Wagner extends a technique of his low-level musical prose or "endless melody" – the interlocking of leitmotivic phrases, textually and/or musically motivated – to larger levels of form, so that endless melody generates "endless," open-ended, centrifugal formal designs.[81] And these, too, involve a continuous interplay of textual and musical motivations.

This tendency of Wagnerian form to open out toward progressively higher levels is precisely what so perplexed the Nuremberg masters in Walther's Trial Song, aside from an incipient tendency to underplay

from A♭ ("O sink' hernieder") to B major, retraces the pitches of the original "desire" motive from the opening of the opera, as has been noted before. On the lines omitted from the original text in the musical setting, see Lorenz, *Der musikalische Aufbau von Richard Wagners "Tristan und Isolde"* (rpt Tutzing, 1966), 120–2. Lorenz is, naturally, most interested in the implications of the original text for "perfect symmetry," although he acknowledges the musical justification of the abridged reprise, noting also that the curtailment of Brangäne's song further supports this logic.

80 Dahlhaus, "Wagners 'Kunst des Übergangs': Der Zwiegesang in *Tristan und Isolde*," in *Zur musikalischen Analyse*, ed. G. Schuhmacher (Darmstadt, 1974), 475–86.

81 Kurth also identified endless melody with the "endlessness of transitions" (*Unendlichkeit der Übergänge*) as "a principle of continuous spinning-out," thus conjoining the idea of melody with the "art of transition" (*Romantische Harmonik*, 453). While he was presumably thinking of the local, moment-to-moment processes with which he was mainly occupied, the idea can easily be extended to a hierarchy of levels, as Wagner's original reference to the whole duet-scene in *Tristan* would imply. Note, incidentally, that what we might describe as the potentially "endless" paratactic *Fortspinnung* of the *Liebestod* idea through the final phase of the duet is also "prefigured" in the text, in a sense: as with the parallel text of Isolde's *Liebestod* (Transfiguration) itself, the text shared by Tristan and Isolde in this climactic phase dispenses with even the basic grammatical parts of speech in favor of a tendentially endless parataxis: "Ohne Wähnen, / sanftes Sehnen; / ohne Bangen, / süß Verlangen; / ohne Wehen, / hehr Vergehen; / ohne Schmachten, / hold Umnachten," etc.

internal "punctuation." Walther is provoked by Beckmesser's surly behavior to "improvise" a contrasting period to each of his *Stollen*, so that what appeared to be an ABA or *Bogen* (rather than *Bar* form) at the point where Beckmesser interrupts him (*Stollen*–contrast–*Stollen*) will in fact become a "new form" of interlocking periods (*Stollen*–contrast–*Stollen*–contrast–*Abgesang*). When the masters despair of ever "finding an end" to Walther's song, it is not for a lack of cadences, which are perfectly clear, or even a consequence of the distention of melodic phrases, which is not excessive. It is simply the fact that he has opened up the accustomed order of things to the threat of endless parataxis. Walther's song represents a simple, even "schematic" paradigm (to be paradoxical) of Wagner's endless melody, or of its potential formal implications. At the same time, the overall process is meant to suggest a natural evolution; it should appear as the product of natural forces, "Wie Vogelgesang im süßen Mai," as Sachs later recalls his impressions of the song. The motivic substance of Walther's song is dictated to him by nature, as the Prize Song is later dictated by a dream. Walther teaches Sachs the imperative of "natural melody," which (like Wagner's forest-melody) lingers in the mind as little motivic fragments of an immeasurable whole. Sachs teaches Walther, on the other hand, the necessary role of artifice in imitating nature. The natural melody dreamt of by Walther, like that dreamt of by Wagner in his utopian fantasies of *Worttonsprache* and the restoration of primal unity, is nonetheless an artificial construction – and so, too, is the natural, organic "evolution" of endless melody, as the history of the *Lauschen* theme in *Tristan* reveals. (It should be evident by now, too, that the formal process I have been describing here is another way of viewing the "poetic-musical period" and its evolutions.) From this perspective, the radical Romanticism of Wagner's endless melody assumes the classical aim of "imitating nature." But it pretends to do so more wholly and perfectly, and at many levels, ranging from imitation of natural emotional utterance or gesture (*Versmelodie*, leitmotif) to the imitation of evolutionary growth.

The secret of such natural appearances, for Wagner, was also the secret of their motivation. Wagner repeatedly insisted that music's formal and expressive credibility, so to speak, depended on the persuasiveness of its "motives" – motives not only in the sense of expressive musical gestures or ideas (leitmotifs), but also the expressive impulse (motivation) behind them, and behind their deployment throughout the drama. Like the evolutions of "endless melody" and like Wagner's fantasies of restoring a primeval immediacy to the language of modern art, his ideal of a genuinely "motivated" new music is – as I will suggest in the final chapter – another dialectic of nature and contrivance, of musical instinct and rhetorical prose.

6

Motives and motivations: leitmotif and "symphonic" drama

Composers of the modern, post-Beethovenian era were, from Wagner's perspective, caught in a dilemma arising from the conflict between inexorable "world-historical" cultural forces and inflexible musical conventions. Wagner shared the view of many contemporaries (as I have proposed throughout earlier chapters) that music, as an art or a "language" of emotional expression, must naturally evolve in its capacity to express a more complex, varied, and "distinct" content. Without sacrificing its status as a "higher language" of feelings, it was nonetheless seen as driven by a natural urge toward articulate communication. But like another group of his contemporaries – mostly anti-Wagnerians, by nature – he also subscribed to the doctrine that instrumental musical forms were constrained to abide by conventional structuring principles inscribed in the very nature of tonality, human perception, and the body, if these forms were to preserve the impression (at least) of autonomous intelligibility. Where he differed from this latter, conservative group was in his conviction that a poetic-dramatic text could serve as a *pretext* for departing from such conventionalized formal principles – offering a poetic license, as it were, for their transgression, and at the same time explaining it. (Here he appeared in his more accustomed role as sponsor of progressive ideals, although it was a role he was more and more loath to assume publicly.) Are the two stances compatible – conservative connoisseur of classical symphonies and radical aesthetic theorist of the avant-garde? Could Wagner, in good aesthetic conscience, promote the dissolution of generic and formal boundaries in the *Gesamtkunstwerk* while at the same time issuing proclamations about the natural limits of instrumental forms, even invoking the "stylistic purity" which non-dramatic composers were obliged to observe? As usual with Wagner, there is no clear answer. Perhaps this theoretical dissonance is, like his musical ones, productively calculated (even if, like them, it is not always obviously under control). Like most forms of artistic experiment, Wagner's were also indebted to a creative friction between the claims of utopian freedom and "natural" conventions.

Wagner was at any rate consistent in upholding this aesthetic double standard, permitting in the musical drama all that was denied to the symphony and its offshoots. While contemporary musicians and critics were celebrating music's conquest of the realm of "ideas" by virtue of a more precise, determinate thematic vocabulary, and a more flexible melodic and formal syntax, Wagner continued to cultivate a cautionary tone. In *Opera and Drama* he castigated Berlioz as a "neo-Romantic" eccentric; in the open letter on Liszt's symphonic poems he offered a guarded and potentially ambivalent appreciation of his benefactor's creative efforts; and in the later essay "On the Application of Music to the Drama" ("Über die Anwendung der Musik auf das Drama," 1879) he continued to polish up old arguments about the inherent limits of "dance-based" instrumental forms, *vis-à-vis* the liberating agency of dramatic text and action.

Warum? (motives to musical form)

Wagner is perhaps most explicit about the grounds of his skepticism toward the formal emancipation of instrumental music in the 1860 brochure *"Music of the Future"* (written in conjunction with the Paris *Tannhäuser*, but conceived as a critical companion-piece to the recently completed *Tristan und Isolde*). Even Beethoven's symphonies, he argues here, are still predicated on the conventional framework of the "dance-melody" and cannot finally afford to let this foundation disappear from view altogether: "Perhaps this is why [he] maintains a certain reserve, keeps his musical expression within certain limits – that is to say, does not sound the note of tragic passion too strongly: emotions and expectations would be aroused compelling the listener to put that unsettling question 'Why?' which the composer cannot satisfactorily answer" (VII, 128).[1]

That unsettling question "Why?" ("jene beunruhigende Frage nach dem Warum") was glossed by Wagner earlier in the 1860 essay as a new variation on the old theme of the historical-aesthetic inevitability of the music drama. Music, he says, tends more and more to exhibit a "need" which only poetry can fulfill (in direct proportion to its striving after the determinate representation of "ideas," we can infer). This need or lack on music's part, which is perhaps to be understood as a corollary of its "feminine" nature, has to do with the indeterminate character of its signs, and the consequent problematics of their hermeneutic provocations. In recalling here the text in which these problems are raised (cited in chapter 2 with reference to Beethoven's implication in them), let us read a little further into the paragraph that follows:

To explain [music's] need we have to remind ourselves of the human mind's ineradicable impulse, when confronted by an impressive phenomenon, to put the

[1] Translation from Robert Jacobs, *Three Wagner Essays* (London, 1979), 39.

question: Why? Even when we are listening to a symphony the question cannot be completely suppressed and, since the symphony is least of all able to provide an answer, the question puts the listener's perceptual faculties, bound to the laws of causality, into a state of confusion. This not only has the effect of disturbing him, it also gives rise to an entirely false judgement.

Only a poet can provide this disturbing yet inescapable question with an answer that would, as it were, by circumvention prevent it from ever being put (*daß sie von vornherein durch Beschwichtigung gewissermaßen eludiert wird*).

(VII, 112; Jacobs, 28)

And only the drama, Wagner goes on to explain, as "actual scenic representation" of meaningful human actions, is able to supplement fully music's "lack" or need of a distinct object for its semantic orientation. The listener-spectator's engagement with this scenic action transports him into an "ecstatic condition" in which he forgets the baleful question ("Why?"), and "one willingly abandons oneself to the guidance of those new laws which enable music to make itself so miraculously comprehensible, those laws which – in a profound sense – provide the only right answer to that 'Why?'" (VII, 112; Jacobs, 29). Typically enough, Wagner has twisted his argument so as to have it both ways. While drama alone is said to motivate, justify, or otherwise excuse innovations of musical form, style, and general behavior, such innovations contain "in a profound sense" (if unspecified) their own excuse, their own answer. (This "profound sense," the mysterious logic of pure music, is perhaps an echo of Schopenhauer's apothegm that music, properly regarded, might constitute "the only true philosophy of things.")[2]

Indeed, we often read that for Wagner *après* Schopenhauer – the Wagner of *Tristan* or the 1870 *Beethoven* essay – the music "explains" the drama rather than the other way around. While the *Beethoven* essay does make a few gestures in this direction, Wagner remained more consistently wedded to the view that all music required some kind of phenomenological motivation or *raison d'être*, and that if this were not provided by highly conventionalized, collectively internalized and relatively simple schematic models (e.g. simple binary or ternary forms and the sonata), then some other motivating force would have to be adduced to explain the musical behavior of a composition (a cardinal point of the Wagnerian poetics of musical form briefly sketched in chapter 2). It is above all in this broadly conceived "theory" of the necessary poetic-dramatic motivation of new or non-schematic forms that Wagner confronted that central music-aesthetic preoccupation of his age, the role of "poetic ideas" in motivating "new musical forms." But again, Wagner set himself apart from most of his fellow progressives by his general unwillingness to concede that music could in and of itself

---

2   A. Schopenhauer, *Die Welt als Wille und Vorstellung* (Zurich, 1977), vol. I, §52, 332.

convey "ideas" or embody a dramatic action, insisting instead on their representation in words and gestures that would at once motivate and interpret music's "new forms." Or at any rate, Wagner remained radically undecided on such fundamental issues of musical form and meaning: whether the symphony might legitimately aspire to drama, or whether opera could be successfully rendered symphonic. A consequence of this critical indecision remains the perennial question as to whether Wagner's own music drama can or should be evaluated according to the canons of "symphonic unity" or coherence, or whether apparent transgressions of symphonic (or merely tonal) coherence in these scores demand the mediation of drama to justify and interpret them. That Wagner was unable to make up his mind whether a Beethoven symphony was fundamentally dramatic or fundamentally un-dramatic may ultimately seem irrelevant to our appreciation of that music.[3] But his indecision does suggest the obverse question pertaining to his own scores: whether they are fundamentally "symphonic" or un-symphonic in conception.

The supposed apologia for Liszt's new orchestral works in 1857 (the "Open Letter on Franz Liszt's Symphonic Poems") remains awkwardly equivocal on related grounds. While Carl Dahlhaus seems always to have accepted the essay as proof that Wagner retracted his theoretical objections to programmatic genres after encountering Liszt's works in the 1850s (and there is no doubt that the music left its mark on him),[4] the case advanced in support of their aesthetic legitimacy in the open letter is fairly tenuous. And much of what Wagner has to say, not surprisingly, serves his own critical agenda better than it does the Lisztian program (in either sense of the word).

The hotly debated topic of program music and the musical representation of ideas, poetic or otherwise, offered Wagner a stimulus to reflect on some broad aesthetic issues of musical form and meaning he had

---

3   Compare, for example, the following, apparently incompatible propositions from *"Music of the Future," Beethoven,* and "On the Application of Music to the Drama," respectively: "The idealized form of dance that would exactly fit [Beethoven's] music is in fact to be found in the *dramatic action*" (VII, 128; Jacobs, 39); "The motion, formation, and variation of these motives [in Beethoven's *Coriolan* overture] not only bear a close analogical relation to the drama, but even the drama itself and the idea it represents can in truth only be completely grasped by means of such motion, formation, and variation of these musical motives" (IX, 106); " . . . even the most intricate complications of thematic-motivic workings of a symphonic movement can never be explained dialectically, in the sense of a dramatic action, but only as the interweaving of ideal dance figures" (X, 179).

4   See for example Dahlhaus, *Nineteenth-Century Music,* 237 ("The [genre of the] symphonic poem that so startled Wagner in 1857, forcing him to modify his aesthetic . . . ") or "Wagner und die Programmusik" (1973), in *Klassische und romantische Musikästhetik,* 414–28.

evidently been turning over in his mind for several years at the time of the 1857 letter. The dichotomy of formal principles he identifies here under the rubrics of "alternation" or contrast (*Wechsel*) and "evolution" or development (*Entwicklung*) has already been alluded to a number of times in the foregoing chapters. The roots of Wagner's concern with this dichotomy are already evident in much of *Opera and Drama*, especially in the organicist discourse of musical form loosely developed across Part III of that work. (The ideological roots of this *Entwicklungsprinzip* have been briefly examined in chapter 3, while I have tried to suggest some of its practical consequences on ideas of "period" and melody, respectively, in the following chapters.) That the actual terms of this dichotomy are first coined in the seemingly out-of-the-way context of a brief article Wagner sent to the *Neue Zeitschrift für Musik* in June of 1854 (to accompany the concert ending he had composed to Gluck's overture to *Iphigénie en Aulide*) may well be explained by the broader biographical context – the recent initiation of the *Ring* composition.[5] The simple "neo-classical" architecture of Gluck's (classical) overture is now surely highlighted, in Wagner's mind, against his recent attempt to invent music that would "evolve" along the lines of drama itself. And when Wagner returned to the dichotomy of *Wechsel* and *Entwicklung* in 1857 not only had his compositional confrontation with the latter principle advanced by several crucial years, he was now also presented with a more challenging point of comparison to his own works, in the form of Liszt's symphonic poems.

What "form" is that? Do Liszt's symphonic forms in fact "evolve" rather than juxtapose melodic periods in patterns of contrast and return? And if they do evolve, what justifies (motivates) that evolution in such a way that the listener can make sense of it and interpret the "idea" behind it? Wagner is equivocal on these points. If Liszt's works were really to convey an idea – such as the trajectory of events, actions, and consequences that constitute a given mythic subject – then they would (Wagner supposes) necessarily dispense with the accustomed patterns of sonata form in favor of some evolving musical process that could be perceived as embodying the outlines of such a myth. On the other hand, the very conception of any "symphonic" movement is, for Wagner, indissolubly linked with the idea of binary or ternary constructions of sonata form, so that it is by no means obvious how an instrumental composition might transcend the boundaries of conventional form and still remain symphonic or musically intelligible at all (the mere musical imitation of some extra-musical scenario is naturally dismissed from serious consideration, at least in the instrumental domain). Wagner

---

5   "Glucks Ouvertüre zu 'Iphigenia in Aulis'," V, 111–22 (see esp. 118–19). See also T. Grey, "Wagner, the Overture, and the Aesthetics of Musical Form."

argues himself into a tight spot by insisting, still, that "autonomously" intelligible musical form is always rooted in conventional (dance-derived) patterns of periodic contrast and return, but then shifting his rhetorical stance to insist that the musical embodiment of "ideas" (automatically construed here as "dramatic" ideas) will naturally cast aside those conventional patterns in favor of some "new form" more adequate to the idea in question.

What, then, would this new form be? – Necessarily that which is demanded in each case by the object and the representation of its development (*durch den Gegenstand und seine darzustellende Entwickelung*). And what would this object be? – A poetic motive. That is – *horribile dictu!* – "program music." (V, 191)

Wagner extricates himself from the corner into which he has argued himself – his claims regarding the immutable constraints of musical-formal autonomy and intelligibility – by indulging in the circular reasoning that characterizes much "idealist" discourse on musical form. Ideas generate their own necessary and natural "form" as if this were somehow genetically encoded within them (Wagner often implies something similar in speaking of drama, or of his dramas). How such a form is decoded from the "idea" remains a mystery of artistic nature, it seems. But the suggestion that an imagined, physically absent object can adequately justify and "explain" a non-conventional musical design, or even non-conventional details within it, is still difficult to square with Wagner's habitual insistence on the immediate presence of a concrete object for music in the form of drama. Can a poetic *Motiv* or subject lodged in the listener's mind fulfill the same function as Wagner's dramatic motives (motivating impulses within the action), textually articulated and visibly enacted? Can such a *Motiv*, that is, really motivate and validate new developmental, non-schematic forms, even on the basis of the listener's merely "abstract" intellectual acquaintance with it?

Wagner's seemingly affirmative answer is still equivocal (essentially: "Why not?"). "I ask you: do the dance or march, and the gestures associated with such actions, constitute a more worthy form-giving motive (*Motiv zur Formgebung*) than, for example, the mental representation of the characteristic principal features of an Orpheus or a Prometheus, their deeds and sufferings? I ask you further: if music depends on a form in order to communicate [a content], as I have tried to explain, would it not increase the nobility and freedom of a work if it were to derive that form from such a conceptual motif as Orpheus or Prometheus rather than from that of a mere dance or march?" (V, 192). Having first stressed the narrow limits of intelligible musical form, Wagner now turns around and dismisses them. All music can move any way it pleases, so long as it has a "motive," a reason, he seems to say. But there is a catch, he admits (without offering any clear solution to it): the trick is to derive from

Warum? *(motives to musical form)*

"such higher, individualized representations *(Vorstellungen)*" a form that can be rendered musically intelligible, even though it has so far seemed impossible to operate outside of conventional musical groupings based on those lower, generalized *Formmotive* (dance, march, or song types).

On this point of poetic "motives" to musical form Wagner's case for Liszt does carry some conviction, at last. But it is the very generality of the poetic-formal "motives" in Liszt's orchestral works which he defends, evidently their appeal to broad, culturally internalized narrative tropes rather than the "prosaic" discursive detail. The Adagio from Berlioz's *Roméo et Juliette* is cited as a foil, the composer charged with failing to process Shakespeare's balcony scene for proper musical digestion. And yet the ostensible apologia for Liszt still falls short. Wagner's sympathy with the Lisztian approach, on a general level, doesn't seem to translate into a wholesale approval of the details. He allows that the *Faust* or *Dante* symphonies, for instance, have stimulated his consciousness of the "problem" of forms and the motives behind them ("mich über das vorliegende Problem erst klar gemacht"), yet says nothing about their having *solved* it.

The wording of this pseudo-apologia continues to suggest that Wagner is reserving the role of musical-historical hero for himself. Music is not held back by any immanent limitations, he says. History merely awaits the artist "possessed of the requisite poetic-musical qualities to grasp a poetic object in such as way as to serve the musician in fashioning musically intelligible forms from it" (V, 193). "And herein lies the real secret and the difficulty, whose solution must have been reserved for just such a highly gifted figure *(nur einem höchst begabten Auserlesenen vorbehalten sein konnte)* who is at once a complete musician and a complete, perceptive poet." We are, of course, to infer from the rhetorical protocol of this "open letter" that Liszt is such an artist. Yet Wagner cannot finally bring himself to say as much, directly. No amount of admiration or gratitude, it seems, could persuade Wagner to cede his role as poetic-musical chosen one *(Auserlesenen)* to another.

Having discharged at least this *gesture* of support for Liszt in the open letter, Wagner would soon turn around and retract it.[6] In *"Music of the Future"* (1860) he goes back to asserting the claims of the musical dramatist over the program musician in no uncertain terms, with respect to the newly formulated hermeneutic dilemma of the Beethovenian symphonic legacy: "A program, which provokes rather than stills the

---

6   I will not attempt to go into the biographical factors that might play a role in Wagner's attitudes toward Liszt and his music, although I by no means deny their possible relevance. The numerous biographies that might be consulted on this question mostly agree that even before the Cosima affair in the mid-1860s, the mutual enthusiasm sustained between Wagner and Liszt through the 1850s had already begun to wane.

311

impulse to put that disturbing question 'Why?', cannot convey the meaning of a symphony. This can only be done by a dramatic action depicted on the stage" (VII, 129; Jacobs, 39). By 1879 ("On the Application of Music to the Drama") Wagner even reverses his long-held dogma of the *tendentially* dramatic Beethovenian symphony in claiming that

even the most intricate complications of thematic-motivic working in a [classical or Beethovenian] symphony can never be explained dialectically in the sense of a dramatic action, but only as the interweaving of ideal dance figures, without the mental imposition of any rhetorical dialectic . . . Here there is no conclusion, no purpose, and no [dramatic] achievement *(keine Konklusion, keine Absicht, und keine Vollbringung)*. (X, 179).

Beethoven's relative caution in harmonic matters (as opposed to his rhythmic-metrical experimentation) is explained as a function of the symphonic genre, which could provide no motivating impulse for truly expanding the frontiers of modulation. A genuine dramatic, tragic action might do so, but a symphony is not a tragedy, nor any kind of drama, Wagner now insisted. The "ideal dance form" of the symphony would merely be confused by gestures of "dramatic pathos," which could only provoke "questions without the possibility of answers" (X, 180) – in other words, the hermeneutic dilemma encapsulated in Wagner's critical query, *Warum?*

The birth of the music drama from the "labor-pains of program music"

Despite this increasingly conservative stance, or pose, regarding the inherent limitations of traditional instrumental music, Wagner did subscribe wholeheartedly to the popular contemporary doctrine, documented in chapters 1 and 2, that music since Beethoven was inexorably evolving toward greater expressive determinacy, nuance of character, and the representation of human actions and interactions – in short, that music "naturally" aspired to the condition of drama. The theorem of the symphony's incapacity to embody real dramatic action thus had a corollary in the historical imperative of music drama. Here opera could be reformed and the symphony could be redeemed at a single stroke. Wagner summarizes this view quite succinctly in "On the Application of Music to the Drama," whose title explicitly refers to the application of programmatic-characteristic musical innovations (judged largely to have misfired as such) to dramatic ends, where they will find more suitable employment:

[P]ure instrumental music was no longer satisfied to remain bound by the strictures of classical symphonic form *(in der gesetzmäßigen Form des klassischen Symphoniesatzes)* and hence sought to stimulate the expansion of its capacities in every respect by means of attempting poetic representations (*dichterischen Vorstellungen*). The reaction against this trend [an allusion to Brahms and his "symphonic revival"] was nonetheless incapable of maintaining the life of these classical forms, and it, too, found itself compelled to absorb thoroughly alien elements, thereby distorting these forms [all the same].

If this first [programmatic] tendency led to the acquisition of new capacities, while the reactionary tendency has merely exposed its own creative impotence, it nonetheless transpired that the boundless aberrations which seemed to threaten seriously the spirit of music through these continued attempts to exploit such new musical capacities could only be avoided by turning them, openly and deliberately, in the direction of *drama*. Here [in drama] that which had been left unspoken could now be stated clearly and distinctly (*deutlich und bestimmt*), while at the same time the "opera" might be redeemed from the stigma of its unnatural origins (*aus dem Banne ihrer unnatürlichen Herkunft*). Here, too, in the "musical" drama, as we might now call it, we can arrive at a clear understanding of the [more fruitful] application of these newly-won musical capacities to the cultivation of noble, inexhaustibly rich artistic forms.   (X, 184)

While the 1879 essay has been repeatedly cited as further evidence of Wagner's unyielding dogma of the sublation of the symphony in the music drama, the defensive re-positioning of his argument here has been little noticed. By 1879 Wagner had seen the symphonic poem become accepted into the international canon of "high" musical genres, and of course he was sensitive to the more recent threat to his musical-aesthetic prognoses by the first two symphonies of Brahms. (Presumably Wagner felt less threatened by the likes of Gade, Rubinstein, or Raff, or by the early symphonies of Dvořák or Tchaikovsky, although he did feel compelled to make disparaging noises about "characteristic" and nationalistic symphonies, more generally, in the "Application" essay.) The covert attacks on Brahms in this essay (as in "On Poetry and Composition" from the same year) have always been recognized. But Wagner also feels compelled here to reduce the symphonic poem and its relations, such as the characteristic or nationalistic symphony, to experimental epiphenomena at the margins of musical drama. The strategy is, once again, to co-opt the critical discourse of "poetic ideas" and determinacy of expression, which already played a considerable role in the historiographical constructions of the Zurich writings, as I have argued. In sketching a context for Wagner's essays of 1879 (mainly "On the Application of Music to the Drama") I would draw attention here to two particular points about this discourse that Wagner could exploit to his own ends, just as he admitted to "exploiting" the results of modern instrumental experiments: first, the underlying conviction that new or substantially modified musical forms, procedures, or styles required some kind of ideational *motivation* in the form of a "poetic object," idea, program, or other textual accompaniment; and second, that many exponents of this discourse – not only Wagner – proposed drama as the most effective source for such motivation and hence as the leading paradigm for the further evolution of modern musical technique and form.[7]

Partisans such as Liszt or Franz Brendel, of course, provided abundant support for the first of these points. Liszt's 1855 essay, "Berlioz and his Harold-Symphony," is perhaps the most familiar example of this literature. (As a critical apologia for his own symphonic project, disguised as an appreciation of Berlioz, it parallels Wagner's letter on Liszt, which, as suggested, tends toward a poorly disguised piece of self-promotion.) A *Grundmotiv* of Franz Brendel's many prolix essays and pamphlets of the 1850s and 60s, promoting Wagner and Liszt alike, is the role of "distinct" poetic ideas (whether in programmatic or dramatic form) in motivating the advancement or "progress" of compositional technique. The natural history of music, as Brendel never tired of proclaiming, lay in an evolution "from the indistinct to the distinct," from abstract *Tonspiel* of fugues and sonatas to the semantically enriched musical language of the symphonic poem and music drama.[8]

Nor were such convictions limited to the "New Germans." They may be found again and again, in countless variations and in all kinds of contexts. (Even if those opposed to these trends were likely to stigmatize them as indices of cultural decline, they nonetheless acknowledged them as all too real preoccupations of the musical present.) To cite just one example, an essay on "Beethoven's Ideals and the Orthodox Criticism," printed in Ludwig Bischoff's conservative *Niederrheinische Musik-Zeitung* and in the *Berliner Musik-Zeitung Echo* (famous as the venue of the Brahms-Joachim manifesto against the New Germans), includes a summary perspective of Beethoven's position along these familiar lines: "The creative output of Beethoven mirrors in this way [i.e., in the development from early to late styles] the whole evolutionary history of music, since its motivating principle is none other than the law whereby art progresses from a play of the senses to the complete expression of human nature."[9] Beethoven's essential innovation, this writer posits, was to transplant the kinds of "spiritual or intellectual motives" (*geistige Motive*) as had previously informed a few exceptional works

---

7   Dahlhaus has often observed that Wagner's dictum about the obsolescence of the symphony was less absurd than it might seem in retrospect, indeed "almost prophetic" in view of its historical context (1849–50) and the dearth of historically "significant" symphonies to emerge across the following quarter century (see for example *Nineteenth-Century Music*, 236). This may satisfy a twentieth-century perspective that feels entitled to distinguish between music-historical "facts" and "rubble," but in his own time Wagner had a much better chance of defending the hubris of such constructions by appealing to the critical discourse of "ideas" and determinacy under discussion here.

8   Brendel, "Programm-Musik," *Anregungen für Kunst, Leben, und Wissenschaft* 1 (1856), 82.

9   [Anon.], "Die Ideale Beethovens und die orthodoxe Kritik," reprinted from *Niederrheinische Musik-Zeitung* in *Berliner Musik-Zeitung Echo* 8 (1858), 225.

(certain overtures and explicitly characteristic or programmatic works) into all of his sonatas, quartets, and symphonies.

An essay in the *Neue Zeitschrift* commemorating the centenary of Beethoven's birth under the rubric "Recent Music and its Application to Cultural Objectives" obligingly confirms Wagner's thesis about the progress of the musical *Zeitgeist* from Beethoven into his own oeuvre through the conduit of dramatic impulses. The writer (one Ferdinand Ludwig) aligns himself with what he calls "the current Beethoven movement" as well as with "that great movement which seeks to locate in the *dramatic* the central point of all the arts."[10] Ludwig takes it upon himself to explain why Beethoven, for all his affinity for music's dramatic potential, should have for the most part avoided specifically dramatic genres. Both the question and the answers he provides surely take their cue from Wagner, as must his assertion that those factors preventing Beethoven, the symphonic composer, from continuing as a composer of opera are precisely the "cardinal point . . . of all questions pertaining to the development of recent music."[11]

An anonymous essayist writing at about this same time on the "musical-poetic object" appears to allude directly to Wagner's musical-hermeneutic query ("Why?") in *"Music of the Future,"* which he interprets as symptomatic of a new interpretive impulse characterizing the modern musical era as a whole (suggesting at the same time the migration of natural-scientific paradigms into the domain of humanistic criticism):

The trademark (*Wahrzeichen*) of the nineteenth century also manifests itself now in the artistic life of the present, which is no longer content to collect answers as to "What?" or register those as to "How?", but in a distinct sense also seeks to learn from the world-spirit an answer to the question "Why?" in every branch of the physical and psychological sciences, and also in art, in order to achieve a clear sense of what route will lead to this goal.[12]

By means of an ever-increasing capacity for characterization and expressive nuance, music inexorably progresses from out of the restricted realm of "lyricism" toward that of epic and drama, he continues. This epic-dramatic turn of modern music (since Beethoven) plays a reciprocal role in stimulating the development of musical means that, in turn, enable the musician to articulate the ideas or emotional designs necessary for the musical representation of dramatic actions:

Epic provides the imagination with the greatest latitude; it not only allows a more eloquent, because more direct, musical language (*Tonvermittlungssprache*), but further gives essential support to the polyphony that raises the significance of

---

10   F. Ludwig, "Die neuere Musik und ihre Anwendung auf die Culturaufgaben" (Part I, Beethoven), *Neue Zeitschrift für Musik* 66:39 (1870), 349 (emphasis added).

11   Ibid., 350.

12   "Musikalische Poesie-Objecte," *Neue Zeitschrift für Musik* 65:16 (1869), 130.

the medium (*das Tonwesen ja besonders hebende Polyphonie*) – that is, a polyphony that is not merely a superficial play of contrary [linear] motions, but a truly contrasted, thought-filled counter-discourse in tones (*contrastirende, gedankenerfüllte Gegenrede in Tönen*).[13]

For instance, while in "lyrical" forms or styles the bass is generally restricted to plucking out harmonic accompaniment ("pflichtschuldige Harmoniereverenzen in Form gewählter Accompagnements-Wendungen") or a few measures of thematic imitation now and then, music with genuine dramatic motives behind it will emancipate all the voices of the texture and grant them speaking roles. The progress from lyrical to epic-dramatic paradigms is given, in fact, a frankly political construction paralleling the progression from an *ancien régime* to the modern republican era – a construction so often found lurking in the background of Beethoven criticism of the period:

> The listener's role is not made any easier in the case of epic compositions (*epische Tondichtungen*); and no one can claim that the layman or dilettante will enjoy calm, untroubled musical pleasure in such epic genres, in which the pace of events may often suggest a somewhat ill-bred character and the music may well permit itself a freely republican manner of speech; one soon realizes that one is no longer on the ground of aristocratic etiquette, and finds oneself instead pressed into a position where one is never for a moment safe from cheeky impositions (*eine Lage . . . , in welcher man keinen Augenblick vor persönlichen Zumuthungen sicher ist*).[14]

Louis Köhler, finally (whom we may recall from his early glosses on the "poetic-musical period" in chapter 4), may be cited to similar effect on the new role of "poetic motives" from his pamphlet on *The New Direction in Music* (published a year before the premiere of *Tristan*): "[Where] earlier composers gave only the general emotional expression of a poetic idea in their music, recent composers give a more detailed account of it, sometimes even choosing poetic motives that are awkward to express in music."[15] But if this new determinacy of musical expression presented new and even "awkward" challenges to composers, the "republican" ethos that informed it (as our anonymous essayist saw it) sought to bring the esoteric language of music into a broader domain of public discourse, for which drama was perhaps the most effective paradigm, as Wagner understood. And again, one does not have to turn only to confirmed

---

13 Ibid., 131. A similar equation between encoded meaning and modern, melodic-motivic (non-imitative) counterpoint was proposed by J. C. Lobe (see "Beethoven's sketches" in chapter 2 above, relating Lobe's text to Wagner's remarks on Beethoven in *Opera and Drama*).

14 Ibid., 131.

15 L. Köhler, *Die neue Richtung in der Musik* (Leipzig, 1864), 46. The section on program music in Köhler's book includes a brief genealogy of the role of "poetic motives" or ideas in music from Beethoven through his own time (48–9).

apostles of the Wagnerian or New German creed to find evidence of this conviction, or of Beethoven's supposed role in instigating this dramatic-representational turn in modern music. Even the notorious conservative, Alexander Ulibishev, claimed (in his 1857 monograph on Beethoven, "his critics, and his *glossateurs*") that the pursuit of "poetic ideas" in recent instrumental music was a response to impulses emanating from the *Zeitgeist*. "One saw this," he continues, "as a means of bringing music closer to the people, in that one tried to endow it with a more distinct, sharply drawn, and tangible character; in this way one hoped to approach the precision of dramatic expression and to achieve thereby a greater effect on the mass of listeners."[16]

While the early Romantic aesthetic of pure, "absolute" music is often characterized as an emancipation of instrumental music from text or extra-musical function, the subsequent "neo-Romantic" generation (as it was often identified) – musicians and critics who, like Wagner, came of age between 1830 and 1848 – was thoroughly caught up in the idea of music's emancipation from its own internal conventions and the putative "laws" and restrictions of classical form. Wagner and his biographers have generally been at pains to dissociate his earlier political enthusiasms from his real artistic calling. But despite this, and despite Wagner's later conservative posturings, there has never been any question of his leading role in the musical *Freiheitskrieg* of the mid-nineteenth century. From the Zurich writings to the time of *Parsifal* his aesthetic theory consistently turns back on the idea of discovering the kind of motivation (in drama) that can free music from the rule of "dance and march forms," those vestiges of the old, obsolete order.

From this perspective, program music and its related species are judged by Wagner as a perfectly natural response to the historical imperative of increasing expressive determinacy and the impulse to liberate music from classical "etiquette" (as our *Neue Zeitschrift* critic put it). But they are also re-interpreted, in 1879, as a transitional phenomenon within the natural history of the music drama. Evidence of the imperfect, transitional nature of such genres is seen in their unstable admixture of inevitable "traces of traditional symphonic construction" (*Spuren der eigentlichen Symphoniesatz-Konstruktion*) with a new "passionate and

---

16 Connecting these phenomena with the impulses underlying Beethoven's "third manner" (as their principal source), Ulibishev continues: "De la sphère des sensations, Beethoven voulut passer dans celle de la perception, combiner l'idée musicale avec une idée sensible ou rationelle, mêler l'élément dramatique à l'élément lyrique, se servir, en un mot, du programme idéal, indécis et variable qui se forme de lui-même dans l'âme des auditeurs, sans qu'ils le cherchent, pour les conduire à la compréhension logique d'un programme arrêté et choisi d'avance" (*Beethoven, ses critiques et ses glossateurs* [Leipzig and Paris, 1857], 103–4).

eccentric character" in the "invention of themes, their expression as well as their contrasts and transformations (*Gegenüberstellung und Umbildung*), from which purely symphonic music ought really to keep its distance" (X, 181). The by-products of this *mésalliance*, however – Liszt's thematic transformations, experiments with augmented or diminished harmonies, and with sequential or prolongational applications of these, or Berlioz's manifold orchestral innovations – all provided valuable resources for the musical drama destined to inherit them (see X, 180).[17] The dissonance of ends and means in "program music" is felicitously resolved in musical drama:

> If this dilemma [the drive to express a "poetic figure or formation" (*dichterische Gestalt oder Gestaltung*) as precisely as possible by means of "eccentric *Charakteristik*"] led naturally to complete musical melodramas with pantomimed action to be supplied by the listener's imagination, or else to instrumental recitatives, then there was really nothing left – while critical opinion swelled with horror at the advent of such rampant formlessness – but to let the new form [i.e., genre] of musical drama to be born from such musical labor-pains.[18]   (X, 181)

Already once engendered by the happy union of poetic father and musical mother, the music drama is accorded a second birth and endowed with an alternative parentage – the more troubled partnership of music and "poetic ideas" (to which the analogous gender identities presumably apply).

But do real, visible action and real, audible text (intelligible or not) really justify what would otherwise be judged formless and eccentric? Does Wotan's distress or Tristan's delirium really "make sense" of progressions or motivic combinations that are otherwise senseless? Early critics were clearly not always satisfied on these points, but criticism in our own day has not often pressed Wagner on such questions. In his own time Wagner could perhaps appeal to a broader version of the criterion of aesthetic autonomy, displacing that of autonomous, "absolute" musical logic: where music transgresses the bounds of conventional behavior, the reasons for this (the motivations) are now right before our eyes – feelings, ideas, and motivations are all "realized" on stage and in the sung text as part of the musical work proper. The *Gesamtkunstwerk* comes with batteries included. Everything is there, musical motives and the dramatic motivations that drive them.

---

17   Wagner had already conceded the "valuable contributions" of *Tonmalerei* to the "sensual capacities" (*sinnliche Vermögen*) of contemporary musical language in *Opera and Drama*, where he otherwise rejected the genre on theoretical grounds (IV, 188).

18   Although "musical melodramas" might refer to the melodrama proper, as accompanied recitation, the reference to an imaginary action ("mit hinzudenkender pantomimischer Aktion") and to "instrumental recitatives" suggests Berlioz's *Roméo et Juliette* (the tomb scene, for example – see below), as well as certain passages of instrumental recitative in Liszt's orchestral works.

The audience needs no manual to explain the musical goings-on (although Wolzogen's *Leitfäden* unfortunately suggested the opposite), provided they know who is singing and what is sung. Yet evidently Wagner and his multi-purpose "motives" do not themselves answer all the questions they raise, nor solve quite so easily all the problems of contemporary aesthetics they engage.

Motif, motive, *Motiv*: dramatic motivations and "symphonic form"

Various orthographic and semantic uncertainties surrounding Wagner's most famous bequest to music history (the leitmotif) can serve to focus attention on some of the critical problems it continues to provoke. Wagner himself, as we know, did not speak of *Leitmotiven*, but employed a variety of other terms and circumlocutions to describe the thing we now know by that name: *melodische Momenten, Themen, Melodien, Grundthemen, Hauptthemen, Grundmotiven, plastische Natur-Motiven, musikalische Motiven*, or simply *Motiven*.[19] This plurality aptly (though not in any systematic sense) reflects the spectrum of his practice: his "leitmotifs" come in many shapes and sizes – some are themes or melodies, some are motives, some are "fundamental," "principal," or "natural," some are not. Without attempting a statistical analysis, it is probably safe to say that, in the Zurich writings, Wagner tended to reserve the word *Motiv* and its compounds to refer to dramatic "motifs" – conceptual themes and motivating causes – as distinguished from the musical melodies, themes, motives, or "elements" (*Momenten*) that might be associated with them. In later contexts, through the 1879 *Bayreuther Blätter* articles, the term *Motiv* becomes more frequently applied to musical ideas, as well (i.e., leitmotifs), while some remnants of the earlier vocabulary still remain. Even from the beginning, however (that is to say from Part III of *Opera and Drama*), Wagner mobilizes the latent ambiguity of the term *Motiv* to signify various interconnected phenomena: broad underlying themes or mythic tropes within the drama (the power of the Ring, its attendant curse, the sibling love of Siegmund and Sieglinde, the emotional pre-history of Tristan and Isolde, or Walther's natural lyric gift would be motives, or "motifs," in this sense), but also the musical figures that attach themselves to these, thereby achieving a certain – or rather uncertain – semantic determinacy as "leitmotifs."

English usage distinguishes (although not consistently) between "motive" and "motif," where German conveniently confounds all senses within a single word. The *Oxford English Dictionary*, for instance, includes

---

[19] Klaus Kropfinger details some of the vagaries of Wagner's terminology in *Wagner and Beethoven*, 91–4; see also 217–19 on "leitmotif."

the following separate definitions, while ultimately allowing for orthographic interchangeability:[20]

Motif sb. 1848 1. In art and literature, a distinctive feature or element of a
design or composition; a particular type of subject; also, the dominant idea of a
work; *Mus.* a leading figure or short phrase, a subject or theme; see also Leitmotiv;
2. *Dress-making.* an ornament of lace, braid or the like, sewn separately on a
dress 1882; 3. Often use instead of Motive, in order to avoid the suggestion of
volition associated with the Eng. word 1874.

Motive sb. 2. That which moves or induces a person to act in a certain way; a
desire, fear, reason, etc. which influences a person's volition: also often applied
to a result or object which is desired; [obs.] 3. A mover, instigator, promoter; 4.
A moving limb or organ (only in Shaks.); 5. In art and literature = Motif 1. 1851.

The *American Heritage Dictionary* similarly includes under the definitions
of "motif" the following: "A recurrent thematic element used in an artistic
or literary work," "A dominant theme," "A short significant phrase in a
musical composition," and "A repeated figure or design in architecture or
decoration," while "motive" has again to do with emotions, desires,
needs, impulses, and behavioral causes.[21] In dealing with Wagner's prose,
these orthographic distinctions are more an inconvenience than an asset.
For while we might perfectly well speak of dramatic or musical "motifs"
in the sense of the first definition-group here (indeed, we are encouraged
to do so), this excludes the substratum of emotional impulse, volition, and
motivation which seems essential to both the theory and practice of
"leitmotifs." The Ring and its Curse are dramatic "motifs" and motivating
impulses at once: they motivate much of the action in Wagner's drama, as
they motivate the incidence of musical ideas attached to them. The
musical motives of *Tristan*, famed for their resistance to (or transcendence
of) semantic determinacy, are more like "motives" in the second sense,
seething beneath the phenomenal surface of things like the perpetual tides
of the Schopenhauerian "Will," whose sounding emblems they are said to
be. Furthermore, the all-important relation of dramatic motifs to musical
leitmotifs is supposed to be one of reciprocal motivation – this is how
Wagner explained the possibility of his musical "forms" in the first place,
as an outgrowth of that long-standing discourse of poetic ideas.

These semantic ambiguities of *Motiv* or motive have traditionally
played a part in music-analytical discourse, more generally critics are
often pleased to assume that musical processes might be set in motion
by forces mysteriously residing in the "motives," which, like seeds,
contain the genetic code according to which a work will "naturally"
unfold. Since these implications of impulse or causal force are themselves encoded within the word "motive," the critic may easily invoke

[20] *Oxford English Dictionary*, shorter edn (Oxford, 1973), s.v. "Motif," "Motive."
[21] *American Heritage Dictionary* (Boston, 1982), s.v. "Motif."

them without incurring the responsibility of proof. The same ambiguities work to Wagner's advantage in *Opera and Drama*, where "motives" can be many things at once, and Wagner, for a change, can't be blamed for the imprecision.[22]

The reciprocity of dramatic and musical motives has always been axiomatic to Wagnerian criticism and, unlike the popular parody of leitmotifs as musical calling cards, this axiom enjoys the sanction of Wagner's theory. The "characteristic sounding" of musical motives in the orchestra, for instance, is said to contribute to our fuller understanding of a situation by assisting in the "interpretation of [dramatic or psychological] motives that are contained in this situation" (*durch Deutung von Motiven, die in dieser Situation wohl enthalten sind*), but which otherwise resist concrete representation (IV, 184). On the other hand, of course, Wagner maintained that musical motives could never achieve the kind of determinate expression so eagerly sought after by his contemporaries without attaching themselves to dramatic motives, characters, situations, and text. "A musical motive," he writes in *Opera and Drama*

can only convey a distinct impression to our mental activity when the feelings expressed in this motive are communicated by a distinct individual with reference to a distinct object and are thus made distinct, that is, precisely conditioned (*von einem bestimmten Individuum an einem bestimmten Gegenstand als ebenfalls bestimmte, d.h. wolhbedingte*). Apart from these conditions a musical motive can only be presented to our feelings as something indistinct (*etwas Unbestimmtes*), and something indistinct may be repeated in the same shape as often as you like, it will amount to nothing more than a repercussive indeterminacy (*es bleibt uns immer ein eben nur wiederkehrendes Unbestimmtes*).

(IV, 185)

The multiplication of the word *bestimmt* (distinct, determinate) and its inversion throughout this passage seems almost calculated to enact for us the very phenomenon Wagner describes: the futility of an endlessly repeated gesture, word, or motive so long as it lacks a meaningful definition or context. Beyond that, the passage drives home my own

---

[22] A citation in the *Oxford English Dictionary* from Wagner's contemporary, John Ruskin, also bridges the two groups of meanings in a suggestive way: "a great [visual] composition," Ruskin says, "always has a leading emotional purpose, technically called its motive, to which all its lines and forms have some relation" (s.v. "Motive"). Having raised this semantic mare's nest, I should perhaps clarify my own – partially arbitrary – usage here. In order to preserve the connotative lability of *Motiv* in Wagner's usage I will attempt to restrict myself, within this section, to the single spelling "motive," even though I have elsewhere permitted myself the distinction between dramatic "motifs" (as conceptual themes or tropes) and musical "motives" (following the more common American usage). On the other hand (as explained in chapter 1), I have chosen to render *Leitmotiv* as "leitmotif" simply for the sake of its isosonorous relation to the German term, and because it reflects the most common British and American usage.

claim that Wagner's motivic theory is conceived as a response to the discourse of a new musical "determinacy" of expression. Until now, he admits, music's forte has been the evocation of "indistinct emotional intimations (*die Anregung unbestimmter, ahnungsvoller Empfindungen*), which, however, became a liability whenever music wanted to determine the significance of these feelings more precisely (*die angeregten Empfindungen auch deutlich bestimmen wollte*)" (IV, 187).

Wagner's theory of motives in *Opera and Drama* is shot through with such appeals to this trope of a new semantic determinacy. At last we will know what music is "talking about," for at last it will be really saying something, rather than just idly humming or gesticulating, as it had been wont to do. But apart from the whole vexed question of how or even if Wagnerian leitmotifs acquire meaning and what their musical contribution to meaning might be (a question I don't intend to tackle here), the reciprocity of dramatic and musical motives brings up another perennial critical problem: how do the motives or motivating impulses within the drama direct the traffic of the musical motives they engender so as to create music of "symphonic" status, if indeed they do so at all?

In two articles of 1989 Carolyn Abbate has sought to deconstruct the "myth" of Wagner's music dramas as essentially symphonic creations.[23] The corrective impulse here is salutary, to resist a "totalizing" analytic habit of seeking out grandly scaled (if often esoteric) coherencies in the guise of long-range tonal or motivic planning that by no means ceased with Lorenz. (Kerman's comment in *Opera as Drama*, cited by Abbate, remains perhaps the most succinct and sensible view of the matter: "As purely musical forms, Wagner's operas succeed as well as any romantic symphonic poems of their length might be expected to succeed; which is to say, none too well."[24]) Given Wagner's own chronic indecision as to the "dramatic" status of the symphony, or consequently the precise nature of his own relation to a symphonic tradition, it is not difficult to build a case either for or against the "symphonic" Wagnerian drama. But for the same reasons, it is just as easy to dismantle them both.

In her essay "Opera as Symphony" Abbate retraces the peregrinations of Wagner's pro- and anti-symphonic discourse throughout the writings, proposing a reading of the "Conspiracy Scene" in *Götterdämmerung* that elegantly mirrors this discursive trajectory: "a metamorphosis from anti-symphonic to symphonic, a balance tipped from an *ethos* of musical symbolization of poetry in the beginning" – where the *Rachebund* motivic

23 C. Abbate, "Opera as Symphony, a Wagnerian Myth," in *Analyzing Opera: Verdi and Wagner*, 92–124, and "Wagner, 'On Modulation,' and *Tristan*."

24 Joseph Kerman, *Opera as Drama* (New York, 1956; 2nd edn, Berkeley and Los Angeles, 1988), 171.

refrain acts as an "alarming intrusion" into the surrounding music – "to music's genuine negligence toward the text in a 'symphonic' end," albeit a negligence born of the *operatic* signals embedded in the text, which instigate the ensemble-singing that ends the scene.[25] The second essay, concerning a fragmentary text "on modulation in pure instrumental music and in drama" and a passage from *Tristan*, grants a larger role to Wagner's anti-symphonic voice and the ways in which his music "may be regarded as driven by poetry to transcend the limited orderliness of absolute music and 'form'."[26] Both essays share the entirely justified premise that Wagner's understanding of the "symphonic" element in his own music was a loose one, grounded in the idea of an overall "web" of motivic relations and transformations and in no way subject to the restrictions of harmonic language and formal design he considered binding for the symphony *per se*. On this point Wagner was certainly consistent: his music absorbs the accumulated means of the symphonic tradition but then emancipates them to utterly different ends. All of the much-cited passages in which he arrogates the "unity of the symphonic movement" to the motivic web of the music drama agree that the drama is free to suspend the canons of harmonic logic and formal symmetry that obtain in the symphony proper.[27] The music drama is always described by Wagner as being *like* the symphony, but at the same time something much more. Nurtured by a hundred years' symphonic development, the music drama is enabled to charge forth recklessly in new directions, rather like the young Siegfried. (Like Siegfried, its true parents are dead, and any remaining false pretenders to the title of symphonist are fit only to be smitten down, like Mime, by Wagner's words and deeds.)

In the *Tristan* essay Abbate opposes a reading of a passage from the Act II *Tagesgespräch* emphasizing local harmonic "modulation" full of poetically inspired fissures, ruptures, unmediated juxtapositions, to putative "symphonic" readings of Wagner that deal in orderly *thematic* patternings, leitmotifs drilled into disciplined symphonic formations. At the same time, the anti- or ultra-symphonic transcendent incoherencies of a poetically liberated harmonic syntax are played off against a conventional "harmonizing" criticism (as it is termed here) that feeds on

---

[25] Abbate, "Opera as Symphony," 115. The terminological irony here, only glancingly acknowledged toward the end of this essay (p. 124), is that the polarity of "opera" and "symphony" collapses, in the larger framework of Wagner's polemics, within the category of absolute music. Such a collapsing of apparent antitheses might pose a threat to the rhetorical terms of Abbate's arguments, were it not to produce a further antithesis (absolute music/music drama), which can then substitute for the first one.

[26] Abbate, "Wagner, 'On Modulation,' and *Tristan*," 37.

[27] For example, *Opera and Drama* (IV, 201–2), *A Communication to My Friends* (IV, 322), and "On the Application of Music to the Drama" (X, 185).

simplistic equations of leitmotif and verbal meaning and limits interpretation to the exegesis of motivic signs. Individually, these critiques
of "symphonic" and "harmonizing" assumptions have some force; but
do *they* harmonize?[28] I would guess that the majority of analyses
proposing to discover symphonic coherence in Wagner's scores, from
Lorenz's time down to ours, have tended to focus on ideas of "tonal
planning" on various levels rather than leitmotif (Abbate herself cites
examples by Robert Bailey, Nors Josephson, and Patrick McCreless,
though with the aim of distinguishing between claims about long-range
or background tonal design and her own interest in the subversive role
of local harmonic detail). Leitmotif, too, can articulate tendentially
autonomous form, especially when it "ignores" the text and goes its own
("symphonic") way. But certainly the most simplistic "harmonizing"
view of leitmotif has always been an embarrassment for symphonically
inclined critics: the notion of Wagner drafting his libretti, inventing a
suitable repertory of leitmotifs, and then matching these up like pieces
of a puzzle is more like a prophetic picture of Cageian aleatorics than
one of classical symphonic *Besonnenheit*.

Even if we accept the corrective impulse behind Abbate's anti-
symphonic or anti-harmonizing polemics, however, they raise another,
fundamental and obvious problem. Once we have identified and catalogued the disruptive, provocatively irrational gestures in a given
passage, what then? Abbate's method – executed with the same
imagination and elegance as the *Götterdämmerung* analysis – is, after all,
to explicate these gestures according to rhetorical details in the text as
poetic and dramatic enunciation; that is, to harmonize music with text
(if on an anti-symphonic, miniaturist level). When Wagner announces
his emancipation from the canons of traditional musical practice by
virtue of his superior dramatic motives, what other, higher set of
guidelines come into play? Why should we accept the idea that a
certain chordal progression (that of the first "Death motive" in *Tristan*,
for instance) will compel us when draped over with a singer's words
and gestures, while it would otherwise remain empty, irrational noise?
Why should the transformation and combination of previously exposed
themes (the climax preceding Tristan's death, or the merging of
harmonically altered Rhine-gold and Valhalla motives cited by Wagner

---

28 The analysis by Dahlhaus of the opening of the *Tagesgespräch* (1974) which Abbate
cites as a counter-example to the standard "harmonizing" criticism, for example,
points up alleged contradictions between music and text only to demonstrate how
structural or "symphonic" criteria – in this case the ideal of a seamless musical
transition – can take precedence over detailed text-setting. It is also surprising to find
Abbate, by the end of her analysis, invoking the same "iconic" status for keys or chords
that she claims to abjure in the case of leitmotif ("E major is once more Wagner's
translation for the word 'light'," 54).

in "On the Application of Music to the Drama") be the prerogative of texted music alone? We all know that Wagner pointed the way to the modernist abyss, but do we really believe that it couldn't possibly have happened without the impetus of Wotan's moral dilemmas or the metaphysical colloquies of Tristan and Isolde? Abbate senses clearly enough the dilemmas her arguments, and Wagner's manifestos, leave unresolved, when she reflects on Wagner's text:

A fundamental difference between pure music and opera: Freedom. Modulation of a sort unjustified without motivation. So the fragment "On Modulation," Wagner's smallest credo. My conversation with this credo, like all conversations, must involve misunderstanding. For instance, what is the motivation that both animates and absolves these impulsive, unacceptable modulations? I understand it . . . as poetry or stage action; but the fragment leaves the question open (57).

The same question as to what "animates and absolves" transgressive modulatory impulses in *Tristan* would apply to the impulses or motivations behind its motivic designs and textures, as well – the motives leading its "leading motives." What makes the resulting music, in either case, "symphonic"? Or – if that is indeed a myth, or a misapprehension – what then makes this music meaningful, expressive, or satisfying at all?

Posed that way, the question may be too broad to be useful. Of course, critics and analysts have been pondering the method behind *Tristan*'s madness for over a century, and come up with answers of all kinds. Abbate's formulations, however welcome their resistance to simplistic reductionism, tend to suggest disquieting conclusions, as she admits. (Wagner's own contention that any self-declared "motivation" will justify the act it engenders, however outrageous or transgressive, has disquieting implications of its own, were it to be translated into an ethical or legal principle that whatever animates also absolves.) They might confirm, for instance, the suspicions harbored by many earlier critics of a regressive Wagnerian *Worttonsprache* that is parasitic on language, having despaired at last of music's ability to further evolve as a meaningful language on its own. There is also a suggestion that the shock-value of certain musical gestures comes to substitute for the "reasoned syntax" of a musical language, in the spirit of the avant-garde: unaccustomed harmonic progressions, motivic contrasts, rhythmic disjunctions signify merely as transgressive acts, without constituting a meaningful alternative discourse of their own. (This is probably an exaggeration with some truth to it, as testified by Wagner's legacy to subsequent generations of modernism, invoked near the end of Abbate's essay.) Yet Wagner was convinced of the linguistic capacities of his music, its *Sprachvermögen*, even if these were to be cultivated through a re-acquaintance of the musical language with that of words. At the same time he conceded that the new capacities of his musical language, while

"animated and absolved" by dramatic text and context, were indebted to
the aesthetically unlicensed transgressions of other composers before
him and their "misguided" efforts to make music speak on its own.

Delirium and death as transgressive motives: "dramatic symphony" and "symphonic drama"

> *A work of Herr Svendsen's provokes R. into speaking about the atrocities of the
> new kind of composer; grimaces, bizarre expressions, . . . strange rhythms are
> used to bring forth a theme which looks forceful but whose melody does not
> stick in one's mind. And everything goes beyond the bounds of instrumental
> music, for one is bound to ask oneself questions about the subject and the
> situation in order to understand all the murders and killings.*
> (CWD, 22 July 1872)

Two of the more extreme moments in the Romantic musical canon are
predicated on similar poetic-dramatic motives: the instrumental scene
of "Roméo au tombeau des Capulets" from Berlioz's *Roméo et Juliette* and
the scene of Tristan's protracted "delirium" and eventual death in Act
III of *Tristan und Isolde*. Both scenes depict their heroes *in extremis*, their
final agonies are interrupted by a frenzied exaltation as they regain their
beloved object for a brief moment prior to death. (Berlioz follows
Garrick's then still-popular version, in which Juliet awakens in time to
exchange a few lines with the stricken Romeo.) Both scenes encompass
the most strident effects and jarring contrasts of their respective scores,
befitting their parallel position as apogee of the respective tragic actions.
Julian Rushton suggests, in fact, that the "hysterical" transformation of
the theme from the adagio *scène d'amour* in the episode of "delirious
joy" within the tomb scene is "the obvious model for the climax of
Tristan's delirium (where Wagner forces his tenderest love-motive into
an Allegro with bars of 5/4)."[29] Indeed, the words and phrases Berlioz
strings together as a kind of programmatic epigraph or resumé of his
instrumental *scena* very nearly spell out the "motives" of Wagner's scene,
as well: *Invocation – Réveil de Juliette – Joie délirante, désespoir, dernières
angoisses et mort des deux amants* (with the exception that it is the male
partner who awakens from apparent death in *Tristan*, and that he alone
undergoes a "final anguish and death," for the time being). Wagner was
surely well aware of other motives his work shared with Shakespeare's
original drama (such as the *Tagesgespräch* between Romeo and Juliet in

[29] J. Rushton, *The Musical Language of Berlioz* (Cambridge, 1983), 191. Rushton is
referring, of course, to the transformation and development of the "slumber" motive
from Act II (what I have dubbed the *Lauschen* theme in the preceding chapter)
immediately prior to Isolde's arrival (at Tristan's lines "Auf des Lagers Bann wie sie
ertragen! Wohlauf und daran, wo die Herzen schlagen!").

Act IV), and we might also recall that Wagner inscribed one of the first three engraved full scores of *Tristan*, upon receiving them in Paris, "Au grand et cher auteur de *Roméo et Juliette*, l'auteur reconaissant de *Tristan et Isolde*."[30] Finally, both of these works invoke the status of drama and symphony at once: Berlioz's as a "dramatic symphony," and Wagner's (at least by critical tradition) as a "symphonic drama."

But both exist only at the margins of "symphonic" coherence, by their authors' own admission. Each composer takes the occasion offered by extreme motives to press the limits of such coherence, and both were well aware of the extremity of their responses. Wagner was shocked and exhilarated at what he had done in the third act, as witnessed by his letter to Mathilde Wesendonck in which he expressed his fears for the sanity of any listener who might hear the thing as its author had really imagined it.[31] Berlioz inserted a note into the first published score of *Roméo* – half sardonic but half-apologetic, it seems – that conductors had best suppress the tomb scene in the probable ninety-nine percent of cases where the audience is not either "extremely familiar with the fifth act of Shakespeare's tragedy with the Garrick *dénouement*" or otherwise endowed with the requisite "very elevated poetic sensibilities."[32] No doubt the remark was provoked by hostile criticisms of the movement; but at the same time it conveys a tacit confession that Berlioz may, in this case, have really been asking too much – either of his music or of his audience. For Wagner, Berlioz's tomb scene must have represented something of the musical "birth pangs" he spoke of in "On the Application of Music to the Drama" as heralds of the nascent music drama. In fact, the text of that passage could well put us in mind not only of Berlioz generally, but of the tomb scene in particular. Wagner refers there to the "passionate and eccentric character" or *Charakteristik* to which certain composers have resorted in order to make themselves as "precisely understood" as possible (*sich sehr präcis vernehmen zu lassen*), leading ultimately to "complete musical melodramas with pantomimed action to be supplied by the listener's imagination, or else to instrumental recitatives" (X, 181). If *Roméo* can be identified with the birth pangs of

---

30 E. Newman, *Life of Wagner*, vol. III (New York, 1941), 15. We might recall, further, that Wagner had heard a performance of Berlioz's "dramatic symphony" in London in 1855, and that he had reflected on the work in his open letter of 1857, just at the time he was turning in earnest to the composition of *Tristan*.

31 "This final act!!! - - - - - - - I fear the opera will be banned – unless the whole thing is parodied in a bad performance – : only mediocre performances can save me! Perfectly good ones will be bound to drive people mad, – I cannot imagine it otherwise. This is how far I have gone!! Oh dear! – " (letter to M. Wesendonck, mid-April 1859: *Selected Letters of Richard Wagner*, 452). Wagner seems to have translated his response to this excess into his punctuation (in letter and music alike – to invoke the critiques of "endless melody" from chapter 5).

32 See *Roméo et Juliette*, ed. D. K. Holoman (Cassel, 1990), 253.

Tristan (we might also recall that intimations of *Tristan*'s melodic chromaticism have often been heard in the instrumental passage headed "Roméo seul – tristesse"), this may justify reading the later work as, among many things, a reflection or commentary on its troubled ancestry (those programmatic "birth pangs"), rather as Tristan reflects on the conjunction of his own birth with the deaths of his parents and the strains of the same *alte Weise* he now hears once again in Act III ("Da er mich zeugt' und starb, / sie sterbend mich gebar").

The literally marginal position of "Roméo au tombeau des Capulets" within Berlioz's dramatic symphony is part of its justification. The scene is played before the curtain of the symphony proper, as it were, as a transition of sorts between the formalized numbers of Juliet's funeral *convoi* and the operatic final tableau. Its lack of tonal closure can be explained superficially according to this transitional function: the opening measures of the Allegro agitato e disperato pick up the key (E minor) and even the repeated pitches of the foregoing litany, and the movement closes with the faintest of cadences in A minor, where the Finale will begin. But the loose overall key structure of the movement (E-minor introduction, C♯-minor "invocation," A-major "delirious joy" and A-minor close) is primarily to be explained in the same way as its disjointed sectional structure, punctuated by wordless "recitatives" and *accompagnato* action music: the movement is stylistically marked from its opening measures as an operatic *scena*, as Berlioz's caustic-rueful footnote makes explicit in referring to "la scène instrumentale." In this instrumental scene, as in the earlier adagio "scène d'amour," Berlioz rejects the option of assigning vocal parts to his leading characters. He explained his reasons for this demurral in an *avant-propos* to the score, with a characteristic mixture of ironic disingenuousness and romantic effusion:

First, and this reason alone would be sufficient, it is a symphony and not an opera. Second, since duets of this nature have been treated vocally a thousand times by the greatest masters, it was wise as well as unusual to attempt another means of expression. It is also because the very sublimity of this love made its depiction so dangerous for the musician that he had to give his imagination a latitude that the positive sense of the sung words would not have given him, resorting instead to instrumental language, which is richer, more varied, less precise, and by its very indefiniteness incomparably more powerful in such a case.[33]

The appeal to the topos of the ineffability of a higher musical language is surely sincere, yet at the same time there is something disingenuous even in this honest effusion. For Berlioz does not merely aim to express vague, "indefinite" emotions, such as love or anguish generally, in these scenes; he clearly means to represent both emotions and "distinct" actions

---

[33] Translation by Holoman (ibid., 383).

in music, to give musical form to specific dramatic motives. Wagner, at least, said as much about the love scene, which he criticized on these grounds in the 1857 letter on Liszt. (The tomb scene was perhaps too easy a target for such criticism.) In both "scenes," but more radically in the later one, Berlioz challenges the ultimate power of a vocal text to either explain or justify the music its "motives" might have engendered. Of course, a vocal text would serve to convey aloud those motives which Berlioz has simply listed in telegraphic form at the head of the tomb scene, and suppressed altogether from the *scène d'amour*. If comprehensible, a text may serve to occupy our attention where the "musical thread" breaks off (as it did for Wagner in the *scène d'amour*), or lend its syntax and rhetoric as support to a music cut loose from its *own* syntactic-rhetorical foundations. But the text will hardly rationalize music, as such, where internal sense and structure are otherwise obscure.

As we may recall, Wagner invokes the *scène d'amour* in the Liszt letter as a foil to Liszt's more generalized or musicalized "poetic ideas." The distinction he draws has since become a standard evaluative means in the criticism of music dealing with "extra-musical" ideas. Berlioz is seen as mapping details of musical form (and motive) directly onto a dramatic model (rather as Wagner was seen by others to do with his leitmotifs). Liszt, on the other hand, has transmuted such prosaic matter into some more generalized poetic *Formmotiv* adapted to the principles of instrumental form (the most common with Liszt is the archetype of suffering-to-triumph; another formal "motive" is the interaction and resolution of conflicting "voices," in Hugo's *Ce qu'on entend sur la montagne*, or of historical-ethical principles – Christians vs. Huns – in Kaulbach's *Hunnenschlacht*).[34] Wagner's reservations about the *scène d'amour* aired in the Liszt letter could easily be transferred to the tomb scene, as I have suggested, and the terms of his critique of the earlier movement are of interest for the way in which they play off, again, the multiple senses of "motive":

[T]he rapture that filled me as I followed the evolution of the principal motive (*Entwickelung des Hauptmotives*) faded, in the course of the movement, into a feeling of real unease; I immediately supposed that once I had lost the musical thread (that is, the logically perceptible alternation of distinct motives) I ought to be guided by scenic motives which, however, I could not recall just then and which were not provided as part of a program. These scenic-dramatic motives are doubtless present in Shakespeare's famous balcony scene; but it was the great failing of the composer to take them over unchanged, in their original disposition, as presented by the poet. Having decided on this scene as the motive

[34] See, for example, Carl Dahlhaus, *Nineteenth-Century Music*, 238–41, as well as the essays, "Dichtung und symphonische Dichtung" and "Liszts Idee des Symphonischen" in *Klassische und romantische Musikästhetik*, 385–92, 392–401.

for a symphonic poem, the composer ought to have realized that the poet uses very different means than the musician to express similar ideas . . . The musician . . . should pay no attention to the events of common life, but instead – cancelling all incidental empirical detail – he should sublimate all this according to its concrete emotional content, which alone may be distinctly conveyed in music.

(V, 194)

Wagner's comparison of Liszt's approach with that of Berlioz, in this movement, is surely not specious, even if we take exception to his critical evaluation. The *scène d'amour* is indeed riddled with provocative gestural features, and Berlioz does explicitly undermine the "logical alternation of distinct motives," after arousing certain expectations in this area. The "motives" behind both phenomena (gestures and form) are easily discovered in the Shakespearian prototype for the scene.[35] But Berlioz exercises a certain logic in separating gestural evocations of visible "action" from the lovers' principal discourse as melodic "song," suggesting through this division the different stylistic levels of accompanied recitative and lyric number, just as he does in the tomb scene.

As in the later scene, the syntactically disruptive, incoherent gestural music of the *scène d'amour* occupies only the margins of the musical form, as articulating pauses or transitions between lyrical, thematic phrases; it punctuates the main symphonic "text" of the movement like so many exclamation points and question marks. But the larger design traced by the properly thematic phrases or periods, which Wagner claimed to find disorienting, could be described as a genuinely "evolutionary" scheme, in which a process of motivic substitution replaces that of simple reprise. This might be crudely represented by the letter scheme (ignoring transitions and interpolations): A–B–A'–B'–C–D–D'–D" (Coda). The repetitions and elaborations of the final D phrase (mm. 274–389) correspond to the protracted leave-taking of Shakespeare's two lovers, while embedded in this parting phrase (D") is a recollection of what has gone before: the characteristic cadential tail of the earlier B phrase commonly identified as the movement's principal "love theme" (see Example 6.1, a and b). By maintaining a coherent, if freely evolving, melodic discourse across the *scène d'amour* as a whole, Berlioz can excuse the provocative gestures he has inserted into the interstices of the form. (In fact, the "coherence" of this larger discourse depends very much on the kind of motivic association and substitution that underwrites the "symphonic web" or *Beziehungszauber* of Wagner's leitmotif technique.) These little agitated motions, accelerations, ritards, and recitative fragments are meant, of course, to conjure dramatic motives in the listener's mind, whether as

---

[35] On the possible correspondence of dramatic "motives" and musical detail in the *scène d'amour*, and the attitudes of Wagner (and other contemporaries) to the piece, see also T. Grey, "Richard Wagner and the Aesthetics of Musical Form," 366–70.

recollections of the Shakespearian text or imaginatively reconstructed for the occasion. Articulating the larger thematic periods, they also serve to "determine" these, rather like the way Wagner's dramatic text is meant to determine his musical motives and their evolutions. Wagner resisted the provocations of Berlioz's music on the theoretical grounds, perhaps, that such motives ought to be fully "realized" (*verwirklicht*) to

Example 6.1   Berlioz, *Roméo et Juliette*, "Scène d'amour" (Adagio): cadential tail to themes B and D
(a) theme B

(b) theme D

the mind and senses alike. From Berlioz's perspective he merely aligned himself with the obtuse "ninety-nine percent" lacking in imagination or culture – the requisite "elevated poetic sensibilities."

"Roméo au tombeau des Capulets" invokes a similar mixture of generic-stylistic gestures, as I have suggested, to distinguish between a coherent musical center (the *Invocation*, as a kind of instrumental *preghiera*) and its rhetorically discursive margins, annotated with quizzical, "incoherent," and fragmentary markings. Only here, those margins become so wide they threaten to engulf the central, coherent text. "The very premises of this movement," as Rushton notes, "are rhythmic, harmonic, and motivic disjunction."[36] Here even Berlioz evidently did not feel he could leave it to the audience to intuit the motives of his music, since, unlike the love scene, he enumerates them at the head of the movement: invocation, Juliet's awakening, delirious joy, despair, final anguish and death of the two lovers. (The old collected edition enters each of these rubrics at the corresponding point in the score, and the original, unpublished version of 1839 included a second vocal "prologue" before the *Convoi funèbre* in which these "motives" of the tomb scene were actually enunciated by the chorus.[37]) The musical realization of this series entails an introductory burst of "action" music as Romeo (presumably) comes rushing breathlessly on to the scene; the quasi-vocal *Invocation* in which English horn, French horn, and two bassoons become the voice(s) of Romeo's meditations before death (the idiom of instrumental dirge recalls the *Symphonie funèbre et triomphale*); a brief passage of instrumental recitative, cutting into the cadence of the preceding section, as the clarinet mimics the re-animation of Juliet's voice awakening from her drugged state; a sudden outburst of fast music (¢, 6/8) in and around A major that defies stylistic classification, notably incorporating a transformation of the earlier "love theme" cited in Example 6.1a and eventually dissolving its cadential tail into isolated fragments; and finally a string of disjointed, forceful gestures ("despair – anguish – death"?), at the end of which the strings seem to portray Juliet's fatal actions and the oboe her dying voice. Of course, one could purge this descriptive catalogue of references to concrete Shakespearian motives; but without these, a description of the musical series and its gestures would justly provoke Wagner's

---

36   Rushton, *The Musical Language of Berlioz*, 131.
37   The text of this *récitatif harmonique*, as it was designated, is reproduced in Wolfgang Dömling, *Hector Berlioz und seine Zeit* (Laaber, 1986), 311–12. The relevant lines read: "Il [Roméo] vole à Verone, il pénètre / dans le sombre tombeau qui dévora son cœur, / et, sur le sein glacé dont vivait tout son être, / il boit la mortelle liqueur! . . . / Juliette s'éveille! / Elle parle! . . . Ô merveille! / Oublieux de sa propre mort, / Roméo, comme dans un rêve, / pousse un cri délirant, cri d'extase d'abord, / qu'aussitôt l'agonie achève!! . . . / Et Juliette au cœur se frappe sans remord" (ellipses in original).

Delirium and death as transgressive motives

Example 6.2 Berlioz, *Roméo et Juliette*, "Roméo au tombeau des Capulets" (mm. 28–48)

[Allegro agitato e disperato]

hermeneutic query (*Warum?*) at every juncture, resulting in a series of musical "questions without answers," in the words of the 1879 essay (X, 180).

Without any "distinct" dramatic motives in mind we could still perhaps read the opening Allegro agitato e disperato simply as an agitated introductory flourish serving as an emphatic frame for whatever is to follow (such as we find in several of Berlioz's early overtures, Beethoven's "Tempest" Sonata, the "Eroica" Finale, or, most famously, the Finale of the Ninth). All of these cases obviously provoke questions of interpretation and formal integration, too. But like Beethoven in the Ninth, Berlioz far exceeds the requirements of a merely rhetorical gesture. What, for instance, are we to make of the screeching halt to this frenzied activity at m. 28 and the following series of sustained chords arbitrarily fixing on the dominant of C♯ minor (see Example 6.2)? What of the uncanny gaping spaces between these chords, multiplied across two pages of the full score by a host of rests and fermatas (glaring off the page like a collection of watchful eyes, silent and forbidding)? Berlioz is, of course, preparing the key of the following *Invocation*; even so, we may reasonably ask why C♯ minor, or why approached so brusquely? Were this an opera, the frenzied introduction might plausibly accompany Romeo's unwilling murder of Paris outside the Capulet crypt, or the sustained chords and gaping spaces might accompany his entry into the gloomy precincts of the crypt itself. ("Cryptic" it all is, by any measure; we might also recall the "homicidal" gestures that usher in the "new theme" of the "Eroica" first movement, and the responses these provoked in Marx and others, cited in chapter 2.) But here Wagner's complaint of absent motives would apply. Some explanatory detail would need to be supplied by the listener's memory or invention, as this particular one is not even contained in Berlioz's summary list. An actual drama, Wagner might further argue, would fill these silent spaces with a visible picture of their motive (the murder of Paris followed by horror at the deed, or the dreadful dark of the crypt?), while otherwise, they only draw our attention to the rupture of a "musical thread," such as had disoriented Wagner in the Adagio.

Other details engage and challenge tenets of the Wagnerian canon of musical-dramaturgical aesthetics. If the brief gestural interlude of Juliet's awakening is prepared by Berlioz's textual cues at the head of the movement (so that Wagner's complaint of an absent program for the Adagio movement is met, at least), what about the enigmatic little chromaticized scale of the cellos that leads into this (Example 6.3a)? It is tempting to think here not only of Romeo quaffing his poison draft, but also of the very similar musical gesture that accompanies the same "motive" in the first act of *Tristan und Isolde* (Example 6.3b). One might press further to suggest that this gesture also serves here to "revoice"

Example 6.3
(a) "Roméo au tombeau des Capulets," mm. 70–3

(b) *Tristan und Isolde* Act I, scene 5 (after drinking, Isolde lets the chalice fall from her hands)

Romeo – for whom the quartet of winds had been speaking in the *Invocation* – into the cello part, which now gesticulates on his behalf during Juliet's awakening. The orchestral (and hence loosely "symphonic") component of Wagner's motivic theory in *Opera and Drama* is predicated on an essential rapport between human and musical gestures (see IV, 173–81). To this extent we might suppose that the gestural motives activating the transgressive music of the tomb scene are justified as gestural impulses. But in theory, the category of gesture Wagner had in mind in *Opera and Drama* was of a more elevated sort: meaningful glances, expressions, and postures that communicate "ineffable" things beyond the grasp of language, analogous to the ineffabilities of musical speech (even though in practice he doesn't scruple to depict poison-quaffing or sword-play, any more in *Tristan* than in the *Ring*). A more serious theoretical objection, however, would be the absence of real, visible gestures to complement their musical presences. In other words, Romeo's stabbing of Paris, his taking the poison, Juliet's reviving voice (which is more gesture than speech), the ensuing moment of "delirious joy," and the culminating deaths only serve to point up the inability of music to articulate "distinctly" the sense of its gestures, however violently it transgresses the norms of symphonic coherence in its desperation to do so (from the perspective Wagnerian theory, at any rate).

The sudden explosion of "delirious joy" that interrupts the voice of the reviving Juliet is a classic example of the unmediated juxtaposition of radically contrasting moods that Wagner identified as characteristic of the "newer French school, in particular, with Victor Hugo at its head"

Example 6.4 Berlioz, *Roméo et Juliette*, "Roméo au tombeau des Capulets," mm. 148–60

in the famous letter to Mathilde Wesendonck on the "art of transition."[38] The transition from delirious joy to "despair and death" at the end of the Berlioz scene is scarcely more mediated than the (non-)transition into that delirium. The radically transformed reminiscence of the Adagio "love theme" (see Example 6.1a) that emerges from the shapeless hubbub of the "delirious" music (mm. 108ff) is abruptly dismembered and cast aside, and succeeded by a polymetrical rumbling in the winds and a few groaning gestures in the trombones, effecting a rough temporary modulation from A to F minor (mm. 148–69; the beginning of this passage is given in Example 6.4). Are these abrupt contrasts flanking the music of "delirious joy" sufficiently motivated? Or is the unexpected reminiscence of the "love theme" in its passionately distorted guise? Wagner admitted in the "art of transition" letter that he himself has always been drawn to the expression of violent emotional extremes, but that the secret of his aesthetic success in *Tristan* was due to his new-found ability to effect convincing and "motivated" transitions between such extremes. Indeed (he added), abrupt, violent contrasts are "often unavoidable and necessary" – but even in such "unavoidable" cases they ought to be "clearly prepared in advance, so that the suddenness of the transition appears . . . as a matter of course."[39] Is this to say that they ought somehow to be "musically" motivated, as well as dramatically? The answer is not self-evident, and it is difficult to see how jarring surprises could or should be "prepared" in a way that makes them sound inevitable, no surprise at all. The strange sounds of Juliet's awakening or of the dismembered "love theme" do create an atmosphere of suspense in which drastic gestures *are* perhaps a more acceptable response than would be a sudden lapse into easy tunefulness or into some form of symphonic rigor. In a sense, the "coherence" of the tomb scene is established by its pattern of transgressive gestures, which is relaxed only for the short lyrical inter-lude of the *Invocation*. Its abrupt non-transitions create a kind of negative consistency for the brief duration of this anti-symphonic essay in dramatic gesture. (The *imprévu*, as Berlioz himself declared in a rare moment of critical self-analysis, was an essential feature of his compositional aesthetic.[40] If individual instances still call for individual motivation, the larger phenomenon might be defended as a stylistic choice.)

---

38 Letter of 29 October 1859: *Selected Letters of Richard Wagner*, 474.
39 Ibid., 475.
40 H. Berlioz, *Mémoires de Hector Berlioz*, ed. P. Citron (Paris, 1969), vol. 2, 233. On the *imprévu* as a stylistic principle, see also Dömling, *Berlioz und seine Zeit*, 147–8, who also identifies it with the poetics of drama (peripeteia) and Hermann Danuser, "Das imprévu in der Symphonik: Aspekte einer musikalischen Formkategorie in der Zeit von C. P. E. Bach bis Hector Berlioz," *Musiktheorie* 1 (1986), 62–81 (esp. 74–7). Danuser selects precisely this example (the tomb scene) to represent the Berliozian poetics of the *imprévu* in its pure form, so to speak. While elements of a classical developmental

"Unavoidable and necessary" – Wagner's concession to what he says has now grown "repugnant" to him (unmediated, violent contrasts of mood) recalls the historiographical dialectics of his interpretation of Berlioz and "program music" in general. The excesses of the tomb scene of *Roméo et Juliette*, like those desperate efforts at articulate speech in Beethoven's late works (in which Wagner recognized the ancestry of Berlioz and his misbegotten experiments) are judged as necessary evils – wrong turns on the path to music drama, but turns which nevertheless generated knowledge indispensable to achieving the final goal. The history of Berlioz's work and the composer's annotations to it – the original second "prologue," the descriptive headings, the caustic footnote – in the margins of this movement (itself on the margins of his dramatic symphony, and nearly engulfed by the "margins" of its own formal design): all of this shows that Berlioz himself was concerned with the problem of absent motives here, if not in the *scène d'amour*. Whatever "motives" Act III of *Tristan* may share with the Shakespeare / Garrick / Berlioz *Roméo*, it obviously differs from the earlier work in much more than the supplemental realization of these dramatic motives as poetic text and stage picture. Its musical extremes are mediated, and hence mitigated to some extent, by Wagner's "art of transition," as he claimed.

But then, the music of *Tristan* is more extreme altogether, and its extreme states are by no means marginal to a more coherent center, but form the very substance of the act. Of all of Wagner's music, this act most deliberately and consistently transgresses the boundaries of symphonic behavior (as construed by Wagner) to explore the outer reaches of "dramatic pathos" that Wagner had posted as off limits to the symphony in *Beethoven* (IX, 99) and the "Application" essay (X, 180).[41] Are the transgressive elements of the *Tristan* idiom justified by the articulation of its "motives" in poetic texts and visible action, by "transitions" that prepare them psychologically and structurally, or simply under the aegis of avant-garde experimentalism and technical progress? Further, is it the deployment of developmental techniques to

"logic" can, of course, be identified within the individual sections of the *scena* (the opening Allegro agitato, for instance), Danuser also comes to the conclusion that, as a whole, this particular movement raises "discontinuity" to a "principle of musical form" (76), by which it adumbrates a condition of musical modernism (where the very possibility of "predictive" listening, hence the effect of the *imprévu* as such, is canceled), while it also reveals certain dilemmas faced by Berlioz in realizing his notion of a "dramatic" symphony. (The contingent status of this movement – the prerequisite of the audience's familiarity with the dramatic "motives" behind it – is perhaps at odds with its crucial position as the dénouement of the dramatic action.)

41 Compare also the further remark in the 1879 essay that "most alien of all to it [the symphonic movement] was, however, drama, which requires infinitely richer forms for its unfolding than those based on symphonic forms (*auf der Basis des Symphoniesatzes*) or dance music" (X, 185).

effect these transitions, the deployment of a consistent network of musical motives, or simply the continuous presence of a large orchestral apparatus that might validate the "symphonic" status of music that Wagner otherwise intimated to be anti- or "ultra"-symphonic? It could fairly be said that Wagner subscribed to the first two propositions of each of these groups (Abbate's two essays of 1989 conclude as much), while the cruder notions of historical progress and expansion of technical means have been supplied by popular traditions of critical thought (transgression as historical imperative, the relentless pursuit of the new).

Abbate contrasts a twentieth-century critical tradition that celebrates the "symphonic" qualities of the *Tristan* score (in particular) and Wagner's own, perhaps ambiguous, protestations to the contrary, that the music is symphonic only in having sublated the symphony into a higher and altogether different musical organism. This discrepancy between Wagner and his latter-day champions is explained, in part, by the history that divides them. Wagner's original audiences were, of course, all too ready to recognize his radical departure from either symphonic or operatic norms. Some celebrated this as liberation, others condemned it as anarchy. But in either case, the nineteenth century's willingness to acknowledge Wagner as a genius of disorder provoked the likes of Karl Grunsky and Alfred Lorenz to rescue his musical reputation by means of patient analysis. Grunsky's choice of the third act of *Tristan* as the object for his demonstration of "Wagner als Symphoniker" should be seen in this context. He doesn't pick *Tristan* because of any wide consensus as to its symphonic qualities. Rather the contrary: up until now, he remarks (writing in 1906), the music of *Tristan* "has been regarded not only by its opponents or unwilling admirers as a kind of narcotic with intoxicating effects, but even its genuine partisans have held it in awe as an untouchable." Then, within the three larger divisions he identifies in Act III, Grunsky chooses the central one, from the reprise of the shepherd's *alte Weise* (corresponding to what Joseph Kerman, in *Opera as Drama*, calls the second "cycle" within the overall scene of Tristan's "delirium"), "since this is generally considered to be the most 'pathological,' almost always abused as an occasion for naturalistic sobbing and raging, and thereby lending credence to the deeply rooted conviction that Wagner's art is unpredictable and hysterical (*unberechenbar, hysterisch*)."[42] (*Tristan* was hardly perceived as the music of patriarchal values and male hegemony, in other words.)

Grunsky's view of the "symphonic" element in this music is probably much closer to Wagner's sense of the term than to ours. While he does briefly suggest analogies to individual symphonic movement-types

---

[42]   Karl Grunsky, "Wagner als Symphoniker," *Richard Wagner-Jahrbuch* 1 (1906), 238.

within the scene, as later "symphonic" readings of Wagnerian drama have sometimes attempted, this is purely incidental to the substance of his comments. He is otherwise entirely concerned with explaining the construction of small musical units (made up mostly of two-, three-, and four-measure groups), their motivic content, and how these small bits articulate gradually larger dynamic shapes of increasing or decreasing intensity. The resulting structures are loose paratactic trajectories with nothing of the overarching hierarchical relations we (or Wagner) would expect of a symphonic form in the strict sense. The very existence of perceptible small-scale units – underlying two- and four-measure groupings, or intelligible patterns of model–sequence–intensification–dissolution – is for Grunsky sufficient evidence of "coherent" musical thought, in conjunction with a network of motives that return, transform, and combine. Granted, such general means as these hardly warrant a close identification of music drama and Beethoven symphony. But Wagner's (or Grunsky's) invocation of the symphonic becomes considerably less problematic when we recognize a simple terminological distinction (one that is implied in Abbate's distinction between Wagnerian and modern-analytical senses of "symphonic," but that deserves to be emphasized). The music drama adopts and transforms procedures that have evolved in the context of symphonic writing, while casting aside the actual structures of the symphony. The relation is adjectival, not substantive: the music drama is *like* a symphony in certain ways (especially in developmental techniques, as we know), but that does not mean it is constructed according to the same principles – the point Wagner emphasized again and again.[43] A challenge it often shared with the symphonic poem was to apply the "advanced" techniques of symphonic development outside the formal framework of the symphony. In both cases – symphonic poem and opera – the composer was challenged to provide a convincing "motivation" for this appropriation and transformation of a technique divorced from its conventional context

[43] The varying emphases of the adjective "symphonic" in Wagner's writings are set out by Wolfram Steinbeck in "Die Idee des Symphonischen bei Richard Wagner: Zur Leitmotivtechnik in *Tristan und Isolde*," in *Bericht über den internationalen musikwissenschaftlichen Kongress* Bayreuth 1981, ed. C.-H. Mahling and S. Wiesmann (Cassel, 1984), 424–35 (see 424–8). On the legacy of Wagner's discourse of symphonic drama, see Annegrit Laubenthal, "Zum Thema 'Form' in der nachwagnerischen Oper: Friedrich Kloses 'Dramatische Symphonie'," in *Geschichte und Dramaturgie des Operneinakters*, ed. W. Kirsch and S. Döhring (Laaber, 1991), 217–25. Surely misreading Wagner, Klose scanned his one-act opera *Ilsebill*, after the Grimms' tale "The Fisherman and his Wife," as a four-movement "symphony" with coda. The conjunction of Klose's determination to impose a rigorous "symphonic form" on his opera and his virulent anti-semitic and reactionary political views (he dismissed "democracy," in the Germany of the 1920s, as "the Eldorado of *Untermenschtum*") might be some cause for reflection, if Wagner didn't already provide enough along these lines.

340

(the symphonic development section). And the poetic or ideational motivation could only convince if the musical results did, too. The level of musical autonomy required for convincing results will naturally vary according to the attitudes of different listeners. (The lack of consensus as to the "sense" of Wagner's later scores, as musical objects, is perhaps just as sure a confirmation of their status as the first emphatic texts of musical "modernism" as are the specific manipulations of chromatic harmony, for example, that are a contributing factor.[44])

In his discussion of the scene of Tristan's delirium, Grunsky cites the "art of transition" letter (he may have been the first to draw attention to it, since the Wesendonck letters had appeared in print just two years earlier). It is not surprising that Grunsky heard the voice of Wagner *als Symphoniker* in this letter, and his remarks point up ways in which this symphonic voice does, in fact, temper the voice that elsewhere promises unlimited freedoms on the authority of dramatic motives and "poetic license." The advice to symphonic poets in the 1857 Liszt letter – that poetic motives should be rationalized with a view to musical imperatives – is brought to bear on Wagner's own case, confirming the now common view of a "symphonic" aesthetic emerging in the *Tristan* period. The letter speaks of abrupt transitions as well as gradual ones. Either might be dramatically motivated. But the preference for gradual transitions, as Grunsky sees it, derives from essentially musical motives:

Aside from the [dramatic] content of the music, the art of transition can already be explained in terms of the musical instincts that manifested themselves in Wagner the closer the relation of poetry and music became; for he seems to have become increasingly aware of the dangers that any vocal music poses to musical form. That which raises dramatic music to the level of the symphonic is to be found precisely in such transitions! Disjunctions (*Schroffheiten*) may indeed be justified by dramatic contrasts, but music desires forms that are not only poetically, but musically founded (*begründet*) . . .[45]

---

[44] Surprisingly little has been written on Wagner's broader aesthetic and ideological legacy to musical modernism (that is, beyond the specific issues of the emancipation or dissolution of tonality and the like). Some provisional thoughts on the subject can be found – already from the perspective of the "post-modern" – in John Deathridge's essay "Wagner and the Post-modern," *Cambridge Opera Journal* 4:2 (July 1992), 143–61.

[45] Grunsky, "Wagner als Symphoniker," 238. Grunsky follows his remarks on the Mathilde Wesendonck letter with a lengthy passage from Lessing (p. 239) that intriguingly anticipates Wagner's ideas about the motivation of extreme emotional contrasts in music and the question of an object or agency of musical expression ("Jetzt zerschmelzen wir mit ihm [dem Musikus] in Wehmut und auf einmal sollen wir rasen? Wie? Warum? Wider wen? Alles das kann die Musik nicht bestimmen; sie läßt uns in Ungewißheit und Verwirrung, wir empfinden, ohne eine richtige Folge unserer Empfindungen wahrzunehmen . . . In der Tat ist diese Motivierung der plötzlichen Übergänge einer der größten Vorteile, den die Musik aus der Vereinigung mit der Poesie, d.h. dem Drama zieht, ja vielleicht der allergrößte")."

True, this is now Grunsky speaking for Wagner (*als Symphoniker*), but as a gloss on the "art of transition" letter, its perceptions ring true. An awareness of both the "dangers" and "desires" involved in the musical idiom of *Tristan* was very much a consequence of Wagner's recent compositional experience. The reciprocity of dramatic and musical motives (as "motifs," themes, ideas) in Wagner's vocabulary is now reflected in a similar reciprocity of formal or procedural *motivations*, dramatic and musical.

The stunningly executed second climax of Tristan's delirium, from the reprise of the *alte Weise* to his momentary relapse into unconsciousness, is an excellent example of this motivational reciprocity. The entire passage can be construed as an extended development of the *alte Weise* itself, which motivates this development not only as a musical theme, of course, but as a complex sign of the dramatic past and present (it summons memories of Tristan's past, while serving as an explicit sign of the unchanging present, as agreed upon between Kurwenal and the shepherd). The passage also constitutes a musical conversation between the shepherd's melody (the *alte Weise*), Tristan, and the orchestra (performing its eminently Wagnerian role as the sounding board of memory). In the process of this three-way conversation the *alte Weise* is dissected in manifold ways, counterpointed with other themes and with itself, as it passes from the shepherd's pipe (English horn) to the orchestral winds and gradually to all parts of the orchestra (in addition to Tristan's vocal line).

There is at least one brusque, seemingly unmediated turn in this conversation at the moment where the orchestra brutally arrogates the *alte Weise* to itself (m. 689, see Example 6.5). This is motivated foremost by a rhetorical turn in the text: Tristan suddenly attempts to retract his reading of the musical sign he hears ("Nein, Ach nein! So heißt sie nicht!") but the attempt founders in confusion, and the melody is ceded one last time to the English horn on stage through a beautiful echo-like stretto of its opening notes. The moment is further prepared as a strong melodic and harmonic cadence to F minor, and by the anticipation of the melody's new turn some lines earlier ("die alte Weise / sehnsuchtbang / zu ihnen wohl / auch klagend drang," mm. 664–70). To this extent Wagner realizes the injunction of his "art of transition" letter not only to motivate but to prepare, psychologically and musically, abrupt contrasts that are otherwise "unavoidable."

From this point up to the climactic peroration, in which Tristan curses the love potion and then himself, the music traces a classic Wagnerian *Steigerung* compounded of many things: intensification of dynamics, texture, harmonic tension – but above all a crowding-in of past motives, especially noticeable against the economy of motive that

Example 6.5 *Alte Weise* arrogated by orchestra (*Tristan und Isolde* Act III, scene 1)

has characterized most of the act until now. This crowding in of motives reflects the process of Tristan's memory, activated by the sound of the *alte Weise*. As he recalls the principal "motives" of his past – the pre-history of his sickness and Isolde's cure, Isolde's voyage to Cornwall, the potion, his wound, his present agonies – this crowding of past and present calls up an accumulating welter of motivic activity in the orchestra. The process begins with the combination of the *alte Weise* and the "Day" motive, followed by a combination of the "Sick Tristan" figure, from Isolde's Act I narration, with the *alte Weise* beneath (Example 6.6) – a combination with which Wagner was very pleased, as he confessed in another letter to Mathilde. Other motives crowd in: the *Sühnetrank* (potion), the "second Death" motive, the heart-clutching gesture that originally followed the drinking of the potion, and of course the omnipresent four-note chromatic cell of "Desire." These are all variously fragmented and combined in "symphonic" developmental style, capped by a truly astounding passage in which the severed members of the *alte Weise* multiply themselves in uncanny fashion and recombine in a nightmarish polyphony, with the chromatic contours of Desire weaving their way beneath it (Example 6.7). The unbearable weight of these accumulating recollections is discharged in the musical and rhetorical peroration of the whole episode ("Ich selbst, ich hab' ihn gebraut"), where a new motive accompanies Tristan's devastating epiphany that he, not any magic potion, is the agency of his present distress (Example 6.8).

Example 6.6   Combinations of *alte Weise*, Day, and Sick Tristan motives (*Tristan und Isolde* Act III, scene 1)

Example 6.7 Recombinations of *alte Weise* segments and Desire cell
(*Tristan und Isolde* Act III, scene 1)

[Tristan: "Für dieser Hitze heißes Verschmachten,

ach keines Schattens kühlend Umnachten!]

Für dieser Schmerzen schrecklicher Pein, welcher Balsam sollte mir Lindrung verleihn?"]

This accumulation of "motives" operates on both dramatic and musical levels, as usual, but there is a further reciprocity of motivation behind the process as a whole. The entire complex of musical intensification, discharge (peroration), and the subsequent dissolution of motive and energy following Tristan's collapse describes a classic developmental trajectory. The motivic accumulation it involves is justified (if not precisely motivated) by the exposition of all this material as independent thematic elements earlier in the opera. The process is motivated, according to Wagnerian theory, by the accumulation of past and present psychological motives, leading to the climactic epiphany (Kerman's reference to the dramatic gesture of the curse as a "purgation" also draws attention to its structural value in the musical process).[46] But the effect succeeds as it does only because of the way in which the developmental process carries the conviction of its own internal musical motivation.

Wagner once observed that in *Tristan* he had felt the need to "let himself rave, musically (*sich musikalisch auszurasen*), as if [he] had written a symphony."[47] If "symphony" were only a paradigm for musical coherence, unity, and control, Wagner's locution would seem to be something of a solecism. But we instinctively understand Wagner's sense here, as we do when he speaks of "endless melody." In particular, we understand the aptness of the expression, with its connotations of both madness and "purgation," to Act III of *Tristan* (though it might also put us in mind of Hans Sachs's stated aim to channel *Wahn* into well-made musical poetry). More particularly, the oxymoronic figure of "symphonic raving" or *Ausrasen* (which could well describe the delirium scene as a whole) captures a quality of the perorational "period" of the second cycle just described, beginning from the introduction of the new ("Curse") motive at "Ich selbst, ich hab' ihn gebraut!" (Example 6.8). Grunsky identifies the "symphonic" logic behind this essentially

Example 6.8 New motive (Curse) at climax of Tristan's delirium

---

[46] Kerman, *Opera as Drama*, 166. Kerman also describes here the process of accumulating memories and motives that leads up to the climax.
[47] CWD, 28 September 1878.

keyless passage, again, in terms of underlying two- and four-measure poetic-musical phrase units, disguised by the compression of the Curse motive into a single measure of 3/2 in the orchestra. Reiterations of the Desire cell, prominently embedded in the texture by the trumpet, press the sequencing Curse motive toward a conclusion, which is initiated by an emphatic, if seemingly random, arrival on an $F^{\sharp 6}_{\sharp 4}$ chord (m. 823, "Verflucht sei, furchtbarer Trank!"). A dense motivic congeries at the word *Trank* (Tristan chord, Desire cell, Curse, *alte Weise* fragment, followed by Day) yields to an abrupt F-minor cadence ("Verflucht, wer dich gebraut") – the rhetorical (if hardly "structural") cadence to the whole cycle, from the reprise of the *alte Weise*. Here is a moment where the drama might well have justified a striking, abrupt contrast: Tristan's relapse into unconsciousness might have motivated an immediate cessation of motion and a complete change of musical motive. Wagner could, for instance, have cut directly into the motionless reprise of the motive-complex of the Act I prelude that occurs some two dozen measures later (Kurwenal: "Bist du nun tot? Lebst du noch"). Instead, the energy built up across the climactic peroration (Tristan's "terrible epiphany") discharges into a continued sequential development of the Curse motive, which undergoes a further series of rhythmic permutations, first accelerating and then gradually pulling back as it sinks in register and dynamic level (Example 6.9).

This "artful transition" can be seen as a response to Kurwenal's text, which moves from shorter to longer exclamations of dismay – "Mein Herr! Tristan!" through "Der Welt holdester Wahn! Wie ist's um dich getan!" – and then to more extended meditations over the body of his prostrate sire. The accumulation and discharge of motivic energy could also be seen in Kurthian terms as tracing a more abstract psychological trajectory, of the kind in which musical and psychological motivations become indistinguishable. While the "symphonic" logic of the passage (Tristan's peroration and its aftermath) is purely developmental, divorced from clearly articulated tonal goals, this development is driven, finally, by dramatic motives of delirium and collapse – by extremes of "pathos" that Wagner would have considered unwarranted as affective or psychological motives to merely instrumental form. But the extremes are tempered, as Wagner claimed, by transition. And the transition – although Wagner might have claimed it to be "poetically pre-construed" (VII, 123) in the form of Kurwenal's text – seems to have been motivated by a psychology as much musical as dramatic. At the same time, while there is an audible logic, even compulsion to this musical process, an awareness of the "poetic motive" or psychology supplements what might still be understood as music's "need" or "lack."

Example 6.9   Aftermath of delirium climax (permutations of new motive)

Dénouements (motivic threads, dramatic plots, musical knots and resolutions)

As in *Tristan*, the extreme motives of the tomb scene in *Roméo* (deriving in part from the *dénouement de Garrick*) also impel a recollection, transformed by delirium: the "love theme" from the Adagio movement of Berlioz's symphony, now become fast and furious, spinning uncontrollably out of its A-major orbit into C and back, before it collapses into fragments and silences (followed by the frenzied, a-thematic gestures of Romeo's death-throes). This transformed recollection is also, like the drastic abruptions that surround it, a transgression of symphonic norms that posit separate thematic identities for separate movements. The transgression of a normal frame has, of course, famous precedents in Beethoven (the finales of the Fifth and Ninth). Like those exceptional cases, it is motivated by the desire to evoke an imagined thread to a normally inaccessible musical past, beyond the fixed boundaries of the movement which traditionally demarcate the temporal frame of a single, continuous musical process. Such reminiscences were more at home in opera, on the other hand, where their motivation was more easily interpreted. In drama, as in narrative, it is entirely natural to posit such threads between events in different acts or chapters, through the reappearance of a character, a setting, an image, or perhaps even a

349

song. Indeed, a story in which such threads are entirely absent or invisible is hardly a story at all.

We might likely be inclined to call the recollection of the "love theme" in the tomb scene a leitmotif, if the impulse were not checked by scruples regarding the anachronism of the label and its inauthenticity even as a Wagnerian term. Certainly this movement transgresses further into the realm of opera than any of the other instrumental movements in Berlioz's "symphony." The recollection and transformation of this leading or principal motive from the *scène d'amour* at this extreme juncture may well have impressed the young Wagner who heard Berlioz's dramatic symphony in Paris, back in 1839, with the possibilities of a more radical approach to motivic "reminiscences" than he had yet conceived of. The gesture is also a perfect paradigm of the symphony's desperate, even self-destructive, attempts to enter the forbidden terrain of "dramatic pathos," as construed by Wagner's subsequent philosophy of modern musical history. Again, much of the gesture's claim to meaning derives from its transgression of temporal boundaries – a point Wagner must have reflected on, whether with regard to this moment, to motivic recall in Beethoven, or to the "reminiscence motives" of earlier Romantic opera. However determinate or indeterminate we consider the expressive value of Berlioz's theme in its original adagio context, its unexpected resurrection in this later context – transformed by tempo and orchestration – commands our attention in a way that reiterations and variations of a theme within a movement normally do not. Like those other gestures of abruption that surround it, this auto-citation functions as a hermeneutic irritant, a goad to interpretation (*Warum?*). But it is not only by historical hindsight that this transformed theme might be brought to bear on the idea of "leitmotif." The critical pre-history of the (pseudo-)Wagnerian terminology, as well as of the "authentic" practice, can be followed back to the dénouement of Berlioz's dramatic symphony and to similar moments of musical-temporal transgression in both symphony and opera.

The invention of the word *Leitmotiv* has traditionally been attributed to the industrious apostle of the Bayreuth cult, Hans von Wolzogen. The authority for this rests partly with Wagner's reference to Wolzogen in the 1879 "Application" essay as "one of my younger friends who has made a comprehensive study of what he calls the 'leitmotifs' [in my operas], but more according to the characteristics of their dramatic significance and effect (as this author was not specifically a musician) rather than their implementation within the musical structure (*ihre Verwertung für den musikalischen Satzbau*)" (X, 186). This, the only Wagnerian text in which the word "leitmotif" actually appears, is at first blush more an anti-text. So it has been deployed, at least. Time and again in the critical literature of the past half-century or so the passage has been adduced to discredit the authenticity of the popular term, to draw attention to Wagner's own understanding of the structural ("symphonic") value of his motives, and to exorcise the entrenched superstition about a dilettantish system of musical ciphers, the notion that the Wagnerian *Orchestermelodie* amounted to an endless game of musical charades. But here – again, and for the last time – we depart from the Wagnerian text to consider some contexts and subtexts.

Wolzogen himself later disavowed the invention of the term "leitmotif" itself (prompted, perhaps, by Wagner's skeptical allusion to it and by an ever-increasing stream of critical ridicule directed at the phenomenon).[48] Of course, he could not and did not disavow his motivic guides, or *thematische Leitfäden*, which were, after all, not designed for students of musical composition or analysis, but to serve the uninitiated as a guiding or leading "thread" through the labyrinth of Wagner's music dramas (hence the title of the inaugural guide of 1876: *Thematische Leitfaden durch die Musik zu Richard Wagners Festspiel "Der Ring des Nibelungen"*). So it would seem that, even if Wolzogen did not himself employ the term "leitmotif" in his guides (he spoke merely of "motives"), he was at least indirectly responsible for it – having inspired it through the wording of his title – and still directly responsible for the naively "materialistic" exegetical practices associated with the term.

Whatever truth there may be to the latter charge, the first turns out to be, again, untrue. John Warrack pointed out that the early Weber scholar, Wilhelm Jähns, had already used the term *Leitmotiv* in his thematic catalogue of Weber's works published in 1871, where he catalogued the reminiscence motives in Weber's operas under this rubric.[49] It would be difficult to determine whether this particular instance exerted any immediate influence on contemporary critical vocabulary at large. In any case, a number of other writers can be found discoursing of Wagner's "leitmotifs" between the time of Jähns's book and Wolzogen's first *Leitfaden* of 1876: Francis Hueffer in 1874 (possibly already in 1872), Heinrich Dorn in 1875, and Ottokar Hostinsky by 1876.[50] And, as it happens, others had been using this word even

---

[48]   Hans von Wolzogen, "Leitmotive," *Bayreuther Blätter* 20 (1897), 313–30: "Legend has it that I am responsible for inventing this word, but I cannot with good conscience admit that I was ever aware of doing so" (313).

[49]   Wilhelm Jähns, *Carl Maria von Weber in seinen Werken. Chronologisch-thematisches Verzeichniss seiner sämtlichen Compositionen* (Berlin, 1871). See Warrack, "Leitmotif", *The New Grove Dictionary*, vol. 10, 644.

[50]   Francis Hueffer, *Richard Wagner and the Music of the Future* (London, 1874), 111 (most of Hueffer's book had appeared as articles in the *Fortnightly Review* in 1872); Heinrich Dorn, "Leitmotive, keine Erfindung der Neuzeit," *Neue Berliner Musik-Zeitung* 29 (1875), 257 (rather than looking to Weber and the post-revolutionary *opéra comique*, as we might expect, Dorn announces the hitherto "overlooked" fact of the consistent

before Jähns: references to Wagner's "leitmotifs" occur in an 1869 review of *Die Meistersinger* in Dresden (by Friedrich Stade in the *Neue Zeitschrift für Musik*) as well as in Eduard Hanslick's review of the 1868 Munich premiere, and even as early as 1860, in an essay on Wagner, Liszt, and their *so-genannte Zukunftsmusik* by A. W. Ambros.[51] (Ambros considers the themes of Liszt's symphonic poems to be "leitmotivic," as well as the principal themes of *Tannhäuser* and *Lohengrin*, which is probably all the Wagner he would have known in 1860.) If none of these earlier instances of the term "leitmotif" could have been inspired by Wolzogen's thematic *Leitfäden*, then what is their etymology?

Wolzogen, evidently, did not conjure up the notion of a motivic *Leitfaden* out of thin air. Not only does the practice of naming Wagnerian motives pre-date Wolzogen (this could hardly be otherwise – and Cosima's diaries attest to the fact that even Wagner was quite willing to call his motives by name, on occasion); it also appears that the image Wolzogen found apposite to mapping the motivic web of Wagner's scores, the *Leitfaden*, already resonated with existing habits of listening to Wagner's music, and much other music as well. Liszt, in his 1855 essay on Berlioz and the program symphony, identified as a symptom of modern musical conditions the public's growing need to be "led through music's labyrinths with the help of an Ariadne's thread" (by this he means the indication of its "poetic ideas" in a title or program) "just as composers have had to learn to provide one."[52] A generation earlier, a reviewer of Beethoven's *fantasia*-like Piano Sonata in A, op. 101, described the experience of the work in terms of some picaresque

deployment of "leitmotifs" in Mozart's operas, "from *Mitridate* through *Tito*"; as evidence he traces Don Giovanni's personal *Sprungmotiv* – an arpeggiated triad – throughout the score of that work!); and Ottokar Hostinsky, *Das Musikalisch-Schöne und das Gesammtkunstwerk vom Standpuncte der formalen Aesthetik* (Leipzig, 1877), 113 (Hostinsky's preface is dated June 1876).

51   Friedrich Stade, "Wagner's 'Meistersinger' auf der Dresdener Hofbühne," *Neue Zeitschrift für Musik* 65 (1869), 62; E. Hanslick, "Die Meistersinger," in *Die moderne Oper* (Berlin, 1875), 304–14 (a slightly revised version of the 1868 review for the *Neue freie Presse*, the original text of which can also be found excerpted in the *Allgemeine musikalische Zeitung* 3 [1868], 225–8); A. W. Ambros, "Der Streit um die so-genannte Zukunftsmusik," in *Culturhistorische Bilder aus dem Musikleben der Gegenwart* (1860; 2nd edn, 1865), 142–3. Hanslick speaks of the "so-called memory- or leitmotifs (*die sogenannten Gedächtniss- oder Leitmotive*), that is, themes that appear in the orchestra each time a certain character appears or a certain event is mentioned," and which are meant to serve not only as a means of characterization, but also as a "life-saving anchor for the ear in the ocean of melodic endlessness" (*Allgemeine musikalische Zeitung* 1868, 227). Some of these texts and their critical implications are discussed further in T. Grey, "Leading Motives and Narrative Threads: Notes on the *Leitfaden* Metaphor and the Critical Pre-History of the Wagnerian *Leitmotiv*," *Bericht über den Kongress der Gesellschaft für Musikforschung*, "Musik als Text" (Freiburg, 1993) (forthcoming).

novelistic experience, "as if following Ariadne's thread through tortuous, labyrinthine twistings and turnings, where one moment a gentle stream whispers to us, the next moment we are face to face with some ragged cliff, here some sweet-smelling, unknown flower entices us, there some thorny trail frightens us off."[53]

Others spoke of "secret threads" or often of a "red thread" running through a composition, threads whose perceptible identity was usually motivic, yet whose continuity was essentially a construction of the listener's imaginative faculties. Locally, it is true, one listened for the melodic "thread" that constituted the logical, intelligible syntax of a harmonic-polyphonic texture. This was as true for the tuneful strains of absolute music as it was for Wagnerian "endless melody" (at least that strand of its sense we interpret as the spinning-out of a single, continuous line through various parts of the orchestral web or fabric). But these other, "secret" or "red" threads are more imagined than immanent, and the figure seems to trade on the "threads" of narrative or dramatic plots rather than the "actual" thread of melodic syntax alone. Weber, for instance (who would clearly have had an ear for such things), admired the "happily conceived" melodic reminiscences running through the score of Spohr's *Faust* (1816) "like subtle threads, and giving it a spiritual coherence" ("einige Melodien [gehen] wie leise Fäden durch das Ganze und halten es geistig zusammen").[54] Ludwig Rellstab supposed that a "secret thread" was woven through Mendelssohn's early String Quartet in A minor, op. 13, by the "poetic content and musical expression" of a small *Lied* the composer placed as an enigmatic preface to the work, even if no literal traces of the melody were to be detected.[55] Theodor Uhlig's response to the recurring *Hauptmotiven* of Wagner's *Lohengrin* (which he knew well from arranging the piano score) recalls Weber on Spohr: "the most important musical ideas," he explains, "run through the opera like a red thread," and in this way, he suggests, compensate for the disintegrating

---

52 Franz Liszt, "Berlioz und seine Harold-Sinfonie," in *Gesammelte Schriften*, vol. IV, 26–7.

53 Review of Beethoven, Sonata in A major, op. 101 (signed "–d–"), *Allgemeine musikalische Zeitung* 19 (1827), col. 687.

54 Carl Maria von Weber, *Kunstansichten. Ausgewählte Schriften*, intro. by Karl Laux (Wilhelmshaven, 1978), 194.

55 Ludwig Rellstab, review of Mendelssohn's String Quartet, op. 13, *Iris im Gebiet der Tonkunst* 1:51 (24 December 1830), n.p. A Viennese critic spoke of the "fantastic humor that runs like a red thread through the entire delicate fabric" of Berlioz's Queen Mab scherzo. While he identifies this thread with the *melodische Hauptthema*, at first, the continuity of this thread across the movement is evidently supplemented by broader aspects of style, instrumentation, and tone. As in the case of the Mendelssohn quartet, the connecting "thread" is more imagined than it is literally present in the musical texture. (Julius Wend, "Berlioz und die moderne Symphonie," *Wiener Allgemeine musikalische Zeitung* 6:43 [1846], 169.)

framework of fixed solo and ensemble numbers.[56] A Viennese review of Verdi's *Forza del destino* in 1864 identifies the arching melody of Leonora's "Deh non m'abbandonar" (though not the opera's rhythmic-melodic "fate" figure) as a "reminiscence motive (*Erinnerungsmotiv*) that constitutes the so-called *red thread* ..." [57] A lengthy and extremely literal gloss on the motivic theory of *Opera and Drama* (from an 1865 monograph on *Tristan* by one Franz Müller) sees fit to supplement its extended citations of Wagner's text with just this figure – "a spiritual red thread" – in evoking the role of the "principal thematic motives" of Wagner's dramas.[58] And, finally, the same critic who spoke of "leitmotifs" in the context of an 1869 review of *Die Meistersinger* heard the "midsummer magic" motive in Act II (first heard after Walther's apoplectic tirade against the Masters is interrupted by the Nightwatchman's horn) as a "red thread" running through the rest of the act, which "seems to have a multiple significance."[59] Unlike the direct metaphor of a melodic thread, this "red thread" (like the general image of a narrative thread, which it connotes) is doubly metaphorical. That is, all the linear terminology of "narrative line and diegesis: dénouement, curve of the action, broken or dropped thread, line of argument, story line" are figurative terms to begin with, as J. Hillis Miller notes.[60] "They do not describe the actual physical linearity of lines of type or of writing" – rather, they describe a construction of the reader's imagination. Wagner's leitmotifs can create a sounding analogue to such imagined threads (even where the "endless melody" is not itself continuous), hence "threads" that are twice metaphorical.

The figure of a secret or "red" thread describes an important characteristic of those leitmotifs in Wagner which do not partake of the

---

56 Theodor Uhlig, "Drei Tage in Weimar" (1850), in *Musikalische Schriften*, 333.

57 This anonymous Viennese reviewer was not, however, favorably impressed by Verdi's theme nor by its implementation as a reminiscence: "Auf ein Erinnerungsmotiv, welches den sogenannten *rothen Faden* bildet, war Verdi auch bedacht, leider ist die Phrase eine solche, die man auf jeder Straße findet" (review of Verdi's *La forza del destino* in Vienna, *Blätter für Musik, Theater und Kunst* 11 [1864], 142–3; emphasis added).

58 "Diese zur einheitlich-künstlerischen Form sich zusammenschliessenden thematischen Hauptmotive der dramatischen Handlung erstrecken sich über das ganze Drama in einem ... organischen Zusammenhange, in welchem sie sich stets klar und bedeutungsvoll – *ein geistig-seelischer rother Faden* – dem Gefühle kundgeben" (F. Müller, *Tristan und Isolde nach Sage und Dichtung* [Munich, 1865], 237; emphasis added).

59 "Diese Melodie ... zieht sich wie ein rother Faden durch den übrigen Theil [des Aufzugs] und scheint eine mehrfache Bedeutung zu haben" (Friedrich Stade, "Wagner's 'Meistersinger'," *Neue Zeitschrift für Musik* 65 [1869], 62).

60 J. Hillis Miller, *Ariadne's Thread: Story Lines* (New Haven, 1992), 20. Miller's first chapter, a reflection on the various linear images applied to literary texts, derives from an earlier article, "Ariadne's Thread: Repetition and the Narrative Line," *Critical Inquiry* 3:1 (Autumn 1976), 57–79. The images of thread and line remain largely

simple semiosis of direct, textual-dramatic identification – a characteristic that also mediates between the idea of a syntactic melodic thread (a stretch of "endless melody") and the musical analogue to a "narrative" or dramatic thread, imaginatively constituted. The "midsummer magic" motive heard by the Dresden critic as a "red thread" woven through the end of Act II of *Die Meistersinger* resembles, in this way, many of the motives in *Tristan*, above all the celebrated motivic complex of mm. 1–21 of the Prelude. Like the *Tristan* motive-group, the "midsummer magic" idea is initially spun out as a small piece of endless melody, meant to evoke a certain nameless *Stimmung*, and resurfaces at certain, calculated nodal points of the ensuing drama. The distinctive musical and expressive qualities of this material ensure that its highlighted recurrences will be felt to tie together the motivic fabric of the work, at least in some very loose sense (Wagner's "symphonic web"). Like the image of the "red thread," some secret, unarticulated meaning seems to attach to these motives. Like the "red thread," they maintain an immanent presence throughout the texture of the work; their intermittent resurfacings are intuitively understood as significant events, orienting us within the web of the musical texture and dramatic text. As an implicit "subtext" they inform our hearing and reading of the text as a whole. (Here the four-note chromatic "Desire" cell of the *Tristan* prelude would be paradigmatic: as the veritable emblem of the score's all-pervasive chromaticism and all that it signifies, the figure may at any moment penetrate the surface of the musical texture, and as an audible, sub-motivic "red thread" it is scarcely ever far from view.)

The analogy between musical motives and the "threads" of a dramatic or narrative plot that implicitly informs the very term "leitmotif" is made explicit by a review of *Das Rheingold*, arranged for piano, four hands, without text. ("A piano score for four hands," exclaims the bemused critic, "that is, Wagner as pure musician!") This reviewer defends (already) Wagner's motives as more than mere sonorous labels:

[T]hey express more by means of their varied positions and relations to one another than simply what is represented by the scenic proceedings (*szenische Vorgänge*); they connect the past and the future with the present, the unfolding action, and indicate the further inner connections among individual characters, the threads of action and mood (*Handlungs- und Stimmungsfäden*), in a way that only music is able to do. Where the word fails, the musical motive carries on, further spinning out its threads (*dichtet das musikalische Motiv fort, spinnt es seine Fäden weiter*), so that it . . . acquires a further dramatic significance. Here is also the origin of that wonderful polyphony, that secret construction of dramatic and musical art . . .[61]

submerged throughout the other chapters, however.
[61] R. Musiol, review of *Das Rheingold*, arr. piano, four hands (Mainz, 1879), *Neue Berliner*

The analogy with the figurative threads of narrative or drama high-lights that feature of the leitmotif that was so crucial for Wagner already in the provisional theory of motives in *Opera and Drama*: its capacity to recall a musical past, to suggest a thread connecting present with past and future.[62] In his 1851 pamphlet on *Lohengrin*, Liszt appears to suggest a similar transference of the threads of a dramatic plot, as figure, to the broad lines or threads traced by musical motives. While the audience of this opera is necessarily prepared to "forgo any of those detached numbers that are simply tied, one after the other, onto the thread of some plot (*engrenés l'un après l'autre sur le fil de quelque intrigue*)," as in the tradi-tional opera, "he will find a singular interest in following throughout three long acts the profoundly considered, astonishingly skillful, and poetically intelligent combination with which Wagner, by means of several principal phrases, has drawn a melodic knot that constitutes [the essence of] his entire drama (*a serré un nœud mélodique qui constitue tout son drame*)."[63] The threads of a dramatic plot, whose knotting and subsequent unknotting generally carry our attention in a drama, are here subsumed within the threads of the motivic web, the "red threads" of those "principal phrases" retrospectively designated as leitmotifs. (Ortrud's sinuously sinister motive, for instance, is described by the linear image of a "venomous serpent that here coils itself about its victims.")[64] Similarly, a critic quoted in *Dwight's Journal* in 1877 allowed that, "at first sight this clinging to fixed *motives* [in the *Ring* operas] seems rich in suggestion, since by this means threads of like thoughts are interwoven through the whole work, knitting all its parts together." But for the better part of the public, he adds, "these over-ingenious thematic interweavings are thrown away," too abstruse of import to communicate anything directly. ("All the time one is forced to ask himself: Motive, what do you want of me?")[65]

In the tomb scene of *Roméo*, Berlioz picks up that very motivic "thread" Wagner had lost track of back in the *scène d'amour*, where he had been unable to match the windings, turnings, and seeming ruptures of the

---

Musik-Zeitung 33 (1879), 132.

[62] In one of the few passages where Wagner specifically alludes to his motivic techniques after beginning the composition of the *Ring*, it is precisely this counterpoint of temporal layers that interests him, the notion of musical threads tying present and past events. Speaking of the theme of reincarnation in his unrealized project for a Buddhist drama, *Die Sieger*, he writes (in *Mein Leben*): "The simple story owed its significance to the way that the past life of the suffering principal characters was entwined in the new phase of their lives as being still present time. I perceived at once how the musical remembrance of this dual life, keeping the past constantly present in the hearing, might be repre-sented perfectly to the emotional receptivities . . . " (*My Life*, 528–9).

[63] F. Liszt, *Lohengrin et Tannhäuser de Richard Wagner* (Leipzig, 1851), 67.

[64] Ibid., 69.

[65] "Musical 'Motives' and Wagner's 'Leit-Motive'," *Dwight's Journal of Music*, 21 July

melodic line to the discursive maze of Shakespeare's (absent) text. The "love theme" is very much a kind of musical "red thread" through the *scène d'amour*, coalescing at first from apparent fragments, and mutating throughout the course of the movement by virtue of its detachable cadential tail. (Its "secret sense," of course, has to do with the here unarticulated passions of the two lovers.) Berlioz momentarily works this thread into the tomb scene in order to link the musical past and present within the bundle of bizarre orchestral gestures that constitute the dénouement of his dramatic symphony. Multiple motives are gathered here so that the dramatic knot, the catastrophe, may be tied and then loosed, or severed. The "dénouement" is completed here by the literal (well, figurative) forceful severing of this very thread, the love theme – an abruptive gesture that is further replicated across the concluding pages of the movement.

Tristan's death occupies, by no surprise, a similarly literal "nodal point" in the score of the musical drama. (Both critical moments are eventually followed, naturally, by a stabilizing catharsis: Berlioz's operatic finale of reconciliation and Isolde's quasi-autonomous Trans-figuration, which at the same time picks up the severed thread of the Act II duet.) As if consciously sensing the metaphorical analogies implicit in his motivic "system," Wagner creates perhaps the thickest motivic knot of his entire, complex score at this last, brief crossing of Tristan and Isolde. Out of the metrical delirium of the transformed "slumber" or *Lauschen* theme (and a fairly straightforward C$^6_4$ prolon-gation) emerges the motive associated with the torch in Act II, scene 1. ("What, do I hear the light?", Tristan asks, and his confusion of modalities suggests that in his final moments he has been made miraculously conscious of the musical signs about him, *as music* – a remarkable transgression of the implicit "conventions" of the music drama itself: Tristan himself tells us he hears a leitmotif.) The "torch" motive, the original "death" motive, and the syncopated line of Tristan's anxious anticipation from the beginning of the scene all converge here, as the whole motivic complex of the Act I prelude wells up portentously one last time (see Example 6.10a). This knot is audibly disentangled during Tristan's final moments. The "red thread" of that enigmatic, "languishing" music is reduced again to a single, fragile thread in the cello line (the "Glance" or *Blick* motive), which is at last severed with exquisite delicacy by a diminished triad, struck on the harp (Example 6.10b). As in the earlier climax of the delirium scene, this last contrapuntal crowding of motives embodies the commingling threads of memory and conscious-ness in Tristan's mind, an "idea" that stimulates a recapitulation of motives far denser than any symphonic context could explicate, even though its terminal position following the last and greatest "wave" of Tristan's delirium conveys a certain formal logic. But the logic of the

Example 6.10   Motivic "dénouement" at Tristan's death (*Tristan und Isolde* Act III, scene 2)   (a)

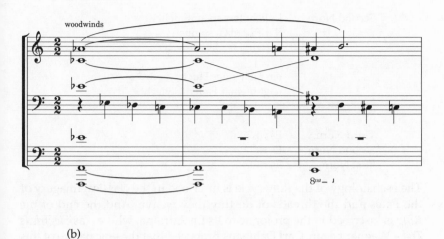

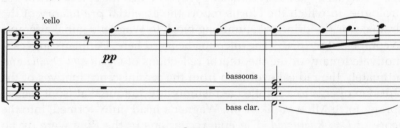

"red thread" resurfacing here (like that of its fleeting but inevitable recrudescence in the opera's last measures) is finally an *in*formal one: it is dramatically motivated, of course, but its structural role can only really be subjected to intuitive verification, as befits the secretive, intuitive, elusive nature of the figure itself.

> First Norn. Die Nacht weicht;
> nichts mehr gewahr' ich:
> des Seiles Fäden
> find' ich nicht mehr;
> verflochten ist das Geflecht.

Second Norn.   [N]icht fest spannt mehr
der Fäden Gespinnst;
verwirrt ist das Geweb':
[...]
ein rächender Fluch
nagt meiner Fäden Geflecht.
[...]

Third Norn.   Es riß!
Second Norn.   Es riß!
First Norn.   Es riß!

The eschatology of the *Ring* cycle is inscribed in the classical imagery of the Fates and the threads of destiny they weave. And the end of the *Ring* is inscribed in the prologue to its final drama, where – as *Siegfrieds Tod* – Wagner began. Carl Dahlhaus proposed that the epic nature of this prologue, in which the Norns report the essential pre-history of the drama, was the principal stumbling block to Wagner's initial attempts to compose it in 1850.[66] The dilemma he faced here, Dahlhaus suggests, motivated many of the theoretical reflections of *Opera and Drama* and ultimately the radical evolution from the reminiscence motives of the Dresden operas to a full-fledged leitmotif technique that (so it seems) sprang forth Minerva-like from Wagner's head, fully formed, into the score of *Das Rheingold*. The epic recitations in the *Ring* were by no means eliminated – rather the reverse, as we know (the Norns' scene is a case in point). But it was precisely the demand posed by these recitations for a musical "past" that could be recalled, or "realized for the senses" in the *Orchestermelodie*, that motivated the development of an extended leitmotif technique, with its capacity to project the intertwining of past, present, and future.

The argument is convincing, especially in view of Wagner's own emphasis in *Opera and Drama* on the possibility of conveying a layered temporal framework by means of motivic recollection and transformation (see also his remarks on *Die Sieger* cited in n. 62). Might the image of the Norns' spinning itself have played some, perhaps subconscious, motivating role here as well? Certainly Wagner spoke often enough of the "form" of his scores in terms of a vast motivic "fabric" not to have missed the allegorical aptness of this image to his own musical methods.[67] And this visual motif of the Norns' spinning is used to much greater

---

1877, 63.

[66] C. Dahlhaus, "Zur Geschichte der Leitmotivtechnik bei Wagner," 17–36 (see esp. 31–6).

[67] Among the several familiar instances of this locution we might recall those in *A Communication to My Friends* ("ein jederzeit charakteristisches Gewebe der Haupt-themen, das sich nicht über eine Szene . . . sondern über das ganze Drama . . . ausbreitete" – IV, 322) and the "Application" essay ("Diese Einheit gibt sich dann in einem das ganze Kunstwerk durchziehenden Gewebe von Grundthemen" – X, 185).

effect in structuring the revised, expanded version of the scene, where the impending end is visualized in the climactic snapping of their thread. (Originally the Norns had just quietly retreated from the scene, threads intact.) If the expansion of this and other passages of epic narration was motivated by the opportunities thus provided for exploiting an allusive motivic network, it is appropriate that Wagner should also have expanded the role of their visual symbol here, as well.

As the Norns weave their threads they sing of what is past, passing, and to come. In doing so, they gather together the motivic threads – dramatic and musical alike – of the imminent dénouement. As these threads proliferate across the scene – especially after the last refrain of the first Norn ("Die Nacht weicht; / nichts mehr gewahr' ich") – the Norns' control of them is progressively eroded, to the point where the cord they form is suddenly severed, the prologue ends, and "the end" begins.[68] The pattern here could also remind us of Tristan's delirium, where the accumulation of motives spun around the central "red thread" of the *alte Weise* – the thread of Tristan's memory – finally yields to its own internal tension (like the Norns' cord), severed by the new motive of Tristan's "Curse" and its development as formal-rhetorical peroration. The variously arpeggiated seventh chord associated with the Norns' spinning (Example 6.11) is identified by Patrick McCreless in terms that precisely recall this "red thread" function, as described earlier: "Its continual appearance, disappearance, and reappearance give the illusion that it is there all the time: like the rope of time it symbolizes, it is continuous."[69] But the presence of this particular aural thread, as refrain, becomes audibly attenuated as the scene progresses. After the third Norn first sings of the impending apocalypse, only brief snatches of this thread are to be heard again, crowded out by other motives. It is as much the accumulation of these diverse musical motives as it is the apocalyptic story they signify that rouses the scene out of the gloomy E♭-minor penumbra of its beginning and into other keys, eventually B minor. The confusion that finally leads to the severing of the Norns' cord is thus precipitated by an influx of motives (we even seem to "hear" Siegfried's horn-call tugging at this motivic thread and the Curse motive slicing through it), and by the tonal destabilization effected by this influx. Both the loss of motivic refrain (the "cord" arpeggio, or arpeggiated chord) and of tonal center give a musical

[68] Patrick McCreless has analyzed the formal *Steigerung* of the scene in terms of the contrast between the more normative tonal-prolongational language of the first two Norns and its disruption by a freer chromatic-linear motion in the music of the third Norn (singing of the future), emanating from manipulations of a "motivic" half-diminished seventh chord (F–A♭–C♭–E♭, later as F♯–A–C–E). See McCreless, "Schenker and the Norns," 276–97 (esp. 288–97).
[69] Ibid., 281.

Example 6.11 Cord motive (*Götterdämmerung* prologue).

meaning to the first Norn's cautionary text: "the threads of the cord I find no more, the braid becomes tangled" ("des Seiles Fäden find' ich nicht mehr; verflochten ist das Geflecht"). The image could express the completed knot of plot lines that only awaits its tragic dénouement.

At the same this knot or tangle of threads could be imagined as the consequence of a confusion of temporal levels on the Norns' part. Even after the third Norn has pointed to the future in her first speech (a proleptic allusion to the motive of Brünnhilde's apocalyptic pyre), the other two cast back to past motives: Alberich (his *Herrschersruf*), the Rhine-gold, the Ring, the Curse. (This is the point where Siegfried's sword and horn-call rush in precipitously – bass trumpet, horn, trumpet – and the motivically overloaded texture collapses.) It is as if the motivic knot the Norns have inadvertently created is the result of tangled time lines, threads leading in too many temporal directions at once. (*Histoire* has been confounded by this three-way *récit*, looking simultaneously forwards and backwards.) Then, where these epic-narrative threads are ruptured, a new melodic thread emerges. The *musical* thread – in the broader sense of a continuous melodic line – that had been abruptly severed is eventually resumed in the long legato cello line that begins the next scene. Over a series of dominant prolongations (V of B, V of B♭, V of E♭) the "new" Siegfried and Brünnhilde motives rise up through the orchestral texture and a new, uncluttered musical present is established, for the time being.

If the Norns' scene is a proleptic vision of the end, using the classical figure of the Fates' thread as a symbolic prop, where is the actual dénouement of the drama? The question is not easily answered. All of *Götterdämmerung* is in some sense an extended dénouement to the tetralogy as a whole, as its title intimates. This is one way of formulating the insight that motivated Wagner to expand *Siegfrieds Tod* into a cycle of four works. Within the original drama of Siegfried's death (*Götterdämmerung*), the beginning of the dénouement might be located at several "nodal points" where a knot of intersecting lines begins to unravel.

The terminology of Aristotle's *Poetics* would place it early. "By Complication," writes Aristotle, with reference to the lineaments of dramatic plot structures, "I mean all from the beginning of the story to the point just before the change in the hero's fortunes; by Dénouement, all from the change to the end."[70] From this perspective the dénouement would begin with Siegfried's arrival at the Gibichung's Hall in Act I, and his drinking of the potion that will erase his memory of Brünnhilde. Or at the very latest, it would begin with the contretemps between Siegfried and Brünnhilde during the nuptials of Act II – the peripeteia of Brünnhilde's discovery of the Ring on Siegfried's hand. By the more common usage that places the dénouement nearer the actual end of things, we would probably look to the opening of the opera's last scene, where Hagen returns with Siegfried's corpse, Gutrune intuits the facts of his murder, and Gunther is killed by Hagen. Or perhaps it actually occurs out of view, during that enigmatic, unseen nocturnal colloquy between Brünnhilde and the Rhine-maidens just before this (the hermeneutic crux for Carolyn Abbate's reading of Brünnhilde's role in this finale),[71] where the plot behind Hagen's plot is somehow revealed to her, and with her omniscience restored, Brünnhilde can return to the scene and calmly set the end in motion. The complete process of dénouement, in any case, continues through Brünnhilde's immolation, of course. The lines of the universal story are not fully unraveled until the Ring returns to the Rhine and the gods have fallen.

If we could speak of a *musical* dénouement, on the other hand, we would likely look to the moment of Brünnhilde's entrance in the final

---

70 *The Rhetoric and the Poetics of Aristotle*, trans. Ingram Bywater [*Poetics*] (New York, 1954), 246.

71 C. Abbate, "Brünnhilde Walks by Night," *Unsung Voices*, 206–49.

tableau. As she enters, the "Sword" motive slices through the chaotic jumble of material accompanying the unseemly squabble (as Brünnhilde characterizes it) that has erupted at Hagen's return; here, too, the descending motive of the "Dusk of the Gods" evokes an almost literal sense of untying or undoing by making explicit its inversional relation to the figure expressing the natural genesis of things that began *Das Rheingold* (Example 6.12).[72] This sense of a musical "undoing" is reinforced by the series of non-functional Neapolitan relationships that give the inverted motive its characteristically deracinated feeling. Furthermore, the death of Gunther immediately preceding this, the uncanny raising of Siegfried's lifeless arm, and Brünnhilde's majestic entrance also constitute a knot of dramatic motives (motifs) that could identify this moment as the initiation of the dramatic dénouement, as well.

Wagner, as we know, was undecided about the details of the overall dramatic dénouement of the *Ring*, or the motives behind it. He tinkered with the words of Brünnhilde's closing speech more than with any other

Example 6.12 Final scene of *Götterdämmerung*: Brünnhilde's entrance and beginning of the (motivic) "dénouement"

[72] Wagner identifies the forces of nature with the image of "weaving" a number of times throughout the *Ring*, for example in the *Waldweben* of *Siegfried*, Act II, or the lines of Loge's narration in *Das Rheingold*, "So weit Leben und Weben (etc.)." On the effect of Brünnhilde's majestic intrusion here and the musical events surrounding it see also Christopher Wintle, "The Numinous in *Götterdämmerung*," 217–19 as well as Abbate, *Unsung Voices*, 220–1.

Dénouements

parts of the *Ring* text, throughout the work's protracted genesis. The different endings have themselves created a famous knot of motives attracting the attentions of countless interpreters eager to untangle the ultimate meaning of the *Ring*'s end, and thus of the whole. One thing is clear: Wagner's leading motive here was that of apocalypse. The author of the *Ring*, like the revolutionist and fledgling anarchist he had lately been, started from the premise that everything must go in the end. The precise mechanisms of apocalypse – social or dramatic – were of secondary concern. The image of his mythical stage-world purified by fire and water took precedence over any details affecting its actual motivation. It was obvious from the beginning that nothing else would do.

To characterize the apocalypse of *Götterdämmerung* as the grandest of all "effects without causes," however, would not be entirely just. While critics have noted its affinity with the spectacular dénouements of grand opera often enough, we should also recall that the motif of the Norse gods' downfall was an authentic part of the mythology, and not merely dreamed up for the occasion.[73] Still, for all the shadings of philosophical and ethical import effected by the various revisions in Brünnhilde's closing speech, the apocalyptic dénouement itself seems to have been above all a dramaturgical imperative (as are the catastrophic final tableaus of grand opera, or the empirically unmotivated deaths of so many operatic heroines in general) and, in a related sense, a musical imperative.[74] The musical imperative, I suggest, has something to do with the radical formal experiment Wagner had undertaken in the leitmotif technique of the *Ring*, and with the metaphorical figures that seem to have informed the technique and the term alike (despite the alleged spuriousness of the latter).

Wagner, we will recall, spoke of the "possibility of a dramatic poem itself providing a counterpart to symphonic form" (VII, 128). By

[73]   See, for example, Elizabeth Magee, *Richard Wagner and the Nibelungs* (Oxford, 1991), 202: "The destruction of the firmament through fire and water at the end of the era of the gods was a standing feature of Eddic mythology, expounded most fully in the *Völsupá* and in the *Snorra Edda*."

[74]   In probing the question "Why Does Isolde Die?" in a paper delivered at the International Conference on Nineteenth-Century Music at the University of Surrey (July 1994), John Deathridge reaches some conclusions about the musical-allegorical significance of Isolde's moment of death and transfiguration similar to those I draw from Brünnhilde's valedictory *scena* (not surprisingly, considering the proximity of these scenes as musical-dramaturgical gestures). For Deathridge, however, the sea of "purely musical" sound that engulfs or consumes Isolde represents an over-mastering "male" symphonic principle erasing the female (vocal) subject, rather than the embodiment of a "female" principle of pure music, as I have suggested in light of the metaphorical codes of *Opera and Drama*. Both women, in any case, are "annihilated" in the process of carrying out their redemptive roles, just as the female representative of "pure music" is (according to *Opera and Drama*) to be "annihilated" in attaining the mutual redemption of music and drama.

reversing the terms of this familiar formula (from *"Music of the Future"*) we can get another perspective on the nature of Wagner's musical experiment, as the "possibility of a symphonic poem itself providing (or generating) a counterpart to dramatic form." The reversal immediately suggests a broad affinity with the concerns of Liszt and other contemporaries. On the other hand, the phrase "symphonic poem" could very well describe the nature of that dramatic text which is a "counterpart to symphonic form," or in which musical form is "poetically prefigured" or "preconstrued," as Wagner also put it in the 1860 essay. The reversal of terms also suggests something of how the figurative background of the "leitmotif" (as motivic thread) informs its musical implementation in Wagner's scores. The formal experiment of the *Ring*, modified in the remaining works, consisted in the re-tracing of the discursive labyrinth of a dramatic text – musically or "symphonically" conceived, in some loose sense – with an evolving network of motivic threads, in hopes that some significant, seemingly cohesive design would result ("all by itself," as Wagner optimistically put it in *Opera and Drama*).[75] The idea was very much a product of Wagner's own, quite astonishing imagination. But to some extent, he also took a cue from contemporary habits of listening as to how characteristic motives might be configured along the lines of the intertwining "threads" of narrative textures or dramatic action.

The structural categories of drama, like those of rhetoric, had always posed inviting analogies to music, which composers like Berlioz and Liszt had begun to explore in various ways. Wagner's experiment was to press these analogies still further. The dialogically structured "evolution" of poetic-musical periods (chapter 4) is one example of this. Another, then, might be loosely construed as a principle of motivic "dénouement," most drastically exemplified in the immolation scene of *Götterdämmerung*. Liszt had already invoked this category in appreciating the design of the *Tannhäuser* overture, remarking that one could not imagine any "symphonic poem . . . of more perfect logic in the exposition, development, and dénouement of its propositions."[76] Evidently it was the grandiose apotheosis of the Pilgrims' Chorus that Liszt regarded as the "dénouement" of the overture, just as he seems to have regarded thematic apotheosis as an imperative of the rhetorical logic of large-scale symphonic form in general. Thus also the imperative of apocalypse in Wagner's monumental tetralogy: the ultimate dramatic gesture of

---

[75]   " . . . the musician, as the one to realize the poet's intent, is to organize these [dramatic]-motifs-become-musical-motives (*zu melodischen Momenten verdichteten Motive*) in the most complete accord with the poetic intent, so that the most perfectly unified musical form will automatically result (*ganz von selbst*) from their reciprocally conditioned repetition (*in ihrer wohlbedingten wechselseitigen Wiederholung*)" (IV, 201).
[76]   Liszt, *Lohengrin et Tannhäuser de Richard Wagner*, 155.

catharsis (a literal "purgation" by fire and water) is also the motive for a vast gathering of the cycle's musical *Grundmotiven*. A description by Eduard Hanslick of the *Meistersinger* prelude and the motivic polyphony of its "dénouement" resonates with this aspect of the immolation scene, which it perhaps better describes: "it [the *Meistersinger* prelude] throws one after another all the leitmotifs of the opera into a flood of chromatic progressions and sequences, in order to whip them up into a veritable musical typhoon (*um sie schließlich in einem wahren Ton-Orcan über und durcheinander zu schleudern*)."[77] So, too, the final tableau of *Götterdämmerung* floods the auditorium with leitmotifs.

Wagner seems to have sensed that the only convincing way to resolve the immense motivic labyrinth of the *Ring* was through a great gathering together of the principal threads running through it, and their final "un-knotting." Each of the two *Hauptsätze* identified by Alfred Lorenz as supporting the triumphal *Bogen* of Brünnhilde's valedictory song (the *Schlußgesang*) is articulated by the march-like "funeral pyre" motive. With each appearance, especially at its return in the great orchestral coda, this motive seems to accumulate an ever-greater array of motivic material in the monumental tread of its path. (My deliberately mixed metaphor draws attention to the characteristic insufficiency of Lorenz's architectonic formal categories: this music is not so ᵢ.ʾuch the triumphal arch itself as it is the parade of motives marching through it *en défilé* – literally "threading" or "unthreading" their way toward the final goal.) At one point Brünnhilde picks up the broken textual-musical thread of the Norns' prologue: "Wißt ihr, wie das ward?" The question-formula of the "Fate" motive that accompanies this constitutes an erratic but persistent refrain punctuating the opening half of Brünnhilde's song (through the great cadence at "Ruhe, ruhe, du Gott!") – another elusive "red thread" through the score, whose connotations have never really been determined beyond a general sense of fateful brooding and unanswered questions. (The cadence at "Ruhe, du Gott" also claims attention as a moment of motivic dénouement, where a complex of early motives from *Rheingold* and *Walküre* relating to Wotan's story are solemnly gathered and sorted, as if to form a kind of musical shroud for the doomed god.) In the second half of the scene this questioning motive disappears: the dénouement involves the answering of questions, the solution of problems, and if this is not wholly accomplished in the text, it can at least be symbolically asserted in the music.

The second large cursus of Brünnhilde's song (Lorenz's second *Hauptsatz*, beginning as Brünnhilde takes the Ring from Siegfried's hand) gathers a welter of elemental motives: water (various Rhine-maiden melodies and the Rhine-gold motive), fire (Loge and the Magic

---

[77] Hanslick, *Die moderne Oper*, 293.

Fire), air (flying Valkyries), as well as the reciprocal pairing of genesis/ apocalypse (Nature/Dusk of the Gods). The end of this second cursus, from the moment where Brünnhilde ignites the pyre, has a detached, perorational quality. (Or, just as *Götterdämmerung* is a series of dénouements, Brünnhilde's valedictory song is a series of perorations: her words to the ravens coincide with a first musical coda to these multiple perorations, and the lighting of the pyre with a second one, also registered as such by Lorenz.) As the flames begin to rise there emerges out of the air, as it were (the leaping Valkyrie music), the famous return of the so-called "Redemption" motive, or Brünnhilde's glorification (as Wagner once identified it).[78] Here indeed is the ultimate red thread of the *Ring* score, a memorable and yet unnameable melody that has remained submerged since its single appearance at the center of the cycle. What motivates its sudden reprise and apotheosis at the end has always been one of the great puzzles of *Ring* exegesis. Whatever the possible relevance of its original context in *Die Walküre* (Sieglinde's ecstatic response to Brünnhilde's "annunciation" that she, Sieglinde, is with child), it is hard to suppress the suspicion that Wagner also recognized in it a melodic inspiration whose potential for uplifting sequential development had never been tapped.[79] Here, at the climax of Brünnhilde's peroration(s), these uplifting sequences seem calculated to evoke thoughts of that most famous of nineteenth-century literary finales, the end of Goethe's *Faust*. The glorification of Brünnhilde – here as in *Die Walküre* – is the glorification of the *ewig Weibliche*, as many of Wagner's remarks on her character would attest (see chapter 3). The upward sequencing, with its fragmentation and overlapping of the motive, also recalls Isolde's Transfiguration, and, like that, presents an unmistakable musical image of "drawing beyond" (*Hinanziehen*), the gesture of redemptive assumption that was Goethe's principal legacy to Wagner.

The "Redemption/Glorification" motive completes its contribution to the process of dénouement in the orchestral coda. Here Wagner deploys his leitmotifs as virtual symbolic agents in tying up the end of the story, all on their own. The Curse (trombones: F♯–A–C–E) is literally cut off as Hagen and the Ring go under; the Rhine-maiden's original, prelapsarian song returns briefly (in its original pitches, like

---

[78] In a letter of 6 September 1875 (in Cosima's hand), as cited by John Deathridge in *19th-Century Music* 5 (1981), 84. Interpreting the whole Immolation scene as a kind of "glorification of Brünnhilde" Abbate emphasizes the fact that this motive was originally directed at and heard (if not sung) by Brünnhilde alone (*Unsung Voices*, 243–4). It does undoubtedly become her musical property here, however we interpret her appropriation of it.

[79] In fact, Wagner admitted nearly as much to Cosima, two days after finishing the developed draft for Act III of *Götterdämmerung*: "I am glad I kept back Sieglinde's theme of praise for Brünnhilde, to become as it were a hymn to heroes" (CWD, 24 July 1872; vol. I, 515).

the Curse); Valhalla chords rise up one last time from D♭ (likewise tonally restored) to intertwine with the Rhine music, until the motives of Siegfried and the Dusk of the Gods signal Valhalla's end. Riding above all this is the Redemption figure (violin 1, flutes), which now acts as an audible melodic thread binding together this larger complex of symbolic-dramatic threads.

We might even say that Wagner enacts here a complicated layering of metaphors symbolic of the role of leitmotif in the music drama altogether: motives with a strongly "determinate" semantic value (Rhine-maiden's song, Valhalla, Curse, Siegfried) combine in symbolic counterpoint with a melodic thread of "pure music" that leads them on (*hinan*) to the end. This indeterminate motive that has re-attached itself to Brünnhilde might be read, like Brünnhilde herself in the last scene of *Siegfried* (see chapter 3), as an allegorical embodiment of "pure music." Both partake of the *ewig Weibliche* as agents of a redemptive closure. This motive effects the last ("purely musical") of *Götterdämmerung*'s many dénouements: it binds together the last symbolic knot of motives and finally loosens this same knot; as "purely musical melody" it arrogates the resolution to the whole drama, taking the repeated plagal cadences of the closing entirely unto itself. Just as the world is returned to its natural state at the end of the *Ring*, music (paradoxically) reverts to its pre-Wagnerian state of indeterminate *Ahnung*, a side-effect of the cosmic catharsis that has just taken place. If the *Ring* contains, as Nattiez has proposed,[80] an allegory of the history of music ("according to Wagner," that is), then it would make sense that its apocalyptic dénouement should signify a reversion of music to its original condition – the "utopia of regression" implied by Wagner's constructs of melody, as interpreted in chapter 5.

In the first adumbrations of the leitmotif idea in *Opera and Drama*, Wagner had explained that the feelings expressed in a given piece of "verse-melody" would be recorded, in a sense, by the accompanying musical line or motive. In this way the feeling will become "the property of pure music" (*Eigenthum der reinen Musik* – IV, 184). But just as Wagner the revolutionary was ambivalent toward the idea of material property, Wagner the aesthetic theorist was undecided about the "property of pure music" – either its rights or its properties, that is. Where traditional aesthetics held that feelings were the inalienable property of pure music, Wagner's music drama and its network of leitmotifs tended to abrogate those claims in favor of language, drama, and fictional human agents (that is, it demanded that musical "feeling" be grounded in these human objects). The dénouement of the *Ring* is

---

[80] Jean-Jacques Nattiez, *Wagner Androgyne*, chapter 3: "The *Ring* as a Mythic Account of the History of Music," 53–90.

about restitution of natural property: cleansed of its history of abuses, the gold is restored to the Rhine and the mythic circle is completed. In composing the end, has Wagner perhaps thought to restore the "property" of pure, absolute music – its innate and ineffable expressive properties – following this epic subjugation of music to the power and abuses of drama (that is, those critical *bêtes-noirs* of declamatory melody and referential leitmotif)? Has the leitmotif, in the end, been forced to yield up its impure, ill-begotten semiotic powers to a mere "pure" bit of uplifting melody?[81]

Perhaps – but probably not. The *Opera and Drama* passage spoke not of the inherent property of pure music, its natural birth right, but of an expressive "property" assigned to it by virtue of a dramatic text and context. It is true that when Wagner departs from the epic drama of the *Ring* for the interior drama of *Tristan* a character of indeterminate (and yet intensified) *Ahnung* becomes again the leading motive of the music, largely, but not entirely, displacing previous attempts to cultivate a new semiotic competence in music. But the end of *Götterdämmerung*, the dénouement to the whole *Ring* cycle, remains emblematic of the formal experiment of the music drama altogether and of the motives behind this experiment, precisely because the form, the textures, and the methods of this ending are (unlike Isolde's Transfiguration) unremittingly leitmotivic. Brünnhilde's *Schlußgesang* has no musical form, to speak of. At best, its music fills out the rhetorical shape of the speech – its commanding tones, its lyrical reminiscences ("Wie Sonne lauter strahlt mir sein Licht"), its violent antitheses ("trog keiner wie Er!"), its articulating pauses, physical gestures, and nested perorations. And yet the result is compelling: we even listen to it shorn of its text, as the "Immolation Scene from *Götterdämmerung*," possibly recollecting the sense of some motives, while imagining that of others. The music remains an impressive palimpsest of the rhetorical form, while the tone-painting of the orchestral coda is able to speak for itself. The point here is not to ascribe such a *telos* of autonomy regained to Wagner's overall musical or philosophical development, but to evoke an aspect of "form" that resembles an accumulating motivic fabric, web, or labyrinth, and an experience of listening that resembles the retracing of

---

81 Wayne Koestenbaum surely speaks for untold numbers in describing his delight at this melody's refractory impression of autonomy and difference with respect to the rest of the score. When Sieglinde first emits this music in *Die Walküre*, he writes, "she embodies [Wagner's] vision of woman [as music?], but she also represents a joy separate from this plan – a pleasure I can loosely wear, like a cape. She subscribes to her body: she votes for thrill over theory" (*The Queen's Throat: Opera, Homosexuality, and the Mystery of Desire* [New York, 1993]). In other words, Sieglinde, in her supreme moment, indulges in a frisson of pure lyric pathos such as we associate with the opera of instinct (Puccini) rather than that of reflection (Wagner).

or threading through such figures. We need not (and probably cannot) hear all of the music as an elaborate and consistent musical code. At the same time, we probably cannot help trying to attach semantic meanings to motivic gestures, harmonic moves, instrumental effects, changing rhythms and meters, and so on, and constructing from all of this the metaphorical threads we use to trace all types of temporal experiences charted by means of the available signs.

The central emblem of Wagner's experiment, of its aesthetic and cultural motives, is the leitmotif. This word and the ideas it comprehends form the center of a knot in which nearly every strand of a Wagnerian critical problematics is somehow entangled. Absolute music, the autonomy or contingency of musical forms, the nature of their motivations, the conflicting claims of symphonic and dramatic structures, the ability of music to express or signify "ideas" (and their relative "determinacy"), the metaphorical nature of all discourse about music, the organizing principles of an "emancipated" melodic syntax and periodic structure, the authority of Wagner's own texts as measured against their critical reception and interpretation – all of these converge in one way or another in the concept of leitmotif. It is a magnet for the compound of fear, loathing, and fascination that characterizes so many responses to Wagner, the beast at the center of the Wagnerian labyrinth. Like the spider, the leitmotif is at the same time the source of the web, the lines, the threads through this maze. Critics fear to name them, yet have no choice. Audiences long to learn the secret of these names and to track their secret meanings. The leitmotif allows Wagner to cut loose from traditional designs and to spin entirely new ones that are, he says, a true map of the drama and all its subterranean corridors. The complex artistry of this sounding maze is offered in place of the arabesques of symphony, quartet, and sonata (or the mosaics of opera), while the motivic threads that trace this maze at the same time absorb the discursive meanings of their dramatic model. But mazes are traditionally ambivalent signs. The complex artistry of the finished product may engender confusion and fear in the subject who experiences it as a process – indeed, this may be an objective.[82] Certainly Wagner's music drama engendered in many of its early listeners a confusion, or other negative responses one might associate with a labyrinthine experience: disorientation, frustration, anger, tedium, impatience. Yet Wagner promised enlightenment, meaning, aesthetic progress, and spiritual redemption for those who succeeded in negotiating his labyrinths. And where the threads of the drama failed to assist this process, Wolzogen's *Leitfäden* offered a supplementary means of negotiation.

[82] See Penelope Doob, *The Idea of the Labyrinth from Antiquity through the Middle Ages* (Ithaca, 1990).

Was this a spurious means, that generated the "spurious" term, leitmotif? If Wagner was hesitant to sanction the term or the naive methodology of its text (the *Leitfäden*), he was obviously powerless to check its influence. The term and its methodology, after all, grew out of an impulse he had created: the impulse to endow music with determinate ideas, poetic intentions, substantial meanings. Or had he created it? The impulse was certainly one Wagner read in the musical culture of his time – the culture which, according to Liszt, was ever more in search of an "Ariadne's thread" through the mazes of modern music, with all its complex harmonies, labyrinthine forms, and portentous motivic signs. Listeners listened for threads of discursive meaning even in symphonies and quartets, as well as operas.[83] The claim that the symphony had been sublated within the music drama was perhaps not pure hubris, since Wagner's music can be said to have subsumed widespread listening practices and offered them a new, richer, more suitable ground for cultivation (so he maintained).

If Wagner never authorized the term "leitmotif" for his most celebrated invention, it is validated by the critical and cultural background of the technique itself, so far as it responds to an existing propensity to listen for or to construct threads of meaning from motivic signs. The situation thus embodies a basic premise of my concerns throughout this book. Wagner's own texts, however voluminous, are necessarily incomplete. No author's texts (imaginative or theoretical) are expected to offer an authoritative key to interpretation – this much has become axiomatic. Even Wagner's nearly endless texts are incomplete without their contexts, which often speak to things he leaves unsaid. We might capture this dialogic relationship of authorial text and context, especially Wagner's to his, in this familiar Wagnerian text describing the poet's relation to "endless melody": "in it you will be voicing what I leave unsaid, for only you can say it; while I, in my silence, will still be saying it all, because it is your hand I am guiding." ("Saying it all" seems apt,

---

[83] See, for example, my essay "Metaphorical Modes," and Arno Forchert's "'Ästhetischer' Eindruck," cited in chapter 1, n. 15. Forchert develops the argument that the programmatic practices of the mid- and later nineteenth century can be seen as a product of listening habits that were already entrenched by the beginning of the century and thus helped to determine the character of a repertoire that would better meet their expectations. We might recall Schindler's claim that audiences read Beethoven's symphonies as *verkappte Opern*, or "operas in disguise." A contemporary review of Lenz's first Beethoven book notes that "one used to go to great lengths in explicating Beethoven's works, especially the symphonies, in words, even reading whole novels into them (*ihnen geradezu vollständige Romane unterzulegen*)" (J. Schäffer, "W. v. Lenz, *Beethoven et ses trois styles*," *Neue Berliner Musikzeitung* 7 [1853], 97). As late as 1891 Chrysander could still maintain that the themes of Beethoven's symphonies act like "personal leitmotifs" – whatever he meant by that (see A. Schering, *Beethoven und die Dichtung*, 83).

if silence does not.) Wagner would readily admit, he spoke most when his prose voice was silent and he composed instead. But the positions outlined in Wagner's writings have guided operatic criticism to a remarkable extent, from his time to our own, even as they inevitably reflect the concerns of the larger musical culture in which he participated. And few can be said to have guided the hand of their entire culture to the extent that Wagner did, whether by persuasion or by mere persistence, through his words and music alike.

Appendix 1

The "poetic-musical period"
(from *Opera and Drama*, Part III, section 3)

[152][1] Alliterative verse [*Stabreim*], as we have seen, already connects speech roots of varied or contrasted expression (such as *Lust* and *Leid*, *Wohl* and *Weh*) so as to make the connection audible to our sense of hearing, and in this way also presents these roots to the feeling as generically related. Imagine, then, to what greater degree of expression these connections can be made sensually perceptible to our feeling with the help of musical modulation. Let us take for example a line of *Stabreim* containing a perfectly unified range of expression: *Liebe gibt Lust zum Leben* [love gives pleasure to life]. Since the alliteration of accented syllables in this line is matched by a perfect congruity of emotional content, the musician would have no occasion to depart from his initially chosen tonality in setting these words; a fully adequate musical setting would need to take account only of the strong and weak syllables, while remaining within a single key, appropriate to the emotional unity of the text. If, on the other hand, we take a line of mixed emotional significance, such as *die Liebe bringt Lust und Leid* [love brings pleasure and sorrow], the musician would need to match the contrasting emotions of the alliterated words by modulating from his original tonality into a contrasting, related one appropriate to the contrasting sense of the final word. The word *Lust*, representing the furthest extreme of the original emotion, seems to press across to the contrasting emotion, and it would acquire in our new phrase an entirely different emphasis than it had in the original line, *Liebe gibt Lust zum Leben*: the note to which the word *Lust* is sung would naturally tend to function as a leading-tone [*Leitton*], determining and necessarily drawing us into the new tonality appropriate to the expression of sorrow [*Leid*]. In their relative positions, *Lust* and *Leid* would be enabled to communicate a particular emotion, the peculiar nature of which would result precisely from their point of contact, the point at which two opposed feelings are represented as mutually conditioned by and thus as related to one another, necessarily belonging together. [153] This kinship can only be communicated through music and its capacity for harmonic modulation, by means of which it exercises a compelling force on our senses and feelings attainable through no other art.

---

[1] The approximate corresponding pagination of the text in the *Sämtliche Schriften*, vol. IV, has been indicated throughout the following translation.

Appendix 1

— Let us consider first how the musical modulation, in conjunction with the poetic verse, is able to lead back to the original feeling. — Suppose that our original line, *die Liebe gibt Lust zum Leben*, were to be followed by a second line: *doch in ihr Weh auch webt sie Wonnen* [but with its pain, it weaves also delight]. Here the word "weaves" [*webt*] would correspond to the leading-tone of the original key, as the second, contrasting emotion would at this point return to the original, yet now enriched key. The poet, by means of his *Stabreim*, can only represent this return to our sensible and emotional faculties as a unified progression from pain [*Weh*] to delight [*Wonnen*], but not as a return to the genus of feeling originally represented by the word "love." The musician, on the other hand, can intelligibly connect the whole pair of lines by returning to the original key, distinctly indicating the familial relationship between the contrasting emotions – an impossibility for the poet, who must continually alternate the alliterative syllables of his *Stabreim*. — The poet indicates such a familial relationship only through the *meaning* of his verse: he still longs to realize this connection for the feelings, and this is precisely the task he sets for the musician [*den verwirklichenden Musiker*]. The musician's procedures would remain unconditioned, and therefore arbitrary and unintelligible, if they were not justified in this way, through the intent of the poet – an intent which the poet himself can only suggest or at best hope to realize in fragmentary fashion through his *Stabreim*. The complete realization of this [poetic] intent is only possible for the musician, in his capacity to apply the inner relation of all notes and tonalities [through modulation] to the perfectly unified communication of the original related emotions to our feeling.

We can best picture for ourselves how immeasurably great is this capacity of the musician if we imagine the content of the above two-line example expanded to a larger scale: suppose that after leaving the original emotion of the first line, instead of returning to it already in the second line, a long series of other lines were to intervene, expressing the most varied [154] intensification and mixture of intermediate emotional stages – some stronger, some more conciliatory – before finally returning to the affective point of departure [*Hauptempfindung*]. In order to realize the poetic intent of these lines the musical setting would modulate through the most varied tonalities; yet every key touched on would appear in its specific relation to the original key, which would condition the particular expressive light shed by these various other tonalities, to some extent making that light possible in the first place. The tonic key [*Haupttonart*], as the foundation of the initially represented emotion, would reveal its original relation to all other keys. For the length of its duration this tonic key would also communicate a determinate emotion in its fullest dimensions; our feeling would be affected only by this emotion and anything relating to it, by means of its expanded scope, and this particular emotion would thereby be raised to an all-encompassing, universally human and unfailingly perceptible level.

In this, we have described the poetic-musical period, as it is determined by a single principal tonality. On that basis, we could provisionally describe the most perfect art-work, viewed as a vehicle of expression, as that in which many such periods are presented in rich profusion, such that each is conditioned by the next in the realization of the highest poetic intent, evolving into a rich overall manifestation of human nature, distinctly and surely communicated to

376

our feeling; this evolution proceeds so as to embrace all aspects of human nature, just as the principal key may be understood to embrace all other possible keys. Such an art-work is the complete drama. In it, the all-embracing human element is communicated to our feeling in a consequential, well-determined series of emotional components [*Gefühlsmomenten*] of such strength and conviction that the action of the drama seems to grow out of all this of its own accord – [155] as the natural product of this rich set of conditions – into a larger, instinctively unified entity [*zu einem umfassenden Gesamtmotiv*], and perfectly intelligible as such.

Before we proceed from the character of the poetic-musical melodic period to examine its effect on the drama, as that emerges from the mutually conditioned evolution of many such necessary periods, we must first determine the factor that conditions the individual melodic period and its expressive value according to the capacity of pure music – and that therefore provides us with the organ of immense connective power essential to the very existence of our complete drama. If we are prepared to bestow on harmony the fullest participation in the creation of the whole art-work we will find this organ generated from its vertical expansion – as I have already referred to it – upwards from its foundations.

[end of Part III, section 3]

Appendix 2

Principal writings of Richard Wagner cited in the text[1]

Date / title, GSD, SSD (translation, PW)

1840 "Über deutsches Musikwesen" (orig. pub. as "De la musique allemande"), I, 149–66 ("On German Music," PW VII, 83–101)

1840 (or 1837–?) "Über Meyerbeers *Huguenotten*," XII, 22–30

1840 "Eine Pilgerfahrt zu Beethoven" (orig. pub. as "Une visite à Beethoven: épisode de la vie d'un musicien allemand"), I, 90–114 ("A Pilgrimage to Beethoven," PW VII, 21–45)

1841 "Über die Ouvertüre" (orig. pub. as "De l'ouverture"), I, 194–206 ("On the Overture," PW VII, 151–65)

1841 "Ein glücklicher Abend" (orig. pub. as "Une soirée heureuse"), I, 136–49 ("A Happy Evening," PW VII, 69–81)

1846 "Programm zur 9. Symphonie Beethovens," II, 56–64; see also XII, 205–7 ("Programme for Beethoven's Ninth Symphony," PW VII, 247–55; see also PW VIII, 201–3)

1849 *Die Kunst und die Revolution*, III, 8–41 (*Art and Revolution*, PW I, 21–65)

1849 (pub. 1850) *Das Kunstwerk der Zukunft*, III, 42–177 (*The Art-Work of the Future*, PW I, 67–213)

1850 "Das Judenthum in der Musik," V, 66–85 ("Judaism in Music," PW III, 79–100)

1850–1 (pub. 1852) *Oper und Drama*, III, 222–320; IV, 1–229 (*Opera and Drama*, PW II, 1–376)

1851 (pub. 1852) "Beethovens 'heroische Symphonie'" (programmatische Erläuterung), V, 169–72 ("Beethoven's *Eroica* Symphony [programmatic commentary]", PW III, 221–4)

[1] Volume and page numbers (as in the body of the text) refer to Wagner, *Sämtliche Schriften und Dichtungen* (SSD), vols. I–XVI (Leipzig, 1911–16). Volumes I–X are equivalent to the *Gesammelte Schriften und Dichtungen* (GSD), vols. I–X (2nd edn, Leipzig, 1887). PW indicates volume and page numbers for the corresponding translation in William Ashton Ellis, *Richard Wagner's Prose Works*, vols. I–VIII (London, 1892–9). Alternative published translations are cited in the main text. For an extensive list of Wagner's published writings, with original publication information, see Jean-Jacques Nattiez, *Wagner Androgyne*, trans. Stewart Spencer (Princeton, 1993), 303–22.

378

Principal writings cited in the text

1851 *Eine Mittheilung an meine Freunde,* IV, 230–344 (*A Communication to My Friends,* PW I, 267–392)

1852 "Beethoven's Ouvertüre zu 'Koriolan'" (programmatische Erläuterung), V, 173–6 ("Beethoven's Overture to *Coriolans*" [programmatic commentary], PW III, 225–8)

1854 "Glucks Ouvertüre zu 'Iphigenie in Aulis': Eine Mittheilung an den Redakteur der 'Neuen Zeitschrift für Musik'," V, 111–22 ("Gluck's Overture to *Iphigénie en Aulide*: A Communication to the Editor of the *Neue Zeitschrift für Musik*," PW 153–66)

1854 "Beethovens Cis moll-Quartett (op. 131)," XII, 350 ("Beethoven's C♯-minor Quartet, op. 131," PW VIII, 350)

1857 "Über Franz Liszts symphonische Dichtungen (Brief an M[arie] W[ittgenstein])," V, 182–98 ("On Franz Liszt's Symphonic Poems" [letter to Marie Wittgenstein]," PW III, 235–54)

1860 (pub. 1861) "*Zukunftsmusik*" (orig. *Quatre poèmes d'opéra traduits en prose français précédés d'une lettre sur la musique par Richard Wagner*), VII, 87–137 ("*Music of the Future*," PW III, 293–345)

1868 "Meine Erinnerungen an Ludwig Schnorr von Carolsfeld," VIII, 177–94 ("My Recollections of Ludwig Schnorr von Carolsfeld," PW IV, 225–43)

1869 *Über das Dirigieren,* VIII, 261–337 (*On Conducting,* PW IV, 289–364)

1870 *Beethoven,* IX, 61–126 (PW V, 57–126)

1871 "Über die Bestimmung der Oper," IX, 127–56 ("On the Destiny of Opera," PW V, 127–55)

1872 *Über Schauspieler und Sänger,* IX, 157–230 (*On Actors and Singers,* PW V, 157–228)

1872 "Über die Benennung 'Musikdrama'," IX, 302–8 ("On the Designation 'Music-Drama'," PW V, 299–304)

1878 "Modern," X, 54–60 (PW VI, 41–9)

1879 "Über das Dichten und Komponieren," X, 137–51 ("On Poetry and Composition," PW VI, 131–47)

1879 "Über das Opern-Dichten und Komponieren im Besonderen," X, 152–75 ("On Operatic Poetry and Composition in Particular," PW VI, 149–72)

1879 "Über die Anwendung der Musik auf das Drama," X, 176–93 ("On the Application of Music to the Drama," PW VI, 173–91)

1880 "Religion und Kunst," X, 211–53 ("Religion and Art," PW VI, 211–52)

1882 "Über das Männliche und Weibliche in Kultur und Kunst," in *Das braune Buch: Tagebuchaufzeichnungen 1865–1882,* ed. Joachim Bergfeld (Zurich, 1975), 245–6 (trans. George Bird, *The Diary of Richard Wagner 1865–1882: The Brown Book* [London, 1980], 204)

[1865–80; orig. pub. 1911] *Mein Leben,* ed. Martin Gregor-Dellin (Munich, 1963; 2nd edn, 1976) (*My Life,* trans. Andrew Gray and ed. Mary Whittall [Cambridge, 1983])

Bibliography

(Periodical literature before c. 1900 is not included in the bibliography.)

Abbate, Carolyn. "Opera as Symphony, a Wagnerian Myth." In *Analyzing Opera: Verdi and Wagner*, ed. C. Abbate and R. Parker, 92–124. Berkeley and Los Angeles: University of California Press, 1989

Unsung Voices: Opera and Musical Narrative in the Nineteenth Century. Princeton: Princeton University Press, 1991

"Wagner, 'On Modulation,' and *Tristan*." *Cambridge Opera Journal* 1:1 (1989), 33–58

and Roger Parker. "Dismembering Mozart." *Cambridge Opera Journal* 2:2 (1990), 187–95

Abegg, Werner. *Musikästhetik und Musikkritik bei Eduard Hanslick*. Regensburg: Bosse, 1974

Ackermann, Peter. "Absolute Musik und Programmusik: Zur Theorie der Instrumentalmusik bei Liszt und Wagner." In *Liszt-Studien* 3, ed. Serge Gut, 21–7. Munich and Salzburg: Emil Katzbichler, 1986

Adler, Guido. *Richard Wagner: Vorlesungen*. 2nd edn, Munich: Drei Masken Verlag, 1923

Adorno, Theodor W. *Aesthetic Theory*, trans. C. Lenhardt, ed. G. Adorno and R. Tiedemann. London: Routledge and Kegan Paul, 1984

In Search of Wagner (*Versuch über Wagner*, 1952), trans. Rodney Livingstone. Manchester: NLB, 1981

Allfeld, J. B. *Tristan und Isolde von Richard Wagner – Kritisch beleuchtet mit einleitenden Bemerkungen über Melodie und Musik*. Munich: C. Fritzsch, 1865

Ambros, August Wilhelm. *Culturhistorische Bilder aus dem Musikleben der Gegenwart*. Leipzig: Matthes, 1860; 2nd edn, 1865

Die Grenzen der Musik und Poesie: Eine Studie zur Ästhetik der Tonkunst. Leipzig: Matthes, 1855/6; rpt Hildesheim: Georg Olms, 1976

Bailey, Robert. "The Genesis of *Tristan und Isolde*: A Study of Wagner's Sketches and Drafts for the First Act." Ph.D. dissertation, Princeton University, 1969

"The Method of Composition." In *The Wagner Companion*, ed. P. Burbidge and R. Sutton, 269–338. New York: Cambridge University Press, 1979

"Wagner's Musical Sketches for *Siegfrieds Tod*." In *Studies in Music History: Essays for Oliver Strunk*, ed. Harold Powers, 459–94. Princeton: Princeton University Press, 1968

(ed.). *Richard Wagner: Prelude and Transfiguration from "Tristan und Isolde."* New York: Norton, 1985

Bibliography

Barzun, Jacques. *Berlioz and the Romantic Century*. 2 vols. New York: Columbia University Press, 1969

Darwin, Marx, Wagner. New York: Random House, 1941; 2nd edn, 1958

Battersby, Christine. *Gender and Genius: Towards a Feminist Aesthetics*. London: Women's Press, 1989

Bekker, Paul. *Richard Wagner: His Life and Work*, trans. M. M. Bozman. New York: W. W. Norton, 1931; rpt Westport: Greenwood Press, 1971

Berlioz, Hector. *A travers chants*. Paris: Michel-Lévy frères, 1862

Bonds, Mark Evan. *Wordless Rhetoric: Musical Form and the Metaphor of the Oration*. Cambridge MA: Harvard University Press, 1991

Borchmeyer, Dieter. *Richard Wagner: Theory and Theatre*, trans. Stewart Spencer. Oxford: Clarendon Press, 1991

Brendel, Franz. *Geschichte der Musik in Italien, Deutschland und Frankreich*. Leipzig: Breitkopf & Härtel, 1851; 5th edn, 1875 (2nd through 4th edns revised)

Die Musik der Gegenwart und die Gesammtkunst der Zukunft. Leipzig: Hinze, 1854

Buelow, George. "The Concept of *Melodielehre*: A Key to Classic Style." In *Mozart Jahrbuch 1978–9*, 191–7. Cassel: Bärenreiter, 1979

Bülow, Hans von. *Ausgewählte Schriften: 1850–1892*, ed. Marie von Bülow (= vol. III of *Briefe und Schriften*). Leipzig: Breitkopf & Härtel, 1896.

Bujic, Bojan, ed. *Music in European Thought 1851–1912*. Cambridge: Cambridge University Press, 1988

Burnham, Scott. "Criticism, Faith, and the *Idee*: A. B. Marx's Early Reception of Beethoven." *19th-Century Music* 13:3 (Spring 1990), 183–92

"On the Programmatic Reception of Beethoven's *Eroica* Symphony." *Beethoven Forum* 1 (1992), 1–24

Cone, Edward T. *The Composer's Voice*. Berkeley and Los Angeles: University of California Press, 1974

Music: A View from Delft (selected essays), ed. Robert P. Morgan. Chicago: University of Chicago Press, 1989

Cooke, Deryck. *I Saw the World End*. Oxford: Oxford University Press, 1979

"Wagner's Musical Language." In *The Wagner Companion*, ed. P. Burbidge and R. Sutton, 225–68. New York: Cambridge University Press, 1979

Cusick, Suzanne G. "Gendering Modern Music: Thoughts on the Monteverdi-Artusi Controversy." *Journal of the American Musicological Society* 46:1 (Spring 1993), 1–25

Dahlhaus, Carl. *Between Romanticism and Modernism: Four Studies in the Music of the Later Nineteenth Century*, trans. Mary Whittall and Arnold Whittall. Berkeley and Los Angeles: University of California Press, 1980

"Eduard Hanslick und der musikalische Formbegriff." *Die Musikforschung* 20 (1967), 145–53

Esthetics of Music, trans. William Austin. Cambridge: Cambridge University Press, 1982

"E. T. A. Hoffmanns Beethoven-Kritik und die Ästhetik des Erhabenen." *Archiv für Musikwissenschaft* 38:2 (1981), 79–92

"Formprinzipien in Wagners *Ring des Nibelungen*." In *Beiträge zur Geschichte der Oper*, ed. Heinz Becker, 95–130. Regensburg: Bosse, 1969

The Idea of Absolute Music, trans. Roger Lustig. Chicago: University of Chicago Press, 1989

Bibliography

Klassische und romantische Musikästhetik (collected essays on musical aesthetics). Laaber: Laaber-Verlag, 1988

Ludwig van Beethoven: Approaches to his Music, trans. Mary Whittall. Oxford: Clarendon Press, 1991

Die Musiktheorie im 18. und 19. Jahrhundert, vol. I. Darmstadt: Wissenschaftliche Buchgesellschaft, 1984

Nineteenth-Century Music, trans. J. Bradford Robinson. Berkeley and Los Angeles: University of California Press, 1989

Realismus in der Musik des 19. Jahrhunderts. Munich: Piper, 1982. (*Realism in Nineteenth-Century Music*, trans. Mary Whittall. Cambridge: Cambridge University Press, 1985)

Richard Wagner's Music Dramas, trans. Mary Whittall. Cambridge: Cambridge University Press, 1979

"Tonalität und Form in Wagners *Ring des Nibelungen.*" *Archiv für Musikwissenschaft* 40 (1983), 165–73

"Wagners Begriff der 'dichterisch-musikalischen Periode'." In *Beiträge zur Geschichte der Musikanschauung im 19. Jahrhundert*, ed. Walter Salmen, 179–94. Regensburg: Bosse, 1965

"Wagners dramatisch-musikalischer Formbegriff." *Analecta musicologica* 11 (1972), 290–303

Wagners Konzeption des musikalischen Dramas. Regensburg: Bosse, 1971

"Wagners 'Kunst des Übergangs': Der Zwiegesang in *Tristan und Isolde.*" In *Zur musikalischen Analyse*, ed. G. Schuhmacher, 475–86. Darmstadt: Wissenschaftliche Buchgesellschaft, 1974

"Der Wahn-Monolog des Hans Sachs und das Problem der Entwicklungsform im musikalischen Drama." *Jahrbuch für Opernforschung* 1 (1985), 9–25

"Zur Geschichte der Leitmotivtechnik bei Wagner." In *Das Drama Richard Wagners als musikalisches Kunstwerk*, ed. C. Dahlhaus, 17–36. Regensburg: Bosse, 1970

"Zur Wirkungsgeschichte von Beethovens Symphonien." In *Gattungen der Musik und ihre Klassiker*, ed. Hermann Danuser, 221–33. Laaber: Laaber-Verlag, 1988

and John Deathridge. *The New Grove Wagner*. New York: Norton, 1984

Danuser, Hermann. "Das imprévu in der Symphonik: Aspekte einer musikalischen Formkategorie in der Zeit von C. P. E. Bach bis Hector Berlioz." *Musiktheorie* 1 (1986), 62–81

Musikalische Prosa. Regensburg: Bosse, 1975

and F. Krummacher (eds.). *Rezeptionsästhetik und Rezeptionsgeschichte in der Musikwissenschaft*. Laaber: Laaber-Verlag, 1991

Daverio, John. *Nineteenth-Century Music and the German Romantic Ideology*. New York: Schirmer Books, 1993

Deathridge, John. "Wagner and the Post-modern." *Cambridge Opera Journal* 4:2 (July 1992), 143–61

with Martin Geck and Egon Voss. *Verzeichnis der musikalischen Werke Richard Wagners* (WWV). Mainz: Schott, 1986

see also Dahlhaus, Carl. *The New Grove Wagner*

Derrida, Jacques. *Of Grammatology*, trans. Gayatri Chakravorty Spivak. Baltimore and London: Johns Hopkins University Press, 1976

Bibliography

Dijkstra, Bram. *Idols of Perversity: Fantasies of Feminine Evil in Fin-de-Siècle Culture.* Oxford and New York: Oxford University Press, 1986

Dömling, Wolfgang. *Hector Berlioz und seine Zeit.* Laaber: Laaber-Verlag, 1986

Donington, Robert. *Wagner's "Ring" and its Symbols.* London: Faber and Faber, 1963

Doob, Penelope. *The Idea of the Labyrinth from Antiquity through the Middle Ages.* Ithaca: Cornell University Press, 1990

Eco, Umberto. *Interpretation and Overinterpretation.* Cambridge: Cambridge University Press, 1992

Elterlein, Ernst von [pseud. of Ernst Gottschald]. *Beethovens Symphonien nach ihrem idealen Gehalt.* Dresden: Adolph Bauer, 1854; 3rd edn, 1870

Evans, Edwin. *Wagner's Teachings by Analogy. His Views on Absolute Music and of the Relations of Articulate and Tonal Speech, with Special Reference to "Opera and Drama."* London: William Reeves, n.d.

Finck, Henry T. *Wagner and his Works.* 2 vols. New York: Charles Scribner's Sons, 1897

Forchert, Arno. "'Ästhetischer' Eindruck und kompositionstechnische Analyse: Zwei Ebenen musikalischer Rezeption in der ersten Hälfte des 19. Jahrhunderts." In *Rezeptionsästhetik und Rezeptionsgeschichte,* ed. H. Danuser and F. Krummacher, 193–203. Laaber: Laaber-Verlag, 1991

Franke, Rainer. *Richard Wagners Zürcher Kunstschriften.* Hamburg: Wagner, 1983

Freud, Sigmund. "The 'Uncanny'." In *On Creativity and the Unconscious,* ed. Benjamin Nelson, 122–61. New York: Harper and Row, 1958

Gatz, Felix. *Musikästhetik in ihren Hauptrichtungen: Ein Quellenbuch der deutschen Musikästhetik von Kant und der Frühromantik bis zur Gegenwart.* Stuttgart, 1929

Gay, Peter. *The Bourgeois Experience: Victoria to Freud.* Vol. I, *Education of the Senses;* vol. II, *The Tender Passion.* New York: Oxford University Press, 1984, 1986

Geck, Martin, and Peter Schleuning. *"Geschrieben auf Bonaparte." Beethovens "Eroica": Revolution, Reaktion, Rezeption.* Hamburg: Rowohlt, 1989

Glasenapp, C. F. *Das Leben Richard Wagners.* 6 vols. Leipzig: Breitkopf & Härtel, 1894–1911

Glass, Frank W. *The Fertilizing Seed: Wagner's Concept of the Poetic Intent.* Ann Arbor: UMI Research Press, 1983

Glatt, Dorothea. *Zur geschichtlichen Bedeutung der Musikästhetik Eduard Hanslicks.* Munich and Salzburg: Katzbichler, 1972

Gregor-Dellin, Martin. *Richard Wagner: Sein Leben, Sein Werk, Sein Jahrhundert.* Munich: R. Piper, 1980. (*Richard Wagner: His Life, His Work, His Century,* trans. J. Maxwell Brownjohn. New York: Harcourt Brace Jovanovich, 1983)

Grey, Thomas S. "Leading Motives and Narrative Threads: Notes on the *Leitfaden* Metaphor and the Critical Pre-history of the Wagnerian *Leitmotiv*." In *Bericht über den Kongress der Gesellschaft für Musikforschung, "Musik als Text"* (Freiburg, 1993), forthcoming

"Metaphorical Modes in Nineteenth-Century Music Criticism: Image, Narrative, and 'Idea'." In *Music and Text: Critical Inquiries,* ed. Steven P. Scher, 93–117. Cambridge: Cambridge University Press, 1992

"Richard Wagner and the Aesthetics of Musical Form in the Mid-Nineteenth Century (1840–60)." Ph.D. dissertation, University of California, Berkeley, 1988

Bibliography

"Wagner, the Overture, and the Aesthetics of Musical Form.'" *19th-Century Music* 12:1 (Summer 1988), 3–22

"A Wagnerian Glossary." In *The Wagner Compendium*, ed. Barry Millington, 230–41. London: Thames & Hudson, 1992

"Wagner's *Lohengrin*, Between *grand opéra* and *Musikdrama*." In *Lohengrin*, ed. Nicholas John, 15–31. London: John Calder, 1993

Grunsky, Karl. "Wagner als Symphoniker." *Richard Wagner-Jahrbuch* 1 (1906), 227–44

Hanslick, Eduard. *Die moderne Oper*, vol. I. Berlin: A. Hofmann & Co., 1875

Vienna's Golden Years of Music (selected music criticism), trans. Henry Pleasants. New York: Alfred Knopf, 1950

Vom Musikalisch-Schönen: Ein Beitrag zur Revision der Ästhetik der Tonkunst. Leipzig: Matthes, 1854; rpt Darmstadt: Wissenschaftliches Buchgesellschaft, 1981. (*On the Musically Beautiful*, trans. and ed. Geoffrey Payzant. Indianapolis: Hackett, 1986)

see also Dietmar Strauß, *Eduard Hanslick: Vom Musikalisch-Schönen*

Hegel, G. W. F. *Werke*, ed. Eva Moldenhauer and Karl Markus Michel. 20 vols. Frankfurt: Suhrkamp, 1969–71

Hepokoski, James. "The Dahlhaus Project and its Extra-Musicological Sources." *19th-Century Music* 14:3 (Spring 1991), 221–46

Herder, J. G. *On the Origin of Language* (*Über den Ursprung der Sprache*, 1772). In *On the Origin of Language: Two Essays*, ed. and trans. Alexander Gode and John Moran. Chicago: University of Chicago Press, 1966

Hinrichs, Friedrich. *Richard Wagner und die neuere Musik. Eine Skizze aus der musikalischen Gegenwart.* Halle: Schrödel & Simon, 1854

Hoffmann, E. T. A. *Schriften zur Musik*, ed. Friedrich Schnapp. Munich: Winkler, 1977

Hollier, Denis (ed.). *A New History of French Literature*. Cambridge MA: Harvard University Press, 1989

Holoman, D. Kern. *Berlioz*. Cambridge, MA: Harvard University Press, 1990

Holub, Robert. *Reception Theory: A Critical Introduction*. New York and London: Routledge, 1984

Horowitz, M. C. (ed.) *Race, Class, and Gender in Nineteenth-Century Culture*. Rochester NY: University of Rochester Press, 1991

Hostinsky, Ottokar. *Das Musikalisch-Schöne und das Gesamtkunstwerk vom Standpuncte der formalen Aesthetik.* Leipzig: Breitkopf & Härtel, 1877

Hueffer, Franz (Francis). *Richard Wagner and the Music of the Future. History and Aesthetics.* London: Chapman and Hall, 1874

Jacobs, Robert L. (ed. and trans.). *Three Wagner Essays*. London: Eulenberg, 1979. ("*Music of the Future*," "*On Conducting*," and "*On Performing Beethoven's 9th Symphony*")

and Geoffrey Skelton (eds. and trans.). *Wagner Writes from Paris . . . (Stories, Essays and Articles by the Young Composer)*. London: Allen & Unwin, 1973

Jahn, Otto. *Gesammelte Aufsätze über Musik.* 2nd edn, Leipzig: Breitkopf & Härtel, 1867

Kamuf, Peggy. "Origins (1754? Rousseau Writes His *Essai sur l'origine des langues*)." In *A New History of French Literature*, ed. Denis Hollier, 455–60. Cambridge MA: Harvard University Press, 1989

Bibliography

Kerman, Joseph. *The Beethoven Quartets.* New York: Alfred A. Knopf, 1967
Opera as Drama. New York: Vintage, 1956; 2nd edn, Berkeley and Los Angeles: University of California Press, 1988
"Taking the Fifth." In *Das musikalische Kunstwerk: Festschrift Carl Dahlhaus zum 60. Geburtstag,* ed. Hermann Danuser, et al., 483–90. Laaber: Laaber-Verlag, 1988
Kivy, Peter. "Opera Talk: A Philosophical 'Phantasie'." *Cambridge Opera Journal* 3 (1991), 63–77
Köhler, Louis. *Die Melodie der Sprache.* Leipzig: J. J. Weber, 1853
Die neue Richtung in der Musik. Leipzig: J. J. Weber, 1864
Kramer, Lawrence. "Culture and Musical Hermeneutics: The Salome Complex." *Cambridge Opera Journal* 2:3 (1990), 269–94
Music and Poetry: The Nineteenth Century and After. Berkeley and Los Angeles: University of California Press, 1984
Music as Cultural Practice, 1800–1900. Berkeley and Los Angeles: University of California Press, 1990
Kropfinger, Klaus. *Wagner und Beethoven: Studien zur Beethoven-Rezeption Richard Wagners.* Regensburg: Bosse, 1974. (*Wagner and Beethoven: Richard Wagner's Reception of Beethoven,* trans. Peter Palmer. Cambridge: Cambridge University Press, 1991)
Kullak, Adolph. *Das Musikalisch-Schöne: Ein Beitrag zur Ästhetik der Tonkunst.* Leipzig: Matthes, 1858
Kunze, Stefan. "Über Melodiebegriff und musikalischen Bau in Wagners Musikdrama." In *Das Drama Richard Wagners als musikalisches Kunstwerk,* ed. Carl Dahlhaus, 111–44. Regensburg: Bosse, 1970
(ed.). *Ludwig van Beethoven: Die Werke im Spiegel seiner Zeit.* Laaber: Laaber-Verlag, 1987
Kurth, Ernst. *Romantische Harmonik und ihre Krise in Wagners "Tristan."* 2nd edn, Berlin, 1923; rpt Hildesheim: Georg Olms, 1975
LaCapra, Dominick and Steven L. Kaplan (eds). *Modern European Intellectual History: Reappraisals and New Perspectives.* Ithaca: Cornell University Press, 1982
Laqueur, Thomas. *Making Sex: Body and Gender from the Greeks to Freud.* Cambridge MA: Harvard University Press, 1990
"Orgasm, Generation, and the Politics of Reproductive Biology." In *The Making of the Modern Body: Sexuality and Society in the Nineteenth Century,* ed. C. Gallagher and T. Laqueur, 1–41. Berkeley and Los Angeles: University of California Press, 1987
Lenz, Wilhelm von. *Beethoven: Eine Kunststudie.* 4 vols. Cassel: Ernst Balde, 1855–60.
Beethoven et ses trois styles (1852). Paris: G. Legouix, 1909; rpt New York: Da Capo, 1982
Leppert, Richard and Susan McClary (eds.). *Music and Society: The Politics of Composition, Performance and Reception.* Cambridge: Cambridge University Press, 1987
Lester, Joel. *Compositional Theory in the Eighteenth Century.* Cambridge MA: Harvard University Press, 1992
Lippmann, Friedrich. "Ein neuentdecktes Autograph Richard Wagners: Rezension der Königsberger 'Norma'-Aufführung von 1837." In *Musicæ*

scientiæ collectanea: Festschrift für Karl Gustav Fellerer, ed. Heinrich Hüschen, 373–9. Cologne: Arno Volk Verlag, 1973

Liszt, Franz. *Gesammelte Schriften über Musik*, ed. Lina Ramann. 6 vols. Leipzig: Breitkopf & Härtel, 1880–3

Lohengrin et Tannhäuser de Richard Wagner. Leipzig: F. A. Brockhaus, 1851

Lobe, Johann Christian. *Compositions-Lehre oder umfassende Theorie der thematischen Arbeit und der modernen Instrumentalformen* (1844). Rpt Hildesheim: G. Olms, 1988

Consonanzen und Dissonanzen. Leipzig: Baumgartner, 1869

Musikalische Briefe. Wahrheit über Tonkunst und Tonkünstler, von einem Wohlbekannten. Leipzig: Baumgartner, 1852; 2nd edn, 1860

Musikalische Compositionslehre. Leipzig, 1844

Lorenz, Alfred. *Das Geheimnis der Form bei Richard Wagner*. 4 vols. Berlin: Max Hessses Verlag, 1924–33; rpt Tutzing: Hans Schneider, 1966

Magee, Elizabeth. *Richard Wagner and the Nibelungs*. Oxford: Clarendon Press, 1991

Mann, Thomas. *Pro and Contra Wagner* (*Wagner und unsere Zeit* [1963], trans. Allan Blunden. Chicago and London: University of Chicago Press, 1985

Marx, Adolf Bernhard. *Die Lehre von der musikalischen Komposition, praktisch-theoretisch*. 4 vols. Leipzig: Breitkopf & Härtel, 1837–47

Ludwig van Beethoven: Leben und Schaffen. 2 vols. Berlin, 1859; Leipzig: Adolf Schumann, 1902

Die Musik des neunzehnten Jahrhunderts und ihre Pflege. Leipzig: Breitkopf & Härtel, 1855; 2nd edn, 1873

Maus, Fred E. "Hanslick's Animism." *Journal of Musicology* 10:3 (1992), 273–92

"Music as Drama." *Music Theory Spectrum* 10 (1988), 56–73

McClary, Susan. *Feminine Endings: Music, Gender, and Sexuality*. Minneapolis: University of Minnesota Press, 1991

"Narrative Agendas in 'Absolute Music': Identity and Difference in Brahms' Third Symphony." In *Musicology and Difference: Gender and Sexuality in Music Scholarship*, ed. Ruth A. Solie, 326–44. Berkeley and Los Angeles: University of California Press, 1993

see also Richard Leppert, *Music and Society*

McClatchie, Stephen. "The Warrior Foil'd: Alfred Lorenz's Wagner Analyses." *Wagner* 11:1 (January 1990), 3–12

McCreless, Patrick. "Schenker and the Norns." In *Analyzing Opera: Verdi and Wagner*, ed. C. Abbate and R. Parker, 276–97. Berkeley and Los Angeles: University of California Press, 1989

Wagner's "Siegfried": Its Drama, History, and Music. Ann Arbor: UMI Research Press, 1982

McGann, Jerome J. *The Romantic Ideology: A Critical Investigation*. Chicago and London: University of Chicago Press, 1983

Miller, J. Hillis. *Ariadne's Thread: Story Lines*. New Haven: Yale University Press, 1992

Millington, Barry. "Nuremberg Trial: Is there Anti-Semitism in *Die Meistersinger*?" *Cambridge Opera Journal* 3:3 (1991), 247–60

Wagner. Princeton: Princeton University Press, 1992

(ed.). *The Wagner Compendium*. London: Thames and Hudson; New York: Schirmer Books, 1992

Moos, Paul. *Richard Wagner als Ästhetiker: Versuch einer kritischen Darstellung.*
Berlin and Leipzig: Schuster & Loeffler, 1906

Müller, Franz. *Tristan und Isolde nach Sage und Dichtung.* Munich: Christian
Kaiser, 1865

Müller, Ulrich and Peter Wapnewski (eds.). *Wagner Handbuch.* Stuttgart: Kröner,
1986. (*Wagner Handbook*, trans. and ed. John Deathridge. Cambridge, MA:
Harvard University Press, 1992)

Nägeli, Hans Georg. *Vorlesungen über Musik mit Berücksichtigung der Dilettanten.*
Stuttgart and Tübingen: Cotta, 1826; rpt Hildesheim: Georg Olms, 1976

Nattiez, Jean-Jacques. *Wagner Androgyne*, trans. Stewart Spencer. Princeton:
Princeton University Press, 1993

Neubauer, John. *The Emancipation of Music from Language: Departure from Mimesis
in Eighteenth-Century Aesthetics.* New Haven: Yale University Press, 1986

Newcomb, Anthony. "The Birth of Music out of the Spirit of Drama: An Essay in
Wagnerian Formal Analysis." *19th-Century Music* 5 (1981), 38–66

  "*Ritornello ritornato*: A Variety of Wagnerian Refrain Form." In *Analyzing
Opera: Verdi and Wagner*, ed. Carolyn Abbate and Roger Parker, 202–21.
Berkeley and Los Angeles: University of California Press, 1989

  "Schumann and Late Eighteenth-Century Narrative Strategies." *19th-Century
Music* 11:2 (1987), 164–74

  "Those Images that Yet Fresh Images Beget." *Journal of Musicology* 2 (1983),
227–45

Newman, Ernest. *The Life of Richard Wagner.* 4 vols. New York: Alfred Knopf,
1933–46; rpt Cambridge: Cambridge University Press, 1976

  Wagner as Man and Artist. New York: Alfred Knopf, 2nd edn, 1924

  The Wagner Operas. New York: Alfred Knopf, 1949; rpt 2 vols. New York:
Harper, 1983

Nietzsche, Friedrich. *The Birth of Tragedy and The Case of Wagner*, trans. with
commentary by Walter Kaufmann. New York: Vintage, 1967

  Der Fall Wagner. Schriften und Aufzeichnungen über Richard Wagner, ed. with
afterword by Dieter Borchmeyer. Frankfurt: Insel Verlag, 1983

  "Nietzsche contra Wagner." In *The Portable Nietzsche*, ed. and trans. Walter
Kaufmann. New York and London, 1968

Oulibicheff [Ulibishev], Alexander. *Beethoven, ses critiques et ses glossateurs.*
Leipzig: Brockhaus, and Paris: Gavelot, 1857.

  *Nouvelle biographie de Mozart suivie d'un aperçu sur l'histoire générale de la
musique.* 3 vols. Moscow: August Semen, 1843

Parker, Roger. "On Reading Nineteenth-Century Opera: Verdi through the
Looking-Glass." In *Reading Opera*, ed. A. Groos and R. Parker, 288–305.
Princeton: Princeton University Press, 1988

  see also Carolyn Abbate, "Dismembering Mozart"

Petersen, Peter. "Die dichterisch-musikalische Periode: Ein verkannter Begriff
Richard Wagners." *Hamburger Jahrbuch für Musikwissenschaft* 2 (1977),
105–24. Response by Carl Dahlhaus, "Was ist eine 'dichterisch-musikalische
Periode'?" *Melos/Neue Zeitschrift für Musik* 4:3 (1978), 224–5.

Porges, Heinrich. *Tristan und Isolde, nebst einem Brief Richard Wagners.* Leipzig, 1906

Raff, Joachim. *Die Wagnerfrage, kritisch beleuchtet*, vol. I (no more published).
Brunswick: F. Vieweg, 1854

Rather, L. J. *Reading Wagner: A Study in the History of Ideas*. Baton Rouge: Louisiana State University Press, 1990

Rehm, Jürgen. *Zur Musikrezeption im vormärzlichen Berlin*. Hildesheim: Georg Olms, 1983

Reicha, Anton. *Traité de mélodie*. Paris: [pub. privately], 1814; 2nd edn, 1832

Roeder, Erich. *Felix Draeseke: Der Lebens- und Leidensweg eines deutschen Meisters*. Dresden: Wilhelm Limpert, 1932

Rosen, David. "Cone's and Kivy's 'World of Opera'." *Cambridge Opera Journal* 4:1 (1992), 61–74

Rothfarb, Lee A. *Ernst Kurth as Theorist and Analyst*. Philadelphia: University of Pennsylvania Press, 1988

Rothstein, William. *Phrase Rhythm in Tonal Music*. New York: Schirmer Books, 1989

Rousseau, Jean Jacques. *Ecrits sur la musique*. Paris: Pourrats, 1838; rpt, ed. Catherine Kintzler, Paris: Stock, 1979

Essay on the Origin of Languages (*Essai sur l'origine des langues*, 1753), trans. John H. Moran (*see* Herder, *On the Origin of Language*)

Rubinstein, Joseph. "Symphonie und Drama." *Bayreuther Blätter* 4 (1881), 53–61

de Ruiter, Jacob. *Der Charakterbegriff in der Musik: Studien zur deutschen Ästhetik der Instrumentalmusik, 1740–1850*. Stuttgart: Franz Steiner Verlag, 1989

Rushton, Julian. *The Musical Language of Berlioz*. Cambridge: Cambridge University Press, 1983

Schäfke, Rudolf. *Geschichte der Musikästhetik in Umrissen*. Berlin: Max Hesses Verlag, 1934; rpt Hildesheim and New York: Georg Olms, 1964

Schering, Arnold. *Beethoven und die Dichtung*. Berlin: Junker und Dünnhaupt, 1936; rpt Hildesheim: Georg Olms, 1973

Schilling, Gustav (ed.). *Enzyklopädie der gesammten musikalischen Wissenschaften oder Universal-Lexikon der Tonkunst*. 6 vols. Stuttgart: F. H. Kohler, 1835–42
Versuch einer Philosophie des Schönen in der Musik, oder Aesthetik der Tonkunst. Mainz: B. Schott's Söhnen, 1838

Schindler, Anton. *Biographie von Ludwig van Beethoven*. Münster: Aschendorff, 1840; 2nd edn, 1845; 3rd edn, 1860

Schlegel, Friedrich. *Schriften zur Literatur*, ed. Wolfdietrich Rasch. Munich: Deutsche Taschenbuch Verlag, 1972

Schleuning, Peter. *See* Martin Geck, "*Geschrieben auf Bonaparte*"

Schmidt, Lothar. "Arabeske. Zu einigen Voraussetzungen und Konsequenzen von Eduard Hanslicks musikalischem Formbegriff." *Archiv für Musikwissenschaft* 46:2 (1989), 91–120

Schopenhauer, Arthur. *Essays and Aphorisms*, trans. R. J. Hollingdale. Harmondsworth: Penguin, 1970
Die Welt als Wille und Vorstellung (1819/1844), ed. Arthur and Angelika Hübscher. 2 vols. Zurich: Diogenes, 1977

Skelton, Geoffrey. *Wagner in Theory and Practice*. London, 1992
see also Robert L. Jacobs, *Wagner writes from Paris . . .* and Cosima Wagner, *Diaries*

Solie, Ruth A. "Whose Life? The Gendered Self in Schumann's *Frauenliebe* Songs." In *Music and Text: Critical Inquiries*, ed. Steven P. Scher, 219–40. Cambridge: Cambridge University Press, 1992

(ed.). *Musicology and Difference: Gender and Sexuality in Music Scholarship*. Berkeley and Los Angeles: University of California Press, 1993

Stein, Herbert von. "Richard Wagners Begriff der dichterisch-musikalischen Periode." *Die Musikforschung* 35:2 (1982), 162–5

Stein, Jack. *Richard Wagner and the Synthesis of the Arts*. Detroit: Wayne State University Press, 1960

Steiner, George. *Real Presences*. Chicago: University of Chicago Press, 1989

Stephan, Rudolph. "Gibt es ein Geheimnis der Form bei Richard Wagner?" In *Das Drama Richard Wagners als musikalisches Kunstwerk*, ed. C. Dahlhaus, 9–16. Regensburg: Bosse, 1970

Strauß, Dietmar. *Eduard Hanslick: Vom Musikalisch-Schönen*. Teil I: *Historisch-kritische Ausgabe*; Teil II: *Hanslick's Schrift in textkritischer Aussicht*. Mainz: Schott, 1990

Stravinsky, Igor. *Poétique musicale*. Cambridge MA: Harvard University Press, 1942. (*Poetics of Music*, trans. A. Knodel and I. Dahl. Cambridge MA: Harvard University Press, 1942)

Strobel, Otto. *Richard Wagner: Skizzen und Entwürfe zur Ring-Dichtung*. Munich: F. Bruckmann, 1930

Sulzer, J. G. *Allgemeine Theorie der schönen Künste*. Leipzig: Weidmann, 1771–4; 4th edn, 1792–9

Tieck, Ludwig, and Wilhelm Heinrich Wackenroder. *Herzensergießungen eines kunstliebenden Klosterbruders* (Berlin, 1797), ed. Richard Benz. Stuttgart: Reclam, 1975

Phantasien über die Kunst für Freunde der Kunst (Hamburg, 1799), ed. Wolfgang Nehring. Stuttgart: Reclam, 1973

Todorov, Tzvetan. *Theories of the Symbol*, trans. Catherine Porter. Ithaca: Cornell University Press, 1982

Uhlig, Theodor. *Musikalische Schriften*, ed. Ludwig Frankenstein. Regensburg: Bosse, [1913]

Ulibishev, Alexander. *see* Oulibicheff

Vischer, Friedrich Theodor. *Ästhetik oder Wissenschaft des Schönen* (5 vols., 1851–7). 2nd edn, ed. Robert Vischer. Munich: Meyer & Jessen, 1923

Voss, Egon. *Wagner und die Instrumentalmusik*. Wilhelmshafen: Heinrichshofen, 1977

Wackenroder, Wilhelm Heinrich. *See* Ludwig Tieck, *Herzensergießungen* and *Phantasien über die Kunst*

Wagner, Cosima. *Cosima Wagner's Diaries* (CWD). 2 vols., ed. Martin Gregor-Dellin and Dietrich Mack, trans. Geoffrey Skelton. New York and London: Harcourt Brace Jovanovich, 1978, 1980

Wagner, Richard. *Beethoven*, trans. Edward Dannreuther. London: William Reeves, 1880

Briefe an Hans von Bülow. Jena: Eugen Diderich, 1916

Briefwechsel zwischen Wagner und Liszt. 2 vols. Leipzig: Breitkopf & Härtel, 1887 (*Correspondence of Wagner and Liszt*, trans. with preface by Francis Hueffer. 2nd edn, London: H. Grevel & Co., 1896)

Gesammelte Schriften und Dichtungen (GSD). Leipzig: E. W. Fritzsch, 1871–3; 2nd edn 10 vols., 1887

Mein Leben, ed. Martin Gregor-Dellin. 2nd edn, Munich: List, 1976. (*My Life*, trans. Andrew Gray and ed. Mary Whittall. Cambridge: Cambridge University Press, 1983)

Richard Wagner's Prose Works, trans. William Ashton Ellis. 8 vols. London: Routledge & Kegan Paul, 1892–9

Sämtliche Briefe. 8 vols. to date (1830–57), ed. G. Strobel and W. Wolf (vols. I–V), H.-J. Bauer and J. Forner (vols. VI–VIII). Leipzig: VEB Deutscher Verlag für Musik, 1967–93

Sämtliche Schriften und Dichtungen (SSD). 16 vols. [Ed. Richard Sternfeld.] Leipzig: Breitkopf & Härtel/C. F. W. Siegel, 1911–16

Selected Letters of Richard Wagner, trans. and ed. Stewart Spencer and Barry Millington. New York: Norton, 1988

Tagebuchblätter und Briefe: Richard Wagner an Mathilde und an Otto Wesendonk, foreword by G. Will. Berlin: Th. Knaur, n.d. [1904]

see also Robert L. Jacobs (ed. and trans.), *Three Wagner Essays* and *Wagner Writes from Paris* . . .

Wallace, Robin. *Beethoven's Critics: Aesthetic Dilemmas and Resolutions During the Composer's Lifetime.* Cambridge: Cambridge University Press, 1986

Wapnewski, Peter. *See* Ulrich Müller, *Wagner Handbuch*

Weber, Carl Maria von. *Kunstansichten. Ausgewählte Schriften*, intro. by Karl Laux. Wilhelmshafen: Heinrichshofen, 1978

Westernhagen, Curt von. "Wagner as a Writer." In *The Wagner Companion*, ed. P. Burbidge and R. Sutton, 341–64. New York: Cambridge University Press, 1979

White, Hayden. *The Content of the Form: Narrative Discourse and Historical Representation.* Baltimore and London: Johns Hopkins University Press, 1987

Whittall, Arnold. "The Music." In *Parsifal*, ed. Lucy Beckett, 61–86. Cambridge: Cambridge University Press, 1981

"Musical Language." In *The Wagner Compendium*, ed. Barry Millington, 248–61. London: Thames & Hudson, 1992

"Wagner's Great Transition?: from *Lohegrin* to *Das Rheingold.*" *Music Analysis* 2:3 (1983), 269–80

Wintle, Christopher. "The Numinous in *Götterdämmerung.*" In *Reading Opera*, ed. A. Groos and R. Parker, 200–34. Princeton: Princeton University Press, 1988

Wolzogen, Hans von. "Leitmotive." *Bayreuther Blätter* 20 (1897), 313–30.

Der Ring des Nibelungen: thematischer Leitfaden durch Dichtung und Musik. Leipzig: G. Esseger, 1911

Wagneriana. Leipzig, 1888

Wörner, Karl. "Beiträge zur Geschichte des Leitmotivs in der Oper." *Zeitschrift für Musikwissenschaft* 14 (1931–2), 151–72

Index

Index

Berlioz, Hector, 46, 71, 78, 109, 113, 228, 306, 318, 334, 352, 353n., 367
Harold en Italie, 46
Roméo et Juliette, 311, 326–38, 349–50, 356–7
Symphonie fantastique, 29, 46
Symphonie funèbre et triomphale, 332
biography (and musical hermeneutics), 11, 123
Bischoff, Ludwig, 269n., 314
Bonds, Mark Evan, 273, 275, 279
Bonnet, Charles, 148
Borchmeyer, Dieter, xii–xiii, 81n., 173n.
Brahms, Johannes, 49, 283, 313
Breig, Werner, 210n., 213n.
Brendel, Franz, 43–5, 111, 269n., 314
Buffon, Georges L. L., 148
Bülow, Hans von, 34, 37, 111, 142n., 252
Burckhardt, Jacob, 11n.
Burnham, Scott, 55, 60n., 65n.

Champfleury (Jules Fleury-Husson), 283n.
Chopin, Fryderyck, 288n.
chorus, orchestra as, 77–9, 81–92
Chrysander, Friedrich, 373n.
Cone, Edward T., 77n., 100n., 230n.
Conrad, Joseph, 144n.
Cooke, Deryck, 234n., 236
Cusick, Suzanne G., 14n.
Czerny, Karl, 52

Dahlhaus, Carl, xi–xiii, xviii, 3, 4n., 5, 6n., 7, 12, 16, 22, 24, 27–8, 31n., 42, 46, 49, 52, 55–7, 60, 181, 184, 190, 206–10, 212, 214, 216, 223–4, 226–7, 232, 253–5, 274, 282–6, 298, 303, 307, 314n., 324n., 360
dance (and absolute-musical forms), 12, 250–1, 253, 271–2, 306, 312
Dante Alighieri, 51–2
Divine Comedy, 51
Danuser, Hermann, 288, 337–8n.
Da Ponte, Lorenzo, 115
Darwin, Charles, 148, 269n.
Origin of Species, 148
Daube, Johann Friedrich, 273–4
Daverio, John, 6n.
Deathridge, John, 196n., 366n., 369n.
de Man, Paul, 267n.
Derrida, Jacques, 260–1, 267
determinacy (distinctness) of musical expression and "idea," 6, 7, 41–2,

42–50, 54, 72–3, 109–11, 305–6, 321–2, 327–8, 334, 372
dialogue, in musical drama, 212–14, 226, 228–39 (*Die Walküre*, "annunciation of death" scene), 296–301 (*Tristan und Isolde*, Act II love duet)
Dijkstra, Bram, 132n., 134
Dömling, Wolfgang, 337n.
Donington, Robert, 154
Donizetti, Gaetano, 11
Dorn, Heinrich, 351
Draeseke, Felix, 251, 275
drama, musical drama (theoretical perspectives on), 14–15, 17, 22, 30n., 38–9, 48–50, 366–7; dramatic "motifs" and "motives" (motivations), 319–49; "dramatic pathos" and instrumental music, 80, 98–100, 306, 312, 348; and instrumental form, 71–80, 307–8, 312, 315–19; and metaphors of gender and biology, 130–1, 138–51 (and chapter 3, *passim*); and the realization of a "poetic intent," 125–9. *See also* dialogue, evolution, gender (as metaphor), leitmotif, "poetic intent"
Dresdener Anzeiger, 102
Dvořák, Antonín, 313
Dwight's Journal, 356

Eco, Umberto, 51, 127
Ellis, William Ashton, 136n., 142
Elterlein, Ernst von (Ernst Gottschald), 62
Evans, Edwin, 99
evolution (*Entwicklung*), as biological and organicist metaphor, 138–51, 171–2, 309, 329–30; as musical-formal principle, 59, 73, 78–80, 83–4, 91, 125, 129, 147–8, 182, 205–11, 226 (and chapter 4, *passim*), 289–90, 304, 309

Feuerbach, Ludwig, 2
Grundsätze einer Philosophie der Zukunft, 2
Finck, Henry T., 254
Forchert, Arno, 9, 373n.
formalism (musical), 3, 5, 19–20, 21n., 30–4
Franke, Rainer, 2, 210n.
Freud, Sigmund, 94–5
Friedheim, Philip, 163n.

Gade, Niels, 313
Galeazzi, Francesco, 273

Index

Index

Mahler, Gustav, 77n., 105n.
Mann, Thomas, xvn., 100n.
Marschner, Heinrich, *Der Vampyr*, 197–204
Marx, A. B., 43–4, 55–6, 59, 60n., 61, 62, 65n., 67–9, 71, 77–8, 92, 110–11, 148, 195, 208, 274–5, 278, 334
Mattheson, Johann, 239, 273, 278
Maurin-Chevillard Quartet, 109, 115
Maus, Fred E., 21n., 29n., 35
McClary, Susan, 8n., 101n.
McCreless, Patrick, 164, 165n., 210n., 324, 361
The Meister, xi
melody, theoretical and aesthetic constructions of, 112–13, 129, 150–1, 241; as basis of musical form, 249–53, 269, 270–304; critical interpretations of "endless melody," 252–6, 279–84, 353–4; criticism of Wagner's "lack of melody," 242–50; melodic line and "outline" as determinants of form, 275–9; original context of the term "endless melody," 248–57; and "punctuation," 243, 248, 275, 279–80, 290, 303–4; Wagner on "operatic" and "absolute" melody, 247–52, 256–7
Mendelssohn, Felix, 41
String Quartet in A minor, op. 13, 353
Meyerbeer, Giacomo, 115, 192, 194–5, 206
Les Huguenots, 199, 203–5, 217
Miller, J. Hillis, 354
Millington, Barry, xvn., 16n.
modulation, aesthetic theories and interpretations of, 64, 86–90, 119–22 (and "poetic-musical period"), 182–210
Monteverdi, Giulio Cesare, 173n.
Mottl, Felix, 180n.
Mozart, Wolfgang Amadeus, 57–8, 61n., 92n., 115, 228, 250, 283, 351–2n.
Symphony in E flat, K. 543, 57
Müller, Franz, 354
musical form, as active "formation" (process), 271, 277–8, 281–2; aesthetic or theoretical perspectives on, 3, 12, 17, 307–11, 366–7; *Bar* form, 233–5, 243, 304; form and content as musical-aesthetic categories, 18–42; relation to "poetic" and "underlying" idea

in Beethoven, 55–7, 59–60, 63–4 (and chapter 2, *passim*). *See also* alternation, dance, evolution
musical prose (as technical term), xiv–xv, 195, 224, 226, 228, 255, 283, 285–6, 288

Nägeli, Hans Georg, 20, 30–2
Vorlesungen über Musik, 30
Napoleon Bonaparte, 62, 65, 70
Nattiez, Jean-Jacques, xii, 4n., 16, 133n., 135, 138, 140–1, 143–4, 146, 152, 156–9, 264n., 266, 370
nature, as source of metaphor and evaluative criteria in Wagner's writings, 130–3, 138–51, 154–7, 160–4, 256–7, 261, 280–1, 304
Newcomb, Anthony, 22n., 207n., 217n.
Newman, Ernest, xi, 169, 205n., 293, 295
Newton, Isaac, 148
Nietzsche, Friedrich, xiii, 4–5, 49, 146, 178n., 191, 246, 248, 258, 284
The Birth of Tragedy, 5, 81n., 97
On the Genealogy of Morals, 4
Nietzsche contra Wagner, 248
Nordau, Max, xv
Novalis (Friedrich Hardenberg), 7

Offenbach, Jacques, *Les Contes d'Hoffmann*, 95
organicism, musical, 6, 11, 33, 112, 130–1, 137–9, 143–5, 147–51, 263–4, 274, 294, 304

Parker, Roger, xi
period, "poetic-musical," 164–5, 180, 181–210 (and chapter 4, *passim*), 269, 279, 280; original text from *Opera and Drama* (translated), 375–7; possible relation to earlier operatic practices, 196–206
Petersen, Peter, 195n., 209, 216
"poetic ideas" (critical tradition of), xiv, 6, 9, 34, 42–50, 52–9 (and chapter 2, *passim*), 155, 157n., 307–15
"poetic intent" (*dichterische Absicht*), 14, 25, 37–8, 48, 108, 114–15, 121–3, 125–9, 130, 131, 137, 138, 190, 194, 297n.; as "fertilizing seed" of music, 141–4
Pohl, Richard, 111
Porges, Heinrich, 116n., 153

Index

Index